# New Demographic Faces of Europe

Springer
*Berlin*
*Heidelberg*
*New York*
*Barcelona*
*Hong Kong*
*London*
*Milan*
*Paris*
*Singapore*
*Tokyo*

T. Kučera O. V. Kučerová
O. B. Opara E. Schaich (Eds.)

# New Demographic Faces of Europe

## The Changing Population Dynamics in Countries of Central and Eastern Europe

With 131 Figures
and 151 Tables

Springer

Dr. Tomáš Kučera
Dr. Olga V. Kučerová
Charles University in Prague
Faculty of Science
Dept. of Demography and Geodemography
Albertov 6
12843 Prague 2
Czech Republic

Dr. Oksana B. Opara
The University of Auckland
Women's Studies
Private Bag 92019
Auckland
New Zealand

Prof. Dr. Eberhard Schaich
Eberhard-Karls-Universität Tübingen
Abt. Statistik, Ökonometrie und Unternehmensforschung
Mohlstr. 36
72074 Tübingen
Germany

ISBN-13: 978-3-642-64131-2 Springer-Verlag Berlin Heidelberg New York

Library of Congress Cataloging-in-Publication Data applied for
Die Deutsche Bibliothek – CIP-Einheitsaufnahme
New demographic faces of Europe: the changing population dynamics in countries of Central and Eastern Europe / ed.: Tomas Kucera ... – Berlin; Heidelberg; New York; Barcelona; Hong Kong; London; Milan; Paris; Singapore; Tokyo: Springer, 2000
ISBN-13: 978-3-642-64131-2



Springer-Verlag Berlin Heidelberg New York
a member of BertelsmannSpringer Science+Business Media GmbH

ISBN-13: 978-3-642-64131-2 e-ISBN-13: 978-3-642-59800-5
DOI: 10.1007/978-3-642-59800-5


Softcover reprint of the hardcover 1st edition 2000



Hardcover-Design: Erich Kirchner, Heidelberg

SPIN 10776857 42/2202-5 4 3 2 1 0 – Printed on acid-free paper

# Preface

The collapse of the communist system ten years ago caused profound changes in the main demographic processes and fostered transformation of population structures in all former communist countries. In most of them, fertility declined dramatically, mortality worsened and migration moved in new directions and intensities. The other processes such as marriages, divorces, and abortions developed completely new characteristics. And, above all, the altered demographic situation is grounded on new and quite different socio-economic foundations. Despite many general trends, however, a great deal of individuality in the transition processes of participating countries is evident.

The *Central and East European Demographic Network (CEDN)* represents an international co-operation of demographers, statisticians and other professionals interested in population development, which was established in view of these dramatic demographic transition processes. The CEDN objectives involve monitoring and analysing recent spatial population distribution and forecasting its future development in the target region. The core activities of this project are the description and analysis of population structures and processes on a sub-national (regional) level through its basic components (fertility, mortality and migration) and their changes in a new economic, social and political context. In particular, the processes' intensity, structural characteristics, dynamics and their interregional differentiation together with the impact on formation of spatial demographic structures are the major focus of the CEDN research inquiry. It is aimed to identify regularities and causalities that would allow comprehensive forecasting. All project activities are directed towards creating the national sets of regional population forecasts, which would describe the probable future development of regional population size and structure according to sex and age.

The first volume through its focus on national population development intends to prepare a comparable informative and cognitive basis for realisation of the central effort of CEDN – further demographic studies on sub-national levels. The sense and need for sub-national population analysis is well illustrated in the last chapter of the volume.

This publication is of specific importance for the described field of research because it presents the recent demographic chronicle of Europe in terms of a new variety of population developments on both sides of the former iron curtain. It elucidates singularities of the demographic situation in different national populations as well as peculiarities in data availability and methods. And most importantly, it presents the evidence that the demographic changes observed in post-communist countries have been more than a simple process of demographic adaptation to so-called Western structures, because Western populations also show a variety of change. Aside from some formal similarities, e.g. some noticeable parallels with fertility development in West Europe, the demographic changes in Central and East Europe seem to be of a different nature.

The target region of the CEDN and of this first volume covers *cum grano salis* the CADSES (Central, Adriatic, Danubian and South East European States) in the sense of the operational EU programme INTERREG II C. This country grouping (classification) is essential for the whole project for the purposes of comparison of Eastern processes *per se*, Western processes *per se* and, particularly, for East-West-comparisons and for testing the hypotheses of East-West convergence. Except Albania, the former Yugoslavia, Greece, and Italy, all countries of the CADSES region are engaged in the CEDN project. To extend further the basis and scope of comparative perspective, the Baltics and the Russian Federation as well as Denmark, with its typical North European structure, are also included into the CEDN target space.

A constitutive element of the CEDN is intensive co-operation of demographers from all involved countries. This organisational principle ensures that pitfalls which may arise from a limited knowledge of the political and legal system, of ethnic peculiarities, of the religious situation or of actual economic developments of the involved countries and similar risks are avoided. This element is also essential to engage the best available data and produce its adequate interpretation. An intensive scientific co-operation within the framework of 17 regionally coherent countries: Austria, Belarus, Bulgaria, the Czech Republic, Denmark, Estonia, Germany, Hungary, Latvia, Lithuania, Moldova, Poland, Romania, Russia, Slovakia, Slovenia, Ukraine, with various infrastructural backgrounds, diverse conceptual and organisational levels of statistical services, distinct definitions of demographic notions and different languages is a great challenge.

The CEDN turned out to be not completely free of some minor complications and obstacles. The composition of the team of scholars was not stable at the beginning of the project and has changed since then. But *Olga Kučerová* and *Tomáš Kučera*, Prague, and their admirable motivation and perseverance managed to overcome all difficulties that arose along the way. At the end, the CEDN co-operation has proved to be successful, focused and efficient enough to offer a hopefully attractive first result despite all technical communication problems. In addition, the CEDN promoted a very good understanding and friendship among all participating authors, which offers an optimistic outlook on further close co-operations.

The principal part of this book consists of the country-specific contributions, i.e. the description and basic analysis of the demographic situation of the CEDN target space countries. The structures of these national studies are not identical. The authors were asked to take into account a list of essentials which was agreed upon in advance and to respect a maximum length of their contributions. All the other components of their papers were left to individual suggestions and judgements. This may reduce the options of detailed multi-country comparisons of numbers, facts and tendencies. On the other hand, it increased the opportunities to describe the characteristics of the demographic situation of the countries in a greater detail. In the last section, a case study on regional differentiation of fertility and mortality in the Czech Republic attempts to demonstrate that sub-national aspects and factors are of great relevance for the new demographic reality in Europe and that they are worth to be investigated in greater detail.

The time span described and analysed in this publication begins mostly in 1989 and ends with the present, according to our agreements. Of course, the relevant demographic processes that began before 1989 and influenced the demographic transition processes of the last decade cannot remain unmentioned. Additionally, it was unavoidable that the definition of the present shows slight variation between countries because of the different performance of statistical services.

This book is a work of a numerous group of persons who contributed to its publication. Among them, *Olga Kučerová*, Prague, and *Oksana Opara*, Auckland, were primarily responsible for the editing and all main editorial activities such as motivating the authors in all participating countries to deliver their raw products (first versions) on time, insisting on the inclusion of essential components and, in some cases, making revisions to improve comparability. In addition, they helped some authors with translation of their texts into English, and *Oksana Opara* took responsibility for the language to make sure that *English* and not *bad English* would be our medium of communication. *Tomáš Kučera*, Prague, is the scientific co-ordinator of the CEDN group. He contributed the main ideas to the CEDN project and has been, together with *Olga Kučerová,* strongly involved in the conceptual foundation and the editorial principles of this publication. He is also the co-author of the chapter devoted to the changes of regional demographic patterns in the Czech Republic. *Eberhard Schaich*, Tübingen, is the organisational co-ordinator of the CEDN and has been responsible for its publishing and financial issues. He wrote the chapter concerning Germany's current demographic situation together with *Jochen Fleischhacker*, Rostock, in an inner-German East-West-co-production to capture most of the latest German demographic peculiarities. *Karin Hummel* and *Katrin Schmidt*, Tübingen, worked hard to optimise the German part of the CEDN, including the contribution about Germany to this volume, in addition to their support in many organisational and financial activities. *Boris Burcin*, Prague, produced and formatted the final version of the volume according to the rules of the publishing house. His competence and patience have been outstanding.

The first stage of the CEDN research project was financially supported by a grant from the European Union in the framework of the operational programme *INTERREG II C (CADSES)*. The authors are grateful for this great support that enabled them to discuss in detail and co-operate at several workshops, and which tremendously helped the CEDN to publish this volume. They also thank the Institut für ökologische Raumentwicklung e.V., Dresden, and the Sächsisches Staatsministerium für Umwelt und Landwirtschaft, Dresden, for their helpful co-operation. Additionally, the *German Research Society (DFG)* supported the first workshop of the CEDN in Tübingen (May 1997). The *Charles University in Prague* contributed financially toward the initial meeting (October 1996) and the second conference held in Zahrádky Castle (July 1998). The *Max-Planck-Institute for Demographic Research*,

Rostock, hosted the final CEDN workshop in November 1999, which concluded work on this first volume and conceived the details of the group's next research steps. We are very grateful for all their support.

Springer-Verlag GmbH & Co. KG Heidelberg, Germany, is the publisher of this first volume. The co-operation with *Dr. Werner A. Müller*, Executive Economics Editor, and his crew was uncomplicated and a great pleasure.

Tübingen, April 15, 2000 Eberhard Schaich

# Table of Contents

# 1

# Current Demographic Trends in Austria[1]

**Isabella Buber and Alexia Prskawetz[2]**

## 1.1 Population Size and Age Structure

Austria's population surpassed the 8 million mark at the end of 1993. High net migration together with an increase in the number of births during the years 1991 through 1994 contributed to the pronounced growth of the Austrian population in the early 1990s. But the new laws on immigration and a reduction in the number of births led to a slowdown in population growth since 1993: from 0.7% in 1993 to 0.2% in 1996.

Since 1981, the number of foreigners has more than doubled and amounted to 730,869 or 9.0% of the Austrian population in 1996 (Table 1.1). But since the naturalisation of foreigners outweighs the natural increase of foreigners, their stock is growing less than their net migration.

**Table 1.1: Population Development, 1981–1996[1]**

| Year | Total population | Foreigners | Population change | | |
|---|---|---|---|---|---|
| | | | Total increase | Natural increase | Net migration |
| 1981 | 7,584,094 | 319,167 | 30,768 | 1,249 | 29,519 |
| 1982 | 7,567,339 | 297,665 | -16,755 | 3,501 | -20,256 |
| 1983 | 7,566,693 | 295,639 | -646 | -2,923 | 2,277 |
| 1984 | 7,574,364 | 299,936 | 7,671 | 768 | 6,903 |
| 1985 | 7,582,160 | 308,829 | 7,796 | -2,138 | 9,934 |
| 1986 | 7,593,818 | 320,937 | 11,658 | -107 | 11,765 |
| 1987 | 7,602,488 | 331,555 | 8,670 | 1,596 | 7,074 |
| 1988 | 7,628,072 | 356,488 | 25,584 | 4,789 | 20,795 |
| 1989 | 7,689,529 | 417,877 | 61,457 | 5,352 | 56,105 |
| 1990 | 7,768,944 | 494,246 | 79,415 | 7,502 | 71,913 |
| 1991 | 7,867,796 | 581,118 | 98,852 | 11,201 | 87,651 |
| 1992 | 7,962,003 | 665,349 | 94,207 | 12,140 | 82,067 |
| 1993 | 8,015,027 | 706,335 | 53,024 | 12,710 | 40,314 |
| 1994 | 8,039,865 | 720,911 | 24,838 | 11,731 | 13,107 |
| 1995 | 8,054,802 | 726,305 | 14,937 | 7,498 | 7,439 |
| 1996 | 8,067,812 | 730,869 | 13,010 | 8,019 | 4,991 |

[1]As of 31 December of a given year
Sources: ACSO, 1996–1998

The age structure of the Austrian population in 1997 (Figure 1.1) represents a mirror image of Austrian history. The baby boom generation is reflected in the bulge around ages 30 to 35, while the losses in the number of births during and after the First and the Second World Wars are manifested in the indentations around ages 80 and 50. The smaller cohorts born during the economic crisis of the 1930s are responsible for the contraction of the age pyramid around age 60. The asymmetry of the male and female age distribution in the ages above 60 is the result of the male population losses during the Second World War and the difference in life expectancy between men and women.

According to the medium projection variant of the Austrian Central Statistical Office, the Austrian population will continue to grow and will reach 8.338 million in 2024 (ACSO, 1997). Immigration as well as a short-term excess of births over deaths will cause this growth. The smaller cohorts of parents after the year 2000 will lead to a continuous decrease in the number of births, and ageing will be the dominant factor of population development in Austria, as illustrated by the right-hand panel in Figure 1.1.

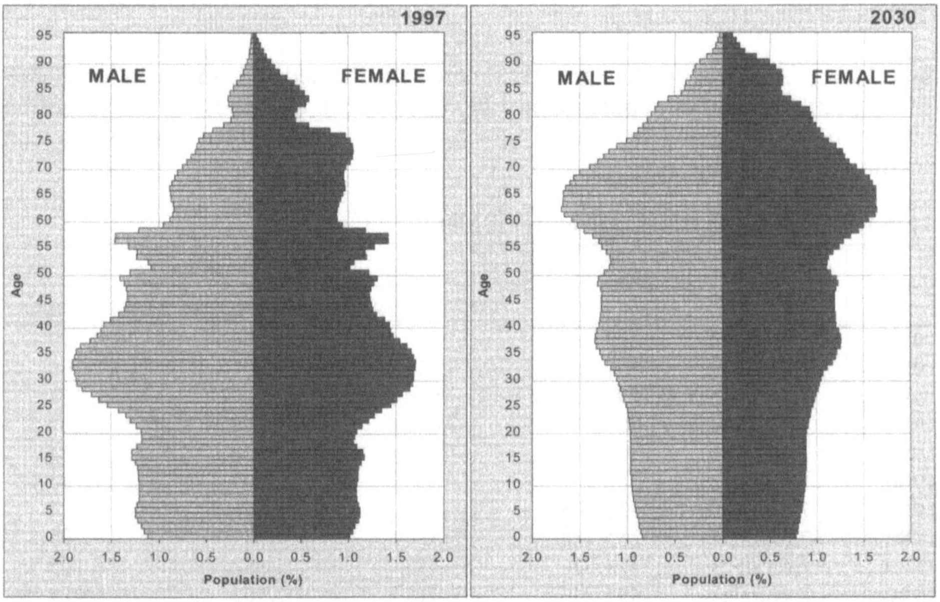


**Figure 1.1: Age Pyramid, 1997 and 2030**
Source: ACSO, 1997

A more dynamic representation of Austrian age structure during the last two decades is given in Table 1.2. The increasing share of the working age population reflects the entrance of the baby boom generation into the labour market during the 1970s and early 1980s and the increase in net migration during the early 1990s. In 1993, the working age population (people aged 15–59 years) surpassed the 5 million mark for the first time. During the last 15 years, the share of the young population (below age 15) has been declining while the share of old people has remained constant at around 20% of the total population. Considering these numbers in terms of dependency ratios gives a similar picture. The old age dependency ratio is around 32% while the young age dependency ratio has declined below 30%[3].

**Table 1.2: Age Structure and Dependency Ratios, 1981–1995, selected years, per cent**

| Year | Proportion of population aged | | | Dependency ratio | |
|---|---|---|---|---|---|
| | 0–14 | 15–59 | 60+ | Young age | Old age |
| 1981 | 20.0 | 60.8 | 19.2 | 32.9 | 31.7 |
| 1985 | 18.3 | 61.9 | 19.8 | 29.6 | 32.1 |
| 1990 | 17.4 | 62.5 | 20.1 | 27.9 | 32.2 |
| 1995 | 17.5 | 62.7 | 19.7 | 28.0 | 31.5 |

Sources: ACSO, 1996–1998

## 1.2 Ethnic Composition

The ethnic composition of the Austrian population during the last decades reflects the distinctive stages of net migration flows of foreigners into Austria (Figure 1.2).

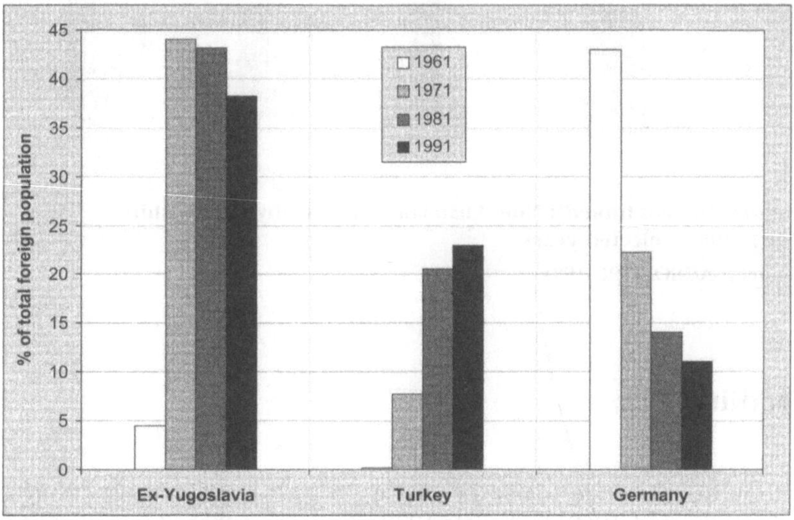


**Figure 1.2: Non-Austrian Nationals by Citizenship, 1961–1991, selected years**

Sources: ACSO, 1996–1998

The immediate post-war period was characterised by a large influx of ethnic Germans from different parts of Central and Eastern Europe. Three major waves of refugees from Hungary in 1956–1957, from Czechoslovakia in 1968–1969, and from Poland in 1981–1982 followed. Most of these refugees later went on to other countries or returned to their home countries. A period of strong economic growth in the 1960s together with demographically caused labour shortages led to the recruitment of foreign workers from Spain in 1962, from Turkey in 1964, and from Yugoslavia in 1966 (Fassmann and Münz, 1995, p. 41)[4]. The fall of the "Iron Curtain" at the end of the 1980s and internal "pull" factors in Austria (strong economic growth) led to an increase in immigration from Eastern European countries. However, as the ethnic composition of the foreign population in Figure 1.2 indicates, traditional flows from the former Yugoslavia and Turkey are still dominant, while migration from Eastern and Central Europe plays only a minor role.

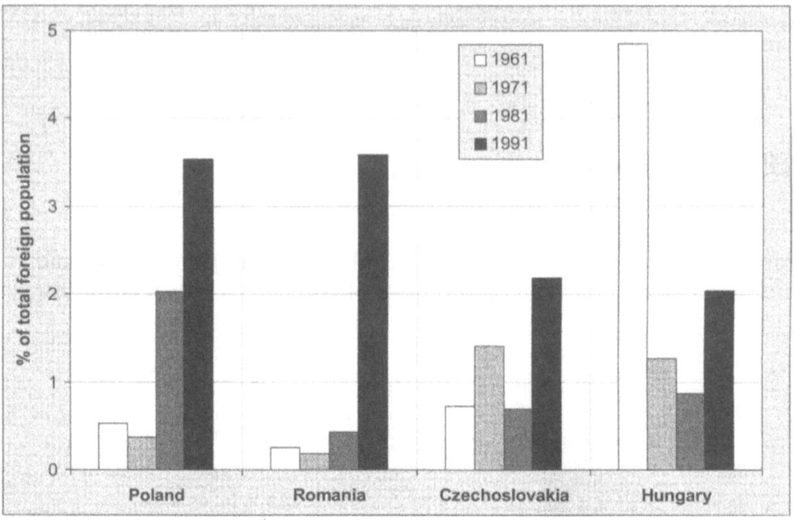


**Figure 1.2 (continued): Non-Austrian Nationals by Citizenship, 1961–1991, selected years**

Sources: ACSO, 1996–1998

## 1.3 Fertility

Similar to most other industrialised countries, Austria experienced a strong drop in fertility from the mid-1960s to the late 1970s. Ever since then, Austria's fertility has remained at a sub-replacement level (Figure 1.3). The lowest level of the TFR was reached in 1997 – 1.37 children per woman. The net reproduction rate decreased to a level of 0.66, which is almost as low as during the 1930s (0.65 in 1937). At the same time, Austria is a country with a strong two-child per family norm, as it was indicated in recent surveys that included questions on the ideal number of children[5].

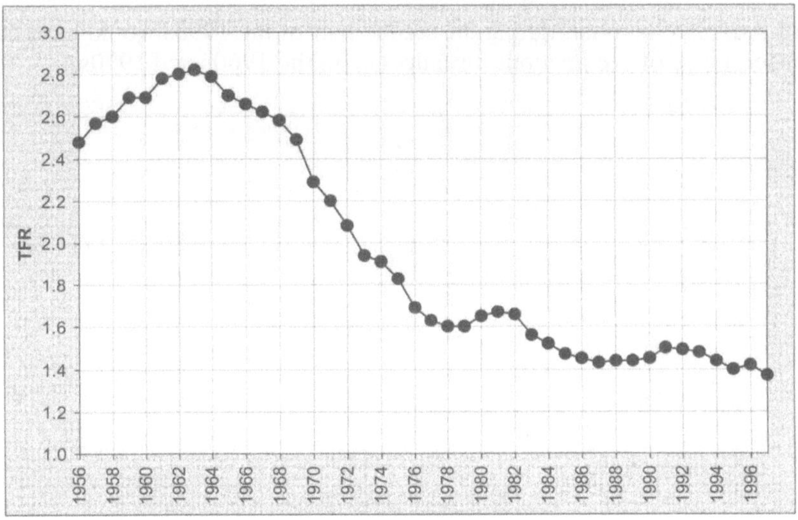


**Figure 1.3: Total Fertility Rate (TFR), 1956–1997**

Sources: ACSO, 1996–1998

**Table 1.3: Main Indicators of Fertility, 1985–1996**

| Year | Live births | Share of live births by non-Austrian nationals (%) | Live births (per 1,000 inhabitants) | Total fertility rate | Net reproduction rate | Mean age of women at childbearing |
|---|---|---|---|---|---|---|
| 1985 | 87,440 | .. | 11.5 | 1.47 | 0.70 | 26.86 |
| 1986 | 86,964 | .. | 11.5 | 1.45 | 0.69 | 26.77 |
| 1987 | 86,503 | .. | 11.4 | 1.43 | 0.68 | 26.92 |
| 1988 | 88,052 | .. | 11.6 | 1.44 | 0.69 | 26.96 |
| 1989 | 88,759 | .. | 11.6 | 1.44 | 0.69 | 27.09 |
| 1990 | 90,454 | 7.3 | 11.7 | 1.45 | 0.70 | 27.23 |
| 1991 | 94,629 | 9.4 | 12.1 | 1.50 | 0.72 | 27.24 |
| 1992 | 95,302 | 12.2 | 12.0 | 1.49 | 0.71 | 27.28 |
| 1993 | 95,227 | 13.6 | 11.9 | 1.48 | 0.71 | 27.34 |
| 1994 | 92,415 | 13.7 | 11.5 | 1.44 | 0.69 | 27.52 |
| 1995 | 88,669 | 13.8 | 11.0 | 1.40 | 0.67 | 27.68 |
| 1996 | 88,809 | 13.6 | 11.0 | 1.42 | 0.68 | 27.82 |

Sources: ACSO, 1996–1998

The slight increase in fertility rates during the early 1990s (Table 1.3) was mainly due to the growing foreign population. Between 1990 and 1995, the share of live births of non-Austrian nationals increased from 7.3% to 13.8%, whereas the number of live births of Austrian nationals, except the years 1991 and 1996, was decreasing. The increased number of resident foreigners during the first half of the 1990s thereby slowed down the decline in the total number of births in Austria. The 7.0% decline in birth numbers between 1992 and 1995 resulted from an 8.7% decline in Austrian births, which was compensated by a 5.8% increase in foreign births. Even without any change in the average number of children per family, the number of births of Austrian nationals during the second half of the 1990s would have declined as a consequence of the previous birth decline in the 1960s and 1970s.

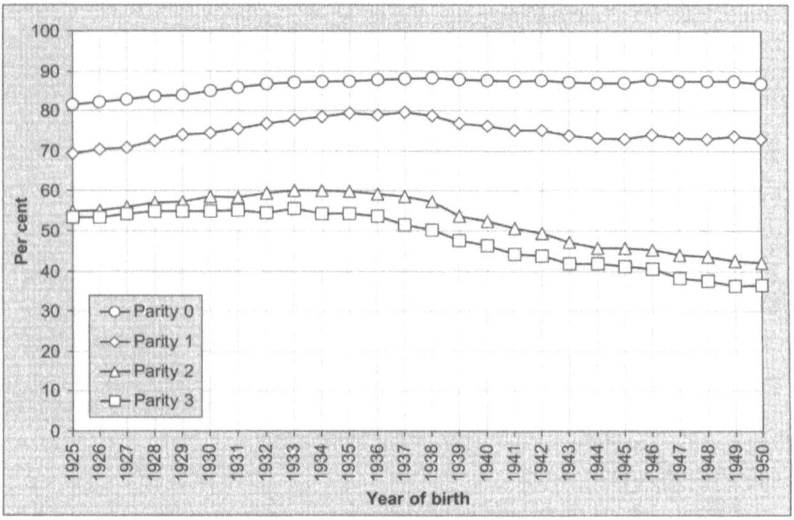


**Figure 1.4: Probability of Having a (Another) Child by Current Parity[1], Austrian Women Born in 1925–1950**

[1]Parity progression ratios at parities 4 and 5 are very close to those for parity 3 and are not shown in the chart
Sources: ACSO, 1996–1998

Cohort parity progression ratios (Figure 1.4) suggest that much of the fertility decline has been concentrated at parities two and above, which means that Austrians have had declining rates for third and higher-order births (Hanika, 1996). Age-specific fertility rates (Figure 1.5) show that the decline in overall fertility is mainly caused by declines in fertility of women below age 30, while fertility rates for women above age 30 have actually increased. Consequently, the mean age at childbearing increased to 27.82 years in 1996.

The pronounced regional variation in fertility (Table 1.4) is peculiar to Austria. In 1996, the TFR in Vorarlberg, the westernmost federal state, was 1.66, while it was only 1.26 in Burgenland, the easternmost federal state.

**Table 1.4: Total Fertility Rate by Federal States, 1996**

| Federal state | TFR | Federal state | TFR | Federal state | TFR |
|---|---|---|---|---|---|
| Vorarlberg | 1.66 | Salzburg | 1.46 | Lower Austria | 1.48 |
| Tyrol | 1.49 | Upper Austria | 1.53 | Vienna | 1.27 |
| Carinthia | 1.42 | Styria | 1.35 | Burgenland | 1.26 |

Source: ACSO, 1997

A further peculiarity of the Austrian fertility pattern is the large proportion of extramarital births. In 1996, 28.0% of all live births were outside marriage, as compared to 12.8% in 1970 and 17.8% in 1980. The percentage of extramarital births is the highest among the first births (41.8% in 1996) and decreases with the birth order (18.9% and 13.1% in 1996 for second and third births, respectively). Because the number of births outside marriage declined less than the number of births within marriage, the percentage of babies born outside marriage increased further to 28.8% in 1997. The proportion of extramarital births in 1996 was the highest in the federal states Carinthia (41.2%), Styria (38.0%), Tyrol (31.5%) and Salzburg (30.9%). In eastern Austria (Burgenland – 14.9%, Lower Austria – 18.3%) and western Austria (Vorarlberg – 21.0%), the share of extramarital births was much lower. These regional differences in fertility outside marriage can be explained by historical and socio-economic factors (see Haslinger, 1982; Kytir, 1993).

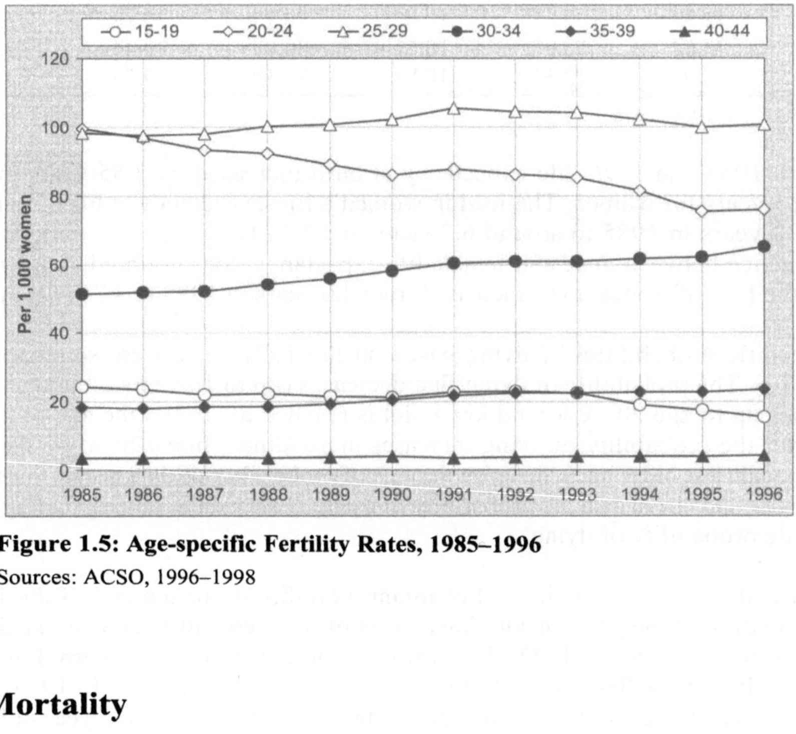


**Figure 1.5: Age-specific Fertility Rates, 1985–1996**

Sources: ACSO, 1996–1998

## 1.4 Mortality

After a sharp decline in mortality in the late 1940s and the 1950s, it seemed that this trend came to an end in the 1960s. However, similar to many Western industrialised countries, Austria experienced a further significant rise in life expectancy during the 1970s and 1980s, which was primarily due to a decline in mortality among old people.

**Table 1.5: Life Expectancy by Sex and Age, 1985–1996, in years**

| Year | Male | | | Female | | |
|---|---|---|---|---|---|---|
| | Life expectancy at | | | Life expectancy at | | |
| | Birth | 1 year | 60 years | Birth | 1 year | 60 years |
| 1985 | 70.38 | 70.31 | 16.96 | 77.34 | 77.05 | 20.99 |
| 1986 | 70.96 | 70.81 | 17.28 | 77.71 | 77.38 | 21.26 |
| 1987 | 71.47 | 71.24 | 17.52 | 78.10 | 77.79 | 21.54 |
| 1988 | 71.95 | 71.58 | 17.73 | 78.58 | 78.18 | 21.80 |
| 1989 | 71.99 | 71.65 | 17.77 | 78.73 | 78.32 | 21.98 |
| 1990 | 72.35 | 71.97 | 17.89 | 78.93 | 78.49 | 22.18 |
| 1991 | 72.41 | 72.02 | 18.03 | 79.05 | 78.57 | 22.21 |
| 1992 | 72.86 | 72.30 | 18.12 | 79.22 | 78.73 | 22.35 |
| 1993 | 72.96 | 72.50 | 18.30 | 79.43 | 78.87 | 22.55 |
| 1994 | 73.34 | 72.85 | 18.62 | 79.73 | 79.18 | 22.79 |
| 1995 | 73.54 | 72.97 | 18.67 | 80.05 | 79.44 | 22.93 |
| 1996 | 73.93 | 73.33 | 18.85 | 80.19 | 79.58 | 23.03 |

Sources: ACSO, 1996–1998

Between 1985 and 1996, life expectancy at birth increased by 3.55 years for men and 2.85 years for women. The lead in women's life expectancy at birth decreased from 7.0 years in 1985 to around 6.3 years in 1996. However, this trend towards convergence between male and female life expectancy does not hold at older ages, where the lead of women even increased from 4.0 years in 1985 to 4.2 years in 1996.

Age-specific probabilities of dying based on the 1991 census are summarised in Figure 1.6. The probability of dying first decreases (up to 10 years of age) and then increases up to age 20. A second low point is reached at around the age of 25, and thereafter the probability of dying increases in an almost linear trend on the logarithmic scale. At older ages, the growth rates of probability of dying start to decline. At all ages, the curve of male probability of dying is above the corresponding curve of female probability of dying.

Austria had a relatively high level of infant mortality up to the end of the 1970s, when one third of the gains in additional years of life were attributable to the decline of infant mortality. Since 1977, the most noticeable decline has occurred in infant mortality during the first week of life, as can be seen in Figure 1.7. In 1996, infant mortality was at a level of 5.1 deaths per 1,000 live births in the first year of life.

Parallel to the increase in life expectancy, the major causes of death shifted from infectious diseases to chronic-degenerative diseases and neoplasm. The main causes of death are now diseases of the circulatory system, neoplasms, and diseases of the digestive system. Moreover, during the last decade the risk of death from several of these diseases has shifted to older ages. Olshansky and Ault (1986) characterised this development as "the stage of delayed degenerative diseases". Evidence of a delay in deaths from specific causes of death in Austria (e.g. malignant neoplasm of digestive organs and peritoneum, heart diseases without acute myocardial infarction, etc.) is summarised in Kytir and Prskawetz (1995).

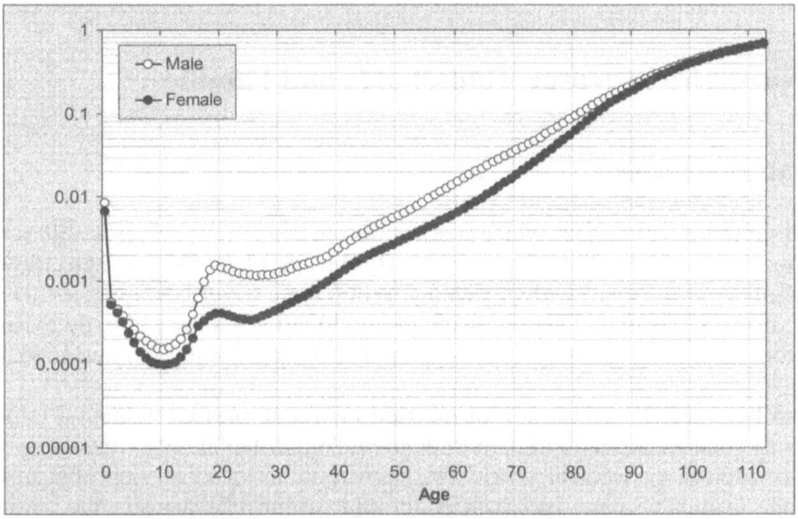


**Figure 1.6: Probability of Dying by Age, 1990–1992**

Sources: ACSO, 1996–1998

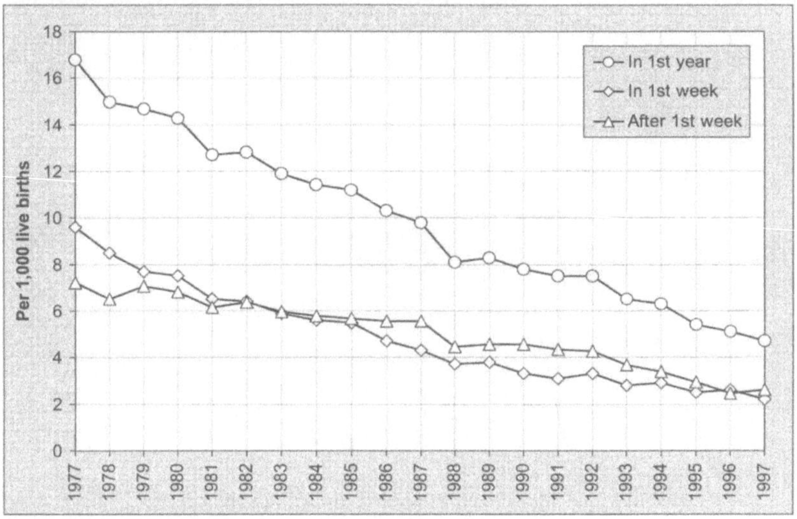


**Figure 1.7: Infant Mortality, 1977–1997**

Sources: ACSO, 1996–1998

Similar to fertility, life expectancy at birth clearly shows regional variation. Among males, in 1996, it was the highest in western Austria (in Vorarlberg – 75.90; in Tyrol

– 75.58; and in Salzburg – 74.70) and the lowest in eastern Austria (in Vienna – 73.01 and in Burgenland – 72.91).

## 1.5 Nuptiality, Divorce, Households and Families

### 1.5.1 Marital Status

According to the last census, which was conducted in 1991, marriage is still a common lifestyle for Austrian adults (Figure 1.8). By the age of 30 (35 for men), fewer than 20% of all women (men) within each age group have never been married. However, 10.0% of the total population in the age group 40–50 years have already experienced a divorce. This is three times as many men and twice as many women as in 1971.

The gap between the proportion of married men and married women at older ages reflects the decreasing ratio of men to women. Higher female life expectancy and the losses of men in the Second World War contribute to the excess number of women in the age groups 65 years and over. At the time of the 1991 census, the sex ratio for the population aged 60 and over was 605 males per 1,000 females and for the population aged 75 and over it was even less – 405 males per 1,000 females. This trend is also manifested in the increasing proportion of widowed women at older ages.

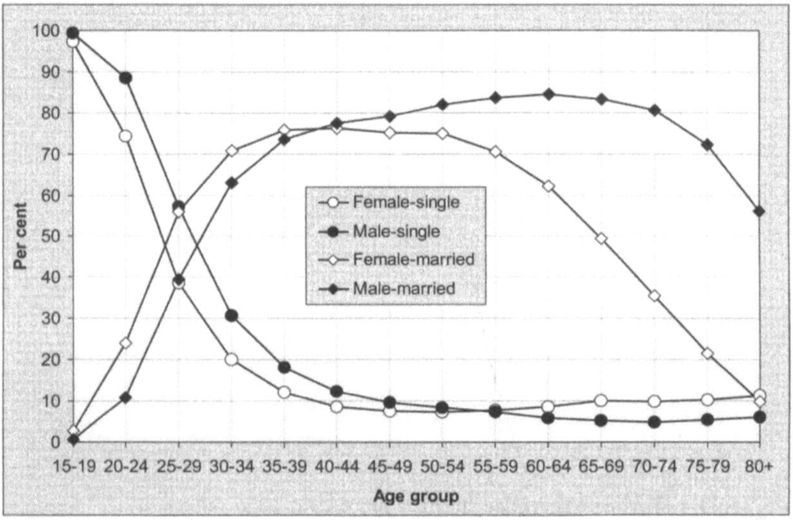


**Figure 1.8: Distribution of Population by Marital Status and Age Group, 1991**

Sources: ACSO, 1996–1998

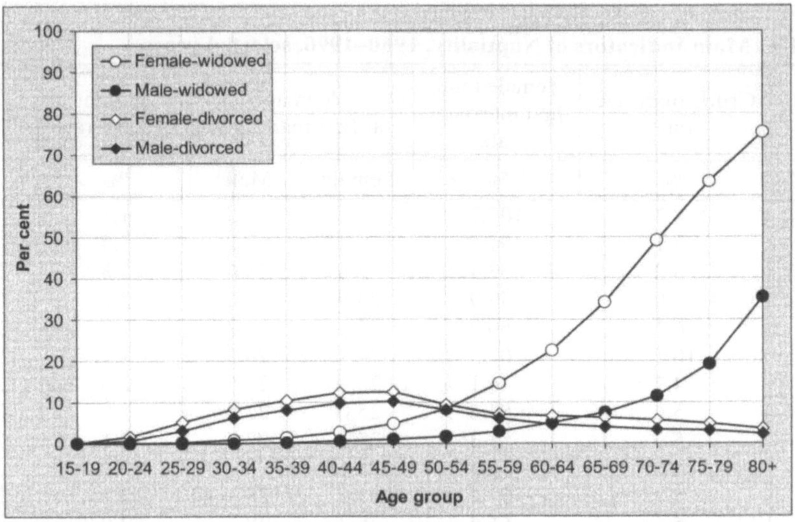


**Figure 1.8 (continued): Distribution of Population by Marital Status and Age Group, 1991**

Sources: ACSO, 1996–1998

### 1.5.2 Divorce

In the 1960s, the years of the post-war baby boom, there was a high propensity to marry; a declining age at marriage and a low propensity to divorce were common. During the 1970s and up to the mid-1980s, this trend had reversed. Marriage rates declined and divorce rates increased (Table 1.6). At the same time, the mean age at first marriage increased to 23.9 years for women and 26.6 years for men in 1985.

The increase in the marriage rate in 1987 was purely the result of the announcement that the marriage allowance was going to be abolished on 1 January 1988. As shown in Table 1.6, the boom was immediately followed by a bust. It seems that this change in legislation only affected the timing of marriages, and it probably had no effect on the proportion of ever-married persons.

The decrease in marriage rates and increase in divorce rates continued in the second half of the 1980s and in the 1990s. If these rates remain at the levels measured in 1996, only about two-third of women eligible to marry will ever do so and every third marriage will end in divorce. In 1996, a pronounced peak of divorce rates was observed in the second to fourth years of marriage, and the mean duration of marriages ending in divorce was 8.8 years. At the same time, marriages are delayed to older ages, as evidenced by the mean age at marriage, which increased from 1985 to 1996 by 3.5 years for women and by 3.3 years for men.

**Table 1.6: Main Indicators of Nuptiality, 1960–1996, selected years**

| Year | Crude marriage rate | Female total first marriage rate | Mean age at first marriage | | Crude divorce rate | Total divorce rate |
|---|---|---|---|---|---|---|
| | ‰ | % | Female | Male | ‰ | % |
| 1960 | 8.3 | 103.2 | .. | .. | 1.1 | 13.9 |
| 1970 | 7.1 | 91.3 | .. | .. | 1.4 | 18.1 |
| 1980 | 6.2 | 67.4 | 22.6 | 25.6 | 1.8 | 26.3 |
| 1985 | 5.9 | 59.9 | 23.9 | 26.6 | 2.0 | 30.8 |
| 1986 | 6.1 | 60.9 | 24.1 | 26.7 | 1.9 | 29.5 |
| 1987 | 10.1 | 107.3 | 24.1 | 26.5 | 1.9 | 29.5 |
| 1988 | 4.7 | 44.1 | 25.0 | 27.5 | 2.0 | 29.5 |
| 1989 | 5.6 | 54.6 | 25.0 | 27.4 | 2.0 | 30.6 |
| 1990 | 5.9 | 58.3 | 25.3 | 27.7 | 2.1 | 32.8 |
| 1991 | 5.6 | 55.5 | 25.6 | 28.0 | 2.1 | 33.5 |
| 1992 | 5.8 | 57.2 | 25.9 | 28.3 | 2.1 | 33.7 |
| 1993 | 5.6 | 56.4 | 26.3 | 28.7 | 2.0 | 34.0 |
| 1994 | 5.4 | 55.3 | 26.7 | 29.1 | 2.1 | 35.4 |
| 1995 | 5.3 | 55.4 | 27.1 | 29.5 | 2.3 | 38.3 |
| 1996 | 5.2 | 55.5 | 27.4 | 29.9 | 2.2 | 38.3 |

Sources: ACSO, 1996–1998

Although non-marital cohabitation has become more prevalent in Austria, only 8.0% of all couples irrespective of age were recorded by the microcensus 1991 as living in consensual unions[6]. One aspect of non-marital cohabitation, pre-marital cohabitation, has been much better documented since 1989. While in 1990 only 44.6% of all marriage license applications displayed the same address for bride and groom, by 1995 this number increased to 53.1%.

### 1.5.3 Households and Families

In 1996, there were 3.2 million private households[7] in Austria. Compared to 1990, this was an increase of 226,900 households, or 7.7%. Since the total population increased by only 3.8% in the same period, the average household size decreased from 2.6 to 2.5 persons. This downward trend was the strongest in Vienna, where only two persons (2.03) lived in an average household.

The decline in household size, which is identifiable in many other industrialised countries as well, can mainly be attributed to a significant increase in one-person households. While the number of private households increased by 7.7% from 1990 to 1996, as mentioned above, the number of one-person households increased by 13.9% from 820,400 to 934,400 in the same period. High rates of one-person households are an urban phenomenon: in 1996 one in four Viennese households was occupied by only one person. The number of private households with two, three or four persons also increased from 1990 to 1996, as can be seen in Figure 1.9. Meanwhile, the number of households with five persons decreased by 4.6% and the number of households with six or more persons dropped significantly – by 13.1%.

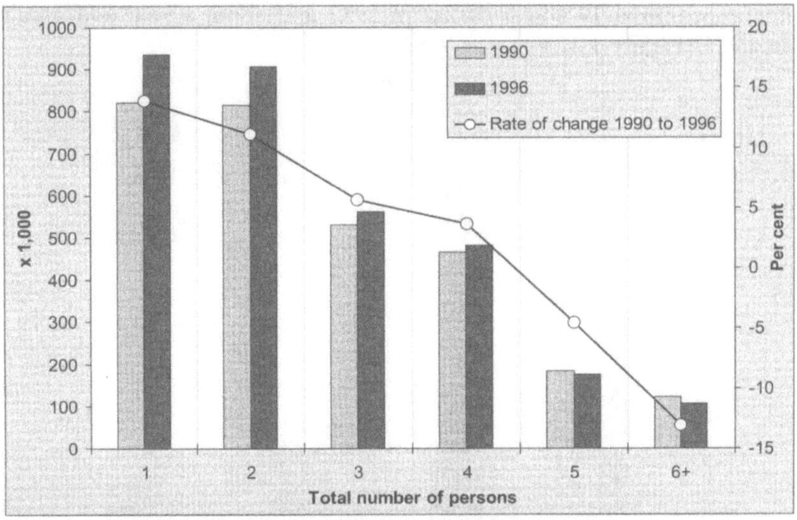


**Figure 1.9: Private Households by Size, 1990 and 1996**

Sources: ACSO, 1996–1998

During 1990–1996, the number of families in Austria increased by 5.3%, to a total of 2,245,700. More detailed analysis reveals that the number of families with no children under age 15 grew by 6.2% and represented a third (32.9%) of all family types in 1996, while the number of families with children rose by only 3.7% (Figure 1.10)[8]. The growth in households with single mothers was the highest of all, with a 6.4% increase.

The average number of children in a household has decreased as a consequence of the decline in birth rates since the second half of the 1960s, and in 1996, the average family[9] had 1.61 children aged under 15. Figure 1.11 illustrates the structure of Austrian families in 1996: every second family had no child, a third of all families consisted of a couple (married or cohabiting) with child(ren), one in ten was a single-mother family and 2% of all families were single-father families.

In family statistics, a person is no longer considered a "child" as soon as he or she marries or moves out. The age at which children leave their parents' household has increased in the last several decades. The main reason for this shift appears to be a longer period of education, which results in a later entrance into the labour market.

In 1991, nearly all persons aged 15 were statistically considered "children" living at parental home. Up to the age 19, the majority of boys tend to stay with the parents or parent, but after that age they become more independent. However, 50% of young men were still living in their parents' household at the age of 24. According to the results of the 1991 census, daughters left their parents earlier, since young women achieved the 50% threshold already at the age of 21, i.e. three years sooner than young men. The intersection point of the curves with the 50% line for both sexes was approximately a year earlier in 1981 and about a year and nine months earlier in 1971 (Figure 1.12).

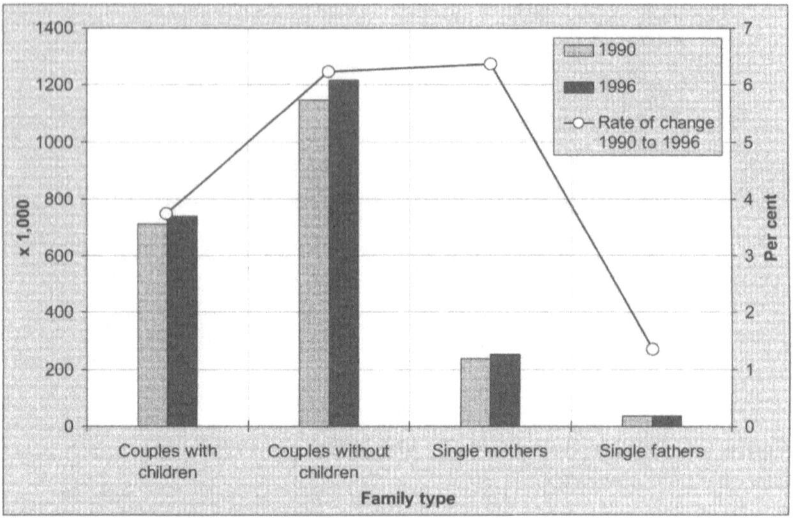


**Figure 1.10: Families by Family Type, 1990 and 1996**

Sources: ACSO, 1996–1998

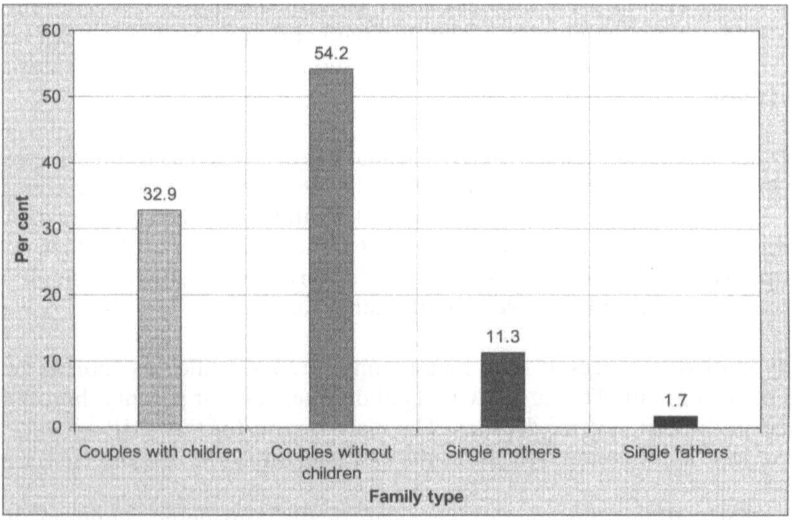


**Figure 1.11: Family Structure, 1996**

Source: ACSO, 1997

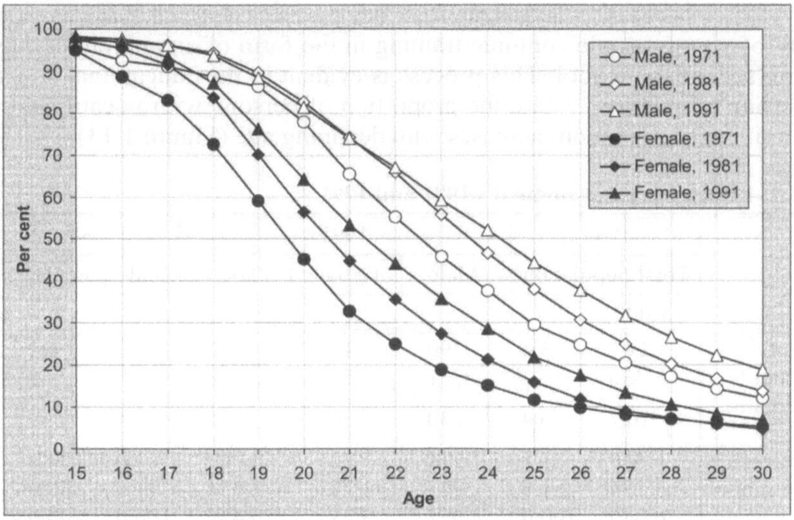


**Figure 1.12: Entrance into Adulthood (Survivor Function), 1971, 1981 and 1991**

Sources: ACSO, 1996–1998

## 1.6 Education

Educational attainment of Austrian population (Table 1.7), according to the results of the 1991 census, had the following structure: four out of ten people aged 15 and older had obtained only primary school education (compulsory education); a third had completed an apprenticeship; one in ten had graduated from an intermediate school; one in ten was a graduate of a high school (and thus eligible to enter university); and 5.0% had a university degree. Between 1981 and 1991, the percentage of university graduates had risen from 3.0% to 5.0%. An international comparison among OECD countries shows that Austria's percentage of university graduates is one of the lowest.

In spite of equal access to education and professional qualification for women and men, gender-specific differences were considerable in 1991: half of the female population had attained only primary school, as opposed to a third of the male population; 21.4% of women versus 44.0% of men had completed an apprenticeship (Table 1.7). Nevertheless, gender-specific differences are decreasing, and women of younger age groups could catch up with men and even "overtake" them.

Since the educational structure of the present population is largely determined by the access to education of former generations, it makes sense to look at the educational attainment of specific age groups. At present, only a minority of adolescents has no further education after the nine years of mandatory school attendance. The majority of young people continue training in the form of an apprenticeship or by attending secondary school. This process is evident in the educational structure of the Austrian population, where the proportion of persons with vocational training and/or university education increases with declining age (Figure 1.13).

**Table 1.7: Educational Attainment[1], 1981 and 1991**

| | 1981 | | 1991 | | | 1991 | | |
|---|---|---|---|---|---|---|---|---|
| | Total population | | Male | Female | Total | Male | Female | Total |
| | 1,000 | % | 1,000 | | | % | | |
| University[2] | 207 | 3.4 | 190 | 142 | 332 | 6.2 | 4.2 | 5.2 |
| High school | 436 | 7.2 | 331 | 297 | 628 | 10.8 | 8.8 | 9.8 |
| Intermediate school[3] | 627 | 10.4 | 230 | 505 | 735 | 7.5 | 14.9 | 11.4 |
| Apprenticeship | 1,640 | 27.1 | 1,344 | 725 | 2,069 | 44.0 | 21.4 | 32.1 |
| Primary school | 3,134 | 51.8 | 962 | 1,713 | 2,674 | 31.5 | 50.6 | 41.5 |
| Total | 6,045 | 100.0 | 3,057 | 3,382 | 6,439 | 100.0 | 100.0 | 100.0 |

[1]Educational attainment is defined as the most advanced level a person has reached in the educational system; all data concerns population at age 15 and older
[2]University includes *Hochschule* and *hochschulverwandte Ausbildung*
[3]Intermediate school stands for *Fachschule*. The final examination does not qualify for entrance to university.
Sources: ACSO, 1996–1998

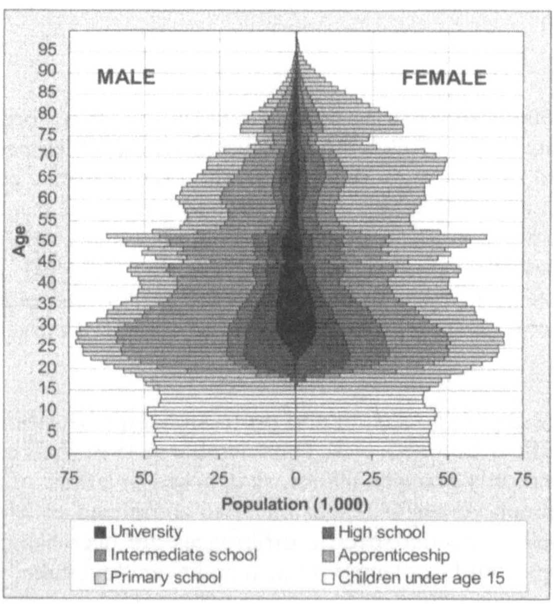


**Figure 1.13: Educational Attainment by Age and Gender, 1991**

Source: based on the 1991 census data

Nevertheless, among persons aged 20 to 29, about one-fifth (22.0%) had only a primary school education. Given that the majority has completed their final level of educational attainment at this age (high school, apprenticeship and intermediate school), this percentage is surprisingly high. This means that one-fifth of all Austrians born in the 1960s did not take advantage of the "expansion of education" (ACSO, 1996, p. T5).

## 1.7 Labour Force Participation

A short summary of the development of the Austrian labour force during the last decades (Table 1.8) highlights the increase in the proportion of foreigners from 1.4% in 1961 to 8.2% in 1991. Labour force participation rates of foreigners were highest during the first wave of immigration in the late 1960s and increased again during the most recent influx of immigrants in the late 1980s and early 1990s. In the meantime, return migration of many foreigners as well as economic downswings have led to a decline in the labour force participation rate of foreigners.

High economic growth during the late 1980s, the increasing labour force participation of women and the entrance of the baby boom generation to the labour market led to an increase in the labour force participation of Austrian nationals to 46% in 1991. As regards gender differences, the gap between male and female rates of labour force participation has decreased for Austrian nationals but widened for non-Austrian nationals.

**Table 1.8: Labour Force and Labour Force Participation Rates by Citizenship and Sex[1], 1961-1991, selected years**

| Year | All population | | | Austrian nationals | | | Non-Austrian nationals | | |
|---|---|---|---|---|---|---|---|---|---|
| | Total | Male | Female | Total | Male | Female | Total | Male | Female |
| | Labour force (1,000) | | | | | | | | |
| 1961 | 3,370 | 2,010 | 1,360 | 3,323 | 1,977 | 1,345 | 47 (1.4)[2] | 33 (1.6) | 15 (1.1) |
| 1971 | 3,133 | 1,930 | 1,203 | 2,996 | 1,834 | 1,161 | 138 (4.4) | 96 (5.0) | 41 (3.4) |
| 1981 | 3,412 | 2,035 | 1,377 | 3,246 | 1,928 | 1,318 | 166 (4.9) | 107 (5.3) | 58 (4.2) |
| 1991 | 3,684 | 2,159 | 1,525 | 3,384 | 1,960 | 1,423 | 301 (8.2) | 199 (9.2) | 10 (6.7) |
| | Labour force participation rate (%)[3] | | | | | | | | |
| 1961 | 47.6 | 61.0 | 36.0 | 47.7 | 61.0 | 36.1 | 46.3 | 58.9 | 31.2 |
| 1971 | 41.8 | 54.6 | 30.4 | 41.2 | 53.9 | 30.0 | 65.0 | 75.0 | 49.6 |
| 1981 | 45.2 | 57.0 | 34.6 | 44.7 | 56.5 | 34.2 | 56.9 | 66.2 | 45.1 |
| 1991 | 47.3 | 57.5 | 37.7 | 46.5 | 56.6 | 37.3 | 58.1 | 67.8 | 45.4 |

[1]1971 including temporary foreign labour force
[2]Numbers in brackets indicate the share of non-Austrian nationals in % of the total labour force
[3]Labour force participation rate indicates the share of population in labour force in % of the total population
Sources: ACSO, 1996–1998; authors' calculations

As evidenced in Table 1.9, the increase in the labour force participation rates during the last decade was accompanied by a steady increase in the unemployment rate.

**Table 1.9: Unemployment Rate[1], 1985 and 1990–1997, per cent**

| | 1985 | 1990 | 1991 | 1992 | 1993 | 1994 | 1995 | 1996 | 1997 |
|---|---|---|---|---|---|---|---|---|---|
| Total | 4.8 | 5.4 | 5.8 | 5.9 | 6.8 | 6.5 | 6.6 | 7.0 | 7.1 |
| Austrian nationals | 5.9 | 5.2 | 5.7 | 5.8 | 6.6 | 6.4 | 6.5 | 6.9 | 6.9 |
| Non-Austrian nationals | 4.8 | 7.8 | 7.1 | 7.4 | 8.9 | 8.0 | 7.7 | 8.4 | 8.4 |

[1]The denominator in the unemployment rate is defined as the sum of employed and registered unemployed workers
Sources: BMAGS; AMS; Main Association of the Austrian Social Security Institutions; authors' calculations

## 1.8 Migration

During the last several decades, interest has been focused on Austria more as a country of immigration, but it has been characterised by emigration throughout its history as well (Neyer, 1996).

Emigration from Austria increased during the decades after the Second World War[10]. While in 1960 about 193,000 Austrians were living abroad in 13 of the most important destination countries, this number had increased to 323,000 in 1990 (Bauer-Fraiji and Fraiji, 1996). The number of Austrians living in Germany increased from 47,000 in 1951 to 183,000 in 1990, and an additional 55,000 Austrians have been naturalised in Germany since 1945. In the second most important country for Austrian emigrants, Switzerland, there were about 22,000 Austrians in 1950. This number had doubled by the 1970s and thereafter decreased to a level of 30,000 in 1990. In addition, about 29,000 Austrians were naturalised in Switzerland, and about 11,500 Austrians have been counted as *Grenzgänger* (people who live in one country and work in the other) in 1993. In contrast, Austrian emigration to typical destination countries like the US and Canada declined after 1945, while emigration to Australia and South Africa increased.

Immigration to Austria since the Second World War (Figure 1.14) can be classified into distinct stages according to the net migration flows of foreigners (Bauböck, 1994; Biffl, 1993; Prskawetz, 1997). The immediate post-war period was characterised by a large influx of ethnic Germans from different parts of Central and Eastern Europe. The geographic location, the neutral status and the Western democratic system made Austria attractive as a transition point from which subsequent migration to larger Western countries could be organised (Bauböck, op. cit.). Three major waves of refugees from Hungary in 1956–1957, from Czechoslovakia in 1968–1969, and from Poland in 1981–1982 followed.

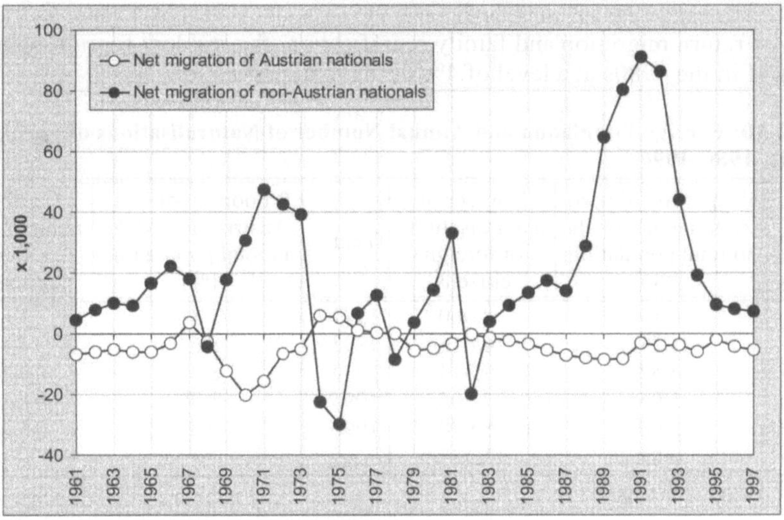


**Figure 1.14: Net Migration[1], 1961–1997**

[1]Migration statistics are only available since 1996. Statistics on net migration, emigration and immigration before 1996 are estimates based on the residual method (censuses, vital statistics and labour statistics)
Source: based on ACSO data

Strong economic growth during the 1960s (from 1962 to 1967, real GDP grew by about 4% per year), the small birth cohorts of the early 1950s, the retirement of large birth cohorts born before 1915 as well as the emigration from Austria led to supply shortages in the Austrian labour market. Additionally, the supply shortage was reinforced by decreasing labour force participation due to increasing educational attainment and improved social security arrangements for older workers, which reduced the level of labour force activity at the beginning and at the end of a working life period. The emigration of Austrian nationals reached a peak in 1970. To increase the labour supply, the so-called "social partners" (employers' representatives and trade unions) agreed upon the recruitment of foreign workers and decided upon specific quotas by region and sector. Agreements were signed with Spain in 1962, with Turkey in 1964, and with Yugoslavia in 1966. This "guest-worker" system reached its first peak at the beginning of the 1970s at the level of 30,000 people per year. During the 1970s and 1980s, as foreign workers started to settle in Austria, the number of naturalisations began to increase (Table 1.10).

Periods of economic stagnation after the first oil price shock of 1973 and the entry of the baby boom generation into the labour market led to a pronounced decrease in "guest-worker" recruitment and to a reduction of immigration, accompanied by increasing emigration. Except for the influx of Polish refugees, net migration was relatively stable during the 1980s. The pronounced decrease in the absolute number and proportion of foreigners in Austria reached its peak in the years 1975 and 1982, with a net migration of foreigners -24,543 and -20,256 people, respectively. After waves of return migration and family reunification, the resident foreign population stabilised in the 1980s at a level of 4% of the total population.

**Table 1.10: Foreign Population and Annual Number of Naturalisations of Foreign Citizens, 1986–1996**

| Year | Proportion of non-Austrian nationals in total population (%) | Number of naturalisations of foreign citizens | Year | Proportion of non-Austrian nationals in total population (%) | Number of naturalisations of foreign citizens |
|---|---|---|---|---|---|
| 1986 | 4.15 | 8,060 | 1992 | 7.87 | 11,656 |
| 1987 | 4.29 | 6,616 | 1993 | 8.63 | 14,131 |
| 1988 | 4.52 | 7,314 | 1994 | 8.89 | 15,275 |
| 1989 | 5.06 | 7,305 | 1995 | 8.90 | 14,366 |
| 1990 | 5.90 | 8,980 | 1996 | 9.00 | 15,627 |
| 1991 | 6.82 | 11,137 | | | |

Sources: ACSO, 1996–1998

Economic growth at the end of the 1980s (in 1988–1990, real GDP grew by about 4% per year) incited the largest inflow of migrants to Austria since 1945–1946. While new "push" factors and emigration opportunities emerged in Eastern Europe after 1989, internal "pull" factors in Austria have also gained strength. This marked increase of labour and refugee immigration brought the share of non-Austrian nationals in the total population from 4.52% in 1988 to 6.82% in 1991 (Table 1.10). The economic downswing of 1993 and more restrictive legal regulations concerning immigration led to a decline in the net migration of foreigners to 44,000. The continued implementation of these restrictive policies led to a continuous decrease of net migration of non-Austrian nationals – down to 13,107 in 1994, and 7,439 in 1995.

## 1.9 Population Policy and Social Expenditures

### 1.9.1 Population Policy

Austria's family and population-related policies include measures to alleviate the financial burden for those who decide to have a child (or children) and to provide access to contraceptives and the option of pregnancy termination[11] for those who do not intend to have a child (in their present situation). One of the policy aims is a redistribution – to level out the financial difference between those who rear children and those who are childless, without privileging a certain type of living (Federal Government of Austria, 1994, p.31).

Paid maternity leave is one of the most frequently discussed measures of family policy. Income-related paid maternity leave of eight weeks before and eight weeks after delivery is now granted to employed women[12]. After this time, "dependently employed"[13] mothers may take parental leave (paid as a lump sum) up to the first birthday of the child. In July 1990, parental leave was extended to the child's second birthday and fathers were also entitled to take parental leave. Moreover, a parent could take part-time parental leave or parental leave could be split up between the parents up to the third or the fourth birthday of the child. As of July 1996, parental leave was reduced to 18 months for one parent and six months for the other parent, and a maximum of three years of part-time parental leave could be taken in a combination with a part-time work.

Such employment-related regulations and family policies aim to ease the double burden of work and family for women with children, especially during the first years of a child's life. Nevertheless, the combination of child rearing and employment remains difficult, due to the inflexibility of the Austrian parental leave system and the lack of a policy oriented to working mothers (Hoem, Prskawetz and Neyer, 1999). At present, political debate is focused on the proposed introduction of paid maternity leave for all women who give birth, irrespective of their employment status.

A comparison among the OECD countries clearly shows that Austria pays the highest family allowances in the form of direct transfers (about 14.2% of the average worker's gross income), but fiscal benefits for children in Austria (about 3.7% of an industrial worker's gross income) are below the OECD average. A comprehensive summary of the instruments and measures aimed at promoting families can be found in the National Report on the Austrian Population (Federal Government of Austria, op. cit.).

At the beginning of the 1990s, population policy discussions centred on immigration to Austria that was being caused by the worsening standards of living in some Central and Eastern European countries and especially by the war in Bosnia-Herzegovina. Since 1992, a new law regulates the immigration of foreigners. Future migration policy will not be motivated exclusively by demographics – it will be determined mainly by the absorption capacity of the domestic labour and housing markets (Federal Government of Austria, op. cit.).

### 1.9.2 Social Expenditures

Based on the criteria of EUROSTAT, social expenditures are registered according to a harmonised system to allow comparative analysis[14]. Austria's social rate[15] increased between 1990 and 1997 from 26.7% to 29.5% of the GDP and in 1995 it was slightly under the EU-mean of 28.4%.

The development of the social rate in Austria (Figure 1.15) reflects the economic growth of the 1980s – with a rise in the social rate during the years of economic recession up to 1987 and a subsequent fall during the economic boom years 1988 and 1989. From 1991 to 1994, the increase in the social rate was caused by structural changes such as the introduction of a second year of paid maternity leave, improvements in legislation concerning the retirement of women, the introduction of tax deductions for children, and nursing allowances. Despite of less favourable economic conditions (e.g. an increase in unemployment), the social rate was stabilised in 1995 as a consequence of the need for budgetary consolidation in order to reach fiscal and budgetary standards set by the European Union.

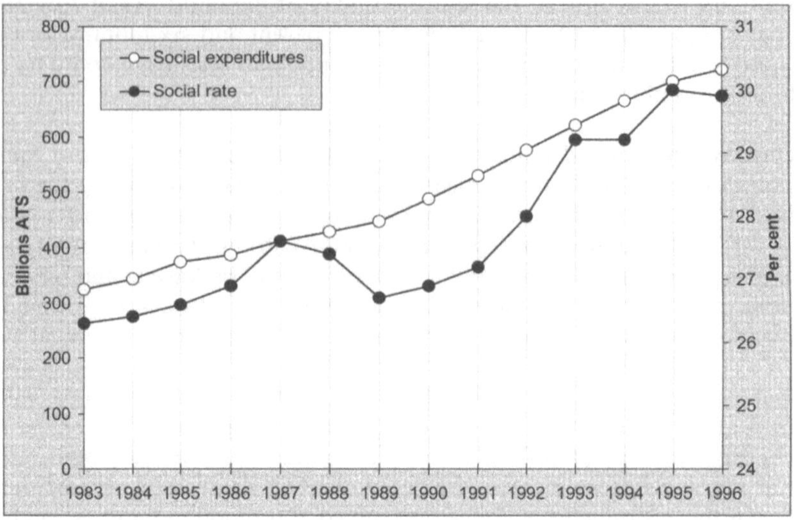


**Figure 1.15: Social Expenditures and Social Rate, 1983–1996**

Sources: Austrian Institute of Economic Research; Main Association of the Austrian Social Security Institutions; ACSO, 1996–1998

Austria's entrance into the European Union in 1996 and the need to comply with EU-criteria, on the one hand, and demographic developments, on the other, led to reduction of social expenditures[16] so as to consolidate the Austrian budget in form of the so-called *Strukturanpassungsgesetz 1995* and the *Strukturanpassungsgesetz 1996* (BMAGS, 1996; 1997). Due to these measures, the social rate remained stable in 1995 and even decreased slightly in 1996 despite an economic recession[17].

The structure of social expenditures in Austria is different from that of most countries in the European Union. While expenditures for aged and other economically dependent persons and families are higher in Austria, expenditures for unemployment payments as well as for illness and handicapped persons are lower (Table 1.11).

Besides economic indicators, demographic shifts and socio-political measures influence the volume of expenditures for social security as well. The impact of demographic effects is evident in the expenditures for ageing persons: in 1997, about three million people received a pension in Austria. These numbers represent a ratio of 620 pensions per 1,000 contributing insured persons, compared to 590 per 1,000 in 1990. Between 1981 and 1991, the number of persons aged 60 to 64 increased from 308,000 to 398,000. This change significantly affected the number of persons receiving retirement payments. Furthermore, there was a structural shift among retired persons, which was caused by a rising number of white-collar pensioners with comparatively higher pensions (BMAGS, 1998).

**Table 1.11: Social Expenditures in Austria and the European Union, 1995, per cent**

| | Percentage of the total social expenditures | | Percentage of the GDP | |
|---|---|---|---|---|
| | Austria | EU-15 | Austria | EU-15 |
| Aged and other economically dependent persons | 48 | 44 | 13.9 | 11.9 |
| Illness, handicapped persons | 33 | 36 | 9.5 | 10.0 |
| Families | 11 | 8 | 3.3 | 2.1 |
| Unemployment | 6 | 8 | 1.6 | 2.3 |
| Others | 1 | 4 | 0.4 | 1.0 |

Sources: EUROSTAT, 1998; BMAGS, 1998, p. 90

The increase in life expectancy described above also affected expenditures for retirement payments. Moreover, the mean age at retirement was decreasing up to the mid-1990s, and then, since 1995, it has remained stable. In 1997, the average person entering retirement was 57.6 years old, whereas women retired, on average, one and a half year earlier than men – at 56.8 years, compared to 58.4 years for men.

By international standards, Austria has an advanced public health system. Nearly the entire population has access to health care. About 99% of the resident population have either individual health insurance or are insured free of charge via a family member. The system is largely financed on the basis of obligatory public health insurance. This is supplemented by an increasing number of private health insurance companies. The decline in births together with the ongoing process of population ageing will result in a shrinking labour force, while the growing number of elderly will raise health-care costs and increase the need for nursing services in the medium and long term (Federal Government of Austria, op. cit.).

### 1.9.3 Poverty

In political and scholarly debates, various definitions of poverty are used. Consequently, the estimated number of poor persons is influenced by the definition one refers to. According to the criteria of EUROSTAT, a person is at risk of poverty if his or her income is below half of the average income per capita. In 1994, between 11% and 14% of the Austrian population were at risk of poverty[18].

Taking only income into account results in an inadequate picture of the actual situation. Non-monetary poverty indicators also have to be considered. Therefore, it can be said that a person lives in poverty if low income is combined with a lack of certain social standards (e.g. a sub-standard dwelling, inability to pay for heating, clothes and food). According to this definition and the budget panel, 5% of the Austrian population in 1994 were affected by poverty. A comparison with the countries of the European Union shows that poverty is relatively low in Austria.

Even if the definition of poverty is arbitrary to a certain extent, the structure of the population affected by poverty remains the same. Among those with a higher risk of getting into a precarious financial situation and thus being excluded from certain social activities are: households of unemployed persons (above all long-term unemployed persons); families of foreign workers; farmers; single mothers or fathers; families with many children; families with only one breadwinner; households of persons working in economic sectors with low wages.

## Notes

1. The authors wish to thank Richard Gisser, Elfriede Hammer, Gerhard Hammer, Alexander Hanika, Hildegard Plha and Andrea Schiel from the Austrian Central Statistical Office for providing relevant data on the Austrian population structure and Karl Brehmer for editorial advice. The present survey is mainly based on the report of the Federal Government of Austria (1994), The Demographic Yearbook of the Austrian Central Statistical Office (1997) and The Social Report of the Federal Ministry of Labour, Health and Social Affairs (1996, 1997 and 1998).
2. The views expressed in this paper are the authors' own views and do not necessarily represent those of the Max Planck Institute for Demographic Research.
3. The old age dependency ratio represents the proportion of people aged 60 or over to the working age population (people aged 15–59). Similarly, the young age dependency ratio is the ratio of persons below age 15 to the working age population.
4. Immigration from Spain was negligible.
5. In the Austrian Family and Fertility Survey (FFS), which was conducted between December 1995 and May 1996, about 49% of all male and about 51% of all female respondents indicated two children as the ideal norm for a family (UNECE/UNPF, 1998)
6. The Austrian microcensus represents a quarterly sample survey of the Austrian population. Dwellings are chosen according to selection criteria. The sample size varies between 28,000 and 30,000 dwellings (about 1.0% of all Austrian dwellings), which are selected to be representative of the Austrian population. Each quarter, 1/8 of the sample is replaced by new addresses.
7. A private household consists of all persons who live together and share costs of food and other essentials (ACSO, 1998). Apart from private households, there are also institutional households, which will not be considered in this contribution due to their negligible numerical significance.

8. Only children under 15 years of age are taken into consideration.
9. This number refers only to families with children.
10. Statistics on emigration numbers have to rely on data available in destination countries since Austria lacks a comprehensive system of migration statistics. A first attempt to quantify emigration from Austria since 1945 is summarised in Bauer-Fraiji and Fraiji, op. cit.
11. At the beginning of 1999, the introduction of Mifegyne was accompanied by impassioned political discussions. According to information provided by the Ministry of Social Affairs, no application for the use of this option has been filed so far.
12. To receive the so-called "Wochengeld", a woman has to be employed at least 13 weeks or three months, and the termination of the last employment has to be within 32 weeks before the start of the leave (Knöfler, 1996, p. 92).
13. These are mainly women with wage and salary income.
14. This system is called "ESSPROS 1996", which stands for European System of Integrated Social Protection Statistics, a system providing a means of analysing and comparing social protection financial flows. Social protection is defined as follows in the ESSPROS Manual 1996: "Social protection encompasses all interventions from public or private bodies intended to relieve households and individuals of the burden of a defined set of risks or needs, provided that there is neither a simultaneous reciprocal nor an individual arrangement involved. The list of risks or needs that may give rise to social protection is fixed by convention as follows: 1. Sickness/health care; 2. Disability; 3. Old age; 4. Survivors; 5. Family/children; 6. Unemployment; 7. Housing; 8. Social exclusion not elsewhere classified" (EUROSTAT, 1998, p. 7).
15. The social rate is the share of social expenditures in the Gross Domestic Product (GDP).
16. For example, reduction of family allowances, reduction of nursing allowances, introduction of cost-sharing in the health system, increases in contributions for pension insurance and social insurance for the self-employed and for farmers, reduction of paid maternity leave to 18 months if only one parent (usually a mother) takes maternity leave (as mentioned above).
17. Some impacts of the *Strukturanpassungsgesetz 1995* and the *Strukturanpassungsgesetz 1996* will be noticed in the coming years, e.g. retirement measures in 2000 and 2003 (a step-by-step rise in the assessment period for retirement dependent on the age of retirement).
18. These calculations are based on the budget panel.

## References

ACSO (Austrian Central Statistical Office) (1996), *Volkszählung 1991. Bildungsstand der Bevölkerung*, Vienna: Österreichisches Statistisches Zentralamt.

ACSO (Austrian Central Statistical Office) (1997), *Demographisches Jahrbuch Österreichs 1996*, Vienna: Österreichisches Statistisches Zentralamt.

ACSO (Austrian Central Statistical Office) (1998), *Mikrozensus Jahresergebnisse 1996*, Vienna: Österreichisches Statistisches Zentralamt.

AMS (Labour Market Service) (1998), *Die Arbeitsmarktlage im Jahr 1997*, Vienna: Arbeitsmarktservice.

Bauböck, R. (1994), Western Europe: Austria, In: S. Ardittis (ed.), *The Politics of East-West Migration*, St. Martin's Press, pp. 155–170.

Bauer-Fraiji, A. and A. Fraiji (1996), Auswanderung von Österreichern und Österreicherinnen nach 1945: Statistische Darstellung, In: T. Horvath and G. Neyer (eds.), *Auswanderung aus Österreich. Von der Mitte des 19. Jahrhunderts bis zur Gegenwart*, pp. 279–321, Vienna: Böhlau-Verlag.

Biffl, G. (1993), The Austrian Migration System, Paper presented at the conference on Migration and International Co-operation: Challenge for OECD-Countries, Madrid.

BMAGS (Federal Ministry of Labour, Health and Social Affairs) (1996), *Bericht über die soziale Lage 1995*, Vienna: Bundesministerium für Arbeit und Soziales.

BMAGS (Federal Ministry of Labour, Health and Social Affairs) (1997), *Bericht über die soziale Lage 1996*, Vienna: Bundesministerium für Arbeit und Soziales.

BMAGS (Federal Ministry of Labour, Health and Social Affairs) (1998), *Bericht über die soziale Lage 1997*, Vienna: Bundesministerium für Arbeit und Soziales.

EUROSTAT (Statistical Office of the European Communities) (1998), *Social Protection Expenditure and Receipts, 1980–1995*, Luxembourg: EUROSTAT.

Fassmann, H. and R. Münz (1995), *Einwanderungsland Österreich?* Vienna: Jugend&Volk.

Federal Government of Austria (1994), *National Report on Population – Austria*, Vienna.

Hanika, A. (1996), Volkszählung 1991: Paritäts-Fruchtbarkeitstafeln, *Statistische Nachrichten*, Vol. 6, pp. 426–431.

Haslinger, A. (1982), Unehliche Geburten in Österreich. Historische und regionale Muster, *Demographische Informationen 1982*, pp. 2–34.

Hoem, J., A. Prskawetz and G. Neyer (1999), *Third births in Austria: the effect of educational attainment and labour-force attachment*, Working Paper WP 1999-002, Rostock: Max Planck Institute for Demographic Research.

Knöfler, M. (1996), *Mutterschutzgesetz und Eltern-Karenzurlaubsgesetz*, Vienna: Verlag des Österreichischen Gewerkschaftsbundes.

Kytir, J. (1993), Unehelich, vorehelich, ehelich: Familiengründung im Wandel, *Demographische Informationen 1992/93*, pp. 29–40.

Kytir, J. and A. Prskawetz (1995), Life expectancy at age 60 – epidemiologic scenarios assuming delayed mortality for selected causes of death, *European Journal of Population*, Vol. 11, pp. 261–273.

Neyer, G. (1996), Auswanderungen aus Österreich: Von der Mitte des 19. Jahrhunderts bis zur Gegenwart, *Demographische Informationen* 1995/96, pp. 60–70.

Olshansky, J.S. and B. Ault (1986), The fourth stages of the epidemiological transition: The age of delayed and degenerative diseases, *The Milbank Memorial Fund Quarterly*, Vol. 64(3), pp. 355–391.

Prskawetz, A. (1997), *Wirtschaftliche Auswirkungen der Migration in Österreich 1961–1995*, Forschungsbericht 17, Vienna: Institute for Demography, Austrian Academy of Sciences.

UNECE/UNPF (United Nations Economic Commission for Europe/United Nations Population Fund) (1998), *Fertility and Family Surveys in Countries of the ECE Region. Standard Country Report. Austria*, New York and Geneva: United Nations.

# 2

# Demographic Development of the Republic Belarus

**Liudmila P. Shakhotska**

## 2.1 Population Size and Growth

The Republic Belarus is one of the 15 new independent states that have emerged as a result of the disintegration of the former Soviet Union. On 27 July 1990, the Supreme Soviet of Belarus adopted the Declaration of Independence, which was granted the status of the state law a year later. The territory of Belarus is of a compact size – 207.6 thousand square kilometres. According to the 1999 census, the population of Belarus is 10.037 million people. By the absolute size of the population, Belarus occupies the fifth position after Russia, Ukraine, Uzbekistan and Kazakhstan. The absolute size of the population of Belarus is 14 times smaller than the population of Russia, 5 times smaller than Ukraine's population but 1.3 times larger than population of the all three independent Baltic States (Lithuania, Latvia, Estonia) combined.

The population density at the beginning of 1999 was 49 people per 1 square kilometre. 69.8% of the total population resides in 102 cities and 110 townships, 30.2% of the total population lives in rural areas. Almost one-quarter of the total population is concentrated in the capital of Belarus – Minsk.

From the end of the Second World War to the beginning of the 1990s, the population of Belarus was growing but at a declining rate (Figure 2.1). The gradual slowing of growth became noticeable in the 1970s and significantly intensified during the 1990s. This was caused by the decline in the natural increase of the population (Table 2.1).

At the end of the 1970s, compared to the 1950s, the natural increase of the population dropped by half. During the second half of the 1990s, the natural increase of the population became negative. The decline of the natural increase of the population was caused not only by the lower number of births, but also by the increase in the number of deaths (Figures 2.2, 2.3 and 2.4). In 1993, for the first time in the history of Belarus the number of deaths was higher than the number of births by 11.2 thousand. This new trend has been growing steadily. In 1994, the difference between the number of births and deaths was 19.4 thousand, in 1995 – 33.6 thousand, in 1996 – 37.6 thousand, in 1997 – 47.1 thousand, and in 1998 – 44.7 thousand.

The current demographic situation in Belarus is a direct result of the republic's population development during previous years. Starting from the 1970s, and the 1960s in the cities, the Republic of Belarus has been experiencing a continuous gradual decline of population growth. The natural increase of the population during these years could be attributed to the age structure of the population. In 1998, the population of Belarus was "replacing" itself only by 60.5%, in the urban areas by 54.6%, and in the rural areas by 81.7%. This trend has caused depopulation.

**Table 2.1: Population Growth, 1950–1997**

| Period | Total population[1] | Total increase | Natural increase | Net migration | Annual growth rate |
|---|---|---|---|---|---|
| | 1,000 | | | | % |
| 1950–1954 | 7,757.2 | 48.2 | 644.9 | -596.7 | 0.1 |
| 1955–1959 | 6,147.4 | 390.2 | 718.7 | -328.5 | 1.0 |
| 1960–1964 | 8,557.9 | 410.5 | 634.8 | -224.3 | 1.0 |
| 1965–1969 | 9,002.3 | 444.4 | 437.6 | 6.8 | 1.0 |
| 1970–1974 | 9,345.2 | 342.9 | 378.8 | -35.9 | 0.8 |
| 1975–1979 | 9,621.8 | 276.6 | 322.1 | - 45.5 | 0.6 |
| 1980–1984 | 9,968.9 | 347.1 | 329.3 | 17.8 | 0.7 |
| 1985–1989 | 10,259.3 | 290.4 | 307.2 | -16.8 | 0.6 |
| 1990–1994 | 10,346.0 | 86.7 | 34.0 | 53.0 | 0.2 |
| 1995–1997 | 10,251.7 | -93.5 | -117.3 | 23.8 | -0.3 |

[1]*De facto* population as of 1 January of a given year
Source: Goskomstat RB, 1998, pp. 58, 69

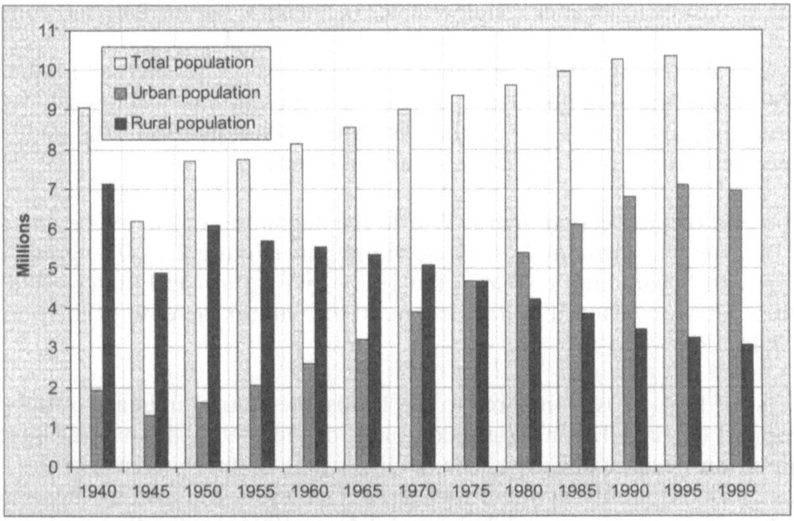


**Figure 2.1: Population, 1940–1999, selected years**
Sources: based on Goskomstat BSSR, 1990; Goskomstat RB, 1999a

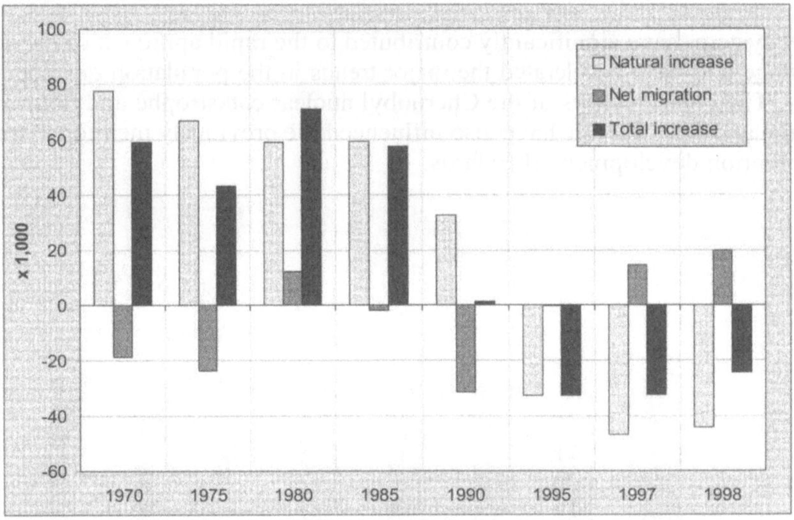


**Figure 2.2: Population Growth by Components – Total Population, 1970–1998, selected years**

Sources: Goskomstat RB, 1999a, p. 70; Goskomstat RB, 1999b, p. 44

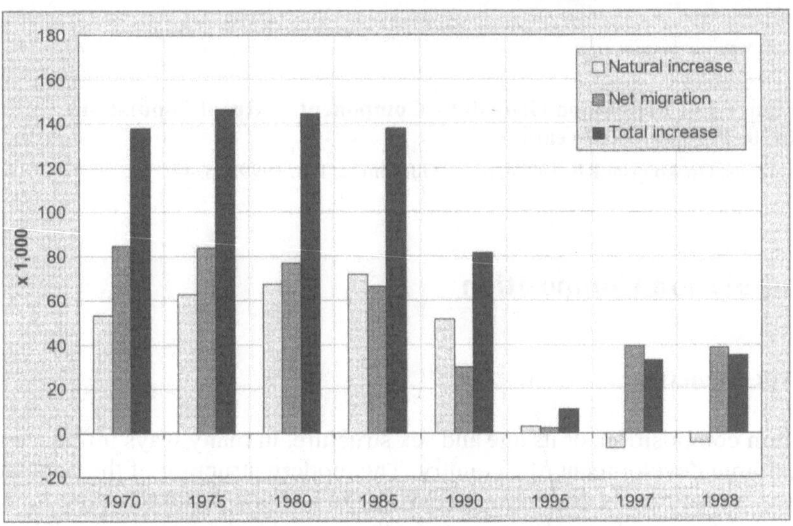


**Figure 2.3: Population Growth by Components – Urban Population, 1970–1998, selected years**

Sources: Goskomstat RB, 1999a, p. 70; Goskomstat RB, 1999b, p. 44

The absolute decline of the population growth in Belarus during 1994–1997 had been determined by the regime of the population growth, which has been already existing over the last 20 years. The socio-economic crisis of the 1980s and 1990s, accompanied by dramatic deterioration of working and living conditions for families as well as the majority of the population, along with the disorganisation of the state health security system, have significantly contributed to the rapid approach of the depopulation stage and have accelerated the major trends in the population development of Belarus. The consequences of the Chernobyl nuclear catastrophe and deformations in the age and sex structure have also influenced the previously mentioned trends in the population development of Belarus.

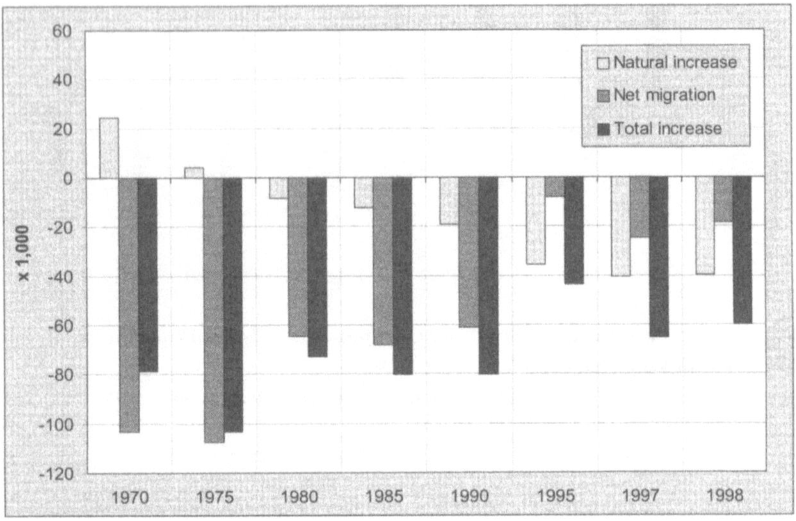


**Figure 2.4: Population Growth by Components – Rural Population, 1970–1998, selected years**

Sources: Goskomstat RB, 1999a, p. 70; Goskomstat RB, 1999b, p. 44

## 2.2 Population Composition

### 2.2.1 Age Structure

Population composition, or its age and sex structure, in many ways influences social and economic development of a country. The modern structure of the population of Belarus is a result of its development during the last one hundred years. It has been very much "deformed" by the wars and other social upheavals of the XX century (see Figure 2.5). The major tendency in the evolution of the age structure has been an ageing of the population (Table 2.2). For example, the proportion of people over the working age has increased from 13.6% in 1960 to 16.9% in 1980 and reached 21.3% at the beginning of 1999. The number of people who are retired have become nearly equal to the number of people younger than 16, but in 1960 the number of children had been 2.3 times higher than the number of people over the working age. The major reason for the ageing population is a dramatic decline in the number of births and the small size of the younger age group in proportion to the total population. In 1960, the proportion of those younger than working age was 31.9%, in 1999 it decreased to 21.4%.

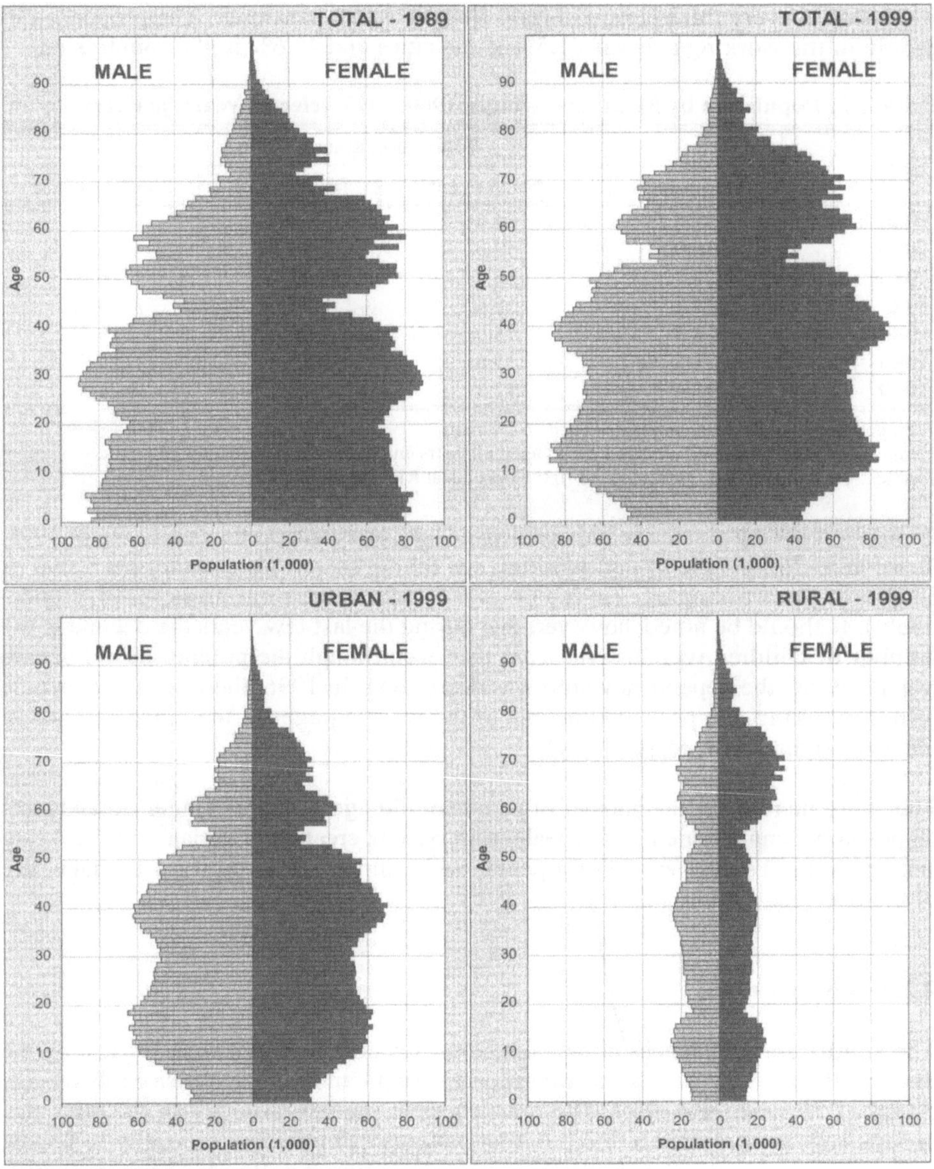


**Figure 2.5: Age Pyramid, 1989 and 1999**[1]

[1]As of 16 February (census)
Source: Goskomstat RB, 1999a

The urban and rural populations in Belarus have dramatically different age structures. At the beginning of 1998, 16.0% of the urban population were elderly people, in the rural areas the proportion of elderly people was twice as high – 33.5%, or in other words every third person in rural Belarus was a pensioner. The proportion of people in the working age was 61.5% in the cities and 45.6% in the countryside.

**Table 2.2: Population by Main Age Groups, 1960–1999, selected years, per cent**

| Year | Population at age | | | |
|---|---|---|---|---|
| | 0–15 years | 16–54(59) years[1] | 16–29 years | 55(60)+ years[2] |
| 1960 | 31.9 | 54.5 | 24.1 | 13.6 |
| 1970 | 30.9 | 52.9 | 19.0 | 16.2 |
| 1980 | 24.7 | 58.4 | 23.7 | 16.9 |
| 1985 | 24.3 | 57.6 | 23.0 | 18.1 |
| 1990 | 24.5 | 55.9 | 20.6 | 19.6 |
| 1995 | 23.5 | 55.6 | 19.3 | 20.9 |
| 1999 | 21.4 | 57.3 | 10.2 | 21.3 |

[1]Females aged 16–54 years and males aged 16-59 years
[2]Females aged 55 years and over and males aged 60 years and over
Sources: Goskomstat RB, 1999a, pp. 61–63; Goskomstat RB, 1999b, p. 38

Population ageing creates an old age dependency problem. At the beginning of 1998, there were 765 people of non-working age (children and old people) per 1,000 of people of the working age (in the cities 627 and in the rural areas 1,193, respectively). It should be noted, however, that during the last few years the decline in the number of children was so significant that even though the number of old people was growing, the dependency ratio was decreasing. In 1996, there were 791 people of non-working age per 1,000 people of the working age (in the cities 650 and in the rural areas 1,211, respectively).

The sharp increase in the number of people of old age demands bigger expenditures on pensions, improvement of the health care system, creation of geriatric medical care and specialised social services for people who cannot live on their own or take care of themselves.

### 2.2.2 Sex Structure

The significant imbalances in the population sex structure that were created by the Second World War have almost disappeared and can only be observed in the age group of 70 years and older. The imbalances in the sex structure in the other age groups can be attributed to the different patterns of births and mortality in female and male populations and also to the structure of migration flows. There are significant differences in the sex structures in urban and rural areas (Figure 2.5).

In cities, the number of males younger than 15 is greater than the number of females of the same age. In the older age groups, females outnumber males. But in rural areas, there are more men than women in the age group of 49 years and younger; however, in the age group of 49 years and older situation is opposite. This situation can be explained by the very high out-migration of young women from rural areas to cities after graduation from high school. As a result, it could be said that there exist a "deficit" of young men in cities and a "deficit" of young women in rural areas.

As some surveys indicate, young women leave rural areas after graduating in order to continue their studies and to search for jobs that accommodate their skills and education. The young men tend to stay, since they expect to be drafted into military service when they reach age 18. Imbalances in the sex structure also exist in some cities. The fluctuations in the sex structures of the working age cohorts impair family formations, negatively influence population growth and also affect employment stability. In the age group 70 years and older, both in the cities and rural areas, the number of men is 2.6 times less than the number of women. This is caused by the high death rate of men during the war years of 1941–1945 and by the much higher death rate for males during non-war years.

### 2.2.3 Ethnic Composition of the Population

The ethnic composition of the population of Belarus can be analysed only by using census data. According to the 1989 census, there were more than 100 ethnic groups in the population. But the majority of the population, more than three-quarters, belongs to the indigenous ethnic group – Belarus (Table 2.3).

**Table 2.3: Population by Ethnic Groups, 1959–1989, selected years**[1]

| Ethnic group | Total numbers 1,000 | | | | Proportion of the total population % | | | |
|---|---|---|---|---|---|---|---|---|
| | 1959 | 1970 | 1979 | 1989 | 1959 | 1970 | 1979 | 1989 |
| Total | 8,065.7 | 9,002.3 | 9,532.5 | 10,151.8 | 100.0 | 100.0 | 100.0 | 100.0 |
| Belarus | 6,532.0 | 7,289.6 | 7,568.0 | 7,904.6 | 81.1 | 81.0 | 79.4 | 77.9 |
| Russian | 660.2 | 938.2 | 1,134.4 | 1,342.1 | 8.2 | 10.4 | 11.9 | 13.2 |
| Polish | 538.9 | 382.2 | 403.2 | 417.7 | 6.7 | 4.3 | 4.2 | 4.1 |
| Ukrainian | 133.1 | 190.8 | 231.0 | 291.0 | 1.7 | 2.1 | 2.4 | 2.9 |
| Jewish | 150.1 | 148.0 | 135.4 | 112.0 | 1.9 | 1.6 | 1.4 | 1.1 |
| Tatar | 8.7 | 10.0 | 10.9 | 12.6 | 0.1 | 0.1 | 0.1 | 0.1 |
| Roma | 4.7 | 6.8 | 8.4 | 10.4 | 0.0 | 0.1 | 0.1 | 0.1 |
| Lithuanian | 8.4 | 8.1 | 7.0 | 7.6 | 0.1 | 0.1 | 0.1 | 0.1 |
| Latvian | 2.6 | 2.7 | 2.6 | 2.7 | 0.0 | 0.0 | 0.0 | 0.0 |
| Estonian | 0.8 | 0.9 | 0.7 | 0.8 | 0.0 | 0.0 | 0.0 | 0.0 |
| Others | 16.2 | 24.6 | 31.2 | 49.9 | 0.2 | 0.3 | 0.4 | 0.5 |

[1]Census data
Source: Goskomstat RB, 1999a, p. 67

According to the 1989 census, there were 10,036.3 thousand ethnic Belarus people in the former Soviet Union, including 7,904.4 thousand (78.0%) living within the territory of Belarus. The remaining 2,131.7 thousand (21.2%) Belarus people lived outside Belarus, mainly in Russia (12.0%), and some in Ukraine (4.4%), Kazakhstan (1.8%), Latvia (1.2%), and in all the other republics of the former Soviet Union – only 1.8% (Goskomstat BSSR, 1990).

During the 1990s, migration flows were to a very large extent differentiated by the ethnic factor. For example, Jewish people were leaving Belarus, and ethnic Belarus people were returning to Belarus from the other republics of the former Soviet Union. More significant than before was the inflow of people of different ethnic groups from the regions of ethnic conflicts and civil wars. As a result, the ethnic composition of the population of Belarus has experienced great changes, which, however, will be fully accounted for and understood only when the 1999 census final results are available.

## 2.3 Changing Fertility Patterns

### 2.3.1 Fertility Trends

The crude birth rate, after its sharp decline during the 1960s and relative stabilisation in the 1970s, increased during the 1980s and started to decrease rapidly during the 1990s. It is now widely understood that the short-lived increase in the crude birth rate during 1983–1986 happened in response to the set of social policy measures put into practice in 1981 and aimed at strengthening government support for families with small children. This increase, however, happened due to changes in the timing of births planned by the family. Social measures did not influence the families' decision about the number of children in the family. This view can be supported by the fact that total fertility rate (Table 2.4) from the end of the 1950s was steadily declining (in 1958–1959 – 2.8; in 1969–1970 – 2.3; in 1978–1979 – 2.1; in 1989–1990 – 2.0 and in 1998 – 1.3 children). The growth of the birth numbers in the 1980s was also positively affected by the age structure of the population.

The decline in fertility rates that has occurred during this period became steeper from the beginning of 1989. Many research publications appeared in response to this trend implicating as its cause mostly social and economic instability of the society (see, for example, Rybakovsky, 1992). Some researchers linked fertility decline with the direct effect of the Chernobyl catastrophe (Zlotnikov, 1991).

Undoubtedly, the slowing of the economy, skyrocketing inflation, destabilisation of the production sphere, increasing unemployment, and impoverishment of the population have influenced the number of births in Belarus. The social and economic crisis has caused people to develop a sense of uncertainty about their future. Furthermore, ecological consequences of the Chernobyl catastrophe, in particular the contamination of the soil with radioactive elements, increased parents' concerns about the health of their children. These concerns were reflected in the number of new births. Parents who had planned to have two or even three children in the family, instead limited the number of children to just one and had postponed having more children until "better times".

**Table 2.4: Fertility Rates, 1958–1998, selected years**

| Period/year | Age–specific fertility rate (per 1,000 women) | | | | | | | TFR |
|---|---|---|---|---|---|---|---|---|
| | -20 | 20–24 | 25–29 | 30–34 | 35–39 | 40–44 | 45–49 | |
| | Total population | | | | | | | |
| 1958–1959 | 16.2 | 146.8 | 177.6 | 120.5 | 71.1 | 22.6 | 4.2 | 2.764 |
| 1969–1970 | 19.6 | 161.6 | 134.5 | 87.0 | 43.2 | 12.3 | 1.3 | 2.331 |
| 1978–1979 | 30.6 | 171.7 | 117.9 | 61.1 | 23.4 | 6.4 | 0.4 | 2.052 |
| 1989–1990 | 41.6 | 178.6 | 103.0 | 47.4 | 17.1 | 3.9 | 0.2 | 1.959 |
| 1995 | 39.0 | 122.8 | 71.7 | 29.5 | 10.6 | 2.3 | 0.1 | 1.386 |
| 1996 | 35.8 | 116.5 | 69.0 | 28.3 | 10.0 | 2.2 | 0.1 | 1.316 |
| 1997 | 33.1 | 105.5 | 66.3 | 28.1 | 9.5 | 2.1 | 0.1 | 1.223 |
| 1998 | 30.4 | 106.9 | 71.2 | 31.2 | 10.3 | 2.0 | 0.1 | 1.265 |
| | Urban | | | | | | | |
| 1958–1959 | 13.3 | 122.1 | 148.4 | 94.0 | 48.9 | 12.1 | 1.5 | 2.154 |
| 1969–1970 | 19.4 | 145.8 | 120.7 | 76.0 | 32.5 | 7.7 | 0.7 | 2.027 |
| 1978–1979 | 27.4 | 155.2 | 110.8 | 56.3 | 18.2 | 4.3 | 0.2 | 1.835 |
| 1989–1990 | 35.7 | 165.4 | 100.7 | 45.3 | 15.3 | 3.1 | 0.1 | 1.828 |
| 1995 | 33.2 | 108.9 | 66.4 | 27.6 | 9.2 | 1.8 | 0.1 | 1.239 |
| 1996 | 30.4 | 103.0 | 63.3 | 26.4 | 9.0 | 1.8 | 0.1 | 1.170 |
| 1997 | 27.2 | 94.2 | 59.8 | 26.3 | 8.4 | 1.6 | 0.1 | 1.088 |
| 1998 | 25.7 | 96.7 | 65.1 | 29.4 | 9.2 | 1.6 | 0.1 | 1.116 |
| | Rural | | | | | | | |
| 1958–1959 | 17.6 | 162.8 | 194.0 | 136.8 | 83.7 | 27.8 | 5.2 | 3.100 |
| 1969–1970 | 19.8 | 192.0 | 152.3 | 99.6 | 51.6 | 15.8 | 1.7 | 2.736 |
| 1978–1979 | 36.7 | 218.4 | 138.9 | 73.2 | 31.7 | 8.8 | 0.5 | 2.629 |
| 1989–1990 | 60.9 | 220.4 | 111.1 | 55.0 | 23.8 | 6.3 | 0.3 | 2.389 |
| 1995 | 56.3 | 171.9 | 88.6 | 36.4 | 15.8 | 4.3 | 0.4 | 1.888 |
| 1996 | 52.5 | 162.2 | 87.9 | 34.3 | 14.0 | 3.6 | 0.1 | 1.770 |
| 1997 | 52.1 | 143.6 | 88.6 | 34.3 | 13.6 | 3.7 | 0.2 | 1.680 |
| 1998 | 46.3 | 141.9 | 93.5 | 37.5 | 14.4 | 3.5 | 0.3 | 1.720 |

Source: Goskomstat RB, 1999a, p. 73

It should also be taken into account that since 1989 the age and sex structure started to change as a result of the accelerated decline in the number of births. During this period, small cohorts that were born in the 1960s started to enter active childbearing age. It is known that almost 70% of all births happen to women in 20–29 years age group. In Belarus at the beginning of 1997, there were only 705 thousand women in this age group, which is 135 thousand (or 16%) less than in 1985. The number of births during the same period (1985–1997) has diminished by 55.6 thousand or by 34%. Therefore, it can be argued that one-third of the decline of the crude birth rate during the 1990s was determined by the structural factors originating from the 1960s.

Some demographers had made predictions ten and even twenty years ago about the increase in the crude birth rate in the middle of the 1980s and the following decline in the 1990s. However, it can be reasonably assumed that if one-third of the decline in the crude birth rate was determined by the population structure, as it was already mentioned, the other two-thirds of the decline was a direct consequence of the social, economic and ecological conditions. This explanation can be illustrated by the decrease in the age-specific fertility rates (Table 2.4) and by the lower proportion of the second and third births, as a result of larger proportion of the first births. It also should be considered that the processes that are described above are specific not only to Belarus but are part of the general trend of the decline in fertility associated with demographic transition.

The issue of if and how ecological situation in Belarus has been affecting fertility is widely discussed by many researchers who often provide very controversial opinions on this matter. Some of them state that the decline in fertility is a direct result of the Chernobyl catastrophe, while others believe that it had only a very small influence. Our view is that the Chernobyl catastrophe had affected fertility, but was not the major significant cause of its decline. This view is justified by the different trajectories of fertility decline in the contaminated regions and relatively "clean" regions.

The results of the sociological survey conducted in a few regions support the hypothesis that the Chernobyl catastrophe had affected fertility patterns. It also provides important information about the differences and changes in opinions about fertility among people living in these areas (Shakhotska, 1996). In particular, respondents in the age group 20–29 years from the regions that are considered relatively "clean" less often stated their concern about the health condition of their future child as a reason not to have a child. This reason was stated by less than 20% of all respondents from "clean" regions compared to 40% of female respondents and 50% of male respondents from contaminated regions.

The majority of all respondents thought that an ideal family should have two or three children. None of the respondents said that family without children could be ideal and only 15% of all respondents said that an ideal family is a family with one child. On the other hand, the majority of respondents indicated that they had fewer children in the family than they thought a family should have, and among those who had one child in the family only 5% planned to have more children.

### 2.3.2 Abortions and Family Planning

It is important to mention that during the 1990s the number of abortions went down in Belarus (Table 2.5). Nevertheless, as the results of the survey conducted by the Ministry of Statistics of Belarus in 1995 show, birth control by the use of abortion is still a widespread practice. Among female respondents who were married, 50% had used abortion as a birth control measure. In particular, 23% of them had one abortion, 18.6% – two abortions and 8.4% three or more abortions (Shakhotska, op. cit.)

**Table 2.5: Births and Abortions, 1990–1998, selected years**

| Year | Births | Total abortions | Induced abortions per 1,000 | |
|---|---|---|---|---|
| | 1,000 | 1,000 | Births | Women aged 15–49 |
| 1990 | 142.2 | 254.7 | 1.791 | 103.1 |
| 1993 | 117.4 | 212.7 | 1.812 | 83.4 |
| 1994 | 110.6 | 207.7 | 1.878 | 80.6 |
| 1995 | 101.1 | 188.7 | 1,866 | 71.2 |
| 1996 | 95.8 | 169.9 | 1.762 | 64.3 |
| 1997 | 89.6 | 149.7 | 1.646 | 56.0 |
| 1998 | 92.6 | 141.1 | 1.524 | 52.5 |

Sources: Goskomstat RB, 1999a, p. 203; Goskomstat RB, 1999b, p. 42

It is widely known that abortions very often have negative effects on women's health and may lead to secondary infertility, which in turn may affect the decline in fertility. According to the same survey, only half of all respondents had been using contraceptives for birth control (57.8% of all respondents in the cities and 22.6% in the rural areas). Even in Minsk, the capital of Belarus and the largest city in the republic, only 60% of all respondents indicated use of contraceptives (Shakhotska, op. cit.).

The most commonly used contraceptive was IUD, as indicated by every third woman respondent in this survey. 13.1% of female respondents said that they had used "natural" methods of birth control, which rely on menstrual cycle. Among the reasons of the low level of the use of contraceptives, respondents mentioned a fear of side effects and the high price of contraceptives.

### 2.3.3 Extramarital Births

In contrast to the declining crude fertility rate, the number of births given by non-married women has been constantly growing and especially rapidly during the 1990s, when the proportion of children born outside marriage more than doubled, increasing from 8.5% in 1990 to 16.2% in 1997 (Table 2.6).

**Table 2.6: Live Births Outside Marriage, 1990–1998, selected years**

| Year | Total numbers | | | Per 100 live births | | |
|---|---|---|---|---|---|---|
| | Total | Urban areas | Rural areas | Total | Urban areas | Rural areas |
| 1990 | 12,131 | 7,656 | 4,475 | 8.5 | 7.5 | 11.2 |
| 1993 | 12,752 | 8,296 | 4,456 | 10.9 | 10.2 | 12.4 |
| 1994 | 13,342 | 8,693 | 4,649 | 12.1 | 11.4 | 13.6 |
| 1995 | 13,631 | 8,962 | 4,669 | 13.5 | 12.8 | 14.9 |
| 1996 | 14,293 | 9,321 | 4,972 | 14.9 | 14.1 | 16.7 |
| 1997 | 14,503 | 9,306 | 5,197 | 16.2 | 15.1 | 18.5 |
| 1998 | 15,730 | 10,111 | 5,619 | 17.0 | 15.6 | 20.2 |

Source: Goskomstat RB, 1999a, p. 72

### 2.3.4 Future Trends in Fertility

The age and sex structure of the population during the 1990s, when cohorts born in the 1970s have been entering childbearing age, will not stimulate further decline in the number of births and will not influence the dynamics of fertility in the republic. Later, when women who were born in the 1980s will be entering childbearing age, structural factors might increase probability of a growth in the number of births. We might also expect stabilisation of the social and economic situation in Belarus, which could facilitate adoption of a more efficient demographic policy that could result in a growth of fertility if a family decides to have the children that had been postponed.

However, taking into consideration "reproductive" views of the families, there is no reason to expect a dramatic increase in the number of children per family. The survey of women aged 18–34, conducted by the Ministry of Statistics of Belarus, showed that an average ideal number of children in the families was 2.17, a desirable number of children was 2.02, and an expected number of children was only 1.02 (Shakhotska, op. cit.).

The fertility decline is a historic process, already characteristic of the majority of the developed European countries. As the experiences of these countries show, there are as of yet no measures available that could change the fertility trends in the opposite direction. Therefore, it is important to acknowledge that in the nearest future Belarus will continue to have low fertility levels that do not allow for population growth. Understanding the possible implications of this situation, it is necessary to look for the ways to deal with it. At the same time, it seems desirable to promote ideas that favour fertility growth.

Significant decline in fertility due to structural changes might be expected to occur in the second decade of the XXI century, when women born in the 1990s will be entering childbearing age. Knowing this fact provides an opportunity to work out beforehand the appropriate measures that would counteract fertility decline and eliminate imbalances in the age structure by shifting timing of births and thus terminate the demographic "wave".

## 2.4 Family Formation and Dissolution

### 2.4.1 Marriages

Since the end of the 1980s, the number of marriages and the marriage rates in Belarus have been declining (Table 2.7). This trend has been influenced by the population age structure. At the same time, Belarus has a relatively high marriage rate. The majority of men and women in every cohort sooner or later marry. According to the

1989 census, in the cohort of people aged 45–49, only 3.6% men and 3.3% women had never been married.

**Table 2.7: Marriages and Divorces, 1959–1998, selected years**

| Year | Marriages | Crude marriage rate | Divorces | Crude divorce rate |
|---|---|---|---|---|
| | Number | Per 1,000 inhabitants | Number | Per 1,000 inhabitants |
| 1959 | 90,734 | 11.2 | 5,011 | 0.6 |
| 1979 | 104,034 | 10.9 | 29,707 | 3.1 |
| 1989 | 97,929 | 9.6 | 34,573 | 3.4 |
| 1990 | 99,229 | 9.7 | 34,986 | 3.4 |
| 1994 | 75,540 | 7.3 | 44,075 | 4.3 |
| 1995 | 77,027 | 7.5 | 42,119 | 4.1 |
| 1996 | 63,677 | 6.2 | 43,089 | 4.2 |
| 1997 | 69,735 | 6.8 | 47,301 | 4.6 |
| 1998 | 71,354 | 7.0 | 47,227 | 4.6 |

Sources: Goskomstat BR, 1999a, p. 68; Goskomstat BR, 1999b, p. 42

During a long period of time, in Belarus the portion of people who married at a young age was rising steadily. This was equally specific for men and for women. In 1960, the proportion of men at the age 20 and younger entering marriage was 2.7%, the proportion of women of the same age group was 12.0%; in 1970, these proportions changed to 3.6% and 22.2%, respectively; in 1979 to 4.0% and 25.5%; in 1989 to 4.1% and 26.2 %; and in 1995 to 5.8% and 28.9%. In the middle of the 1990s, this trend has changed and the proportion of those married at the age 20 and younger started to decrease. In 1997, the proportion of men marrying at the age 20 and younger was 4.5% and the proportion of women marrying at the age 20 and younger dropped to 23.8%. The proportion of first-married people at the age 20 and younger was even higher; however, this proportion also started to decline. In 1991, the proportion of first-married men at the age 20 and younger was 6.9%, while in 1997 it dropped to 6.1%. The proportion of first-married women had changed from 37.3% in 1991 to 31.6% in 1997 (Goskomstat RB, 1998).

### 2.4.2 Consensual Unions

The growing number of consensual unions has become a prevalent trend in many developed countries. This trend is also present in Belarus. One of the indicators of the increasing number of non-registered unions might be the growing number of births outside marriage that are registered by the mutual application of both parents. The survey conducted in Minsk in 1997 showed that 5.4% of all respondents were living in a factual not officially registered marital union (*Current Statistics 1998*, 1999, p. 176).

### 2.4.3 Widowhood

Significant changes have occurred in the processes of marital dissolution. Marriages can dissolve through either of two events, divorce or death of a spouse. In a long-term perspective, increase in longevity and life expectancy that has been taking place in Belarus from the beginning of this century has significantly lowered the probability of a marital dissolution as a result of a spouse's death. However, during the last 20–30 years, because of the rise in mortality the probability of widowhood had increased again.

In general, the probability of widowhood in Belarus is relatively high. According to the 1989 census, in the age group 40–44 years 4.1% of women and 0.7% of men, and in the age group 50–54 years 12% and 2.3 %, respectively, were widowed. The higher rate of widowhood among women is caused, on the one hand, by their longevity and the higher mortality of men and, on the other hand, by the higher rate of remarriage among men. In the mean time, the sex difference in the rate of remarriage has been slowly diminishing.

### 2.4.4 Divorces

The overall trend of probability of marital dissolution as a result of divorce is clearly increasing in Belarus. In 1959, from every 1,000 married couples 2.7 got divorced. In 1970, the number was almost three times higher – 8.5, reaching 13.4 divorces per 1,000 married couples in 1989. Another measurement of divorce – crude divorce rate – also shows the upward tendency: there were 1.9 divorces per 1,000 of the total population in 1970; 3.2 in 1980; 3.4 in 1990; 4.1 in 1995; 4.6 in 1997 and 4.6 in 1998 (see Table 2.7).

In 1998, there were 71.3 thousand officially registered marriages and 47.2 thousand officially registered divorces. Therefore, the increase in the number of married couples during 1998 was only 24.1 thousand, not taking into account marriage dissolution as a result of widowhood.

### 2.4.5 Family Size and Composition

The average size of a family in Belarus is declining. During the last 30 years, it has decreased from 3.7 people in 1959 to 3.2 in 1989 and has reached 3.1 in 1998. The proportion of small families consisting of 2–4 members has been growing and the proportion of big families with 5 and more members has been decreasing. The majority of two-person families belong to the so-called "empty nest" family category. These are the families that consist of a married couple, whose adult children have left the family home. Single-parent families also form a big proportion of the two-person families.

The most prevalent type of family in Belarus in 1998 was a family consisting of one married couple with children or without them (simple nuclear family). 73.0% of all families fell into this category (Figure 2.6).

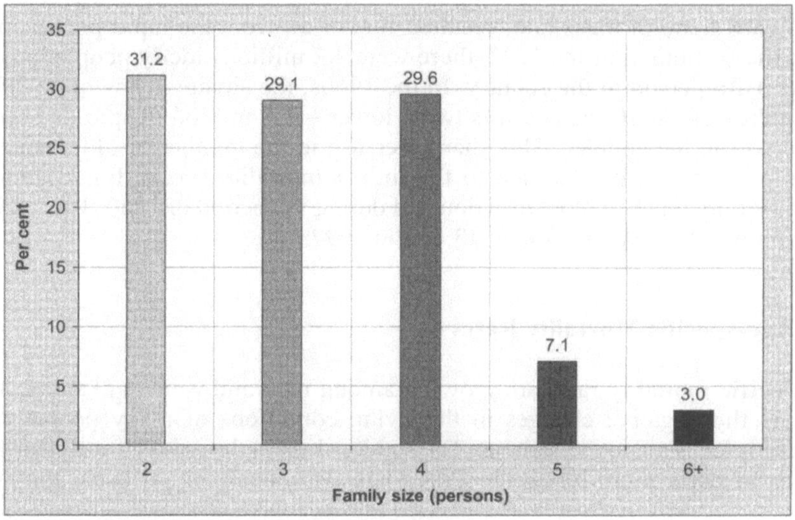


**Figure 2.6: Family Structure by Size, 1989**

Source: based on the 1989 census data (Goskomstat BSSR, 1990)

Families, consisting of one parent (more often it is a mother) with a child (non-complete nuclear family), make 12.1% of all families. At the beginning of 1998, according to our estimations, the proportion of single-parent families reached 12.9% and their absolute number was 382.3 thousand.

In 1989, according to the census data, 42.5% families did not have children younger than 18 years, 27.7% families had a one child and 24.7% – two children. From the total number of 2,796 thousand families, only 143 thousand families had three or more children. These families comprised 5.1% of the total number of families. On average, there was less than one child per family in Belarus in 1989. During the 1990s, the number of children per family has continued to drop and the number of families without children or with only one child has been on the rise.

## 2.5 Mortality

The health of the population is one of the most precious commodities of society. Judgements about the state of the health of the population may be formed only on the basis of information about illnesses, mortality and life expectancy. The state of a population's health depends on the social and economic development of the country, its material well being, living conditions and quality of health care. From the beginning of the 1960s, the absolute number of deaths as well as the crude mortality rate have been increasing.

The upward trend of these rates resulted first of all from the rapid population ageing. At the beginning of the 1997, there were 2.2 million elderly people in Belarus, or every fifth person in the country. In the 1960s, the situation was quite different. The number of elderly people was twice lower – 1.1 million people or every seventh person in the country. This sharp increase in the number of old people in the population undoubtedly had led to the higher mortality levels. For example, the crude mortality rate had more than doubled during the period of 1960–1997, climbing from a moderate 6.6‰ in 1960 to 13.4‰ in 1997.

### 2.5.1 Age-specific Mortality Rates

Age-specific mortality rates are growing among men and women (Table 2.8). One reason is the negative changes in the living conditions of many people and the poor ecological situation in Belarus. The sudden drop in the material well being of the majority of population during the 1990s has also negatively affected the public's health.

**Table 2.8: Age-specific Mortality Rates, 1980–1997, selected years, per 1,000 inhabitants**

| Age group | Male | | | | Female | | | |
|---|---|---|---|---|---|---|---|---|
| | 1980–1981 | 1990 | 1995 | 1997 | 1980–1981 | 1990 | 1995 | 1997 |
| Total | 10.5 | 11.2 | 14.3 | 14.8 | 9.2 | 10.3 | 11.9 | 12.1 |
| 0–4 | 4.8 | 3.2 | 3.4 | 6.1 | 3.5 | 2.4 | 2.4 | 2.3 |
| 5–9 | 0.6 | 0.5 | 0.4 | 0.4 | 0.3 | 0.3 | 0.3 | 0.3 |
| 10–14 | 0.5 | 0.4 | 0.4 | 0.4 | 0.3 | 0.3 | 0.2 | 0.2 |
| 15–19 | 1.1 | 1.2 | 1.4 | 1.2 | 0.4 | 0.5 | 0.5 | 0.5 |
| 20–24 | 2.2 | 2.3 | 2.6 | 2.6 | 0.5 | 0.6 | 0.7 | 0.6 |
| 25–29 | 2.8 | 2.6 | 3.5 | 3.5 | 0.7 | 0.6 | 0.8 | 0.8 |
| 30–34 | 3.8 | 3.2 | 4.5 | 4.6 | 1.0 | 0.9 | 1.1 | 1.1 |
| 35–39 | 5.9 | 4.6 | 6.3 | 6.2 | 1.6 | 1.3 | 1.6 | 1.7 |
| 40–44 | 7.5 | 6.4 | 9.2 | 8.9 | 2.3 | 2.1 | 2.5 | 2.5 |
| 45–49 | 10.6 | 10.4 | 13.6 | 13.3 | 3.6 | 3.8 | 4.2 | 4.1 |
| 50–54 | 13.5 | 14.8 | 21.4 | 19.8 | 5.1 | 5.1 | 6.8 | 6.5 |
| 55–59 | 18.1 | 20.7 | 27.6 | 28.3 | 7.8 | 7.9 | 9.6 | 9.7 |
| 60–64 | 26.2 | 29.0 | 38.0 | 39.5 | 11.7 | 11.9 | 14.4 | 14.2 |
| 65–69 | 38.6 | 39.7 | 50.3 | 54.1 | 19.4 | 19.7 | 21.8 | 22.2 |
| 70+ | 92.3 | 102.4 | 109.2 | 106.9 | 65.5 | 77.8 | 80.6 | 78.3 |

Source: Goskomstat RB, 1999a, p. 74

### 2.5.2 Life Expectancy

Life expectancy at birth in Belarus after steady growth (it had increased from 38 years in 1897 to 72.9 years in 1968–1969) had stabilised during the second half of the 1970s and the beginning of the 1980s and then it had started to decline, reaching 70.8 years in 1983–1984. After a slight rise in 1986–1987, the life expectancy at birth experienced a steady decline (Table 2.9).

**Table 2.9: Life Expectancy at Birth, 1958–1998, selected years, in years**

| Period/ year | Both sexes | Male | Female | Period/ year | Both sexes | Male | Female |
|---|---|---|---|---|---|---|---|
| 1958–1959 | 70.3 | 66.2 | 73.5 | 1993 | 69.2 | 63.8 | 74.4 |
| 1970–1971 | 72.5 | 68.1 | 76.0 | 1994 | 69.0 | 63.5 | 74.3 |
| 1978–1979 | 71.4 | 66.3 | 75.9 | 1995 | 68.6 | 62.9 | 74.3 |
| 1989 | 71.8 | 66.8 | 76.4 | 1996 | 68.6 | 63.0 | 74.3 |
| 1990 | 71.1 | 66.3 | 75.6 | 1997 | 68.5 | 62.9 | 74.3 |
| 1991 | 70.7 | 65.5 | 75.5 | 1998 | 68.4 | 62.7 | 74.4 |
| 1992 | 70.3 | 64.9 | 75.4 | | | | |

Sources: Goskomstat RB, 1999a, p. 87; Goskomstat, 1999b, p. 48

As a result, life expectancy dropped lower than the 1958–1959 level and in 1998 was only 68.4 years. The worsening public health can be attributed to poor working conditions, low economic well being, poor nutrition, polluted environment, stress, transport congestion in cities, lack of economic and social stability, lack of fitness activities and a low level of medical care. These social developments are also reflected in the rise of the cause-specific death rates (cancer, endocrine abnormalities, immune system illnesses, accidents, homicides and suicides).

### 2.5.3 Causes of Death

The structure of the cause-specific mortality rates in Belarus is similar to the structure in developed countries; however, the rates are much higher. In 1997 638.5 people per 100,000 died from the heart and vascular diseases, 189.7 people per 100,000 died from cancer and 145.9 people per 100,000 died from accidents, poisoning and traumas.

The health of a population strongly depends on people's life styles and their self-protecting behaviour. In Belarus, neither the dominant life style nor the self-protecting behaviour is boosting public health. People do not take personal responsibility for their own health. For instance, 54.0% of all men aged 16 and older smoke, 4.8% of all women smoke. The average number of cigarettes a person smokes per day is 14 for men and 8 for women (*Current Statistics 1998*, 1999)

Consumption of alcohol is growing even among schoolchildren. According to children's responses, by the year 9 at school, 2.6% of them drink alcohol 3–4 times or more per month (4.2% boys and 1.8% girls) and by the year 11 at school, 9.9% do the same (13.5% boys and 7.3% girls). Among adult population, the use of alcohol is much heavier (*Current Statistics 1998*, 1999).

Furthermore, people in Belarus do not usually exercise or participate in sports. Children also are not actively involved in sports. Only 17.7% of them regularly go to sport sessions, 32.0% occasionally go to the swimming pool, 43.0% do some exercises only at school at physical culture lessons, and 7.3% do not practice sports or physical exercises at all. Adult population is even less active in sport and fitness. Only 20.2% of men and 11.0% of women aged 16 and older practice sports (*Current Statistics 1998*, 1999).

The modern regime of mortality and life expectancy in Belarus and its dynamics are worrisome. The negative trends, as we have already mentioned, are the consequences of the current economic development of the republic. But the biggest concern is the fluctuation of life expectancy and mortality rates during last 25 years. Life expectancy has been also lagging behind the economically developed countries. This situation is not new, however. The high mortality trends that we described above have continued to hold since the beginning of the 1960s.

The current social and economic crisis and the deteriorating ecological situation negatively affect population health and mortality levels. Mortality is likely to stay at high levels long into the future. A downward trend might be expected only beyond the first decade of the XXI century. To bring about this change, effective preventive measures against premature deaths are needed. Not only stagnation but also the degradation of the population's health should be dealt with. A one time centralised action will not be enough. There is a need for a long-term government programme that would address protection and support of the population's health.

The draft of the programme "*Health*" has already been developed. According to this programme, the state should provide basic medical services and emergency medical help, monitor and deal with infectious and other serious diseases, and support health care for mothers and children. The state also should create wide opportunities for every citizen to actively engage in the protection of his or her own health (free choice and availability of a physician, hospital, method of treatment, quality of medical care, etc.). With the understanding that the complex goal of improving the population health cannot be achieved solely by reforming the health care system, the government programme also plans to promote healthy life styles in which people are responsible for their own health and their children's health. The programme also plans to ameliorate the ecological situation in Belarus.

In view of the crisis situation that Belarus has lately been experiencing, it is very important not to lose previously achieved standards of the medical care. That is why the government programme "*Health*" includes urgent measures to resolve problems existing in epidemiological services, first aid and emergency medical care, and aims to guarantee supply of the basic medicines to population. Measures geared at resolution of the ecological problems are also included into programme. But the biggest issue that puts the implementation of this programme under threat is that the government lacks necessary financial and other resources to support the programme.

## 2.6 Migration

During the 1980s and in the beginning of the 1990s, Belarus had experienced radical changes in the volume, intensity and direction of migration flows. The changes were caused by the start of the transformation ("perestroika") of the economic and social life in the republic and, in addition, by the Chernobyl catastrophe in 1986. The collapse of the former Soviet Union in December 1991 had the biggest impact on migration trends. Internal inter-republic migration of the population of the former Soviet Union after its dissolution has become an international migration phenomenon.

As a result of the collapse of the former Soviet Union, the amount of migrations due to economic, family and study motives has decreased, but migration caused by crisis or stress situations has skyrocketed.

The dissolution of the former USSR, the economic and political crisis, military conflicts in some parts of the former Soviet Union, the Chernobyl catastrophe and other events have determined the growth of migration flows of repatriates, refugees and illegal immigrants. The net migration has fluctuated significantly during the last years in both directions. In 1992, net migration was positive – plus 53.6 thousand people, in 1993 it was plus 32.4 thousand. After that it had been negative during two years: minus 3.3 thousand in 1994 and minus 0.2 thousand in 1995; and then it became again positive: plus 9.4 thousand in 1996 and plus 14.7 thousand in 1997 (Council of Europe, 1998, p. 445). The net migration had peaked during 1992 and 1993 years.

### 2.6.1 Internal Migration

The most intensive migration in Belarus was internal. In 1997, 190.6 thousand people migrated within the republic. In particular, 114.1 thousand people moved within one district, 76.4 thousand people moved from one region to the other, and 100.1 thousand people migrated within their region: moving from district to district, from town to town or from rural area to the city. However, the main direction of the migration streams was from rural areas to the cities (Goskomstat RB, 1998).

### 2.6.2 International Migration

During the 1990s, international migration streams in Belarus were not as big as internal streams. In 1997, 31.4 thousand people arrived to Belarus and 16.7 left it, making the net migration 14.7 thousand (Council of Europe, op. cit., p. 444). There are currently two major flows of international migration in Belarus: the first one is directed to and from the countries of the Commonwealth of Independent States (CIS) and the Baltic states and the second – to and from the countries that are not part of the CIS or the Baltic States. The first flow during the 1990s had steady positive net migration (Figure 2.7); the second flow had a negative net migration. During seven years from 1991 to 1997, the biggest number of migrants came to Belarus from Russia – 68.8 thousand people and from the Baltic States – 40.8 thousand people. The relatively big number of migrants arrived from Kazakhstan – 20.5 thousand, from Ukraine – 20.2 thousand, from the republics of Central Asia – 17.9 thousand, from Caucasian states – 15.1 thousand and from Moldova – 2.6 thousand (Goskomstat RB, 1999a).

In 1997, 29.9 thousand people came to Belarus from the CIS and the Baltic States and 9.7 thousand people left Belarus in the opposite direction. Seven thousand people moved out of Belarus and beyond the borders of CIS and the Baltic States to the so-called "far abroad", and 1.5 thousand people arrived in Belarus from the "far abroad" (Goskomstat, 1999a).

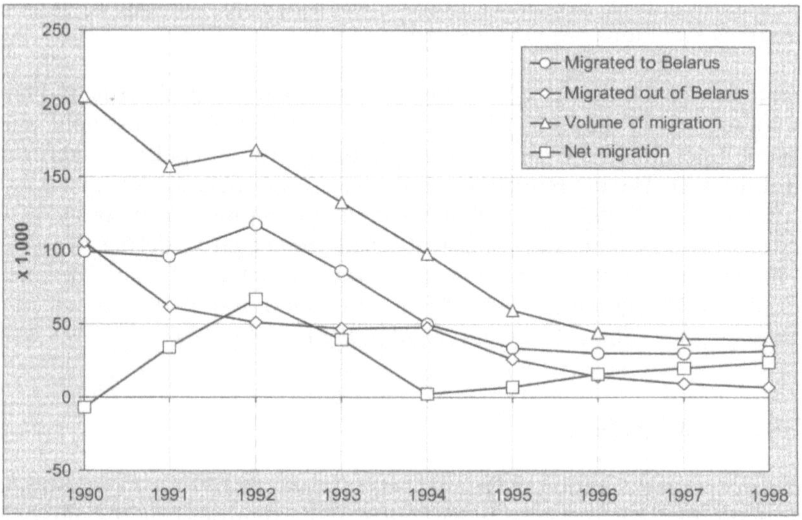


**Figure 2.7: Migration Between Belarus and the CIS and the Baltic States, 1990–1998**

Sources: Goskomstat RB, 1999a, pp. 89–95; Goskomstat RB, 1999b, pp. 49–51

### 2.6.3 Repatriation of Ethnic Belarus

The repatriation of Belarus people had started in the 1980s, but during the 1990s it has become more intensive. Ethnic Belarus people are returning to Belarus: 40–50% of all registered immigrants identified themselves as ethnic Belarus. The largest proportion of ethnic Belarus was in the stream of migrants from the Baltic States –

more than 50%. During seven years (1990–1997), 236.8 thousand people, identifying themselves as ethnic Belarus, came to Belarus from the CIS and the Baltic States. This is more than 10% of all ethnic Belarus that lived in the former Soviet Union outside of Belarus. Repatriation of Belarus people was caused by many factors, among which the dissolution of the former Soviet Union and interethnic conflicts in many parts of the CIS are the strongest. The immigration to Belarus from all republics of the former Soviet Union peaked in 1992; after that year the volume of this flow decreased. During 1996, 50.2 thousand Belarus people returned to Belarus from the countries of the CIS, and during 1997 – 13.5 thousand people (Council of Europe, op. cit., p. 444).

### 2.6.4 Emigration Beyond the Borders of the CIS and the Baltic States

The dramatic economic and social crisis along with critical ecological situation in the republic, as well as liberalisation of life and reform of the emigration legislation contributed to the growth of the emigration flow at the end of the 1980s and beginning of the 1990s (Figure 2.8). According to the data of the Ministry of Internal Affairs of Belarus, in 1989, 14.7 thousand people were granted permission to travel abroad, while in 1990 this number increased more than twice and reached 34.1 thousand. Later, the volume of this flow has declined and has relatively stabilised: in 1991 – 22.0 thousand people; in 1992 – 9.7 thousand people; in 1993 – 6.9 thousand people; in 1994 – 7.0 thousand people; in 1995 – 8.8 thousand people, in 1996 – 8.9 thousand people; and in 1997 – 8.9 thousand people.

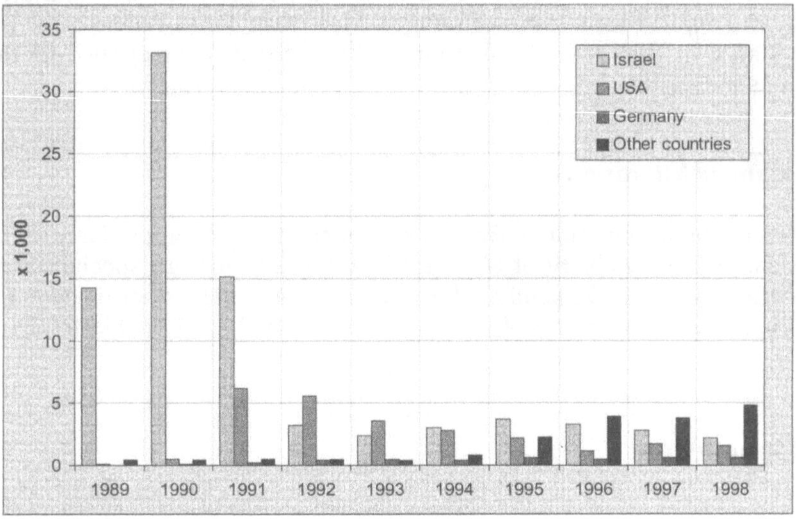


**Figure 2.8: Emigration from Belarus, 1989–1998**

Sources: Goskomstat RB, 1999a, p. 94; Goskomstat RB, 1999b, p. 51

### 2.6.5 Ecological Migration

The critical ecological situation in Belarus, a direct result of the Chernobyl catastrophe, strongly affected the volume and destinations of internal migration. People are migrating from Gomel and Mogilev regions. During 1996, from the contaminated zones of the immediate relocation 1,582 people (720 families) have moved and in 1997 – 1,261 people (498 families), respectively.

### 2.6.6 Illegal Migration

Illegal migration is a very new phenomenon for Belarus. According to the estimations of some specialists, there are around 100–300 thousand people who came illegally to Belarus from the countries of CIS, Asia, Africa and Middle East. Illegal immigrants are coming to Belarus as tourists, transit passengers, business or private visitors. Very often, illegal immigrants are coming as refugees. The majority of the illegal immigrants use Belarus as a transit point for their further illegal migration to the countries of Western Europe.

### 2.6.7 Refugee Migration

Massive forced migration and growing number of refugees during the 1990s became a new and very serious issue for Belarus. During 1992–1997, the Government Migration Department registered 31.2 thousand people from CIS and the Baltic States, who applied for a status of refugee. More than 35% of them came from the Baltic States. In 1997, 158 people from the "far abroad" have applied for the refugee status in Belarus.

### 2.6.8 Labour Migration

Registered labour migration in Belarus has a small but growing volume. According to the data of the Ministry of Statistics in 1995, 225 foreign specialists came to work officially and 1,692 people left Belarus officially to work elsewhere. In 1996, this figures were 371 and 1,894; and in 1997 – 457 and 3,226, respectively.

## 2.7 Conclusion

The current demographic situation in Belarus creates concerns regarding the future development of the country. These concerns are not only about the decreasing absolute size of the population, but more about the fact that Belarus is losing a previously achieved standard of living for its population. The material well being of the population, availability and quality of education and medical care are declining, physical and moral health of the population is deteriorating, opportunities to have even a small number of children are narrowing. The major complex demographic problems of the coming 20–25 years thus will have not only quantitative, but a mostly qualitative character.

## References


Council of Europe (1998), *Recent Demographic Developments in Europe 1998*, Strasbourg: Council of Europe.

*Current Statistics 1997. Collection of research articles*, (1998), Minsk.

*Current Statistics 1998. Collection of research articles*, (1999), Minsk.

Goskomstat BSSR (State Committee on Statistics of the BSSR) (1990), *Chislennost, vozrastnaia struktura, sostoianie v brake, chislo I razmer semei, natsionalni sostav, uroven' obrazovania i istochniki sredstv suschestvovania naselenia Belorusskoi SSR. Po dannym perepisi naselenia 1989 goda*, Minsk: Goskomstat BSSR.

Goskomstat RB (State Committee on Statistics of the Republic of Belarus) (1998). *Statistical Yearbook of the Republic of Belarus 1998*, Minsk: Goskomstat RB.

Goskomstat RB (State Committee on Statistics of the Republic of Belarus) (1999a). *Statistical Yearbook of the Republic of Belarus 1999*, Minsk: Goskomstat RB.

Goskomstat RB (State Committee on Statistics of the Republic of Belarus) (1999b). *The Republic of Belarus in Figures 1999*, Minsk: Goskomstat RB.

Rybakovsky, L. (1992), Demographicheckie posledstviya avarii na Chernobylskoi AES, *Sociologicheskie Issledovaniya*, No. 9.

Shakhotska, L. (1996), *Naselenie Respubliki Belarus v kontse XX veka*, Minsk.

Zlotnikov, A. (1991), *Gomelchane v ekstremal'nych usloviyah: social'no psyhologicheskii klimat v postchernobylskyi period*, Gomel.

# 3

# Population Development in Bulgaria

**Dimiter Philipov**

## 3.1 Introduction

In 1962, Bulgaria celebrated the birth of its eight millionth inhabitant. I remember that it was a boy, born in the countryside. His parents got presents and their names were in the newspapers. But how was it possible to trace that he was exactly the eight millionth person? The answer is obvious – with very crude approximation. This baby was selected by chance. A case was created to celebrate a growing population in conditions of victorious socialism. In 1985, the population reached 8.5 million, but there were no celebrations. They were postponed for the 9 millionth person. Some were impatient waiting for the appearance of the 10 millionth Bulgarian citizen. After the population reached its maximum of 8,992 thousand in 1989, one would expect that the 9 million mark would be reached in 1990, but by then nobody was thinking of such solemnities. Instead, in the 1990s the demographic change has been often described as a "catastrophe".

The year 1989 was a turning point in the population changes that will be discussed in this paper. The year 1990 marked a decrease in the population, because deaths exceeded births for the first time in the history of Bulgaria, except for in wartime years. A huge number of emigrants who left the country were accounted for only in the 1992 population census, which was carried out in December of that year. Half a million people were lost. During the next several years, deaths increasingly exceeded births, thus natural increase decreased steadily below the zero mark. The emigration continued, although at a lower speed. Table 3.1 illustrates these changes.

**Table 3.1: Population Change, 1989–1996**

| | 1989 | 1990 | 1991 | 1992 | 1993 | 1994 | 1995 | 1996 |
|---|---|---|---|---|---|---|---|---|
| Crude rates (per 1,000): | | | | | | | | |
| Births | 12.5 | 11.7 | 10.7 | 10.2 | 10.0 | 9.4 | 8.6 | 8.6 |
| Deaths | 11.9 | 12.1 | 12.3 | 12.4 | 12.9 | 13.2 | 13.6 | 14.0 |
| Natural increase | 0.6 | -0.4 | -1.6 | -2.2 | -2.9 | -3.8 | -5.0 | -5.4 |
| Emigration (1,000) | 218.0 | 87.9 | 40.2 | 65.2 | .. | .. | .. | .. |
| Population (1,000)[1] | 8,767[2] | 8,669[2] | 8,595[2] | 8,485 | 8,460 | 8,427 | 8,385 | 8,340 |

[1]As of 31 December of a given year

[2]Estimations done on the basis of the 1992 population census results

Source: based on the data of National Institute of Statistics (NIS)

This article discusses the basic constituents of these changes, such as fertility, mortality, external migration, and family formation and dissolution, as a result of changed demographic behaviour.

## 3.2 Basic Demographic Processes

### 3.2.1 Population Change and its Components

Changes in the total population were briefly described above. Here I discuss what happened with the components of these changes – fertility, mortality, and external migration. They are preceded by descriptions of other changes in population structures. I first consider the basic demographic structure – the age and sex composition. Figure 3.1 below presents the age pyramid of the population observed in 1992, a population census year.

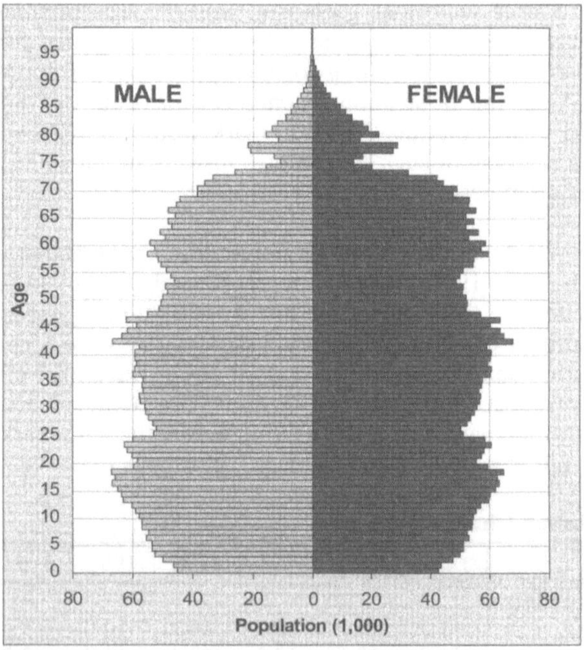


**Figure 3.1: Age Pyramid on 31.12.1992**

Source: author's calculations based on census tabulations

The pyramid tells a brief story of the Bulgarian population. It reflects the decrease in the number of births during the 10–15 years preceding 1992. The decrease in the last two years is notable. The population pyramid also reflects a temporary increase in natality that began in 1973 and in 1968. This was due to the pronatalist policy, which was adopted in 1967 and improved in 1972. The increase of the number of people around ages 40–45 was due to the compensating increase in births after the Second World War. It was preceded by a decrease in natality during the war. Finally, the effect of the First World War and the preceding wars in the Balkans substantially narrowed the pyramid because of a decreased number of births.

The sex distribution is typical for a population where females live longer. The pyramid is a little bit "swelled" on the right side beyond around age 60. Beyond this age, females outnumber males by about 12%. This difference is primarily due to the longer life expectancy of females.

In order to get a quantitative impression on the age composition and its change, I consider three age groups: 0 to 14 years of age, 15 to 64, and 65 and over. The table below gives their shares observed in 1985, 1992 and 1996, for the total population of the state, as well as for the urban and the rural population. In addition, data for males and females is given for 1996.

**Table 3.2: Population by Age Group and Sex, 1985, 1992 and 1996, per cent**

| Age group | 1985 | 1992 | 1996 | | |
|---|---|---|---|---|---|
| | Total | Total | Total | Male | Female |
| | | | Total | | |
| 0–14 | 22 | 19 | 17 | 18 | 16 |
| 15–64 | 67 | 67 | 67 | 68 | 67 |
| 65+ | 11 | 14 | 15 | 14 | 17 |
| | | | Urban | | |
| 0–14 | 23 | 20 | 18 | 19 | 17 |
| 15–64 | 69 | 70 | 71 | 71 | 70 |
| 65+ | 8 | 11 | 12 | 10 | 13 |
| | | | Rural | | |
| 0–14 | 19 | 17 | 16 | 17 | 16 |
| 15–64 | 63 | 61 | 61 | 63 | 59 |
| 65+ | 18 | 22 | 23 | 20 | 26 |

Source: NIS, 1996

Table 3.2 refers to a very short period of time when changes in the population age structure were occurring. Still, these 11 years vividly mark the process of population ageing. It can be seen that the share of aged persons increases rapidly because of a decrease in the share of youngsters. The share of adults remains relatively constant. The same trend would be observed if a longer period of time was considered.

The Bulgarian population has been ageing for several decades. Population projections indicate that this process will continue into the future. International comparisons show that it will be one of the most aged populations in Europe at the beginning of the next century (Stolnitz, 1992).

The ageing of the total population is due to decreased fertility. International migration has only a limited impact. The distribution of the ageing population in urban and rural settings is completely different. Table 3.2 shows that the share of aged persons in the rural areas is significantly higher than in urban settlements. In many rural communities the population consists of aged people only. The population pyramid in such areas is "T"-shaped. This territorial difference is due to the domination of the rural-urban internal migration flow. It was the strongest during the 1950s and the 1960s when the spreading industrialisation needed a labour force.

The sex structure in these three age groups, given for 1996 in Table 3.2, exhibits a larger number of aged women than men. This indicates an important social problem – the number of aged women living alone is very large, especially in rural settlements. By using Tables 3.1 and 3.2, one can estimate approximate changes in the labour force, which is the population aged 15 to 64. In 1985, it was 5,997 thousand. In 1992, it decreased to 95% of that number, and in 1996 to 92% of that in 1985. Hence, the demographic change caused a trend towards a decrease in the labour force. This process is rapid, given the decline by 8% in just 11 years.

The demographic burden can be estimated by using the data in Table 3.2. These are two types of dependency ratios. Dividing the aged (old) by the adult population forms a ratio that is a measure of the demographic burden on the adults with respect to aged people. Dividing the sum of aged and young to the adult (measure of full demographic burden) forms another ratio. Both are given in Table 3.3.

**Table 3.3: Age Dependency Ratios, 1985, 1992 and 1996**

| | 1985 | 1992 | 1996 |
|---|---|---|---|
| Age dependency ratio, 1st variant[1] | 0.17 | 0.21 | 0.23 |
| Age dependency ratio, 2nd variant[2] | 0.49 | 0.50 | 0.48 |

[1]Population aged 65 and over as a percentage of population aged 15–64
[2]Population aged 0–14 and 65 and over as a percentage of population aged 15–64
Source: author's calculations

While the full demographic burden hardly changes during the 11 years, the ratio of aged to adults increases considerably. These observations indicate, in general, that transfers in the social system must take place in the direction from young to aged people. The future social system will heavily be engaged with problems of the aged persons. Economic policy will inevitably have to consider the specific consumption patterns of the aged and their need for certain goods, such as pharmaceutical products. The most important problem is whether there will be enough working people to make up for the pensions of the aged. Thus, one of the major problems in the reform of the contemporary pension security system is to consider these demographic difficulties that will inevitably increase in the next couple of decades.

### 3.2.2 Marital Status

The marital status structure of the Bulgarian population is analysed by using population censuses. The last census of 1992 will be considered here. It shows the population distribution by sex and four marital categories: single, married, divorced, and widowed. The latter three can be combined into the category of ever-married. It is exhibited in Figure 3.2.

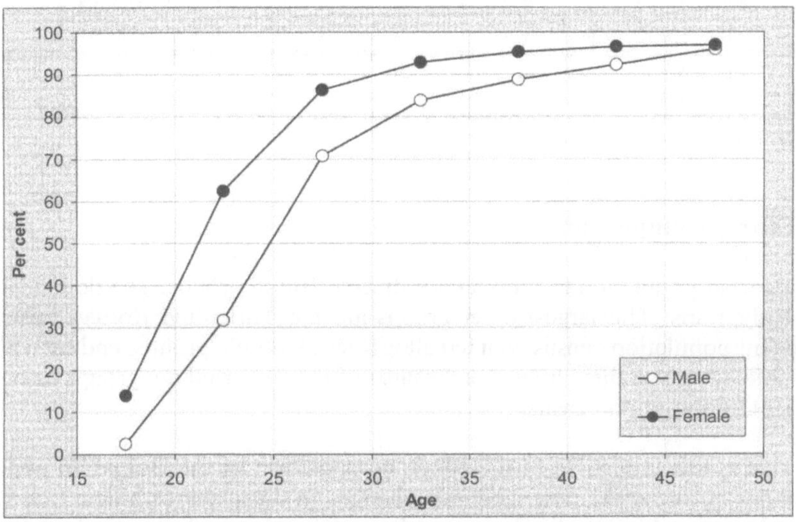


**Figure 3.2: Distribution of Ever-married Males and Females by Age, 1992**

Source: author's calculations based on census tabulations

The Figure 3.2 shows that ultimately all males and females have ever entered into a marriage, independently of whether they were married, widowed, or divorced at the time of the census. The data shows that 96–98% of people over 50 was ever-married. The available data is grouped into 5-year age groups until age 40 and 10-year age groups at higher ages. Still, it can be judged that the top 10 percentile interval is reached at about age 40 for males, and at age 30 for females. The singulate mean age approximates the mean ages of entry into first marriage (see J. Hajnal, 1953). This number is equal to 26.5 for males and 22.2 for females. It refers to a period of several decades rather than to a particular year.

Table 3.4 gives data for the marital composition by four marital categories. It reveals that the divorced population is a small fraction of the total. A major reason is that divorcees remarry. Their fraction would remain small if the age distributions were considered. This fraction is higher for females because their number at older ages is higher.

The category of widowed reveals a large number of widows with respect to widowed men. It is again the longer length of life for females that explains this difference. For example, at ages beyond 80, nearly 80% of all females are widows, while the number of widowed men equals approximately the number of married men beyond the same age.

**Table 3.4: Population by Sex and Marital Status, 1992**

| | Total | Single | Married | Divorced | Widowed | Total |
|---|---|---|---|---|---|---|
| | 1,000 | % | % | % | % | % |
| Male | 4,166 | 38 | 56 | 2 | 4 | 100 |
| Female | 4,313 | 30 | 54 | 4 | 12 | 100 |

Source: NIS, 1992

### 3.2.3 Ethnic Composition

The Bulgarian population is a mixture of diverse ethnic groups. The dominant group is the Bulgarians. The largest other groups are the Turks and Roma/Gypsies. The most recent population census counted altogether 29 ethnic groups, ending with "others". Table 3.5 gives the numbers and shares of the major ethnic groups as observed in the 1992 population census.

These shares are indicative of the ethnic composition of the Bulgarian population for decades before 1992. The moderate changes in these shares hide a rich story of diverse demographic trends. Turks and Roma/Gypsies traditionally have a higher fertility and mortality than Bulgarians. Large groups of Turks have left the country following bilateral agreements with the neighbouring Republic of Turkey.

**Table 3.5: Population by Main Ethnic Groups, 1992**

| | Total | Bulgarians | Turks | Roma | Others |
|---|---|---|---|---|---|
| Number (1,000) | 8,487 | 7,271 | 800 | 313 | 103 |
| Proportion (%) | 100.0 | 85.7 | 9.4 | 3.7 | 1.2 |

Source: NIS, 1992

Among the "others" of specific interest, are ethnic groups such as the Karakachans (of Greek origin), Cherkez, Gagauz (of proto-Bulgarian origin), Wallachians, and Tartars. Studies about their origin are often controversial.

## 3.3 Fertility

The abrupt fall in fertility began in 1989. While the total number of live births in 1985 was 118,995 and 117,440 in 1988, it fell down to 112,272 in 1989, and as low as 72,188 in 1996. In discussing fertility changes, I will focus separately on the levels of fertility, age differentials and birth order.

### 3.3.1 Fertility Level

The demographic transition in Bulgaria finished around the end of the 1950s and the beginning of the 1960s. Then fertility and mortality fell to about zero population growth. In 1965, fertility was for the first time below replacement level, although the population growth was positive. This trend caused the adoption of the famous pronatalist policy in 1967 with a highly effective political instrument being the ban of abortions. Fertility rose for a couple of years, but then fell down again. In 1972 and several times during the next decade, the pronatalistic policy was improved and a moderate rise in fertility could be maintained. During the 1980s, the total fertility rate (TFR) was close to replacement level (approximately equal to 2.1). These changes are illustrated in Figure 3.3.

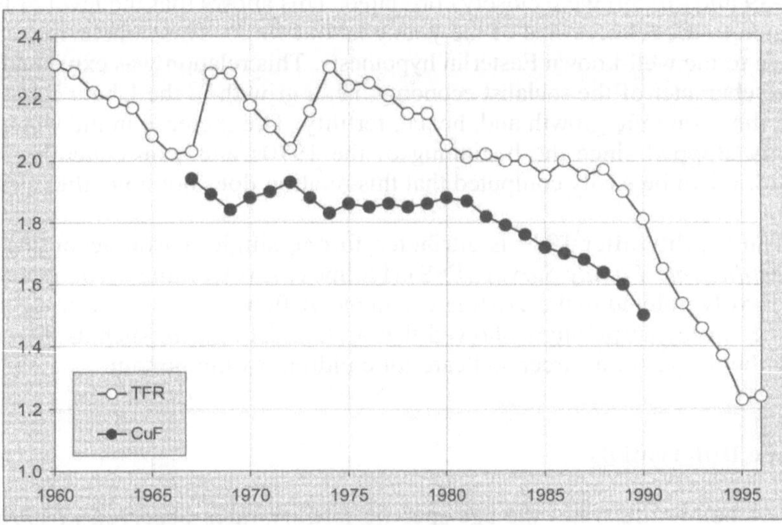


**Figure 3.3: Total Fertility Rate (TFR) and Cumulated Fertility (CuF) at Age 30[1] of the Cohort Born Between 1944–1966**

[1]Cumulated fertility at age 30 represents 90% of completed fertility. It is centred at the mean age of childbearing, 24 for each cohort

Source: author's calculation

The figure illustrates the abrupt fall in fertility that began in 1989. The TFR dropped down from 1.97 in 1988 to 1.23 in 1996 (Table 3.6). Beside TFR, the figure exhibits the values of partially completed fertility (CF) of cohorts born in 1944–45, through 1966. A restriction is imposed at the age of 30, when nearly 90% of all fertility has already been completed. This restriction makes it possible to comprise a larger number of cohorts. In the figure, the CF is placed at the mean age of childbearing, which is approximately 24 years. Thus the CF for the first cohort born in 1944 is placed in

1968. It can be seen that the CF changes moderately in comparison with the TFR. Its values are close to replacement level.

**Table 3.6: Total Fertility Rate (TFR), 1989–1996**

| | 1989 | 1990 | 1991 | 1992 | 1993 | 1994 | 1995 | 1996 |
|---|---|---|---|---|---|---|---|---|
| TFR | 1.87 | 1.74 | 1.71 | 1.59 | 1.47 | 1.37 | 1.23 | 1.23 |

Source: NIS, 1996

Surveys have been used in order to gain a deeper insight into the reasons for the fertility change in the 1970s and 1980s. Researchers point to the following major reasons: the high level of female employment; the rising educational level of women; housing problems; rising consumerism and material aspirations (Atanasov, 1987).

Carlson (1994) revealed that during the period 1947–1989, the deviation from the mean TFR and that of the ratio of young to aged within the labour force (age intervals 15–39 and 40–59) were closely correlated. This shows that the level of fertility was related to the relative size of the young labour force. This conclusion is in fact an inverse to the well-known Easterlin hypothesis. This relation was explained by the extensive character of the socialist economy, i.e. a growth in the labour force would increase the economic growth and, hence, fertility. The increase in the labour force practically stopped since the beginning of the 1970s and, consequently, fertility decreased. It can be easily computed that this relation does not hold after 1989.

The fall in fertility after 1989 is attributed to one single reason according to the 1998 *Fertility and Family Survey* (FFS) (Philipov, forthcoming). The interviewed women mostly pointed to the existing economic difficulties for not wanting another child. The survey surprisingly showed that a classical reason, such as the conflict between the desire for a career and care for children is unimportant.

### 3.3.2 Age Differentials

Figure 3.4 below illustrates the age-specific fertility rates observed in 1996. This age schedule is typical for fertility that begins at an early age, when compared with other European populations. It is also typical for an early completing of births. Indeed, beyond age 30, there is only a small fraction of the overall area under the curve. A third characteristic is that a large portion of the area under the curve is situated within a narrow age interval. These observations are quantified by the values for the mean age of childbearing and its standard deviation. They are 24.3 years and 5.1, respectively. This pattern of age-specific fertility was characteristic for a couple of decades preceding 1989. The most important observed change was the fall in the births of higher orders, reflected in a shift of the curve to the left.

Only slight changes were specific to the period after 1989. First, there was a slight increase in the mean age at childbearing, corresponding to a small movement of the curve to the right (Figure 3.4). Second, the standard deviation increased a little, which shows that the dispersion of births throughout ages has increased, although just a little. Third, there was a rise in adolescent fertility. This is, however, not evident from the figure. It is due to diverse reasons. For example, low education contributes to low sexual education and a lack of knowledge about modern contraceptives.

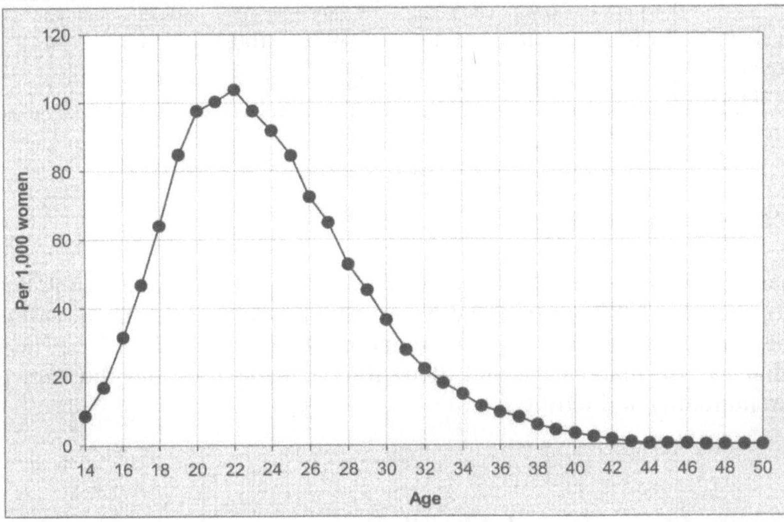


**Figure 3.4: Age-specific Fertility Rates, 1996**
Source: author's calculations

### 3.3.3 Birth Order

The order-specific TFR denoted by TFR(i) for the i-th child allows for the study of both level and distribution of fertility by birth order. It is computed by dividing the number of births of i-th order whose mothers are at age x, by all females aged x. Hence, the sum by i of TFR(i) is equal to TFR. The computed values are given for 1985 and 1996 in Table 3.7.

The TFR(1) for 1985 shows that nearly all women are expected to have at least one child. Most of them are expected to have a second child as well. Higher order births are much more rare. Their share is 15% of the total, as it can be estimated from the last row of the table. Hence, the two-child model was established among the Bulgarian families. The slight fall in fertility during the 1970s and the 1980s was mainly due to a fall in the births of order higher than the second.

In 1996, the situation was completely different. Two-thirds of all women had a first child, and two-thirds of those had a second child. The two-child model does not hold any more. The decrease in fertility was due to a decrease in births of second and first order. The number of women who will remain childless or with only one child increased substantially.

**Table 3.7: Fertility Indicators by Birth Order, 1985 and 1996**

| | 1985 | | | | 1996 | | | |
|---|---|---|---|---|---|---|---|---|
| | Total | 1st child | 2nd child | 3rd child | Total | 1st child | 2nd child | 3rd child |
| TFR(i) | 1.97 | 0.91 | 0.77 | 0.18 | 1.23 | 0.66 | 0.42 | 0.09 |
| Proportion (%) | 100 | 46 | 39 | 9 | 100 | 54 | 34 | 7 |
| Mean age of women at birth | 23.9 | 21.8 | 25.1 | 26.7 | 24.3 | 22.5 | 25.7 | 27.2 |

Sources: NIS, 1985 and 1996

### 3.3.4 Extramarital Births

Extramarital births before 1989 were, for decades, at the level of around 10 per 100 births. In the year 1989, a new trend began here as well. The share of extramarital births began increasing, and by 1996, it had gradually reached 28.2%. There is no doubt that its rise marked the end of traditional behaviour and the start of new norms in nuptiality and fertility.

## 3.4 Family Planning and Abortion

The low level of fertility was mostly achieved by the use of traditional methods of birth control such as the calendar method, coitus interruptus, and abstinence. The use of modern contraceptives has been limited. It has partially spread among women living in urban areas. Knowledge about modern devices was purposefully restricted during the totalitarian regime in order to assure the success of the pronatalist policy. Now, family planning is spreading. It is expected to improve knowledge, distribution and use of modern contraceptives among the entire population.

Bulgaria is known as a country with a large number of abortions, along with Russia and Romania. For decades, it has been known that more than one abortion corresponds to one birth. This ratio was about 1.15 before 1989. Since then it began increasing: first to 1.3 in 1992 and then to the level of about 1.3 in 1995 and 1996. The number of abortions in 1996, for example, was 93,540 while the number of live births was 72,188. Regretfully, this method of birth control prevails among the population primarily because of the low sexual culture and lack of knowledge about modern contraceptives. An important reason is also the high price of the latter.

## 3.5 Mortality

Mortality is described here by the average life expectancy at birth. It is given for the two sexes in Table 3.8.

**Table 3.8: Life Expectancy at Birth by Sex, 1980–1996, selected years, in years**

| | 1980 | 1985 | 1989 | 1990 | 1991 | 1992 | 1993 | 1994 | 1995 | 1996 |
|---|---|---|---|---|---|---|---|---|---|---|
| Male | 68.4 | 68.1 | 68.3 | 68.3 | 68.4 | 68.1 | 67.6 | 67.3 | 67.4 | 67.4 |
| Female | 73.9 | 74.2 | 74.9 | 75.0 | 74.8 | 75.1 | 75.2 | 74.9 | 74.9 | 74.6 |

Sources: NIS, 1985 and 1996

Since the end of the 1960s and until the end of the 1980s, the life expectancies for both sexes did not change substantially. However, causes of death did change during this period of time. Some causes, such as contagious diseases, decreased their impact on the overall mortality level. The primary causes of death were cardiovascular and cerebrovascular diseases, as well as respiratory and circulatory illnesses. The impact of malignant neoplasms also rose significantly.

Infant mortality decreased during this period, but remained high, when compared to other European countries. In 1990, its level was 14.8 per 1,000 births, the lowest level ever achieved in Bulgaria. During the following years, it increased, but an important reason for this trend was a change in the registration of these events. It was adjusted according to the international recommendations of the World Health Organization. In 1996, its level was 15.6 per 1,000 births. After 1989, life expectancy at birth did not change as abruptly as it did in some ex-socialist countries. During the period 1989–1996, males lost about a year of their life. Life expectancy at older ages demonstrates how this happened. The estimated life expectancies at certain ages are given in Table 3.9.

**Table 3.9: Life Expectancy at Certain Ages by Sex, 1990 and 1996, in years**

| Age | 1990 | | 1996 | |
|---|---|---|---|---|
| | Male | Female | Male | Female |
| 0 | 68.3 | 75.0 | 67.4 | 74.6 |
| 1 | 68.4 | 75.0 | 67.7 | 74.6 |
| 15 | 55.0 | 61.4 | 54.2 | 61.0 |
| 45 | 27.5 | 32.6 | 26.6 | 32.2 |
| 65 | 12.9 | 15.4 | 12.6 | 15.1 |

Source: author's calculations

The life expectancy at age 1 shows that if the impact of infant mortality was eliminated, males would live longer, especially in 1996. It can be seen that the loss of a year of life expectancy among the males in 1996 occurred in adult ages. Indeed, at age 65, both life expectancies in 1990 and in 1996 are close, but this is not the case at age 45. Mortality among adult males has increased during the last few years because of stress and an unhealthy way of life, especially smoking and inadequate consumption of food. Bulgaria ranks first in Europe, with respect to smoking.

The age-specific mortality curves for males and females, as observed (without smoothing) in 1996, are presented in Figure 3.5. Both mortality schedules have shapes that do not differ from those observed in many other populations.

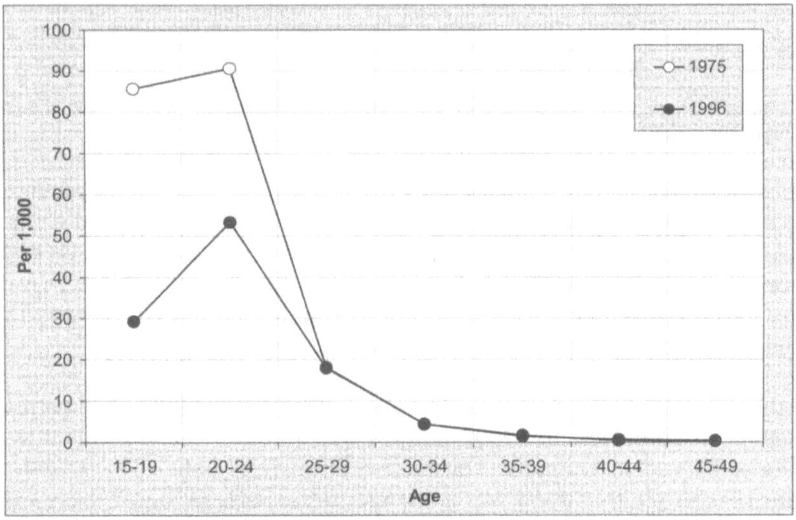


**Figure 3.5: Age-specific Death Rates, 1996**

Source: author's calculations

The most important difference between the two schedules is an excess mortality of males with respect to females at adult ages. It is vividly depicted in the figure. In 1989, the adult mortality ratio for males to females was 2 to 1, while in 1994 it rose to 3 to 1. The reasons for this were mentioned above.

Standardised mortality rates by cause of death from the World Health Organization show that in 1991 Bulgaria's males ranked first in the world according to deaths due to blood circulation diseases. Females ranked second. The total population ranked first in regard to mortality due to brain-vessel diseases. Malignant neoplasm ranked after these causes of death (NIS, 1995). During the most recent years, mortality increased primarily due to a rise in cardiovascular and digestive diseases.

It should be noted that mortality differentials by ethnic groups are substantial. Experts are of the opinion that life expectancy of Roma/Gypsies is not higher than about 60 years (no data is available). Author's personal (unpublished) estimations show that in 1993 life expectancy for Turks was about 64 for males and 71 for females. The Bulgarian ethnic group would have then a life expectancy that is about one year higher than that of the total population.

## 3.6 International Migration

Until 1989, the only significant emigration flow was that of people from the Turkish ethnic group who moved to Turkey, in accordance with bilateral agreements. Ethnic migration was particularly strong in 1989 and 1990, when more than 300,000 Turks left Bulgaria. This flow began spontaneously, following the repression by the totalitarian regime of the Turkish minority group. About 100,000 came back about one year later.

The statistics of emigration are still being developed and, for the time being, there is no official statistical data about the size of annual emigration available. Estimates show that it is about 35 thousand per year (NIS, 1995).

Immigration is considerably smaller and insignificant if demographic change is considered. Illegal emigration and immigration is wide-spread. The most preferred countries for emigration are the USA, Germany, and Canada. Turks have a definite preference for Turkey.

Bulgarians living abroad are not united into ethnic communities, unlike emigrants of some other countries. Hence, the emigration network has not been developed. It is expected that future emigration flows will remain at the magnitudes estimated today, i.e. during the next 10 years, a quarter of a million to half a million people will leave the country.

## 3.7 Family Formation and Dissolution

This section gives a statistical description of nuptiality and divorces followed by a description of the prevailing pattern of family formation.

### 3.7.1 Marriage and Divorce

Table 3.10 shows that the total number of marriages per year has been decreasing since 1975. An abrupt decline was observed after 1989. It cannot be explained by demographic statistical change such as a decrease in the number of persons eligible to marry. New behaviour patterns likely began to develop.

The study of the marital status in the first section revealed that nearly all men and women have ever entered into a marriage. This inference is proven also by period data for first marriages. The sum of the age-specific first marriage rates is the total first marriage rate, denoted here by TFMR. Table 3.10 shows the values for the TFMR in selected years.

**Table 3.10: Main Indicators of Nuptiality, 1965–1996, selected years**

| Year | Marriages | | | Divorces | | |
|---|---|---|---|---|---|---|
| | Number | TFMR[1] | Mean age at first marriage | Number | TDR[2] (under 50) | Mean age at divorce (under 50) |
| 1965 | 65,893 | 0.92 | 21.4 | 8,679 | 0.13 | 30.3 |
| 1975 | 74,947 | 1.00 | 21.4 | 11,030 | 0.16 | 30.2 |
| 1985 | 66,682 | 0.93 | 21.4 | 14,361 | 0.22 | 31.1 |
| 1989 | 63,263 | 0.93 | 21.5 | 12,636 | 0.20 | 32.2 |
| 1990 | 59,874 | 0.87 | 21.4 | 11,368 | 0.18 | 32.1 |
| 1991 | 48,820 | 0.70 | 21.5 | 11,044 | 0.18 | 32.0 |
| 1992 | 44,806 | 0.66 | 21.6 | 9,465 | 0.15 | 34.6 |
| 1993 | 40,022 | 0.58 | 21.9 | 7,324 | 0.12 | 34.5 |
| 1994 | 37,910 | 0.58 | 22.3 | 7,990 | 0.13 | 32.3 |
| 1995 | 36,795 | 0.56 | 22.1 | 10,661 | 0.18 | 32.5 |
| 1996 | 35,723 | 0.54 | 22.4 | 10,014 | .. | .. |

[1]Total first marriage rate (TFMR) is the probability of first marriage for a person if s/he to pass through her/his lifetime conforming to the age-specific first marriage rates of a given year; it is computed by the summation of age-specific first marriage rates, generally up to age 49, observed in a given year
[2]Total divorce rate (TDR) is the probability of divorce for a married person if s/he to pass through her/his marriage years confirming to the duration-specific divorce rates of a given year; it is computed by the summation of divorce rates by duration of marriage, generally up to 30 years, observed in a given year
Sources: based on NIS data and author's calculations

Until 1989, its value was close to 1. That is the case for years not included in the table. Hence, nearly all women will eventually marry. After 1989, this inference did not hold. The percentage of women who will ever marry decreased drastically in 1996. Therefore, many women will remain never-married if the patterns of marriage revealed by the age-specific first marriage rates prevail for long time. In short, nuptiality has decreased significantly during the 1990s.

Table 3.10 gives additional information on nuptiality through the mean age at first marriage. Its rise by nearly one year is evident. This can be observed since 1990. The reasons for the postponement of marriages are not well known. In a few years, with the accumulation of statistical information answer could be found, but now we remain only with speculations.

The changes in the TFMR through time are illustrated by the age-specific first marriage rates for 1975 and 1996, given in Figure 3.6.

The TFMR is the area under the curve. This area is considerably smaller in 1996, and the difference is due to the decrease in first marriages through age 25. After this age, there is virtually no change in the age-specific rates. Does this mean that younger people do not marry? Once again, this question cannot be answered till later. One possibility is that there is a complex cohort change that is masked by the period data studied here. Another possibility for the answer is that young people have decided not to marry. Then extramarital unions should have increased.

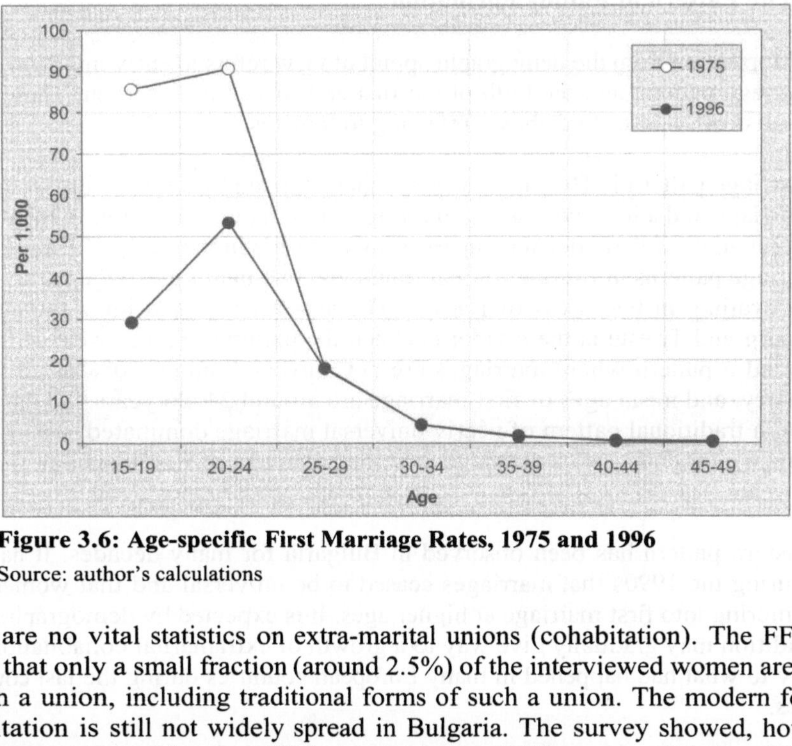


**Figure 3.6: Age-specific First Marriage Rates, 1975 and 1996**
Source: author's calculations

There are no vital statistics on extra-marital unions (cohabitation). The FFS data shows that only a small fraction (around 2.5%) of the interviewed women are living in such a union, including traditional forms of such a union. The modern form of cohabitation is still not widely spread in Bulgaria. The survey showed, however, that women accept this type of living arrangement (Philipov, op. cit.). Possibly, during the next few years it will spread quickly through a large part of the population.

The change in the number of divorces per year is diverse. Divorces are heavily dependent on the legislative system. The changes in the latter in Bulgaria are usually in the direction of increasing divorce taxes. The last increase in the end of 1991 made this tax many times higher than the previous one. Hence, divorces decreased for just three years. During these years, inflation made the tax small, so divorces increased again.

The total divorce rate is a better index than absolute numbers. It is defined analogously to the TFMR. Its values for selected years are given in Table 3.10 above, computed for divorces of females under age 50. The TDR had been decreasing during the 1990s until 1995, when, most probably, a compensation increase began. Thus, through the years, the decrease has been smaller than that observed for marriages. The mean age at divorce for females under age 50 is also given in Table 3.10. Its rise is evident. The temporary rise observed in 1992 and 1993 was probably due to the imposition of the higher tax, which in turn possibly caused postponement of divorce by younger couples.

### 3.7.2 The Pattern of Family Formation

Family formation from the demographic point of view refers to entry into marriage, or the marriage pattern, and the birth of the first and successive children. These events were statistically described above, referring to females.

The marriage pattern in Bulgaria has been characterised by a nearly universal entry into marriage and a low mean age at marriage for females, compared to many European populations. International comparisons were made in the study of Hajnal (1965) on marriage patterns in Europe. Hajnal found that two major marriage patterns have been prevailing in two areas of Europe. The abstract line that links the cities St. Petersburg and Trieste is the divider between the patterns. To the west of this line dominated a pattern where marriages are not universal, about 70% of all women ever marry, and mean ages of first marriage are around 24–26 years. To the east of the line, a traditional pattern of nearly universal marriage dominated, where nearly all women ever enter into a marriage, and the mean age of first marriage is around 20–22 years.

The eastern pattern has been observed in Bulgaria for many decades. It has been only during the 1990s that marriages ceased to be universal and that women have been entering into first marriage at higher ages. It is expected by demographers that this tradition may gradually give way to a growth of extramarital cohabitation analogously to what had happened in many European countries during the last couple of decades.

The demographic patterns of childbearing are very similar to those of marriage. It is common in most populations, where traditions prevail, that the first child is born around a year after the marriage. This should also have been expected to be the case with the Bulgarian population. However, vital statistics data indicates a different inference. Table 3.7 and Table 3.10 show that the difference between the mean age at first marriage and mean age at birth of a first child was 0.4 of a year in 1985 (i.e. about 5 months), and only 0.1 of a year in 1996. The difference is less than 9 months. The FFS data exhibits a completely different relationship. The mean age at first marriage is 19.9 years, and the first child was born 2.4 years later (Philipov, op. cit.).

While vital statistics show a too small difference between mean age at first marriage and mean age at birth of a first child, according to the survey, it is quite large. Other surveys indicate the same inference. This contradiction makes difficult the generalisation of these observations without further detailed work that is beyond the scope of this study. We may only conclude the following. The survey data refers to many cohorts, hence its mean ages refer to a long period of time, not just a particular year. They should describe traditional behaviour. The period data shows a decrease in the difference between the two mean ages. Most probably that during the 1990s, there has been an increase in the number of first marriages that followed the first pregnancy in which the woman decided to deliver. The lack of data allows for diverse speculations based on this observation. It may be concluded though, that there is a shift away from the traditional behaviour.

## 3.8 Current Changes in Demographic Behaviour

The previous sections presented quantitative aspects of recent population change. Here, the discussion focuses on behaviour. Why did fertility fall? Why did the number of marriages fall? Why did the mean ages at marriage and childbearing rise? Such questions need behavioural answers once statistical indicators have outlined the major trends.

The political and economic changes since 1989 brought about numerous changes in the way of life. With respect to changes in demographic behaviour, they form two major groups. The first one refers to the diffusion of behaviour that exists in other populations. The second refers to the adaptation of people to their changing conditions of life.

### 3.8.1 Diffusion of New Forms of Demographic Behaviour

The decline of nuptiality and fertility, a rise in their mean ages, and increase in divorces were observed in nearly all populations in Europe at different time periods. Significant changes of this kind began in the middle of the 1960s. They spread quickly through most of Western, Northern and Southern Europe during the 1970s and the 1980s. These changes were defined by some demographers as the "Second demographic transition" (Cliquet, 1991; Lesthaeghe, 1992; van de Kaa, 1987). An important trend that characterised the second demographic transition was the spread of non-marital cohabitation. As it was already mentioned, extramarital cohabitation has been rare as of yet in Bulgaria, but is expected to grow. Hence, the major demographic changes in Bulgaria today look, at least statistically, like those that developed in Europe one or two decades ago. Is this diffusion? In order to answer this question, one needs to compare the causes of demographic changes in Bulgaria to those of the second demographic transition. The latter are identified as ideational shifts and breaks in traditional behaviour, and economic autonomy of women, among others.

Such a study was carried out by the author (Philipov, 1997; Philipov *et al.*, 1997). It stated that demographic changes until 1989 in Bulgaria, as well as in the other ex-socialist countries, could be closely connected to the domination of the totalitarian regime, where new forms of behaviour had little chance of diffusion. Hence, ideational shifts could hardly break through. Economic autonomy of women was indeed achieved during those years, when labour force participation rates for women rose significantly. It was also found to be doubtful that significant changes in behaviour such as ideational shifts could have developed within just a few years after the fall of the totalitarian regime. The study is inconclusive, finding insufficient evidence as to whether there was a diffusion of new forms of demographic behaviour.

### 3.8.2 Adaptation to Changing Conditions of Life

Since 1989, life in Bulgaria changed drastically in all its spheres: notably political, cultural, economic, and social. A concise description follows.

The well-known political change includes the fall of the totalitarian regime. What followed, though, is difficult to define. Democracy came to predominate through freedom of speech and the press, the free market and new forms of property. Two political powers dominate, making the political system undesirably bipolar. During nine years, none of several governments were able to carry out a full term. The National Assembly needs to adopt hundreds of new laws necessary for the functioning of the new political order. However, the most difficult change to occur is a change within the minds of the people. Many still preserve old habits and understandings that are inconsistent with a democratic society. Aged people dominate among the latter.

The economic changes in Bulgaria were especially difficult. The gross domestic product (GDP) in 1997 was 10.2 billion US dollars, which makes US$1,227 per capita. Given an index of 100 at 1990, industrial production in 1997 was 58.8 (UN ECE, 1999, p. 11, 121).

Privatisation began late. The first wave of mass privatisation was carried out in 1995–1996. Paid privatisation is slow because of a lack of buyers. Most of the enterprises continue to be state property. Very few large companies were privatised. Most of the privatised units are small enterprises and shops. Foreign payment for the privatised objects during the period 1992–1997 was only about 1%. Restitution of land is also slow.

Restructuring is the major economic shift at the level of both sectors and property. Its effect on labour is particularly negative. Unemployment has risen substantially ever since 1990. In November 1997, 534 thousand persons were unemployed, which is 15% of the total labour force. A negative feature of unemployment is its long duration. In November 1997, 308 thousand persons had been unemployed for more than one year. Unemployment is larger among people with low qualifications, among women and the younger population (ILO, 1998). Especially high is the unemployment level among Roma/Gypsies, as well as among the Turkish minority.

Inflation was strong during this period. Its peak was in January 1997, when hyperinflation was reached. It was stopped by a change of the government. During the period 1990–1997, the consumer price index increased nearly 1,000 times. Being 100 in 1990, it was 2,296 in 1994; 3,722 in 1995; 8,300 in 1996; and 98,132 in 1997 (as of 31 December of each year). The largest increase was from 1996 to 1997 – by more than eleven times (UN ECE, 1998).

Liberalisation of prices was perhaps one of the few successful large-scale economic changes. It began in 1990, leaving practically no controlled prices today. Ceiling prices are used for basic primary products. Foreign investment is scarce in comparison to other ex-socialist countries of Central Europe. Its volume during the period 1991–1995 was only 530 million US dollars. Perspectives for its increase are unclear.

The improvement of the economic environment was underway during 1997, after the adoption of a steady exchange course of 1 DM per 1,000 Leva (known as "exchange board"). Inflation as a result has decreased; even deflation was reached for a short period of time.

This difficult economic situation had a negative impact on incomes and social security. For example, the purchasing power of the household decreased nearly twice during the period 1994–1997. It was estimated that at the end of 1996 an inhabitant of Sofia needed 40,235 Leva monthly just for food, while his/her average income was only 15,831 Leva. The difference can be explained by the necessity for people to use up their savings. Unofficially, because of a lack of data, there is the explanation that many people have undeclared income. The black economy is supposed to be very large.

Social policy is lagging behind the needs that it should meet. Social security has been only about 11.1% of the GDP during recent years, and health care – only 3.4%. There still exists a wide social net that covers many people, but the coverage is often below the minimum subsistence level. So are pensions, which size was hardly adjusted until recently.

This brief picture of the Bulgarian political and economic life reveals difficulties that people have to face. Under the need to assure their own personal existence, it may well be supposed that they should postpone marriage and births for later times, hoping for an improvement in their welfare. Postponement of births often leads to their denial. This is a short explanation of the adaptation to changing conditions of life. It may explain why fertility falls, and why mean age of childbearing rises. To the question in the FFS study "Why do you not want to have any more children?" the majority of the respondents (52%) in Bulgaria replied that "care for children is expensive" (Philipov, op. cit.).

However, people who do not experience economic difficulties also postpone marriage and births. All people face a substantially increased set of choice alternatives for study or work. In conditions of increased uncertainty, they decide to postpone such time-consuming and life-changing events as marriage and births.

Diffusion or adaptation? This short discussion reveals that either one can be the basis of changed demographic behaviour if only quantitative changes are considered. Where causes of change are considered, adaptation seems to be dominant. The impact of diffusion may be stronger in the future. Hence, it may be expected that fertility will remain at low levels for at least a decade ahead. This is the basis for hypotheses of low fertility levels in population projections (see Appendix).

## 3.9 Population-related Policy

The first pronatalist population policy (called demographic in Bulgaria) was introduced in 1966. It was dominated by such restrictive policy instruments as a ban on induced abortions, the introduction of a bachelor' tax, etc. It proved to be ineffective: people found ways to go around the restrictions. In 1973, the enlarged set of policy instruments was introduced, adding to the previous ones child allowances, mothers' leaves, and other encouraging measures. This demographic policy was legalised through an Act of the State Council. Such an Act in the legal system of Bulgaria is at a level below laws and has only temporary significance – until a law replaces it. This has not happened yet as of today. This Act remains a legal basis of the demographic policy, even though the State Council has not existed for 8 years. The Act ("for the encouragement of natality") has been reconstructed many times since its first announcement.

After 1989, the rapid inflation made child allowances an ineffective policy instrument. Several times the National Assembly raised their level, but inflation made such adjustments ineffective very quickly. The last corrections were introduced in November 1999. A monthly child allowance now equals 90% of the wage earned by the woman, but cannot be lower than the minimum wage. The same amount is paid to women during 135 days of mother's leave. A longer leave with a decreased payment is also available. These policy instruments do not depend on the order of the birth.

The long-lasting instruments of the demographic policy have become a social necessity. They are accepted by society and no government would dare make unpopular changes. Some changes are indeed discussed, but they are expected by society. For example, it is suggested that people with high incomes would not be eligible to get allowances.

The legal basis of the demographic policy is also under discussion. There exist at the moment two basic opinions. One is that all law texts referring to children and the family, which affect the demographic policy, should be gathered into a single specialised act. The other is that texts should stay where they are (in laws such as the

Code of the Family, the Law for persons and the family, and many others), but be improved according to the requirements of the transition to a democratic society.

Women's organisations and trade unions are most active with respect to the improvement of the legal system. These organisations are pushing the National Assembly to take up discussions on several projects of laws. Such projects refer to a Code of the Child and others that should legalise a system of family planning as well as provide incentives for higher fertility.

## 3.10 Conclusion

Where demographic statistics are considered, there is extensive information that reveals substantial changes in demographic behaviour in Bulgaria. Where causes for change are considered, our knowledge is modest. We are left to let time elapse to help us in understanding what is going on. There is little doubt that the worsened economic conditions of life as well as the diffusion of new behaviour have a major impact on peoples' decisions to form families. Scientific research has to identify the population groups where each one of these, and possibly other, causes of change, have their dominant effect.

# Appendix

## Forecast of the Population of Bulgaria According to Three Fertility Scenarios

This forecast is based on a cohort projection. The key assumption is that cohorts born after 1984 will have a completed fertility at the level of 1996 in Scenario 1; equal to 1.67 in Scenario 2; equal to 2.10 in Scenario 3. The initial year is 1996. The forecast was done by the author.

**Table 3.A1: Scenario 1: Completed Fertility Remaining Constant at the Level Observed in 1996**

| | 1996 | 2000 | 2005 | 2010 | 2015 | 2020 |
|---|---|---|---|---|---|---|
| | Total | | | | | |
| Young[1] (%) | 17.45 | 15.66 | 13.64 | 12.71 | 12.54 | 12.09 |
| Working[2] (%) | 64.00 | 64.96 | 66.61 | 66.73 | 65.70 | 65.05 |
| Old[3] (%) | 18.55 | 19.38 | 19.75 | 20.56 | 21.76 | 22.85 |
| Number (1,000) | 8,362 | 8,179 | 7,906 | 7,606 | 7,282 | 6,927 |
| CBR[4] | 8.63 | 7.97 | 7.91 | 7.85 | 7.22 | 6.45 |
| CDR[5] | 14.00 | 14.84 | 16.28 | 17.06 | 17.64 | 18.16 |
| Natural growth | -5.37 | -6.86 | -8.37 | -9.21 | -10.43 | -11.71 |
| TFR[6] | 1.23 | 1.11 | 1.13 | 1.18 | 1.21 | 1.23 |
| | Male | | | | | |
| 0–14 (%) | 18.30 | 16.53 | 14.55 | 13.69 | 13.57 | 13.12 |
| 15–64 (%) | 68.15 | 69.07 | 71.09 | 72.09 | 71.30 | 70.95 |
| 65+ (%) | 13.55 | 14.39 | 14.35 | 14.22 | 15.13 | 15.93 |
| Number (1,000) | 4,090 | 3,982 | 3,833 | 3,677 | 3,513 | 3,335 |
| | Female | | | | | |
| 0–14 (%) | 16.64 | 14.84 | 12.78 | 11.80 | 11.59 | 11.14 |
| 15–59 (%) | 60.02 | 61.05 | 62.38 | 61.71 | 60.47 | 59.58 |
| 60+ (%) | 23.34 | 24.11 | 24.84 | 26.50 | 27.94 | 29.28 |
| Number (1,000) | 4,272 | 4,197 | 4,073 | 3,929 | 3,769 | 3,592 |

**Table 3.A2: Scenario 2: Completed Fertility[7] Equal to 1.67**

| | 1996 | 2000 | 2005 | 2010 | 2015 | 2020 |
|---|---|---|---|---|---|---|
| | | | Total | | | |
| Young[1] (%) | 17.45 | 15.71 | 14.09 | 14.07 | 15.05 | 15.37 |
| Working[2] (%) | 64.00 | 64.92 | 66.26 | 65.68 | 63.83 | 62.77 |
| Old[3] (%) | 18.55 | 19.37 | 19.65 | 20.24 | 21.12 | 21.85 |
| Number (1,000) | 8,362 | 8,184 | 7,948 | 7,726 | 7,502 | 7,244 |
| CBR[4] | 8.63 | 8.26 | 9.24 | 10.07 | 9.67 | 8.74 |
| CDR[5] | 14.00 | 14.83 | 16.22 | 16.84 | 17.19 | 17.43 |
| Natural growth | -5.37 | -6.57 | -6.98 | -6.77 | -7.52 | -8.68 |
| TFR[6] | 1.23 | 1.15 | 1.32 | 1.51 | 1.61 | 1.65 |
| | | | Male | | | |
| 0–14 (%) | 18.30 | 16.58 | 15.04 | 15.14 | 16.24 | 16.61 |
| 15–64 (%) | 68.15 | 69.03 | 70.69 | 70.88 | 69.11 | 68.21 |
| 65+ (%) | 13.55 | 14.39 | 14.27 | 13.98 | 14.65 | 15.18 |
| Number (1,000) | 4,090 | 3,985 | 3,855 | 3,734 | 3,628 | 3,501 |
| | | | Female | | | |
| 0–14 (%) | 16.64 | 14.88 | 13.20 | 13.07 | 13.94 | 14.22 |
| 15–59 (%) | 60.02 | 61.02 | 62.08 | 60.81 | 58.88 | 57.69 |
| 60+ (%) | 23.34 | 24.10 | 24.71 | 26.12 | 27.18 | 28.10 |
| Number (1,000) | 4,272 | 4,199 | 4,093 | 3,986 | 3,874 | 3,744 |

**Table 3.A3: Scenario 3: Completed Fertility Equal to 2.10**

| | 1996 | 2000 | 2005 | 2010 | 2015 | 2020 |
|---|---|---|---|---|---|---|
| | | | Total | | | |
| Young[1] (%) | 17.45 | 15.74 | 14.50 | 15.33 | 17.37 | 18.38 |
| Working[2] (%) | 64.00 | 64.89 | 65.94 | 64.72 | 62.10 | 60.67 |
| Old[3] (%) | 18.55 | 19.36 | 19.56 | 19.95 | 20.53 | 20.95 |
| Number (1,000) | 8,362 | 8,187 | 7,986 | 7,841 | 7,717 | 7,558 |
| CBR[4] | 8.63 | 8.51 | 10.48 | 12.21 | 12.03 | 10.84 |
| CDR[5] | 14.00 | 14.83 | 16.16 | 16.64 | 16.77 | 16.77 |
| Natural growth | -5.37 | -6.32 | -5.68 | -4.43 | -4.74 | -5.93 |
| TFR[6] | 1.23 | 1.18 | 1.49 | 1.83 | 2.02 | 2.08 |
| | | | Male | | | |
| 0–14 (%) | 18.30 | 16.62 | 15.47 | 16.48 | 18.71 | 19.79 |
| 15–64 (%) | 68.15 | 69.00 | 70.33 | 69.76 | 67.08 | 65.71 |
| 65+ (%) | 13.55 | 14.38 | 14.20 | 13.76 | 14.21 | 14.50 |
| Number (1,000) | 4,090 | 3,987 | 3,875 | 3,800 | 3,740 | 3,664 |
| | | | Female | | | |
| 0–14 (%) | 16.64 | 14.91 | 13.58 | 14.25 | 16.12 | 17.06 |
| 15–59 (%) | 60.02 | 60.99 | 61.81 | 59.99 | 57.40 | 55.93 |
| 60+ (%) | 23.34 | 24.09 | 24.61 | 25.76 | 26.48 | 27.01 |
| Number (1,000) | 4,272 | 4,200 | 4,111 | 4,041 | 3,977 | 3,894 |

**Glossary** (based on *Recent Demographic Developments in Europe 1998*, Strasbourg: Council of Europe, pp. 463–464):

[1]The total population at working age; it is computed by the summation of males and females at working age (these are the ages 15 to 64 for males, and 15 to 59 for females).

[2]The population aged 0 to 14 completed years of age.

[3]The total population beyond working age; it is computed by the summation of males and females beyond working age.

[4]Crude birth rate (CBR) measures the relative frequency of births within the population as a whole in a given year; the ratios are expressed per 1,000 inhabitants.

[5]Crude mortality rate (CMR) measures the relative frequency of deaths within the population as a whole in a given year; the ratios are expressed per 1,000 inhabitants.

[6]Total fertility rate (TFR) measures the average number of children that would be born alive to a woman during her lifetime if she to pass through her childbearing years conforming to the age-specific fertility rates of a given year.

[7]Completed fertility (CF) measures the average number of children born to a cohort of women up to the end of their childbearing age.

## References

Atanasov, A. (1987), Reproductive functions of the family, In: C. Kjuranov (ed.), *The Contemporary Bulgarian Family*, Sofia.

Carlson, E. (1994), The economic context of past and future Bulgarian fertility, *European Journal of Population*, Vol. 10(1), pp. 69–86.

Cliquet, R.L. (1991), The Second Demographic Transition: Fact or Fiction? *Council of Europe Population Studies*, Vol. 23, Strasbourg: Council of Europe.

Council of Europe (1998), *Recent Demographic Developments in Europe 1998*, Strasbourg: Council of Europe.

Hajnal, J. (1953), Age at marriage and proportion marrying, *Population Studies*, Vol. 7, pp. 111–132.

ILO (International Labour Organisation) (1998), *Yearbook of Labour Statistics (various issues)*, Geneva: ILO.

Lesthaeghe, R. (1992), Der Zweite Demographische Übergang in den Westlichen Ländern: Eine Deutung, *Zeitschrift für Befölkerungswissenschaft*, Vol. 18(3), pp. 313–354.

NIS (National Institute of Statistics) (1985), *Demographic Yearbook Naselenie 1985*, Sofia: NIS.

NIS (National Institute of Statistics) (1992), *Demographic Yearbook Naselenie 1992*, Sofia: NIS.

NIS (National Institute of Statistics) (1995), *The Child, the Family, the Society*, Sofia: NIS.

NIS (National Institute of Statistics) (1996), *Demographic Yearbook Naselenie 1996*, Sofia: NIS.

Philipov, D. (1997), Family formation in Bulgaria and the impact of totalitarian regime, *Sociologicheski problemi*, No. 1–2, Sofia: Institute of Sociology.

Philipov, D. (forthcoming), *The International Research Project "Fertility and Family Survey"*, Sofia: Naselenie, Bulgarian Academy of Sciences.

Philipov, D. *et al.* (1997), *The Second Demographic Transition and Demographic Changes in Bulgaria*, Sofia: Institute of Demography, Bulgarian Academy of Sciences.

Stolnitz, G.J. (ed.) (1992), *Demographic Causes and Economic Consequences*, New York: United Nations.

UN ECE (United Nations Economic Commission for Europe) (1998), *Economic Survey of Europe 1998, No. 1*, New York and Geneva: United Nations.

UN ECE (United Nations Economic Commission for Europe) (1999), *Trends in Europe and North America. The Statistical Yearbook of the Economic Commission for Europe*, New York and Geneva: United Nations.

van de Kaa, D.J. (1987), Europe's Second Demographic Transition, *Population Bulletin*, Vol. 42(1), pp. 1–58.

# 4

# Population Development in the Czech Republic in the 1990s

**Miroslava Mašková and Leona Stašová**

## 4.1 Introduction

In January 1993, the Czech Republic has started its independent existence after the dissolution of the Czechoslovakia. Since the beginning of the 1990s, the population of the Czech Republic has been experiencing a new phase of development: a completely new tendencies in demographic behaviour of the Czech population have appeared.

The levels of nuptiality and fertility have rapidly dropped during the past several years and the intensity of induced abortions has markedly decreased as well. The number of divorces has increased to an unprecedented level. Mortality rates, that were stagnating or only slightly improving during the last thirty years, have positively changed in a relatively short time. Consequently, the relation between numbers of births and deaths has also changed. The natural increase has reached negative values for the first time in the post-war period.

The most important implication of the current situation, however, is not a tendency towards a population decrease but, instead, a shrinking of the base of the age pyramid. This will cause irregularities in the age structure and affect relations between children and adults as well as between economically active and non-active population in the future. The progressive population ageing can be expected.

The changes in demographic behaviour in the 1990s have undoubtedly been the result of the new political, economic and social conditions of the population development that have arisen as a part of the economic and social transformation after the November 1989 "Velvet Revolution". The liberalisation of economic conditions and changes in the labour market, especially the emergence of private entrepreneurs and the pressure to have higher qualifications, have played an important role in the economic sphere. Young people, particularly those who are not under the pressure of the past historical experience and for whom it is less difficult to adapt life plans to a new situation, have reacted to these changed conditions.

The transition to a market economy has brought not only positive implications by broadening the spectrum of individual possibilities and decisions. It has been also accompanied by a rise of various social risks, for example, unemployment. A richer variety of opportunities for personal development, on the one hand, and increasing unemployment among young people or threat of it, on the other, have led a majority of young people to change their patterns of marriage and parenthood, to delay marriage and childbearing plans.

While total unemployment rate in 1997 was about 5.5%, among those aged 15–19 it reached 20.2%. In the age groups 20–24 and 25–29, the figures were 7.3% and 6.1%. The unemployment rate was slightly higher for women than for men. One-third of unemployed persons in the age group under 25 years were looking for a job for more than 6 months. In April 1999, the total unemployment rate rose further to 8.2% and its continual increase is expected (Kuchařová and Tuček, 1999; Hajný, 1999).

The changes in the demographic behaviour of young people have also been conditioned by an insufficient housing construction together with a rise in the prices of existing dwellings and the difficulties in finding rental accommodation, especially in large cities. A slow increase in real incomes of employees that only returned to their 1989 level in 1996 has been another important factor, although the higher quality of goods and services available should also be taken into account. Since 1995, the average annual rate of inflation remained just under 10% (UN ECE, 1999, p. 120), and the official minimum income and the social welfare benefits linked with it, including pensions, were adjusted accordingly. The degree of poverty, as judged by objective standards, remained low, although the relative poverty rose as income differences increased (Večerník, 1998).

The necessary transformation processes turned out to be more complicated than had originally been thought, placing a greater burden on the general population. The results of the 1998 parliamentary elections confirmed the changing preferences for existing political parties in response to the increasing criticism of political, economic and, especially, social development. The deregulation of energy and housing rental prices in 1998 has contributed to the stagnation of real incomes, to the increase of inflation and to the rise of anxiety about economic well being. The anxiety has been especially high among young families who are only beginning to decide about the number of children they will have and the timing of births (Kuchařová and Tuček, op. cit.).

Thus, the population climate has substantially worsened under the current social circumstances and young people, except young businessmen, cannot expect any greater improvement of their situation in the meantime. The changes in the reproduction of the population represent an example of pragmatic behaviour that reflects clearly the risks young people face under current situation if they decide to marry and bear children. This situation has not been changed by the valorisation of social and family benefits. On the other hand, the relatively stable social security of elderly people in combination with improved health care was probably one of the reasons for the improved level of mortality among the elderly.

## 4.2 Total Population and Its Structures

During the 1990s, the population of the Czech Republic on its territory of 78,864 square kilometres has remained stable – slightly above 10.3 million (i.e. 131 inhabitants per square kilometre). In 1994, the first decline in the number of inhabitants in modern times was recorded (Table 4.1). Since then, the number of births has not been compensating for the number of deaths. Net migration, even though positive, has not been sufficient to eliminate the losses due to negative natural increase. The falling birth rate means that this trend can be expected to continue over the coming years.

**Table 4.1: Population Change, 1991–1998**

| | 1991 | 1992 | 1993 | 1994 | 1995 | 1996 | 1997 | 1998 |
|---|---|---|---|---|---|---|---|---|
| | Total numbers | | | | | | | |
| Live births | 129,354 | 121,705 | 121,025 | 106,579 | 96,097 | 90,446 | 90,657 | 90,535 |
| Deaths | 124,290 | 120,337 | 118,185 | 117,373 | 117,913 | 112,782 | 112,744 | 109,527 |
| Natural increase | 5,064 | 1,368 | 2,840 | -10,794 | -21,816 | -22,336 | -22,087 | -18,992 |
| Immigrants | 14,096 | 19,072 | 12,900 | 10,207 | 10,540 | 10,857 | 12,880 | 10,729 |
| Emigrants | 11,220 | 7,291 | 7,424 | 265 | 541 | 728 | 805 | 1,241 |
| Net migration | 2,876 | 11,781 | 5,476 | 9,942 | 9,999 | 10,129 | 12,075 | 9,488 |
| Total increase | 7,940 | 13,149 | 8,316 | -852 | -11,817 | -12,207 | -10,012 | -9,504 |
| | Crude rates (per 1,000 inhabitants) | | | | | | | |
| Natural increase | 0.5 | 0.1 | 0.3 | -1.0 | -2.1 | -2.2 | -2.1 | -1.8 |
| Net migration | 0.3 | 1.1 | 0.5 | 1.0 | 1.0 | 1.0 | 1.2 | 0.9 |
| Total increase | 0.8 | 1.3 | 0.8 | -0.1 | -1.1 | -1.2 | -1.0 | -0.9 |

Sources: ČSÚ, 1999; KDGD, 1999b, Appendix, Table 1; authors' calculations based on ČSÚ, op. cit.

In spite of stagnation in the total population in the 1990s, there have been changes in the proportions of the main age groups. Due to a low birth rate in the 1980s and its further fall in the first half of the 1990s, the number of children diminished both in absolute and relative terms. Between 1991 and 1999, the proportion of persons aged 0–14 fell from 21.1% to 17.0% and thus reached a historical minimum (Table 4.2).

As the large number of those born during 1969–1974, a period of a temporary increase in the birth rate, entered productive ages, the proportion of people aged 15–64 increased. Between 1991 and 1999, it grew from 66.3% to 69.3%. During the same period, the number of persons over the age of 65 remained almost unchanged at about 13% of the total population, since the numbers of those born in the 1930s during depression were relatively low. The process of population ageing at the top of the age pyramid thus temporarily slowed. Despite the fact that limited changes in the proportion of the elderly in the population had occurred, the ageing process continued.

**Table 4.2: Population by Age, 1991–1999[1]**

| | 1991 | 1992 | 1993 | 1994 | 1995 | 1996 | 1997 | 1998 | 1999 |
|---|---|---|---|---|---|---|---|---|---|
| | Number of persons (1,000) | | | | | | | | |
| 0–14 | 2,176 | 2,121 | 2,065 | 2,010 | 1,948 | 1,893 | 1,843 | 1,795 | 1,752 |
| 15–64 | 6,827 | 6,876 | 6,933 | 6,981 | 7,029 | 7,056 | 7,078 | 7,103 | 7,127 |
| 65+ | 1,302 | 1,316 | 1,328 | 1,343 | 1,372 | 1,372 | 1,388 | 1,401 | 1,411 |
| Total | 10,305 | 10,313 | 10,326 | 10,334 | 10,333 | 10,321 | 10,309 | 10,299 | 10,290 |
| | Proportion of total population (%) | | | | | | | | |
| 0–14 | 21.1 | 20.6 | 20.0 | 19.5 | 18.8 | 18.3 | 17.9 | 17.7 | 17.0 |
| 15–64 | 66.3 | 66.7 | 67.1 | 67.6 | 68.0 | 68.4 | 68.7 | 69.0 | 69.3 |
| 65+ | 12.6 | 12.7 | 12.9 | 13.0 | 13.1 | 13.3 | 13.4 | 13.6 | 13.7 |
| Total | 100.0 | 100.0 | 100.0 | 100.0 | 100.0 | 100.0 | 100.0 | 100.0 | 100.0 |
| | Indicators of the age structure | | | | | | | | |
| Mean age | 36.3 | 36.5 | 36.6 | 36.8 | 37.0 | 37.3 | 37.6 | 37.9 | 38.3 |
| Median age | 35.4 | 35.6 | 35.9 | 36.0 | 36.2 | 36.4 | 36.6 | 36.8 | 37.0 |
| Ageing index[2] | 59.8 | 62.0 | 64.3 | 66.8 | 69.6 | 72.3 | 75.3 | 78.1 | 80.5 |
| | Dependency ratios (%) | | | | | | | | |
| Young[3] | 31.9 | 30.8 | 29.8 | 28.8 | 27.7 | 26.8 | 26.0 | 25.3 | 24.6 |
| Old[4] | 19.1 | 19.1 | 19.2 | 19.2 | 19.3 | 19.4 | 19.6 | 19.7 | 19.8 |
| Total[5] | 50.9 | 50.0 | 49.0 | 48.0 | 47.0 | 46.3 | 45.6 | 45.0 | 44.4 |

[1]As of 1 January of a given year
[2]Ageing index is a number of persons aged 65+ per 100 children aged 0–14
[3]Population aged 0–14 as a percentage of population aged 15–64
[4]Population aged 65 and over as a percentage of population aged 15–64
[5]Population aged 0–14 and 65 and over as a percentage of population aged 15–64
Source: KDGD, 1999b, p. 10

During 1991–1999, the index of ageing was steadily rising from 59.8 to 80.5 (Table 4.2). The average age of the total population rose by two years during the period 1991–1999 to 38.3 years – the highest level in the Czech history. The median age changed in a similar way, too. At present, the Czech population ages from the base of the age pyramid because of low birth rates. Ageing will speed up again very rapidly at the beginning of the next century when numerous post-war generations reach retirement age.

The above-mentioned trends in the age structure influenced also the economic burden placed on economically active population. The values of the young, the old and the total dependency ratios reflected the declining proportion of children, the stability in the number of the elderly and the slight rise in the proportion of persons in the productive age group. While in 1991 there were 50.9 dependent persons per 100 people aged 15–64, in 1999 it was only 44.4 (Table 4.2) as primarily caused by the decline in the proportion of children in the population. This trend will remain unchanged until the end of the century but will be reversed shortly after the year 2000, when the economic burden of the working age population is expected to rise sharply mainly due to the shifts in the age structure. The development of fertility and further mortality gains are the other factors that will speed up ageing after the turn of the century (KGDG, 1999b, pp. 59–60).

**Table 4.3: Feminity Index[1], 1991 and 1999[2]**

| Year | Age group | | | | | | | Total |
|---|---|---|---|---|---|---|---|---|
| | 0–14 | 15–29 | 30–44 | 45–59 | 60–69 | 70–79 | 80+ | |
| 1991 | 95.3 | 95.7 | 98.4 | 105.6 | 129.8 | 165.4 | 240.7 | 106.0 |
| 1999 | 95.1 | 95.7 | 97.2 | 103.8 | 123.1 | 164.4 | 240.0 | 105.6 |

[1]Number of women per 100 men
[2]As of 1 January of a given year
Sources: KDGD, 1999a, p. 17; ČSÚ, op. cit.; authors' calculations based on ČSÚ, op. cit.

Another important characteristic of the population is its sex structure. It is affected both by biological factors of human reproduction and by the social environment. The slightly larger number of boys at birth is gradually balanced out by the higher level of male mortality, thus from the age of about 45 women outnumber men in the population. This predomination of women quickly rises with age. In the highest age groups it reaches extreme values (Table 4.3). While in 1999 there were about 123 women per 100 men among those aged 60–69, in the age group 70–79 the ratio was 164:100 and above the age of 80 the number of women was more than twice as high as the number of men (240:100).

This imbalance can be explained by a relatively significant difference between the level of male and female mortality in the period before 1990, and partly by the losses of men through war, and by higher intensity of emigration of men during 1948–1989. The less pronounced differences between male and female mortality in the 1990s have meant that the imbalance between the sexes is no longer worsening. In the higher age groups, the disproportion has become even smaller.

The changes in demographic behaviour and the shifts in age structure are reflected in the composition of the population according to marital status. During the last several years, the biggest changes have been seen in the numbers of young people aged 20–34, the age group with the highest intensity of nuptiality and fertility. Between 1991 and 1999, their number rose by 12%. However, this generation shift was accompanied by a decreasing level of nuptiality, as well as by an increase in the average age at first marriage. Consequently, the proportion of single people in the age group 20–34 rose dramatically: their number increased by 484,000 or by 77%; thus a great reserve of potential bridegrooms and brides appeared in the population. The changes in numbers and proportions according to marital status in the age group 35–59 were of lesser importance (KGDG, 1999b.)

The declining mortality influenced the situation among the elderly – the proportion of married people increased while that of widowed persons dropped. Because of the stable high level of divorces, the proportion of divorced persons in the population in the age group above 25 rose continuously. These changes in the population structure according to marital status and age are likely to continue in the coming years unless marriages, which are being postponed, finally take place. Only then the relative proportions of young single and married persons would change. The proportion of divorced persons can be expected to rise further, while the percentages of widowed persons could fall due to the decline of old age mortality, especially male mortality (KGDG, 1999a).

## 4.3 Family Formation and Dissolution

Until the end of the 1980s, the patterns of marriage were relatively stable. The high level of nuptiality (90% among men and 95% among women) and the prevailing low average age at first marriage (21–22 for men, 18–20 for women) were common (Rychtaříková, 1995). Since the beginning of the 1990s, a real upheaval has started both in the total level of nuptiality and in the structure of this process. One-third fewer marriages were registered in 1998 than in 1989, with the greatest drop between 1993 and 1994 (Table 4.4). A similar decrease occurred in the crude marriage rate. According to nuptiality tables for 1998, only 72% of single men and 78% of single women would enter marriage before the age of 50 (KGDG, 1999b). It means that, if the situation that existed in 1998 continued unchanged over the long term, more than one-fourth of men and one-fifth of women would remain single at the age of 50.

**Table 4.4: Marriages, 1989–1998, selected years**

| | 1989 | 1993 | 1994 | 1995 | 1996 | 1997 | 1998 |
|---|---|---|---|---|---|---|---|
| Marriages | 81,262 | 66,033 | 58,440 | 54,956 | 53,896 | 57,804 | 55,027 |
| Crude marriage rate | 7.8 | 6.4 | 5.7 | 5.3 | 5.2 | 5.6 | 5.3 |
| First marriages | 55,958 | 46,107 | 39,538 | 36,756 | 35,900 | 36,866 | 35,896 |
| Net nuptiality rate – male[1] | 89.2 | 81.8 | 76.4 | 73.2 | 71.4 | 73.1 | 72.0 |
| Net nuptiality rate – female[1] | 95.3 | 87.9 | 82.5 | 80.0 | 77.1 | 78.7 | 78.0 |

[1]Calculated from nuptiality tables (the percentage of persons who have ever been married by the age of 50)
Sources: KGDG, 1999b, pp. 15, 17; ČSÚ, op. cit., p. 74; Kučera and Šimek, 1999, p. 175

The decisive majority of people entering first marriage are below the age of 30. In the first half of the 1990s, a dramatic drop in first marriage rates took place in all age groups between 16 and 29 years, the lower the age the greater the drop. In 1997, the probabilities of first marriage for women aged 20 and under, for example, fell by more than 67% and for men aged 22 and under, by 57%. In the age group 24–30, the decrease was not as great – only by one-third (KGDG, 1999a, p. 25). The similar tendency can be found among men despite the shortening of military service to one year and the introduction of civil service as an alternative. The highest level of first marriage rate among men has shifted to 24 years and to 23 years among women. The decline of first marriage rates was accompanied by a lesser concentration of marriages into a narrow age interval. Currently, the highest rates among women have been diffused to 5–7 units of age, while in the 1980s it was only 3–4 units (KGDG, 1999b; Rychtaříková, 1995).

Single people are postponing the first marriage until higher ages. This tendency is very strong and represents an important factor in the transformation of nuptial behaviour. It can be demonstrated by the mean age at first marriage (Table 4.5). In the period 1989–1998, the mean age of men increased from 24.6 to 28.2 years and that of women from 21.8 to 25.8 years. The sharper increase of the mean age of brides decreased the age difference at first marriage between partners from 2.8 to 2.4 years.

The reduction of the total level of nuptiality after 1989 was also influenced by the drop in remarriage rates. The marriage rates of divorced men and women decreased in all age groups, particularly in the age group below 30 (KGDG, 1999a, p. 28). Due to an overall fall in nuptiality in all categories within the population – among single persons as well as among divorced and widowed persons – the structure of marriages according to the marital status of partners has not much changed.

**Table 4.5: Mean Age at First Marriage, 1989–1998**

| | 1989 | 1990 | 1991 | 1992 | 1993 | 1994 | 1995 | 1996 | 1997 | 1998 |
|---|---|---|---|---|---|---|---|---|---|---|
| Male | 24.6 | 24.0 | 24.7 | 24.8 | 25.4 | 26.2 | 26.7 | 27.1 | 27.6 | 28.2 |
| Female | 21.8 | 21.4 | 22.2 | 22.5 | 23.2 | 23.9 | 24.6 | 24.9 | 25.4 | 25.8 |
| Index – male | 100 | 97 | 100 | 101 | 103 | 106 | 109 | 110 | 112 | 115 |
| Index – female | 100 | 98 | 102 | 103 | 106 | 110 | 113 | 114 | 116 | 118 |

Sources: KDGD, 1999b, p. 17; Kučera and Šimek, op. cit., p. 174

The future developments in nuptiality in the Czech Republic decisively will be influenced by the speed with which the new model of marriage patterns will stabilise and when and whether young people who are not entering into marriage now will eventually marry. The question of special interest is a dynamics and demographic consequences of cohabitation. The absence of reliable data does not enable to estimate to what extent consensual unions in the Czech Republic are an alternative or a substitution for legal marriages. At present, it appears that no favourable conditions exist for the broader expansion of cohabitation neither culturally (marriage is still considered an important part of traditional values), nor technically (a massive increase is not possible due to shortages in available affordable housing). Most likely, cohabitation serves as a form of a trial for marriage in the future.

The Czech Republic has long had one of the highest divorce rates in Europe. It reflects acceptance of the phenomena of divorces and divorced people both in the legislative norms and in society's attitudes. The high divorce rates were also a consequence of very high levels of nuptiality before the beginning of the 1990s. Many of these marriages were formed under conditions that later became reasons for crisis in the marriage (e.g. pregnancy of the bride, low age at marriage and living together with the parents of one of the partners etc.) During 1990–1998, there were no substantial changes in the numbers of divorces (Table 4.6). They oscillated around 30,000 yearly, reaching their highest level in 1996 – over 33,000. In 1998, the total divorce rate reached its historical maximum – 42%.

**Table 4.6: Divorces, 1990–1998**

| | 1990 | 1991 | 1992 | 1993 | 1994 | 1995 | 1996 | 1997 | 1998 |
|---|---|---|---|---|---|---|---|---|---|
| Divorces | 32,055 | 29,366 | 28,572 | 30,227 | 30,939 | 31,135 | 33,113 | 32,465 | 32,363 |
| Crude divorce rate | 3.09 | 2.85 | 2.77 | 2.93 | 2.99 | 3.01 | 3.21 | 3.15 | 3.14 |
| Index of divorce | 35.2 | 40.8 | 38.6 | 45.8 | 52.9 | 56.7 | 61.4 | 56.2 | 58.8 |
| Divorces per 1,000 married women[1] | 12.4 | 11.5 | 11.2 | 11.9 | 12.2 | 12.4 | 13.3 | 13.1 | 13.1 |
| Total divorce rate | 38.0 | 34.8 | 33.9 | 36.2 | 37.5 | 38.4 | 41.7 | 41.9 | 42.0 |

[1]As of 1 July of a given year
Sources: KDGD, 1999b, p. 21; Kučera and Šimek, op. cit., p. 175

The highest divorce rates can be found in the age group 20–29. On average, 30 out of 1,000 married men or women are divorced. The rates decrease with age. In 1997, in the age group 30–39, approximately 20 out of 1,000 married men and women were divorced, while in the age group 40–49, about 10 out of 1,000 married men and women were divorced, and in the age group over 60 the rates drop to levels close to zero (KGDG, 1999b, p. 22). Besides the age pattern, the other important criterion for evaluating the structure of divorces is the length of the marriage. The highest rates of divorce, about 3%, were in the third and fourth years of marriage at the beginning of the 1990s; in the second half of the 1990s it also included the fifth year. On the other hand, the divorce rates in the first and second years of marriage slightly fell, reflecting probably new marriage patterns – the postponement of marriages until higher ages. At present, almost 12% of marriages are dissolved within the first 5 years of marriage duration and over 20% within the first 10 years after marriage. This proportion rises to 30% within the duration of 15 years. During last three years, the divorce rate for marriages lasting less than 5 years has decreased while the proportion of dissolved marriages after 5 years of duration has increased (KGDG, 1999b, p. 23). This indicates that marriages formed during the period of a relatively high level of nuptiality are less stable. It also indicates that society is becoming more tolerant towards divorces.

## 4.4 Natality and Abortions

Until the end of the 1980s, natality and fertility rates in the Czech Republic were still reaching relatively high levels. The majority of the first children were born soon after marriage; the preferred fertility model was a two-child family with only a small age difference between the children. Over 90% of children were born in wedlock, albeit many were conceived beforehand (about 55% of all conceptions). A usual reaction to such situation was to marry. That is why the proportions of extramarital births reached very low level – around 8–9% (KDGD, 1999b, p. 28). This fertility regime corresponded to the most favourable time for childbearing (birth timing) in the view of the given social and pronatalist population policy measures of the government, and to the almost full employment of women, including those with young children.

Only after the political changes at the beginning of the 1990s, did substantial changes in reproductive behaviour occur. An unprecedented deep drop in fertility levels has been a part of this transformation. It has been very intensive and quick compared to other European countries, where a similar drop occurred 20–25 years earlier. Fertility rates have decreased very deeply below the replacement level, to where marriage and family have lost their former function. Births are being postponed to when the age of the mother is higher, to a later time; and now more and more children are being born outside of marriage.

**Table 4.7: Main Indicators of Fertility, 1990–1998, selected years**

| | 1990 | 1993 | 1994 | 1995 | 1996 | 1997 | 1998 |
|---|---|---|---|---|---|---|---|
| Live births | 130,564 | 121,025 | 106,579 | 96,097 | 90,446 | 90,657 | 90,535 |
| Stillbirths | 530 | 445 | 336 | 300 | 317 | 273 | 294 |
| Total births | 131,094 | 121,470 | 106,915 | 96,397 | 90,763 | 90,930 | 90,829 |
| Live births per 1,000 inhabitants | 12.7 | 11.8 | 10.3 | 9.3 | 8.8 | 8.8 | 8.8 |
| Stillbirths per 1,000 live births | 4.0 | 3.7 | 3.1 | 3.1 | 3.5 | 3.0 | 3.2 |
| Live births outside marriage | 11,167 | 15,323 | 15,507 | 14,947 | 15,288 | 16,125 | 17,209 |
| Proportion of live births outside marriage (%) | 8.6 | 12.7 | 14.6 | 15.6 | 16.9 | 17.8 | 19.0 |
| Total fertility rate | 1.89 | 1.67 | 1.44 | 1.28 | 1.18 | 1.17 | 1.16 |
| Total rate of pregnancies | 3.62 | 2.82 | 2.34 | 2.10 | 1.96 | 1.91 | 1.88 |
| Proportion of first children born within 8 months of marriage | 54.4 | 54.5 | 54.0 | 50.8 | 49.0 | 48.1 | 47.6 |
| Mean age of women at childbearing | 24.8 | 25.0 | 25.4 | 25.8 | 26.1 | 26.4 | 26.7 |
| Mean age of women at first birth | 22.5 | 22.6 | 22.9 | 23.3 | 23.7 | 24.0 | 24.3 |
| Net reproduction rate | 0.91 | 0.80 | 0.69 | 0.61 | 0.57 | 0.56 | 0.56 |

Sources: KDGD, 1999b, p. 28; ČSÚ op. cit.; Kučera and Šimek, op. cit., p. 177

The period of economic and social transformation in the Czech Republic has been accompanied by a continuous decrease in the number of births, although the population age composition was favourable. Numerous generations born in the first half of the 1970s have entered the reproductive age. In 1998, there were only 90,535 live births in comparison with 1990 when the number was 30% higher (Table 4.7). It is an unprecedented low number in the history of the Czech Republic. At present, the Czech Republic – along with Latvia and Spain – has reached its lowest total fertility rate. Between 1990 and 1998, the total fertility rate dropped from 1.89 to 1.16. In no other post-communist state, except Bulgaria, has the fall of the total fertility rate been so fast and so deep.

Until the end of the 1980s, fertility was concentrated within the age group 20–24 years because of a low first marriage age. The mean age of women at first birth was consequently low – around 22 years (Rabušic, 1996). Since the beginning of the 1990s, the intensive fall of fertility rates has been occurring, especially among women aged under 24. During the 1990s, fertility rates fell by more than 60% in the age group 15–19 and by more than 50% in the age group 20–24 (Table 4.8). A 20% decline took place in the age group of 25–29 years. The mean age of women at first birth increased to more than 24 years (Tables 4.7 and 4.9). This trend may be explained by the decline of nuptiality at younger ages.

**Table 4.8: Age-specific Fertility Rates, 1990–1998 (per 1,000 women)**

| Age group | 1990 | 1991 | 1992 | 1993 | 1994 | 1995 | 1996 | 1997 | 1998 |
|---|---|---|---|---|---|---|---|---|---|
| 15–19 | 44.6 | 46.7 | 44.7 | 42.8 | 32.6 | 24.9 | 20.0 | 17.9 | 16.4 |
| 20–24 | 174.3 | 171.3 | 154.0 | 145.6 | 121.8 | 102.3 | 91.0 | 85.5 | 80.0 |
| 25–29 | 105.2 | 101.1 | 94.8 | 94.3 | 85.6 | 81.4 | 79.2 | 82.7 | 84.8 |
| 30–34 | 37.4 | 36.5 | 35.1 | 37.1 | 35.8 | 35.2 | 35.1 | 36.2 | 37.5 |
| 35–39 | 11.2 | 11.1 | 10.3 | 11.2 | 10.7 | 10.6 | 11.0 | 12.0 | 12.7 |
| 40–44 | 1.6 | 1.8 | 1.8 | 1.8 | 1.8 | 1.7 | 1.7 | 1.7 | 1.8 |

Source: KDGD, 1999b, p. 30

A more important reason is, however, the postponement of childbearing to older ages (Figure 4.1). The Czech population is gradually passing to the model of reproductive behaviour common among the countries of Western Europe. The level of fertility in the age groups above 30 years of age has not changed much because it concerns births of higher orders. The total fertility rate can be expected to be mainly influenced by the level of fertility reached by women in the age interval 25–34 years. The gradual transition of the main childbearing period to higher ages has manifested itself in an increase of the mean age of women at childbirth. Between 1990 and 1998, it rose from 24.8 to 26.7 years (Tables 4.7 and 4.9).

**Table 4.9: Mean Age of Women at Childbearing by Birth Order, 1990–1998**

| Birth order | 1990 | 1991 | 1992 | 1993 | 1994 | 1995 | 1996 | 1997 | 1998 |
|---|---|---|---|---|---|---|---|---|---|
| 1st child | 22.5 | 22.4 | 22.5 | 22.6 | 22.9 | 23.3 | 23.7 | 24.0 | 24.3 |
| 2nd child | 25.6 | 25.7 | 25.8 | 25.9 | 26.1 | 26.4 | 26.8 | 27.1 | 27.4 |
| 3rd or later child | 29.7 | 30.0 | 29.9 | 30.1 | 30.3 | 30.5 | 30.8 | 31.0 | 31.3 |
| Total | 24.8 | 24.7 | 24.8 | 25.0 | 25.4 | 25.8 | 26.1 | 26.4 | 26.7 |

Sources: KDGD, 1998, p. 42; KDGD, 1999a, p. 41; authors' calculations based on ČSÚ, op. cit.

The fall of total fertility rate was caused by the decline in marital fertility (Table 4.10). On the other hand, extramarital fertility rates have been rising. Since 1990, the level of marital fertility in the 20–29 age group has been falling, while in the youngest age group 15–19 the level of marital fertility has started to drop significantly only since 1994. The marital fertility rates in the age groups over 30 have remained almost stable. This trend is partly caused by the postponement of birth of a first child and increasingly frequently by the postponement of birth of the second children. The first years after marriage are starting to become a period of childlessness for the gradually growing proportion of young married couples (Rabušic, 1996).

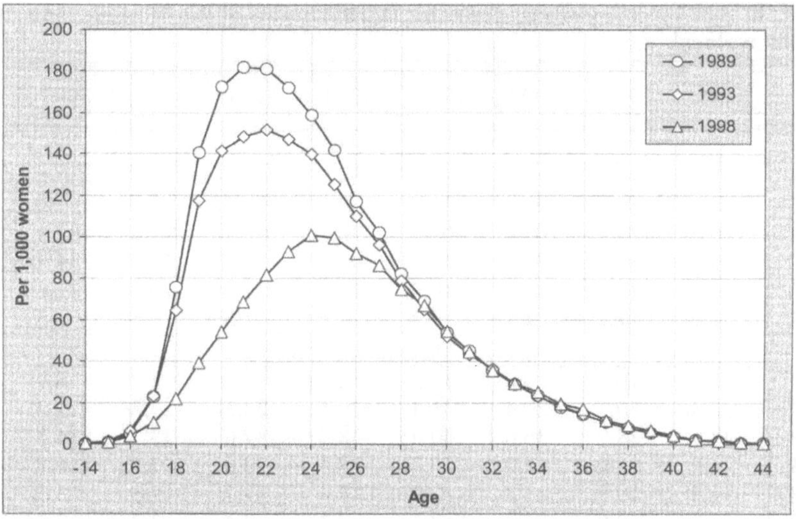


**Figure 4.1: Age-specific Fertility Rates, 1989, 1993 and 1998**
Sources: KDGD, 1999b, p. 29; ČSÚ, op. cit., p. 280

At the same time, in about 50% of all first marriages the bride is pregnant at the time of marriage. In the view of the fall in fertility rate among very young women due to the increased use of contraception, it can be assumed that these premarital conceptions are supposedly planned rather than unwanted. Upon analysis of the development of the age-specific marital fertility rates, it may be concluded that the main cause of the fall of the total fertility rate has been the postponement of marriages and childbearing to higher ages with the two-child family model being maintained. A departure from this model, however, could happen in cases when the postponement of childbearing transforms into a decision not to have a second child at all.

While the number of marital births dropped by 38% in the period 1990–1998, the number of extramarital births increased by 54% and represented almost 19% of total live births in 1998. The highest extramarital fertility rate could be found in the 25–29 age group. Up to 1993, the level of extramarital fertility was rising, but since 1994, the rate of extramarital fertility has been more or less the same, showing an increase again in 1997, primarily among women aged 25–29 (KDGD, 1999b, p. 32). Due to absence of the necessary data, it is not possible to estimate what percentage of mothers, who are having children out of wedlock, cohabitates or lives alone. The number of wanted extramarital births is likely to rise because of easy access to various forms of contraception, as well as to induced abortions that help prevent unwanted births. But the low intensity of extramarital fertility, as compared with its level in some countries of Western Europe, shows that marriage is still considered as an important condition for bearing children by the majority of the population. Another factor affecting the low level of extra-marital fertility is probably the difficulty in finding independent affordable housing for young cohabiting couples.

**Table 4.10: Age-specific Fertility Rates by Marital Status of the Mother, 1990–1998, per 1,000 women**

| Age group | 1990 | 1991 | 1992 | 1993 | 1994 | 1995 | 1996 | 1997 | 1998 |
|---|---|---|---|---|---|---|---|---|---|
| | Married women | | | | | | | | |
| 15–19 | 507.1 | 514.1 | 518.1 | 515.8 | 454.5 | 443.7 | 443.0 | 454.8 | 464.2 |
| 20–24 | 263.5 | 260.1 | 241.4 | 236.8 | 210.9 | 194.5 | 189.7 | 197.9 | 203.5 |
| 25–29 | 120.6 | 115.1 | 108.6 | 108.1 | 98.7 | 95.3 | 95.4 | 102.3 | 108.5 |
| 30–34 | 39.8 | 38.6 | 37.1 | 38.8 | 37.3 | 37.0 | 37.0 | 38.7 | 40.2 |
| 35–39 | 11.3 | 11.2 | 10.1 | 10.9 | 10.4 | 10.5 | 10.7 | 11.6 | 12.3 |
| 40–44 | 1.6 | 1.7 | 1.7 | 1.7 | 1.6 | 1.5 | 1.5 | 1.5 | 1.7 |
| | Unmarried women | | | | | | | | |
| 15–19 | 8.6 | 10.1 | 10.0 | 11.5 | 10.6 | 9.4 | 8.7 | 8.9 | 8.9 |
| 20–24 | 27.6 | 30.3 | 29.4 | 31.4 | 29.1 | 24.5 | 23.3 | 22.0 | 22.3 |
| 25–29 | 34.1 | 38.9 | 36.6 | 40.0 | 38.7 | 37.0 | 33.7 | 34.2 | 33.5 |
| 30–34 | 25.0 | 25.4 | 25.0 | 29.0 | 28.7 | 27.6 | 27.8 | 26.7 | 27.9 |
| 35–39 | 11.0 | 10.9 | 11.2 | 12.9 | 12.3 | 11.1 | 12.3 | 13.5 | 14.2 |
| 40–44 | 2.0 | 2.0 | 2.3 | 2.3 | 2.3 | 2.4 | 2.2 | 2.5 | 2.3 |

Source: KDGD, 1999b, p. 30

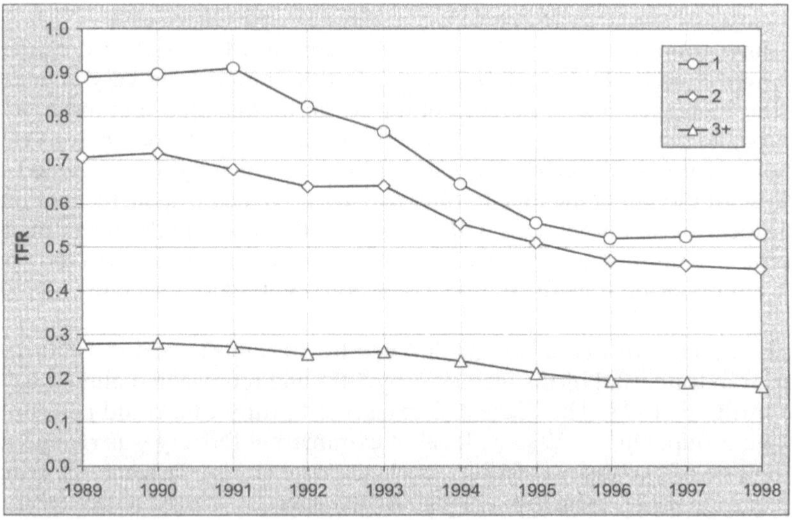


**Figure 4.2: Total Fertility Rate (TFR) by Birth Order, 1989–1998**

Sources: KDGD, 1999b, p. 30; authors' calculations based on ČSÚ, op. cit.

The decline in the abortion rate has been also an important part of gradual transformation of reproductive behaviour after 1989. It has been caused predominantly by the drop of the number of induced abortions. While in 1990 the total induced abortion rate reached 1.51 abortions per 1,000 women, in 1998 the rate dropped to only

0.57. The reduction of abortion rates occurred in all age groups, the greatest reduction being 60% in the age group 20–29 (KDGD, 1999b, pp. 36–37). The drop in the level of induced abortions is witness to the fall in unwanted pregnancies. This trend was influenced by several factors including the introduction of payments for abortions performed for other than health threat reason, the increased availability of quality contraception and overall changes in the attitudes of the population towards the forms of risk demographic behaviour.

## 4.5 Mortality

Until about 1960, Czechoslovakia, and so the today's Czech Republic as a part of it, belonged to the countries with a steady decline in the level of mortality and an increase in life expectancy. This trend was primarily helped by well-organised system of free national health insurance, and particularly by childcare system, which successfully reduced infant and child mortality.

At the turn of the 1950s and 1960s, the life expectancy in the Czech Republic was at the tenth place among the countries of Europe and on the same level as, for example, in France. During the 1960s, this positive development had come to an end, and over the next thirty years life expectancy stagnated at the level of 66–67 years for males and at 73–74 for females (KDGD, 1999b, p. 41). Thus, the Czech Republic started to lag behind the developed countries of Western Europe, where levels of life expectancy were 4–5 years higher and where male mortality rates were more favourable. Only in the second half of the 1980s did the situation start to improve slightly.

**Table 4.11: Indicators of Mortality, 1990, 1993–1998**

| | 1990 | 1993 | 1994 | 1995 | 1996 | 1997 | 1998 |
|---|---|---|---|---|---|---|---|
| Deaths | 129,166 | 118,185 | 117,373 | 117,913 | 112,782 | 112,744 | 109,527 |
| Crude death rate (‰) | 12.5 | 11.4 | 11.4 | 11.4 | 10.9 | 10.9 | 10.6 |
| | Life expectancy at birth (in years) | | | | | | |
| Male | 67.5 | 69.3 | 69.5 | 70.0 | 70.4 | 70.5 | 71.1 |
| Female | 75.4 | 76.4 | 76.6 | 76.9 | 77.3 | 77.5 | 78.1 |
| Difference | 7.9 | 7.1 | 7.1 | 6.9 | 6.9 | 7.0 | 7.0 |

Sources: KDGD, 1999a, p. 51, 1999b, p. 42

The causes of this long-term stagnation are well-known: the unhealthy life style of the majority of the population (poor nutrition structure, widespread smoking, insufficient attention to personal health), unsatisfactory working conditions (especially in industry), deterioration of the natural environment, stagnation of the state health care system, ineffective health education, as well as the stress produced by feelings of dissatisfaction and disbelief in better personal and country's future prevalent among a great part of the population. At the end of the 1980s, life expectancy was approximately 68 years for males and 75 years for females (KDGD, 1999b, p. 41).

After 1990, an apparent long-lasting process of improvement in the health status of the population began and a decline in mortality rates and a rise in life expectancy have been one of its consequences (Table 4.11). The number of deaths fell from 129,166 in 1990 to 109,527 in 1998. During the first half of the 1990s, a drop in the number of infant deaths occurred mostly due to the significant fall in the fertility level. The decline in mortality levels at higher ages, as well as the overall shrinking of differences between male and female mortality levels, however, had the decisive influence. In 1998, the male life expectancy was 3.6 years and the female life expectancy was 2.7 years longer than in 1990.

The Czech Republic stands out from the majority of the other post-communist states because mortality levels of its population are falling. This trend may be explained by the fact that social and economic changes in the Czech Republic have been happening in a relatively peaceful manner and without complete disintegration of the health care system. Although the reorganisation of this system has not been fully successful, the quality of medical care has not been compromised. Moreover, the major changes in health care system, such as the introduction of a right to choose a doctor, upgraded equipment in surgeries and hospitals, a wider availability of more effective drugs and, most of all, a more responsible approach by the majority of doctors towards their patients and increasing responsibility to care for one's own health on the part of the population, represent considerable advancement, which can not be undermined by the shortcomings in the organisation of health care.

The steady fall in the level of mortality has been linked with the continuing reduction of infant mortality. It declined from 10.8 in 1990 to 5.2 infant deaths per 1,000 live births in 1998 (Table 4.12). At the same time, more than one-third of infant deaths occur between the age 4 weeks and 1 year, thus indicating there are reserves for improvement of the care for infants in the family. The decline of infant mortality, particularly when accompanied by the drop of the birth rate, has had an almost negligible effect on the overall level of mortality. In 1998, the number of infants dying before reaching first year of age represented only 4.3 ‰ of the total number of deaths. Between 1989 and 1997, the decline of infant mortality rather significantly contributed to the rise of life expectancy of both sexes – by more than 0.2 years (KDGD, 1999a, p. 54).

As far as the age-specific aspect of mortality development in the 1990s is concerned, the decline of male mortality between the ages 45–69 and female mortality between the ages 65–84 were the most important. The probabilities of dying in these age categories declined by 10–20%. The falling level of mortality of people aged 45 and over was the main cause of the rise of life expectancy at birth. The stability of inter-year decline in the intensity of mortality in given age groups indicates that there has been a stable decrease in the level of mortality rather than a temporary improvement. This decline could be foreseen because it had been the level of mortality in later middle and early elderly age which was the main reason of the backwardness of the

Czech Republic in the context of the developed world. According to the level of mortality at younger ages, the differences between the Czech Republic and developed countries are relatively small albeit the level reached in the Czech Republic still does not correspond to that found in western countries. Moreover, the death rates at certain years can be influenced by random variations, particularly in the case of children under 15 years of age.

**Table 4.12: Infant Mortality, 1990–1998**

| | 1990 | 1991 | 1992 | 1993 | 1994 | 1995 | 1996 | 1997 | 1998 |
|---|---|---|---|---|---|---|---|---|---|
| Deaths under 1 year | 1,410 | 1,343 | 1,204 | 1,028 | 847 | 740 | 547 | 531 | 472 |
| Deaths under 28 days | 1,003 | 902 | 749 | 692 | 505 | 475 | 347 | 326 | 289 |
| Deaths between 28 and 364 days | 407 | 441 | 455 | 336 | 342 | 265 | 200 | 205 | 183 |
| Infant mortality rate (per 1,000 live births) | 10.8 | 10.4 | 9.9 | 8.5 | 7.9 | 7.7 | 6.0 | 5.9 | 5.2 |
| Neonatal mortality rate (per 1,000 live births) | 7.7 | 7.0 | 6.2 | 5.7 | 4.7 | 4.9 | 3.8 | 3.6 | 3.2 |
| Post-neonatal mortality rate (per 1,000 live births) | 3.1 | 3.4 | 3.7 | 2.8 | 3.2 | 2.8 | 2.2 | 2.3 | 2.0 |
| Deaths under 28 days (per 100 infant deaths) | 71.1 | 67.2 | 62.2 | 67.3 | 59.6 | 64.2 | 63.4 | 61.4 | 61.2 |
| Infant deaths (per 100 total deaths) | 1.09 | 1.08 | 1.00 | 0.87 | 0.72 | 0.63 | 0.49 | 0.47 | 0.43 |

Sources: KDGD, 1999a, p. 53; authors' calculations based on ČSÚ, op. cit.

The decline of mortality rates has been relatively more pronounced among males than among females. Thus, the former great differences in the level of mortality according to sex have reduced. Nevertheless, they still are not negligible. For example, between the ages of 15 and 69, the level of male mortality is more than twice that of women, and in the 20–29 age group it is three times higher. The level of mortality in these ages is, however, very low and thus, it does not contribute substantially to the total difference between male and female life expectancy. In 1997, age groups between 50 and 80 years were the main contributors to this difference reaching 7 years (Figure 4.5). As far as causes of deaths are concerned, the male higher mortality level due to circulatory diseases contributed almost 3 years to this difference and further 2 years of it are connected with higher intensity of male mortality due to cancer. External causes of death, being the third most important contributor, were responsible for 1.3 years of the difference. Especially in these causes of deaths there is a considerable room for improvement.

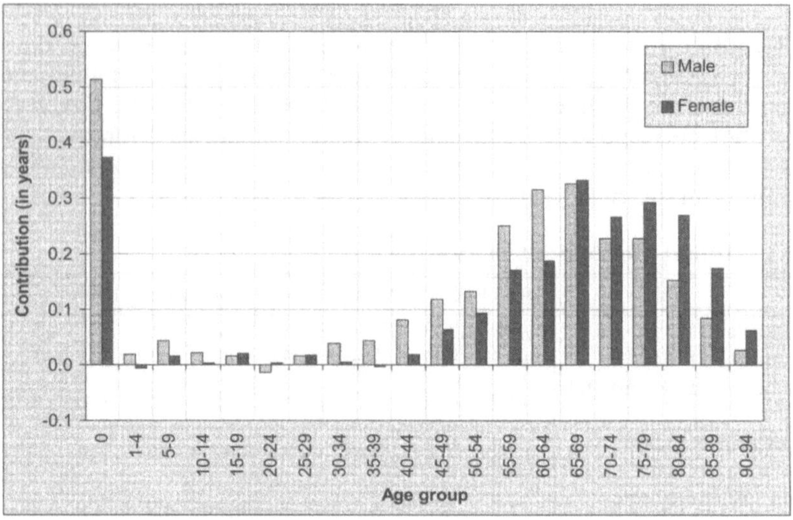


**Figure 4.3: Contribution of Age Groups to the Rise of Life Expectancy at Birth Between 1987 and 1997**

Source: based on calculations done by B. Burcin (unpublished)

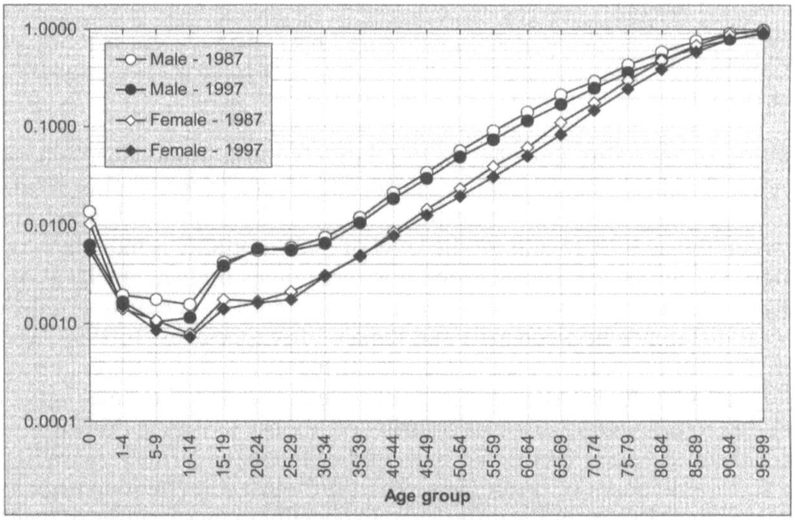


**Figure 4.4: Probability of Dying by Sex and Age, 1987 and 1997**

Source: based on calculations done by B. Burcin (unpublished)

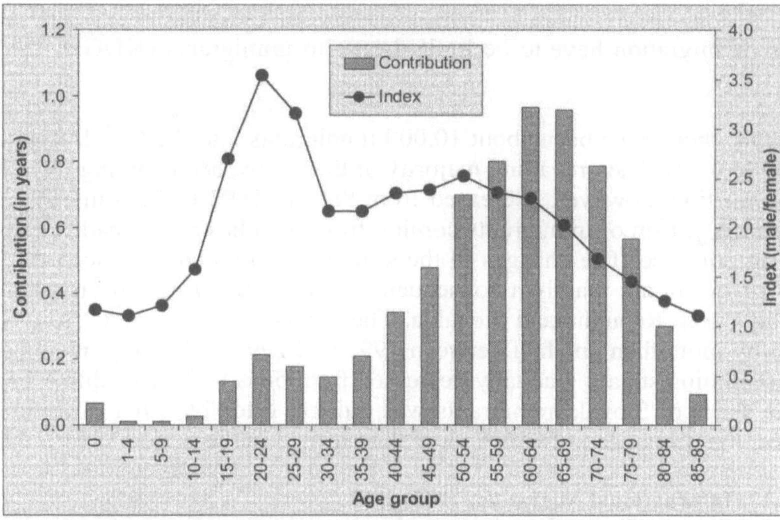


**Figure 4.5: Male Mortality Excess, 1997**

Source: based on calculations done by B. Burcin (unpublished)

## 4.6 Migration

One of the demographic processes that also has experienced a significant change after 1989 is migration. The opening of the borders has made migration possible both in and out of the Czech Republic. The split of the former Czechoslovakia has changed also the pattern of migration between the Czech and Slovak Republics: the formerly considered internal migration has become international.

The establishment of the Czech Republic in 1993 was accompanied by an increased intensity of migration across the newly founded border. During 1992–1993, when the migration wave reached its peak, there were 33,000 registered migrations across the shared border. At the same time, migration (especially, immigration streams) has been reflecting geopolitical changes and the socio-economic situation in Europe and some other parts of the world. According to official statistics, during the period 1993–1997, there were over 57 thousand immigrants and almost 10 thousand emigrants in the migration balance (KDGD, 1999b, p. 49). The official data on emigrants, however, is not complete. Only a very limited number of emigrants were registered: those who returned their identity cards before emigration. By comparing of the Czech emigration statistics with those of the countries of destination, it can be estimated that 4–5 thousand emigrants yearly are not registered. The numbers of immigrants also include people who gained permission for permanent (not long-term, however) residence in the Czech Republic. Those people, particularly in the case of later emigration, are not officially registered as emigrants. Thus, any further analyses of migration have to be limited only to immigrants (KDGD, 1999b, pp. 49–50).

Since 1994, there have been about 10,000 immigrants into the Czech Republic per year (Table 4.13). The prevailing majority of them have been coming from Europe. Their proportion, however, decreased from 88% in 1993 to 72% in 1997. On the other hand, a stream of immigrants coming from Asia has been steadily growing in relative importance. The changes in the structure of immigration according to the country of origin are mainly a consequence of decreasing migration relations between the Czech Republic and Slovakia. The number of immigrants from Slovakia dropped by more than one half between 1993 and 1997 and their percentage in the total immigration stream gradually decreased from 56% to 24% (Table 4.14). However, the share of Slovak immigrants was quickly filled by other post-communist countries, the proportion of which more than tripled in the period 1993–1997.

**Table 4.13: International Migration, 1993–1997**

| | Number of migrants | | | | |
|---|---|---|---|---|---|
| | 1993 | 1994 | 1995 | 1996 | 1997 |
| Immigration from Slovakia | 7,276 | 4,076 | 3,845 | 3,450 | 3,088 |
| Immigration from other countries | 5,624 | 6,131 | 6,695 | 7,407 | 9,792 |
| Total immigration | 12,900 | 10,207 | 10,540 | 10,857 | 12,880 |
| Emigration to Slovakia[1] | 7,232 | 56[2] | 140[2] | 213[2] | 260[2] |
| Emigration to other countries[1] | 192 | 209 | 401 | 515 | 545 |
| Total emigration[1] | 7,424 | 265 | 541 | 728 | 805 |
| Net migration with Slovakia[1] | 44 | 4,020 | 3,705 | 3,237 | 2,828 |
| Net migration with other countries[1] | 5,432 | 5,922 | 6,294 | 6,892 | 9,247 |
| Total net migration[1] | 5,476 | 9,942 | 9,999 | 10,129 | 12,075 |

[1]Incomplete numbers
[2]According to the data of the Slovak Statistical Office – 3,144; 1,497; 993 and 867 Czech immigrants, respectively
Source: KDGD, 1999b, p. 49

In 1997, the strongest stream came from the countries of the former Soviet Union, representing 22% of all immigrants to the republic. Out of these countries, the Ukraine holds the leading position and it can be expected that it will remain a very important source of migrants to the country in the future because of the high level of commuting to the Czech Republic. Another strong stream comes from Vietnam, reaching 13% of all immigrants. Similar growth trend can be seen in arrivals of immigrants from Southeast Europe, including the former Yugoslavia (KDGD, 1999b, p. 51). During the first half of the 1990s, besides Slovakia, the gradual decline in the proportion of immigrants coming to the Czech Republic from Germany, Switzerland and Canada took place as the wave of return migration of Czech nationals, who emigrated during the 1948–1989 period, began to slow down.

Along with the shifts in the structure of source countries of immigrants, the other structural characteristics of the migrant flows have changed too. Because of a gradual increase in economic migration, the proportion of men among immigrants, as well as persons in the working age, began to rise. Moreover, their educational structure is very favourable, better than that of the Czech population at the beginning of the 1990s. In 1997, more than 80% of immigrants were in the productive age group and more than one-quarter of them were university graduates. Relatively lower educational qualifications are present among immigrants from Vietnam and Romania: only 6% and 2% of them are university graduates (KDGD, 1999b, p. 51).

**Table 4.14: Immigrants into the Czech Republic by Country/Region of Origin, 1990, 1993 and 1997**

| Region | 1990 | | 1993 | | 1997 | |
|---|---|---|---|---|---|---|
| | Number | % | Number | % | Number | % |
| Total | 12,411 | 100.0 | 12,900 | 100.0 | 12,880 | 100.0 |
| Europe | 11,653 | 93.9 | 11,283 | 87.5 | 9,255 | 71.9 |
| Asia | 238 | 1.9 | 407 | 3.2 | 2,331 | 18.1 |
| America | 383 | 3.1 | 794 | 6.2 | 677 | 5.3 |
| Africa | 52 | 0.4 | 210 | 1.6 | 142 | 1.1 |
| Australia and Oceania | 82 | 0.7 | 191 | 1.5 | 119 | 0.9 |
| Not specified | 3 | 0.0 | 15 | 0.1 | 356 | 2.8 |
| Slovakia | 10,073 | 81.2 | 7,276 | 56.4 | 3,088 | 24.0 |
| Former Soviet Union | 175 | 1.4 | 781 | 6.1 | 2,863 | 22.2 |
| Former Yugoslavia | 87 | 0.7 | 277 | 2.1 | 1,230 | 9.5 |
| Other European post-communist countries | 385 | 3.1 | 240 | 1.9 | 688 | 5.3 |
| Other non-European post-communist countries | 169 | 1.4 | 227 | 1.8 | 1,814 | 14.1 |
| Post-communist countries, total | 10,889 | 87.7 | 8,801 | 68.2 | 9,683 | 75.2 |
| Post-communist countries excluding Slovakia | 816 | 6.6 | 1,525 | 11.8 | 6,595 | 51.2 |

Source: KDGD, 1999b, p. 50

In the 1990s, the role of international migration in the population reproduction began to rise. It was not, however, a result of increasing numbers of migrants, net migration or intensity of migration. Migration plays a significant role in the total balance of the population. In spite of the under-registration of the emigrants, it can be assumed that the net migration is positive and thus significantly moderates negative population growth resulting from natural change, as well as slows the process of population ageing.

## 4.7 Population-related Policy

Although the Government formed by the Social democrats in 1998 has put into effect some new measures in the sphere of social policy, the basic concept of this policy has not been substantially changed: the low level of fertility and negative natural increase has only a marginal position in it. In addition, the leading political parties have yet to achieve consensus whether and how to influence the downward nuptiality and natality trends. On the one hand, social democrats acknowledge the need for the state pronatalist population policy, on the other, conservatives (Civil Democratic Party) consider the number of children in a family to be a private issue of individual. The position of other parliamentary parties, Christian Democratic Union and Union of Liberty, are somewhere in between.

Pronatalist population policy therefore still remains a set of political proclamations by certain politicians rather than a present-day reality. At the same time, more and more families with children are experiencing the decline of the living standards, particularly due to continuously increasing unemployment and inflation. In April 1999, the level of unemployment was 8.2%, while the estimation for 31 December 1999 was set at about 11% (Hajný, op. cit.). More vulnerable to the risk of unemployment are foremost women with young children, people with low qualifications, handicapped people and young people without professional experience. Unemployment of spouse or partner in the family might not only lower its living standard but could also alter the decision-making regarding the timing and number of births. In some cases, motherhood may, however, become a "solution" to a woman being under a threat of possible unemployment.

Since 1 October 1999, the maximum level of unemployment allowance has been increased by 56% in case of requalification, and by 67% in other cases (although the mechanism that ties the increase of the allowance according to the level of the previous earnings has not been yet approved). It appears that the state policy in relation to unemployment continues to be oriented towards solving an emerging unemployment and its implications rather than at prevention of its rise and acceleration. At present, the state social policy in the sphere of employment is based on The National Plan of Employment in the Czech Republic. This plan emphasises the necessity of elimination of discrimination in the professional sphere, including discrimination by family status or gender.

Generally, in recent years the efforts to eliminate discrimination in the professional sphere have become more apparent. In 1998, the Government adopted a resolution about the status of women in society, while the Ministry of Labour and Social Affairs established a special department dealing with the issues of gender equality.

During 1999, the minimal salary was raised twice – in January and in July. It is expected that the minimal salary will continue to slightly exceed the minimum living standard income, which was recalculated before the elections of 1998. It is used to define the living standards of families that are in need of social support by the state and the family income level at which family can qualify for such social support as housing or transport allowance, social allowance, or children allowances. Since the beginning of 1999, due to changes in legislation, more families with children have had legal possibilities to apply for children allowances and use them for longer period of time (Kuchařová and Tuček, op. cit.).

Although there is a variety of social allowances provided currently by the state, they do not constitute an important item in family budget. Their levels are not significant enough to influence the living standard of families as well as decision-making about number of children in the family. This theoretical observation is supported by the results of the survey conducted in the second half of 1998 by Sofres-Factum, a well-recognised public opinion agency. According to the survey results, 63% of respondents did not agree that the family or children allowances might influence the decisions about childbearing. More than 50% of respondents even suggested that such allowances might be used as a form of the state control over families (Štěpánová, 1999).

An important development in the sphere of family policy was the reform of family legislation and introduction of a new Family Law in August 1998, which replaced the 1963 Family Law. Some new regulations have been adopted, particularly in relation to family formation and dissolution. For example, the divorce rules for families with children became tougher, while possibilities for joint custody wider. A notion and definition of "parent responsibility" was introduced, the procedure of marriage was reconsidered, and the conditions for adoption and guardianship were substantially changed. There was active both professional and public discussion about the reform of the Family Law, especially in relation to parents' and children's rights, indicating a remarkable extension of public concern from children's rights and interests to parents' rights and responsibilities. It is expected that emerging problems could be resolved through the new Law on Children, which was adopted in November 1999 and deals specifically with the issues of social and legal protection of children. In accordance with the new Family Law, the Civil Law has been also revised.

Like in many other countries, rapid population ageing and its potential implications for the sphere of social security have provoked live policy debates about the solvency of the current pension system, the need to reform it and about the level of retirement age. In 1993, the parliament accepted the law defining the gradual increase of retirement age during the period up to 2007 for men by two years (from 60 to 62 years) and for women by four years (from 53–57 to 57–61 depending on number of children). These changes reflect both the longer life expectancy at higher ages and the attempt of the Government to anticipate the worsening relation between the number of pensioners and economically active population.

Policy makers from the right side of political spectrum suggest reforming the whole pension system. The new system is proposed to be based on three principles: primarily on compulsory individual capital savings for old age, on fixed pensions guaranteed by the state and on voluntary extra savings. Special pension funds for voluntary savings with state per capita contributions have already come to existence. Left-oriented parties suggest the pay-as-you-go system to be continued in spite of the fact that it would lead to higher taxes or deficit of the state budget. However, only a very limited attention is given by politicians to health care expenditures, which can be expected to rise as a result of faster population ageing and increasing number of the aged after the turn of century.

To summarise above-mentioned, despite the fact that some family-related measures in the sphere of social policy have been adopted, all together they do not represent a systematic family policy, not saying about pronatalist policy. Under present social system, families have to resolve emerging problems by relying mostly on their own resources and possibilities, and this undoubtedly has an impact on current demographic behaviour too.

## 4.8 Conclusion

The current transformation of the demographic behaviour in the Czech Republic is not without precedent. It resembles the so-called second demographic transition that has started in the second half of the 1960s in Western Europe and in other countries with prevalence of inhabitants of European origin. In Western democracies, the second demographic transition was a result of long-term gradual development in the sphere of policy, economics, employment, social security, the standard of living, technologies as well as of cultural norms and behavioural patterns (van de Kaa, 1987). The rapid changes in reproductive behaviour in the Czech Republic appear also to be a reaction of population to political and economic pressures (Rychtaříková, 1998).

According to the level of demographic rates, the Czech Republic's position is approximately in the middle of the process of the second demographic transition. Until recently, the declining numbers of marriages and births have been explained as being the result of the postponement of marriage and childbearing until later years due to contemporary unfavourable conditions for population reproduction. Demographers cannot yet give any definite conclusions about the current situation and the future development (see, for example, *Demografie* 40(4), pp. 247–280). Without a detailed survey it is difficult to say whether the downward trend in nuptiality and fertility rates would turn around after the conditions change, or whether current postponement of childbearing is going to lead to further decisions not to have children.

Due to the low numbers of births, the base of the age pyramid has radically narrowed and a deep incorrigible distortion of the age structure has started to form. It will affect the level of natality in the future, as well as the speed of population ageing and the age structure. After the turn of the century, rapid population ageing can be expected. It is an unavoidable trend influenced by both generation (numerous post-war generations will retire) and period effects – increasing life expectancy at higher ages and very low level of fertility in the 1990s (Burcin and Kučera, 1995).

Fast upward growth of the retired population accompanied by even faster upsurge of the number of people aged over 80 will put a severe strain on health care system and retirement insurance. In the near future expenditures on health care and particularly on old-age pensions are likely to rise at such unprecedented rate that the social security system could collapse unless it is radically changed. The state fiscal demands will inevitably soar. Consequently, the economic burden of the economically active population could expand beyond only direct taxation to include also indirect taxes to cover individual expenditure on health care, everyday health and social care for elderly or ill people in the family and, most importantly, the costs of personal pensions. The changes in relationships between the generations and in the organization and functioning of society as a whole will acquire an extreme importance in this situation.

The character of the anticipated developments of the demographic structures is deeply rooted in the past, but it is being shaped by the changes in reproductive behaviour occurring at present, during the period of economic and social transition, as well. The features of the future population development that are inherently linked with the existing age structure cannot be changed, but others, particular future fertility level and pattern, could to some degree be altered by social policy. It is important therefore that both the present and forecasted population developments are seriously considered at all levels and stages of economic and social reform.

## References

Burcin, B. and T. Kučera (1995), *The Current State and Future Prospects of Population Development in the Czech Republic to the Year 2020*, Praha: KDGD, PřF, Univerzita Karlova.

ČSÚ (Czech Statistical Office) (1999), *Pohyb obyvatelstva v ČR 1998*, Praha: ČSÚ.

Hajný, J. (1999), Státní politika zaměstnanosti v roce 1999, *Sociální politika* 25(4), pp. 7–14.

KDGD (Department of Demography and Geodemography) (1998), *Populační vývoj České republiky 1997*, Praha: KDGD, PřF, Univerzita Karlova.

KDGD (Department of Demography and Geodemography) (1999a), *Populační vývoj České republiky 1998*, Praha: KDGD, PřF, Univerzita Karlova.

KDGD (Department of Demography and Geodemography) (1999b), *Population Development in the Czech Republic 1999*, Praha: KDGD, PřF, Univerzita Karlova.

Kuchařová, V. and M. Tuček (1999), *Sociálně ekonomické souvislosti rodinného chování mladé generace v České republice*, Praha: Studie národohospodářského ústavu Josefa Hlávky, 1/1999.

Kučera, M. and M. Šimek (1999), Pohyb obyvatelstva v České republice v roce 1998, *Demografie* 41(3), pp. 169–183.

Rabušic, L. (1996), O současném vývoji manželského reprodukčního a rodinného chování v České republice, *Demografie* 38 (3), pp. 173–180.

Rabušic, L. (1997), Polemicky k současným změnám charakteru reprodukce v ČR (sociologická perspektiva v demografii), *Demografie* 39(2), pp. 173–179.

Rychtaříková, J. (1995), Sňatečnost svobodných v České republice dříve a dnes, *Demografie* 37(3), pp. 157–172.

Rychtaříková, J. (1996), Současné změny charakteru reprodukce v České republice a mezinárodní srovnání, *Demografie* 38(2), pp. 77–89.

Rychtaříková, J. (1998), Česká republika a druhý demografický přechod? *Geografické rozhledy* 2, pp. 39–42.

Štěpánová, L. (1999), Přídavky na děti z pohledu veřejného mínění, *Sociální politika* 25(2), pp. 5–12.

(1998), Současné trendy a vzorce demografického chování – Evropa a my, XXVIII. konference České demografické společnosti, *Demografie* 40(4), pp. 247–280.

UN ECE (United Nations Economic Commission for Europe) (1999), *Trends in Europe and North America 1998/1999. The Statistical Yearbook of the Economic Commission for Europe*, New York and Geneva: United Nations.

van de Kaa, D.J. (1987), Europe's Second Demographic Transition, *Population Bulletin*, Vol. 42(1), pp. 1–58.

Večerník, J. (ed.) (1998), *Zpráva o vývoji české společnosti 1989–1998*, Praha: Academia.

# 5

# A Review of Some Current Danish Population Trends

**Hans Oluf Hansen**

## 5.1 Introduction

Before reviewing the Danish population trends and prospects, we consider briefly some issues of the institutional, political and economic background of the current population development.

### 5.1.1 Some Highlights of the Institutional and Political Background

Denmark is a constitutional monarchy reigned by Queen Margrethe II. As a political entity and a national state, the present Danish society dates one thousand years back in time. Since 1380, Greenland and the Faroe Islands have been part of the Kingdom. Important events in the evolution towards the modern welfare state are the land reforms of 1788; the abolishment of absolute monarchy in 1848; introduction of parliamentarianism in 1905; and the conversion of entailed estate into fee simple in 1919. The latest revision of the constitution (Da. *Grundloven*) took place in 1953. By the constitutional amendment Denmark passed from a two-chamber system to a one-chamber system (Da. *Folketinget*). Moreover, parliamentarianism became established in the revised constitution of 1953.

Denmark has been a member of NATO since 1949. By the referendum of 2 October 1972, Denmark joined the European Economic Community (EEC). Up to now, Denmark has been a reticent and somewhat sceptical member of the EEC. Referenda regarding extended political integration with the EEC were taken in 1986, 1992, 1993 and 1998. At the referendum of 2 June 1992 the voters turned down the Maastricht Treaty. Supplemented with four reservations embodied in the so-called Edinburgh Decision, the Maastricht Treaty was subsequently accepted by the referendum of 18 May 1993. Denmark has not yet joined the European Monetary Union with the EURO introduced on 1 January 1999.

The country is divided into 14 counties (Da. *amter*) plus the communes of Copenhagen and Frederiksberg; this administrative division being split up in 276 primary communes. To strengthen public participation in the political process, a wide range of social tasks have been delegated from Folketinget to local government based on this administrative framework.

### 5.1.2 Features of the Economic Background

Excluding Greenland and the Faroe Islands in the North Atlantic, the territory of Denmark is 43,094 square kilometres with 5.26 million inhabitants as of 1996. Up to 1960, the population traditionally has been ethnically homogeneous. This issue will be discussed in more detail later.

The basic economic resources include a rich farmland with an Atlantic climate, oil resources in the North Sea, and fishery. Manufacturing and trade are extremely important activities. As a small open economy, Denmark remains excessively vulnerable to fluctuating economic conditions abroad. The GDP per capita amounted to DKR 212,500 or US$32,600 in 1997 (Økonomiministeriet, 1998) placing Denmark among the richest countries in the world. In 1999, the tax burden was expected to be at the level of 49.9% of the GDP. The rate of unemployment amounted to 6.4% in 1998. In the same year, the transfer payments amounted to 17.8% of the GDP. In other terms, a very high proportion of the GDP is currently redistributed via the public sector to the benefit of persons with social needs and health problems. Medical care and education are fully subsidised by the state. Heavy taxation, combined with rapid income progression in the taxation, secures a considerable degree of equalisation in the economic distribution within families and across households. A Scandinavian "welfare system" of this type obviously may have some drawbacks on the economic efficiency of the society. On the other hand, this does not necessarily have to be so: the Danish welfare system undeniably confers economic self-determination and personal responsibility to the individual from an early age. Such qualities, combined with systematic build-up of competitive human capital, are obvious assets in a changing international environment.

The reality tends to be less ideal, however: the moral and social responsibility of some members of the resident citizen groups sometimes give way to selfish interests directed against the public good. To accommodate public transfers to cover justified social needs and to cope with social malpractice and pilfering, a public system of administration and control has been developed, which, on the other hand, at times may impose rather tight bureaucratic restrictions on individual initiative and behaviour.

Recurrent economic and political issues facing Denmark include maintaining a realistic educational and professional standard, efficiency and a competitive cost level in the international markets.

## 5.2 Current Population Trends in Denmark

A process is a sequence of events. We see demographic events as outcomes of complex, commonly interactive stochastic processes in continuous time. Demographic processes are normally defined on finite state spaces. A pioneering contribution over the past 30 years in identifying the modern statistical framework of conventional demographic concepts and measures has been provided by the Norwegian statistician and actuary, Jan M. Hoem (see, for example, Hoem and Funck Jensen, 1982).

Measurement of recorded demographic behaviour in the framework of relevant stochastic modelling has been gaining increasing importance in modern demographic research. Micro-economic theory, and the so-called New Home Economics in particular, provide a sophisticated and relevant body of consistent thinking regarding the motivation and determinants of social behaviour resulting in demographic events. Over the past more than 25 years, a large body of demographic research based on these ideas has been produced at the Institutes of Statistics and Economics of the University of Copenhagen.

### 5.2.1 Population Growth and Its Principal Demographic Components

The development of the size of the population since the early 1930s is shown in Figure 5.1. The population has gone up from 3.6 million in the early 1930s to 5.26 million in 1996. However, the population growth slowed down markedly from 1975 to the late 1980s.

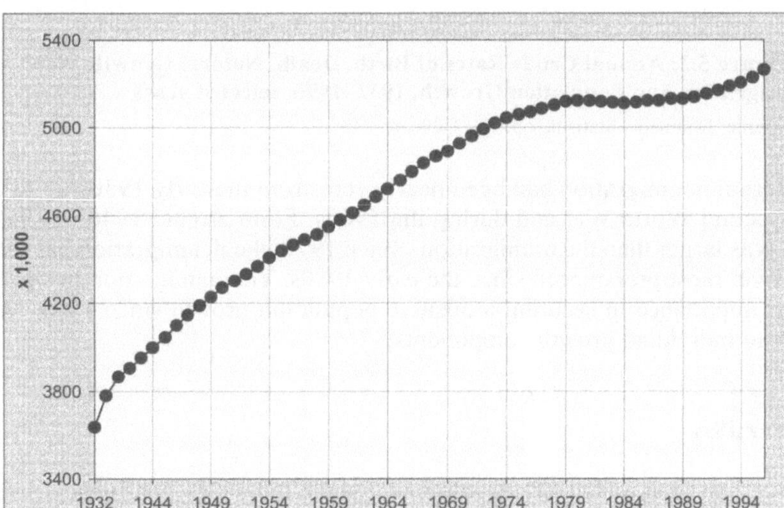


**Figure 5.1: Annual Mean Population, 1932–1996, selected years**

Source: Danmarks Statistik, 1998, Table 4

In terms of conventional definitional macro-level approach, the background of these developments becomes evident from Figure 5.2. The cohorts born in the years 1944 through 1946 were extraordinarily large. Except the temporary upsurge during 1960–1966, the annual birth cohorts had been diminishing since the post-war years up to 1983. From then on, up to around 1995, the birth numbers were increasing again. With a few setbacks, the crude death rate has been slowly increasing since 1948. Consequently, the natural population growth had been falling from 13.2‰ in 1946 to zero growth in about 1980. It hovered around zero up through the 1980s and it has been slightly greater than zero ever since.

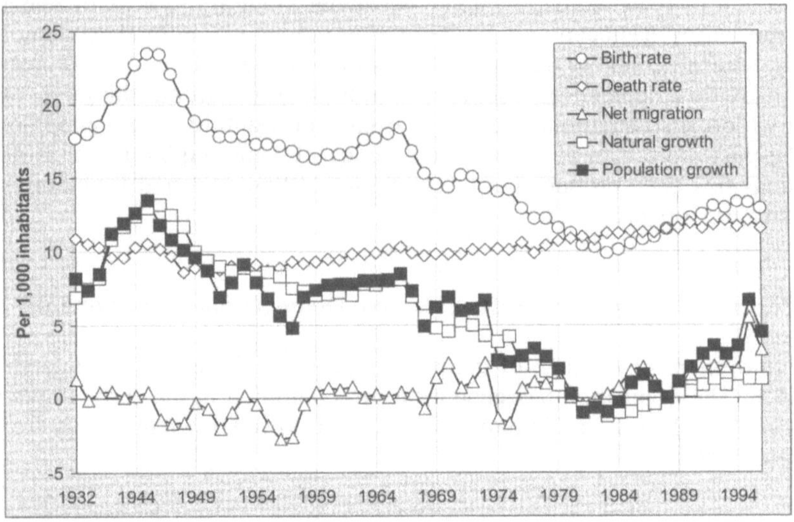


**Figure 5.2: Annual Crude Rates of Birth, Death, Natural Growth, Net Migration and Population Growth, 1932–1996, selected years**

Source: Danmarks Statistik, op. cit., Table 4

The external net migration had been nearly zero from the early 1930s up to the end of the Second World War and during the 1960s. From around 1946 to 1959, emigration was larger than the immigration. Since 1970, the net migration has tended to be positive, most pronounced since the early 1980s. The immigration has gained increasing importance in securing a positive population growth since 1989. We now turn to the individual growth components.

### 5.2.2 Fertility

To convey an idea of fertility development since the 1930s, we present indices in terms of estimates of the total fertility rates and the net reproduction rates (Figure 5.3). For the period from 1930 through 1944, the graphs are based on five-year averages.

The population of Denmark was below the level of reproduction in the beginning of the 1930s and has been so since 1969, although for very different reasons than in the early 1930s. Interestingly, on a cross-sectional basis, fertility has been subject to a substantial and steady increase from 1983 to 1995. This development has many parallels to contemporary Swedish fertility trends (Hansen, 1995).

The European *Family and Fertility Survey* (FFS) was not implemented in Denmark. The latest modern fertility survey in Denmark dates back to 1975. In the absence of such data, we have very little direct up-to-date knowledge regarding important micro-demographic behaviour of the Danish population. Modern fertility surveys were conducted in Sweden in 1981 and in 1992–1993. The comparison of the Swedish and Danish experience in this situation becomes all the more important from a Danish point of view.

**Figure 5.3: Cross-sectional Estimates of the Total Fertility Rate (TFR) and the Net Reproduction Rate (NRR), 1932–1996, selected years**

Source: Danmarks Statistik, op. cit., Table 6

The recent Scandinavian fertility increase may be seen as a delayed implementation of latent personal and familial preferences moulded by the process of complex social and societal change since the 1960s (Hansen, 1995; Hansen and Rohrmann, 1985).

Being based on reproductive experience from cross-sections of maternal birth cohorts (synthetic cohorts), the natural cohort interpretation of indices – like those presented in Figure 5.3 – will be subject to restrictive and unrealistic *ceteris paribus* assumptions of stationarity. To overcome this problem we have compiled graphed estimates of the age-cumulated cohort fertility of Danish women born after the year 1900 (Hansen, 1993).

The maternal cohorts born before 1940 tend to have more or less the same completed fertility at a level of 2.2 to 2.4 live births per woman; however, the timing of live births has been subject to considerable variation over the maternal life cycles. In the early

1930s, during the deep economic recession, women clearly postponed childbirth. The younger women caught up with this loss after 1943. The trend-effect resulting in the big birth cohorts from 1944 to 1947 is also clearly discernible (Hansen, 1993).

The most dramatic change occurred after 1967. From then on, women in the ages below 25 experienced a fertility decline, which has been going on up to now. It is quite evident that women born after the early 1940s and entering their reproductive age after 1960 will never reach the completed fertility of the preceding maternal birth cohorts. We see, also, that women in the mature reproductive ages (after age 26) in the latter half of the 1980s tended to have slight increases in their fertility. This trend has continued into the 1990s.

The Danish fertility decline since the late 1960s has been associated with a perceptible fall in the inclination to enter first marriage, in particular in the ages below 25. It appears that the decline of entering first marriage came to a halt among the women born after 1960 and entering the marriageable ages in the 1980s. The fact that many more women now tend to stay out of marriage does not mean that they live in celibacy or do not have children. Fertility among non-married women has been subject to an enormous increase (Hansen, 1993). This development started in the older reproductive ages among the cohorts born since the late 1930s; it has spread downward to age 20 in the subsequent birth cohorts. In 1996, 46.3% of all live births took place outside marriage (Danmarks Statistik, op. cit.).

According to the Swedish FFS, the prevalence of non-marital cohabitation in 1992–1993 was 43% against 28% in Norway. The fact that non-marital cohabitation has gained such popularity in Scandinavia does not mean that a status of being formally married has become unimportant. Nonetheless, marital status was excluded from the latest Danish fertility survey of 1975. Fertility appears to be much higher among married women than among women living out of marriage and possibly in non-marital (consensual) unions (Hansen, 1993).

The contraceptive pill was released for public use in the mid-1960s, and induced abortion was legalised in 1973. These innovations coincided with substantial decrease of marital fertility in the ages below 20. Like with the first-marriage rates, the decrease of marital fertility appears to have levelled off among the female cohorts born after 1961.

As a crude indication of the divorce trends in the 1980s, cross-sectional estimates of the age-specific divorce rates for 1981 and 1989 are presented in Figure 5.4. There has been little change in ages below 30, but a considerable increase in the ages above 35. Increasing divorce numbers since the 1960s clearly became an important factor behind the profound changes in the family formation and reproductive behaviour.

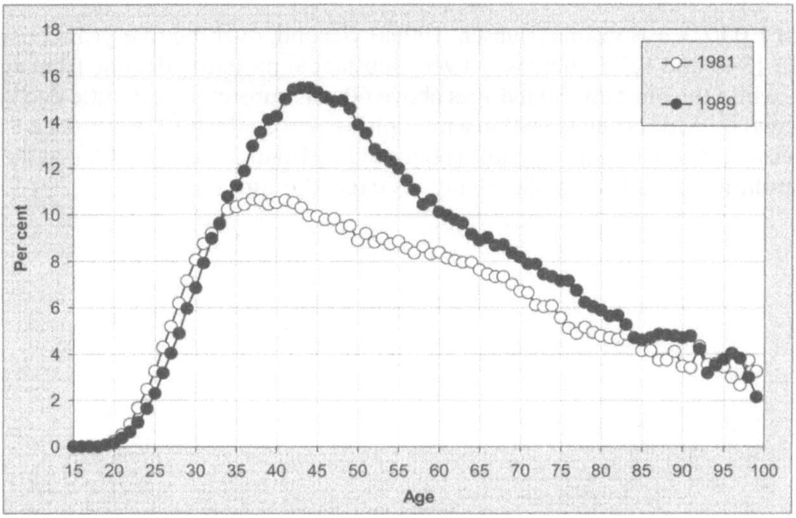


**Figure 5.4: Proportion of Divorced Among Danish Women, 1981 and 1989**

Source: Ponzi *et al.*, 1999, p. 43

### 5.2.3 Mortality

As in the case of fertility and family formation, evaluating mortality and survivorship on a cross-sectional basis is a dubious undertaking; the reason being, of course, heterogeneity in the risk sets. In many situations the heterogeneity will be poorly observed – if observable at all. This is tantamount to saying that contemporary demographic phenomena may be poorly understood if detached from their historical prerequisites. Nonetheless, calculating life table statistics under *ceteris paribus* assumptions of stationarity, using cross-sectional intensities in terms of central demographic rates, is firmly established in traditional descriptive demography.

The current development of Danish survivorship has caused some concern in the public and in political circles. In terms of cross-sectional life expectancies evaluated at age 0, it is frequently asserted that mortality has been stagnating or even increasing during recent years. This assertion is not supported by available official statistics which are normally too crude to allow for unbiased measurement of survivorship in the extreme ages. In order to overcome this problem, we have truncated the underlying synthetic life tables by age 85. The results are exhibited in Figure 5.5.

Women have much lower mortality than men do. However, in terms of life expectancies at age 0, during the period from 1981 through 1996, female mortality decreased rather slowly in the ages (0,85), while men have gained around 1.6 years in expected life. What are the main factors behind this development? First, since 1987, there has been a substantial decline in infant mortality; this decline being associated with an almost linear increase of 50 grams in expected birth weight in the weight range of 1,000–4,499 grams (Hansen, 1996a). Second, over the five-year cohorts born between 1840 and 1875, there was a very substantial mortality decline from age 20 to age 60, while the mortality in the ages above 60 was subject to very little decline. This was shown by Mortensen (1994) in a multiplicative reanalysis of occurrence/exposure data recovered with cohort life tables published by Matthiessen (1970), and the historical population census data underlying his exposure times.

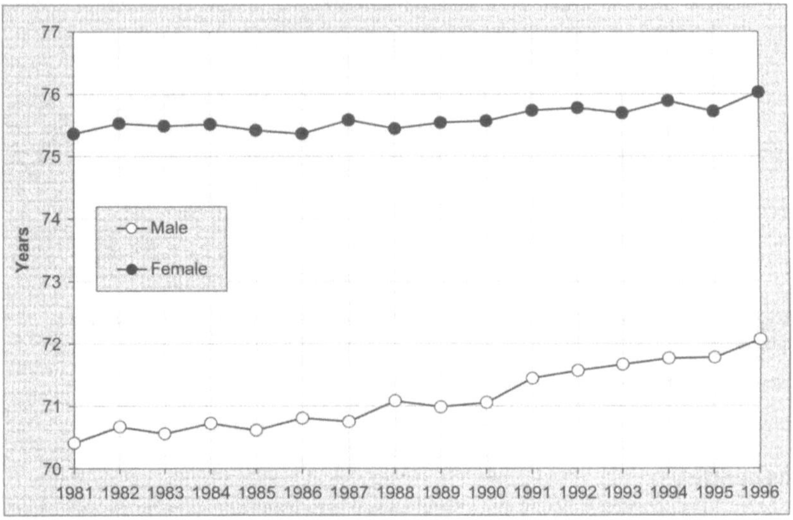


**Figure 5.5: Annual Cross-sectional Estimates of Life Expectancy at Birth, Truncated by Age 85, 1981–1996**

Source: Author's calculations with DEMOPACK based on the EXTRACT System (see Hansen, 1998)

The relatively small changes in contemporary old-age mortality may plausibly be explained by changing heterogeneity in the corresponding risk sets: declining cohort mortality in the ages 20 to 60 may entail postponement of transition to death, meaning that the risk sets of birth cohorts having reached old age by the end of the 20th century, come to include relatively higher and increasing proportions of weak or frail lives than cohorts born further back in time. Using fairly simple statistical modelling, it is easy to see that the processes of health and morbidity work this way. To conclude, any informed discussion of the current changes in Danish longevity must be based on much more careful cohort studies than have been published up to now.

Third, while awaiting more informative national cohort-based survivorship studies, it may be useful to conduct some preliminary comparisons of cause-specific, cross-sectional death risks across national populations. Comparing Sweden and Denmark, we see that the annual cross-sectional life expectancies over age period of (0,85) years were somewhat higher in Sweden than in Denmark from 1981 through 1993 (Table 5.1). Danish infant mortality is now approaching the Swedish level of very low infant mortality (Table 5.2). Cancer mortality is much higher in Denmark than in Sweden (Table 5.3). This is also true for mortality associated with motor vehicle accidents and suicide. However, mortality caused by suicide decreased considerably during the period from 1981 to 1993 in both populations, probably due to improved medical treatment. Danish mortality caused by suicide has a simple multiplicative structure (Dørum, 1995).

**Table 5.1: Estimated Annual Life Expectancies at Birth for the Age Segment (0, 85) Years, Denmark and Sweden, 1981–1994**

| Year | Denmark | | Sweden | |
|---|---|---|---|---|
| | Male | Female | Male | Female |
| 1981 | 70.41 | 75.36 | 71.39 | 76.40 |
| 1982 | 70.67 | 75.53 | 71.72 | 76.61 |
| 1983 | 70.56 | 75.49 | 71.98 | 76.69 |
| 1984 | 70.73 | 75.51 | 72.20 | 76.83 |
| 1985 | 70.62 | 75.42 | 72.32 | 77.12 |
| 1986 | 70.81 | 75.37 | 72.28 | 76.88 |
| 1987 | 70.76 | 75.58 | 72.43 | 77.15 |
| 1988 | 71.08 | 75.44 | 72.57 | 77.15 |
| 1989 | 70.99 | 75.54 | 72.54 | 77.09 |
| 1990 | 71.06 | 75.57 | 73.01 | 77.47 |
| 1991 | 71.45 | 75.74 | 73.04 | 77.33 |
| 1992 | 71.57 | 75.78 | 73.18 | 77.34 |
| 1993 | 71.66 | 75.69 | 73.61 | 77.70 |
| 1994 | 71.76 | 75.88 | .. | .. |

Source: Author's calculations with DEMOPACK based on the CD-ROM "Statistics across Borders" published by the Nordic Central Bureaus of Statistics

**Table 5.2: Estimated Death Intensity at Age (0,1) Years, Based on Cross-sectional Experience, Denmark and Sweden, 1981–1994**

| Year | Denmark | | Sweden | |
|---|---|---|---|---|
| | Male | Female | Male | Female |
| | Deaths per 1,000 person-years | | | |
| 1981 | 8.47 | 6.71 | 8.21 | 5.78 |
| 1982 | 9.53 | 6.85 | 7.42 | 6.55 |
| 1983 | 8.70 | 6.44 | 7.15 | 6.57 |
| 1984 | 9.27 | 6.21 | 6.96 | 6.96 |
| 1985 | 9.08 | 7.04 | 7.09 | 5.39 |
| 1986 | 8.91 | 7.65 | 7.09 | 6.18 |
| 1987 | 10.09 | 6.54 | 6.52 | 5.11 |
| 1988 | 8.36 | 7.22 | 6.45 | 5.37 |
| 1989 | 9.34 | 6.99 | 6.49 | 4.92 |
| 1990 | 8.70 | 6.42 | 6.36 | 4.76 |
| 1991 | 8.18 | 6.52 | 6.63 | 5.28 |
| 1992 | 7.71 | 5.70 | 6.61 | 5.61 |
| 1993 | 6.06 | 4.78 | 6.00 | 4.60 |
| 1994 | 6.24 | 4.81 | .. | .. |

Source: Author's calculations based on official statistics (see Table 5.1)

**Table 5.3: Estimated Expected Loss of Lifetime[1] of a Live-born Child in the Age Segment (0, 85) Years, Caused by a Given Death Risk in Absence of All Other Death Risks, Denmark and Sweden, 1981 and 1993, in years**

| Causes of deaths by groups[2] | Denmark | | | | Sweden | | | |
|---|---|---|---|---|---|---|---|---|
| | Male | | Female | | Male | | Female | |
| | 1981 | 1993 | 1981 | 1993 | 1981 | 1993 | 1981 | 1993 |
| 1 | 4.68 | 4.69 | 3.76 | 3.83 | 3.62 | 3.35 | 2.96 | 2.76 |
| 2 | 5.66 | 4.00 | 2.35 | 1.88 | 5.59 | 4.00 | 2.28 | 1.73 |
| 3 | 1.69 | 1.58 | 1.16 | 1.13 | 1.62 | 1.40 | 1.15 | 0.88 |
| 4 | 0.63 | 0.47 | 0.23 | 0.17 | 0.47 | 0.34 | 0.19 | 0.14 |
| 5 | 0.62 | 0.58 | 0.27 | 0.30 | 0.71 | 0.48 | 0.23 | 0.15 |
| 6 | 1.09 | 0.74 | 0.56 | 0.35 | 0.78 | 0.56 | 0.32 | 0.25 |
| 7 | 4.70 | 5.17 | 3.01 | 3.34 | 4.36 | 3.83 | 2.80 | 2.33 |
| 8 | 14.59 | 13.34 | 9.64 | 9.31 | 13.61 | 11.39 | 8.60 | 7.30 |

[1]est. ${}_{85}\overset{0}{\overline{e}}_{0}$
[2]Code $i$ =
1 Cancer, all types
2 Heart diseases
3 Circular and vascular diseases
4 Motor vehicle accidents
5 Other accidents
6 Suicide
7 All other causes of death
8 All deaths
Source: Author's calculations with DEMOPACK based on CD-ROM "Statistics across Borders" published by the Nordic Central Bureau of Statistics

### 5.2.4 External Migration

As the fourth and last component of population growth, we now consider external migration and some of its impacts on the ethnic heterogeneity of the resident population. A suitable multistate model featuring the essentials of this process has been proposed by Hansen and Maxim (1996) and Hansen (1996b). The state space of the model is shown in Figure 5.6.

Treating resident citizen group as a background variable, we see that fertility may be expressed as a function of age $x$ and a wide range of a person's characteristics included in a covariate vector $\boldsymbol{Z}$. A resident foreign national may become naturalised after a sojourn in Denmark of at least seven years. External migration and mortality may likewise depend on age and citizenship and other personal characteristics. In published Danish official statistics the covariate vector has been unobserved up to now.

As we have seen, up to 1960, the resident population was ethnically rather homogeneous. The subsequent net influx of foreign citizens, sometimes with a very different cultural and ethnic background, has caused a growing concern in the public and in the political debate: what are the expected impacts of differential reproduction and differential external migration? First, as indicated by Figure 5.7, fertility is highly differential with regard to ethnicity. Fertility tends to be much higher among immigrants from the former Yugoslavia, Turkey, Eastern Europe, Africa, Pakistan, and all other Asian countries, as compared to the fertility of Danish nationals and resident citizens from the other Nordic countries. Second, emigration tends to be lower among the citizen groups with high fertility and high among citizen groups with low to moderate fertility. Resident Danish citizens not surprisingly have relatively low emigration (Figure 5.8).

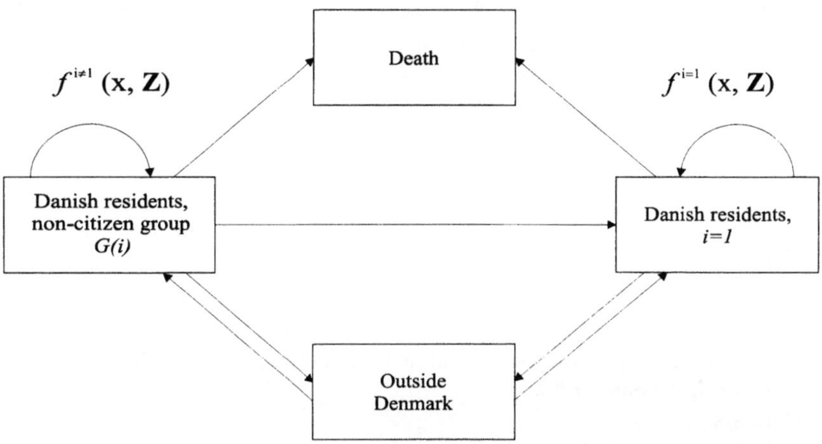


**Figure 5.6: State Space of Survival, Reproduction, Naturalisation and External Migration Among Resident Citizen Groups G(i), i = 1...12**

Source: Hansen, 1996b

Immigrants from high-fertility countries are likely to have a negative relation between the level of their fertility and their sojourn in Denmark. The cross-sectional fertility of resident citizens groups for which this hypothesis is true, consequently, may be quite sensitive to variation in the distribution with regard to sojourn in Denmark, i.e. to external migration. Up to now, convincing empirical studies regarding the relationship between fertility and sojourn in Denmark, however, do not exist. This obviously should be taken into account while considering the results presented in Figures 5.7 and 5.8.

To elucidate the importance of external migration in the presence of below-replacement reproduction among resident Danish citizens we may proceed as follows. We may project the population under the general *ceteris paribus* assumptions of differential fertility and differential external migration, altogether as of the beginning of the 1990s. Mortality is taken to be the same for all citizen groups. We consider the following three scenarios: A) Presence of external migration; B) Absence of external migration; C) Presence of emigration but absence of immigration. The likelihood of scenario C is, of course, close to nil, its main function being to convey an impression of the importance of immigration as a factor in future Danish population development, through comparison with scenarios A and B.

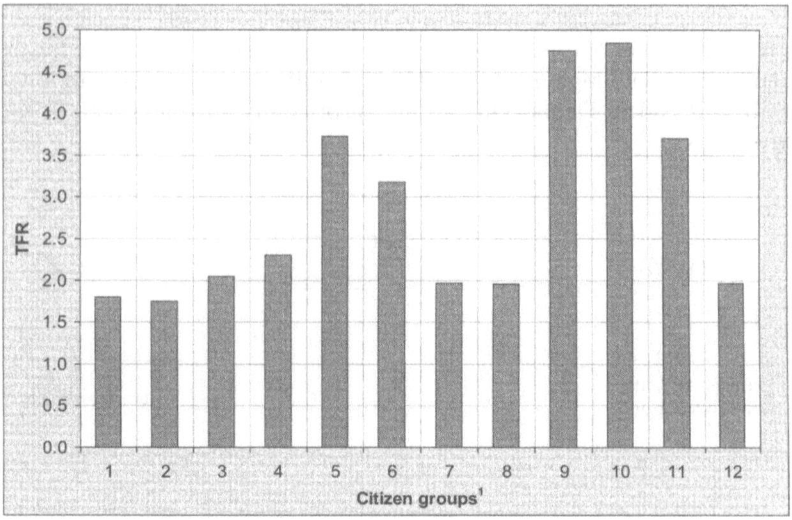


**Figure 5.7: Estimated Age-cumulated Total Fertility Rate (TFR) by Citizenship Groups, 1992**

[1]Citizenship groups:
1 Denmark and Faroe Islands and Greenland
2 All other Nordic countries except group 1
3 All other EU-countries except group 1
4 Yugoslavia
5 Turkey
6 European countries (except groups 1–4)
7 USA and Canada
8 Latin and South American countries
9 Africa
10 Pakistan
11 Asian countries except group 5 and 10
12 Australia, New Zealand and Oceania (Pacific region) and all other countries
Source: Author's calculations based on official statistics

In the presence of below-replacement reproduction since the late 1960s (Figure 5.3), external migration (Figure 5.2), differential fertility and differential external migration (Figures 5.7 and 5.8) are likely to have a dramatic impact on Danish population growth over the coming decades (Table 5.4). Under scenario A, the total population is anticipated to increase by 281,000 residents over the period 1994–2044; this increase will be due to foreign nationals.

Conversely, if the borders were to remain closed, the total population would decrease by 643,000 residents, mainly because of naturalisation. It is assumed in the projections that, upon naturalisation, foreign citizens acquire the same fertility as Danish-born nationals. By picturing the combined effects of naturalisation and absence of immigration, scenario C, *ceteris paribus*, provides a crude illustration of the enormous potential impact of immigration on current and future Danish population development, comparatively to scenario A.

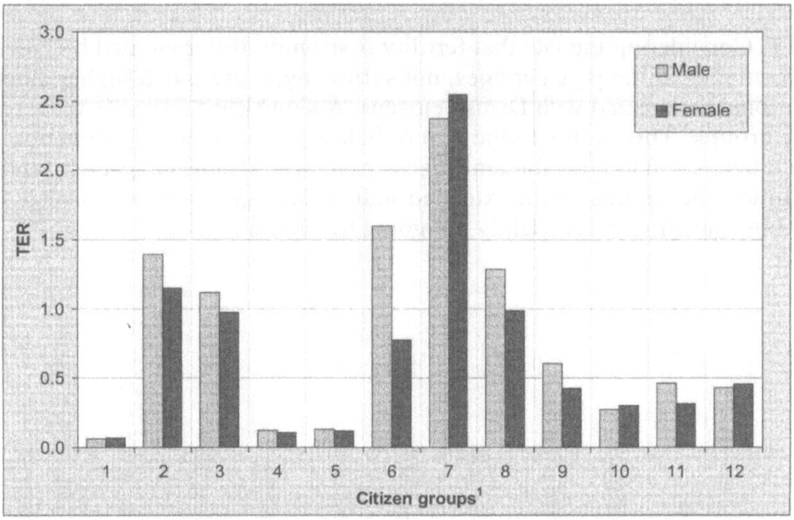


**Figure 5.8: Estimated Age-cumulated Total Emigration Rate (TER), by Citizenship Groups, 1992**

[1]Citizenship groups: see Figure 5.7
Source: Author's calculations based on official statistics

**Table 5.4: Observed and Expected Number of Resident Danish and Foreign Citizens, According to Scenario A, B, and C[1], 1994, 2024 and 2044**

| Year | Resident Danish citizens, by scenario | | | Resident foreign citizens, by scenario | | | Proportion of foreign citizens (%), by scenario | | |
|---|---|---|---|---|---|---|---|---|---|
| | A | B | C | A | B | C | A | B | C |
| 1994 | 5,016,441 | 5,016,441 | 5,016,441 | 189,014 | 189,014 | 189,014 | 3.6 | 3.6 | 3.6 |
| 2024 | 5,077,588 | 4,846,857 | 4,081,200 | 441,781 | 140,274 | 77,981 | 8.0 | 2.8 | 1.9 |
| 2044 | 4,986,895 | 4,451,407 | 3,208,806 | 500,040 | 110,522 | 55,528 | 9.1 | 2.4 | 1.7 |

[1]General assumptions: non-differential mortality; differential fertility and external migration as of the early 1990s. Special assumptions: (A) Presence of external migration; (B) Absence of external migration; (C) Presence of emigration, but absence of immigration.
Source: Author's calculations based on official statistics

In 1994, about 3.6% of the total resident population were foreign citizens. By European standard, such a percentage is rather low. Under scenario A, the proportion of resident foreign citizens is expected to reach 9.4% in 2044. Under the same scenario, the percentage of live births of resident foreign nationals is anticipated to increase from around 10 % in the late 1990s to more than 17% around 2020 (Figure 5.9). It is quite evident that the ethnic heterogeneity of population, in terms of resident foreign citizens, naturalised citizens and their descendants, is bound to increase very considerably in a foreseeable future.

The structural age differentials of external migration are also anticipated to be considerable. This is demonstrated by the proportional age distributions in Figures 5.10

and 5.11. Considering the fact that fertility is strongly differentiated by citizenship, the percentages in the younger ages, not surprisingly, are much higher among foreign nationals compared with Danish citizens. A significant ageing is to be expected in both groups. This is due to the severe below-replacement reproduction among Danish citizens. Up to now, foreign citizens have been relatively sparsely represented in the older age groups. With extended individual sojourn in the Danish society, maybe until death, this is certainly not going to remain so.

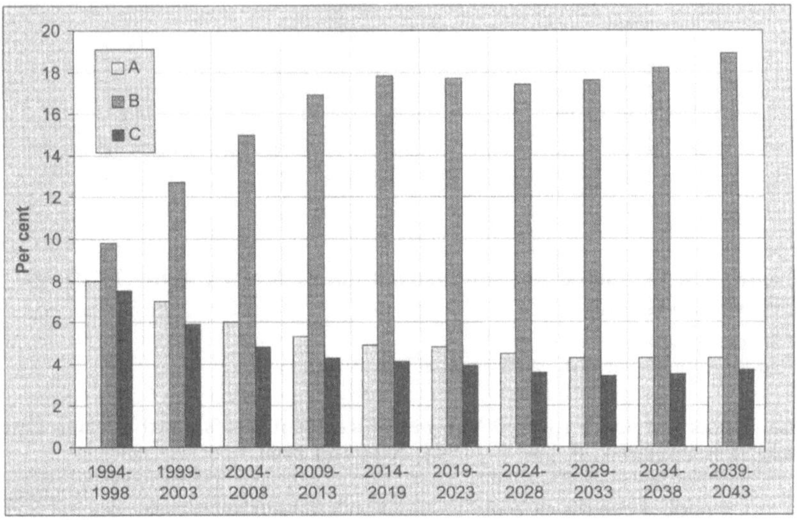


**Figure 5.9: Expected Proportion of Live Births Delivered by Resident Foreign Citizens, According to Scenario A, B, and C[1], 1994–2044**

[1]General assumptions: see Table 5.4
Source: Hansen, 1996b

As a further illustration of the increasing ethnic heterogeneity of the resident population, age-specific prevalence rates of the resident foreign population, as of 1994 and as foreseen by 2044 under scenarios A, B, and C, are shown in Figure 5.12. The effects of this course of events are beginning to be seen, for example, in habitation, in the schooling system, in the social system, and in the labour market. As the groups of resident foreigners become more numerous, they are likely to seek political influence in these and other areas (Rasmussen, 1998).

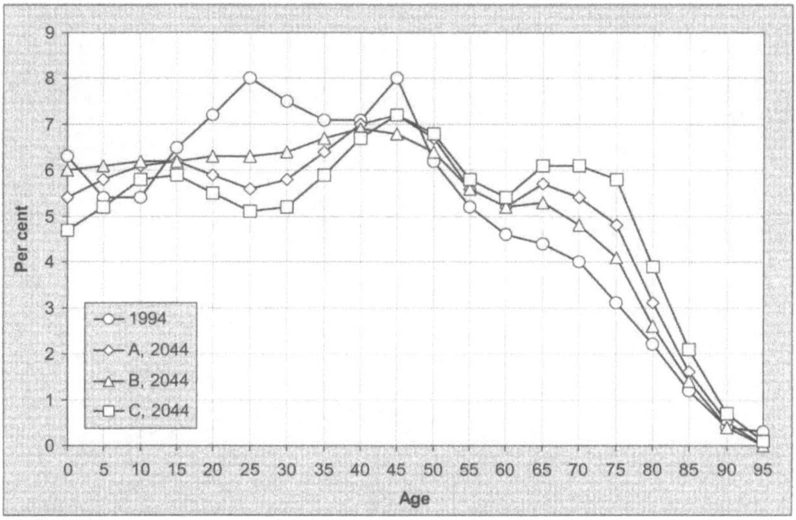


**Figure 5.10: Proportion of Resident Danish Citizens by Age, According to Scenario A, B, and C[1], 1994 and 2044**

[1]General assumptions: see Table 5.4
Source: Hansen, 1996b

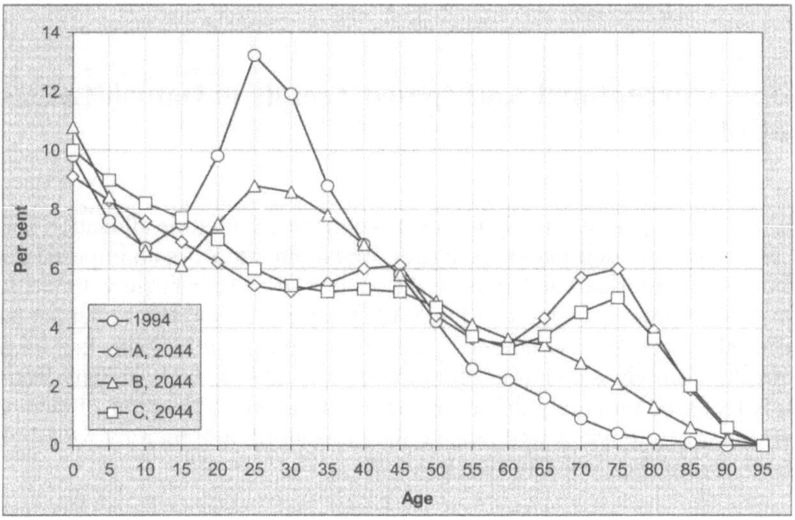


**Figure 5.11: Proportion of Resident Foreign Citizens by Age, According to Scenario A, B, and C[1], 1994 and 2044**

[1]General assumptions: see Table 5.4
Source: Hansen, 1996b

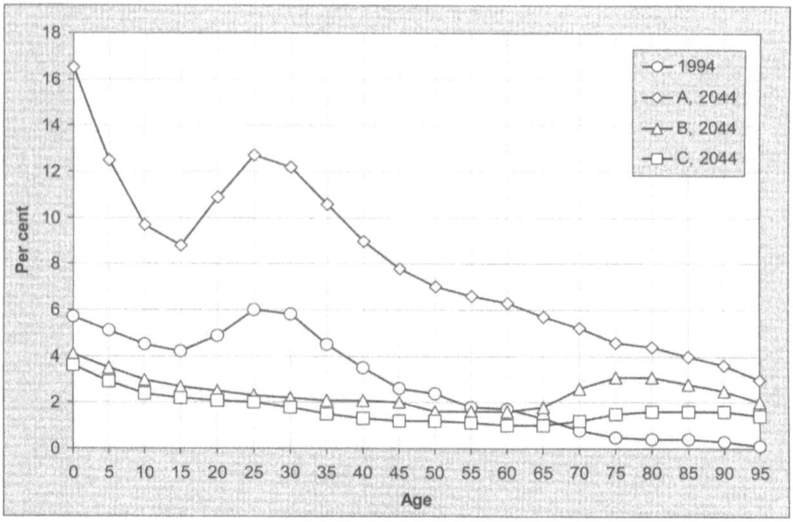


**Figure 5.12: Prevalence of Resident Foreign Citizens in a Given Age Group, According to Scenario A, B, and C[1], 1994 and 2044**

[1]General assumptions: see Table 5.4
Source: Hansen, 1996b

## 5.3 Some Current and Anticipated Trends in Danish Labour Supply

In economic theory, labour supply is closely connected with time allocation between a variety of market and non-market activities. As labour supply is an important element of wellbeing of individuals and, thus, of the general welfare in society, time allocation decisions are of great importance to individual agents and to the society at large. In conventional macro-theory, labour is considered one of the basic factors of economic production while common economic micro-theory, such as New Home Economics, is focussed on family formation, labour division and transfer of income, with implications for time use in and outside the household, and thereby for labour supply and labour market mobility (Becker, 1991).

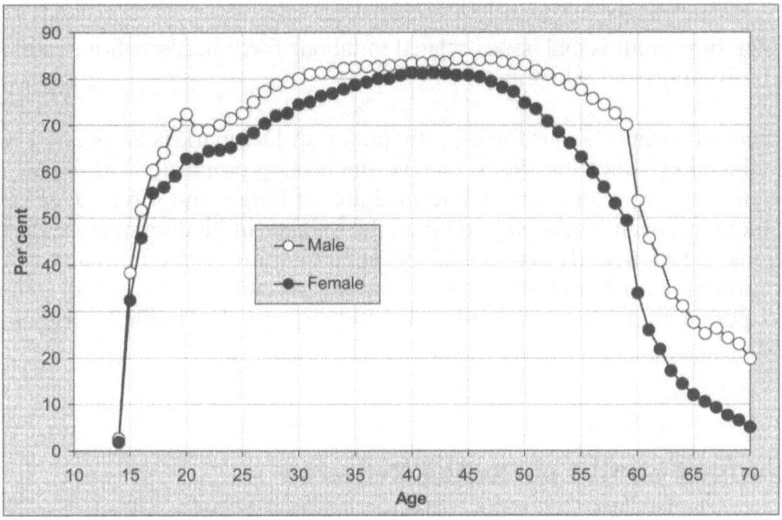


**Figure 5.13: Economically Active Population by Age and Sex, 1993**

Source: Author's calculations based on official statistics

Like in the other Scandinavian welfare countries, Danish labour force participation is high. The labour force participation of women has increased considerably over the past four decades, and it is now approaching the labour force participation of men (Figure 5.13). It is, however, difficult to document the motivations behind this recorded behaviour: Danmarks Statistik has not published detailed panel data on national labour force movements since 1988. The latest available data set (gross flow basis) relates to the period from November 1983 to November 1984. For obscure reasons, Danmarks Statistik up to now has refused to provide labour market information to the Luxembourg Employment Study (LES).

Can the Danish labour force growth, and the observable labour force participation from 1985 through 1996, in the context of the above-mentioned background, be adequately described in terms of the estimable labour force mobility using the published gross flow data for 1983–1984? Or do the observable changes indicate substantial time dependency in the (latent) intensities of labour force transitions since 1985? Are the differentials in the labour force participation, for example, related to foreign nationals with residence in Denmark? These questions were considered by Hansen and Gustafsson (1997). Their project entailed recovering intensities embedded in estimated probabilities in the framework of a generalised life model.

The main results are as follows. After a massive increase in the female labour force participation across the cohorts born since the beginning of the 1950s, it has levelled off and virtually come to a halt since the beginning of the 1980s. The population development and the Danish labour force participation were converging towards stationarity by the mid-1990s. Danish labour force participation is strongly differential with regard to ethnicity, with foreign citizens having much lower participation rates than Danish citizens. This result has implication for multistate projection of a wide range of current social issues related to labour force participation, employment, external migration and ethnicity.

The increased female labour force participation in Denmark is associated with improved education. Since the 1960s, the ever-increasing proportions of female cohorts have been entering education of intermediate or longer duration. Over the same period, there has been a massive growth in the number of kindergartens and childcare institutions. Being heavily tax-subsidised, such institutions are normally run by the local communities. The old-age pensions, as well as care institutions for elderly and disabled persons unable to look after themselves, are also publicly organised and financed.

## 5.4 Summary and Concluding Remarks

As in many other European nations, Danish population reproduction has been below replacement for several decades. This development has perceptible implications, not least in the form of severe demographic ageing. Some major political and public concerns, caused by the current and expected ageing, are the following: will the future labour force be large enough to accommodate the increasing dependency burden? Will the old-age pensions keep up their values? And what will happen to the national economy when the future larger numbers of pensioners start spending their savings?

Given that the dependency burden is commonly calculated as the ratio of the number of persons in the ages below 20 and above age 65 to the number of persons in the so-called occupationally active age span in between, the question regarding the size of the labour force seems to be ill posed. First, people do neither enter the labour market at some fixed age, nor withdraw from the labour market at one and the same age. Second, not all people in the working ages are in the labour force. Third, not all persons in the labour force are gainfully employed. With a rate of unemployment of 6.4% of the Danish labour force in 1998, how can anyone speak of insufficient labour supply in quantitative terms? True enough, moderate to massive unemployment may not rule out the existence of shortage of manpower with specialised skills and particular occupational know-how.

The "bottleneck" problem, however, is primarily a question of inadequate supply of a flexible manpower with sufficient education and realistic build-up of human capital. In a society subject to rapid technological change and increasing internationalisation, the issues of the quality of the labour force are likely to matter much more for sustained economic and social development than sheer quantity of the labour force. In many contemporary societies, including Denmark, the negative correlation between economic efficiency and educational incapability is becoming evermore manifest and critical. If the education and distribution issues can be mediated, there should be little reason for fearing the immediate and upcoming economic impacts of the current below-replacement reproduction in a foreseeable future.

Denmark does not have any explicit population policy aiming at influencing the growth of the population. However, most of the economic and social policies in a modern welfare society have numerous implicit behavioural impacts, resulting in demographic events on the level of individuals, families and households.

Is external migration an asset to the Danish society, given below-replacement reproduction? Obviously, there are no simple answers to such a question. Again, this is an issue not only of quantity but rather more of quality. Can the payment transfer problem, commonly associated with population ageing, be solved or alleviated through immigration? And how do issues of human capital relate to this problem? Empirical experiences of traditional immigration countries like USA, Canada, and Australia suggest that persons admitted through immigration tend to work harder than natives; to be more educated than native people; to have a higher level of self-employment than the natives in the country of immigration; and to use fewer transfer payments than do native families (Simon, 1989). It seems questionable, however, whether the experiences of immigration to overseas countries would be relevant and applicable to the current European welfare societies. Competitive social research based on data of better quality could throw new light on such questions in Denmark.

To find political ways to deal with the issues of human capital and other social impacts of external migration and below-replacement reproduction in a responsible and balanced, yet realistic manner, presents some of the most important challenges to the Danish society at the beginning of the third millennium.

## Acknowledgement

Enlightening discussions and constructive criticisms from Ulla Funck Jensen are gratefully acknowledged; the responsibility for any shortcoming or error rests with the author.

## References

Andersen, Th.B. (1996), *"New Home Economics", arbejdsudbud samt alternative fremskrivninger af den danske arbejdsstyrke fordelt på køn og alder*, Copenhagen: Copenhagen University, Dept. of Economics, unpublished master thesis.

Becker, G.S. (1991), *A Treatise on the Family*, Enlarged Edition, Cambridge, MA: Harvard University Press.

Danmarks Statistik (1998), *Befolkningens bevægelser 1996*, Copenhagen: Danmarks Statistik.

Dørum, K. (1995), *En analyse af selvmordets demografi og epidemiologi, Danmark 1981–1993*, Copenhagen: Copenhagen University, Dept. of Economics, unpublished.

Gustafsson, L. (1997), *En komparativ studie af arbejdsudbuddet på de skandinaviske arbejdsmarkeder*, Copenhagen: Copenhagen University, Dept. of Economics, unpublished master thesis.

Haahr, K. (1988), *Nogle praktiske og teoretiske aspekter ved udvalgte danske arbejdsmarkedsfremskrivninger*, Copenhagen: Copenhagen University, Dept. of Economics, unpublished master thesis.

Hansen, H.O. and D. Rohrmann (1985), Fertility and Family Formation. Some trends among Danish female cohorts born between 1932 and 1967, *Scandinavian Population Studies*, Vol. 7, pp. 34–47.

Hansen, H.O. (1993), *Elementær demografi*, Copenhagen: Akademisk forlag.

Hansen, H.O. (1995), Formation of Families of Danish Women born after 1931 with a Review of some Current Fertility Trends, In: Ch. Lundh (ed.), *Demography, Economy, and Welfare*, pp. 45–61, Lund, Sweden: Lund University Press.

Hansen, H.O. (1996a), Social and Biological Issues in Infant Survivorship among Danish cohorts born between 1982 and 1990, *Scandinavian Population Studies*, Vol. 11, pp. 82–100.

Hansen, H.O. (1996b), Some Demographic Impacts of Current Regional and Ethnical Differentials in Denmark, In: M.C. Debernardi (ed.), *Evolution or Revolution in European Population*, pp. 129–144, Milano: Franco Angeli.

Hansen, H.O. and P.S. Maxim (1996), Some patterns and social impacts of external migration on a below-replacement population: Denmark by the turn of the Millennium, *Yearbook of Population Research in Finland*, Vol. 33, pp. 136–149.

Hansen, H.O. and L. Gustafsson (1997), *Analysis of the Danish Labour Force Mobility 1985–1996*, unpublished conference paper.

Hoem, J.M. and U. Funck Jensen (1982), Multistate Life Table Methodology: A Probabilist Critique, In: K.C. Land and A. Rogers (eds.), *Multidimensional Mathematical Demography*, New York: Academic Press.

Matthiessen, P.C. (1970), *Some Aspects of the Demographic Transition in Denmark*, Copenhagen: Akademisk forlag, Ph.D. thesis.

Mortensen, M. (1994), *Begrebet 'demografisk transition' i kritisk belysning*, Copenhagen: Copenhagen University: Dept. of Economics, unpublished master thesis.

Ponzi, A., B. Gottardi and L. Cocchi (1999), *National and regional issues of fertility and reproduction in Italy 1980–93 – with a comparison of Italian fertility 1993 and Danish fertility 1994*, Copenhagen: Copenhagen University, Dept. of Economics, unpublished manuscript.

Rasmussen, L. (1998), *Nogle samfundsmæssige konsekvenser af den danske befolknings heterogenitet særlig m.h.t. statsborgerskab*, Copenhagen: Copenhagen University: Dept. of Economics, unpublished master thesis.

Simon, J. (1989), *The Economic Consequences of Immigration*, Oxford: Basil Blackwell.

Strandmark (1983), Den danske arbejdsstyrkes bevægelser på årsbasis 1972–79 belyst ved hjælp af erhvervsoverlevelsestavler, *Økonomi og politik*, Vol. 4.

Økonomiministeriet (Ministry of Economics) (1998), *Økonomisk oversigt*, Copenhagen: J.H. Schultz Information A/S.

# 6

# Demographic Development of Estonian Population: Recent Changes in the Context of the Long-term Trends

**Kalev Katus, Luule Sakkeus, Allan Puur and Asta Põldma**

## 6.1 Introduction

Estonia, the northernmost of the three Baltic countries, has an area of 45,215 square kilometres and a population of 1,565.7 thousand (census 1989) (EKDK, 1996–1999). Estonian people have lived on the present territory for more than 5,000 years, so Estonia may be considered one of the oldest nations in Europe in that respect. At the beginning of the 13th century, the country lost its independence after twenty years of fighting against combined attacks by Germans, Danes, Swedes, and Russians. Since then, Estonia began to serve as a dividing line between the Roman Catholic and Orthodox worlds, a division, which has maintained its importance until today. Although the geopolitical dividing line was moved westwards due to the victory of Russia in the Northern War (1700–1721), the Baltic provinces secured substantial autonomy under the Russian Empire.

After being ruled by various powers for nearly 700 years, Estonia declared its independence on 24 February 1918. In the Independence War (1918–1920) the young Republic defended itself against the Russian Federation as well as German military forces, which had been established in the region after the capitulation to *Entente*. During the course of the Second World War, Estonia fell to Soviet occupation for the first time in 1940. The occupation by the Germans (1941–1944) was followed by the second Soviet occupation, which lasted for almost fifty years. In 1944, the Soviet Union unilaterally established new borders, transferring parts of Estonia to the Russian Federation. The new regime introduced a forceful rearrangement of the entire societal organisation, which was implemented by means of terror and mass deportations. In contrast to Central Europe, the loss of statehood in Estonia involved not only the absence of independent policies but also the dismantling of national institutions. Estonia regained its independence in 1991 and since then has been working to re-establish civil society, rebuild the institutional framework, and restore its position in the international community.

## 6.2 The Timing of the Demographic Transition

The demographic transition is a universal process, however, its timing has varied to a large extent among nations. This different timing has had tremendous impact on the human and political development of European nations and is still influential in the modern world. Even before the transition era, the European marriage pattern was widely acknowledged as a major demarcation line in human development (Hajnal, 1965). Since at least the 18th century, Estonia formed the easternmost area of the European marriage pattern, characterised by relatively late marriages and a high proportion of people who never marry (Palli, 1988).

In Estonia, the beginning of the demographic transition could be traced back to the mid-19th century. Judging by the spread of the parity-specific family limitation and other characteristics, the emergence of the modern type of population reproduction in Estonia has been synchronous with that in Northern and Western European countries (Katus, 1994). For example, in the 1880s, the countries with the lowest overall fertility such as Sweden, Switzerland, and Norway demonstrated up to a twenty per cent higher marital fertility compared to Estonia. During the same period, France – the leading nation in the fertility transition – was the only other European country having both an overall and marital fertility lower than Estonia. Belonging to the pioneering nations in the fertility transition, Estonia had already reached under-replacement fertility and a slow turnover of generations by the 1920s (Katus, 1989).

Mortality transition progressed alongside with fertility decline: the male life expectancy increased from 41.9 years in 1897 (the earliest census based life table) to 53.1 in 1934, the corresponding female figures being 45.5 and 59.6 years, respectively. The endogenous causes of death had already taken the lead by the 1930s (Katus and Puur, 1992). Although Estonia did not belong to the forerunners of the mortality transition as it had in fertility development, in the mid-20th century the country was characterised by one of the most advanced levels of life expectancy in Central Europe (Krumins, 1990). When compared to Northern and Western Europe, Estonia lagged behind primarily in the decrease of infant mortality.

In terms of population reproduction, the demographic transition in Estonia followed the so-called French model. Mortality and fertility declined practically simultaneously and, as a result, population increase appeared markedly small compared to neighbouring countries. Following this decline in population fertility and mortality, Estonia entered a stage of mobility transition in the last quarter of the 19th century. During that stage, the acceleration of population growth brought about a build-up of migration potential which, in the case of Estonia, resulted in intensive emigration (mostly to frontiers of the Russian Empire) and to a lesser extent, internal urbanisation. The First World War marked the cessation of emigration and after the war the already-decreasing migration potential was channelled to the development of the country's urban settlement system. By the eve of the Second World War, the migration processes in Estonia had begun to stabilise.

## 6.3 Population Growth and Structure

The present demographic development of Estonia has been to a great extent influenced by the changes in the population composition that occurred during and after the Second World War. On one hand, in the course of the war and the ensuing successive occupations, Estonia lost four out of five national minorities (Germans were repatriated in 1939–1941, Jews were exterminated by 1942, Swedes escaped in 1944, Russians and Latvians living in mixed-populated areas were annexed by the Soviet Union in 1945) (Katus *et al.*, 1997a). Altogether, the combined losses from the war and post-war sovetisation accounted for at least 17.5% of total population, and even currently, the number of native-born population is about 10 % lower than its pre-war level.

On the other hand, these losses were exceeded in numbers by mass immigration from different parts of the Soviet Union, mainly from Russia. As a result, Estonia has developed from a socially and nationally homogeneous country (in 1945 Estonians formed 97.3 % of population), into a country with residents of more than a hundred different ethnic backgrounds. According to the 1989 census, the foreign-born population including the second generation comprised 36% of the total population (Katus and Sakkeus, 1993). The post-war immigrants to Estonia originated from the regions located East of the Hajnal line, and compared to native-born population, featured about a fifty-year lag in the timing of demographic transition (Vishnevsky and Volkov, 1983). Sometimes, these dissimilarities between sub-populations have been misinterpreted as ethnic inequalities and used as a political argument. Studies on various dimensions of population development have revealed that regardless of the decades passed since the completion of transition and the half-century of unifying Soviet rule, native- and foreign-born background is still the most important characteristic for explaining the heterogeneity of demographic and social behaviours in Estonia (EKDK 1995; UN ECE 1999a; UN ECE, 1999b).

Similarly, as in other dimensions of demographic development, the discontinuity introduced by the emergence of an immigrant population is essential for understanding the trends in age composition and population growth. Belonging to the pioneering nations in demographic transition, Estonia's continuous progress of population ageing had resulted in one of the most advanced degrees of the process by the Second World War. For example, even at the time of the 1941 census, the percentage of elderly (population aged 60 and over) had reached 16% (Katus, 1995). After the war, the expansion of immigrant population with a remarkably high prevalence of young individuals halted the general ageing trend for almost fifty years: the ageing of native-born population which peaked in the 1970s was counterbalanced by a continuously increasing number of immigrants. In the long run, understandably, this effect did not prove to be sustainable, and the ageing process resumed in the 1980s. In the 1990s, a rapid fertility decline and a decrease in migration flows (mortality stagnation has limited the process from the bottom of age pyramid) have considerably accelerated the ageing process and this trend is expected to progress further in the coming decades (Figure 6.1).

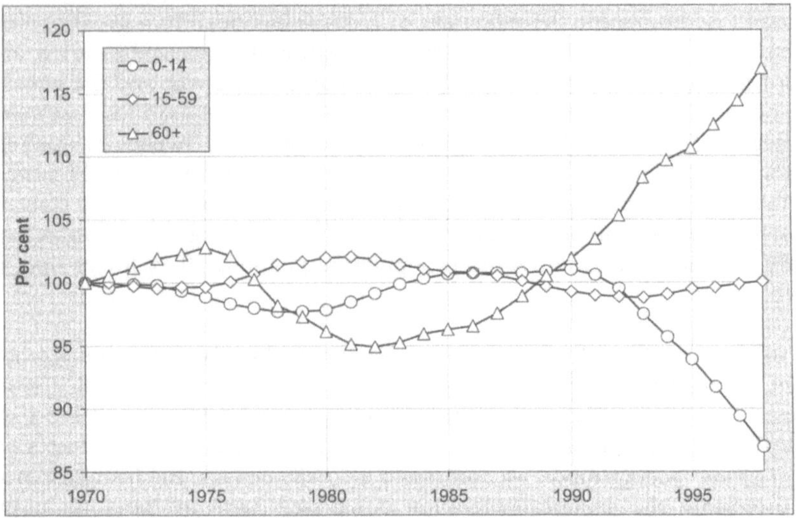


**Figure 6.1: Change in the Proportion of Main Age Groups, 1970–1998 (1970 = 100%)**

Source: Estonian Population Databank

As regards to the size of the population, a continuously positive migration balance assured population growth throughout the post-war period, both directly and indirectly through maintenance of a younger age structure. Due to rapid fertility decline starting in 1991, however, a natural decrease of population has been observed in Estonia. It should be noted that without the contribution of immigration, this natural decrease would have occurred by the 1970s (as is the case for the native-born population). Currently, the drop in fertility combined with advanced population ageing and a relatively low life expectancy translates into one of the world's most rapid population declines. Still, considering the demographic statistics for Estonia in the 1990s, one should be aware of significant deterioration of data quality which has resulted from unaccomplished reform of the statistical system, discussed in detail elsewhere (Anderson *et al.*, 1994; Katus *et al.*, 1997b). Responding to the situation, the Statistical Office has recently issued alternative estimates for population size and age structure, which yield a difference from official figures of 5% in total population, and in specific age groups the difference between the two estimates is over 10% (ESA, 1998). Understandably, the uncertainty related to the denominator leaves no population-based indicator untouched.

## 6.4 Fertility and Reproductive Health

Belonging to the nations advanced in fertility decline, the Estonian population reached below-replacement fertility in the 1920s. As an exception to the general European trend (Festy, 1984; Gillis *et al.*, 1992), no baby boom occurred and fertility also remained below replacement level during the post-war decades, with a total fertility rate (TFR) of 1.9 to 2.0 in the 1940s–1950s. In this period, Estonia most likely featured the lowest fertility level in Europe. At the end of the 1960s, however, this fertility trend changed. The period fertility of the native-born population increased more than 17% in four years (1971 compared to 1967). This increase proved to be of a long-term nature, affecting the cohort indicators and lasting for nearly a generation (Figure 6.2). Taken together, the relatively early demographic transition, the absence of a baby boom, and the fertility increase resulted in remarkable stability of post-transitional fertility trends in Estonia (Katus, 1997).

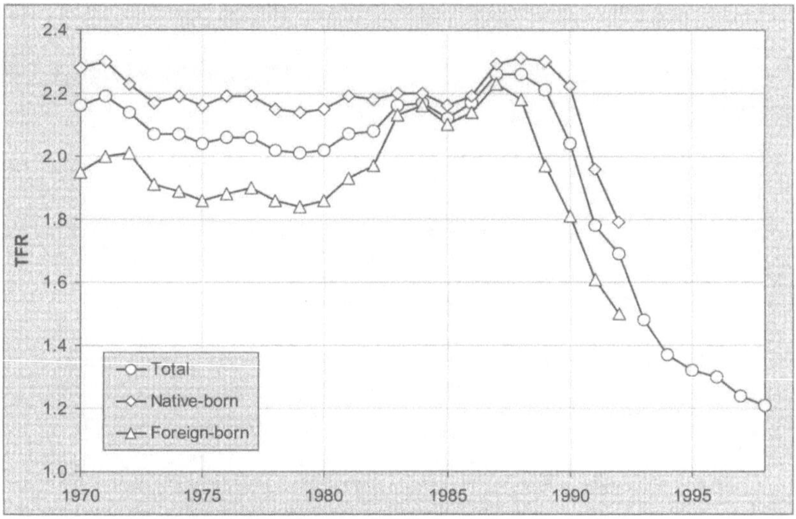


**Figure 6.2: Total Fertility Rate (TFR), 1970–1998**

Source: Estonian Population Databank

The fertility level reached a peak in 1988, when the population of an immigrant origin caught up with the level of the native-born population. For a couple of years, the TFR even exceeded 2.2. This level, the highest recorded in Estonia during the past 80 years, was followed by a sharp decline in the 1990s: by 1997, the TFR had dropped to below 1.3 with clear signs of slowing in recent years. The decline occurred virtually in all subgroups of the population. In terms of parity, the biggest reduction occurred with the second and third child. Still, despite several years of very low fertility, it is not yet clear to what extent the recent decline reflects a new pattern of lower and/or delayed reproductive behaviour, and to what extent it should be regarded as a period effect. Regardless of its origin, the fertility decline has already caused a serious discontinuity in the age structure of the population.

Extramarital fertility in Estonia has closely followed the Scandinavian pattern, and as in Iceland, Sweden, Norway, and Denmark, the proportion of extramarital births in Estonia is currently close to 50% (Figure 6.3). In contrast to these countries, the level of extramarital fertility was already very high during the sovetisation period 1945–1955 (0.5 of total rate), declined through the mid-1960s, and then grew again (Katus, 1992). Notably, the sharp fertility decline of the 1990s has been influenced solely by marital fertility. The nearly stable extramarital fertility only slightly decreased in recent years. Additionally, among first births, more than four-fifths are conceived before the official registration of a union. At the same time, very high extramarital fertility does not necessarily mean a growth of birth to single (non-cohabiting) mothers. The latter has remained at the level of 7–10% across the whole period of post-transitional fertility (EKDK, 1995).

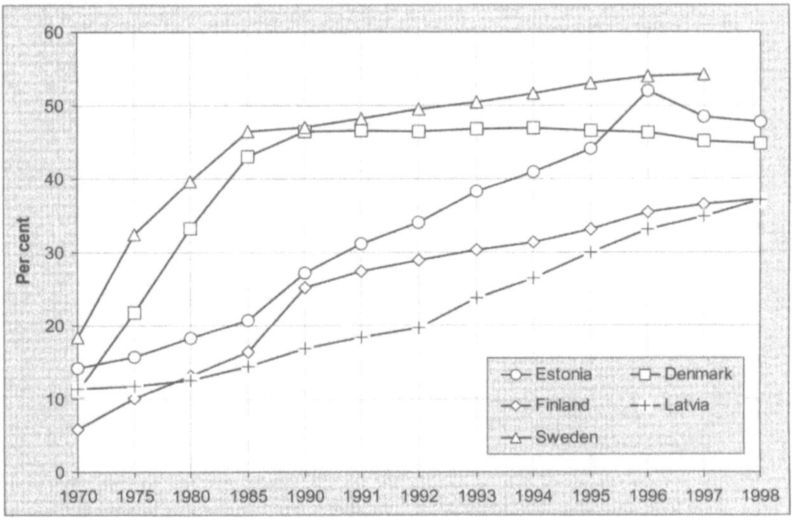


**Figure 6.3: Proportion of Extramarital Births, 1970–1998**

Sources: European Population Databank; Council of Europe, 1998

The fertility transition and the under-replacement fertility level were achieved in Estonia through traditional methods of family planning. During the Soviet period, the unavailability of contraceptives and a lack of relevant education resulted in an increasing reliance on abortion as a method of fertility control. As a result, the number of abortions exceeded the number of live births and the extremely high number of abortions became the major reproductive health issue in Estonia (Anderson *et al.*, 1993). From another perspective, for example, among women born in the 1940s, the total abortion rate (average number of abortions over lifetime) exceeded 1.8. In recent years, easier access to modern contraceptives has led to a rapid change in the patterns of family planning. Younger cohorts, particularly the native-born population, are becoming less exposed to the risk of abortion. Nevertheless, the decline in fertility has proven to be yet more rapid, and the abortion ratio had even increased in the first half of the 1990s.

## 6.5 Mortality

The transitional mortality decline in Estonia proceeded until the end of the 1950s. At that time, the country ranked quite favourably by mortality indicators, featuring one of the highest levels of life expectancy in Central Europe. The following decades, however, did not show the continuation of earlier trends and can be briefly characterised as mortality stagnation. In the 1960s, when the stagnation of general mortality had begun, there had been only a negligible improvement of life expectancy at birth, caused mainly by the improvement of infant mortality, which continued to decline for about a decade (EKDK, 1994). The pattern of mortality combining a relatively advanced infant mortality with a relatively high adult mortality, which became established three decades ago, appears atypical in respect to both the Coale-Demeny and UN model life tables (Katus and Puur, 1992). Actually, the mortality stagnation during 1959–1989 was not characterised by an absence of progress in mortality levels, but rather by deterioration in the age-specific pattern, particularly for males aged 20–55. Although this phenomenon has been well documented and addressed by extensive scientific discussion, its ultimate cause still remains unidentified (Bourgeois-Pichat, 1984; Meslé and Vallin, 1993). Compared to Central European countries with similar experiences, in Estonia the early demographic transition has contributed to the particular length of mortality stagnation.

The structure of causes of death in Estonia broadly reflects the patterns generally found in developed countries: non-infectious diseases along with accidental and violent deaths account for 90% of all deaths (Leinsalu, 1993). For all main causes, however, these deaths occur at significantly younger ages compared to Western countries. Cardiovascular mortality has increasingly become a problem of middle-aged men and has not begun to show any decline. The trends in cancer mortality also have not revealed any substantial progress over the past 25 years (Thomson *et al.*, 1996). In comparative perspective, the most distinctive feature of causal mortality in Estonia is the persistently high proportion of accidental and violent deaths. For example, the suicide rate for males has been one of the highest in Europe since the 1960s (Värnik, 1997). Yet another notable feature of the pattern is the extensive gender gap in life expectancy. Ranging between 10 and 12 years, it has strongly unbalanced the proportion of males and females among the elderly, putting an additional strain on social policies (Sakkeus, 1995).

Turning to the most recent developments in Estonia, the population's health situation has worsened and life expectancy has decreased in the 1990s (Figure 6.4). Between 1989 and 1994, life expectancy for males dropped from 66.1 to 61.6 years and from 75.0 to 74.2 for females (the extent of the decline partly reflects the deterioration of data accuracy). Contrary to some expectations, the biggest increase in mortality appeared not among the groups traditionally most vulnerable (children and the elderly), but rather was concentrated in the active age-span, particularly among middle-aged men. The sharpest increase was related to the already high number of violent deaths, with rates more than doubling in six years. On the other hand, however, the general mortality pattern remained unchanged, and therefore, the observed decline in life expectancy can be regarded simply as an aggravation of old tendencies, rooted in the 30-year mortality stagnation. This similarity also suggests that the same causal mechanisms, which led to stagnation, are most likely responsible for the recent increase rather than some principally new processes emerging from societal transitions (Katus and Zakharov, 1997; Leon *et al.*, 1997).

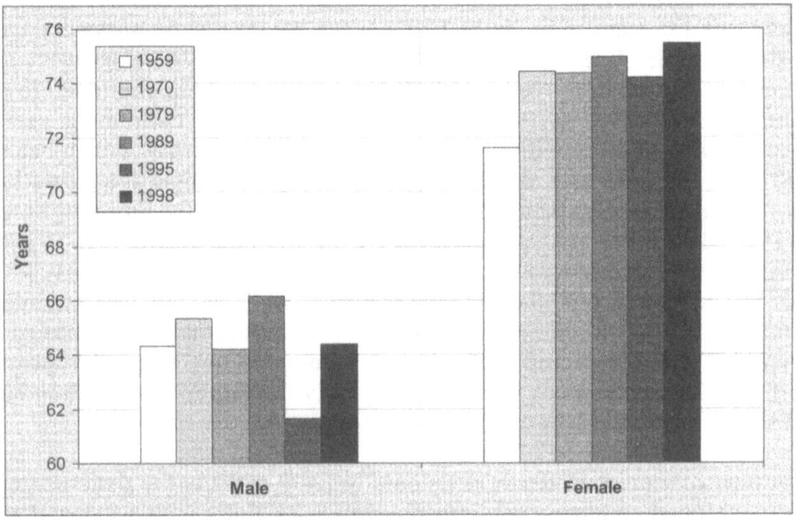


**Figure 6.4: Life Expectancy at Birth, 1959–1998, selected years**

Source: Estonian Population Databank

In 1995, without any noteworthy intervention by governmental institutions, mortality began to decrease at a relatively high rate (Katus and Puur, 1997). It is most likely that the present advancement has been bringing the life expectancy back to the "stagnation level" rather than introducing a rapid improvement and entry into the fourth stage of epidemiological transition (see Olshansky and Ault, 1986). This suggestion is consistent with the basic features of post-transitional mortality, according to which deaths due to endogenous causes result from a gradual accumulation of adverse impacts of the social environment. These accumulation mechanisms are particularly relevant for cardiovascular diseases and cancer, accounting for more than three-fourths of all deaths under the modern mortality regime. From another perspective, these mechanisms draw attention to the particular importance of cohort effects, related to a varying duration and intensity of environmental impacts. If this hypothesis holds true, it is realistic to expect it will take several decades to overcome completely the legacy of mortality stagnation, regardless of the speed of societal normalisation and advancement of economic opportunities. The principal improvement is likely to start in the younger age groups, as is suggested by the recent decline in infant mortality to a level of around 10‰.

## 6.6 Marriage and Divorce

In the 1930s, the mean age at first marriage was around 29 years for males and 26 for females. The proportion of single persons at ages 40–49 had increased, confirming that the late marriage/low prevalence marriage pattern was present in Estonia before the Second World War. During the post-war period, this pattern was replaced by a tendency towards higher marriage rates and earlier family formation. In the 1960s, the total first marriage rate approached 1.0, and suggesting a sharp drop in the age of marriage, exceeded that level in the second half of the decade. In the 1980s, the total first marriage rate stabilised at the level of 0.9, and the decline of mean age at first marriage stopped around 24–25 years for males and 22–23 years for females (Vikat, 1994).

The 1990s have witnessed a sharp decline in annually registered marriages (Figure 6.5). The total first marriage rate has fallen to 0.35 for Estonia in 1996, and is, along with Iceland, Latvia, Norway and Sweden, among the lowest in Europe (Council of Europe, op. cit.). A sharp drop to very low levels of total first marriage rate has occurred due to the postponement of marriage as well as the increase in non-marital cohabitation. Although consensual unions have increasingly gained popularity, it is unlikely that more than half a generation would remain unmarried, which would occur if the very low current marriage rate continues for a generation. It is more likely that the marriage rate will recover when the level of later marriages has reached equilibrium, though it would probably never reach the high level observed in the 1970s.

Considering family formation in a broader context, the decline in marriage rates has, however, not implied a decrease in partnerships. Among the native-born population, the matrimonial behaviour has traditionally paralleled the Scandinavian pattern. Cohabitation has shown a steady increase since the 1960s and, among women born in the early 1970s, it accounts for approximately 95% of first unions (EKDK, 1995). Younger cohorts of the native-born population have entered consensual unions at a rate comparable with Sweden, a country well-known as the forerunner of new family behaviour. Marriage follows later, usually after the birth of a child. By removing the former mechanisms of housing distribution and providing young couples the access to modern contraceptives, these recent societal changes have contributed to further establishment of cohabitation as a distinct life cycle stage. Among immigrant population, marital behaviour appears to be more traditional and non-marital cohabitation is much less common.

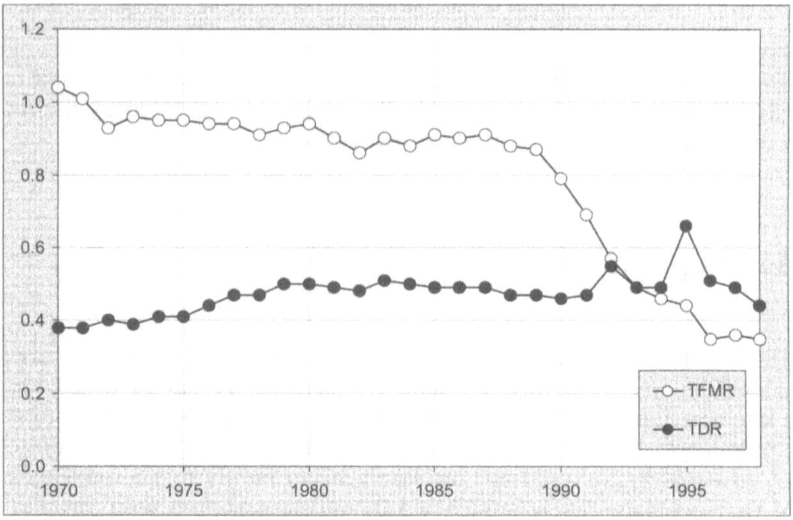


**Figure 6.5: Total First Marriage (TFMR) and Total Divorce Rates (TDR), 1970–1998**

Source: Estonian Population Databank

The frequency of divorces steadily increased until the 1980s to a relatively high rate (Figure 6.5). The level of the total divorce rate indicates that about half of marriages end in divorce. In Europe, comparably high divorce rates can be found only in Denmark, Latvia, and Sweden. In the 1990s, the sharp decline in the marriage rate, together with some changes in divorce regulations, resulted in unique situation in which divorces outnumbered registered marriages in 1995–1996. One should be aware, however, that statistics on legal divorce do not account for the complete picture of family dissolution because an increasing number of partnerships occurs as consensual unions. Based on the evidence from the Estonian *Family and Fertility Survey* (FFS), about one-third of all first unions are broken up after ten years (Vikat, 1997). From a life course perspective, this implies a growing diversity of living arrangements and household patterns.

## 6.7 International Migration

In the post-war period, Estonia, similar to other nations of post-transitional demographic development, transformed from an emigration to an immigration country. However, due to geopolitical changes stemming from the incorporation of Estonia into the Soviet Union, immigration to Estonia began earlier and in extremely high volumes. Immigration originated mostly from the European part of Russia, which had entered mobility transition. The realisation of a high migration potential was strengthened by societal rearrangements.

Estonia's external migration experienced two major migration waves (Sakkeus, 1991). The first occurred in the immediate post-war period, and consisted mostly of forced migration (administrative and military immigration from the Soviet Union, deportations of local population etc.). After some decrease, the second wave of immigration had emerged in the late 1960s, followed by a gradual decline in migration intensity. The main characteristic of migrations between Estonia and the USSR had been that an overwhelming majority of immigrants used Estonia as a temporary residence. According to available data, approximately only one out of seven immigrants remained in Estonia. Such a high turnover is related to the extensive military component of migration as well as to a small family component. Since a large part of military moves went unrecorded in statistics, the turnover could have been even higher.

The societal transition of the 1990s was accompanied by a rapid reduction in the migration volume between Estonia and the former Soviet Union. According to official records, immigration flows began to decrease sharply in 1989, at first due to cessation of drafting the conscripts from Estonia. Since 1990, the data on international migration has shown a negative balance, which reached a peak shortly after the dissolution of the USSR. However, statistics on migration should be used with great caution, as the picture may have been strongly affected by the outflow from formerly closed military territories whose inhabitants had not been counted in official statistics upon their arrival into Estonia. In other words, the observed reversal in net migration could prove to be, to a considerable extent, a statistical artefact (Sakkeus, 1996).

Post-war immigration has left Estonia with a disproportionately large stock of immigrant population. According to the 1989 census, 26% of the population of Estonia is foreign-born, and 35%, including the second generation, are of immigrant origin. These indicators are among the highest in Europe (Figure 6.6). In other words, out of 602 thousand non-Estonians, only 38 thousand are members of an ethnic minority, while the remainder is comprised of immigrants and their second generation (Katus and Sakkeus, op. cit.). In contrast to other European immigration countries, the second generation of the foreign-born has not displayed noticeable signs towards adaptation or integration in spite of a very low intention to return to the homeland. As a result, the currently high heterogeneity of the population is likely to persist and will have a strong bearing on societal development in Estonia.

Moreover, it must be pointed out that the foreign-born population of Estonia has 1.2–1.5 million family members and relatives living in countries of the former Soviet Union, who may be considered potential immigrants in case these families wish to reunify. For Estonia, this poses a possible further increase of heterogeneity, adding to an already high burden on social and population-related policies.

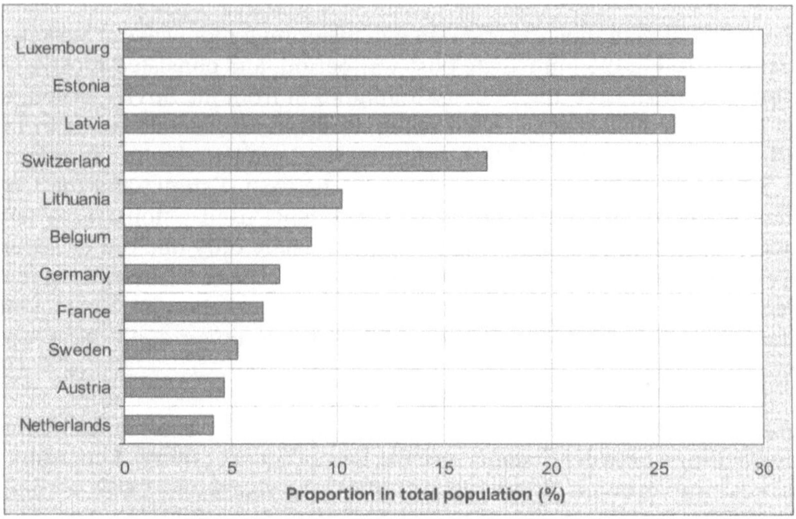


**Figure 6.6: Foreign-born Population in Selected Countries Between 1990 and 1995**

Source: Estonian Population Databank; Council of Europe, 1998

## 6.8 Population-related Policies

Population-related policies have been characterised by the process of formulation in Estonia during the 1990s (Põldma, 1995, 1997). In contrast with many countries of Central and Eastern Europe, the economic transition in Estonia coincided with the restoration of statehood. Hence, the entire set of sectoral policies had to be reconsidered in parallel with market economy institutions. To a considerable extent, the formulation of social and population-related policies has been shaped by the imbalance between demographic and economic development. From population perspective, the high proportion of elderly, acute depopulation, prevalence of chronic illnesses, developing individualism and the changed nature of intergenerational relations imply a considerable need of resources for pensions, health care and other social expenditures. From an economic perspective, however, the country belongs to the developing rather than to developed nations. The liberal economic policies which Estonia introduced at the beginning of the 1990s, have resulted in comparatively rapid transformation of central planning to a market economy, but at the same time, have put tight fiscal restrictions on the implementation of social population-related policies (Figure 6.7).

A comprehensive and integrated population policy still needs to be introduced. However, several elements of social policy should be considered in the context of population policy as well. In regard to family and fertility, the system of comprehensive child allowances exists in Estonia. According to the present scheme, monthly allowances are paid until the child reaches age 16 (in case the child is studying, until age 19). The amount of benefits is progressively dependent on the number of children, and benefits are paid to all children irrespective of the income of their parents. Given the economic constraints, the rates of allowances are relatively scanty and cover only a quite small proportion of child-rearing costs. Among target groups of family policy, the implemented policies have paid relatively little attention to young families. Thus, there is no comprehensive system of subsidised housing loans. Loans offered by commercial banks are affordable to a relatively small stratum of young families.

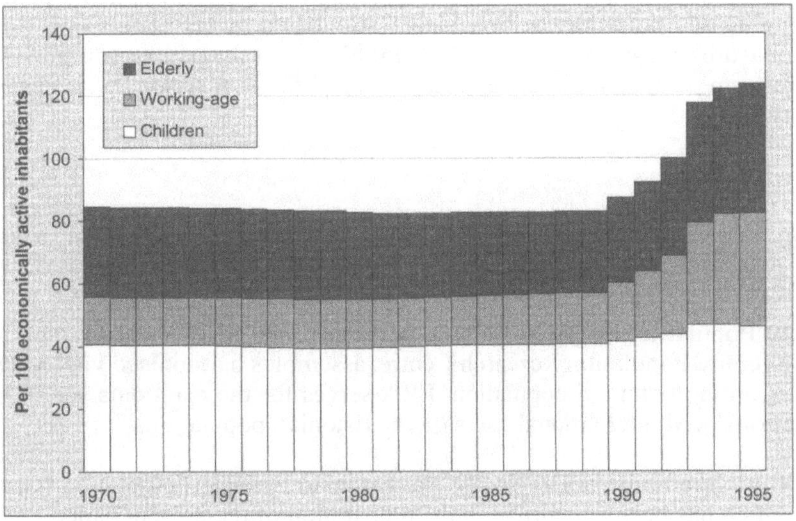


**Figure 6.7: Economic Dependency Ratio, 1970–1995**

Source: Estonian Population Databank

The paid maternity leave consists of 56 days before and 56 days after delivery (in special cases it can be extended up to 70 days after delivery). During that period, the amount of compensation accounts for 100% of the woman's salary. After maternity leave, one of the parents may take paid parental leave for a maximum period of up to the child's third birthday. The amount of compensation during the period is related to the child's age: under age two, the payment is four times the rate of child benefit; between age two and three, the payment is reduced to two times the rate of child benefit. There are also other provisions of family, related support but with a more limited coverage/entitlement period.

The core of the policies dealing with population ageing, the pension system, has undergone repeated modifications. In the early 1990s, the implementation of the previous pension formula was temporarily suspended and flat-rate benefits for all old-age pensioners were introduced. In 1993, the flat-rate scheme was revised and a limited differentiation according to length of employment was re-introduced. More important was the decision to increase the statutory retirement age by five years, to

65 for males and 60 for females, raising the previous limit by 0.5 years each year during the period 1994–2003. Subsequently, the plan was revised and the retirement age for both sexes is expected to converge at age 63.

In June 1998, the Parliament adopted the reform programme which aims at the three-pillar pension system, consisting of the present pay-as-you-go element, supplemented with compulsory scheme based on funding principle, and voluntary pension insurance. The role of the first pillar would be to secure a minimum standard of living for all groups of the elderly population, while the second is meant to introduce differentiation based on a person's lifetime contributions. The third pillar would aim at encouraging additional saving for old age, stimulated by tax deductions. However, these measures are unlikely to reduce the pressure on the pay-as-you-go system in medium-term perspective and may result in a call for an increase in the general taxation level.

## Notes

Estonian Population Databank (ERA), developed and maintained by the Estonian Interuniversity Population Research Centre, assembles harmonised vital and census statistics on the Estonian population. ERA serves for the main data warehouse for both national and international users on the Estonian population.

The authors gratefully acknowledge the Estonian Science Foundation (Grant No. 2901) which has been supportive in the preparation of the present paper.

## References

Anderson, B., K. Katus, A. Puur and B. Silver (1993), Characteristics of Women Having Abortions in Estonia, *Proceedings of the International Population Conference*, Vol. 1, pp. 215–234, Montreal: IUSSP.

Anderson, B., K. Katus and B. Silver (1994), Developments and prospects for population statistics in the countries of the former Soviet Union, *Population Index*, Vol. 60 (1), pp. 4–20.

Bourgeois-Pichat, J. (1984), Mortality trends in the industrialized countries, *Mortality and Health Policy*, pp. 196–217, New York: United Nations.

Council of Europe (1998), *Recent Demographic Developments in Europe 1998*. Strasbourg, Council of Europe.

EKDK (Estonian Interuniversity Population Research Centre) (1994), *Infant Mortality: Counties 1965–1993*, RU, Series C, No. 5, Tallinn: EKDK.

EKDK (Estonian Interuniversity Population Research Centre) (1995), *Estonian Family and Fertility Survey. Standard Tabulations*, RU, Series C, No. 6, Tallinn: EKDK.

EKDK (Estonian Interuniversity Population Research Centre) (1996–1999), *Reviewed Population Vital and Census Statistics*, RU, Series C, No. 9–12, Tallinn: EKDK.

ESA (Statistical Office of Estonia) (1998), *Social Trends*, Tallinn: Statistical Office of Estonia.

Festy, P. (1984), *Fertility in Western Countries from 1870 to 1970*, Bangkok: United Nations.

Gillis, J., L. Tilly and D. Levine (1992), *The European Experience of Declining Fertility, 1850–1970*. Cambridge.

Hajnal, J. (1965), European Marriage Patterns in Perspective, In: D. Glass and D. Eversley (eds.), *Population in History*, Chicago.

Katus, K. (1989), *Demographic Development in Estonia through Centuries*, RU, Series B, No. 10, Tallinn: EKDK.

Katus, K. (1992), Trends in Non-Marital Fertility in Baltic Region, Paper presented at the EAPS/BIB Seminar on Demographic Implications of Marital Status, Bonn.

Katus, K. (1994), Fertility Transition in Estonia, Latvia and Lithuania, In: W. Lutz, S. Scherbov and A. Volkov (eds.), *Demographic Trends and Patterns in the Soviet Union before 1991*, pp. 89–111, London and New York: IIASA.

Katus, K. (1995), *General Trend of Population Ageing in Estonia*, RU, Series B, No. 27, Tallinn: EKDK.

Katus, K. (1997), Post-Transitional Fertility: Case of Estonia, In: K. Katus, V. Stankuniene and A. Vikat (eds.) *Demographic Development in Baltic Countries. Special Issue of Revue Baltique*, pp. 49–63.

Katus, K. and A. Puur (1992), *Eesti rahvastiku suremustrend elutabelite analüüsi põhjal*, RU, Series B, No. 14, Tallinn: EKDK.

Katus, K. and A. Puur (1997), *Mortality Development and Economic Transition: Case of Estonia*, RU, Series B, No. 35, Tallinn: EKDK.

Katus, K. and L. Sakkeus (1993), *Foreign-born Population in Estonia*, RU, Series B, No. 19, Tallinn: EKDK.

Katus, K., A. Puur and L. Sakkeus (1997a), *Development of National Minorities: Republic of Estonia up to 1944*, RU, Series B, No. 34. Tallinn: EKDK.

Katus, K., A. Puur and L. Sakkeus (1997b), *Comparability of Population Data in the previous USSR: Case of Estonia*, RU, Series B, No. 30. Tallin: EKDK.

Katus, K. and S. Zakharov (1997), Demographic Adaptation to Socio-Economic Changes in the USSR Successor States, Paper presented at the IUSSP XXIII General Population Conference, Beijing.

Krumins, J. (1990), Stanovlenie sovremmenogo tipa smertnosti naselenia Latvii, *Izvestia AN Latvii*, No. 8, pp. 75–84.

Leinsalu, M. (1993), Surmapõhjused Eestis aastail 1965–1990, *Eesti Arst*, No. 1, pp. 18–31.

Leon, D.L. *et al.* (1997), Huge variation in Russian mortality rates 1984–1994: Artefact, alcohol or what? *The Lancet*, Vol. 350, pp. 383–388.

Meslé, F. and J. Vallin (1993), Developpement economique et esperance de vie: la transition sanitaire au tournant des annees soixante, *Proceeding of the International Population Conference. Vol. 2*, pp. 365–383, Montreal: IUSSP.

Olshansky, J.S. and B.A. Ault (1986), The fourth stage of epidemiological transition: the age of the delayed degenerative disease, *The Milbank Quarterly*, Vol. 64(3), pp. 355–391.

Palli, H. (1988), *Otepää rahvastik aastail 1716–1799*, Tallinn: Valgus.

Põldma, A. (1995), *Social and Population-Related Policies in Estonia*, RU, Series B, No. 26, Tallinn: EKDK.

Põldma, A. (1997), Population-related policies in Estonia in the Baltoscandian context, In: K. Katus, V. Stankuniene and A. Vikat (eds.), *Demographic Development in Baltic Countries. Special Issue of Revue Baltique*, pp. 165–185.

Puur, A. (1994), *The 1989 Estonian Population and Housing Census. Microdata Description: Variable Definitions and Coding Schemes II*, RU, Series A., No. 36, Tallinn: EKDK.

Sakkeus, L. (1991), *Post-War Migration Trends in Estonia*, RU, Series B, No. 15, Tallinn: EKDK.

Sakkeus, L. (1995), *Marital Status and Living Arrangements of the Elderly in Estonia*, RU, Series B, No. 24, Tallinn: EKDK.

Sakkeus, L. (1996), Estonia, In: T. Frejka (ed.), *International Migration in Central and Eastern Europe and the Commonwealth of Independent States*, pp. 57–65, New York and Geneva: United Nations.

Thomson, H., M. Rahu, T. Aareleid and K. Gornoi (1996), *Cancer in Estonia 1968–1992. Incidence, Mortality, Prevalence, Survival*, Tallinn: Institute of Experimental and Clinical Medicine.

UN ECE (United Nations Economic Commission for Europe) (1999a), *Fertility and Family Surveys in the Countries of the ECE Region. Standard Country Report. Estonia*, New York and Geneva: UN ECE.

UN ECE (United Nations Economic Commission for Europe) (1999b), *Dynamics of Population Ageing in the Countries of the ECE Region. Standard Country Report. Estonia*. New York and Geneva: UN ECE.

Vikat, A. (1994), *Family Formation in Estonia*, Finnish Demographic Society, No. 15, Helsinki.

Vikat, A. (1997), Recent trends in partnership formation and dissolution in Estonia, In: K. Katus, V. Stankuniene and A. Vikat (eds.), *Demographic Development in Baltic Countries. Special Issue of Revue Baltique*, pp. 78–89.

Vishnevsky, A. and A. Volkov (eds.) (1983), *Vosproizvodstvo naselenya v SSSR*, Moscow.

Värnik, A. (1997), *Suicide in the Baltic Countries and in the Former Republics of the USSR*, Stockholm: Karolinska Institute.

# 7

# The Current Demographic Shape of Germany: Similarities and Differences in Eastern and Western Population Processes

**Eberhard Schaich and Jochen Fleischhacker**

## 7.1 Historical Background of the Current Situation

The far-reaching political changes in Central and Eastern Europe in the early 1990s brought forth a reunified Germany with unique demographic characteristics: two significantly different populations of 63.3 million in the former Federal Republic of Germany ("West Germany") and 16.1 million in the former German Democratic Republic ("East Germany") were melted together. A main consequence of this development is a dichotomy in Germany's new population structure, which continues to prevent demographic analysis on an aggregate basis. For this reason, demographic phenomena are generally reported and analysed mainly separately for West and East Germany in this contribution.

There exist five main features pertinent to Germany's current demographic situation:

1. A lasting low fertility level and a favourable mortality rate give West Germany the typical structure of an ageing Western population that has its second demographic transition in the sense of *van de Kaa* behind it (van de Kaa, 1987). A further main structural element connected with the fertility decline is the ongoing dissolution of traditional patterns of marriage and family life.
2. Up until 1990, East Germany's population revealed similarities to but also substantial differences from the population of West Germany; however, it held some differences from typical Eastern European structures as well. Indeed, East Germany exhibited some qualities of a demographic mix of Western and Eastern characteristics.
3. The dynamic demographic changes in East Germany since 1990 include two major components:
   - The take-over by West Germany's economic and social system has correlated with a demographic assimilation process in several main dimensions. This process is now in an advanced phase.
   - The new and unaccustomed personal freedom for East Germany's population caused several dramatic developments attributing to East Germany the role of a world-wide demographic outlier which has not yet faded.

4. Unlike in typical Western populations, immigration flows to Germany include:
   - ethnic Germans, especially persons leaving the Russian Federation or Kazakhstan ("Aussiedler");
   - foreigners, especially refugees from civil wars and other crisis regions of the world asking for asylum in the Federal Republic of Germany.
5. Within Germany, there is an ongoing noticeable migration from East to West; however, it has begun to decrease.

## 7.2 Population Structure

### 7.2.1 Population Size, Age and Sex Structure

At present, Germany's population is still growing – although, at a decreasing rate as shown in Table 7.1. The current annual increase of 200,000 persons results from immigration, thereby hiding a considerable surplus of deaths. The increase is situated exclusively in West Germany; East Germany's population is declining.

**Table 7.1: Annual Average Population Size, 1990–1997, in thousands**

| Year | West Germany | East Germany | Total |
|---|---|---|---|
| 1990 | 63,254 | 16,111 | 79,365 |
| 1991 | 64,074 | 15,910 | 79,984 |
| 1992 | 64,865 | 15,730 | 80,594 |
| 1993 | 65,534 | 15,645 | 81,179 |
| 1994 | 65,858 | 15,564 | 81,422 |
| 1995 | 66,156 | 15,505 | 81,661 |
| 1996 | 66,444 | 15,451 | 81,896 |
| 1997 | 66,647 | 15,405 | 82,052 |

Source: Statistisches Bundesamt, 1999c, p. 44

The development of the age structure can be seen in Table 7.2. It is determined by several processes, which are discussed in detail later. The rising percentage of people over the age of 60 demonstrates the general ageing tendency. Figures for 1997 reveal that this process is similarly advanced in East Germany.

By the end of 1997, the proportion of women in the total population was 51.26% in all Germany, 51.27% in West Germany, and 51.23% in East Germany. For each age group up to 57, there is a higher proportion of men; the age groups that follow show a majority of women, which increases with rising age (Statistisches Bundesamt, 1999c, pp. 55, 59).

**Table 7.2: Population by Main Age Groups, 1990–1997[1]**

| Year | Under 18 years | | 18–59 years | | 60 years and over | | Total |
|---|---|---|---|---|---|---|---|
| | 1,000 | % | 1,000 | % | 1,000 | % | 1,000 |
| 1990 | 15,344 | 19.24 | 48,147 | 60.57 | 16,263 | 20.39 | 79,753 |
| 1991 | 15,522 | 19.34 | 48,368 | 60.25 | 16,385 | 20.41 | 80,275 |
| 1992 | 15,713 | 19.41 | 48,762 | 60.22 | 16,499 | 20.37 | 80,975 |
| 1993 | 15,840 | 19.47 | 48,904 | 60.12 | 16,593 | 20.40 | 81,338 |
| 1994 | 15,872 | 19.47 | 48,793 | 59.84 | 16,874 | 20.69 | 81,539 |
| 1995 | 15,903 | 19.44 | 48,706 | 59.53 | 17,209 | 21.03 | 81,817 |
| 1996 | 15,921 | 19.41 | 48,535 | 59.18 | 17,556 | 21.41 | 82,012 |
| 1997 | 15,887 | 19.36 | 48,244 | 58.79 | 17,927 | 21.85 | 82,057 |
| Of which: | | | | | | | |
| West Germany | 12,946 | 19.41 | 39,155 | 58.71 | 14,587 | 21.87 | 66,688 |
| East Germany | 2,940 | 19.13 | 9,089 | 59.14 | 3,340 | 21.73 | 15,369 |

[1]As of 31 December of a given year
Source: Statistisches Bundesamt, 1999c, pp. 58–59

### 7.2.2 Marital Status, Families and Households

Marriage is still the dominant lifestyle for German adults. At the end of 1995, 61.0% of the over-20 population were married in Germany; for West and East Germany, the percentages are 60.5 and 63.4, respectively (Grünheid and Mammey, 1997, p. 431).

**Table 7.3: Changes in Family Structure, 1991–1997, in thousands**

| | 1991 | 1992 | 1993 | 1994 | 1995 | 1996 | 1997 | Change (%) 1997/1991 |
|---|---|---|---|---|---|---|---|---|
| | | | | Germany | | | | |
| Married couples | 19,492 | 19,633 | 19,703 | 19,662 | 19,658 | 19,590 | 19,617 | 0.6 |
| – childless | 8,394 | 8,601 | 8,755 | 8,889 | 9,039 | 9,182 | 9,318 | 11.0 |
| – with children | 11,098 | 11,032 | 10,948 | 10,773 | 10,619 | 10,408 | 10,299 | -7.2 |
| Single parents | 2,540 | 2,586 | 2,647 | 2,696 | 2,736 | 2,772 | 2,797 | 10.1 |
| Total | 22,032 | 22,219 | 22,350 | 22,358 | 22,395 | 22,363 | 22,414 | 1.7 |
| | | | | West Germany | | | | |
| Married couples | 15,517 | 15,712 | 15,836 | 15,851 | 15,897 | 15,887 | 15,913 | 2.6 |
| – childless | 6,706 | 6,890 | 7,037 | 7,167 | 7,316 | 7,445 | 7,550 | 12.6 |
| – with children | 8,811 | 8,822 | 8,799 | 8,684 | 8,581 | 8,442 | 8,383 | -4.9 |
| Single parents | 1,858 | 1,904 | 1,949 | 1,982 | 2,005 | 2,024 | 2,049 | 10.3 |
| Total | 17,375 | 17,616 | 17,785 | 17,833 | 17,902 | 17,911 | 17,981 | 3.5 |
| | | | | East Germany | | | | |
| Married couples | 3,975 | 3,921 | 3,867 | 3,811 | 3,761 | 3,703 | 3,704 | -6.8 |
| – childless | 1,687 | 1,711 | 1,718 | 1,722 | 1,723 | 1,737 | 1,768 | 4.8 |
| – with children | 2,288 | 2,210 | 2,149 | 2,089 | 2,038 | 1,966 | 1,916 | -16.3 |
| Single parents | 682 | 682 | 698 | 715 | 732 | 749 | 748 | 9.7 |
| Total | 4,657 | 4,603 | 4,565 | 4,526 | 4,493 | 4,452 | 4,433 | -4.8 |

Source: Dorbritz and Gärtner, 1998, p. 414

In West Germany, this rate is nearly stable, whilst East Germany shows a rather strong decrease. In both parts of Germany, the ratio of divorced persons to the total population is rising slightly. The number of persons living in a consensual union rose from 1.393 million in April 1991 to 1.982 million in April 1998 (Statistisches Bundesamt, 1999c, p. 64).

Table 7.3 shows the changes in family structures during 1991–1997. The data is drawn from the microcensus, based on an annual 1% sample of Germany's population performed in April of a given year. The number of married couples with children is decreasing steadily, whereas the number of married couples without children is rising, as is that of single parents. These processes can be seen in both parts of Germany but with different levels of intensity. Family structure is connected with the development of households, as is shown in Table 7.4.

**Table 7.4: Distribution of Households by Size, 1991–1997[1], per cent**

| Year | Households 1,000 | Household size (persons) | | | | |
|---|---|---|---|---|---|---|
| | | 1 | 2 | 3 | 4 | 5+ |
| | | | Germany | | | |
| 1991 | 35,256 | 33.6 | 30.8 | 17.1 | 13.5 | 5.0 |
| 1992 | 35,700 | 33.7 | 31.3 | 16.9 | 13.3 | 4.9 |
| 1993 | 36,230 | 34.2 | 31.4 | 16.6 | 13.0 | 4.9 |
| 1994 | 36,695 | 34.7 | 31.7 | 16.1 | 12.7 | 4.8 |
| 1995 | 36,938 | 34.9 | 32.1 | 15.8 | 12.4 | 4.7 |
| 1996 | 37,281 | 35.4 | 32.3 | 15.5 | 12.2 | 4.6 |
| 1997 | 37,457 | 35.4 | 32.6 | 15.3 | 12.1 | 4.6 |
| | | | West Germany | | | |
| 1991 | 28,584 | 35.1 | 30.5 | 16.4 | 12.8 | 5.3 |
| 1992 | 29,043 | 35.0 | 31.0 | 16.2 | 12.6 | 5.2 |
| 1993 | 29,496 | 35.3 | 31.2 | 16.0 | 12.4 | 5.2 |
| 1994 | 29,907 | 35.8 | 31.5 | 15.4 | 12.2 | 5.1 |
| 1995 | 30,144 | 35.9 | 31.9 | 15.2 | 12.0 | 5.0 |
| 1996 | 30,471 | 36.4 | 32.0 | 14.8 | 11.9 | 4.9 |
| 1997 | 30,609 | 36.3 | 32.3 | 14.6 | 11.9 | 4.9 |
| | | | East Germany | | | |
| 1991 | 6,672 | 27.6 | 32.0 | 20.0 | 16.5 | 4.0 |
| 1992 | 6,657 | 28.1 | 32.5 | 19.6 | 16.0 | 3.8 |
| 1993 | 6,734 | 29.3 | 32.6 | 19.1 | 15.4 | 3.6 |
| 1994 | 6,788 | 30.1 | 32.7 | 18.9 | 15.0 | 3.4 |
| 1995 | 6,794 | 30.4 | 33.1 | 18.8 | 14.4 | 3.3 |
| 1996 | 6,810 | 30.8 | 33.5 | 18.6 | 13.7 | 3.3 |
| 1997 | 6,848 | 31.2 | 35.9 | 16.9 | 13.4 | 3.3 |

[1]As of 31 December of a given year
Source: Dorbritz and Gärtner, p. 411

In both parts of Germany, single households are becoming more and more numerous. In East Germany, two person households are still the most frequent, but single households increased by 3.6 percentage points from 1991 to 1997. The percentage of households with three or more persons is decreasing in both parts of Germany. In East Germany, the proportion of households with three and four persons ranges remarkably above and of those with five and more persons significantly below the corresponding values in West Germany. As a whole, household structures in East and West Germany are converging despite some slight changes in tendencies in East Germany during 1997.

### 7.2.3 Germans and Foreigners

Population size and age structure is significantly influenced by the persons of foreign citizenship. Table 7.5 shows the percentage of foreign inhabitants since 1990 in total and subdivided by the most common regions of origin. Of course, the abrupt increase in EU foreigners and subsequent decrease in non-EU Europeans in 1994 is connected with the entry of Austria and Sweden into the European Union. Turkey, the EU and non-EU Europe – in particular the countries of Central and Eastern Europe – make up about a quarter of the foreign population each. Since 1994, only the shares of the Asian population have shown a noticeable increase.

**Table 7.5: Foreign Population by Citizenship Groups, 1990–1998[1]**

| Year | Foreigners | | EU | Turkey | Europe | Asia | Africa | Others |
|---|---|---|---|---|---|---|---|---|
| | 1,000 | % | % | % | % | % | % | % |
| 1990 | 5,343 | 6.73 | 26.9 | 31.7 | 24.7 | 8.8 | 3.7 | 4.1 |
| 1991 | 5,882 | 7.35 | 25.3 | 30.3 | 27.0 | 9.4 | 4.0 | 4.0 |
| 1992 | 6,496 | 8.06 | 23.2 | 28.6 | 30.8 | 9.2 | 4.4 | 3.9 |
| 1993 | 6,878 | 8.47 | 22.3 | 27.9 | 32.3 | 9.4 | 4.4 | 3.7 |
| 1994 | 6,991 | 8.59 | 25.5 | 28.1 | 29.1 | 9.5 | 4.2 | 3.7 |
| 1995 | 7,174 | 8.78 | 25.3 | 28.1 | 29.2 | 9.8 | 4.1 | 3.6 |
| 1996 | 7,314 | 8.93 | 25.2 | 28.0 | 28.9 | 10.2 | 4.1 | 3.7 |
| 1997 | 7,366 | 8.98 | 25.1 | 28.6 | 27.8 | 10.6 | 4.1 | 3.7 |
| 1998 | 7,320 | 8.92 | 25.3 | 28.8 | 27.0 | 10.9 | 4.1 | 3.8 |

[1]As of 31 December of a given year

Sources: Grünheid and Mammey, p. 448; Statistisches Bundesamt, 1998, p. 66; Statistisches Bundesamt 1999c, p. 65

Germany has a considerable regional concentration of foreigners. First, in East Germany, the percentage of the population with foreign citizenship is much lower than in the West. In 1995, an overall value of 8.78% of foreign population for all of Germany was reported with numbers ranging from 1.1% (Thüringen) and 2.5% (Brandenburg) in East Germany to 16.1% (Hamburg), 13.6% (Hessen), 12.4% (Baden-Württemberg) and 11.0% (Nordrhein-Westfalen) in West Germany. Second, the foreign population is largely concentrated in the cities. At the beginning of 1995, ratios of persons of foreign citizenship of 29.0% in Frankfurt, 23.8% in Stuttgart, 21.6% in München and 19.0% in Mannheim were reported. The most numerous nationalities were Yugoslavs and Turks (see, for example, Grünheid and Mammey, pp. 453–454).

The age structure of the foreign population is younger than that of the Germans. In 1995, the age-specific proportions of male foreigners were, for instance, 13.2% in the age group 0–4 years, 12.5% (15–19 years), 16.8% (20–24 years), 14.7% (25–29 years) and 12.5% (30–34 years). These values exceed the overall average of 10.1% male foreigners by far, while the values for higher age groups are noticeably lower (Grünheid and Mammey, pp. 450–451).

### 7.2.4 Labour Force Participation and Unemployment

In Germany's official statistics, participants of the labour force are defined as those who have a job or are seriously seeking one. The development of labour force participation since 1991 is shown in Table 7.6.

In Germany, labour force activity rates for men are decreasing – even for men aged 15 to 64, whereas those rates for women have remained stagnant since 1991 at a level of about 41%, respectively 62% for women aged 15–64. In East Germany, the proportion of men participating in the labour force is lower than in West Germany, while for women it is significantly higher. This results from the labour force participation patterns of females in the former German Democratic Republic. However, a tendency towards convergence of Eastern and Western structures is emerging.

**Table 7.6: Labour Force Activity Rates by Sex and Age Group, 1991–1998, per cent**

| Year (April) | Population | Germany | | West Germany | | East Germany | |
|---|---|---|---|---|---|---|---|
| | | Male | Female | Male | Female | Male | Female |
| 1991 | Total | 60.0 | 41.1 | 60.0 | 38.8 | 59.9 | 50.0 |
| | 15–64 years | 82.9 | 62.1 | 82.2 | 58.4 | 86.0 | 77.2 |
| 1992[1] | Total | 59.2 | 41.2 | 59.8 | 39.4 | 56.7 | 48.5 |
| | 15–64 years | 82.0 | 62.5 | 82.2 | 59.5 | 80.8 | 74.8 |
| 1993 | Total | 58.6 | 41.0 | 59.3 | 39.3 | 55.7 | 47.7 |
| | 15–64 years | 81.3 | 62.3 | 81.9 | 59.6 | 78.6 | 73.3 |
| 1994 | Total | 58.3 | 41.1 | 58.7 | 39.4 | 56.6 | 48.3 |
| | 15–64 years | 81.3 | 62.7 | 81.8 | 60.0 | 79.2 | 73.8 |
| 1995 | Total | 57.8 | 40.9 | 58.0 | 39.2 | 57.1 | 48.4 |
| | 15–64 years | 81.0 | 62.6 | 81.3 | 59.9 | 79.2 | 73.9 |
| 1996 | Total | 57.3 | 40.9 | 57.4 | 39.2 | 57.0 | 48.1 |
| | 15–64 years | 80.3 | 62.3 | 80.5 | 59.7 | 79.3 | 73.3 |
| 1997 | Total | 57.4 | 41.3 | 57.3 | 39.6 | 57.6 | 48.5 |
| | 15–64 years | 80.3 | 62.8 | 80.5 | 60.3 | 79.7 | 73.6 |
| 1998 | Total | 57.2 | 41.4 | 57.0 | 39.7 | 58.2 | 48.6 |
| | 15–64 years | 80.2 | 63.0 | 80.2 | 60.5 | 80.2 | 73.5 |

[1]May
Sources: Allafi, 1999, pp. 164–165; Statistisches Bundesamt, 1997a, pp. 152, 261, 349

The general drop in labour force participation is indirectly connected with the increase in unemployment, which finally reached a plateau at a level of 4.5 million in

1998. Table 7.7 shows the rise in the number of the unemployed persons and in the unemployment rates from 1991 to 1998. In East Germany, the rates of unemployment are much higher than in the West. In addition, there is a great amount of regional variation among the *Länder*. In West Germany, Baden-Württemberg and Bayern have the lowest and Berlin (West) and Bremen – the highest level of unemployment, whilst in East Germany the rates are lowest in Sachsen and highest in Sachsen-Anhalt and Mecklenburg-Vorpommern. The dramatic rise in unemployment can be seen in Figure 7.1.

**Table 7.7: Annual Average Number of Unemployed Persons by Sex and Region and Unemployment Rate, 1991–1998**

| Year | Male | Female | Total | Rate[1] | Regional range |
|---|---|---|---|---|---|
| | 1,000 | 1,000 | 1,000 | % | % |
| | | | Germany | | |
| 1991 | 1,280.6 | 1,321.6 | 2,602.2 | 7.3 | 3.7–12.5 |
| 1992 | 1,411.9 | 1,566.7 | 2,978.6 | 8.5 | 4.4–16.8 |
| 1993 | 1,691.6 | 1,727.6 | 3,419.1 | 9.8 | 6.3–17.5 |
| 1994 | 1,863.1 | 1,835.0 | 3,698.1 | 10.6 | 7.1–17.6 |
| 1995 | 1,850.6 | 1,761.3 | 3,611.9 | 10.4 | 7.0–16.5 |
| 1996 | 2,111.5 | 1,853.5 | 3,965.1 | 11.5 | 7.9–18.8 |
| 1997 | 2,342.4 | 2,042.1 | 4,384.5 | 12.7 | 8.7–21.7 |
| 1998 | 2,273.0 | 2,007.0 | 4,279.0 | 12.3 | 8.0–21.7 |
| | | | West Germany | | |
| 1991 | 897.7 | 792.7 | 1,689.4 | 6.3 | 3.7–10.7 |
| 1992 | 982.8 | 825.5 | 1,808.3 | 6.6 | 4.4–11.1 |
| 1993 | 1,277.1 | 993.3 | 2,270.3 | 8.2 | 6.3–12.4 |
| 1994 | 1,461.6 | 1,094.3 | 3,556.0 | 9.2 | 7.1–13.7 |
| 1995 | 1,463.7 | 1,101.2 | 2,564.9 | 9.3 | 7.0–14.3 |
| 1996 | 1,616.5 | 1,179.7 | 2,796.2 | 10.1 | 7.9–15.7 |
| 1997 | 1,740.7 | 1,280.2 | 3,020.9 | 11.0 | 8.7–17.3 |
| 1998 | 1,641.0 | 1,264.0 | 2,804.0 | 10.5 | 8.0–17.9 |
| | | | East Germany | | |
| 1991 | 382.9 | 530.0 | 912.8 | 10.3 | 9.1–12.5 |
| 1992 | 429.1 | 741.1 | 1,170.3 | 14.8 | 13.6–16.8 |
| 1993 | 414.5 | 734.3 | 1,148.8 | 15.8 | 14.9–17.5 |
| 1994 | 401.4 | 740.6 | 1,142.1 | 16.0 | 15.3–17.6 |
| 1995 | 386.9 | 660.0 | 1,047.0 | 14.9 | 14.2–16.5 |
| 1996 | 495.0 | 673.8 | 1,168.8 | 16.7 | 15.9–18.8 |
| 1997 | 601.7 | 761.9 | 1,364.0 | 19.5 | 18.4–21.7 |
| 1998 | 632.0 | 743.0 | 1,375.0 | 19.5 | 18.3–21.7 |

[1]Unemployment rate relates to both sexes
Sources: Statistisches Bundesamt, 1994, pp. 128–129; Statistisches Bundesamt, 1998, pp. 123–125; Statistisches Bundesamt, 1999a, pp. 9–10

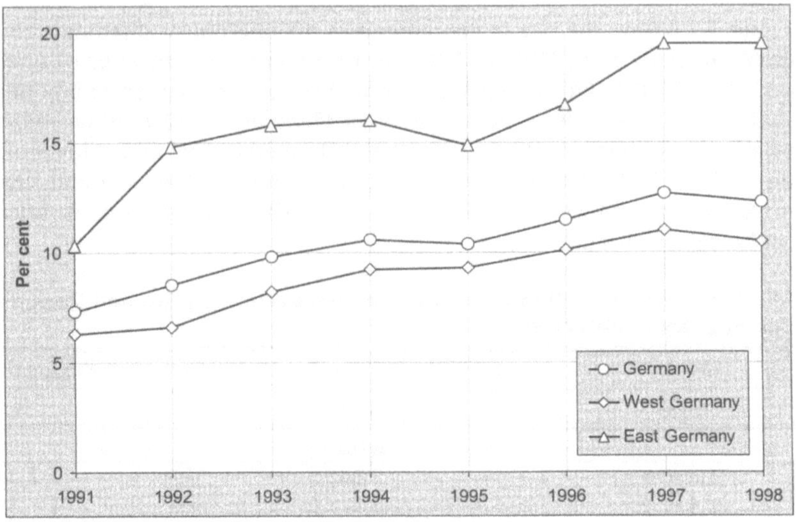


**Figure 7.1: Unemployment Rates, 1991–1998**

Sources: based on Statistisches Bundesamt, 1994, pp. 128–129; Statistisches Bundesamt, 1998, pp. 123–125; Statistisches Bundesamt, 1999a, pp. 9–10

## 7.3 Fertility Developments

Fertility trends in post-war Germany show a great deal of parallels between East and West, with some minor differences. These differences result partly from different attitudes and to a certain extent from pronatalist measures introduced by the GDR Government in the 1980s (Fleischhacker, 1998); the total fertility rates of 1.45 and 1.52 in East and West Germany in 1990 exhibited almost no difference.

Since 1990, West Germany has seen a further decline in the total fertility rate (TFR) down to 1.33 in 1995 (see Table 7.8), but it cannot be viewed as an outlier, however, when compared with Southern or Eastern European countries. The TFR in East Germany, on the other hand, has been consistently below 1.0 since 1991 – experiencing a dramatic international record of 0.77 in 1994, which represents a reproduction level of only about 36%. It has been recovering since 1994 very slowly. But at the moment, East Germany's fertility rate does not seem to be undergoing a direct adaptation to the West German level. Figure 7.2 shows the TFRs in East Germany in comparison with the values in West Germany and the aggregate values for Germany as a whole.

A causal analysis of the collapse of fertility in East Germany is difficult. Münz and Ulrich (1994) propose three different possible explanations of the phenomenon. First, pessimistic views of young women as a consequence of their hard economic situation, the unsatisfactory labour market and reductions in the public nursing facilities have reduced fertility to a drastic extent. Second, the new socio-economic structure with the "blessings" of a Western society and the opportunities it offers for high level consumption and for high-income careers, that Eastern Germany citizens were suddenly confronted with, in an extremely short period of time has challenged dramatically their willingness to have children. Finally, the East German population has rapidly adjusted and accepted an individualistic, Western lifestyle, which presupposes privacy and personal control over decisions regarding number of births and their spread during lifetime of women. In particular, the tendency of West German women to have children at a much higher average age was adopted instantaneously, which caused the so-called "fertility gap".

**Table 7.8: Fertility Development, 1990–1997**

| Year | Live births (1,000) | | Live births per 1,000 inhabitants | | Total fertility rate | | |
|---|---|---|---|---|---|---|---|
| | West | East | West | East | West | East | Germany |
| 1990 | 727.2 | 178.5 | 15.5 | 11.1 | 1.45 | 1.52 | 1.45 |
| 1991 | 722.3 | 107.8 | 11.3 | 6.8 | 1.42 | 0.98 | 1.33 |
| 1992 | 720.8 | 88.3 | 11.1 | 5.6 | 1.40 | 0.83 | 1.29 |
| 1993 | 717.9 | 80.5 | 11.0 | 5.1 | 1.39 | 0.78 | 1.28 |
| 1994 | 690.9 | 78.7 | 10.5 | 5.1 | 1.35 | 0.77 | 1.24 |
| 1995 | 681.4 | 83.8 | 10.3 | 5.4 | 1.34 | 0.84 | 1.25 |
| 1996 | 702.7 | 93.3 | 10.5 | 6.0 | 1.40 | 0.95 | 1.32 |
| 1997 | 711.9 | 100.3 | 10.7 | 6.5 | .. | .. | .. |

Sources: Statistisches Bundesamt, 1996a, pp. 34–37, 111; Guibert-Lantoine and Monnier, 1997, p. 1210; Sommer, 1998, pp. 232, 235; Statistisches Bundesamt, 1999b, pp. 163*–164*

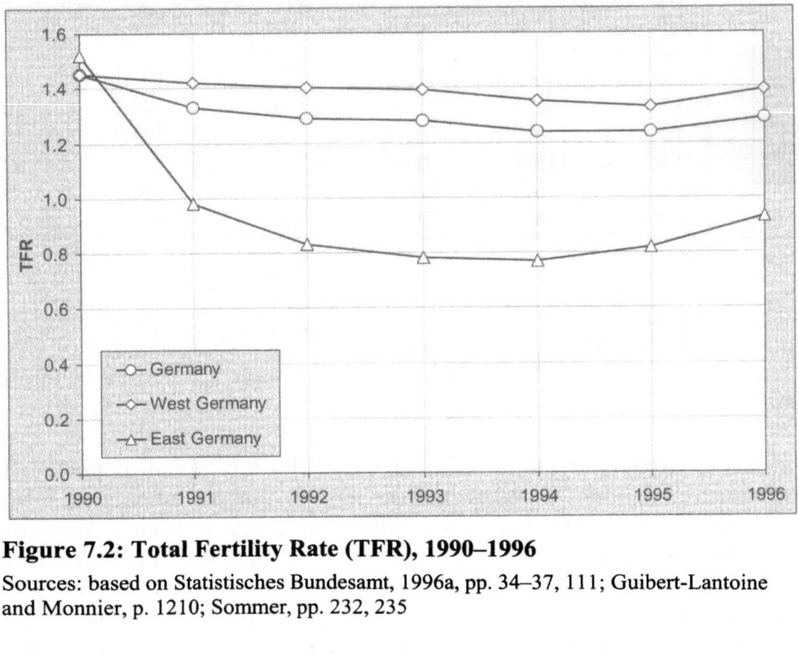


**Figure 7.2: Total Fertility Rate (TFR), 1990–1996**

Sources: based on Statistisches Bundesamt, 1996a, pp. 34–37, 111; Guibert-Lantoine and Monnier, p. 1210; Sommer, pp. 232, 235

This latter hypothesis has been favoured recently as an explanation in the analyses of completed fertility rates (see, for example, Lechner, 1998). However, one should be careful not to reduce the explanation of the phenomenon uniquely to a rapid adoption of West German behaviour. Circumstances of life in both parts of Germany differ greatly. There are dissimilarities in marriage and family patterns as well (Schaich, 1998).

## 7.4 Mortality Developments

The number of deaths showed a certain degree of stagnation, hiding however a significant and increasing excess of deaths over births. This phenomenon is largely caused by the fertility breakdown in East Germany, which generated mortality surpluses of up to -6.7‰ in 1993. At the same time, this indicator showed values in the range from 0.4‰ in 1992 to -0.4‰ in 1995 in West Germany and from -0.2‰ in 1990 to -1.5‰ in 1995 in Germany, as a whole (Sommer and Voit, 1998, p. 971). The actual excess figures are given in Figure 7.3.

**Table 7.9: Deaths and Natural Increase, 1990–1997, in thousands**

| Year | Germany | | West Germany | | East Germany | |
|---|---|---|---|---|---|---|
| | Deaths | Natural increase | Deaths | Natural increase | Deaths | Natural increase |
| 1990 | 921.4 | -15.8 | 713.4 | 13.9 | 208.1 | -29.6 |
| 1991 | 911.2 | -81.2 | 708.8 | 13.4 | 202.4 | -94.7 |
| 1992 | 885.4 | -76.3 | 695.3 | 25.5 | 190.2 | -101.9 |
| 1993 | 897.3 | -98.9 | 711.6 | 6.3 | 185.6 | -105.1 |
| 1994 | 884.7 | -115.1 | 703.3 | -12.4 | 181.4 | -102.7 |
| 1995 | 884.6 | -119.4 | 706.5 | -25.1 | 178.1 | -94.3 |
| 1996 | 882.9 | -86.8 | 708.3 | -5.6 | 174.5 | -81.2 |
| 1997 | 860.4 | -48.2 | 692.8 | 19.1 | 167.6 | -67.3 |

Source: Sommer and Voit, p. 971

Obviously, Germany is among those countries that have a negative natural increase of the population. Specifically, this amounts to about 1‰ in the case of Germany. In other words, the population increase described in part 7.2.1 results entirely from immigration.

As regards life expectancy, West Germany exhibits the typical characteristics of Western industrial nations. Mortality in East Germany, on the other hand, is not typically Eastern European. Life expectancy in East Germany is closer to Western structures. Total life expectancy for men is about 2 to 3 years lower in East Germany than in West Germany, with only a slow tendency towards reaching the Western level. The gap in life expectancy for women decreased from 2.3 years in 1991–1993 to 1.2 years in 1995–1997. Infant mortality in 1995 was 5.3‰ in the West, 5.4‰ in the East, and in 1996, 4.9‰ and 5.3‰, respectively (Guibert-Lantoine and Monnier, p. 1202). Indeed, it is slightly higher in East Germany but not to such an extent that it could partially explain the differences in overall life expectancy.

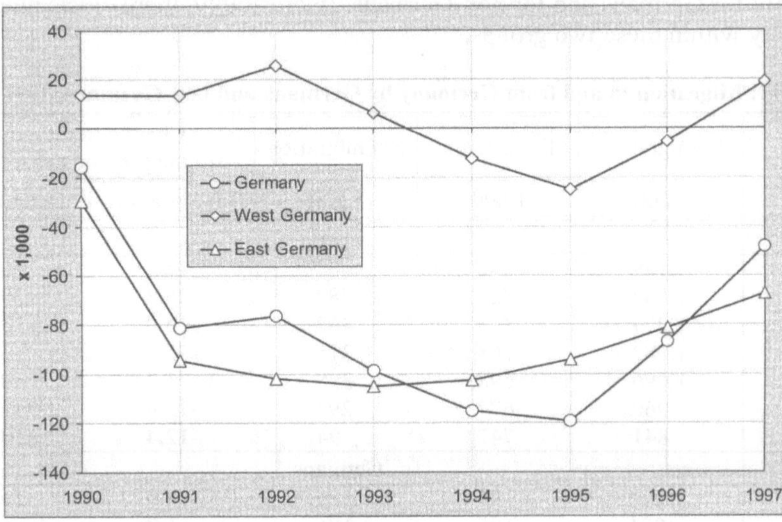


**Figure 7.3: Natural Increase, 1990–1997**

Source: based on Sommer and Voit, p. 971

**Table 7.10: Life Expectancy at Birth, 1986–1997, selected periods, in years**

| Germany | | | West Germany | | | East Germany | | |
|---|---|---|---|---|---|---|---|---|
| Period | Male | Female | Period | Male | Female | Period | Male | Female |
| 1986–1988 | 71.7 | 78.0 | 1988–1990 | 72.6 | 79.0 | 1988–1989 | 70.0 | 76.2 |
| ... | ... | ... | 1990–1992 | 72.9 | 79.3 | 1992 | 69.8 | 77.1 |
| 1991–1993 | 72.5 | 79.0 | 1991–1993 | 73.1 | 79.5 | 1991–1993 | 69.9 | 77.2 |
| 1992–1994 | 72.8 | 79.3 | 1992–1994 | 73.4 | 79.7 | 1992–1994 | 70.3 | 77.7 |
| 1993–1995 | 73.0 | 79.5 | 1993–1995 | 73.5 | 79.8 | 1993–1995 | 70.7 | 78.2 |
| 1994–1996 | 73.3 | 79.7 | 1994–1996 | 73.8 | 80.0 | 1994–1996 | 71.2 | 78.6 |
| 1995–1997 | 73.6 | 80.0 | 1995–1997 | 74.1 | 80.2 | 1995–1997 | 71.8 | 79.0 |

Sources: Statistisches Bundesamt 1993, p. 82; Statistisches Bundesamt 1994, p. 82; Statistisches Bundesamt 1995, p. 76; Statistisches Bundesamt 1996b, p. 77; Statistisches Bundesamt 1997b, p. 76; Statistisches Bundesamt 1998, p. 75; Statistisches Bundesamt 1999c, p. 74; Guibert-Lantoine and Monnier, p. 1213

## 7.5 Migration Processes

The drastic political changes in Central and Eastern Europe since 1989, the lasting tensions in the former Yugoslavia since the early 1990s, along with the new policies restricting immigration into Germany, have produced elements of instability in migration processes. The population flows into and out of Germany are composed of several heterogeneous sub-populations. Table 7.11 shows migration processes separately for Germans and for non-Germans. Interestingly, there exists much heterogeneity within these two groups.

**Table 7.11: Migration to and from Germany by Germans and non-Germans, 1991–1997**

| Year | Immigration | Emigration | Net migration | Change in relation to the previous year (%) | |
|---|---|---|---|---|---|
| | 1,000 | 1,000 | 1,000 | Immigration | Emigration |
| | | | Total | | |
| 1991 | 1,199 | 596 | 603 | -5.3 | 0.2 |
| 1992 | 1,502 | 720 | 782 | 25.3 | 20.7 |
| 1993 | 1,277 | 815 | 462 | -15.0 | 13.2 |
| 1994 | 1,083 | 768 | 315 | -15.3 | -5.9 |
| 1995 | 1,096 | 698 | 398 | 1.3 | -9.1 |
| 1996 | 960 | 677 | 292 | -12.4 | -3.0 |
| 1997 | 841 | 747 | 94 | -12.4 | 10.3 |
| | | | Germans | | |
| 1991 | 274 | 99 | 175 | -35.9 | -23.0 |
| 1992 | 291 | 105 | 186 | 6.3 | 6.3 |
| 1993 | 288 | 105 | 183 | -1.1 | -0.5 |
| 1994 | 305 | 138 | 167 | 6.1 | 32.1 |
| 1995 | 303 | 131 | 173 | -0.6 | -5.5 |
| 1996 | 252 | 118 | 133 | -17.0 | -9.4 |
| 1997 | 225 | 110 | 115 | -10.5 | -7.2 |
| | | | Non-Germans | | |
| 1991 | 925 | 498 | 428 | 10.3 | 6.5 |
| 1992 | 1,211 | 615 | 596 | 30.9 | 23.6 |
| 1993 | 990 | 711 | 279 | -18.3 | 15.6 |
| 1994 | 771 | 629 | 148 | -21.5 | -11.5 |
| 1995 | 793 | 567 | 225 | 2.0 | -9.8 |
| 1996 | 708 | 559 | 149 | -10.7 | -1.5 |
| 1997 | 615 | 637 | -22 | -13.1 | 14.0 |

Source: Sommer and Voit, p. 972

For both Germans and non-Germans, there has been existed a permanent immigration surplus, which has reached its peak in 1992. Since then, this excess has decreased remarkably, showing a first negative number for non-Germans in 1997. In most of the years, the difference for non-Germans exceeds the difference for Germans; the percentage change of the latter has been swiftly declining since 1992.

With regard to the external migration of Germans, one should distinguish between native Germans born in Germany, those who have adopted German citizenship and ethnic Germans arriving from the Russian Federation and from Kazakhstan. Table 7.12 presents data on external migration of Germans (as defined above) and shows the high numbers of the ethnic Germans from the former Soviet Union in the immigration flows. The number of all immigrants (in 1990, almost 400,000) has dropped, however, to almost 50% of this maximum level.

**Table 7.12: Immigration and Emigration of Germans by Country of Origin/Destination, 1996 and 1997, in thousands**

| Origin/ destination | Immigration | | | Emigration | | | Net migration | |
|---|---|---|---|---|---|---|---|---|
| | 1996 | 1997 | Change | 1996 | 1997 | Change | 1996 | 1997 |
| EU-countries | 28.9 | 28.8 | -0.2 | 37.1 | 38.4 | 1.2 | -8.2 | -9.6 |
| Poland | 13.9 | 14.4 | 0.5 | 7.2 | 8.9 | 1.7 | 6.7 | 5.5 |
| Romania | 2.2 | 2.3 | 0.1 | 0.5 | 0.5 | 0.0 | 1.7 | 1.7 |
| Russia | 51.5 | 42.4 | -9.1 | 2.6[1] | 1.7[1] | -0.9 | 48.9 | 40.7 |
| USA | 10.9 | 10.5 | -0.3 | 13.4 | 14.3 | 0.8 | -2.5 | -3.7 |
| Kazakhstan | 79.7 | 68.6 | -11.1 | 9.4[1] | 6.1[1] | -3.3 | 70.3 | 62.5 |
| All countries | 251.7 | 225.3 | -26.4 | 118.4 | 109.9 | -8.5 | 133.3 | 115.4 |

[1]Numbers are probably too high, due to inaccuracy of migration statistics
Source: Sommer and Voit, p. 973

Refugees fleeing from civil wars and asylum-seekers are the main contributors to non-German migration into Germany. Their number was extremely high in 1992 (around 450,000); in the meantime, however, it has fallen to about 100,000 in 1998 (Statistisches Bundesamt, 1998, p. 67; 1999c, p. 66). Table 7.13 shows the main countries of origin and destination of migrating non-Germans. An increase in population due to immigration of non-Germans stems mainly from the EU-countries, Turkey and non-European countries, particularly from Asia. The contribution of the former Yugoslavia, which was remarkable a few years ago, has decreased significantly.

**Table 7.13: Immigration and Emigration of non-Germans, 1996 and 1997, in thousands**

| Origin/ destination | Immigration | | | Emigration | | | Net migration | |
|---|---|---|---|---|---|---|---|---|
| | 1996 | 1997 | Change | 1996 | 1997 | Change | 1996 | 1997 |
| EU-countries | 172.5 | 151.7 | -20.8 | 153.9 | 159.6 | 5.7 | 18.6 | -7.9 |
| Bosnia and Herzegovina | 11.1 | 6.9 | -4.2 | 27.2 | 83.9 | 56.7 | -16.1 | -77.0 |
| Serbia | 42.9 | 31.2 | -11.7 | 34.3 | 44.5 | 10.2 | 8.6 | -13.3 |
| Croatia | 12.3 | 10.0 | -2.3 | 17.3 | 18.9 | 1.7 | -5.0 | -8.9 |
| Poland | 77.4 | 71.2 | -6.2 | 71.7 | 70.2 | -1.5 | 5.7 | 1.0 |
| Romania | 17.1 | 14.2 | -2.8 | 16.6 | 13.6 | -3.1 | 0.4 | 0.7 |
| Slovenia | 2.2 | 1.8 | -0.3 | 2.4 | 2.3 | -0.2 | -0.3 | -0.5 |
| Turkey | 73.2 | 56.0 | -17.2 | 43.5 | 46.0 | 2.4 | 29.7 | 10.0 |
| Hungary | 16.6 | 11.2 | -5.4 | 17.0 | 15.1 | -1.9 | -0.4 | -3.9 |
| Other countries | 181.7 | 167.7 | -14.0 | 106.2 | 118.6 | 12.4 | 75.5 | 49.1 |
| Total | 708.0 | 615.3 | -92.7 | 559.1 | 637.1 | 78.0 | 148.9 | -21.8 |

Source: Sommer and Voit, p. 974

The internal migration process between East and West Germany exhibits similarities to the external migration processes: after a phase characterised by a high level of migration, the volume of migration has declined noticeably. In the long run, the more favourable labour market in West Germany could lead to a moderate loss of population in East Germany due to migration westward.

**Table 7.14: Migration Flows Between West Germany and East Germany, 1990–1997, in thousands**

| Year | West-East | East-West | Difference |
|---|---|---|---|
| 1990 | 36.2 | 395.3 | -359.1 |
| 1991 | 80.3 | 249.7 | -169.5 |
| 1992 | 111.3 | 199.2 | -87.8 |
| 1993 | 119.1 | 172.4 | -53.3 |
| 1994 | 135.8 | 163.0 | -27.3 |
| 1995 | 143.0 | 168.3 | -25.3 |
| 1996 | 152.0 | 166.1 | -14.0 |
| 1997 | 157.4 | 167.8 | -10.4 |

Source: Sommer and Voit, p. 973

## 7.6 Processes Concerning Marriage and Family

### 7.6.1 Marriages and Marriage Dissolutions

The radical political changes in East Germany resulted in dissimilarity between East and West Germany's marital patterns and divorce trends. This process parallels the drop in East Germany's fertility discussed in part 3 of this article.

Table 7.15 shows a time series of numbers of marriages and marriage dissolutions. In West Germany, the number of marriages is decreasing over the given period of time. The balance of marriages and dissolutions of marriage has been negative since the early 1970s with the exception of 1990; in 1996, there was a surplus of 65,309 dissolved marriages, the highest since the mid-1980s. The reasons for this development are a declining number of marriages and a rise in the number of divorces. The numbers of marriage dissolutions because of the death of one of the partners have been stagnating at about 285,000 since 1990, whereas divorces have been increasing from 122,869 in 1990 to 152,798 in 1996. As a result, the proportion of divorces in all marriage dissolutions increased by almost five percentage points (Table 7.16).

The development in East Germany is clearly influenced by the German reunification. There has been also a negative balance of marriages and marriage dissolutions for years, but marriages and divorces per thousand have been exceeding the West German values. After the reunification, both numbers decreased significantly: in 1991, marriages fell to about 50% of last year's number, marriage dissolutions to 78%.

One reason for the number of marriages to decline is the fact that economic advantages for married couples no longer applied. The sharp drop in divorces in 1991 was partly due to the adoption of West German Law, which complicated the process of getting divorced. Since 1991 and, respectively, since 1992, both values have been rising again but without reaching the former level (cf. Table 7.15 and Table 7.16). As the decrease in number of marriage dissolutions by death of one partner has been less intense, the balance of marriages and marriage dissolutions has risen from about -10,000 in the 1980s to almost -40,000 in 1996, with its maximum of -44,633 in 1993.

**Table 7.15: Marriages and Marriage Dissolutions, 1990–1996, in thousands**

| Year | West Germany | | | East Germany | | |
|---|---|---|---|---|---|---|
| | Marriage | Marriage dissolutions | Balance | Marriage | Marriage dissolutions | Balance |
| 1990 | 414.5 | 411.5 | -3.0 | 101.9 | 115.6 | -13.8 |
| 1991 | 403.8 | 414.5 | -10.7 | 50.5 | 90.2 | -39.7 |
| 1992 | 405.2 | 406.8 | -1.6 | 48.2 | 87.4 | -39.2 |
| 1993 | 393.4 | 425.8 | -32.5 | 49.3 | 93.9 | -44.6 |
| 1994 | 387.8 | 427.7 | -39.9 | 52.4 | 96.3 | -43.9 |
| 1995 | 376.4 | 434.4 | -58.0 | 54.2 | 94.0 | -39.8 |
| 1996 | 373.2 | 438.6 | -65.3 | 54.1 | 93.4 | -39.4 |

Source: Grünheid and Mammey, p. 385

**Table 7.16: Dissolution of Marriage by Cause and Divorce Rate, 1990–1996**

| Year | West Germany | | | East Germany | | |
|---|---|---|---|---|---|---|
| | Marriage dissolution by | | Divorce rate | Marriage dissolution by | | Divorce rate |
| | Divorce | Death | | Divorce | Death | |
| | 1,000 | 1,000 | % | 1,000 | 1,000 | % |
| 1990 | 122.9 | 188.5 | 29.9 | 31.9 | 83.7 | 27.6 |
| 1991 | 127.3 | 287.0 | 30.7 | 9.0 | 81.2 | 10.0 |
| 1992 | 124.7 | 281.9 | 30.7 | 10.3 | 77.1 | 11.8 |
| 1993 | 138.1 | 287.5 | 32.4 | 18.4 | 75.5 | 19.6 |
| 1994 | 143.1 | 284.2 | 33.5 | 22.9 | 73.4 | 23.8 |
| 1995 | 148.0 | 285.9 | 34.1 | 21.5 | 72.5 | 22.9 |
| 1996 | 152.8 | 285.1 | 34.8 | 22.8 | 70.7 | 24.4 |

Source: Grünheid and Mammey, p. 397

The marriage decline is also evident, when one considers the number of marriages per thousand persons (see Table 7.17). Another indicator that reflects the low marriage level is the total first marriage rate (TFMR) (see Figure 7.4). Similar to the absolute numbers of marriage, it shows a downtrend in West Germany and a drastic fall in East Germany in 1991 followed by a slow increase. Despite this trend, the values are still obviously lower than the West German ones, showing also a greater difference between the rates for men and women. On the other hand, the mean age at first marriage (see Table 7.17) reveals that in this respect an assimilation process of East to West Germany is at a very advanced stage, almost close to completion. Within a limited number of years, the mean age increased by about 3 years for both females and males in East Germany.

**Table 7.17: Crude Marriage Rate and Mean Age at First Marriage, 1990–1996**

| Year | Crude marriage rate (‰) | | | Mean age at first marriage (years) | | | | | |
|---|---|---|---|---|---|---|---|---|---|
| | | | | Male | | | Female | | |
| | Total | West | East | Total | West | East | Total | West | East |
| 1990 | 6.5 | 6.6 | 6.3 | .. | 28.4 | 25.8 | .. | 25.9 | 23.7 |
| 1991 | 5.7 | 6.3 | 3.2 | 28.5 | 28.7 | 26.6 | 26.1 | 26.2 | 24.5 |
| 1992 | 5.6 | 6.2 | 3.1 | 28.8 | 29.0 | 27.1 | 26.4 | 26.5 | 25.1 |
| 1993 | 5.5 | 6.0 | 3.1 | 29.2 | 29.3 | 27.6 | 26.8 | 26.9 | 25.5 |
| 1994 | 5.4 | 5.9 | 3.4 | 29.4 | 29.6 | 28.0 | 27.1 | 27.2 | 26.0 |
| 1995 | 5.3 | 5.7 | 3.5 | 29.7 | 29.9 | 28.5 | 27.3 | 27.5 | 26.4 |
| 1996 | 5.2 | 5.6 | 3.5 | 30.0 | 30.1 | 29.0 | 27.6 | 27.7 | 26.7 |

Source: Grünheid and Mammey, p. 386

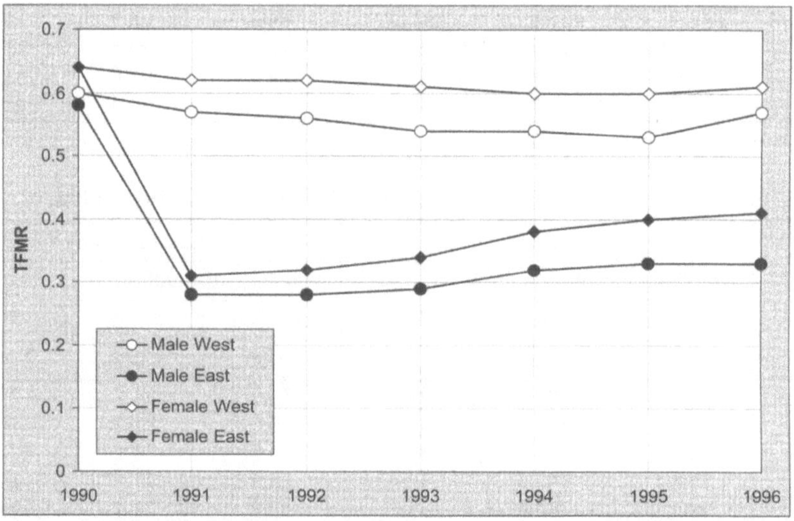


**Figure 7.4: Total First Marriage Rate by Sex (TFMR), 1990–1996**

Source: based on Grünheid and Mammey, p. 386

### 7.6.2 Extramarital Births

One striking change within East Germany's population is the sudden rise in the percentage of extramarital children – up to about 42%. In West Germany, a rise can be observed as well, but at a more moderate rate and resulting in a lower proportion. For 1997, the figures were 14.3% in West Germany and 44.1% in East Germany (Statistisches Bundesamt, 1999b, pp. 163*–164*). No process of assimilation is visible at the moment. The obvious reasons for this are the nearly equal legal treatment of children born within and outside marriage and the low inclination on the part of many to marry. However, it should be taken into consideration, that about 35% of all children born outside marriage in the West and 50% respectively in the East are legitimated by a subsequent marriage (Grünheid and Mammey, p. 407).

### 7.6.3 Abortions

Developments in the number of reported abortions vary greatly in the two parts of Germany. In West Germany, the number of abortions in relation to the number of live births and stillbirths did not rise too much yet showed a sharp increase in 1996. The corresponding figures for East Germany were more than four times as high as in the beginning of the 1990s, but then went down to about the double level of West Germany (Table 7.18).

Certainly, the data regarding abortions should be analysed within the context of recent reforms. In particular, it should be noted that: (1) there was no harmonisation of abortion laws in East and West Germany before 1 October 1995; (2) on 1 January 1996, new guidelines for the reporting of abortions were introduced; (3) in East Germany, abortions have been traditionally more accepted by society than in West Germany.

**Table 7.18: Total Reported Abortions and Index of Abortion, 1990–1997**

| Year | Reported abortions (1,000) | | | Index of abortion (per 10,000 births) | | |
|---|---|---|---|---|---|---|
| | Germany | West | East | Germany | West | East |
| 1990 | 145.3 | 78.8 | 66.5 | 1,598 | 1,080 | 3,709 |
| 1991 | 124.4 | 74.6 | 49.8 | 1,494 | 1,029 | 4,605 |
| 1992 | 118.6 | 74.9 | 43.8 | 1,461 | 1,035 | 4,934 |
| 1993 | 111.2 | 79.1 | 32.2 | 1,389 | 1,087 | 4,392 |
| 1994 | 103.6 | 77.4 | 26.2 | 1,341 | 1,103 | 3,668 |
| 1995 | 97.9 | 73.8 | 24.1 | 1,287 | 1,066 | 3,171 |
| 1996 | 130.9 | 101.4 | 29.5 | 1,637 | 1,436 | 3,147 |
| 1997 | 130.9 | 103.4 | 27.5 | 1,604 | 1,446 | 2,728 |

Source: Dorbritz and Gärtner, p. 392

This leads to the conclusion that, up until 1995 and to some extent for the years since then, the estimated number of unreported abortions in West Germany must have been much higher than in East Germany. Therefore, the difference in the number of abortions per 10,000 births in East and West may be exaggerated and a process of assimilation between East and West is to be expected.

## 7.7 The Political and Social Background

As East Germany's population amounts to about 25% of the population of reunited Germany and in view of a certain degree of westernisation of East Germany's population (age structure; fertility pattern; household size; employment rate), policy decisions with demographic relevance tend to be focussed on a typical Western population. In most cases, this has yielded and will continue to yield measures, which will improve East Germany's population structure and its volatile elements. Policies to improve the situation of families are a good example of this.

There are present, however, specific German peculiarities in regard to policies aimed at influencing demographic trends directly. For historical reasons, population policies are inadequate in Germany. Policies are typically directed towards some structural improvements and yield more or less positive demographic consequences as part of the bargain, as it were. The most important current policy actions are aimed at counterbalancing future negative effects of ongoing demographic processes. There exist several main areas of current German policies with more or less indirect demographic intent or consequences.

### 7.7.1 The Ageing German Society

In 1996, 21% of the German population was aged 60 or older, while for 2025, the projection is 32%, a level close to the highest in the world (33% for Italy and Japan) (see, for example, Vaupel, 1997, p. 13). This increase in longevity, coupled with the reduction in fertility, is already putting severe strains on the state pension system. This will surely lead to smaller pensions and, perhaps, even to a major reform of the system. These problems were intensified by pension payments to retired East Germans and to immigrants of German nationality from Eastern Europe. Reductions in the rate of increase of pension payments, payments to the health insurance system on the part of pensioners and discussions on retirement age represent first steps towards alleviating the situation. Further-going discussions are aimed at fostering individual, private financing of old-age pensions funds and at introducing tax-financed (and lower) standard annuities for everyone. Radical changes are not yet immanent; but the incorporation of the demographic factor in the formula for calculating pensions was in discussion during the former Kohl Government, but is now questioned by Schröder Cabinet.

The ageing population is also causing severe problems for the system of health insurance. Limited subsidies for the payments to physicians and for drugs and hospital treatments for the patients have been introduced. In addition, a new compulsory insurance for elderly patients in need of permanent nursing care has been introduced. This new insurance has already led to a certain degree of upheaval in the traditional nursing care for the elderly.

On a positive side, immigration to Germany serves to reduce the severity of the effects of an ageing German population: the age structure of immigrant groups is much younger and thus far more favourable than that of the German population and the fertility of immigrants is higher as well.

### 7.7.2 Family and Fertility

For reasons stated above, there exists no direct policy in Germany for stabilising fertility despite the dramatically low reproduction rates – especially in East Germany – within the last several years. But it is widely accepted that there is a need to create and to cultivate circumstances that are favourable for families, particularly young families. A major problem, however, is the fact that in East Germany, the new political situation has reduced dramatically the comfort of young families as compared to their lot in the former socialist system. So, despite direct payments for children ("Kindergeld", "Baukindergeld"), decent opportunities for young parents to devote time to child-rearing without losing their job ("Erziehungsurlaub") and guaranteed admission to public kindergartens at the age of three, the infrastructure for young families is often subjectively viewed as being insufficient.

Clearly, budgetary restrictions are the main reasons for reductions in this area. On the other hand, there is certain evidence that in a western developed society such as Germany, there is no direct correlation between the financial circumstances of young families and the number of children they have. Whether or not one decides to have children is obviously more a question of attitudes than of financial or other concerns. In January 1999, the Federal Constitutional Court ("Bundesverfassungsgericht") came to the conclusion that the tax benefits which may be claimed by unmarried couples raising children but not by married couples are contradictory to the Constitution and decided that the German Government is obliged to correct this part of the tax system by 2002.

### 7.7.3 Reduced Stability of Family Structures

In a nearly global process, the role and stability of families have been challenged by modern attitudes of personal independence and freedom, but also, for instance, by the complexities that two professional careers entail for a married couple, or by the mobility requirements of rapidly changing labour markets. This has clearly left its mark on the younger generation in both parts of Germany, where in cities single-person household is the most frequent type. There is, at this time, no evidence that this tendency is abating – nor is this the case for the increasing number of consensual unions and rising divorce rates.

### 7.7.4 Immigration of Germans and Foreigners

There has been much discussion about the need for an immigration law to overcome the current situation of affluence of Germans and non-Germans from many parts of the world without clear rules. A fundamental political change, not yet in view at this time, is, however, possible under the new Federal Government. But many small steps towards slowing down the immigration of ethnic Germans from Russia and Kazakhstan – e.g., establishing programmes to improve their situation in their homeland so that they give up plans to migrate – have already reduced the immigration of ethnic Germans.

### 7.7.5 The Central Role of Unemployment

For almost all processes with demographic implications, there exist links to the labour market in Germany, which, at this time, includes 3.8 to 4.5 million unemployed persons – with a relatively high concentration in East Germany. Unemployment, in turn, caused a great part of the financial shortages in the public insurance system and poverty in families; it has also instigated new policy measures to reduce immigration so as not to load additional problems onto the labour market and has reinforced the increasing role of the "shadow economy" (including illegal, unregistered employment), as well as many other hardships. Presently, there is not much hope that unemployment will be drastically reduced soon.

There is, however, a lot of effort being expended in this area. Examples are the promotions of part-time jobs, setting up public work projects, and retraining unemployed persons. In addition, several measures for reducing the high costs of German labour are under discussion. Together with a new system of enterprise taxation, they should make Germany more attractive for global investors. Of course, a major consequence of this process will be a noticeable reduction in the social welfare system, which, eventually, may influence demographic structures in some unforeseeable way.

## 7.8 Concluding Remarks: The Need for Regionalised Analyses

Many of the demographic structures we have discussed here show noticeable regional differences unrelated to the East-West dichotomy. Convincing explanations for these phenomena as well as regionalised measures for addressing them are still not at the centre of attention because this would require detailed knowledge and forecasts on a sub-national level, which are not yet available.

## Notes

The authors like to thank Katrin Schmidt, Tübingen, for helpful discussions about the main topics and for her assistance in collecting the data and producing the manuscript.

## References

Allafi, S. (1999), Erste Ergebnisse des Mikrozensus 1998, *Wirtschaft und Statistik*, Vol. 3, pp. 163–170.

de Guibert-Lantoine, C. and A. Monnier (1997), La conjoncture démographique: l'Europe et les pays développés d'outre-mer, *Population*, Vol. 52(5), pp. 1187–1216.

Dorbritz, J. and K. Gärtner (1998), Bericht 1998 über die demographische Lage in Deutschland mit dem Teil B "Ehescheidungen – Trends in Deutschland und im internationalen Vergleich", *Zeitschrift für Bevölkerungswissenschaft*, Vol. 23(4), pp. 373– 458.

Fleischhacker, J. (1998), *Die Frauen-, Familien- und Bevölkerungspolitik in der ehemaligen DDR – ein sozialer Großversuch mit geringen Erfolgsaussichten* (unpublished manuscript).

Grünheid, E. and U. Mammey (1997), Bericht 1997 über die demographische Lage in Deutschland, *Zeitschrift für Bevölkerungswissenschaft*, Vol. 22(4), pp. 377–480.

Lechner, M. (1998), Eine empirische Analyse des Geburtenrückganges in den neuen Bundesländern aus der Sicht der neoklassischen Bevölkerungsökonomie, *Zeitschrift für Wirtschafts- und Sozialwissenschaften*, Vol. 118(3), pp. 463–488.

Münz, R. and R. Ulrich (1994), Was wird aus den Neuen Bundesländern? In: *Demographie aktuell*, Berlin: Lehrstuhl für Bevölkerungswissenschaft, Institut für Soziologie, Humboldt University.

Schaich, E. (1998), Der Geburteneinbruch in den neuen Bundesländern seit 1990 und einige Hypothesen zu seiner Erklärung, *Jahrbücher für Nationalökonomie und Statistik*, Vol. 217(1), pp. 93–107.

Sommer, B. (1998), Eheschließungen, Geburten und Sterbefälle, *Wirtschaft und Statistik*, Vol. 3, pp. 232–238.

Sommer, B. and Voit, H. (1998), Bevölkerungsentwicklung 1997, *Wirtschaft und Statistik*, Vol. 12, pp. 971–977.

Statistisches Bundesamt (Central Statistical Office) (1993–1995) *Statistisches Jahrbuch 1993–1995*, Stuttgart.

Statistisches Bundesamt (Central Statistical Office) (1996a), *Fachserie 1, Reihe 1 (Gebiet und Bevölkerung 1994)*, Wiesbaden.

Statistisches Bundesamt (Central Statistical Office) (1996b), *Statistisches Jahrbuch 1996*, Stuttgart.

Statistisches Bundesamt (Central Statistical Office) (1997a), *Fachserie 1, Reihe 4.1.1 (Stand und Entwicklung der Erwerbstätigkeit)*, Wiesbaden.

Statistisches Bundesamt (Central Statistical Office) (1997b), *Statistisches Jahrbuch 1997*, Stuttgart.

Statistisches Bundesamt (Central Statistical Office) (1998), *Statistisches Jahrbuch 1998*, Stuttgart.

Statistisches Bundesamt (Central Statistical Office) (1999a), *Fachserie 1, Reihe 4.3 (Erwerbstätigkeit und Arbeitsmarkt)*, Wiesbaden.

Statistisches Bundesamt (Central Statistical Office) (1999b), *Wirtschaft und Statistik, Vol. 3, Tabellenteil*, Wiesbaden.

Statistisches Bundesamt (Central Statistical Office) (1999c), *Statistisches Jahrbuch 1999*, Stuttgart.

van de Kaa, D.J. (1987), Europe's Second Demographic Transition, *Population Bulletin*, Vol. 42(1), pp. 1–58.

Vaupel, J.W. (1997), Demographic Analysis of Aging and Longevity, Paper presented at the XXXIIIrd IUSSP General Population Conference, Bejing, October 1997.

# 8

# Demographic Situation and Population Policies in Hungary

László Hablicsek

## 8.1 Population Structures and Processes

### 8.1.1 Population Structures

The Hungarian population development can be examined from two basic perspectives. The first, and the most important, frame for analysis is the theory of demographic transitions. It is well known that the first transition from the agrarian population to the industrial one, and the second transition, which characterises the post-industrial populations, are core processes of the 20th century. Transition from high to low fertility and mortality along with the significant population growth and the ageing process are the most important characteristics of population development.

In the 1880s, Hungary had within its current territory a population of 5 million. An average number of children in the family varied around 6 at that time, while life expectancy at birth was about 30 years. The share of elderly did not exceed 6% of the total population. After a century, in the early 1960s, the population size reached 10 million; life expectancy at birth for both sexes achieved 70 years. However, total fertility rate fell to 1.8, the lowest level in the world then, and proportion of those aged 60 and over exceeded 15%. The population development in the last decades showed the elements of the second demographic transition (see van de Kaa, 1987). Fertility continued to fluctuate on the deep below-replacement level, especially in the 1990s.

The second perspective of analysis of the Hungarian population development over recent decades is less theoretical. It entails focus on population size and its determinants. The modern history of population development in Hungary can be divided into two distinct periods: the first one is a period of population increase at moderate rates that lasted until 1980 and the other is a period during which an actual population decline occurred in 1981 and has persisted since then.

The population size of the country peaked in 1980, when it reached 10.710 million. Then it decreased by 3.1% from 1980 to 1990 and by a further 2.7% between 1990 and 1999. The 1999 estimation of the total population size was 10.092 million inhabitants (Table 8.1).

The decrease has been the most significant among those of early age and the young, and moderate among the middle-aged. Since 1980, the number of people under aged 15 fell from 2.3 million to 1.7 million, the proportion of them – from 22% to 17%. On the other hand, the number of those aged 60 and over has increased over the last decade. Their number was 1.8 million in the early 1980s and grew to 2 million in 1999. Consequently, the population decline is taking place along with a further ageing of the population. The share of those aged 60 and over just reached 20%. The differences between males and females are especially remarkable in the older age groups. The number of men aged 60 and over is 40% less than the number of women (Table 8.1).

**Table 8.1: Population by Age and Sex, 1980–1999, selected years[1]**

| Age | Number (1,000) | | | | Percentage | | | |
|---|---|---|---|---|---|---|---|---|
| | 1980 | 1990 | 1995 | 1999[2] | 1980 | 1990 | 1995 | 1999[2] |
| | Total population | | | | | | | |
| 0–14 | 2,341 | 2,131 | 1,870 | 1,745 | 21.8 | 20.5 | 18.3 | 17.3 |
| 15–39 | 3,832 | 3,687 | 3,672 | 3,561 | 35.8 | 35.6 | 35.8 | 35.3 |
| 40–59 | 2,706 | 2,597 | 2,718 | 2,809 | 25.3 | 25.0 | 26.5 | 27.8 |
| 60+ | 1,830 | 1,960 | 1,986 | 1,977 | 17.1 | 18.9 | 19.4 | 19.6 |
| Total | 10,709 | 10,375 | 10,246 | 10,092 | 100.0 | 100.0 | 100.0 | 100.0 |
| | Male | | | | | | | |
| 0–14 | 1,205 | 1,091 | 956 | 894 | 23.2 | 21.9 | 19.5 | 18.6 |
| 15–39 | 1,942 | 1,866 | 1,864 | 1,811 | 37.5 | 37.4 | 38.0 | 37.5 |
| 40–59 | 1,284 | 1,241 | 1,230 | 1,349 | 24.7 | 24.9 | 26.5 | 28.0 |
| 60+ | 758 | 787 | 784 | 764 | 14.6 | 15.8 | 16.0 | 15.9 |
| Total | 5,189 | 4,985 | 4,904 | 4,818 | 100.0 | 100.0 | 100.0 | 100.0 |
| | Female | | | | | | | |
| 0–14 | 1,136 | 1,040 | 914 | 851 | 20.6 | 19.3 | 17.1 | 16.1 |
| 15–39 | 1,890 | 1,821 | 1,808 | 1,750 | 34.2 | 33.7 | 33.9 | 33.2 |
| 40–59 | 1,422 | 1,356 | 1,418 | 1,460 | 25.8 | 25.2 | 26.5 | 27.7 |
| 60+ | 1,072 | 1,173 | 1,202 | 1,213 | 19.4 | 21.8 | 22.5 | 23.0 |
| Total | 5,520 | 5,390 | 5,342 | 5,274 | 100.0 | 100.0 | 100.0 | 100.0 |

[1]As of 1 January of a given year
[2]Preliminary data
Source: HCSO, 1997

The ageing process shows itself as being in a developed phase in Hungary. Some experts have the opinion that the level of ageing in Hungary is higher than the level of overall modernisation of the country. However, there are still some resources in the age structure, especially the generations born in the 1970s (Figure 8.1).

According to the most recent population projections, the size of the population of Hungary will continue to decrease in the long run. Assuming a stabilised level of fertility, a very significant improvement in survival and positive net migration, the population size can be estimated to be only around 8 million in the middle of the next century (Figure 8.2). Another characteristic feature of development will be a new "wave" of ageing. The growing life expectancy together with the low reproduction will produce a duplication of the share of elderly. It is not impossible, that the proportion of those aged 65 and over will exceed 30% in the next half century. This group of the population will show also a dramatic increase in its absolute size – in period of the population decline (Figure 8.3).

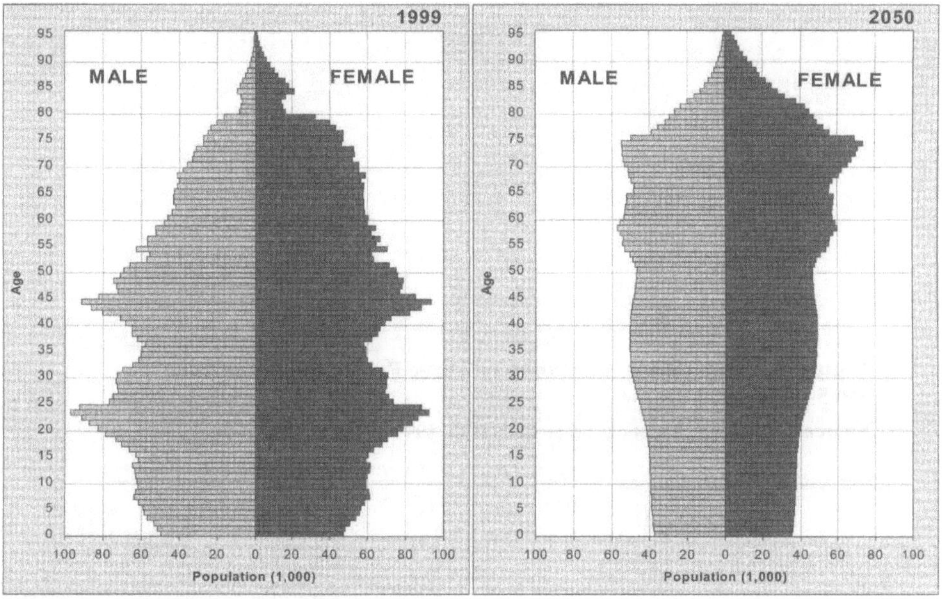


**Figure 8.1: Age Pyramid, 1999 and 2050**

Sources: author's calculations based on HSCO, 1997a; HSCO/DRI, 1998

Coming back to the processes of the past, Table 8.2 shows the population by marital status. It is well known that demographic transitions cause basic changes in nuptial behaviour. Increasing number of never married, widowed and divorced population has been overturning the longstanding dominance of married people.

With regards to urbanisation, the share of the population living in villages has been falling from 51% to 37% during the last eighty years. The most populated part of Hungary is Budapest and its suburbs. Although the number of inhabitants in capital of Hungary has been declining recently, it still remains a "watershed" of the country (Table 8.3).

Changes in economic activity in Hungary are also characteristic of the other countries in transition. After the period of proclaimed full employment, the size of economically active population fell dramatically in the first half of the 1990s. Labour force activity rate has become lower than the level of Western countries: it just exceeded 50% in 1997. Unemployment rate varied over 10% over the recent years, before it came to a more favourable level of 8.7% in 1997. The distinct feature of the Hungarian population economic activity is that the unemployment rate of females is much lower than that of males (Table 8.4).

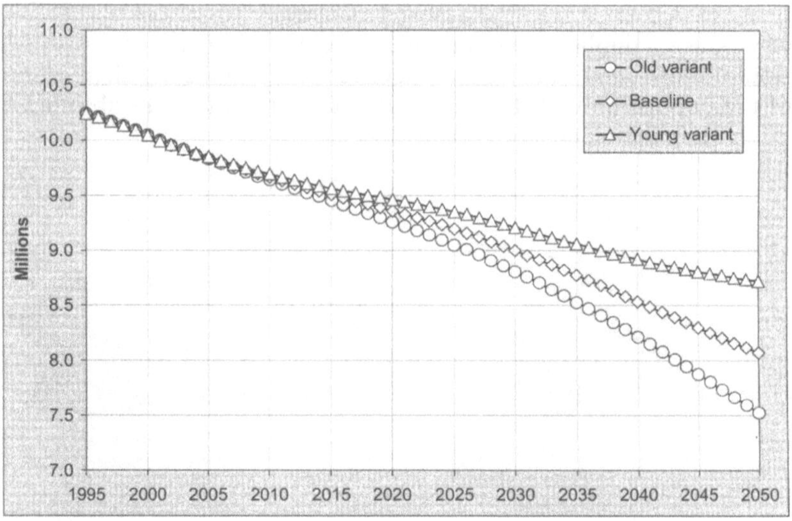


**Figure 8.2: Population According to Three Projection Scenarios, 1995–2050**

Sources: author's calculations based on HSCO, 1997a; HSCO/DRI, 1998

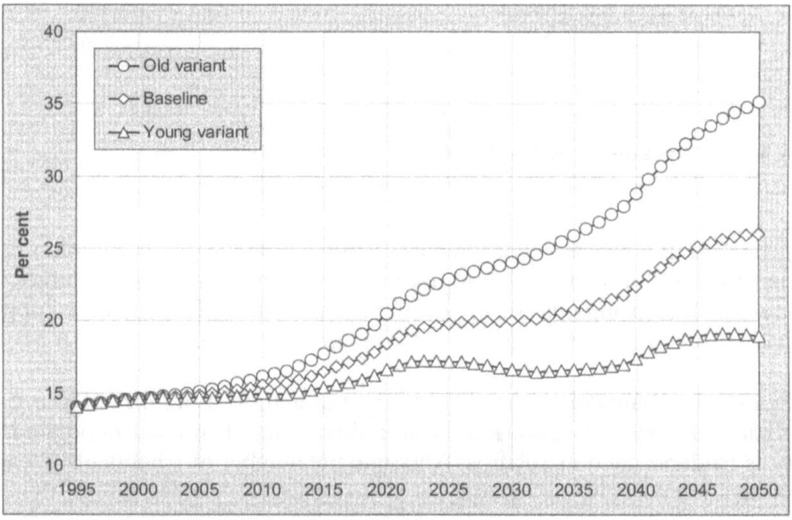


**Figure 8.3: Proportion of Population Aged 65 and Over According to Three Projection Scenarios, 1995–2050**

Sources: author's calculations based on HCSO, 1997; HSCO/DRI, 1998

**Table 8.2: Population Aged 15 and Over by Marital Status, 1980–1997, selected years[1]**

| Year | Never married | Married | Widowed | Divorced | Total | Never married | Married | Widowed | Divorced |
|---|---|---|---|---|---|---|---|---|---|
| | 1,000 | | | | | % | | | |
| | | | | | Total | | | | |
| 1980 | 1,479 | 5.638 | 856 | 396 | 8,369 | 17.7 | 67.4 | 10.2 | 4.7 |
| 1990 | 1,672 | 5,041 | 924 | 607 | 8,244 | 20.3 | 61.2 | 11.2 | 7.4 |
| 1991 | 1,744 | 4,996 | 930 | 622 | 8,291 | 21.0 | 60.2 | 11.2 | 7.5 |
| 1992 | 1,814 | 4,940 | 936 | 638 | 8,328 | 21.8 | 59.3 | 11.2 | 7.7 |
| 1993 | 1,881 | 4,878 | 944 | 649 | 8,352 | 22.5 | 58.4 | 11.3 | 7.8 |
| 1994 | 1,943 | 4,812 | 948 | 663 | 8,366 | 23.2 | 57.5 | 11.3 | 7.9 |
| 1995 | 2,000 | 4,744 | 954 | 678 | 8,376 | 23.2 | 56.7 | 11.4 | 8.1 |
| 1996 | 2,046 | 4,678 | 955 | 697 | 8,376 | 24.4 | 55.9 | 11.4 | 8.3 |
| 1997 | 2,094 | 4,609 | 955 | 714 | 8,372 | 25.0 | 55.1 | 11.4 | 8.4 |
| | | | | | Male | | | | |
| 1980 | 875 | 2,819 | 140 | 149 | 3,983 | 22.0 | 70.8 | 3.5 | 3.7 |
| 1990 | 979 | 2,515 | 151 | 249 | 3,894 | 25.1 | 64.6 | 3.9 | 6.4 |
| 1991 | 1,017 | 2,492 | 152 | 255 | 3,916 | 26.0 | 63.6 | 3.9 | 6.5 |
| 1992 | 1,053 | 2,465 | 153 | 262 | 3,933 | 26.8 | 62.7 | 3.9 | 6.7 |
| 1993 | 1,087 | 2,435 | 154 | 266 | 3,942 | 27.6 | 61.8 | 3.9 | 6.8 |
| 1994 | 1,120 | 2,400 | 154 | 272 | 3,946 | 28.4 | 60.8 | 3.9 | 6.9 |
| 1995 | 1,148 | 2,368 | 154 | 277 | 3,947 | 29.1 | 60.0 | 3.9 | 7.0 |
| 1996 | 1,172 | 2,333 | 153 | 286 | 3,944 | 29.7 | 59.2 | 3.9 | 7.2 |
| 1997 | 1,196 | 2,301 | 152 | 292 | 3,941 | 30.4 | 58.4 | 3.9 | 7.4 |
| | | | | | Female | | | | |
| 1980 | 604 | 2,819 | 716 | 246 | 4,385 | 13.8 | 64.3 | 16.3 | 5.6 |
| 1990 | 693 | 2,526 | 773 | 358 | 4,350 | 15.9 | 58.1 | 17.8 | 8.2 |
| 1991 | 727 | 2,503 | 778 | 367 | 4,375 | 16.6 | 57.2 | 17.8 | 8.4 |
| 1992 | 760 | 2,475 | 783 | 376 | 4,394 | 17.3 | 56.3 | 17.8 | 8.6 |
| 1993 | 793 | 2,444 | 790 | 383 | 4,410 | 18.0 | 55.4 | 17.9 | 8.7 |
| 1994 | 823 | 2,410 | 795 | 392 | 4,420 | 18.6 | 54.5 | 18.0 | 8.9 |
| 1995 | 851 | 2,377 | 799 | 401 | 4,428 | 19.2 | 53.7 | 18.0 | 9.0 |
| 1996 | 874 | 2,343 | 802 | 412 | 4,431 | 19.7 | 52.9 | 18.1 | 9.3 |
| 1997 | 899 | 2,309 | 803 | 421 | 4,432 | 20.3 | 52.1 | 18.1 | 9.5 |

[1]As of 1 January of a given year
Source: based on HSCO data

The great majority of the population of Hungary belongs to the Hungarian ethnic group. The Gypsies are the second largest group. A significant part of the Gypsy population bears characteristics of an earlier stage of the demographic transition (e.g. relatively high fertility and young age structure). The overall increase of social inequalities in Hungary during the first period of economic transformation strikes the Gypsies among others (Table 8.5).

**Table 8.3: Rural and Urban Population, 1920–1997, selected years[1]**

| Year | Budapest | Other urban areas | Rural areas | Total | Budapest | Other urban areas | Rural areas | Total |
|---|---|---|---|---|---|---|---|---|
| | 1,000 | | | | % | | | |
| 1920 | 1,232 | 2,696 | 4,059 | 7,987 | 15.4 | 33.8 | 50.8 | 100.0 |
| 1930 | 1,443 | 2,902 | 4,340 | 8,685 | 16.6 | 33.4 | 50.0 | 100.0 |
| 1941 | 1,713 | 3,120 | 4,483 | 9,316 | 18.4 | 33.5 | 48.1 | 100.0 |
| 1949 | 1,590 | 3,039 | 4,576 | 9,205 | 17.3 | 33.0 | 49.7 | 100.0 |
| 1960 | 1,783 | 3,515 | 4,662 | 9,961 | 17.9 | 35.3 | 46.8 | 100.0 |
| 1970 | 2,001 | 3,984 | 4,337 | 10,322 | 19.4 | 38.6 | 42.0 | 100.0 |
| 1980 | 2,059 | 4,551 | 4,099 | 10,709 | 19.2 | 42.5 | 38.3 | 100.0 |
| 1990 | 2,017 | 4,567 | 3,791 | 10,375 | 19.4 | 44.0 | 36.6 | 100.0 |
| 1997 | 1,886 | 4,539 | 3,749 | 10,174 | 18.5 | 44.6 | 36.9 | 100.0 |

[1]As of 1 January of a given year
Source: based on HCSO data

**Table 8.4: Labour Force Activity by Sex, 1993–1997**

| | 1993 | 1994 | 1995 | 1996 | 1997 |
|---|---|---|---|---|---|
| | Participation rate | | | | |
| Male | 64.0 | 62.4 | 61.7 | 61.1 | 60.4 |
| Female | 48.5 | 46.3 | 43.8 | 43.4 | 42.8 |
| Total | 56.0 | 54.0 | 52.4 | 51.8 | 51.2 |
| | Unemployment rate | | | | |
| Male | 13.2 | 11.8 | 11.3 | 10.7 | 9.5 |
| Female | 10.4 | 9.4 | 8.7 | 8.8 | 7.8 |
| Total | 11.9 | 10.7 | 10.2 | 9.9 | 8.7 |

Source: HSCO, 1997b

**Table 8.5: Population by Ethnic Group, 1941–1990, selected years**

| Year | Total | Hungarian | Slovak | Romanian | Croatian | German | Gipsy | Other |
|---|---|---|---|---|---|---|---|---|
| | Total number (1,000) | | | | | | | |
| 1941 | 9,316 | 8,918 | 17 | 8 | 4 | 302 | 27 | 40 |
| 1949 | 9,205 | 9,104 | 8 | 8 | 4 | 3 | 38 | 40 |
| 1960 | 9,961 | 9,837 | 14 | 12 | 15 | 9 | 56 | 18 |
| 1980 | 10,709 | 10,639 | 9 | 9 | 14 | 11 | .. | 27[1] |
| 1990 | 10,375 | 10,142 | 10 | 11 | 14 | 31 | 143 | 24 |
| | Percentage | | | | | | | |
| 1941 | 100.0 | 95.8 | 0.2 | 0.1 | 0.0 | 3.2 | 0.3 | 0.4 |
| 1949 | 100.0 | 99.0 | 0.1 | 0.1 | 0.0 | 0.0 | 0.4 | 0.4 |
| 1960 | 100.0 | 98.8 | 0.1 | 0.1 | 0.1 | 0.1 | 0.6 | 0.2 |
| 1980 | 100.0 | 99.3 | 0.1 | 0.1 | 0.1 | 0.1 | .. | 0.3[1] |
| 1990 | 100.0 | 97.8 | 0.1 | 0.1 | 0.1 | 0.3 | 1.4 | 0.2 |

[1]Including the Gipsy ethnic group
Source: HSCO, 1997a

### 8.1.2 Demographic Processes

The inclination to marry has been on a gradual decline since the mid-1970s but had fallen sharply over the few past years. The demographic aspects of this trend are many-folded. The marriage rates have dropped considerably both among those marrying for the first time and among those re-marrying.

In 1980, over 80 thousand marriages were formed which means that at least half of the non-married adult population had a wedding at that time (Table 8.6). The recent numbers are very low: number of marriages is under 50 thousand; marriage rate (per 1,000 non-married adults) among females in 1997 was just 21.9‰.

**Table 8.6: Main Indicators of Nuptiality, 1980, 1990–1998**

| Year | Marriages | | | | Average age at marriage | |
|---|---|---|---|---|---|---|
| | Total number | Per 1,000 inhabitants | Per 1,000 non-married persons aged 15+ | | | |
| | | | Male | Female | Male | Female |
| 1980 | 80,331 | 7.5 | 68.7 | 51.1 | 27.2 | 24.2 |
| 1990 | 66,405 | 6.4 | 47.4 | 35.9 | 27.4 | 24.4 |
| 1991 | 61,198 | 5.9 | 42.3 | 32.3 | 27.4 | 24.4 |
| 1992 | 57,005 | 5.5 | 38.3 | 29.3 | 27.4 | 24.4 |
| 1993 | 54,099 | 5.3 | 35.4 | 27.2 | 27.6 | 24.5 |
| 1994 | 54,114 | 5.3 | 34.6 | 26.7 | 28.1 | 25.0 |
| 1995 | 53,463 | 5.2 | 33.5 | 25.8 | 28.3 | 25.3 |
| 1996 | 48,930 | 4.8 | 30.1 | 23.3 | 28.5 | 25.4 |
| 1997 | 46,905 | 4.6 | 28.3 | 21.9 | 29.7 | 26.6 |
| 1998[1] | 45,500 | 4.5 | 27.0 | 20.9 | .. | .. |

[1]Preliminary data
Source: HSCO, 1997a

At the same time, the increasing average age at marriage is evident. It appears that a new pattern of marriage is forming, which is similar to that one in the Western countries. After the fall of the "Iron Curtain" another well-known East-West "border", also known as Hajnal's line of different demographic patterns (Hajnal, 1965), started to disappear at the end of the century.

However, the number of divorces still remains to be rather high in Hungary (Table 8.7) and regional differences in fertility level still form an East-West divide in Hungary.

Over the past decades, the fertility level has shown – though with fluctuations – a basically downward trend. After the Second World War it was in Hungary where, for the first time in Europe, fertility dropped below-replacement level, and this situation has lasted longer than anywhere else for already over thirty five years. In 1997, total fertility rate of 1.38 and the completed fertility of generations with an average number of children between 1.85 and 1.90 were by about 35% and 10%

below-replacement level, respectively (yet this present fertility level does not belong to the lowest ones in Europe).

**Table 8.7: Main Indicators of Divorce, 1980, 1990–1998**

| Year | Divorces | | | | Average age at divorce | |
|---|---|---|---|---|---|---|
| | Total number | Per 1000 | | | Male | Female |
| | | Married couples | Inhabitants | Marriages | | |
| 1980 | 27,797 | 9.9 | 2.6 | 346.0 | 35.7 | 32.6 |
| 1990 | 24,888 | 9.9 | 2.4 | 374.8 | 36.7 | 33.8 |
| 1991 | 24,433 | 9.8 | 2.4 | 399.2 | 36.7 | 33.7 |
| 1992 | 21,607 | 8.8 | 2.1 | 379.0 | 36.7 | 33.8 |
| 1993 | 22,350 | 9.2 | 2.2 | 413.1 | 36.8 | 33.9 |
| 1994 | 23,417 | 9.8 | 2.3 | 432.7 | 37.2 | 34.3 |
| 1995 | 24,857 | 10.5 | 2.4 | 464.9 | 37.2 | 34.3 |
| 1996 | 22,590 | 9.7 | 2.2 | 461.7 | 37.7 | 34.8 |
| 1997 | 24,992 | 10.9 | 2.5 | 532.8 | 38.0 | 35.1 |
| 1998[1] | 25,500 | 11.3 | 2.5 | 560.4 | .. | .. |

[1]Preliminary data
Source: HSCO, 1997a

As in the case of nuptiality, fertility also exhibits a pattern of change. Along with the decline of the level of fertility, very significant changes in age-specific fertility rates can be observed. Fertility rates among women aged under 25 have dropped drastically, while there has been a significant increase of birth intensity among women over 30. This change of pattern may explain partly the fall in total fertility rate (Table 8.8 and Figure 8.4). However, it is not clear, how much this overall postponement of childbirth would decrease the completed fertility in the birth cohorts mostly affected by the economic transformation.

It should be noted that during the first five years (1990–1995) of the political, social and economic transformation fertility had not dropped so drastically in Hungary as in the other countries of the ex-Soviet block. This can partly be attributed to a stable family policy, preserving the former allocations even at the expense of considerable budget expenditures, and partly to the strongly children-oriented scale of values of the Hungarian society. The effectiveness of family policy is well reflected in Figure 8.5.

It can be seen that completed fertility of birth cohorts grew, after the system of family allowances was introduced in the middle of the 1960's. Moreover, according to family planning surveys, there is practically no deliberate childlessness in Hungary: a great number of surveys made in Hungary and abroad have produced evidence that extremely high value is set on children and bringing up children in Hungary (HCSO/DRI, 1999).

As a consequence of low nuptiality level and increasing popularity of cohabitation, the proportions of those living together without marriage and of children born out of wedlock are on the rise; the present 25% proportion is the highest in this century.

**Table 8.8: Main Indicators of Fertility and Demographic Reproduction, 1980, 1990–1998**

| Year | Live births | | Total fertility rate | Average age of mother | Live births out of wedlock | Average of birth order | Net reproduction rate |
|---|---|---|---|---|---|---|---|
| | Total number | Per 1,000 inhabitants | | | % | | |
| 1980 | 148,673 | 13.9 | 1.92 | 24.5 | 7.1 | 1.82 | 0.909 |
| 1990 | 125,679 | 12.1 | 1.84 | 25.2 | 13.1 | 1.88 | 0.889 |
| 1991 | 127,207 | 12.3 | 1.86 | 25.2 | 14.1 | 1.88 | 0.885 |
| 1992 | 121,724 | 11.8 | 1.77 | 25.2 | 15.6 | 1.90 | 0.839 |
| 1993 | 117,033 | 11.4 | 1.69 | 25.3 | 17.6 | 1.93 | 0.804 |
| 1994 | 115,598 | 11.3 | 1.64 | 25.4 | 19.4 | 1.95 | 0.784 |
| 1995 | 112,054 | 11.0 | 1.57 | 25.5 | 20.7 | 1.95 | 0.750 |
| 1996 | 105,272 | 10.9 | 1.46 | 25.6 | 22.6 | 1.94 | 0.693 |
| 1997 | 100,350 | 9.9 | 1.38 | 25.7 | 25.0 | 1.96 | 0.655 |
| 1998[1] | 97,500 | 9.6 | 1.33 | .. | 26.4 | 1.94 | .. |

[1]Preliminary data
Source: HSCO, 1997a

A specific feature of the Hungarian demographic situation is that mortality – compared to the socio-economic and cultural level of the country – is unacceptably high. The mortality level had gradually improved until the mid-1960s, but since then, has significantly deteriorated, especially in the male population (Table 8.9).

**Table 8.9: Main Indicators of Mortality, 1980, 1990–1998**

| Year | Deaths | | Deceased under 1 year | | Life expectancy at birth | |
|---|---|---|---|---|---|---|
| | Total number | Per 1,000 inhabitants | Total number | Per 1,000 live births | Males | Females |
| 1980 | 145,355 | 13.6 | 3,443 | 23.2 | 65.45 | 72.70 |
| 1990 | 145,660 | 14.1 | 1,863 | 14.8 | 65.13 | 73.71 |
| 1991 | 144,813 | 14.0 | 1,989 | 15.6 | .. | .. |
| 1992 | 148,781 | 14.4 | 1,714 | 14.1 | .. | .. |
| 1993 | 150,244 | 14.6 | 1,458 | 12.5 | .. | .. |
| 1994 | 146,889 | 14.3 | 1,335 | 11.5 | .. | .. |
| 1995 | 145,431 | 14.2 | 1,195 | 10.7 | .. | .. |
| 1996 | 143,130 | 14.0 | 1,148 | 10.9 | 66.06 | 74.70 |
| 1997 | 139,434 | 13.7 | 989 | 9.9 | .. | .. |
| 1998[1] | 141,000 | 13.9 | 950 | 9.7 | .. | .. |

[1]Preliminary data
Source: based on HSCO data

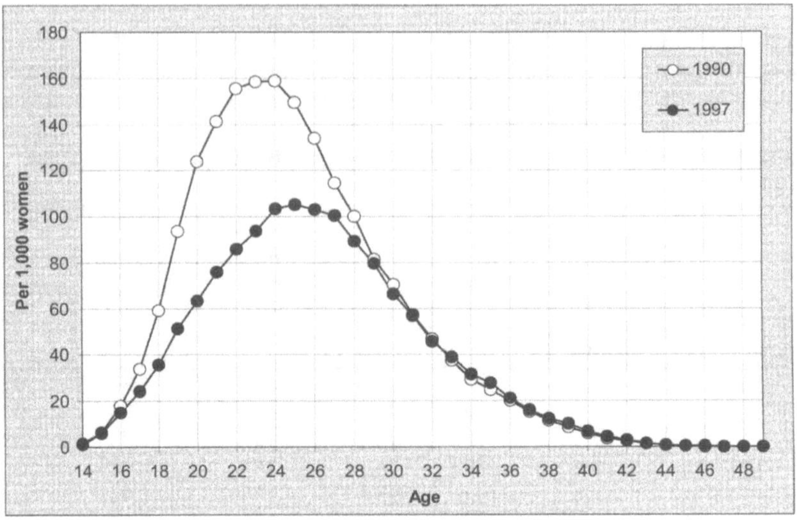


**Figure 8.4: Age-specific Fertility Rates, 1990 and 1997**
Source: author's calculations based on HSCO data

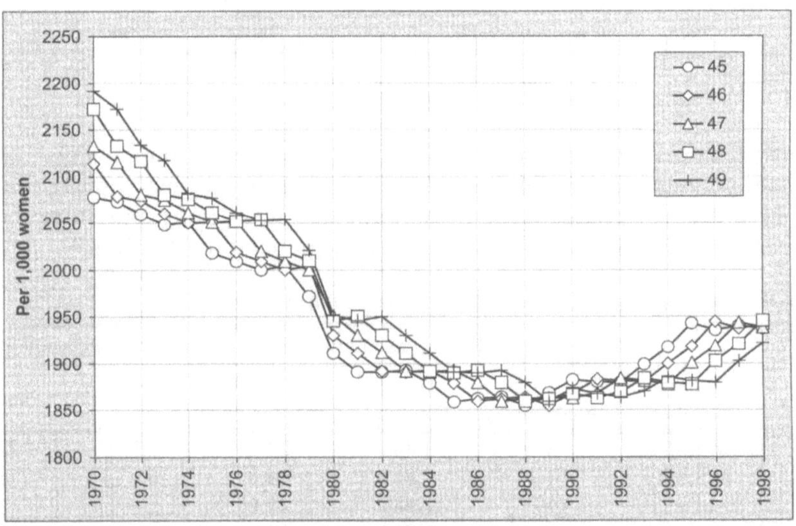


**Figure 8.5. Completed Fertility Rate for Women Aged 45–49, 1970–1998**
Source: author's calculations based on HSCO data

Between 1960 and 1993, the crude mortality rate increased by almost 50% and life expectancy at age 30 for males fell by 4 years. Recently, only the half of newly born boys can expect to survive up to age 65. In certain age groups, increase of mortality rates reached 300% (Figure 8.6).

In the early 1990s, the mortality indicators signalled a new trend of deterioration with a culminating point, i.e. mortality rate of 14.6‰ in 1993. Since then, the mortality rates have improved moderately but continuously. The mortality rate in 1997 was lower by over 6% compared to that of 1993. The average life expectancy of males at birth in 1997 was 66.4 years, which exceeded the 1993 level by 1.9 years; however it was still below the best year ever, i.e. 1966, by over a year. The average life expectancy of females, which in 1997 was 75.1 years, has been rising continuously in the recent years but, nevertheless, compared to developed countries it is still rather low.

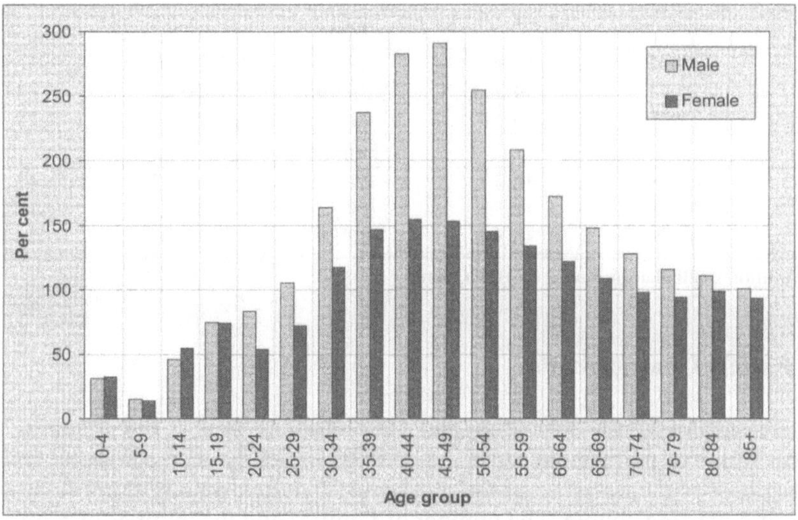


**Figure 8.6: Age-specific Mortality Rates by Sex, 1993 (1961–1965 average values = 100)**

Source: based on HSCO data

However, the internal differences in mortality remain highly pronounced. There is a difference in life expectancy at birth of 5–10 years between groups of population depending on a number of socio-demographic features such as regional, cultural, occupational and ethnic characteristics. Table 8.10 shows the differences in life duration by marital status. It can be seen that the differences significantly exceed 10 years. The life expectancy gap in a married couple with husband aged 35 and wife aged 30 is 12 years, which is the main cause of the development of an "old widow" phenomenon in Hungary.

Infant mortality has gradually decreased over the past decades. However, the special regional and cultural mortality differentials are still significant. It is favourable phenomenon that in the recent years a health-conscious approach has become more common – at least in certain groups of the society.

To address the consequences of the demographic processes on the population size and structure it is necessary to consider population projections. All variants of the population projections expect a further lasting and significant population decline and further certain and considerable ageing process. Due to peculiarities of the age composition of the population and to demographic processes, the decrease of the population size has become a self-generating process. However, demographically sensitive social policy measures and international migration could still influence the extent.

**Table 8.10: Life Expectancy at Certain Ages by Marital Status, 1992**

| Age | Never-married | Married | Widowed | Divorced | Total |
|---|---|---|---|---|---|
| | | | Male | | |
| 30 | 30.30 | 38.96 | 29.11 | 30.40 | 36.74 |
| 35 | 26.25 | 34.35 | 24.99 | 26.21 | 31.31 |
| 40 | 22.70 | 29.91 | 21.29 | 22.84 | 28.15 |
| | | | Female | | |
| 30 | 41.29 | 46.33 | 41.91 | 43.32 | 45.31 |
| 35 | 36.86 | 41.55 | 37.32 | 39.03 | 40.57 |
| 40 | 32.57 | 36.89 | 32.89 | 34.82 | 35.99 |

Source: author's calculations based on HSCO data

### 8.1.3 Family Characteristics

The processes of family formation and dissolution as well as the changing role of different forms of partnership cause major shifts in family characteristics. One of the main features is the decrease in the number of families, among them families consisting of a married couple. The number of families and the number of family members achieved its peak at 3 and 8 million in 1980, respectively. Due to high divorce and low re-marriage rates, the number of one-parent families grew rapidly. The increase in number of consensual unions did not yet counterbalance the decline in the number of married couples. However, the share of families without children did not rise in the last two decades. It is expected that the total number of families would decrease further in the future. Contrary, the spread of cohabitation is expected to increase markedly, while the number of one-parent families would remain around half a million (Table 8.11).

The very special feature of Hungarian families is that the average number of children in families with children is higher in consensual unions than in families of married couples. This phenomenon may be regarded as a consequence of the relatively big heterogeneity of the demographic characteristics across Hungary, but also partly as an effect of ethnic differences (Table 8.12).

The observations show that in Hungary the general demographic changes (population decline and ageing) develop in a way that the number of units playing primary role in the population reproduction (married people, families with married couple, family households) decreases, while the number of units playing lesser role in reproduction (non-married people, families without married couple, single people) increases. This trend could further contribute to a low level of fertility and continuous population decline.

**Table 8.11: Families by Family Structure, 1949–1996, selected years**

| Year | Families | Married couples or consensual unions | | | One-parent family with children | | |
|---|---|---|---|---|---|---|---|
| | Total | Total | Without children | With children | Total | Single fathers | Single mothers |
| | | | | Total number (1,000) | | | |
| 1949 | 2,385 | 2,078 | 640 | 1,439 | 307 | 39 | 268 |
| 1960 | 2,757 | 2,388 | 849 | 1,539 | 366 | 33 | 336 |
| 1970 | 2,891 | 2,598 | 874 | 1,623 | 293 | 37 | 256 |
| 1980 | 3,028 | 2,686 | 1,066 | 1,621 | 341 | 56 | 285 |
| 1990 | 2,896 | 2,446 | 992 | 1,454 | 450 | 89 | 361 |
| 1996 | 2,880 | 2,433 | 956 | 1,477 | 447 | 68 | 379 |
| | | | | Percentage | | | |
| 1949 | 100.0 | 87.1 | 26.8 | 60.3 | 12.9 | 1.6 | 11.2 |
| 1960 | 100.0 | 86.6 | 30.8 | 55.8 | 13.4 | 1.2 | 12.2 |
| 1970 | 100.0 | 89.8 | 33.7 | 56.1 | 10.2 | 1.3 | 8.9 |
| 1980 | 100.0 | 88.7 | 35.2 | 53.5 | 11.3 | 1.9 | 9.4 |
| 1990 | 100.0 | 84.5 | 34.3 | 50.2 | 15.5 | 3.1 | 12.5 |
| 1996 | 100.0 | 84.5 | 33.2 | 51.3 | 15.5 | 2.4 | 13.1 |

Source: based on HCSO data

**Table 8.12: Average Number of Children in Family by Family Arrangement, Age of Children and Settlement, 1990 and 1996**

| Family arrangement | All children | | | | Children under age 15 | | | |
|---|---|---|---|---|---|---|---|---|
| | Total | Budapest | Other urban areas | Rural areas | Total | Budapest | Other urban areas | Rural areas |
| | | | | 1990 | | | | |
| Consensual unions | 1.78 | 1.60 | 1.78 | 1.89 | 1.28 | 1.11 | 1.28 | 1.37 |
| Married couples | 1.69 | 1.61 | 1.69 | 1.72 | 1.14 | 1.03 | 1.16 | 1.17 |
| | | | | 1996 | | | | |
| Consensual unions | 1.75 | 1.57 | 1.78 | 1.82 | 1.24 | 1.05 | 1.27 | 1.32 |
| Married couples | 1.70 | 1.62 | 1.68 | 1.75 | 1.02 | 0.86 | 1.03 | 1.07 |

Source: based on HSCO data

Thus, we can conclude that an urgent elaboration of a new family policy is needed, which prefers strongly stable pair-connections taking long-term responsibility for having children. Special attention has to be paid to family formation by the cohorts born in the 1970s, because for the Hungarian population, it is the only chance in a long time to limit the population decline by using internal resources.

The population problems in Hungary are well known. The great majority of the public regards the population decline as an unfavourable process that should be stopped in the future. More than 70% of the interviewed persons gave the opinion that the government should continue with the well-elaborated family policy measures (HSCO/DRI, 1999). The popularity of families with two and more children remains very high; 78% of the adult population agree that the happiness of having children compensates the hard work and costs of childbearing (Table 8.13).

**Table 8.13: Public Attitudes Towards Families with Different Number of Children, 1989, 1995 and 1997, per cent**

| Number of children in a family | Preferences | | |
|---|---|---|---|
| | 1989 | 1995 | 1997 |
| No child | 16 | 17 | 13 |
| One child | 62 | 57 | 51 |
| Two children | 78 | 77 | 78 |
| Three children | 65 | 58 | 68 |
| Four or more children | 39 | 34 | 40 |

Source: HSCO/DRI, 1999

## 8.2 Population-related Policies and Programmes

### 8.2.1 Principles and Characteristics of Population Policy

In Hungary, the population policy is designed to influence the demographic processes. It already has a long history. After the Second World War, the former regime elaborated the so-called mid- and long-term population policy concepts several times, e.g. the Government decrees of 1953, 1973 and 1984. Apart from the decree of 1953, which is basically known for liberalisation of abortions, the various sets of measures together formed the Hungarian family policy system.

The first Government after the change of regime in 1990 established some new measures in 1990–1992 and adopted a resolution on principles and improvement of population policy in 1994.

During the period from 1994 to 1998, family policy has shifted to a "poverty prevention" policy based on allowance system. The allowance system, which made financial support available mainly for low-income families, created therefore financial disincentives for the middle class people in respect to bringing up children. The new allowance restrictions, which were introduced in 1996, had a clear resonance in the trend of the number of births. The 100,000 births in 1998 represented the lowest level ever in history.

The Government position established in 1998 is that the country's demographic situation represents a national and social issue of great importance, the solution of which calls for all-governmental responsibility and joining of forces of the society.

Among the population-related aims of the Government are: to moderate and, subsequently, to stop the process of population decline and – later on – to achieve a modest population increase, along with an age structure of the population becoming more favourable. Achieving an increased and stabilised level in fertility, improving mortality conditions and strengthening the financial and social situation of families are also regarded as important tasks. These aims are to be achieved by continuous, wide-ranging and co-ordinated, well-timed measures.

Of course, implementation of a new policy requires the corresponding financial means. The resources to be used for social, family and population policy purposes are partly subject to the economic position of the country, the present and future performance of the economy and partly to the enforcement of the priorities identified by the Government.

Two actions that the Government established in 1998 and 1999 should be mentioned. First, family allowance was restored as a citizen's right in 1998. Second, the Ministry for Social Affairs and Family Issues elaborated a new concept of family policy. This concept suggests first of all the renewal of a childcare fee, which will be income related according to suggestions.

In the interest of the most effective use of resources and of best arrangements, the Government assists research that provides a basis for the population and family policy, and efforts aiming at the harmonisation of the research activities furthering comparisons on international level. The Board for Population Policy, which is chaired by the President of Hungary, was established on a high government level.

### 8.2.2 International Migration Policy

Since the last third of the 1980s, the phenomenon of migration has obviously been a challenge for Hungary, the Hungarian politics, the Government, the society, the public and also statistics. After the former isolation for several decades, migration has become an essential process of the Hungarian society. When travel restrictions were lifted in 1998, the economic, political and social situation of the neighbouring countries and the ethnic conflicts have produced unprecedented migration processes and situation in Hungary. For some immigrants, Hungary became a destination country, for others – a transit point.

An increasing number of immigrants arrived in Hungary from the middle of the 1980s till 1990. At the beginning of the economic, social and political changes in the Eastern European countries, the number of migrants rapidly increased then began to decrease and it has become consolidated on a low yearly level of a few thousand. In the early immigration phase, mainly people of the Hungarian minorities living in the neighbouring countries moved to Hungary. The total number of emigrants, i.e. Hungarian citizens living abroad legally, is estimated at over 100 thousand.

By setting up the fundamental elements of political democracy, the Hungarian Government abolished the restrictions of the freedom of movement first in its 1989 Emigration Act, according to which no administrative restrictions are imposed on Hungarian citizens travelling from and to Hungary. Pursuant to the constitution, each person, staying legally in the country, has the right of the freedom of movement, of free choice of domicile and the freedom of leaving the residence (country). It was followed in 1993 by the acts on citizenship and on entry into and residence in Hungary of foreigners and on immigration. Both acts follow the practice of strict control of immigration currently present in Europe.

In respect to refugees, Hungary was signatory to the 1989 Geneva Convention on refugees. The Act on Refugees was passed by the Parliament in 1997 and entered into force in March 1998. This act abolished the geographical restrictions. Joining of the Schengen Convention by Hungary will probably result in further severe tightening of the conditions of migration to Hungary and the circumstances of border crossings in the future.

### 8.2.3 Family Policy and Measures Related to Fertility

In the past decades, numerous measures have been adopted in Hungary in order to promote readiness to have children and to improve the financial situation of families with children. The major part of the costs of the support is covered by the state budget, while a smaller part is provided for by social insurance and employees. The local self-governments play a significant role in social support and in the maintenance and support of children's institutions.

The most important elements of the support system include: maternity allowance (transformed first to pregnancy allowance, later on to maternity aid); childbirth and maternity leave; family allowance; tax and work-related benefits; allowances for those living in unfavourable conditions; and family-related social services (children's preschool institutions; mother and child health care services, and so on). *Maternity allowance* was called pregnancy allowance in 1993 and in 1996 was transformed into maternity aid. It is a one-time payoff, which equals 1.5 of the minimum old-age pension, being valid at the date of delivery. Mothers using the benefit of *childbirth leave* receive 70% of their previous wages and can stay at home for the purpose of childcare, as they would be on sick leave. Moreover, *additional leave* up to a few days is provided on yearly basis for working mothers having child under 16.

Hungary was the first country where a *childcare allowance* was provided for. A specified amount is paid to a parent staying at home for child-care till the age 3 of a child. In 1985, a new element in the family support system, i.e. the *childcare fee*, was introduced. This measure made possible for mothers to stay at home to take care of children until the age of 2 and to receive 75% of their average earnings preceding childbirth. It was cancelled in 1996 and is going to be re-introduced from 2000. Furthermore, from 1993 on, *childbearing support* allows a mother to stay at home if she cares for three or more children in her own household and the youngest of them is aged 3 to 8 years. The monthly sum of the support is equal to that of the minimum monthly old-age pension.

*Family allowance* is the major general instrument of regular monthly financial support of families. In 1998, the Parliament re-established the family allowance system as a citizen's right and made it conditional upon school attendance by children of school age.

In Hungary, there is a strict personal income tax. To support families with children through the tax system, a *tax benefit system for families* was developed. It was cancelled in 1995 and it is going to be re-established again. Taking into consideration the social situation of the family, local governments can also lower the fees to be paid for attendance of pre-school institutions by children.

If mother or father is caring for a sick child, she/he is entitled to a *"sick child" allowance*. As well, a *system of mother and child health care services* is extraordinarily diverse and well developed. An expectant mother is under medical supervision throughout the whole duration of her pregnancy and can resort to pregnancy-consultation whenever she finds it necessary. Prenatal care is free of charge and favourable working conditions are usually provided for pregnant women in employment. Throughout the country, a well-organised network of district nurses is operating. Medical health care for infants and children is also free of charge.

Having a financial contribution from the Hungarian Government, local governments may provide regular and occasional support in cash or kind for families, depending upon their financial situation. The local governments also grant support for the families to finance the costs of housing, depending on their financial situation.

### 8.2.4 Regulation of Induced Abortion and Contraception

The regulation of abortion is stipulated by the 1992 act on the protection of foetal life. The standard basis of the law is protection of foetal life, the right of self-determination for the woman, her right of private life, founding of a family and of family life. Abortion is tolerated only within set limits and is not accepted as means of birth control and family planning. Prior to that, the Constitutional Court of Hungary had declared that both the complete ban on, and unlimited availability of abortion is anti-constitutional. The legislation had to decide upon the conditions under which the abortion could be performed.

Since abortion as means of family planning is considered unacceptable, prevention is important. It would be desirable that no woman gets pregnant against her will. The means of birth control should be contraception. A basic element of social consent is the applicability and availability of all accepted methods of contraception.

### 8.2.5 Health Policy

The Constitution of the Republic of Hungary recognises the right to health and physical fitness among civil rights. The Law on Health adopted in 1997 regulates health protection, the conditions and framework of health care system.

The legislation aims at the improvement of the state of health of individuals and thus of the population by regulating the conditions and means affecting health. The law emphasises the importance of establishing equal opportunity in respect of the availability of health services. The law includes general professional conditions and guarantees of health services. The legislation recognises the enforcement of personal freedom and of the right to self-determination as a basic principle. The cornerstone of the law is that the primary means of improvement of the state of health are preservation of health and prevention of diseases.

## 8.3 Some Principles of Population Policy for the Next Decades

To achieve the long-term demographic goals, some long-range principles of population policy can be emphasised for the forthcoming decades.

The most important population-policy task should be to increase the readiness to have children. To increase fertility, a social atmosphere and a wide-ranging set of measures are to be created which could make it possible that the number of births ensures the sustaining population development. In particular, better assistance should be provided to parents to help them fulfil their double commitments, i.e. in the workplace and at home.

In the future, the readiness to have and bring up children should be supported in a more definite, co-ordinated and target-oriented way than before. Thus, in addition to the improvement of the housing conditions of families with children and to ensuring the financial and institutional conditions for child care, it is necessary to improve the working conditions of mothers in the labour market: make flexible working hours and part-time jobs available; provide for safety in the workplace for mothers back from childcare leave; and encourage parents to divide work at home in a more balanced way.

Furthermore, it has to be a basic principle and to be ensured by all means that the number of planned and wanted pregnancies increases and the numbers of unplanned and unwanted decrease.

In order to reduce the number of abortions and to achieve conscious family planning, a wider use of modern contraceptives – including also the promotion of methods of natural family planning – has to be ensured. In addition to sexual education and development of the family planning network, a fast and easy access to modern contraceptives, covered partly by social insurance, should be provided widely free of charge.

Legal instruments should also be used for the purpose of improving the stability of marriages. Among others, the number of juvenile marriages is to be decreased and a possible reconciliation of couples in case of a ruined marriage is to be promoted not only by means of family law.

For reducing mortality, proper set of measures including progress of preventive medicine, modernisation of therapeutic measures and remedies, and wider access to care systems is to be established in order to decrease fatal diseases, which are frequent at the present. To prevent diseases causing death or long-term grave illness and to increase the general availability of the screening services, it seems to be necessary also to set up a screening system on a wide scale.

Besides the improvement of prevention and of treatment, a change in life-style has to be achieved by proper education, propaganda, direct government measures as well as joining of the forces of the society. For this purpose, it is required to limit harmful habits, i.e. excessive smoking, alcohol consumption, unhealthy eating habits, lack of physical exercise and overwork.

The health status of old people is to be improved by proper care, establishing suitable conditions for co-existence of several generations and the conditions of intergenerational provision of care and support. In this way, old people could live a long life – due to an increased life expectancy – in good health. Moreover, a special emphasis is to be laid on an increased rehabilitation of population, incapacitated for whatever reason, thus on re-integrating them into the society and also on improvement of their living, working and environmental conditions.

Finally, to ensure gender equality in all spheres of societal life, new legal rules, promoting equal socio-economic and political rights for men and women – including the responsibility of parents for bearing the family – are to be adopted.

## References

Hablicsek, L. (1995), *The First and Second Demographic Transition in Hungary and East Central Europe*, Working paper No. 54, Budapest: HCSO DRI.

Hajnal, J. (1965), European Marriage Patterns in Perspective, In: D.V. Glass and D.E.C. Eversley (eds.), *Population in History*, London.

HCSO (Hungarian Central Statistical Office) (1997a), *Demographic Yearbook*, Budapest: HCSO.

HCSO (Hungarian Central Statistical Office) (1997b), *Statistical Yearbook*, Budapest: HCSO.

HCSO/DRI (Hungarian Central Statistical Office/Demographic Research Institute) (1998), *Population Scenarios up to 2050*, Budapest: HCSO/DRI.

HCSO/DRI (Hungarian Central Statistical Office/Demographic Research Institute) (1999), *National Concept for Family Policy. Demographic Backgrounds,* Budapest: HCSO/DRI.

(1998), *National Report of Hungary for the Regional Population Conference*, Budapest.

van de Kaa, D.J. (1987), Europe's Second Demographic Transition, *Population Bulletin*, Vol. 42(1), p. 1–58.

# 9

# Population Development in Latvia

**Atis Berzins and Peteris Zvidrins**

## 9.1 Historical Development of the Population

Latvia has experienced an unusual pattern of population development. The demographic transition in the Baltic provinces of Russia began earlier than in other parts of tsarist Russia. Here, the demographic trends have been historically West-European rather than East-European. A notable decrease of fertility, including marital fertility, as well as of the natural growth of population, began in the last third of the 19th century. Since the middle of the 1920s, fertility has been under replacement level.

The annexation and incorporation of Latvia into the Soviet Union was followed by the deportation or extermination of about one-tenth of the population. Thousands fled to the West. The emigration of the bulk of intelligentsia seriously depleted country's demographic potential. The relative population losses in Latvia in the 1940s were among the largest in the world. The establishment of the Soviet regime opened an era of a vast influx of Soviet immigrants. Immigration accounted for the greatest part of the population growth up to the regaining of independence. This influx of migrants was the main cause of anxiety for ethnic Latvians who were facing the threat of becoming a minority in their own country. On 21 August 1991 Latvia regained its independence.

### 9.1.1 Social and Economic Situation

Latvia has entered a complex transition period to a free market economy, which entails substantial political, economic, and social changes. There are inevitable difficulties caused by the transition to basically new principles in a national economy.

Starting from 1991, the gross domestic product (GDP) in Latvia was rapidly falling. In 1995, the GDP per capita on average was 26.0% lower than in 1980. However, some positive results of the reforms in the economy of Latvia became apparent in the second part of the 1990s. In 1996, the GDP increased by 3.3%, and in 1997 – even by 8.6%. Since the middle of 1998, the GDP growth has become lower, and in 1998 it was only 3.6% (Central Statistical Bureau, 1999b, p. 27). Partly it is connected with the financial crisis in Russia. However, for several years the inflation in Latvia (8.4% in 1997 and 4.7% in 1998) has been lower than that of the neighbouring countries Lithuania and Estonia (LR Ekonomikas ministrija, 1998, p. 24). Many international credit and financial institutions positively evaluate the course of Latvia towards the improvement of basic macro-economic indicators. Latvia was granted a rather high credit rating.

### 9.1.2 Education

The post-war period up through 1989 has been characterised by the rapid growth in the proportion of literate population. In 1989, it was already 99%. The number and proportion of people with higher and secondary education has been growing and the number and proportion of people with low level of education has been decreasing. In 1989, compared to 1959, the number of people with a high level of education increased 4.1 times, those with secondary education 4.2 times, but the number of those with a low level of education has decreased by 37.6%. While in 1959 only 4.3% of the population were highly educated, in 1989 this number reached 13.8%; 14.3% of the population in 1959 and 46.6% in 1989 had a secondary level of education. The proportion of the population with a low level of education was 81.4% in 1959 and 39.6% in 1989 (Zvidrins *et al.*, 1998, p. 7).

The political and economic transformation in the 1990s has radically affected the system of education. Decentralisation has opened the way for forms of education to emerge that were not permitted under the earlier Soviet centralised educational system. Since 1991, there has been an opportunity to open private education schools, schools for ethnic minorities, and alternative schools. At the same time, since 1990 some negative developments were observed; among them an increase in the number of children not attending school.

### 9.1.3 Employment

During the Soviet period, the level of employment in Latvia was amongst the highest in the world, particularly among women. In the 1990s, several new trends have been observed in employment. The number of employed persons and their proportion in the total population has substantially decreased. Along with structural changes in production there is a gradual shift in the types of activities of employed persons. The proportion of persons employed in industry gradually decreases while the share of employed in services and similar type of activities is growing.

The acute problem nowadays is unemployment. In 1991, a process of downsizing and lay-off has begun. Persons who were close to the retirement age were made redundant first. People were laid-off primarily from the occupations that Soviet economic planners had expanded to serve the aims of their centralised administration (UNDP, 1997, p. 35).

In October 1999, the level of unemployment in Latvia reached 9.3%, which was the highest among the Baltic States and the other republics of the former USSR, but much lower than in most countries undergoing transition. However, the officially registered rate of unemployment in Latvia compared to other European countries is not very high. Research indicates that the real level of unemployment is much higher than the officially reported level. According to data from a labour survey, 13.8% of the economically active population were looking for work in November 1998 (Central Statistical Bureau, 1999b, p. 81). In the eastern regions of the country, the rate of unemployment is fairly high. The majority of unemployed are women, but their proportion is gradually decreasing. This is due to the development of service industries in the country.

### 9.1.4 Urban and Rural Population

A rapid growth of the urban population was one of the features of the Soviet period. As a result of the forced pace of industrialisation and city-oriented immigration from the other Soviet republics, the urbanisation rate jumped from 35% in 1939 to 52% in 1959, and to about 70% in the 1980s (Central Statistical Bureau, 1999b, p. 49). Larger cities grew at a faster rate.

The capital city, Riga, has an outstanding position in regard to its disproportionate share of the population of Latvia. Before the war, one-sixth of Latvia's population was concentrated in Riga. By the end of the 1970s, the concentration was up to over 33%, or over one half of the country's entire urban population. Such concentration of a large proportion of total population of a country in a single city is a very unusual case in the world.

The situation has changed since the restoration of Latvia's independence. The proportion of urban and rural population has not changed substantially (69% and 31%, accordingly), but the number of Riga's inhabitants (797 thousand at the beginning of 1999) is systematically decreasing (Central Statistical Bureau, 1999a, p. 40). Agricultural reforms and restitution of the land promote and encourage the return of former rural inhabitants to the countryside.

### 9.1.5 Housing

During the Soviet period, housing construction had increased steadily. Nevertheless, due to an exceptional influx of immigrants into Latvia, the average living space per person actually decreased. In the 1990s, substantial changes in housing construction and population supply with dwellings have taken place. There has been a rapid decrease in the amount of newly built housing. This particularly concerns housing construction financed by the state or local government enterprises and organisations. It has a negative impact on the improvement of housing conditions, especially for people with low income. However, due to a sharp decrease of the population (more than 200,000 people) in the 1990s, the average total floor space per capita has grown by 2.0 square meters reaching 21.8 square meters in 1998 (Central Statistical Bureau, 1999b, p. 121).

According to a household budget survey, in 1997 the majority of the population lived in tenement houses and one-fourth – in private homes or individual farms. About 4% of respondents, living in tenement houses, lived in communal flats. More than a third of households fell into a category of the so-called overcrowded dwellings, in which the number of occupants exceeds the number of rooms. Almost half of the families lived in two-room flats.

### 9.1.6 Ethnicity, Citizenship and Religion

The Latvian population has always consisted of representatives from different nationalities and ethnic groups. According to the last pre-war population census, in 1935 the total population of Latvia consisted of 77% Latvians and only 8.8% Russians. Permanent minorities in Latvia have been Jews (in 1935 – 4.9%) and Germans (3.3%). The proportion of other nationalities was insignificant (6%). During the period from the Soviet invasion in 1940 up to the first post-war national census in 1959, the number of Latvians in Latvia decreased from 1.5 million to 1.3 million people, which is about 200,000 less than before the Second World War. Up to the present time, this loss has not been made up for either by natural or migration growth or assimilation of minorities (Zvidrins, 1998). This is a unique case in the history of nations with a million and more people. Just after the war, the proportion of Latvians was rather high, exceeding 80–85% of the total population. This was due to the repatriation of Germans before the war as well as the extermination of Jews and Gypsies during the war.

Post-war deportations, particularly of Latvians and the immigration of newcomers from other Soviet republics, had a substantial impact on the ethnic composition of the population in Latvia. Latvia is distinguished among European states by a high proportion (26% in 1989) of foreign-born populations. Among non-Latvians the proportion was even higher – 51%. The number of Latvians gradually increased from 1,298,000 in 1959 to 1,387,000 in 1989, but it was still 79,000 less than in 1935. The proportion of Latvians in the total population had decreased from about 80% in 1940 to 52% in 1989. There was a rapid increase of the Slavonic population in Latvia (Ukrainians – 3.1 times, Belarus – 1.9 times, Russians – 1.6 times).

In the 1990s, the changes in the ethnic composition have been of another character. For the first time after the Second World War, the proportion of Latvians tended to increase gradually reaching 56% in 1998, but the number and the proportion of Russians, Belarus, and Ukrainians has decreased. In 1999, compared to 1989, there was a decrease of Russians by 117.1 thousand, or 12.9%, of Belarus by 24.1 thousand people, or 20.1%, and of Ukrainians by 21.3 thousand people, or 23.1%. The proportion of these nationalities has decreased from 41.9% to 39.1% (Central Statistical Bureau, 1999a, p. 38).

The institution of Latvian citizenship was restored in 1992. According to the Law on Citizenship adopted by the Saeima (the Parliament of Latvia) on 22 June 1994, with a few exceptions, only persons who were citizens of Latvia at the time of the

Soviet annexation in 1940 and their descendants are automatically entitled to Latvian citizenship. However, most of the other persons resident in Latvia could become citizens through naturalisation.

According to data based on the Latvian Population Register, there is still a high proportion of the resident population who are not citizens of Latvia (26.7% in 1999). Russians make up 66% of this group, Belarus – 12%, and Ukrainians – 9%. The proportion of ethnic Latvians among non-citizens is less than 2%.

Latvia is a multiconfessional country. The state legislation ensures freedom of consciousness and religious faith for members of various religious communities. The church is separated from the state. Due to historical development, the main religious confessions in Latvia are Lutheran, Catholic, Orthodox, Old-believers, and Baptists. In the late 1980s and early 1990s, the number of parishes in Latvia grew rapidly, particularly Lutheran and Catholic ones. Almost every second Latvian citizen belongs to a church. From the total membership of parishes, 42% are Lutherans, 42% – Catholics, 8% – Orthodox believers, 6% – Old-believers and 0.5% are Baptists.

## 9.2 Age and Sex Structure

Ageing of the population structure is taking place in Latvia both from the bottom of the population age pyramid (as a result of the decline of fertility) and from the top (the increase of the proportion and number of the population in older groups). The population aged 50 and older is growing more rapidly than the total population. Already in 1950, one out of four inhabitants, or 25.4%, was over the age of 50. In the following years, this indicator increased to 30.3% in 1990, and to 32.0% in 1999 (Central Statistical Bureau, 1999a, pp. 31–32). According to the forecasts of the Centre of Demography, University of Latvia, this indicator will continue to increase rapidly because numerous baby boom generations born in the post-war period will reach the age of 50 in the next few years. The proportion of the population over 60 has increased from 15.0% in 1959 to 20.3% in 1999. Correspondingly, the proportion of individuals over 70 increased from 6.8% to 9.4%, but those over 80 – from 1.4% to 2.5 %. Latvia has one of the highest proportions of elderly in Eastern Europe. Since 1996, the share of population aged 60 and over has exceeded that of children and adolescents aged 0–14 years. The mean age of the total population increased from 34.8 years in 1959 and 36.3 years in 1989 to 37.5 years in 1998 (Demografijas centrs, 1998, p. 5).

Until the 1990s, a considerable influx of immigrants of a working age was characteristic in Latvia, which perceptibly delayed ageing of the population, partially compensated the influence of low fertility on the population age structure, and diminished the threat of depopulation. In the 1990s, the directions of migration processes have radically changed, and the number of emigrants systematically exceeds the number of immigrants.

Women make up a greater part of the elderly. In 1999, there were 162 women for every 100 men in the age group of 50 and older. Among the elderly the disproportion of sexes is even higher, and among those over 80, this ratio is 324 (Central Statistical Bureau, 1999a, p. 33). The mean age of women has exceeded 40 years.

Because of the ageing of the population, a gradual increase of the demographic burden on the population of working age should be expected in Latvia as well as an aggravation of different problems which directly result from ageing – an increase in the proportion of pensioners, the problems of social protection, and health care for these people.

## 9.3 Family and Household Structure

Approximately 85% of the population live in families. In the period up to 1989, the number of families continuously grew. In 1989, compared to 1959, the number of families grew more rapidly (34.2%) than the population (28.2%), but the average family size dropped from 3.18 persons in 1959 to 3.12 persons in 1989. In the 1990s, the number of families has gradually decreased due to the population emigration to other countries. The number of one-parent families has been growing rapidly.

The concept of a household was not used in the population censuses from 1959 to 1989. However, the concept of a family closely resembled the household one. According to calculations of the Centre of Demography, University of Latvia, the number of households in 1989, compared to 1959, had increased by 25.2%. Meanwhile, the average size of a household remained almost unaltered and fluctuated between 2.3 and 2.4.

There is a relatively high proportion of single persons in this country. In 1989, 9.4% of the population had no families. According to the latest available data of the Central Statistical Bureau of Latvia, the proportion of single persons in 1998 was about 12%. The proportion of one-person households in the total number of households has reached 30% in 1998.

According to the results of the *Fertility and Family Survey* (FFS) conducted in Latvia in 1995, 65.0% of interviewed women and 67.9% of men lived with a partner. In terms of generations, the proportion of women living with a partner varies from 26.8% in the cohort born in 1975–1977 up to 75.0% in the cohort born in 1955–1960 (Demografijas centrs, 1996a; Zvidrins *et al.*, op. cit.).

Among the interviewed women living with a partner, 87.4% had children. In the group of women who have children and live in a partner relationship, 90.8% were legally married but 9.2% lived in non-marital cohabitation (including 5.8% who had been previously married). On the whole, among about twenty countries participating in the FFS, Latvia is at the bottom of the intermediate group with a prevalence of cohabitation similar to that in Belgium and East Germany. In Italy and Poland this level is much lower, but in Scandinavian countries, the Netherlands and France it is considerably higher (Klijzing and Macura, 1997, p. 889).

## 9.4 Nuptiality and Divorce

The reported crude marriage rate in Latvia was very high through the end of the 1980s (9.5‰ in 1986–1988). However, since 1989 it has been decreasing constantly (7.2‰ in 1992 and 3.9‰ in 1996–1998). The total marriage rate (at the age of 16–59) in 1990 for women was 1.25 and for men 1.21, but in 1998, correspondingly 0.54 and 0.52 (Central Statistical Bureau, 1999a, p. 146). Among European countries, Latvia is distinguished by a rapid decrease of the number of first marriages, and total female and male first marriage rates have dropped below 0.4, indicating that at present intensity of registered marriages at least a half of women and men will never marry.

A complex structure of different social, economic and cultural forces has caused the decreasing attractiveness of marriage (Manting, 1994). The shift in individual preferences has accompanied an increase of opportunities for young women and men. In part, the yearly number of marriages has decreased because young people tend to postpone marriage. Evidence of this is the rising average age of entering the first marriage. It has increased from 22.2 years in 1991 to 24.0 years in 1998 for women and from 23.9 to 26.0 for men, respectively (Central Statistical Bureau, 1999a, p. 143). On the other hand, the decline of marriage rates can also be explained by the emergence and wider spreading of consensual unions (cohabitation).

Judging from the FFS data, almost one-third of the interviewed women (29.3%) had begun their first partnership by the age of 19 years. From those respondents, 15.8% legally married without preceding cohabitation but 13.5% experienced non-marital cohabitation. In the cohort born in 1970–1975, more than two-fifths had a partnership relationship (Zvidrins *et al.*, op. cit.). This proves the tendency that in the 1990s there has been a shift in the attitude of young women towards non-marital cohabitation.

A high level of divorce has been one of the most prevalent demographic problems since the mid-1960s. It has been one of the highest in the world, reaching 5.5 divorces per 1,000 inhabitants in 1979 and 1992 (Figure 9.1). The divorce ratio per 100 marriages reached 50 or more since the early 1970s. However, after 1992, the total divorce rate has decreased from 0.84 for males and 0.79 for females in 1992 to slightly under 0.5 since 1995. Out of the total number of divorces, two-thirds of divorced partners had children. Over the recent years, the average number of common children in all divorced families was less than one (0.90 in 1998), and among them, 1.4 children in families, which had at least one child.

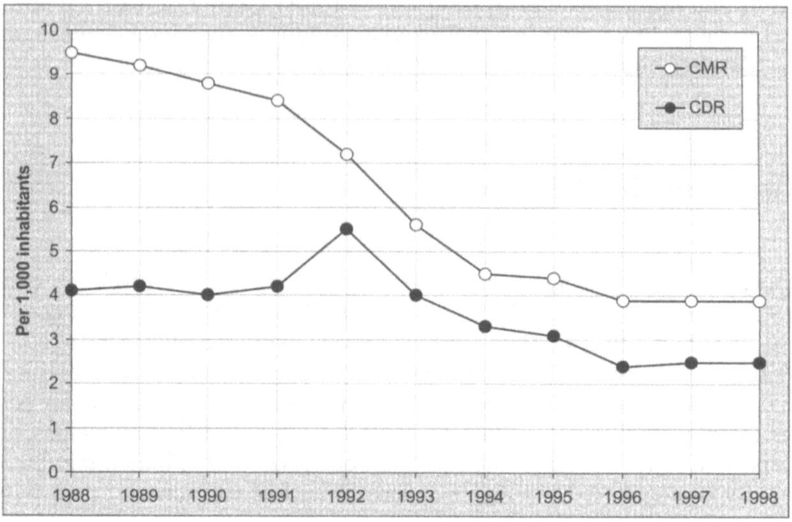


**Figure 9.1: Crude Marriage (CMR) and Divorce (CDR) Rates, 1988–1998**

Source: Central Statistical Bureau, 1999a, p. 63

## 9.5 Fertility

During many decades since the middle of the 1920s, the level of fertility in Latvia was not even sufficient for simple generation replacement. Only in the second part of the 1980s, after the introduction of some measures for stimulating fertility, it increased perceptibly and was slightly above the European average. The total fertility rate (TFR), which had fluctuated between 1.7 and 1.9 for an extended time period, again rose above 2.0 in the mid-1980s, and in 1986–1988 reached a maximum of 2.15.

In the 1990s, the situation has aggravated rapidly. Since 1988, the indicators of the number of births and also the special indicators of fertility have been falling. The TFR decreased from 2.11 in 1988 to 1.09 in 1998 (Central Statistical Bureau, 1999a, p. 88). Never before in Latvia's history has the fertility rate been as low as it is now. As a result, Latvia has one of the lowest fertility rates in the world. Thus, low fertility is currently the key national population problem.

The mean age at childbearing in Latvia has remained almost unchanged and fluctuated between 25 and 26 years from 1980 to 1990, and then slightly decreased. However, since 1994 it has increased again. A little less than 23 years is the mean age of women at birth of their first child. Most children are born to mothers who are 21 years old. About 12.5% of children are born to mothers aged 19 years and younger and only 7% to those aged over 35. The number of births out of wedlock continues to rise. In 1980, the percentage of live births out of wedlock was 12.5. It reached 16.9% in 1990; and in 1997–1998 it exceeded the one-third (37.1% in 1998) of the total number of live births (Central Statistical Bureau, 1999a, pp. 63, 89).

According to the Latvian FFS data, the desirable number of children in families of the respondents was on average 2.1. For different cohorts, it fluctuated from 2.0 to 2.3. A fairly small number of respondents wanted to have three or more children in their family (on average, only every fifth respondent).

There is an increase in extramarital fertility, especially in case of a first childbirth. Among the female respondents 17.0%, and 12.2% of the male respondents were not legally married at the time of their first childbirth. The proportion of mothers having their first child and living in a consensual union was 7.4%, while 9.6% of mothers lived without a partner. In younger age groups, birth out of wedlock was rather widespread. At the time of the first childbirth, 5.8% of women born in 1951–1955 and 16.8% of those born in 1971–1975 lived without a partner (Demografijas centrs, 1999b; Zvidrins *et al.*, op. cit.).

In younger cohorts, a relatively large proportion of women at the time of their first childbirth was living in consensual union. The proportion of women aged 20–24 years and having their first child while living in consensual unions was 10.6%, but 72.6% of the women were married. For respondents aged 18–19 years, the corresponding proportions were 14.3% and 57.1%.

For respondents in the age group under 20 years, the fertility rate systematically increases when we look at different generations. It shows that over the long-term life courses, a definite process of fertility renewal was going on. For the generation born in 1970–1975, the age-specific fertility rate was 229 births per 1,000 women compared to 106 births for the generation born in 1945–1950.

Many researchers have shown that there is no strong link between development indicators and fertility (Bongaarts and Watkins, 1996, p. 641). But it is clear that cardinal social and economic development changes in Latvia in the 1990s have substantially influenced the fertility decline. A high inflation rate combined with a slowdown of production, and increasing unemployment has had a negative impact on fertility transition. We also consider that demographic policy changes should be taken into account.

Analysis of the FFS data shows that most respondents support more substantial government involvement in stimulating fertility, as it was in the second half of the 1980s. They approve many measures aimed at fertility increase, but indicate that the most important are allowances and facilities for children's education, and improved housing conditions. In Latvia, values of marriage and children on life values scale are high enough, and two children are still considered to be the most desirable family model. Therefore, there are certain grounds to predict that by the turn of the century the fertility might begin to increase.

In Latvia, up to present, the most commonly used fertility regulation method was induced abortion. The high number of abortions per every 100 births evidences this. In the 1990s, this number has repeatedly exceeded the number of births (in 1998, it was 107 per 100 births). Lately, more than 70% of induced abortions were performed on women aged 20–35. From every 100 abortions, eight were done at the ages of 17–19 years. Still, there is a very limited awareness about fertility regulation and insufficient use of contraceptive methods in Latvian families.

## 9.6 Mortality and Natural Increase

Until the Second World War, the statistics on morbidity and mortality, as well as the average life expectancy in Latvia, were comparable to or were even slightly better than the average figures for Europe. Even at the end of the 1950s, male life expectancy in the Baltic region generally remained higher than in Eastern and Southern Europe, on the whole. For females, it was higher than the average level in Europe. However, during the following decades this position was lost. Only from 1990 until 1995, the life expectancy decreased by four years for males and by two years for females. It has been increasing slightly since 1995. In 1998, the average life expectancy at birth in Latvia was 64.1 years for males and 75.5 years for females (Central Statistical Bureau, 1999a, p. 123).

More than 80% of the total life expectancy decrease in 1991–1994 was due to increase of mortality among people of working age. The increase in male mortality was larger than that of female, and in the urban population larger than in the rural population. Diseases of the circulatory system contributed to a decrease of life expectancy by almost 50%; accidents, poisonings and injuries contributed – 36% for males and 29% for females (Krumins, 1997, p. 123). Probability per 1,000 of eventually dying from injury or poisoning in Latvia for males (about 200) and females (65–70) are among the highest in Europe.

Excessively high rates of cardiovascular disease, lung cancer, respiratory illnesses, and accidents are attributed to the high prevalence of risk factors such as smoking, consumption of alcohol and highly saturated fats, inadequate nutrition, and environmental pollution in some areas of the country. Mortality in rural areas remains very high, especially among younger people. A pattern of excess mortality is common in regions located further from the capital Riga, especially in Eastern Latvia.

Infant mortality in the Baltics had always been lower than in the rest of the tsarist Russia or in the USSR. By 1988–1989, the infant mortality rate had fallen to 11 per 1,000 and this value was close to the level in many developed countries. But the Soviet definition of infant mortality differed from that recommended by the WHO, and the rate should have been increased by between 20 and 25% to make them comparable. In the 1990s, infant mortality rate has increased considerably, reaching 15.8‰ in 1996 and 14.9‰ in 1998. Transition to the registration of infant deaths according to recommendations of the WHO produced about half of the increase, but the second half of this growth was due to an actual increase in infant mortality (Krumins and Zvidrins, 1992, p. 264).

A sharp decline of fertility and a slight increase of mortality during the first half of the 1990s determined a rapid decrease of the intensity of reproduction. The net reproduction rate decreased from 0.96 in 1989–1990 to 0.54 in 1996, and to 0.52 in 1998 (Central Statistical Bureau, 1999a, p. 88).

Due to the rapid decrease of fertility and growth of mortality, the natural population increase in Latvia has been negative since 1991 (Figure 9.2). For ethnic Latvians, it has been negative starting from 1992. During the 1990s, a natural increase has occurred only in the Gypsy population.

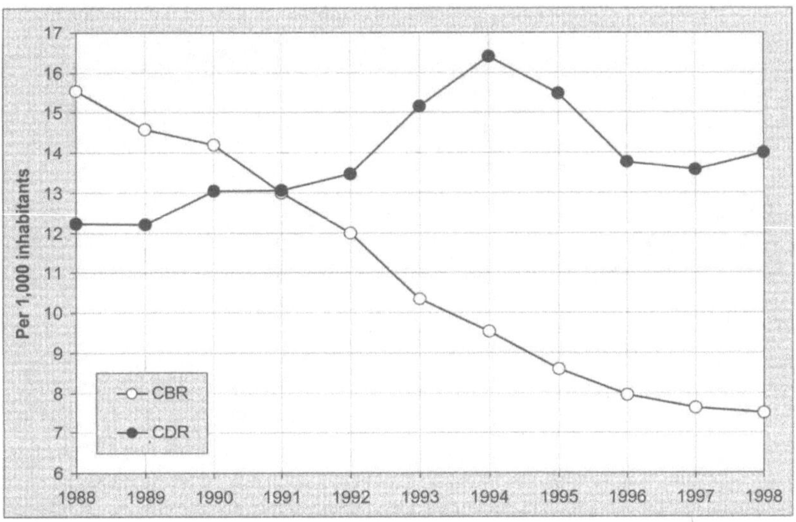


**Figure 9.2: Crude Birth (CBR) and Death (CDR) Rates, 1988–1998**

Source: Central Statistical Bureau, 1999a, p. 63

The negative natural increase reached 17,306 people in 1995 and then it slightly decreased to 15,790 in 1998. However, the negative rate (-6.5 per 1,000) is still one of the highest in the world. In 1995–1998, in all 33 administrative-territorial units (regions and cities) the depopulation could be observed (Central Statistical Bureau, 1999a, pp. 63–70). This situation is especially severe in Eastern Latvia. Moreover, the most likely variant of projections is that the population reproduction in the nearest future will be substantially below the level needed for a simple replacement of generations and the balance between births and deaths will be negative (Demografijas centrs, 1999, p. 11).

Summing up the analysis of the population reproduction processes, we may conclude that at present, a deep depopulation exists in Latvia. Never before have the fertility and population reproduction levels been so low. This is the people's response to economic and social hardship, as well as to the inactivity of the authorities in the field of population development (Demografijas centrs, 1996b, p. 15).

## 9.7 International Migration

Since the restoration of independence, Latvia has experienced drastic changes in both direction and intensity of migration. Some attempts to restrict immigration from the other Soviet republics were undertaken at the end of the 1980s. By 1989, there was already a sharp drop in arrivals, and net-migration has become negative since 1990 (Figure 9.3).

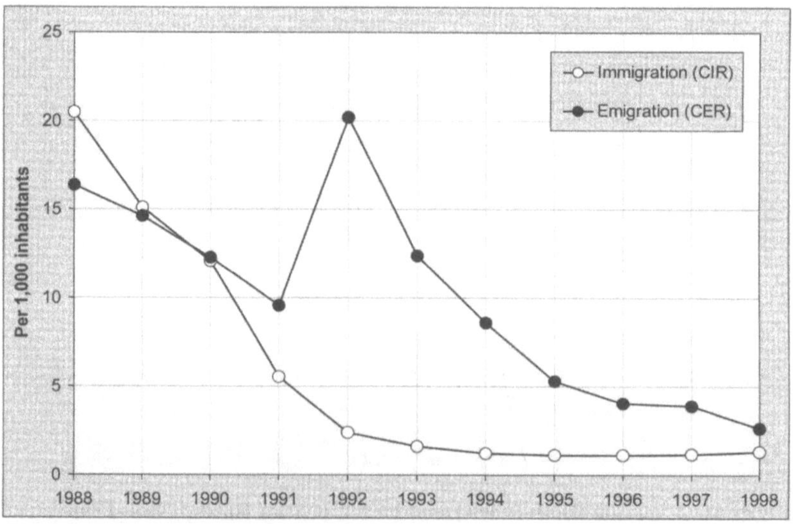


**Figure 9.3: Crude Migration Rates, 1988–1998**

Source: Central Statistical Bureau, 1999a, p. 25–26, 154

The level of emigration and repatriation reached its peak in 1992, when the former Soviet military forces and their family members left the Baltic States. The total number of people who left Latvia since 1990 amounts to about 200 thousand, but the net migration to about minus 130 thousand. One-third of immigrants were people who had previously emigrated from Latvia. The number of immigrants, mainly from the Commonwealth of Independent States (CIS), since 1995 has been less than 3 thousand per year. Migration has gradually lost its decisive role in changes of the total size of population.

The majority of emigrants go to the CIS, mainly to Russia, but also to Ukraine and Belarus, while only one-fifth go to other countries. Since Latvia regained political independence, emigration to the West has increased, but it has not acquired a mass character. The main destinations of emigration are Germany, Israel, and the USA. Latvia has a negative migration balance with neighbouring Lithuania, while with Estonia it is close to zero.

According to the opinions of demographers and other specialists in population studies surveyed by the Centre of Demography, University of Latvia, in the mid-1998, in the near future the net migration rate will be negative, however the values of rate will decrease. That situation, including the natural decrease of the population, inevitably will lead to a fall of the total size of Latvia's population.

## 9.8 Population Policy

Already in 1980, when Latvia had the status of a constituent part of the USSR, the authorities in Latvia approved a complex set of measures to improve the demographic situation, and particularly to stimulate fertility and natural increase of population. The programme "Population of Latvia in 1986–2000" was accepted in 1986. In addition, some other resolutions on the improvement of the demographic situation and the regulation of migration processes were introduced in the second half of the 1980s (Zvidrins, 1996, pp. 164–165).

The governments of Latvia in the 1990s had no specified objectives for population growth. Expressing appreciation of the effectiveness of the programme's approach to the regulation of population development, the first government of independent Latvia issued in December 1990 a decision to develop a new national programme on population. The following governments also had such intentions, but any government, mainly because of economic difficulties, never accepted this programme.

In December 1992, the Supreme Council of Latvia formed a Demographic Commission to draft and implement a demographic policy, but the work on it was ceased when a new parliament was elected in June 1993. A special governmental Demographic Committee was set up in early 1994, when preparations for the 1994 International Conference on Population and Development began. The government also formed a Commission on the Protection of Children's Rights.

In July 1995, the Cabinet of Ministers adopted regulations "On improvement of the demographic situation". In the mid-1995, the government also approved a list of national programmes to be elaborated, as well as overall conditions for their implementation. The programme "Population of Latvia (The Health and Social Security of the Nation)" was included in this list. The Minister of Welfare was given responsibility for the programme, however the programme was narrowed to actions to be taken by departments of the Ministry, and in reality it had a little effect on improving the demographic situation (Eglite, 1998, pp. 4–5).

Currently, the state undertakes part of the costs of support for children through various financial subsidies and monthly allowances. The state ensures the social protection of motherhood during pregnancy and the rearing of children. In recent years, a number of government decisions on financial resource assignment to improve family planning and to restrict abortions were passed. Nevertheless, the reproductive health-care system in general is deficient. Since Latvia regained independence, the government has pursued a policy of zero net migration, except for specific categories of the population.

## References

Bongaarts, J. and S.C. Watkins (1996), Social interactions and contemporary fertility transition, *Population and Development Review*, Vol. 22(4), pp. 639–682.

Central Statistical Bureau of Latvia (1999a), *Demographic Yearbook*, Riga.

Central Statistical Bureau of Latvia (1999b), *Statistical Yearbook of Latvia*, Riga.

Demografijas centrs (1996a), *Gimene un dzimstiba Latvija*, Riga.

Demografijas centrs (1996b), *Latvijas iedzivotaju paaudzu nomaina*, Riga.

Demografijas centrs (1998), *Muza otra puse Latvija*, Riga.

Demografijas centrs (1999), *Latvijas demografiskas attistibas prognozes: 1998–2025 gads*, Riga.

Eglite, P. (1998), Declared and undeclared population policy in Latvia, Paper presented at the international conference on Regularities and Inconsistencies of Demographic Development: Preconditions for the Replacement of Generations, Vilnius, 8–9 October 1998.

Krumins, J. (1997), Health and mortality during a transition to a market economy: case of Latvia, *Revue Baltique*, No. 10, pp. 114–129.

Krumins, J. and P. Zvidrins (1992), Recent mortality trends in the three Baltic States, *Population Studies*, Vol. 46, pp. 259–273.

Klijzing, E. and M. Macura (1997), Cohabitation and extra-marital childbearing: early FFS evidence. In: *International Population Conference Beijing*, Vol. 2, pp. 885–901.

LR Ekonomikas ministrija (1998), *Zinojums par Latvijas tautsaimniecibas attistibu*, Riga.

Manting, D. (1994), *Dynamics in Marriage and Cohabitation: An Inter-Temporal, Life Course Analysis of First Union Formation and Dissolution*, Amsterdam: Thesis Publishers.

UNDP (United Nations Development Programme) (1997), *Latvia. Human Development Report*, Riga.

Zvidrins, P. (1996), A note on the demographic situation and population policy in Latvia, *Studia Demograficzne*, No. 1–2 (123–124), pp. 161–172.

Zvidrins, P. (1998), *Latvijas iedzivotaju etniska sastava izmainas 90 gados*, Riga.

Zvidrins, P. *et al.* (1998), *Fertility and Family Surveys in countries of the ECE Region. Standard Country Report. Latvia*, New York and Geneva: UN.

# 10

# Recent Population Development in Lithuania

**Vlada Stankuniene**

## 10.1 Introduction

In Lithuania, like in the other East and Central European countries, the demographic development during the last ten years has been highly specific. The fundamental trends of demographic processes, which have many similarities in their features and trajectories of change, are quite diverse in the intensity of their manifestation. However, Lithuania noticeably stands out from the post-communist countries with similar recent demographic trends, by the most insignificant degree of its demographic changes.

## 10.2 Population Growth and Structure

### 10.2.1 Population Decline

From a standpoint of national perspective, the present demographic situation in Lithuania, characterised by a decreasing population, is frightening for the public at large and baffling for the academic circles. In Lithuania, the population has been decreasing since 1992, and this is the first time in the country's history when a drop has been caused not by external factors (war, change of territory, etc.) but resulted from demographic processes.

The recent population decline was provoked and accelerated by the high level of emigration of the early 1990s. After its peak in 1990–1993, the emigration wave later ebbed away and since 1997 emigration-immigration flows have been balanced with no further impact on the changes in the population number. Since 1994, when the subsided emigration flows and the beginning of a natural decrease of the population became the key processes, the latter has had the foremost responsibility for the decline of the population.

Before the onset of the recent changes, Lithuania had retained higher rates of natural increase and net reproduction longer than the neighbouring Baltic countries. Up until the beginning of the demographic decline of the early 1990s, the reproduction regime of the country was close to the replacement of generations. Roughly fifteen years prior to the present demographic decline, the net reproduction rates of Lithuania were fluctuating in the range of 0.935–1.012 (Statistics Lithuania, 1999).

The demographic decline, which occurred in the post-communist countries in the late 1980s – early 1990s, started in Lithuania some years later and until today has been slightly less pronounced than in the neighbouring countries with a similar fate. Up to 1994, Lithuania's population still had experienced a natural increase. With mortality rates exceeding those of fertility, the sharpest decline of the population was observed in 1994–1996. Over that period, the natural decrease rate stood at 1.1 per 1,000 inhabitants. Since 1997 this indicator has been slightly improving (Table 10.1). However, due to the continuing, albeit at a lower pace, drop of fertility, the net reproduction rate has been still going down. In 1990, the net reproduction rate was 0.969, in 1996 – 0.682, and in 1997 – 0.658 (Statistics Lithuania, 1999).

In 1992–1998, population of Lithuania dropped by 45,000 reaching 3,702,000 in early 1999. During this period emigration was responsible for the decrease by 40,700 people.

### 10.2.2 Age and Sex Composition

The three decades (1959–1989) preceding the demographic decline were the defining period in the demographic development of Lithuania. Due to the country's swift industrialisation and urbanisation, the demographic transition had been proceeding at a high speed culminating in its final stage, and had resulted in a rapid population ageing, narrowing "bottom" and widening "top" of the age-sex pyramid.

**Table 10.1: Population Change, 1989–1997**

| | 1989 | 1990 | 1991 | 1992 | 1993 | 1994 | 1995 | 1996 | 1997 |
|---|---|---|---|---|---|---|---|---|---|
| Population[1] (1,000) | 3,675 | 3,708 | 3,736 | 3,747 | 3,736 | 3,724 | 3,718 | 3,712 | 3,707 |
| | Crude rates (per 1,000 inhabitants) | | | | | | | | |
| Births | 15.1 | 15.3 | 15.0 | 14.3 | 12.7 | 11.4 | 11.1 | 10.5 | 10.2 |
| Deaths | 10.3 | 10.7 | 11.0 | 11.1 | 12.3 | 12.5 | 12.2 | 11.6 | 11.1 |
| Natural increase (decrease) | 4.8 | 4.6 | 4.0 | 3.2 | 0.4 | -1.1 | -1.1 | -1.1 | -0.9 |
| Net reproduction rate | 0.944 | 0.969 | 0.935 | 0.903 | 0.789 | 0.729 | 0.710 | 0.682 | 0.658 |
| Immigration | 47.4 | 38.6 | 14.2 | 6.6 | 2.9 | 1.7 | 2.0 | 3.0 | 2.5 |
| Emigration | 36.1 | 30.9 | 22.8 | 28.8 | 16.0 | 4.3 | 3.8 | 3.9 | 2.4 |
| Net migration | 11.3 | 7.7 | -8.6 | -22.2 | -13.1 | -2.9 | -1.8 | -0.9 | 0.1 |

[1]As of 1 January of a given year

Sources: Lietuvos Gyventojai, 1990; Statistics Lithuania, 1996 and 1998

Due to specific mortality pattern, typical for Lithuania, as well as for almost all the other former Soviet republics, and distinguished by an increasing gap between male and female mortality and life expectancy rates, the age-sex pyramid was acquiring an increasingly asymmetrical character: at older ages the male side of the pyramid was becoming thinner than the female side. Thus, on the eve of the demographic decline in 1989, the age-sex pyramid had a shape that was indicative of an advanced population ageing, particularly among women.

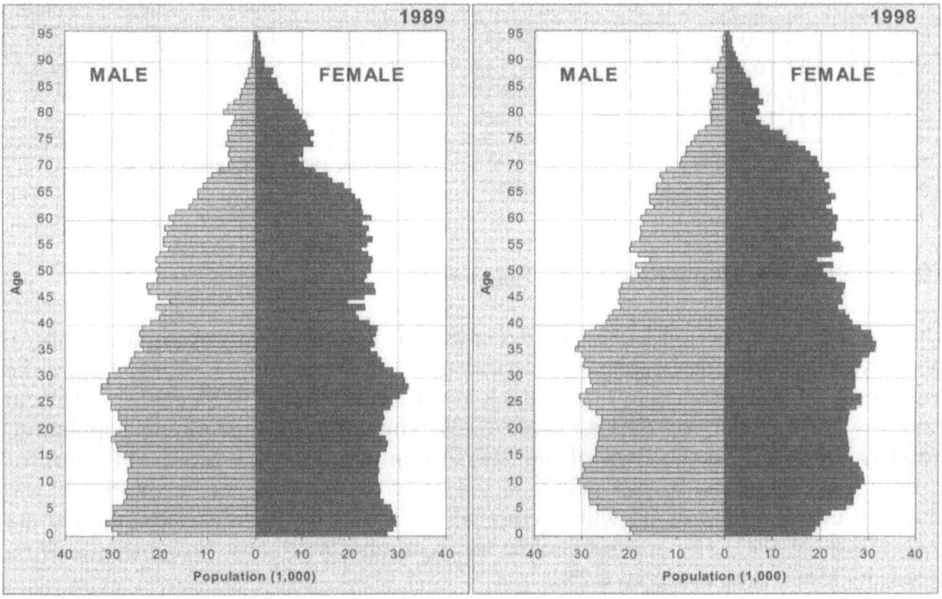


**Figure 10.1 Population by Age and Sex, 1989 and 1998**

Source: author's calculations based on data of Statistics Lithuania, 1996–1998

Since the early 1990s, the new trends of all demographic processes – fertility, mortality, and migration – have significantly altered the age structure of the population. Due to the sharply decreased fertility, accompanied by a rapid shrinking of the proportion of children in the overall population, the age-sex pyramid of the present resembles a tree cut down halfway. Since 1992, the proportion of elderly people has been clearly on the rise. During 1992–1998, the share of population aged 65 and over increased from 11.3% to 12.7%, while the share of children aged 0–14 dropped from 22.6% to 20.8%. The 15–64 age group experienced minor changes over the period and stayed close to 66%. Total dependency ratio shifted insignificantly as well (ranged between 50 and 51). Thus, with the shrinking proportion of economically yet inactive children and the growth of the share of already inactive senior citizens, the child dependency ratio fell from 34.1 to 31.3, and the elderly dependency ratio rose from 17 to 19.1 (Table 10.2). All these figures are indicative of the considerable internal modifications of age structure.

**Table 10.2: Population by Main Age Groups and Dependency Ratio, 1985–1998, selected years**

| Year | Age group | | | Total population | Dependency ratio (%) | | |
|---|---|---|---|---|---|---|---|
| | 0–14 | 15–64 | 65+ | | Young | Old | Total |
| 1985 | 814,080 | 2,350,872 | 363,746 | 3,528,698 | 34.6 | 15.5 | 50.1 |
| 1989 | 832,163 | 2,451,334 | 391,232 | 3,674,802 | 33.9 | 16.0 | 49.9 |
| 1995 | 814,683 | 2,463,075 | 439,976 | 3,717,734 | 33.1 | 17.9 | 51.0 |
| 1998 | 771,197 | 2,462,109 | 470,655 | 3,703,961 | 31.3 | 19.1 | 50.4 |

Source: Author's calculations based on data of Statistics Lithuania, 1996–1998 and Demographic Data Collection of Estonia, Latvia and Lithuania, 1998

### 10.2.3 Ethnic Composition of the Population

During the Soviet period Lithuania, in contrast to the neighbouring Baltic countries, preserved its ethnic homogeneity. According to 1989 census data, shortly before the regaining of independence, Lithuanians constituted 79.6%, Russians – 9.4% and Poles – 7.0% of the population (Table 10.3). The emigration of Slavic population, notably Russians, to the East, of the Jewish population to the West, and return of Lithuanians from the former USSR in the early 1990s have further increased the share of ethnic Lithuanians, who accounted for 81.6% of the total population at the beginning of 1997. The greatest decline has been observed in the proportion of Russians. In 1997, they made up 8.2%.

**Table 10.3: Population Composition by Ethnic Groups, 1970, 1989 and 1997, per cent**

| | 1970 | 1989 | 1997 |
|---|---|---|---|
| Lithuanians | 80.1 | 79.6 | 81.6 |
| Russians | 8.6 | 9.4 | 8.2 |
| Poles | 7.7 | 7.0 | 6.9 |
| Other | 3.6 | 4.0 | 3.3 |

Source: Statistics Lithuania, 1998

## 10.3 Basic Demographic Processes

### 10.3.1 Fertility

The decline of fertility in 1992 terminated the previously stable fertility pattern of at least a 10-year long duration. For some time before 1992, the crude birth rate had been close to 15 per 1,000 inhabitants. It then dropped below this level and in six years approached 10 per 1,000 inhabitants in 1997. The number of births fell from 56.2 thousand in 1991 to 37.0 thousand in 1998, i.e. roughly by 33% (Statistics Lithuania, 1999). Although the drop in fertility rates seems impressive, nevertheless, the crude rates are not enough for the analysis of the extent and character of the fertility change.

The total fertility rate (TFR) in Lithuania remained at a higher level and boasted a more consistent trend than in the countries of a similar fate. Prior to the recent demographic changes, the fertility rate of Lithuania stood close to 2.0, i.e. equal to the level that was sufficient for the replacement of generations. Furthermore, while in the late 1980s – early 1990s the TFR in the entire East and Central European post-communist countries was already decreasing, in Lithuania it still was rising slightly (Macura, 1995). This temporary increase just before its critical fall was conditioned by the highly specific circumstances of Lithuania: quite important measures of family policy were adopted in 1989 and the euphoric atmosphere of national revival exalted family and children as a guarantee for national survival. Besides, in the period of revival and shortly after independence was proclaimed young men tried to skip serving in the Soviet army. One of the legal ways to avoid obligatory military conscription was to marry and to have small children in need of parental support. Therefore it may be reasonably assumed that in 1988–1991 some young people married very early and had children partly for these reasons.

Although the TFR in Lithuania started to fall in 1992, an acceleration of the fall began only in 1993. The years 1993–1994 were in particular marked by the steepest drop of the TFR: it fell from 1.89 in 1992 to 1.52 in 1994 (Statistics Lithuania, 1999). Although the decline of fertility continued into later years, the momentum of the initial period was lost, and the rate stabilised at 1.4 (in 1998, it was 1.36). It should be mentioned that even at its reduced level the fertility in Lithuania was still considerably higher than in the neighbouring Baltic States.

In recent years, the shape of the age-specific fertility curves has been experiencing quite contradictory changes. Although fertility rates have declined in all reproductive age groups, the decline was most pronounced in the best, from the medical point of view, reproductive period for women – in the 20–25 years age group. The latter fact might be considered the most important feature of the recent changes.

Apart from losing height, age-specific fertility curves also lost their pronounced peak, thus acquiring a shape characteristic for postponed fertility, with the first signs of compensated fertility. The maximum of fertility rates is stretched over age 21–26 (Figure 10.2). The "ageing" of fertility has also been signalled by the mean age at first birth, which increased from 22.7 years in 1993 to 23.6 in 1998 (Statistics Lithuania, 1999).

However, during 1989–1997 the changes of age-specific fertility rates were quite inconsistent. Immediately before the decline, reproductive activity of women aged 18–21 had increased in 1990–1991, which was the outcome of the previously mentioned changes in the matrimonial behaviour of the young people.

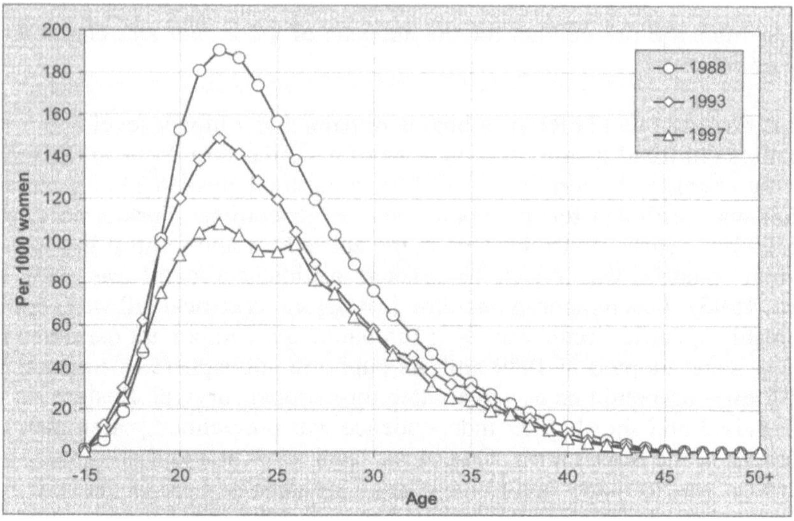


**Figure 10.2: Age-specific Fertility Rates, 1988, 1993 and 1997**
Source: Statistics Lithuania, 1998

The rapidly decreasing fertility in Lithuania has been accompanied by another phenomenon of the changing fertility pattern, i.e. the increase of extramarital births. For a prolonged period, the number of extramarital births was quite stable in Lithuania. According to the available data, the proportion of extramarital births during this century ranged between 3% and 7% (except for the period of Resistance movement directly after the Second World War). However, in the recent years of decreased fertility, the share of extramarital births has grown by more than twice in Lithuania: from 7% in 1990 to 16.5% in 1997 (Statistics Lithuania, 1998). The increase was most pronounced in the 16–19 age group, the earliest years of reproductive age. Extramarital births have also been increasing in older reproductive age groups. However, if a comparison of the development of this phenomenon in three Baltic States is made, it could be argued that in Lithuania it is still in its initial stage, for in 1997 the proportion of extramarital births in Latvia was 34.8% and in Estonia – 51.6% (Council of Europe, 1998).

The recent years in Lithuania have not witnessed any spectacular changes in a parity of births. The births of every order have been on the decrease. During 1991–1994, in the structure of the births according to their order a slight decline of the second and even less pronounced of the third and an insignificant increase of the first births has been observed. Thus, the decrease of fertility rates has been affected to a significant degree by the decrease of the second and subsequent births.

The available data shows that before the recent changes abortion rates in Lithuania were considerably lower than in other post-communist East European countries. In the current decade, the pace of the decrease of the abortion rate has been faster in Lithuania. The abortion rate per 1,000 women aged 15–49 decreased from 43.5 in

1991 to 22.4 in 1998 (Statistics Lithuania, 1999). Over the period, the rates of spontaneous miscarriages remained on the same level.

The results of the surveys conducted in 1988, 1990, and in 1994–1995[1] suggest that the current decade has witnessed marked changes in the fertility preferences as well. The desired number of children went down from 2.8 in 1988 and 1990 to 2.1 in 1994–1995. The ideal number of children has also been affected to the same degree: it declined from 3.1 to 2.9 and to 2.3, correspondingly. Furthermore, the 1994–1995 survey results demonstrate that attitudes of preference for voluntary childlessness have started spreading in the youngest cohorts. About 10% of women and men aged 18–19 indicated that they would not like to have a child at all (UN ECE/UNFPA, 1998).

### 10.3.2 Mortality

From the mid-1960s onwards, in Lithuania, just like in the other former Soviet republics, negative trends of mortality indicators have been expressed, with certain variations, more and more clearly, and they became even more conspicuous due to cardinal societal changes of the current decade. The mortality indicators were rapidly deteriorating in 1990–1994. The number of deaths grew from 38.1 thousand in 1989 to 46.5 thousand in 1994. The crude death rate increased correspondingly from 10.3 to 12.5 per 1,000 inhabitants. During 1989–1994, life expectancy at birth for males diminished by 4.2 years (from 66.94 to 62.73), and for females – by 1.4 years (from 76.33 to 74.89) (Statistics Lithuania, 1997).

Infant mortality during this period was unstable. In 1990, the infant mortality rate was 10.3‰, in 1991 it increased considerably and reached 14.3‰[2]. Infant mortality rate at a level over 14.0‰ still persisted during 1992–1994, however later it started going down again reaching 9.2‰ in 1998 (Statistics Lithuania, 1999).

A pronounced increase of mortality rates during the period of 1990–1994 was primarily determined by increasing mortality among middle-aged men (Figures 10.3 and 10.4). Over 1989–1994, life expectancy of men at 15 years declined by 4.2 years, at 45 – by 3 years, at 60 – by 1.6 years (Table 10.4).

**Table 10.4: Life Expectancy by Sex and Age, 1989, 1994 and 1997, in years**

| Age | 1989 | | 1994 | | 1997 | |
|---|---|---|---|---|---|---|
| | Male | Female | Male | Female | Male | Female |
| 0 | 66.94 | 76.33 | 62.73 | 74.89 | 65.90 | 76.80 |
| 1 | 66.74 | 76.06 | 62.67 | 74.82 | 65.67 | 76.48 |
| 15 | 53.34 | 62.49 | 49.19 | 61.21 | 52.09 | 62.79 |
| 45 | 27.24 | 34.05 | 24.29 | 32.92 | 26.20 | 34.19 |
| 60 | 16.71 | 21.10 | 15.16 | 20.54 | 16.15 | 21.36 |
| 65 | 13.55 | 17.06 | 12.54 | 16.69 | 13.27 | 17.33 |

Sources: Statistics Lithuania, 1996 and 1998

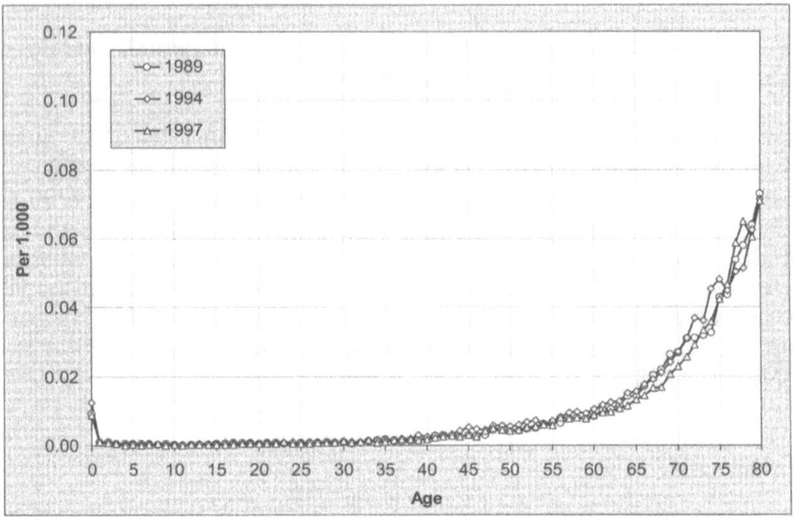


**Figure 10.3: Age-specific Mortality Rates, 1989, 1994 and 1997, female**
Source: Author's calculations based on data of Statistics Lithuania, 1996 and 1998

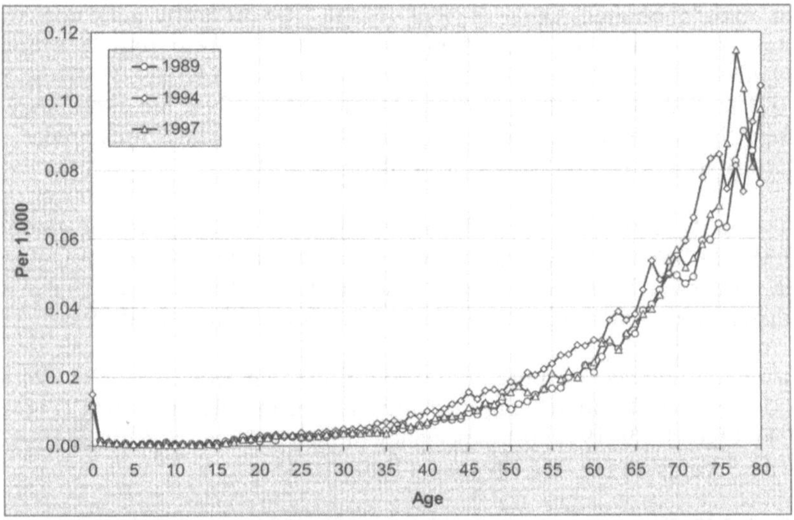


**Figure 10.4: Age-specific Mortality Rates, 1989, 1994 and 1997, male**
Source: Author's calculations based on data of Statistics Lithuania, 1996 and 1998

The growth of mortality was mostly caused by accidents and cardiovascular diseases. Deaths caused by homicide and, in particular, by suicide have risen sharply and are still experiencing an upward trend. In recent years, Lithuania has suddenly topped world rates of deaths caused by suicide. The number of suicides per 100,000 population rose from 26 in 1990 to 44 in 1997 (Statistics Lithuania, 1998). Mortality from infectious diseases, which had been going down for a number of decades, has risen as well in the present decade.

Since 1995, mortality of population in Lithuania has been going down again. In 1997, the number of deaths decreased to 41.1 thousand. Crude death rate has also fallen considerably, and was 11.1 per 1,000 inhabitants in 1997 (Statistics Lithuania, 1998). Mortality among the population groups which have displayed the most negative trends, i.e. young and middle-aged men, has recently fallen slightly as well.

### 10.3.3 Migration

To begin with, it should be noted that statistical data of the last years on migration flows is rather inaccurate. It is merely an illustration of legal migration. However, different expert evaluations indicate that the volumes of illegal migration might surpass the legal migration by several times. Regardless of some inaccuracies in the data on migration flows, several generalisations can be proposed.

Over the recent decade, migration trends and volumes have been spectacular in Lithuania. The year 1990 deserves to be called the turning point of migration trends. The volumes and characteristics of immigration were the first to start changing. In 1990, arrivals, particularly from the territory of the former Soviet Union, which had conditioned negative net migration volumes, fell sharply. In 1989, 47.4 thousand people arrived in Lithuania, but only 14.7 thousand in 1990 (Demographic Data Collection of Estonia, Latvia and Lithuania, op. cit.). In later years, immigration volumes continued to shrink and approximately two or three thousand people arrive annually since 1993.

The largest wave of emigration rolled over the country in 1992–1993, with the East being its main direction. In 1992, which was the peak year of emigration, 28.9 thousand people left the country. With sharply diminishing arrivals and growing departures, net immigration has turned into net emigration since 1990. The largest net emigration was observed in Lithuania in 1992, totalling 22.2 thousand (Statistics Lithuania, 1999). Since 1994 the volumes of emigration have noticeably decreased, and since 1997 the emigration and immigration flows are practically running on parallel lines, thus bringing the net migration rates of 1997–1998 close to zero. However, general indicators of immigration and emigration represent several migration flows different in volumes and trajectories of trends.

Until the late 1980s, a period of radical political changes, according to Statistics Lithuania's unpublished migration data files, Lithuania had high immigration and emigration rates: for example, in 1985 immigration rate was 14.2 and emigration rate was 11.6 per 1,000 inhabitants. However, these were essentially migration flows within the former USSR alone, with departures and arrivals related to the obligatory service in the army dominating the flows. Gross migration rate rose above 25, and net immigration rate was 2–3 per 1,000 inhabitants.

With the beginning of the national revival, due to the avoidance of serving in the army, departures started to decrease in 1989. And upon the regaining of independence in 1990, the former flow of the army recruits vanished altogether. Correspondingly, the immigration flow conditioned by the same circumstances also has changed, but with a lag of 1–2 years. Owing to an unstable political situation caused by the national revival, which acted as a brake on migration "pull" factors, arrivals in Lithuania started decreasing in the late 1980s. Labour migration, notably to military factories, institutes and Soviet political institutions started diminishing. However, as early as the late 1980s, upon the liberalisation of the Soviet migration policy, the emigration of the Jewish population to the West had surged.

After the international recognition of Lithuania's independence in 1991 and the withdrawal of the Soviet troops from Lithuania, which started in 1992 and was accompanied by the remigration of the Slavic population to their homeland, the wave of departures to the East went up. The early 1990s were also marked by the continued Jewish emigration to the West. Departures to the East reached a peak in 1992 and to the West in 1990. However, after the earlier prevalent emigration flows had ebbed, the new flows of the current decade, intensive as they were, even at their peak were in match with the flows of the Soviet times.

Until the recent changes, gross migration rate was about 25.0, in 1990–1992 – about 10.0, and in 1996–1998 – under 2.0 per 1,000 inhabitants (author's calculations based on unpublished migration data files from Statistics Lithuania). During 1990–1997, total volume of emigration from Lithuania was 58 thousand people, with 52 thousand heading for the East and about 6 thousand for the West (Statistics Lithuania, 1998).

## 10.4 Family Formation and Dissolution

### 10.4.1 Nuptiality

During recent years, the changes in family demographics in Lithuania were first manifested in the transformation of marriage patterns. The number of marriages went down from 36.3 thousand in 1990 to 18.8 thousand in 1997, i.e. nearly by half. Crude marriage rates dropped correspondingly from 9.8‰ to 5.1‰ (Statistics Lithuania, 1998).

The most important feature of the recent trend in age-specific marriage rates for both men and women was an obvious and continuous decrease of the rates in all age groups. Some fluctuations in the marriage rates have been observed in recent years. Matrimonial behaviour of men and women aged under 20 became a spectacular exception in the overall changes of marriage rates. As mentioned above, matrimonial activity of this age group, affected by the attempts of men to escape service in the Soviet army, was considerably higher in the late 1980s – early 1990s. At that time, age-specific marriage rates of men had risen twice as high, those of women about 3–4 times higher. Owing to the same causes, the age-specific marriage rates had slightly risen in the age group of 20–24 years as well. However, since 1993, age-specific marriage rates of this age group have been rapidly falling for both sexes. In 1990, the marriage rate for men under 20 was 19‰, for women – 66‰. In 1997, both rates dropped, correspondingly, to 9‰ and 31‰, i.e. decreased by more than half, to levels lower than those before the recent changes (Demographic Data Collection of Estonia, Latvia and Lithuania, op. cit.; Statistics Lithuania, 1998). The marriage rate among men and women aged 20–24 experienced a similar decline: for men the rate fell from 125 to 61‰, for women – from 117‰ to 61‰. With the exception of the age group 25–29 years, the marriage rates of all the other groups have been following the downward trend, which started at the beginning of the 1990s.

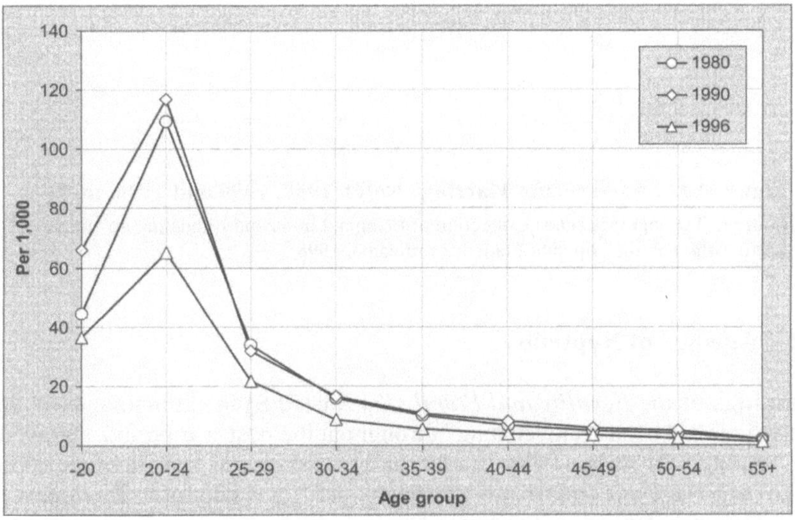


**Figure 10.5: Age-specific Marriage Rates, 1980, 1990 and 1996, female**

Sources: Demographic Data Collection of Estonia, Latvia and Lithuania, op. cit; Statistics Lithuania, 1998; Lietuvos gyventojai, op. cit.

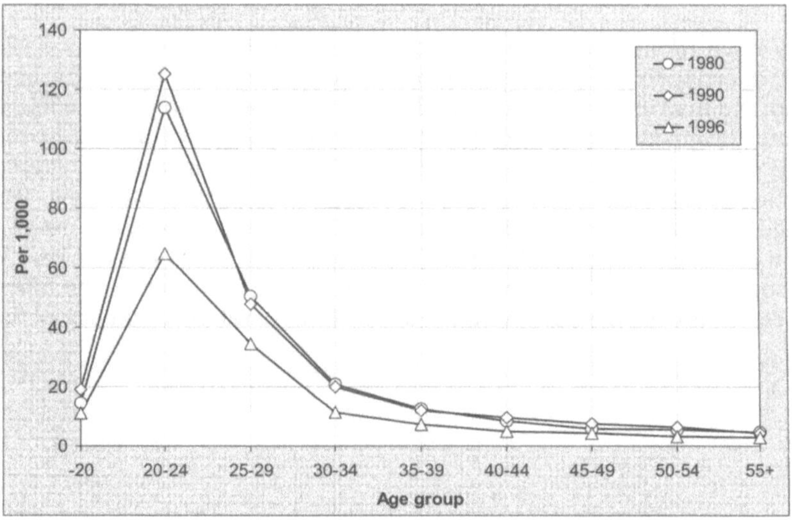


**Figure 10.6: Age-specific Marriage Rates, 1980, 1990 and 1996, male**

Sources: Demographic Data Collection of Estonia, Latvia and Lithuania, op. cit.; Lietuvos gyventojai, op. cit.; Statistics Lithuania, 1998

### 10.4.2 "Ageing" of Nuptiality

The findings of the *Fertility and Family Survey* (FFS) in Lithuania show that marriages, which had been "rejuvenating" throughout the post-war period, started to experience "ageing" during the 1990s. Increasingly fewer people start families upon reaching legal marriage age; marriages are postponed for a later age. In some way, this trend is counterbalanced, in the quantity sense, by the spread of consensual unions, which follow quite different course patterns among young men and young women.

The greatest changes in the matrimonial behaviour are observed among the young people born in the early 1970s (1971–1975). Only 30% of the men born in 1971 had married by the age of 24, whereas in all the older cohorts more than 60% had already been married by the age of 24 (Stankuniene and Baublyte, 1996). When the recent socio-economic changes had started, a considerable proportion of single men born in the late 1960s (1966–1970) had also postponed their marriage. Thus, at the age of 29, 75% of men born in 1966 were married, whereas in all the older cohorts about 85% of men had been married by the age of 29 (Stankuniene and Baublyte, op. cit.).

In recent years, the behaviour of women concerning family formation has also changed significantly, however, in a different way from men. Two distinct groups of matrimonial behaviour may be seen. At present, a number of women marry very early in life, even earlier than before, and the others postpone family formation for a later age. The results of the FFS have shown that young females who do not study or find employment upon finishing school marry much earlier. They do not find a job after marriage either. Possibly, in this manner a new social group of housewives, that did not and could not exist in the Soviet period of full employment, is being formed.

The spread of this phenomenon among young women might be a result of behaviour predetermined by the attitudes of personal self-expression. However, the fact that before marriage a sizeable proportion of these women were unemployed or laid off indicates that their decision and choice of life path might have been also influenced by a negative impact of social environment. Conversely, young women who pursue education and professional careers are in no hurry to marry. Only 53% of women born in 1971 had married by the age of 24, whereas over 70% of women in all the older cohorts had married by that age (Stankuniene and Baublyte, op. cit.).

### 10.4.3 Consensual Unions

A considerable proportion of young people postponing marriage, and especially the youngest of those who reached legal marriage age, enters consensual unions. In Lithuania, the spread of the alternative way of family life has lately acquired the character of an explosion: in every successive young cohort more and more individuals start living together by cohabiting. As the FFS data indicates, 15% of men and 16% of women born in 1971 had lived in consensual unions by the age of 24. In contrast to this, in the cohort twenty years older only 8% of men and 6% of women had an experience of such a union by the age of 24. Those respondents whose parents divorced more frequently started cohabitation in their early years. As many as 20% of them started by cohabiting, while only 10% of respondents who had grown up with both parents had such an experience of family formation. It is obvious that apart from the current socio-economic conditions the spread of consensual unions has been stimulated, in face of the more liberal environment, by the increasing instability of marriages of the few last decades.

### 10.4.4 Divorce

Although divorces are frequent in Lithuania, until the recent changes their prevalence was quite stable. Only in the early 1990s, the number of divorces had increased. In the late 1980s, the annual number of divorces was 11–12 thousand, in 1991 it was 15 thousand, in 1992–1993 it was 14 thousand, and since 1994, the annual number is around 10–11 thousand (Statistics Lithuania, 1999). However, fictitious divorces, which had become more frequent at the initial stage of the privatisation of dwellings, might have been responsible for the short rise in divorce numbers in the early 1990s. Thus, the fluctuation of divorce rates of the recent years may hardly be related to the natural development of demographic processes.

Crude divorce rates of the 1980s were close to 3‰ (3.1–3.3‰). In 1991, the crude divorce rate was the highest in Lithuania and constituted 4.1‰. Later, it went down and in 1998 amounted to 3.1‰ (Statistics Lithuania, 1999). However, while comparing Lithuanian divorce rates with other countries it should not be forgotten that until recently the traditional way of family formation, i.e. exclusively by marriage, was predominant in the country. Therefore, in Lithuania quite a precise register of family formation and dissolution was kept. Consequently, the comparison of the Lithuanian indicators with the ones of the countries with widely spread consensual unions (which are indeed not entered into register) would be not quite correct.

## 10.5 The Current Changes in Demographic Behaviour

The rapid and radical political and socio-economic changes of the recent years are followed in Lithuania by a break in the long-term evolution of demographic trends. The national revival, which began in the late 1980s, the regaining of independence in 1990, and the subsequent reforms towards democratisation of the society and market economy were marked by demographic changes – huge in their size and fundamental in content. All demographic processes – fertility, mortality, and migration – have experienced major changes over the last ten years. However, from the very beginning of their manifestation, the changes have been inconsistent and controversial in character, which might be explained by the fact that the demographic processes have been simultaneously affected by numerous factors diverse in their origin, duration and intensity.

Certain factors are long-term and have been exerting further pressure on demographic processes in the current period of fundamental changes. The others are new and with a short record of influence over demographic development. Yet some are short-lived and have been noticed since they were responsible for the fluctuations of demographic trends or the emergence of long-term demographic trends. The only thing to be stated with certainty is that all the factors are closely intertwined with a varying influence on different strata of the society.

The dramatic changes that have occurred in political, economic, social and cultural spheres of society over a short period of time force people to adapt to transformed life environment. New conditions liberate them from previous legislative and social norms and provide favourable milieu for self-expression and personal choice in various spheres of life, thus affecting life-style, behaviour and values. Furthermore, national revival and consolidation of statehood did and still continues to stimulate the determination to preserve Lithuanian ethnic cultural features and traditions. However, it is important to note that some attitudes and attributes of life-style developed during the Soviet period have demonstrated their viability, and due to social inertia, continue to exercise influence over demographic development.

The liberal political climate, especially a newly opened and long-awaited opportunity to join the European Union and world community, has become a strong incentive for adopting the technologies, life-styles, norms, attitudes, and the material, cultural and spiritual values of western societies. On the other hand, Lithuania, like any other previously isolated and less-developed country, lacking social immunity upon opening of its borders after a prolonged period, has become susceptible to the invasion of mass culture, illegal business and other potentially destructive social phenomena. Moreover, Lithuania as a "transit country" is exposed to some extra invasions, different in their nature and effect. In real life, all these processes are closely intertwined and have a considerable impact on demographic development, occasionally acquiring an apocalyptic character (e.g. highly increased number of suicides).

### 10.5.1 Migration

Migration of the population, which generally exhibits quick reaction to the new environment, became the first of the demographic processes in Lithuania to experience the utmost alterations of trends, directions, and composition. Migration trends in Lithuania are a synthesis of two, highly different processes: migration flows with the East (the former USSR territory) and with the West.

With the collapse of the USSR, dissolution of the socialist centrally planned economic system, and removal of the closed-door migration policy, the Soviet-period international migration pattern suddenly vanished. Revolutionary political changes (not of a lesser importance because of the peaceful nature of the "Singing Revolution") and regaining of independence have weakened the "pull" factors for migration from the former USSR greatly and even have become the "push" factors for inhabitants of non-Lithuanian origin, in particular, for Soviet immigrants or their descendants, who did not desire or were not capable of integrating into the ethnic cultural environment of the country.

After the restoration of Lithuania's independence and in the course of the de-sovietisation process and the withdrawal of the Soviet army underway, migration processes with the former USSR acquired features typical of decolonisation. A wave of return migration to the former USSR, notably to Russia, rose and subsided over a very short period. The new political climate of Lithuania and the new migration policy, backed by a public sentiment to restrict these flows, resulted in a rapidly decreasing flow of immigration from the East. Migration flows with the former USSR became weak in both directions. Thus, following the transitional migration pattern caused by decolonisation, a new pattern of moderate and balanced migration flows is being formed.

The new geopolitical setting of Lithuania has fundamentally affected the migration flow potential with the West. The removal of the "Iron Curtain" and reformed, more liberal migration policy of Lithuania have lessened the strength of the flow-forming factors and have provided, on the national level, prerequisites for migration flows with the West. Political reforms, which have changed conditions for international migration, have not become, after all, a factor stimulating migration with the West. They have mainly dismantled barriers, which during the Soviet period had restrained migration and accumulated emigration potential with no opportunity to realise it.

The new political situation has also triggered new fundamental migration factors of economic and social nature: foremost, the difference in living standards between East and West. However, the migration policy of the western countries, which is highly restrictive and selective in many respects, has quite a blocking effect on the realisation of one's emigration aspirations. Legal ways to realise desire to emigrate to the West are in fact very limited and have been mostly available for the Jewish population. Thus, when an emigration potential of the small community of Lithuanian Jews had been exhausted, legal migration flows with the West have also become thin and balanced.

It should be emphasised that these conclusions are based on official data alone. Different surveys and expert evaluations have revealed the existence of a large emigration potential and, moreover, quite a substantial illegal emigration to the West. It appears that Lithuania has lately become one of the routes for trafficking illegal migrants from Asia to Western Europe, the extent of the latter type of migration being rather obscure.

### 10.5.2 Mortality

The major features of the specific "Soviet" mortality pattern (including a rising mortality among young and middle-aged men and an increasing gap between male and female mortality), which in Lithuania, as well as in the other former Soviet republics, prevailed from the 1960s onwards, were particularly strengthened in the first years of independence. The deepening health crisis of the Soviet years was further aggravated by the transitional period to market economy.

The collapse of the economy in the early 1990s, instigated by the break-up of the economic ties with the former USSR, caused the spread of unemployment, hyperinflation, decline of social guarantees and health care provisions. Rapid deterioration of living standards brought uncertainty and instability into all spheres of life and had a destructive effect on public health and mortality. In addition, a higher mobility of people, intensive and diverse international migration flows (legal, illegal, temporal, commercial, etc.) and some negative factors operative in a transit country (contraband of alcohol, drugs, etc.) also took a heavy toll.

In the early 1990s, the negative mortality trends of the previous period became pronounced even more. However, since the economic recovery started in the mid-1990s, mortality trends have been slightly improving. Nevertheless, they still retain many features of the "Soviet" mortality pattern and have acquired the worst features in the dynamics of suicide.

### 10.5.3 Fertility and Family

The fundamental social, economic and cultural changes, which started at the beginning of the current decade, have conditioned the transformation of the family institution. Traditional family features have been vanishing; features characteristic to western societies are taking root; the strategy of family formation has been changing. Over the last few years, a shift in marriage timing has occurred: marriages, which had been rejuvenating for a long period (a transition from a late marriage, which had predominated in Lithuania until the mid-century, to an early one), have started ageing. The phenomenon of postponed marriages has emerged. The recent social and economic reforms as well as difficulties of economic recession served as an impetus for these changes. However, a universal character of their dynamics has mostly been determined by transition to a democratic society with market economy, which seemingly lies at the bottom of all changes.

Until recently, the Lithuanian population was characterised by a conservative Catholic matrimonial behaviour, a distinguishing feature of which was to start family by marriage (it was almost a universal phenomenon). Cohabitation was ill tolerated by the society. But now fewer and fewer families are formed in the traditional way, i.e. by marriage, while more and more couples start family life by consensual unions. This type of behaviour became already typical for a considerable proportion of representatives of the younger, and particularly, the youngest generations. Public attitudes of the rapidly westernising society towards consensual unions have been getting more liberal too; overt intolerance of the previous years has been disappearing. Currently, consensual unions in the country are mostly short-lived, and either serve as a prelude to marriage or as a temporary alternative to a registered union. However, in the conditions of rapidly westernising Lithuanian society, this kind of matrimonial behaviour could soon turn into a norm and consensual unions could become a permanent phenomenon.

In general, the decline of marriage, its postponement for a later age, and the recent spread of consensual unions have been predetermined both by temporal factors typical to the transitional and crisis period, and by fundamental ones, which appear alongside the market relations in economy, liberal attitudes and deepening individualisation. The impact of the former has been strong recently and brought about the shift of marriage indicators and ageing of marriage, while the fundamental factors are mostly responsible for family transformation and development of a new family pattern. Nevertheless, in the transition period of the society both types of transforming factors have been operative in their close interaction.

The strengthening of the housing market and the skyrocketing prices for housing (in 1994, they exceeded the 1990 level by 106 times) (Seimos Politikos Koncepcija, 1995) not only made the problem of housing acquisition more acute, but for some families made it out of question in any foreseeable future. The deep crisis of the early 1990s; hyperinflation (inflation index of 1992 was 1,163%) (*Main Macroeconomic Indicators of Lithuania*, 1997); emergence of unemployment, which hit young people the hardest and co-exists with very high unofficial employment; the increase of wealth differentiation in the society; impoverishment of a part of the population; and an inadequate provision of social security guarantees in terms of timing and the type of support, have drastically increased social risk, especially among those who have just entered labour market (UNDP, 1996). These conditions, without any doubt, considerably affect the matrimonial behaviour of young people.

To summarise, the country is obviously moving towards the family formation norms and attitudes, which have for the last three decades been observed in western countries. Features of the second demographic transition (van de Kaa, 1987) expressed through family transformation are evolving in Lithuania at what might be called a revolutionary speed. This is most of all reflected in the changes of fertility: fertility has been rapidly declining and ageing at the same time, extramarital births have been increasing, while social intolerance for this phenomenon, typical to Catholic society, has been subsiding. Irrespective of the objections on the part of church and on the part of the society, the spread of modern contraception methods has been changing matrimonial, reproductive and sexual behaviour. And young people entering legal marriage age increasingly distance themselves from the traditional norms of family formation.

## 10.6 Population-related Policy and Programmes: Experience and Strategy

Having survived the major and controversial changes of the recent years, the population-related policy of Lithuania is still being continuously redefined and readjusted. For tackling problems of the population, different measures are planned along the lines of the main demographic processes: family policy, health policy and migration policy. To date, family policy is the best systematised and conceptualised.

As far back as the late 1980s, in the years of national revival, some foundations for independent population-related policy, notably family policy and migration policy, were laid in Lithuania. Using political instability in the USSR and the situation of "restructuring" (perestroika) and a "new way of thinking", the Lithuanian Government practised no commitment to the centralised Soviet legislation still in force, and adopted on the national level decisions about family assistance and, on the regional level, the regulations of external migration.

### 10.6.1 Family Policy

The idea to advance family policy was born with the liberation movement in Lithuania. Turbulent changes, which started in all spheres of life of the republic in 1988, national revival with an emphasis on the importance of demographic factors for the survival of the nation, reverence of family and children as national values, all this called for the development of a targeted family policy. Although at that time Lithuania still was a constituent part of the USSR and had no right of pursuing independent family policy, the concept of family policy was already initiated in 1988, and in

1989 the first independent national decision was adopted in the field. In 1989–1990, the task to formulate and define a family policy strategy was included into the set of goals of the Programme Population of Lithuania.

In 1989, the Lithuanian Government adopted measures on family assistance, which provided for a partially paid parental leave extension from one year to a year and a half, and for an extension of unpaid leave – from one year and a half to three years. Furthermore, these measures established that women could preserve an uninterrupted work record if they stayed at home to look after a child until his/her eighth birthday. The decision also provided for measures to improve pre-school establishments, acquisition of housing, and conditions for women's paid employment. The support for families raising a disabled child was increased. The principle measures of the decision moderated and amended some laws on labour relations, which had hampered the combination of parenthood and professional activity. Nevertheless, all these measures were in fact an extension of a paternalistic system in the field of assistance to family.

The Programme Population of Lithuania held a much more wide-ranging view on family policy. Financial support to the family was already treated as one of possible ways of family policy development. The Programme provided for measures to improve family planning, to decrease abnormal births, etc. Further, it reached beyond exclusive support to families raising children. Measures to develop a system of assistance to the elderly and disabled were planned as well. In general, the main provisions of the Programme were designed to achieve the specific goals of the family policy: to create favourable conditions for family self-expression and autonomy.

However, the implementation of the Programme Population of Lithuania lacked consistency. Since 1990, in the first years of independence, family policy was advanced without taking into consideration the accumulated conceptual expertise and was populist in character, with paternalistic attitudes overemphasised. In 1990–1992, assistance to family was mainly focussed on financial support and different types of benefits were established. Inflation being at its worst, the efforts were taken by the Government to adjust the amount of benefits accordingly, but nevertheless those benefits could not keep up with the fast rising costs of living. Furthermore, in the atmosphere of a total denial of everything that was related to the Soviet past, many preschool institutions were closed down, first of all, in the countryside. Shift of public attitude towards preference for raising children at home was being forged, while ideas on the necessity for women to go back to the family and "handle the hearth", and on the ban of abortion were revived.

The system of assistance to the family developed at that time was rather complicated and expensive. Because of its unilateral character and over-stressed orientation towards financial support, the essence of the family policy remained ill defined. Such provisions of family policy as flexible employment arrangements and social services remained beyond the range of its interests. Moreover, when in 1993 restructuring of the benefit system for families was finally started, the realisation arrived that the family policy devised in the early 1990s could be psychologically justified only in the period of state building. Thus, in 1993–1994 the poorly designed benefit system for families was given up. In particular, the priorities of financial support were transferred to the socially most disadvantaged families (however, in parallel, the reorganisation of the pre-school institutions, which offered different types of activities, was started too).

In 1994, the elaboration of the Concept of Family Policy was renewed. In the Concept of Family Policy approved by the Government in 1996, the goals, principles and actions for the support for families were elaborated. Obligations of the government and society to create a family-friendly environment, as well as development of responsibility on the part of families in solving their problems, were seen as the main goals of family policy (*Family Policy in Lithuania: Principles and Actions*, 1996).

The overall goals of family policy were specified through the actions and measures for family support. The system of family support was oriented towards the solution of problems, which arise at different stages of life course, and the creation of favourable conditions for families to fulfil their functions. The actions of family policy included the following basic elements: economic basis of family viability (benefits, employment guarantees, housing arrangements); family stability; maternal and child health; family planning; child care; child protection; elderly people; disabled people; gender equality and equity.

Although the family policy of Lithuania is still in process of being established, the few last years have reflected the denouncement of the old stereotypes of family support and the transition to the modern pattern of family assistance, aimed mainly at the creation of conditions stimulating activity of families themselves.

### 10.6.2 Health Policy

Health policy in recent years has pursued very controversial trends and has experienced multiple failures. At present, health policy is advanced by way of programmes. The Government of Lithuania has approved the National Health Programme, the provisions of which are defined in specialised sub-programmes such as alcohol control; AIDS prevention; improvement of nutrition of babies and children under three years of age; immunisation; tuberculosis prevention and control; mental disease prevention; dissemination of healthy life messages at schools, etc.

### 10.6.3 Migration Policy

Regardless of the fact that until now Lithuania did not have a conceptually defined and officially approved policy for international migration, general attitudes on the issue are reflected in the decisions of its government.

As far back as the late 1980s, in the revival period, the policy of restriction on immigration from the Soviet Union was initiated. The policy decisions were implemented at the local level in the governmental structure. In 1989, local councils of many large cities (Vilnius, in the first place) and later local councils of some medium-sized towns adopted decisions to restrict the registration (Soviet "propiska" procedure for applicants for permanent residency) and to increase the registration fees for persons arriving from elsewhere.

Upon regaining independence, the Constitution of the Republic of Lithuania (1992) and the Law on Citizenship (1991) established the basic attitudes of Lithuania on international migration and its regulation. In 1992, the Laws on Emigration and Immigration regulating the procedure of arrivals and departures were passed. These documents declared liberal principles of Lithuania on international migration and on granting citizenship to the immigrants of the Soviet period and their children. Only a few restrictions on emigration were set (e.g. for persons with legal or property liabilities, etc.). Immigration quotas were established for every year to regulate the number of migrant arrivals. Some restrictions on arrivals related to health conditions (bearers of dangerous infection diseases), harmful habits (drug addiction), availability of subsistence means, etc. were imposed. In 1992 and 1994, a set of measures was adopted for providing better opportunities for rehabilitated political prisoners, deportees and their descendants' families to return from the former USSR and integrate into the life of Lithuania.

When the phenomenon of illegal transit migration surfaced in Lithuania, the laws were introduced that were based on international documents addressing this specific type of migration.

Although the migration policy pursued by Lithuania is a liberal one, it, nevertheless, contains a general attitude of not becoming a country of "vast emigration" and "mass immigration" (*National Report on Population: Lithuania*, 1993).

## Notes

1. The Department of Demography of the Institute of Economics of the Lithuanian Academy of Sciences carried out the surveys in 1988 and 1990. In 1988, 2,880 employed people were surveyed and in 1990 – 1,540 people aged 18 and over. In 1994–1995, the Department conducted the survey that was a part of the international project *Fertility and Family Surveys in Europe* initiated and coordinated by the Population Activities Unit, United Nations Economic Commission for Europe.
2. In 1991, the WHO definition of stillbirth was introduced and since then has been used in Lithuania.

## References


Council of Europe (1998), *Recent Demographic Developments in Europe 1998*, Strasbourg: Council of Europe.

(1998), *Demographic Data Collection of Estonia, Latvia and Lithuania*. Tallinn.

(1996), *Family Policy in Lithuania: Principles and Actions*. Vilnius.

(1990), *Lietuvos Gyventojai*. Vilnius.

Macura, M. (1995), Fertility and nuptiality changes in Central and Eastern Europe: 1982–1993, *Studia Demograficzne*, Vol. 4.

(1997), *Main Macroeconomic Indicators of Lithuania 1996*. Vilnius.

(1993), *National Report on Population: Lithuania*, presented at the International Conference on Population and Development, Cairo, 1994.

(1995), *Seimos Politikos Koncepcija*. Vilnius.

Stankuniene V. and M. Baublyte (1996), *Lithuanian Family and Fertility Survey. Standard Tabulations and Main Data*. Vilnius: Lithuanian Institute of Philosophy and Sociology.

Statistics Lithuania (1996), *Demographic Yearbook 1995*, Vilnius.

Statistics Lithuania (1997), *Demographic Yearbook 1996*, Vilnius.

Statistics Lithuania (1998), *Demographic Yearbook 1997*, Vilnius.

Statistics Lithuania (1999), *Demographic Yearbook 1998*, Vilnius.

UNDP (United Nations Development Programme) (1996), *Human Development Report 1999. Lithuania*, Vilnius.

UN ECE/UNFPA (United Nations Economic Commission for Europe/United Nations Population Fund) (1998), *Fertility and Family Surveys in Countries of the ECE Region. Standard Country Report. Lithuania*, New York and Geneva: United Nations (unpublished manuscript).

van de Kaa, D.J. (1987), Europe's Second Demographic Transition, *Population Bulletin*, Vol. 42(1), pp. 1–58.

# 11

# Past and Present Population Development in the Republic of Moldova

**Maria Bulgaru, Oleg Bulgaru, Tomáš Sobotka and Kryštof Zeman**[1]

## 11.1 Introduction

The Republic of Moldova – the second smallest country among the republics of the former USSR – is situated in the south of Eastern Europe, between Romania and Ukraine. Located in the area surrounded by deltas of Nistru, Prut and Danube rivers, it has experienced frequent changes in borders and territory size. Moldova was part of the Russian Empire until 1918, then it declared independence and united with Romania. The newly formed Union of the Soviet Socialist Republics refused to recognise this unification and in 1924 established Moldavian Autonomous Soviet Socialist Republic (MASSR) by partitioning the ethnically mixed part of Ukraine located by the Nistru river, although the share of Moldovan population in this region was only 30% (O'Loughlin *et al.*, 1998). During the Second World War, in August 1940, the Moldavian Soviet Socialist Republic was established in its present borders. Later, the territory was annexed by Romania and then again by the USSR at the end of the Second World War. During the post-war period an intense Russification of Moldavan society took place. Russian language was introduced into everyday life and the Cyrillic alphabet replaced traditional Latin alphabet in Moldavan language, which is similar to Romanian language.

After the first democratic elections held in February-March 1990, the new government took power in May 1990 and introduced series of radical changes – the major being the declaration of the sovereignty in June 1990, and the change of the republic's name first to the Soviet Socialist Republic of Moldova and then to the Republic of Moldova in May 1991. Subsequently, two inner regions declared their own independence: The Republic of Gagauzia (in August 1990) and the Transdniester Soviet Socialist Republic (in September 1990). The Gagauzian region is located in the rural south of the country and is mainly inhabited by an ethnic group of a Turkic origin known as the Gagauz, whose main religion is Orthodox Christianity. The Transdniester Moldovan Republic, with the capital Tiraspol, is located in the so-called Transnistria, on the east bank of the river Nistru, and is populated mostly by Slavonic people.

Following the collapse of the 1991 August coup d'etat in the former Soviet Union, the Republic of Moldova declared its independence from the Soviet Union on 27 August

1991. The political situation in Transdniestria gradually escalated into a violent and armed conflict with casualties. As a result of peace negotiations between Moldovan, Ukrainian, Russian and Romanian authorities, in 1992 the conflict was ceased. Since then, Transdniestria has remained a separate "pseudo-state" ("Transdniester Moldovian Republic") with its own government, currency and parliament. In contrast with the Republic of Moldova, where Latin alphabet was reintroduced, law punishes its use in Transdniestria and people of the Moldovan nationality, despite being the largest ethnic group, are persecuted and discriminated there. In contrast, the Gagauz reached a compromise with the Moldovan Government in 1994, and at present this region has a special non-autonomous status.

## 11.2 Social and Economic Development

The population of Moldova is 4.3 million people living on the territory of 33.8 thousand square kilometres, which makes the population density about 127 people per km$^2$. The capital of Moldova is Chişinău, with 752 thousand inhabitants. The majority of population, 54%, lives in rural areas, what makes Moldova, besides Albania and Bosnia-Herzegovina, the least urbanised country of Europe. Almost 50% of the population are employed in agriculture, which uses plentiful rich black soils ("chernozem"). In the past, Moldova was often called "the garden of the Soviet Union" and agricultural products, especially wine, are still the principal export products.

The dissolution of the Soviet Union brought the loss of trade connections, export destinations and secession of industrial Transdniestria. General backwardness of economy as well as slow and chaotic implementation of economic reforms has resulted in continuing economic decline, high inflation and increase of poverty. During the period 1989–1996, the GDP officially declined by 65% and reached the value of US$590 per capita, which makes Moldova the poorest country in Europe. The legal economy was step by step substituted by "shadow economy", which reached alarming proportions. According to expert estimates, the size of the "shadow economy" is equal to 70% of the official GDP derived from legal economic activities (UNDP, 1998). Although the real wages are extremely low (average monthly salary was 220 Moldovan Lei, i.e. US$44, in 1997), the situation of unemployed people, retired persons and families with many children is even worse. The official unemployment rate was only 1.5% in 1997, but unofficial estimate was 25%. Two-thirds of Moldovan population had the average income under 90 Moldovan Lei per month (US$18) in 1997, and 77% of inhabitants lived under the minimum subsistence level (UNDP, 1998).

The deterioration of the living standards of the population accelerated by the price liberalisation has been the most severe consequence of the economic transition. According to estimates, the real income per capita declined 3.5 times during six years of economic transition since 1991 (UNDP, 1998).

## 11.3 Population Structures

### 11.3.1 Age Composition

The age pyramid (Figure 11.1) illustrates disproportional population growth during the last 50 years. The periods of fertility decline (final years of the Second World War and the short subsequent period of famine, first half of the 1960s, following abortion liberalisation, and the 1990s) alternated with the periods of baby boom (in the mid-1950s and mid-1980s). A disproportional age structure is present among the older population. Due to higher male mortality, the proportion of women aged 60 years and over is substantially larger than that of men (there is, for instance, almost twice more women than men among people aged 70 years and over).

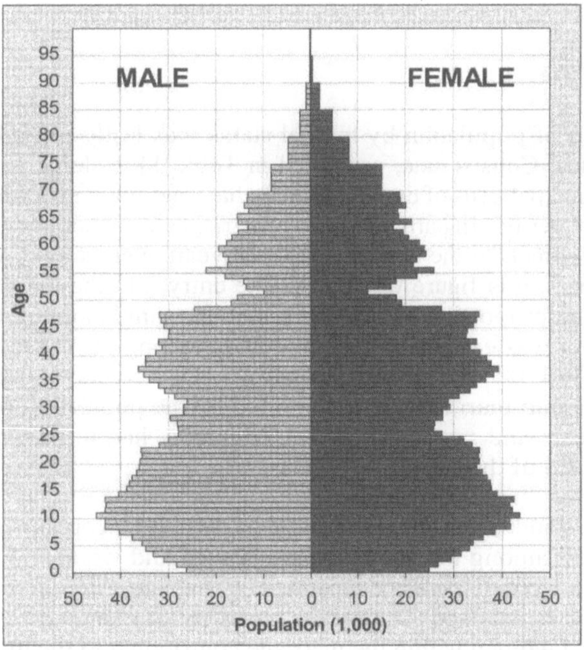


**Figure 11.1: Age and Sex Structure of Population on 1 January 1997**

Source: based on DASS, 1998

Although Moldova is experiencing demographic ageing and the share of older people is slowly increasing, in comparison with other European countries this process is relatively slow due to rather high level of fertility combined with rather high level of mortality in the past. The proportion of children (0–14 years) was 25.8% of the total population in 1997, which is 6% more than the average value for the Eastern European countries, and the share of old people aged 65 and over was only 9.1%, compared with the average of 13% for Eastern Europe and 15% for Western Europe

(Population Reference Bureau, 1998). Besides Albania and Macedonia, the Moldova's population is the youngest one in Europe (Table 11.1).

**Table 11.1: Population by Main Age Groups, 1959–1997, selected years, per cent**

| Age group | Total | | | | | Male | Female |
|---|---|---|---|---|---|---|---|
| | 1959 | 1970 | 1979 | 1989 | 1997 | 1997 | 1997 |
| 0–14 | 33.3 | 32.2 | 27.0 | 27.9 | 25.8 | 27.5 | 24.2 |
| 15–59 | 59.0 | 58.1 | 62.2 | 59.5 | 60.9 | 61.6 | 60.3 |
| 60+ | 7.7 | 9.7 | 10.8 | 12.6 | 13.3 | 10.9 | 15.5 |
| 65+ | .. | .. | 7.6 | 8.1 | 9.1 | 7.2 | 11.0 |
| 80+ | .. | .. | 1.0 | 1.2 | 1.2 | 0.8 | 1.6 |

Sources: DASS, 1996, 1997a, 1998; *Itogi vsesoyouznoi perepisi naselenia 1989 goda po SSR Moldova*, 1990

### 11.3.2 Marital Status

The composition of population by marital status was lastly provided by the 1989 population census. Census data, presented in Table 11.2, demonstrates the prevalence of traditional patterns of demographic behaviour among Moldovan population during the Soviet period. In particular, early marriages were common among women: only 27.8% of women in the age group 20–24 years were single, while in the age group 25–29 years, this figure was 8.8%. The entry into the marriage was almost universal, and the proportion of persons remaining single among the people aged 40 years and over was extremely low, especially among men. Among people aged 45–49 years, only 1.1% of men and 3.3% of women were never married. Early and universal entries into marriage were supported by the population policy measures: men aged 18 years and more, who remained single, had to pay special so-called "bachelor" tax (7% of the salary).

During the 1970s and 1980s, the proportion of divorced people increased. In 1989, it was the highest among the 40–44 years old men and women: 4.7% of men and 10.1% of women were divorced or separated by that age. After divorce, women had lower chance for remarriage. The excess mortality of men and the age difference between men and women within the marriage contributed to the high proportion of widowed women among old people. In the age group 70 years and over, only 28.8% of men were widowed, compared to 74.2% of women.

**Table 11.2: Population by Marital Status, 1989, per cent**

| Age group | Single | Married | Divorced | Widowed | Unknown |
|---|---|---|---|---|---|
| | | | Male | | |
| 16–17 | 99.3 | 0.7 | 0.0 | 0.0 | 0.0 |
| 18–19 | 95.0 | 3.7 | 0.0 | 0.0 | 1.3 |
| 20–24 | 58.0 | 39.9 | 1.0 | 0.1 | 1.0 |
| 25–29 | 14.2 | 82.5 | 2.8 | 0.2 | 0.3 |
| 30–34 | 5.1 | 91.0 | 3.5 | 0.3 | 0.1 |
| 35–39 | 2.6 | 92.9 | 3.9 | 0.5 | 0.1 |
| 40–44 | 1.7 | 92.6 | 4.7 | 0.9 | 0.1 |
| 45–49 | 1.1 | 92.4 | 4.5 | 1.9 | 0.1 |
| 50–54 | 0.8 | 91.9 | 3.9 | 3.3 | 0.1 |
| 55–59 | 0.6 | 91.0 | 3.0 | 5.3 | 0.1 |
| 60–69 | 0.5 | 86.5 | 2.1 | 10.7 | 0.2 |
| 70+ | 0.4 | 69.6 | 0.9 | 28.7 | 0.4 |
| 16+ | 18.1 | 75.4 | 2.7 | 3.5 | 0.3 |
| | | | Female | | |
| 16–17 | 95.7 | 4.1 | 0.1 | 0.0 | 0.1 |
| 18–19 | .. | .. | .. | .. | .. |
| 20–24 | 27.7 | 67.8 | 3.5 | 0.5 | 0.5 |
| 25–29 | 8.8 | 84.4 | 5.7 | 0.9 | 0.2 |
| 30–34 | 4.9 | 86.0 | 7.3 | 1.7 | 0.1 |
| 35–39 | 3.8 | 84.0 | 8.8 | 3.3 | 0.1 |
| 40–44 | 3.6 | 80.3 | 10.1 | 5.9 | 0.1 |
| 45–49 | 3.3 | 76.5 | 9.8 | 10.3 | 0.1 |
| 50–54 | 3.3 | 72.6 | 8.5 | 15.5 | 0.1 |
| 55–59 | 3.7 | 65.9 | 6.4 | 23.8 | 0.2 |
| 60–69 | 3.0 | 51.8 | 4.6 | 40.3 | 0.3 |
| 70+ | 1.7 | 22.4 | 1.6 | 73.8 | 0.5 |
| 16+ | 12.5 | 65.5 | 6.0 | 15.7 | 0.3 |

Source: *Itogi vsesoyouznoi perepisi naselenia 1989 goda po SSR Moldova*, op. cit.

### 11.3.3 Ethnic Composition

Ethnic structure of the population provides a mixed picture (Table 11.3). The Moldovans form only weak majority of 64.5% inhabitants (according to the 1989 census) in their country, and there are large regional disparities in the ethnic composition of the population, which are, in turn, the principle source of ethnic tensions since the breakdown of the Soviet Union. Russians and Ukrainians, with the share of 13.0% and 13.8% respectively are, besides Moldovans, the most numerous ethnic groups.

In total, Slavonic nationalities make up a majority in Transdniestria (29% Russians and 29% Ukrainians compared with 33% Moldovans in 1995) (O'Loughlin *et al.*, op. cit.) and live mostly in urban areas, where Moldovans compose less than half of the total population (46% Moldovans, 24% Russians and 19% Ukrainians in 1989). The Russians were the most rapidly growing nationality in Moldova, especially in the

1950s and 1960s, when "a large segments of Russian and Ukrainian population were established in Moldova through forced and incentive-induced migration" (UNDP, 1995). Another important nationalities in 1989 were the Gagauz (3.5%), the Bulgarians (2.0%) and the Jews (1.5%).

**Table 11.3: Population by Ethnic Groups, 1959–1996, selected years**

| Ethnic group | 1959 | 1970 | 1979 | 1989 | 1996[1] |
|---|---|---|---|---|---|
| | | | Number (1,000) | | |
| Moldovans | 1,886.6 | 2,303.9 | 2,525.7 | 2,794.7 | 2,986.4 |
| Ukrainians | 420.8 | 506.6 | 560.7 | 600.4 | 559.1 |
| Russians | 292.9 | 414.4 | 505.7 | 562.1 | 511.5 |
| Gagauz | 95.9 | 124.9 | 138.0 | 153.4 | .. |
| Jews | 95.1 | 98.1 | 80.1 | 65.8 | .. |
| Bulgarians | 61.7 | 73.8 | 80.7 | 88.4 | .. |
| Others | 31.5 | 47.2 | 58.9 | 70.5 | 277.4 |
| Total | 2,884.5 | 3,568.9 | 3,949.8 | 4,335.3 | 4,334.4 |
| | | | Percentage | | |
| Moldovans | 65.4 | 64.6 | 63.9 | 64.5 | 68.9 |
| Ukrainians | 14.6 | 14.2 | 14.2 | 13.8 | 12.9 |
| Russians | 10.2 | 11.6 | 12.8 | 13.0 | 11.8 |
| Gagauz | 3.3 | 3.5 | 3.5 | 3.5 | .. |
| Jews | 3.3 | 2.7 | 2.0 | 1.5 | .. |
| Bulgarians | 2.1 | 2.1 | 2.0 | 2.0 | .. |
| Others | 1.1 | 1.3 | 1.5 | 1.6 | .. |
| Total | 100.0 | 100.0 | 100.0 | 100.0 | 100.0 |

[1]Estimate (UNICEF, 1998)
Source: *Itogi vsesoyouznoi perepisi naselenia 1989 goda po SSR Moldova*, op. cit.

In 1959, the Jews, along with the Gagauz, were the fourth and the fifth largest ethnic groups, but due to unfavourable age structure and since the 1970s especially due to intensive emigration to Israel, the size of Jewish population has been shrinking considerably. The emigration of Jews had intensified in the 1989–1991 period, and then continued, although less intensively. Since 1989, at least 50 thousand Jews from 65 thousand enumerated by the census have emigrated and, as a result, this nationality almost disappeared from Moldova.

Large migration flows since 1989 have caused the increase of ethnic homogeneity of Moldovans in Moldova and of Russians and Ukrainians in Transdniestria. Although there are no official statistics, the estimate of ethnic structure for 1996 shows considerable increase of the share of Moldovans in population from 64.5% in 1989 to 68.9% in 1996 (UNICEF, 1998).

### 11.3.4 Urban – Rural Differences

The regional population differences in Moldova are substantial. Besides large differences between the Transdniestria and the rest of Moldova, there are also large differences between the south, the centre and the north of the country. Even more visible are differences between urban and rural areas. The rural areas are more ethnically homogenous (80% of inhabitants were of Moldovan nationality in 1989) and more traditional in the sense of higher fertility of women (the crude birth rate in 1996 was 13.8‰ in rural areas and 9.8‰ – in urban ones), earlier entries of women into marriages, lower share of extramarital births (12.9% against 17.2% in urban areas in 1996) and lower share of divorced persons.

The level of mortality also differs in urban and rural areas. Already in 1985, the life expectancy at birth in rural areas was by 5.1 years lower than in urban areas, i.e. 64.1 years. The deterioration of mortality patterns in the 1990s was more distinct in urban areas and the urban-rural differences in the life expectancy at birth decreased only to 1 year for men and 2 years for women in 1996 (1.5 years for both sexes – the life expectancy at birth was 66.0 in rural and 67.5 in urban areas). Better access to the food supplies in rural areas may have played the role, as the malnutrition due to low income became a serious problem for many people.

### 11.3.5 Economic Activity

As the full participation of women in the "labour process" was part of the official ideology of the Soviet regime, the share of women in the productive workforce increased from 35% in 1945 to 51% in 1971 (*Itogi vsesoyouznoi perepisi naselenia 1989 goda po SSR Moldova*, op. cit.). This share remained stable till the mid-1990s. The inefficient economy experienced permanent deficit of the employees and high participation of women was necessary for its functioning: especially in services, women still form significant majority of the workforce, more than two-thirds (68.3%) in 1994 (UNICEF, 1997). In 1990, the share of economically active women was by 6–12% lower than the share of economically active men in all corresponding age groups. The highest labour force participation was between 25 and 44 years: 82% women and 94% men were economically active in that age group. The lower share of women is mainly caused by their participation in the child-rearing during the maternity leave period.

### 11.3.6 Religion

Despite 45 years of atheistic ideology under the communism, the population preserved its religious traditions. In 1997, 94.2% people declared their affiliation with the Christian Orthodox church, 2.7% with other religions and only 3.1% claimed no religious affiliation – 5% in urban and 1% in rural areas (UNFPA, 1998).

## 11.4 Population Development

### 11.4.1 Basic Components

The demographic behaviour of the population in Moldova was traditional in comparison with other European countries till the end of the 1980s. The crude birth rate was especially high, ranging around 20‰. As the crude death rate was varying between 7‰ and 11‰, the rate of natural increase was approximately 1% a year since the 1960s until the 1980s. The mobility of population was strongly regulated and with the exception of partly forced labour migration, rather intensive during the 1950s and 1960s, the population was almost closed.

The total population size jumped from 2.89 million in 1959 to 4.34 million in 1989. All the basic components of the population movement changed dramatically during the 1990s (Table 11.4). Between 1989 and 1996, the crude birth rate decreased from 18.9‰ to 12.0‰, the crude death rate slightly increased to 11.5‰ and natural increase fell almost to the zero level. Population increase had reversed into net population loss due to negative migration balance since 1991, but the total number of population decreased only slightly from 4.36 million in 1991 to 4.32 million in 1997. The population decrease was severe in Transdniestria, where the negative natural increase was combined with the negative migration balance. According to the statistics presented by O'Loughlin *et al.* (op. cit.), the population of Transdniestria dropped between 1991 and 1997 by 10.4%, from 731 to 657 thousand.

**Table 11.4: Main Indicators of Population Development, 1960–1997, selected years**

| Year | Population[1] | Urban population | Live births | Deaths | Natural increase | Marriages | Divorces |
|---|---|---|---|---|---|---|---|
| | 1,000 | % | Per 1,000 inhabitants | | | | |
| 1960 | 2,967.7 | 22.3 | 29.3 | 6.4 | 22.8 | 9.3 | 0.9 |
| 1970 | 3,568.9 | 31.7 | 19.4 | 7.4 | 12.0 | 9.4 | 2.1 |
| 1980 | 3,987.2 | 39.3 | 19.8 | 10.1 | 9.8 | 11.5 | 2.8 |
| 1990 | 4,361.6 | 47.5 | 17.7 | 9.8 | 7.9 | 9.4 | 3.0 |
| 1991 | 4,366.3 | 47.5 | 16.5 | 10.5 | 6.0 | 9.1 | 3.2 |
| 1992 | 4,359.1 | 47.1 | 16.0 | 10.2 | 5.8 | 9.0 | 3.4 |
| 1993 | 4,347.8 | 46.9 | 15.2 | 10.7 | 4.5 | 9.1 | 3.3 |
| 1994 | 4,352.7 | 46.8 | 14.3 | 11.8 | 2.4 | 7.8 | 3.2 |
| 1995 | 4,347.9 | 46.8 | 13.0 | 12.2 | 0.8 | 7.5 | 3.4 |
| 1996 | 4,334.4 | 46.2 | 12.0 | 11.5 | 0.5 | 6.0 | 3.1 |
| 1997 | 4,320.0 | 46.2 | .. | .. | .. | .. | .. |

[1]As of 1 January of a given year
Sources: Council of Europe, 1998; DASS, 1996, 1997a, 1998

### 11.4.2 Migration Balance

The relaxation of the rigid migration laws and the dissolution of the Soviet Union have induced large migration movements since the end of the 1980s (Table 11.5). The largest migration flows out of Moldova were registered in 1990–1992, when, according to incomplete official statistics, 144 thousand people (mostly of non-Moldovan nationality) emigrated to the countries of the former Soviet Union, and 42 thousand people to other foreign countries. On the other hand, 123 thousand people emigrated to Moldova from the other areas of the former Soviet Union, most of them ethnic Moldovans. The migration balance has been negative during the whole period since 1990. The population loss due to emigration in 1990–1996 was 105 thousand people, according to official statistics, and 163 thousand people (3.7% of the population registered in 1990), according to expert estimates (Council of Europe, op. cit.). Besides the former Soviet Union, the principle emigration destination was Israel, where officially 42 thousand people have emigrated since 1990.

**Table 11.5: External Migration, 1990–1996**

| | 1990 | 1991 | 1992 | 1993 | 1994 | 1995 | 1996 |
|---|---|---|---|---|---|---|---|
| Immigration | 155,958 | 133,524 | 104,896 | 86,165 | 68,374 | 60,963 | 57,441 |
| Emigration | 162,690 | 149,165 | 130,628 | 94,504 | 83,233 | 78,061 | 73,915 |
| Net migration[1] | -6,732 | -15,641 | -25,732 | -8,339 | -14,859 | -17,980 | -16,474 |
| Net migration[2] | -30,000 | -33,400 | -36,400 | -15,100 | -14,800 | -17,100 | -16,500 |
| | Emigration by country/region of destination | | | | | | |
| Former USSR | 48,304 | 43,153 | 53,171 | 29,374 | 28,342 | 27,653 | 26,425 |
| Israel | 15,230 | 14,768 | 3,441 | 2,308 | 2,596 | 2,266 | 1,762 |
| USA | 672 | 2,418 | 2,366 | 2,814 | 1,918 | 1,379 | 1,482 |
| Germany | 634 | 799 | 1,088 | 1,166 | 1,729 | 1,625 | 1,286 |

[1]According to official statistics
[2]According to expert estimates (Council of Europe, op. cit.)
Sources: DASS, 1997b; Council of Europe, op. cit.

### 11.4.3 Fertility

The number of live births reached a peak in the mid-1980s at 94.7 thousand in 1986, and then it was declining continually to 51.9 thousand in 1996. Up to the end of the 1980s, the level of fertility in Moldova was the highest in the European part of the Soviet Union and in the mid-1980s was the second highest in Europe after Albania.

First large-scale reduction in fertility occurred after the legalisation of abortions in 1955, in particular between 1960 and 1965 (see Table 11.6). Total fertility rate (TFR) dropped from 3.6 in 1958 to 2.7 in 1965 and then remained between 2.4 and 2.6 until the beginning of the 1980s. These figures refer in reality to the two-year periods, 1958–1959 and 1965–1966, as the TFR in the USSR was published before 1986 for the two-year periods. The decline of the number of births of the higher birth orders was characteristic for this period. If in 1965, 32% of births were of the fourth or subsequent birth order (biological birth order during reproductive life of mother), in 1980, their share was only 8% (Figure 11.2). Reduction of fertility of higher ranks influenced the average age of women at childbearing, which dropped from approximately 29 to 26 years.

**Table 11.6: Main Indicators of Fertility, 1960–1996, selected years**

| Year | Live births | Crude birth rate (‰) | Total fertility rate | Mean age at childbearing | Live births out of wedlock (%) |
|---|---|---|---|---|---|
| 1960 | 87,910 | 29.3 | 3.20[1] | 29.0[1] | .. |
| 1965 | 67,996 | 20.4 | 2.68 | 29.0 | .. |
| 1970 | 69,778 | 19.4 | 2.58[2] | 28.2[2] | .. |
| 1975 | 79,169 | 20.6 | 2.55[3] | 27.2 | .. |
| 1980 | 79,580 | 19.8 | 2.39 | 26.5 | 7.4 |
| 1985 | 90,453 | 21.5 | 2.75 | 26.4 | 8.8 |
| 1986 | 94,726 | 22.3 | .. | .. | .. |
| 1987 | 91,762 | 21.4 | 2.73 | 26.5 | .. |
| 1988 | 88,568 | 20.5 | 2.64 | 26.4 | .. |
| 1989 | 82,221 | 18.9 | 2.78 | 25.6 | .. |
| 1990 | 77,085 | 17.7 | 2.39 | 25.4 | 11.0 |
| 1991 | 72,020 | 16.5 | 2.26 | 25.0 | 11.8 |
| 1992 | 69,654 | 16.0 | 2.21 | 25.0 | 11.6 |
| 1993 | 66,179 | 15.2 | 2.10 | 25.0 | 11.2 |
| 1994 | 62,085 | 14.3 | 1.95 | 25.0 | 12.3 |
| 1995 | 56,411 | 13.0 | 1.76 | 24.9 | 13.3 |
| 1996 | 51,865 | 12.0 | 1.61 | 25.0 | 14.6 |

[1]1961
[2]1969
[3]1974
Sources: DASS, 1996, 1997a, 1998; Council of Europe, op. cit.

The first half of the 1980s was a period of a moderate baby boom, which occurred as a reaction to the population measures implemented for the stimulation of higher birth order fertility. These measures were especially successful in stimulation of the third births (total number of the third births increased by 73% between 1980 and 1986), particularly also of the second (increase by 34%) and fourth and subsequent births (25% increase). The TFR increased from 2.4 in 1980 to 2.8 in 1985. In 1990, the TFR was 2.39, and fertility was mostly concentrated in the younger ages of women between 19 and 24 years, peaking at the age of 20 years (Figure 11.3). As in the other post-communist countries, the TFR dropped extensively after 1989 to the level of 1.61 in 1996.

Current fertility level in Moldova still remains somewhat higher than in the other Eastern European countries, but contrary to many of them, there are no signs of post-ponement of fertility to higher ages of women. The reduction of age specific fertil-ity rates between 1990 and 1996 was rather equal within all age groups (30–40%), only somewhat more moderate between 24–28 years (reduction by 20–30%). Sur-prisingly, the fertility of the 15–17 years old women increased and those of 18 years old women decreased only by 6%. The mean age of women at childbearing remained low (25.0 years in 1996, i.e. 0.4 years less than in 1990) and the mean age of women at first birth (22.2 years) was the lowest in Europe, although not far from the other Eastern European countries. In comparison with other countries, the level of fertility of teenage girls stands out: 16.9% of total births and 31.5% of first births occurred among women under 20 years in 1996 (based on DASS data).

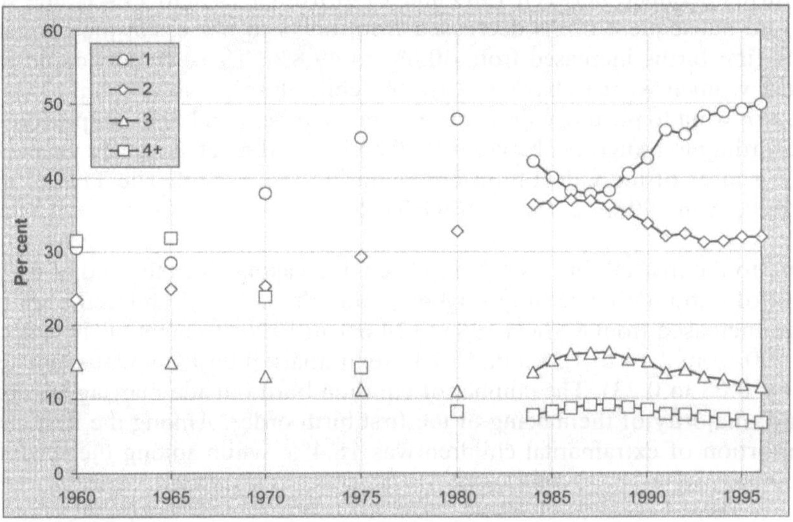


**Figure 11.2: Proportion of Live Births by Birth Order, 1960–1996, selected years**

Source: Council of Europe, op. cit.

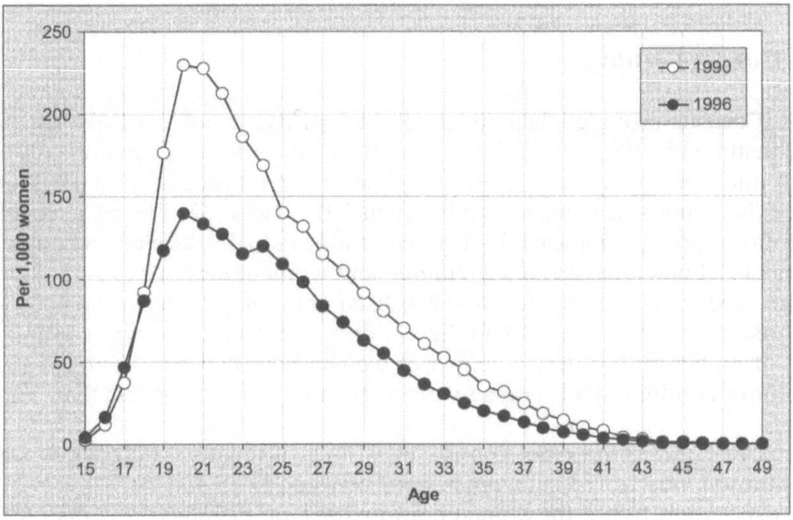


**Figure 11.3: Age-specific Fertility Rates, 1990 and 1996**

Source: based on DASS data

The fertility decline was more intensive among the third and subsequent birth orders. Their share increased after implementation of the population policy measures at the beginning of the 1980s. Due to the economic crisis and hyperinflation, these measures have lost their efficiency. The share of third births among the total number of births declined between 1989 and 1996 from 15.4% to 11.4%, the share of fourth and subsequent births decreased from 8.9% to 6.8%. On the contrary, the share of first births increased from 40.6% to 49.8%. These figures could indicate that most women want to have at least one child despite the economic crisis, and they do not want to postpone these births. On the other hand, the composition of the TFR according to birth order between 1990 and 1996 did not show any visible changes in the shares of individual birth orders during this period. The TFR of the first rank was 0.63 in 1996, i.e. 45.5% of the TFR.

Opposite to the marital fertility that has been decreasing since the end of the 1980s, the level of extramarital fertility stagnated, and the share of children born outside marriage increased from 8.8% in 1985 to 14.6% in 1996. The marital TFR decreased since 1990 from 2.14 to 1.38, but TFR for extramarital births in fact stagnated (decrease by 0.03 to 0.23). The number of children born outside marriage is around 8 thousand, majority of them being of the first birth order. Among the first children, the proportion of extramarital children was 18.4%, while among the second ones only 10.4%.

In 1997, the average ideal number of children was 2.2 (see UNFPA, op. cit.). This number indicates that despite traditionally higher fertility, the family with two children is considered an ideal family model in Moldova.

### 11.4.4 Cohort Fertility

The 1989 census provided data about cohort fertility, which confirms some of the trends illustrated by the period fertility data. If we take into consideration only women aged 35 and over, who had almost completed their reproduction in 1989, we can compare the cohorts of women born between 1919 and 1953. The basic conclusions are as follows. First, completed fertility decreased gradually, as women born between 1919 and 1924 had on average 3.2 children and women born in 1946 – 2.2 children. Then the level of completed fertility stabilised and younger generations of women up to those ones born in 1954 had 2.2 children. Second, there was continuous reduction of higher birth orders: a quarter of women born between 1919 and 1924 had five or more children, while among women born in 1953 it was less than 5%.

Furthermore, among the older cohorts of women ultimate childlessness was also more common, nearly 15% of women born between 1919 and 1928 were childless, the corresponding figure for women born in 1951 or 1952 was less than 8%. This trend may have been influenced by the improvement of health care, which could have reduced the female sterility, but also by the perceived decrease of the social value of childless women combined with population policy (all women who were married and childless had to pay tax of 6% of their salary). If the estimates of women infertility are accurate, the share of infertile women was the same as the share of the childless women born at the beginning of the 1950s – so almost every woman, who could have a child, had at least one. Step by step, the model of family with two children was asserted: around 45% among the women born in the first half of the 1950s had two children, almost 20% had three children, 18% had one child, 11% had four or more children and only 8% were childless (Figure 11.4).

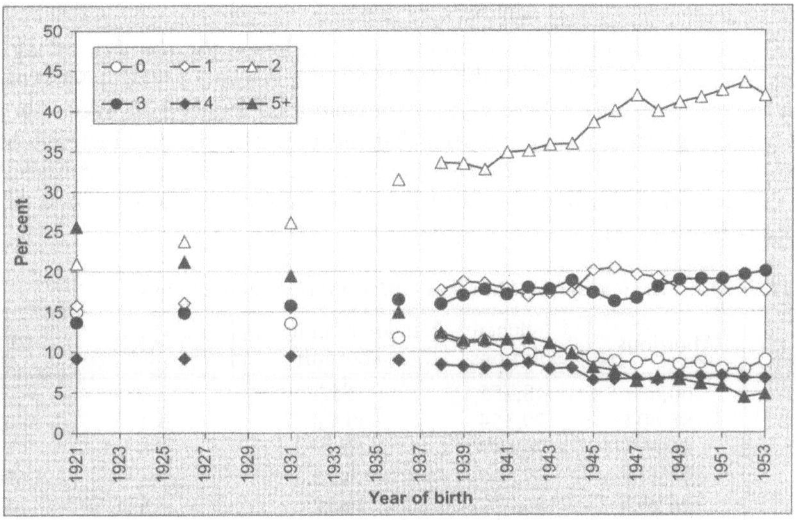


**Figure 11.4: Proportion of Women Born Between 1921 and 1953 According to Number of Live-born Children, selected generations**
Source: *Itogi vsesoyouznoi perepisi naselenia 1989 goda po SSR Moldova*, op. cit.

## 11.5 Abortions, Contraception and Reproductive Health

After the re-legalisation of abortions in the USSR in 1955, which allowed abortions to be performed on demand through the first trimester of pregnancy, induced abortions became a principal means of fertility regulation. Although some modern contraceptive devices were available – especially condoms and since the 1960s also the intrauterine device (IUD) – their use was limited. The supply of condoms was several times lower than the potential demand and the availability of chemical contraceptives (pills) was extremely scarce as they were officially considered threatening to woman's health (and the brands available in the USSR really were, at least till the 1970s). Together with the absence of appropriate sexual education and general lack of information, "the only easily accessible method of family planning was induced abortion, which was permitted on the basis of social background" (Popov, 1991).

The statistics of induced abortions are based on incomplete figures and estimates, as the surgical induced abortions were registered separately from the vacuum aspirations: statistics on vacuum aspirations (miniabortions) were incomplete and, on the other hand, the statistics of total abortions included spontaneous abortions. Moreover, inclusion of the illegal abortions could further increase the number of abortions by 13%, according to official estimates, and by 50–70%, according to independent estimates (Popov, op. cit.).

According to our estimates, based on official statistics, the number of legal abortions had increased sharply until the mid-1960s when around 80 thousand abortions were performed annually (Table 11.7). Estimated total induced abortion rate (TIAR) was 3.1, the highest since the abortion legalisation. The parallel increase of TIAR between 1960 and 1965 (from 2.0 to 3.1) and decrease of the total fertility rate from 3.6 to 2.7 confirms the hypothesis of the use of abortions as a method of family planning (Figure 11.5).

**Table 11.7: Main Indicators of Abortion, 1960–1996, selected years**

| Year | Abortions | Induced abortions[1] | Index of induced abortion[2] | TIAR[3] | TCR[4] |
|---|---|---|---|---|---|
| 1960 | 60,687 | 48,755 | 55.2 | 2.0 | 6.0 |
| 1965 | 88,604 | 79,354 | 115.8 | 3.1 | 6.2 |
| 1970 | 86,093 | 76,598 | 108.9 | 2.8 | 5.8 |
| 1975 | 93,334 | 82,558 | 102.9 | 2.6 | 5.6 |
| 1980 | 96,283 | 85,423 | 106.2 | 2.5 | 5.3 |
| 1985 | 102,661 | 90,283 | 98.9 | 2.7 | 5.9 |
| 1986 | 110,011 | 97,113 | 101.6 | .. | .. |
| 1987 | 112,426 | 99,921 | 107.9 | 2.9 | 6.1 |
| 1988 | 94,998 | 82,930 | 92.8 | 2.4 | 5.5 |
| 1989 | 90,860 | 79,674 | 96.2 | 2.7 | 5.9 |
| 1990 | 81,931 | 71,441 | 91.9 | 2.2 | 4.9 |
| 1991 | 73,454 | 63,771 | 87.9 | 2.0 | 4.5 |
| 1992 | 71,430 | 61,773 | 88.0 | 1.9 | 4.4 |
| 1993 | 64,178 | 55,242 | 82.9 | 1.7 | 4.1 |
| 1994 | 58,777 | 50,380 | 80.5 | 1.6 | 3.8 |
| 1995 | 57,181 | 49,460 | 87.0 | 1.6 | 3.6 |
| 1996 | 46,010 | 38,901 | 74.4 | 1.2 | 3.1 |

[1]Including non-specified and criminal abortions (estimations until 1990)
[2]Per 100 births
[3]Authors' estimation
[4]Total conception rate (TCR) is computed by the summation of the total fertility rate (TFR), total induced abortion rate (TIAR) and total spontaneous abortion rate (TSAR); expert estimation
Sources: ASM, 1998; Council of Europe, op. cit.; DASS data

During the period between 1960 and 1989, the estimated total conception rate (including spontaneous abortions) was ranging between 5.3 and 6.2 conceptions per woman during her reproductive life and the TIAR after moderate decrease stabilised around 2.5 since the mid-1970s. This decrease could be caused by the spread of IUD, which was used by more than 20% women in reproductive age at the end of the 1980s.

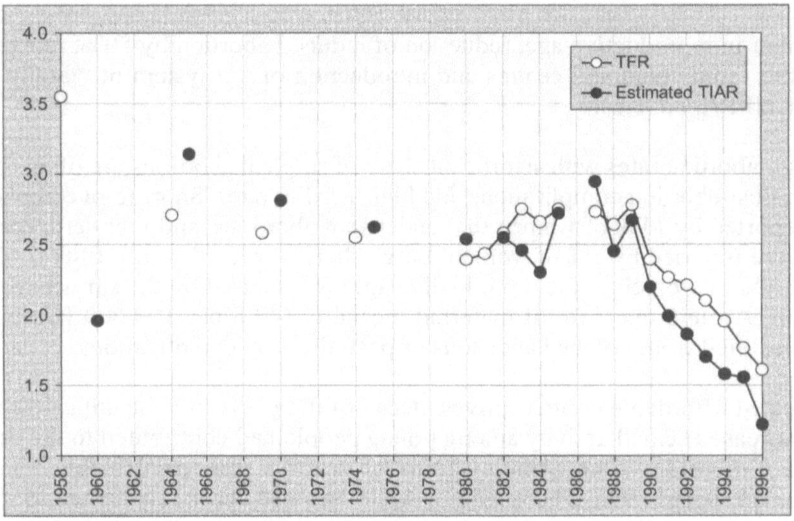


**Figure 11.5: Total Fertility Rate (TFR) and Estimated Total Induced Abortion Rate (TIAR), 1958–1996, selected years**

Sources: ASM, op. cit.; Council of Europe, op. cit.; DASS data

The official figures indicate decrease in the number of induced abortion during the last ten years. According to this data, the TIAR fell from 2.7 in 1989 to 1.2 in 1996. The real number of induced abortions was higher than 39 thousand registered in 1996. There is under-registration of "miniabortions", and abortions performed in private clinics and out of the hospitals are not reported at all. The under-registration of the vacuum aspirations is signalled by the disproportion between the share of vacuum aspirations in the total number of induced abortions according to official figures (25% in 1996) and according to the reproductive health survey (39%, UNFPA, op. cit.). Opposite to the official numbers, the data from the survey indicates increasing share of the vacuum aspirations, which do not endanger the health of women as much as the surgical abortions: from 12% in 1988 to 39% in 1996.

As in the times of the Soviet Union, abortions are still used mostly by the married women, who already reached desired number of children. The large majority of women have liberal attitude towards abortion, with only 1.2% responding that abortion is quite unacceptable and 18.2% responding that abortion is acceptable under some circumstances (UNFPA, op. cit.).

The insufficient prevalence of modern contraceptives is slowly eliminated with the help and technical assistance of international family planning organisations. The use of modern contraceptives remains inadequate: in 1997, only 50% of women who were married or in union used modern contraceptive devices (38.4% IUD, 5.9% condom, 3.4% were sterilised and only 2.1% used chemical contraception) and another 23.6% practised traditional methods (21.6% – coitus interruptus and 2.0% – calendar method). The Moldovan Government formulated in 1998 target goals for the year 2003, among them the increase in the oral contraception use to 15%

of women in reproductive age, reduction of induced abortion by 50%, reorganisation of the family planning centres and introduction of the system of "family education" (UNFPA, op. cit.).

The high abortion rates with significant share of surgical abortions are often connected with post-abortion complications and high sterility rates. Short-term complications were reported by 11% of women that underwent abortions, and long-term complications were reported by 5% of women. Large share of recorded infertility (officially, around 8% of women in the reproductive age) was caused by the surgical or illegal abortion. Around one-fifth of maternal mortality (40.8 per 100,000 live births in 1995) resulted from botched abortions or post-abortion complications.

The lack of affordable contraceptives, decay of the preventive health care and possibly increased sexual activity among young people had contributed to the dramatic growth of morbidity from syphilis – from 7.1 to 200.1 cases per 100,000 inhabitants between 1989 and 1996. The spread of AIDS has also accelerated since 1995.

## 11.6 Family Formation and Dissolution

### 11.6.1 Nuptiality

The annual number of marriages was around 40 thousand between 1985 and 1993, then it dropped to 26 thousand in 1996. The singulate mean age at marriage (SMAM), first introduced by J. Hajnal (1953) and computed from the proportion of ever-married people by age group, was 23.8 years for men and less than 21 years for women, according to the 1989 census.

As in the case of fertility, the level of nuptiality dropped between 1990 and 1996, the female total first marriage rate (TFMR) declined from 1.13 to 0.62 and male TFMR – from 1.10 to 0.64 (Table 11.8). The timing of the first marriages did not change during this period; the mean age at first marriage in 1996 was 21.6 years for women (-0.1 year compared to 1990) and 24.2 years for men (+0.4 year). The mean age at first marriage for Moldovan women is currently the lowest in Europe. The reduction of the first marriage rates was strongest at the ages of highest nuptiality, between 21 and 24 years for men (-42%) and between 18 and 21 years for women (-45%). On the other hand, the first marriage rate of 16 and 17 years old women increased (see Figure 11.6). Strong decline in nuptiality of young men and women could be the sign of the postponement of marriages to a later age. Despite this reduction, the age of highest nuptiality remained at 19 years for women and at 22 years for men. Majority of women still marries in a narrow age span: 42% – between 16 and 19 years and another 44% – between 20 and 24 years.

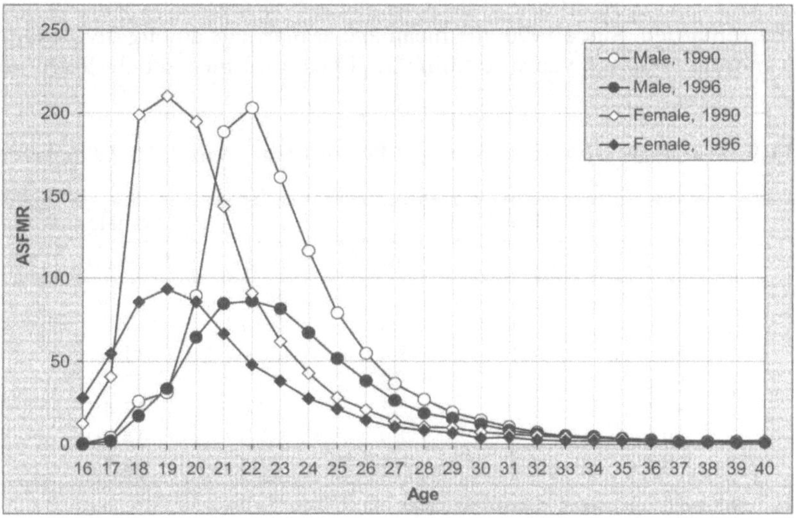


**Figure 11.6: Age-specific First Marriage Rates (ASFMR), 1990 and 1996**

Source: based on DASS data

**Table 11.8: Main Indicators of Nuptiality, 1960–1996, selected years**

| Year | Marriages | Crude marriage rate (‰) | Total first marriage rate, female[1] | Mean age at first marriage, female[1] | Divorces | Crude divorce rate (‰) | Total divorce rate |
|---|---|---|---|---|---|---|---|
| 1960 | 27,963 | 9.3 | .. | .. | 2,660 | 0.88 | .. |
| 1965 | 22,871 | 6.9 | .. | .. | 3,554 | 1.07 | .. |
| 1970 | 33,692 | 9.4 | .. | .. | 7,472 | 2.08 | 0.21 |
| 1975 | 40,596 | 10.6 | .. | .. | 8,655 | 2.25 | 0.23 |
| 1980 | 46,083 | 11.5 | 1.11 | 22.2 | 11,273 | 2.81 | 0.28 |
| 1985 | 40,901 | 9.7 | 1.06 | 21.7 | 11,176 | 2.65 | 0.27 |
| 1990 | 40,809 | 9.4 | 1.13 | 21.7 | 13,135 | 3.01 | 0.30 |
| 1991 | 36,609 | 9.1 | 1.05 | 21.5 | 13,879 | 3.18 | .. |
| 1992 | 39,340 | 9.0 | 1.03 | 21.3 | 14,821 | 3.40 | .. |
| 1993 | 39,469 | 9.1 | 1.03 | 21.2 | 14,468 | 3.33 | 0.33 |
| 1994 | 33,742 | 7.8 | 0.85 | 21.3 | 13,811 | 3.17 | 0.32 |
| 1995 | 32,775 | 7.5 | 0.80 | 21.5 | 14,617 | 3.37 | 0.34 |
| 1996 | 26,089 | 6.0 | 0.62 | 21.6 | 13,440 | 3.11 | 0.31 |

[1]Authors' estimation

Sources: Council of Europe, op. cit.; DASS, 1997a.

The proportion of marriages of divorced people in the total number of marriages is slowly increasing (Table 11.9). In 1996, 18.0% of grooms and 15.5% of brides were divorced. The share of marriages among widowed persons has stabilised at 3% for both men and women during the last twenty years. Between 1990 and 1996, the total marriage rate for divorced people did not drop as sharply as the total first marriage and was 0.11 for females and 0.14 for males. If this level of remarriage would sustain for long period, almost half of divorced men and more than third of divorced women would be remarried. Since 1990, the mean age at marriage among divorced men and women increased by 0.6 years, reaching 33.4 years for men and 34.9 for women in 1996.

**Table 11.9: Marriages by Marital Status of Persons Marrying, 1975–1996, selected years**

| Year | Male | | | Female | | |
|---|---|---|---|---|---|---|
| | Single | Divorced | Widowed | Single | Divorced | Widowed |
| 1975 | 86.1 | .. | .. | 90.0 | .. | .. |
| 1980 | 85.6 | 11.1 | 3.3 | 89.7 | 7.7 | 2.6 |
| 1985 | 82.5 | 14.1 | 3.4 | 85.6 | 11.3 | 3.1 |
| 1990 | 81.3 | 15.4 | 3.3 | 84.5 | 12.3 | 3.2 |
| 1994 | 81.3 | 15.9 | 2.8 | 83.6 | 13.4 | 3.0 |
| 1995 | 79.2 | 17.9 | 2.9 | 82.3 | 14.9 | 2.8 |
| 1996 | 78.9 | 18.0 | 3.1 | 81.4 | 15.5 | 3.1 |

[1]Category "widowed" includes also unknown cases
Source: DASS, 1996, 1997a, 1998

Although the proportion of children born outside marriage has been increasing during the 1990s, consensual unions are still rare in traditional Moldovan society. The marriage is considered to be one of the most important events during the life cycle, especially in rural areas, and the extent of pre-marital cohabitation is still negligible. According to data from the reproductive and health survey of 1997 (UNFPA, op. cit.), only 2.2% women of reproductive age were living in a consensual union.

### 11.6.2 Divorces

The annual number of divorces at the beginning of the 1960s was 2.7 thousand and the crude divorce rate was as low as 0.89. Since then, both had been continually increasing and peaked in 1992 at 14.8 thousand and 3.40, respectively. The divorce became quite common, and the total divorce rate exceeded 30% during the 1990s.

## 11.7 Mortality

The situation in mortality worsened after 1990 (see Table 11.10). Life expectancy according to official data was the highest around 1970, when it was 66.4 years for men and 71.8 years for women. Afterwards, life expectancy at birth for men slowly declined and that for women stagnated, so in 1990 it was 65.0 and 71.8, respectively. In the 1990s, the situation did not improve, and, after reaching the lowest level in 1995, life expectancy at birth slightly rose in 1996, when it was 62.9 for males and 70.4 for females. The female life expectancy at birth in Moldova at that time was the lowest in Europe, while the male life expectancy at birth was the fourth lowest after Russia, Ukraine and Belarus. The deterioration of mortality is also apparent in the values of age-specific mortality rates, as shown in the Table 11.11.

**Table 11.10: Main Indicators of Mortality, 1958–1996, selected years**

| Year/ period | Life expectancy at age | | | | | | | | Infant mortality rate (‰) | Deaths | Crude death rate (‰) |
|---|---|---|---|---|---|---|---|---|---|---|---|
| | 0 | | 1 | | 15 | | 30 | | | | |
| | M | F | M | F | M | F | M | F | | | |
| 1958–59 | 65.6 | 69.8 | .. | .. | 57.2 | 60.9 | 18.5 | 20.7 | .. | .. | .. |
| 1969–70 | 66.4 | 71.8 | .. | .. | .. | .. | .. | .. | .. | .. | 8.4 |
| 1980 | 62.4 | 68.8 | 64.1 | 70.5 | 51.2 | 57.3 | 11.9 | 14.3 | 35.1 | .. | .. |
| 1985 | 63.1 | 69.5 | 64.2 | 70.2 | 51.2 | 56.9 | 11.7 | 17.1 | 30.8 | 46,075 | 10.9 |
| 1990 | 65.0 | 71.8 | 65.4 | 72.0 | 52.1 | 58.6 | 12.5 | 14.8 | 19.2 | 42,427 | 9.7 |
| 1991 | 64.3 | 71.0 | 64.7 | 71.3 | 51.4 | 57.8 | 14.7 | 17.7 | 20.0 | 45,849 | 10.5 |
| 1992 | 63.9 | 71.9 | 64.3 | 72.3 | 51.1 | 58.8 | 15.1 | 18.3 | 18.6 | 44,522 | 10.2 |
| 1993 | 64.3 | 70.9 | 64.7 | 71.5 | 51.3 | 57.8 | 14.5 | 17.3 | 21.5 | 46,637 | 10.7 |
| 1994 | 62.3 | 69.8 | 63.0 | 70.4 | 49.7 | 56.8 | 13.8 | 16.6 | 22.9 | 51,514 | 11.8 |
| 1995 | 61.8 | 69.7 | 62.6 | 70.1 | 49.1 | 56.5 | 13.6 | 16.4 | 21.5 | 52,969 | 12.2 |
| 1996 | 62.9 | 70.4 | 63.3 | 70.7 | 50.0 | 57.2 | 13.9 | 16.9 | 20.5 | 49,748 | 11.5 |

Sources: Council of Europe, op. cit.; DASS, 1996, 1997a, 1998

Between 1990 and 1996, high infant mortality rate had negatively influenced the life expectancy at birth for men and was responsible for the 6.3% of its decline. Large contribution to the decline had also all ages over 40. The ages over 70 contributed 22.0% of the decline. In the case of women, the contribution of age 0 was not significant (2.0%), while the contribution of ages over 70 was almost 50%.

High infant mortality is still a persistent phenomenon in Moldova. The situation did not change in the 1990s, and infant mortality rate is still around 20 deaths per 1,000 live births during the first year of life (among European countries, only Romania has higher rate). Consequently, the life expectancy at age one is still higher than the life expectancy at birth. In urban areas, the situation remains unchanged as well: the infant mortality rate was 18.7‰ in 1996, compared to 21.1‰ in rural areas.

The gap between male and female mortality broadened from 6.8 years in 1990 to 8 years in 1992 and 7.5 years in 1996. The first age group contributed 6.2% to this gap, while the other important "contributors" were the age group 50–54 (11%) and the older age groups.

The medical care in Moldova depends on the economic situation, which has been deteriorating since the breakdown of the USSR. In 1996, there were 250 inhabitants per one doctor and 82 persons per one hospital bed. These numbers are higher than in the Western European countries, what indicates the poor efficiency of medical care in Moldova. In the comparison with developed Western European countries, for example with the Netherlands, mortality conditions of Moldovan men are much worse at the age 0 and at ages over 40. Moldovan women have also higher mortality at the age 0 and at ages over 55, particularly above 70.

**Table 11.11: Age-specific Death Rates, 1990 and 1995, per thousand**

| Age group | 1990 | | 1995 | |
|---|---|---|---|---|
| | Male | Female | Male | Female |
| 0–4 | 1.28 | 0.98 | 1.36 | 0.99 |
| 5–9 | 0.18 | 0.10 | 0.20 | 0.10 |
| 10–14 | 0.12 | 0.08 | 0.12 | 0.10 |
| 15–19 | 0.28 | 0.15 | 0.32 | 0.11 |
| 20–24 | 0.65 | 0.18 | 0.55 | 0.17 |
| 25–29 | 0.69 | 0.18 | 0.78 | 0.22 |
| 30–34 | 0.80 | 0.27 | 1.08 | 0.35 |
| 35–39 | 1.12 | 0.44 | 1.49 | 0.50 |
| 40–44 | 1.60 | 0.71 | 2.34 | 0.94 |
| 45–49 | 2.59 | 1.29 | 3.20 | 1.40 |
| 50–54 | 3.80 | 2.01 | 5.08 | 2.41 |
| 55–59 | 5.19 | 3.20 | 6.68 | 3.87 |
| 60–64 | 7.98 | 4.55 | 9.57 | 5.61 |
| 65–69 | 10.62 | 6.91 | 13.40 | 8.55 |

Source: DASS, 1996–1998

The structure of causes of death (Table 11.12) did not change much, except that the share of the circulation system diseases increased up to 50% of all deaths in 1996. The death rates for malignant neoplasms are much higher in the north of the country, which is close to the Chernobyl nuclear power plant (UNICEF, 1997).

**Table 11.12: Causes of Death, 1990 and 1996**

| Cause of death | 1990 | | 1996 | |
|---|---|---|---|---|
| | Death rate | Proportion | Death rate | Proportion |
| | Per 100,000 | % | Per 100,000 | % |
| Total | 972.20 | 100.0 | 1,149.65 | 100.0 |
| Of which caused by: | | | | |
| Infection and parasitic diseases | 10.77 | 1.1 | 16.75 | 1.5 |
| TBC or expiratory diseases | 4.61 | 0.5 | 10.93 | 1.0 |
| Diseases of the circulatory system | 419.27 | 43.1 | 576.56 | 50.2 |
| Acute myocardial infarction | 21.60 | 2.2 | 22.95 | 2.0 |
| Malignant neoplasms | 131.37 | 13.5 | 132.65 | 11.5 |
| Diseases of the respiratory system | 64.55 | 6.6 | 70.37 | 6.1 |
| Pneumonia | 20.94 | 2.2 | 24.13 | 2.1 |
| Diseases of the digestive system | 91.98 | 9.5 | 103.05 | 9.0 |
| Cirrhosis of liver | 69.89 | 7.2 | 78.50 | 6.8 |
| Diseases of the nervous system | 8.30 | 0.9 | 11.07 | 1.0 |
| Others | 143.71 | 14.8 | 131.63 | 11.4 |
| External causes | 102.25 | 10.5 | 107.57 | 9.4 |

Source: DASS, 1997a

From 1987 to August 1998, out of around 5 million people tested for HIV, 828 were tested positively. The proportion of those who tested positively had been gradually increasing: in 1996 it was 21.3 per 100,000 tested, in 1997 – 145.3, and in the first 8 months of 1998 – 223.2. Out of 828 tested positively, 792 were citizens of Moldova. The main cause of infection were use of drugs (84%) and heterosexual relationship (15%). 60% of HIV positive persons were 20–29 years old, 21% aged 30–39, and 73% of all who tested positively were men. 88% of all cases were concentrated in four towns: Bălţi, Chişinău, Tiraspol and Bendery.

In 1996, there were 773 suicides in Moldova (17.9 per 100,000 inhabitants) and 586 homicides (13.5 per 100,000), what are not extreme values, although the number of homicides rose by about 50% since 1990.

## 11.8 The Background of Current Changes in Demographic Behaviour

Current changes in demographic behaviour are above all the result of the economic crisis after the dissolution of the Soviet Union.

Moldovan economy, which was rather backward even during the Soviet era, faced one of the steepest declines among Eastern European countries during the 1990s. Securing of the basic needs, especially of the food supplies, became the principal concern for most inhabitants. As the value of maternity leave provisions, child allowances and other family income supplements depreciated due to high inflation, childbearing became an expensive and financially risky "undertaking" and, therefore, a problematic choice for many. Majority of young women in the reproductive age reduced their fertility plans to one or two children, and if the current situation would continue unimproved, large part of women will likely remain childless.

On the other hand, the demographic picture of Moldova would be incomplete if we would explain all the current changes only as a consequence of the economic crisis in traditional society. Already during the Soviet times, there were "progressive" changes in demographic behaviour, which were similar to those in Eastern Europe. Differently from Western Europe, where the changes were generated by the spreading of the new cultural norms and patterns, which then were reflected in the liberal reform of the legislation, the changes in the demographic behaviour of Moldovan population occurred mostly as a consequent reaction to the legislative changes. The liberalisation of abortion in 1955 and easy access to divorce since 1965 were the major legislative norms that enabled spread of induced abortions and increase in family dissolution.

Both processes are considered to be a sign of the second demographic transition (van de Kaa, 1987, 1997). However, besides these two processes, no other changes associated usually with the second demographic transition were observed in Moldova before the end of the 1980s. There were extremely limited possibilities for the free choice of career, independent activities or travelling abroad and there was no space for alternative lifestyles similar to those appearing in the West. All these possibilities were the engine for the processes typical for the second demographic transition like cohabitation, postponement of births, increase in the share of children born outside marriage or increase in the voluntary childlessness – none of them were occurring in Moldova till the end of the 1980s – beginning of the 1990s.

Some of the demographic changes in the 1990s can be interpreted as the signs of the new demographic behaviour. The fall of the total fertility rate and the total first marriage rate, continual increase of the share of extramarital births or certain increase in the use of the modern contraceptives, are changes connected with changing lifestyles. On the other hand, we must take into consideration that up to now these changes mostly occurred as the consequences of the economic crisis and not as the results of the spread of "western values" or new cultural patterns. This hypothesis is supported by the persistence of very low mean ages of women at marriage and at childbearing, currently the lowest in Europe.

## 11.9 Population-related Policies and Programmes

At present, the social and population policy is very weak, and the real value of grants and allowances depreciated since the beginning of the economic crisis. The deficits of the state budget do not allow improvements in the social security system or significant increase of the real value of grants, allowances and other social provisions.

The system of the legislation on the family, social welfare and labour under the Soviet era can be divided into measures that were openly pronatalist and into measures, which were more social welfare measures than a deliberate pronatalist incentives. Openly pronatalist were two measures, which were already mentioned: special tax for men remaining single after they reached 18 years (7% of their salary) and similar tax for women remaining childless after they got married (6% of their salary). These taxes were abolished around 1990.

Other measures were introduced primarily as social provisions, but they also served as fertility incentives since the beginning of the 1980s. Rather complicated system of grants and allowances (see, for example, Heer, 1977; Weber and Goodman, 1981) consisted of maternity leave, maternity grants, family income supplements and child allowances, from which only maternity leave and child allowances were important.

Postnatal maternity leave was gradually extended up to 1.5 years after the childbirth, but initially it was unpaid. Partially paid leave (35 Roubles per month at the time when 1 Rouble was officially around US$1.5) was introduced in the first half of the 1980s. Family income supplements for low-income families were first introduced in 1974 for families with low per capita income; this programme provided an allowance for each child under the age of 8 (12 Roubles). The child allowances, granting women a lump sum payment, originally did not begin until the birth of the third child (20 Roubles) and gradually increased till the birth of the eleventh child (250 Roubles). Since 1981, families were getting 50 Roubles upon the birth of the first child and 100 Roubles upon the birth of the second and third child. Single mothers received additional money until the child reached the age of 12. Non-existent regular child allowances (with mentioned exceptions) were substituted by providing free of charge education including pre-school institutions and boarding schools.

The improvements in the first half of the 1980s were introduced after a long period of discussions concerning fertility decline and "critical manpower shortage" in the USSR. They were designed to encourage births of the second and third birth order, and in achieving this goal they were relatively successful. Generally, the economic pronatalism was typical for the Soviet population policy since the 1970s. Even more obscure was the fear of the loss of the country's position in the world due to slow population increase (Heer, op. cit.).

Most of the population policy measures implemented during the Soviet era remained valid up to the present times. Only the real value of the social transfers depreciated and, moreover, a large part of allowances has been paid with long delay or has not been paid at all. Mother gets a one-time payment of 148 Lei (US$1 was equal approximately 9 Lei in 1998) after the childbirth, and in addition to the fully-paid maternity leave of 56 days before and 56 days after the birth, women can take up to 18 months of partly-paid maternity leave (in 1998, the average payment was only 26.8 Lei per month). Mothers can spent another 18 months on unpaid maternity leave, which makes total of 3 years of a maternity leave after the birth with the reservation of their work place. However, this advantage is only theoretical, as many workplaces are lost or reorganised during this three years period. The provisions for single mothers as well as the provisions for the poor families with children aged from 1.5 to 16 are negligible, reaching on average 9.3 Lei (US$1) per month (UNDP, 1998).

The most important change of social policy is the proposed increase of the retirement age. Until 1998, the retirement age was 60 years for men and 55 years for women. Although the share of old people in Moldova is low in European context, there was the pressure from the World Bank and other international institutions, which called for the pension reforms. In 1998, the Moldovan Parliament ratified the law establishing the increase of the retirement age by 0.5 years per year during the period 1999–2008. At the end of the year 2008, the retirement age will be 60 years for women and 65 years for men. The difference of five years between men and women remained unchanged in favour of women, although post-soviet republics are countries with the highest difference between life expectancy of men and women in the world (again, in favour of women). In 1996, women in Moldova had 7.5 years longer life expectancy at birth than men. Paradoxically, the current level of male life expectancy at birth (62.9 years in 1996) is lower than proposed retirement age of 65 years in 2008.

## 11.10 Summary

Until the end of the 1980s, the demographic behaviour of Moldovans was rather traditional: almost all men and women entered the marriage at an early age and almost all women had at least one, mostly two or three children. During the 1990s, the patterns did not change radically, but the levels of demographic processes did. Total fertility rate and total first marriage rate declined considerably, while the timing of births and marriages remained unchanged. The structure of births was changing slowly, the main trend being the increase of the proportion of extramarital births and the increase of the share of first births. Due to rather intensive emigration and steep decline of natural increase, the high population increase recorded till the end of the 1980s turned into moderate population decrease. The health care and health conditions of the population deteriorated since 1989 and life expectancy declined, although not as dramatically as in Russia. With the help of some international institutions and organisations, sexual education was introduced, and expanded availability of modern contraceptives enabled to reduce high levels of induced abortion rates. Most of the recent demographic changes resulted from the serious decay of the quality of life, while the influence of Western cultural norms and behavioural patterns was negligible.

### 11.10.1 Data Reliability

Although most of the data used in the article is correct and reliable, we were confronted many times with incomplete or less authentic data. Some unreliability is caused by the incomplete data on the age structure of the population: the age structure was corrected after the 1989 population census, but large migration flows of the first half of the 1990s, which were not recorded in full, brought some inaccuracy to present official estimation of the population age and sex structures.

Moreover, there was an important change in the recording of the population movement: until the end of the 1980s, statistical data was processed centrally for the whole Soviet Union and only since the independence of Moldova all the data has been processed in Moldova. Some of the currently available data covers therefore only short period between 1990 and 1996. Furthermore, due to some methodological changes, there are some inconsistencies between the figures for the 1980s and for the 1990s.

While interpreting the data, we took the possibility of inaccuracy into consideration, however we did not comment some changes caused, in our opinion, by age structure incompleteness or by the changes of methodology, especially in the period 1988–1990. For instance: the increase of the TFR between 1988 and 1989 despite decrease in the total number of births by 6 thousand (7%), the sudden increase of the fertility rate among young women aged 15–19 years in 1990 in parallel with the drop of fertility rates among women aged 25 years and over, etc.

Then, there is a problem of an ambiguous meaning of some data. For example, the data concerning female nuptiality (see, for instance, Council of Europe, op. cit.) indicates a very high level of female total first marriage rate. However, it may be the case that total marriage rate includes also data on remarriages. On the other hand, we know that data for the last few years (at least, for the years 1994–1996) indicates the real total first marriage rate. Finally, when there were concerns about data validity and reliability, we had to use estimates or to handle these data very carefully. All data concerning abortions belongs to this category.

Another problem was caused by the secession of Transdniestria. Until 1996, the data for Transdniestria was obtained by the Moldovan Department of Statistical and Sociological Analysis through the Russian Institute for Statistics (Goskomstat) in Moscow. Up to April 1999, the data for Transdniestria for the years 1997 and 1998 was not available. That is why our analysis mostly ends up with the year 1996.

## Notes

1. The research work of T. Sobotka and K. Zeman in Moldova was supported by the Open Society Fund, Prague.

## References

ASM (Academy of Sciences of the Republic of Moldova) (1998), *Probleme actuale medico-sociale şi demografice ale familiei*, Chişinău: Academia de Ştiinţe a Moldovei.

Council of Europe (1998), *Recent Demographic Developments in Europe 1998*, Strasbourg: Council of Europe.

DASS (Department of Statistical and Sociological Analysis of the Republic of Moldova) (1996), *Republica Moldova în cifre 1996*, Chişinău: Departamentul Analize Statistice şi Sociologice.

DASS (Department of Statistical and Sociological Analysis of the Republic of Moldova) (1997a), *Republica Moldova în cifre 1997*, Chişinău: Departamentul Analize Statistice şi Sociologice.

DASS (Department of Statistical and Sociological Analysis of the Republic of Moldova) (1997b), *Migraţia populaţiei Republicii Moldova în anii 1990–1996. Buletin statistic*, Chişinău: Departamentul Analize Statistice şi Sociologice.

DASS (Department of Statistical and Sociological Analysis of the Republic of Moldova) (1998), *Republica Moldova în cifre 1998*, Chişinău: Departamentul Analize Statistice şi Sociologice.

Hajnal, J. (1953), Age at marriage and proportion marrying, *Population Studies*, Vol. 7, pp. 111–132.

Heer, D. (1977), Three issues in Soviet population policy, *Population and Development Review*, Vol. 3, pp. 229–252.

(1990), *Itogi vsesoyouznoi perepisi naselenia 1989 goda po SSR Moldova. Statisticheski sbornik*, Kishinev.

O'Loughlin, J., V. Kolossov and A. Tchepalyga (1998), National construction, territorial separatism, and post-Soviet geopolitics in the Transdniester Moldovan Republic, *Post-Soviet Geography and Economics*, Vol. 39(6), pp. 332–358.

Popov, A. (1991), Family planning and induced abortion in the USSR: Basic health and demographic characteristics, *Studies on Family Planning*, Vol. 22(6), pp. 368–377.

Population Reference Bureau (1998), *1998 World Population Data Sheet*, Washington, D.C.: Population Reference Bureau.

UNDP (United Nations Development Programme) (1995), *Human Development Report. Republic of Moldova 1995*, Chişinău: UNDP.

UNDP (United Nations Development Programme) (1998), *Human Development Report. Republic of Moldova 1998*, Chişinău: UNDP.

UNICEF (1997), *Situaţţia Mamei si a Copilului în Republica Moldova*, Chişinău: UNICEF and Guvernul Republicii Moldova.

UNICEF (1998), *Children at Risk in Central and Eastern Europe. Regional Monitoring Report No. 5*, Florence: UNICEF.

UNFPA (United Nations Population Fund) (1998), *Studiul Sănătăţii Reproducerii în Moldova 1997*, Chişinău and Atlanta: UNPFA.

van de Kaa, D.J. (1987), Europe's Second Demographic Transition, *Population Bulletin*, Vol. 42(1), p. 1–58.

van de Kaa, D.J. (1997), *Options and Sequences of Europe's Demographic Patterns*, Nethur-Demography Paper No. 39, The Hague.

Weber, C. and A. Goodman (1981), The demographic policy debate in the USSR, *Population and Development Review*, Vol. 7(2), pp. 279–295.

# 12

# Population Development in Poland

**Petra Vojtěchovská**

## 12.1 Introduction

Since the early 1990s, Poland, similarly to other Eastern and Central European countries, has experienced a rapid transformation in population development, which resulted first of all in the declining propensity to marry, declining fertility with increasing proportion of extramarital births, very slowly decreasing mortality and strongly increasing volume of international migration. The crucial changes in the demographic phenomena have been occurring in the course of the social and economic transformation of society accompanied by high unemployment and growing poverty among selected groups of population. Hence, it may be argued that the changes in demographic behaviour have been also inspired by major socio-economic pressures as well as by the present level of material well-being.

Until the mid-1980s, Poland belonged to a group of countries characterised by high dynamics of population growth reaching 9‰ per year. In the early 1990s, the rate of annual population increase was 2.6‰. In 1995–1997, this rate has maintained a stable level and currently fetches below 1‰ that is the lowest increase during the whole post-war period (see Table 12.1).

**Table 12.1: Main Demographic Indicators, 1980–1997, selected years**

| Year | Average population | Live births | Deaths | Natural increase | Net migration | Total increase | Natural increase | Net migration | Total increase |
|---|---|---|---|---|---|---|---|---|---|
| | 1,000 | | | | | | Per 1,000 inhabitants | | |
| 1980 | 35,578 | 695.8 | 353.2 | 342.6 | -21.2 | 321.4 | 9.6 | -0.6 | 9.0 |
| 1985 | 37,203 | 680.1 | 384.0 | 296.1 | -18.9 | 277.2 | 7.9 | -0.5 | 7.4 |
| 1990 | 38,119 | 547.7 | 390.3 | 157.4 | -15.8 | 141.6 | 4.1 | -0.4 | 3.7 |
| 1991 | 38,245 | 547.7 | 405.7 | 142.0 | -16.0 | 126.0 | 3.7 | -0.4 | 3.3 |
| 1992 | 38,365 | 515.2 | 394.7 | 120.5 | -11.6 | 108.9 | 3.2 | -0.3 | 2.9 |
| 1993 | 38,459 | 494.3 | 392.3 | 102.0 | -15.4 | 86.6 | 2.6 | -0.4 | 2.2 |
| 1994 | 38,544 | 481.3 | 386.4 | 94.9 | -19.0 | 75.9 | 2.5 | -0.5 | 2.0 |
| 1995 | 38,588 | 433.1 | 386.1 | 47.0 | -18.2 | 28.8 | 1.2 | -0.5 | 0.7 |
| 1996 | 38,618 | 428.2 | 385.5 | 42.7 | -13.1 | 29.6 | 1.1 | -0.3 | 0.8 |
| 1997 | 38,650 | 412.7 | 380.2 | 32.5 | -11.8 | 20.7 | 0.9 | -0.3 | 0.6 |

Source: GUS, 1998a

## 12.2 Population and Its Structures

### 12.2.1 Demographic Structure

The population of Poland is demographically young, as compared to other European populations. Median age stands at 31.8 years for men and at 35.3 years for women. Urban population is however older than the rural: median age for urban areas is 34.8 years and for rural – 31.6. Figure 12.1 shows the structure of Poland's population by sex, age and the place of residence as of 1 January 1998. The effects of the two world wars as well as imbalances in the birth rate have determined the highly irregular age composition. The cohort born during the First World War, period of low natality, is now disappearing from the group of retirement age, but there was the notable decline of the birth rate during the Second World War, followed by high birth rate in the post-war period. The age pyramid also reflects a decrease in the number of births in the late 1950s and 1960s. The subsequent widening of the age pyramid represents the echo of the post-war baby boom. With a fall in birth rate in the mid-1980s, the base of the pyramid began to narrow again.

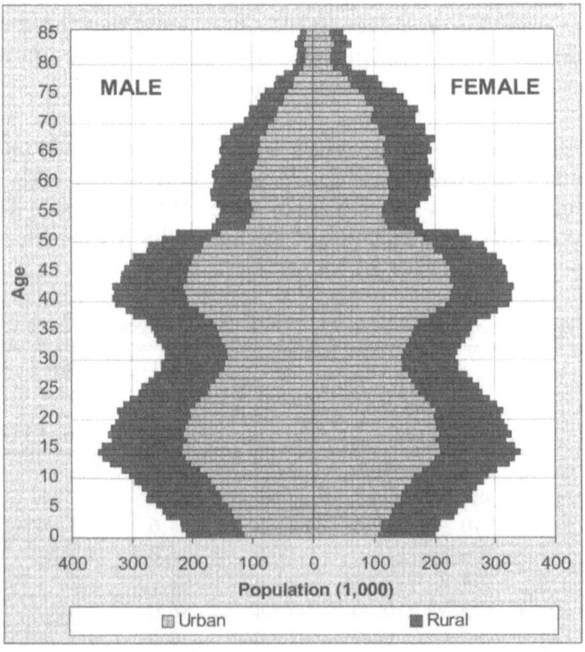


**Figure 12.1: Age Pyramid on 1 January 1998**

Source: GUS, 1998a

The changes of demographic behaviour occurred in the last decades have affected the age structure of population. The decreasing birth rate since the mid-1980s has reduced the number of children in both absolute and relative terms. Between 1985 and

1997, the proportion of the population aged 0–14 fell from 25.6% to 21.1%. In absolute terms, it was a decrease of 1.4 million. On the other hand, the size of the age group 15–59 had risen in the same period, reaching 62.7% of the total population in 1997. The proportion of the population aged 60 and over increased too; in 1997, this age group represented 16.2%. The process of demographic ageing is undergoing both at the top and the base of the population pyramid. Between 1990 and 1997, the index of ageing rose steadily from 60.1 to 76.7. In gender terms, female population has older age structure than the male population.

**Table 12.2: Population by Main Age Groups, 1980–1997, selected years[1]**

| Age group | 1980 | 1985 | 1990 | 1995 | 1996 | 1997 | | |
|---|---|---|---|---|---|---|---|---|
| | | | | | | Total | Male | Female |
| | 1,000 | | | | | | | |
| 0–14 | 8,707 | 9,558 | 9,523 | 8,678 | 8,446 | 8,170 | 4,184 | 3,985 |
| 15–59 | 22,304 | 22,572 | 22,933 | 23,803 | 23,990 | 24,221 | 12,110 | 12,111 |
| 60+ | 4,724 | 5,211 | 5,728 | 6,129 | 6,203 | 6,269 | 2,507 | 3,763 |
| Total | 35,735 | 37,340 | 38,183 | 38,609 | 38,639 | 38,660 | 18,801 | 19,859 |
| | % | | | | | | | |
| 0–14 | 24.4 | 25.6 | 24.9 | 22.5 | 21.9 | 21.1 | 22.3 | 20.1 |
| 15–59 | 62.4 | 60.4 | 60.1 | 61.6 | 62.1 | 62.7 | 64.4 | 61.0 |
| 60+ | 13.2 | 14.0 | 15.0 | 15.9 | 16.0 | 16.2 | 13.3 | 18.9 |
| Total | 100.0 | 100.0 | 100.0 | 100.0 | 100.0 | 100.0 | 100.0 | 100.0 |
| Index of ageing[2] | 54.2 | 54.5 | 60.1 | 70.6 | 73.4 | 76.7 | 59.9 | 94.4 |

[1]As of 31 December of a given year
[2]Population aged 60 and over as a percentage of population aged 0–14
Sources: GUS, 1997 and 1998b

The changes in the age structure have had, however, much more bearing on the economically active population. In 1990, for every 100 persons in the labour force, there were 74 dependent persons, while by 1997 this number has fallen to 68 (Table 12.3). This was primarily due to the fall in the proportion of children in the population. Although the number of dependent older persons had risen by 1.5 for every 100 economically active persons between 1990 and 1997, the number of dependent children declined by 7.3 at the same time (GUS, 1997 and 1998b).

The sex structure of the population is affected both by biological factors in reproduction and the influence of the environment. The slightly higher number of boys among new-born is gradually balanced out by the higher level of male mortality in all age groups. The number of males surpasses the number of females below age 40 and vice versa above this age. Among people aged 60 and over, the number of women is significantly higher than that of men. In particular, among those aged 60–69, there were 127 women for every 100 men and among people aged 80 and over this number rose as high as 235 in 1997. For several years, the sex ratio has maintained a constant level of about 105. The figure for urban population stands at 109, whereas the rural areas experience a biased situation (Table 12.4).

**Table 12.3: Dependency Ratios and Index of Economic Burden, 1980–1997, selected years, per cent[1]**

| | 1980 | 1985 | 1990 | 1995 | 1996 | 1997 |
|---|---|---|---|---|---|---|
| Dependency ratio I[2] | 48.5 | 50.9 | 51.5 | 47.0 | 45.6 | 44.2 |
| Dependency ratio II[3] | 19.9 | 20.6 | 22.3 | 23.5 | 23.7 | 23.8 |
| Index of economic burden[4] | 68.5 | 71.5 | 73.9 | 70.5 | 69.3 | 68.0 |

[1]As of 31 December of a given year
[2]Population aged 0–17 as a percentage of the working-age population (men aged 18–64, women aged 18–59)
[3]Old-age population (men aged 65+, women aged 60+) as a percentage of the working-age population (men aged 18–64, women aged 18–59)
[4]Population aged 0–17 and the old-age population (men aged 65+, women aged 60+) as a percentage of the working-age population (men aged 18–64, women aged 18–59)
Sources: GUS, 1997 and 1998b

As regards the structure of population by marital status, in 1995, more than one-fifth of women aged 15 and over were single, 60% of them were married, 16% were widowed and 4% were divorced. In case of males, single men accounted for almost 30%, married males stood at about 65%, widowed and divorced at about 3% each (data from microcensus carried out in 1995).

**Table 12.4: Sex Ratio[1] by Age Groups and Urban/Rural Settlement, 1997[2], per cent**

| | Age group | | | | | | | | Total |
|---|---|---|---|---|---|---|---|---|---|
| | 0 | 15–29 | 30–39 | 40–49 | 50–59 | 60–69 | 70–79 | 80+ | |
| Total | 93.8 | 96.1 | 97.9 | 101.6 | 110.5 | 127.4 | 169.8 | 234.6 | 105.6 |
| Urban | 93.7 | 98.7 | 105.5 | 108.9 | 113.8 | 130.1 | 175.5 | 260.3 | 109.2 |
| Rural | 93.9 | 92.0 | 86.6 | 87.8 | 104.3 | 123.3 | 162.8 | 207.4 | 100.0 |

[1]Sex ratio indicates the number of women per 100 men of a given age group
[2]As of 31 December
Source: GUS, 1998a

### 12.2.2 Ethnic and Religious Structure

The population of Poland is quite homogeneous if measured by either nationality or religion. Although detailed data on the current distribution of the population by nationality is not available, some estimates can be provided on the basis of the existing data on membership in national and ethnic associations in Poland. It is assumed that Poles now make up about 95% of the population, while the remaining 5% is composed of minorities such as Germans, Ukrainians, Belarus, and Lithuanians.

Similarly, data on the distribution of Poland's population by religion affiliation is indirect. Estimates made by the Central Statistical Office show that the vast majority of people are members of the Roman Catholic Church (95.6% in 1997). These estimates are based on the number of persons baptised as Roman Catholics. Among other religions, the most important are Orthodox Church, Protestant Church, Greek Catholic Church and Jehovah Witnesses (GUS, 1998b).

### 12.2.3 Education, Labour Force Participation and Urbanisation

In Poland, as in many other European countries, the educational attainment of women is now equal to that of men. In 1997, 1.1 million of men and 1.2 million of women aged 15 and over had completed university or an equivalent degree granting institution. The similar situation was among persons with a secondary-level education. In absolute terms, 8.5 million men and 8.3 million women had completed secondary or basic vocational education (GUS, 1998b). As social and economic conditions changed, education acquired value in itself. Not only did the number of students rise year by year but a growing number of private schools appeared at all levels of education. Recently, however, the reforms in economy have produced some financial barriers that may negatively affect the access to the education for the lower income strata of society.

Labour force participation of men as well as women became very high in Poland following the Second World War. Both genders, however, experienced decline in their labour force activity rates during the 1990s. In 1997, the labour force activity rate was 4.3% below the level of the 1992 and 7.9% below the level of 1988 (Table 12.5).

**Table 12.5: Labour Force Activity Rates[1], 1988–1997[2], selected years, per cent**

| | 1988 | 1992 | 1993 | 1994 | 1995 | 1996 | 1997 |
|---|---|---|---|---|---|---|---|
| Total | 65.3 | 61.7 | 61.2 | 59.2 | 58.4 | 57.9 | 57.4 |
| Male | 74.3 | 70.0 | 69.6 | 67.0 | 66.5 | 65.9 | 65.5 |
| Female | 57.0 | 54.2 | 53.6 | 52.2 | 51.1 | 50.6 | 50.0 |

[1]Labour force activity rate indicates the total number of employed and registered unemployed persons as a percentage of population aged 15 and over
[2]Data for 1988 is from the census, data since 1992 is based upon labour force surveys conducted in November of a given year
Sources: GUS, 1993, 1997, 1998b

As regards the distribution of employed persons by sectors of the national economy, 27.4% worked in primary, 29.5% in secondary and remaining 43.1% in tertiary sector in 1997 (GUS, 1998b). Unemployment was not reported until the beginning of the 1990s. The unemployment rate for 1990 showed a level of 6.5%, and it rose sharply thereafter. It peaked at 16.4% at the end of 1993. At that time, in absolute terms, almost 3 million people were without jobs. The following four years brought decline in both the number of unemployed persons and the rate but the latter was still as high as 10.5% at the end of 1997 (Table 12.6).

In the 1990s, around 62 out of 100 Poles resided in towns or settlements, which had administrative status as urban areas, while the remainder resided in rural areas. The absolute number of urban dwellers at the end of 1997 was 23,925 thousand. In recent years, around 50% of the urban inhabitants and 30% of the whole population has been living in towns of more than 100,000 inhabitants but there is a tendency of the both proportions to decline slightly. Poland has only one city – the capital city of Warsaw – with a population over one million (GUS, 1998a).

**Table 12.6: Registered Unemployed Persons and Unemployment Rate, 1990–1997[1]**

| | 1990 | 1991 | 1992 | 1993 | 1994 | 1995 | 1996 | 1997 |
|---|---|---|---|---|---|---|---|---|
| Registered unemployed persons (1,000) | 1,126 | 2,156 | 2,509 | 2,890 | 2,838 | 2,629 | 2,360 | 1,826 |
| Unemployment rate | 6.5 | 12.2 | 14.3 | 16.4 | 16.0 | 14.9 | 13.2 | 11.9 |

[1]As of 31 December of a given year
[2]Unemployment rate indicates number of registered unemployed persons as a percentage of the economically active population (excluding persons in active military service and employees of budgetary entities of the Ministry of National Defense and the Ministry of Interior and Administration)
Sources: GUS, 1997 and 1998b

## 12.3 Demographic Behaviour and Population Issues

### 12.3.1 Family Formation and Dissolution

The absolute number of marriages has been declining constantly since the early 1980s. The trend towards fewer marriages has continued also in the 1990s, although the number of young persons reaching the legal marriage age was growing. Almost 20% fewer marriages took place in 1996 than in 1990, but a slight increase was registered in 1997. The changes in the number of first marriages, which represented about 87% of newly-weds in the beginning of the 1980s, were the driving force behind the sizeable decrease in the total number of marriages: between 1990 and 1996, the number of marrying single people fell by 19% in relative and by 41 thousand in absolute terms (Table 12.7).

**Table 12.7: Main Indicators of Nuptiality, 1980–1997, selected years**

| | 1980 | 1985 | 1990 | 1995 | 1996 | 1997 |
|---|---|---|---|---|---|---|
| Marriages (1,000) | 307.4 | 266.8 | 255.4 | 207.1 | 203.6 | 204.8 |
| Crude marriage rate (‰) | 8.6 | 7.2 | 6.7 | 5.4 | 5.3 | 5.3 |
| First marriages (1,000) | 268.8 | 227.2 | 218.5 | 179.8 | 177.2 | 177.4 |
| Proportion of first marriages (%) | 87.5 | 85.1 | 85.6 | 86.8 | 87.0 | 86.6 |
| Total first marriage rate – female | 0.89 | 0.89 | 0.90 | 0.66 | 0.64 | 0.61 |
| Mean age at first marriage – female | 22.0 | 22.1 | 21.7 | 22.1 | 22.3 | 22.5 |

Sources: GUS, 1986 and 1998a; Council of Europe, 1998

Before 1990, nuptiality of Poland's population followed the traditional pattern characterised by the high proportion of people entering the first marriage and low mean age at first marriage. At the beginning of the 1990s, marriage pattern in Poland began to change. For females below age 50, the total first marriage rate dropped from 0.90 in 1990 to only 0.61 in 1997. This means that if the 1997 level is maintained, it can be expected that 39% of women will reach age 50 without marrying. Mean age of females entering their first marriage rose slightly from 21.7 to 22.5 years during the period from 1990 to 1997 (Figure 12.2).

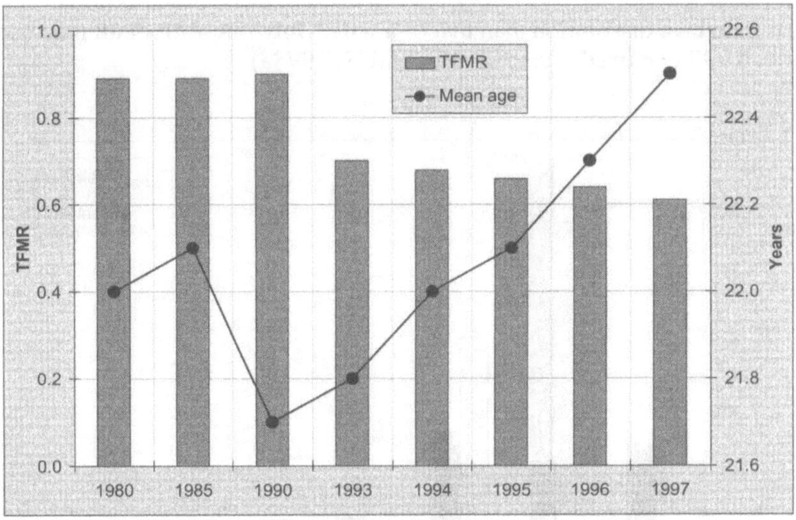


**Figure 12.2: Total First Marriage Rate (TFMR) and Mean Age at First Marriage, 1980–1997, selected years, female**

Source: Council of Europe, op. cit.

The majority of people marrying for the first time do so by the age 30. In 1997, about 87% of all single grooms were under the age 30, as were 94% of brides entering their first marriage (Figure 12.3). The marriage rate of this group (aged under 30) has therefore a major influence on the total level of nuptiality. The age-specific first marriage rates were highest below age 25 for women and at ages 20–29 for men. These rates moved distinctly downward in the early 1990s for both females and males (GUS, 1998a).

The official data on consensual unions in Poland is not available and that from surveys is very limited. The Polish *Fertility and Family Survey* (FFS) carried out in 1991 revealed that cohabitation was not very popular at the beginning of the 1990s and the predominant choice was to start the partnership with marriage, without pretest in consensual union (Holzer and Kowalska, 1997). Another survey conducted by Duch-Krzystoszek in 1989 showed that although only a tiny minority decided to cohabit, the Polish society had rather liberal attitude towards consensual unions (Duch-Krzystoszek, 1998). It is highly probable, nevertheless, that cohabitation was adopted by some groups of population in the 1990s. The growing number of persons reaching the legal marriage age and continuously falling number of marriages at the same time suggest the evidence that consensual unions become more common, leading to postponement or abandonment of the decision to marry.

In 1993, the number of dissolved marriages exceeded the number of registered marriages for the first time in the post-war history of Poland. The balance remained negative in four successive years. In 1997, there were 10.1 thousand more marriage dissolutions than new marriages. The major reason behind the marriage dissolution remains the death of one spouse; the death of a husband is three times more frequent cause of marriage dissolution than that of a wife. Only one-fifth of all marriage dissolutions in 1997 occurred due to divorce (GUS, 1998a).

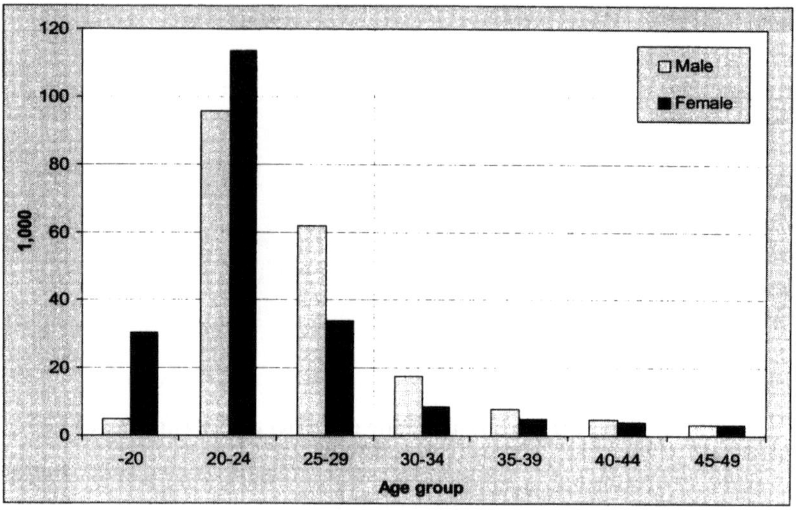


**Figure 12.3: First Marriages by Sex and Age Group, 1997**

Source: GUS, 1998a

Divorces are less frequent in Poland than in most other European countries. The absolute number of divorces peaked in 1984 (52.9 thousand) and then moved distinctly down until 1993 when 27.9 thousand divorces were reported. After 1993, the number began to rise again, reaching 42.6 thousand in 1997, i.e. over 3 thousand more than in the previous year (see Table 12.8). The index of divorce has been rising since 1993, both due to the fall in the number of marriages and rise in the number of divorces. The crude divorce rate stood at 1.1‰ in 1997. The divorce rate differed significantly between urban and rural areas: the rate for rural areas was 0.5‰, while that for urban areas reached 1.5‰. The balance between the numbers of contracted and dissolved marriages was highly negative in urban areas, but it remained positive in rural parts of the country.

**Table 12.8: Divorces, 1980–1997, selected years**

| | 1980 | 1985 | 1990 | 1995 | 1996 | 1997 |
|---|---|---|---|---|---|---|
| Divorces (1,000) | 39.8 | 49.1 | 42.4 | 38.1 | 39.4 | 42.5 |
| Crude divorce rate (‰) | 1.1 | 1.3 | 1.1 | 1.0 | 1.0 | 1.1 |
| Index of divorce[1] | 13.0 | 18.4 | 16.6 | 18.4 | 19.4 | 20.8 |

[1]Divorces per 100 marriages
Source: GUS, 1998a

Age-specific divorce rate was the highest in the 20–24 age group for both sexes, followed by the 25–29 age group for men and the group aged less than 20 years for women. About 20% of marriages were terminated within the first four years of marriage and 45% – during the first nine years. The main causes of divorce in Poland are: irreconcilable differences between spouses, extramarital affair, alcohol abuse and objectionable relation towards family. The average number of children per divorced couple was 1.05 in 1997. This means that some 44.6 thousand children "lost" one of the parents through a divorce in that year. Only one-third of couples breaking up their marriage in 1997 did not have children aged under 18, while 6.5% had three or more children (Figure 12.4).

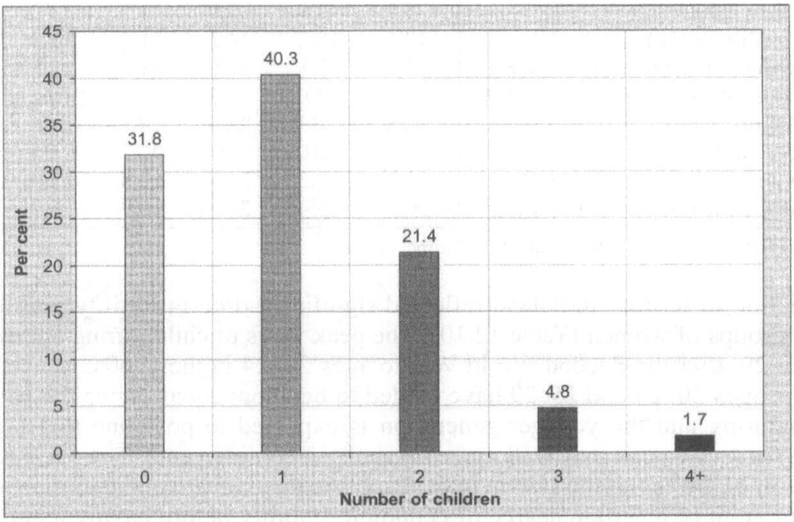


**Figure 12.4: Divorces by Number of Children Aged Under 18, 1997**
Source: GUS, 1998a

### 12.3.2 Fertility

The number of births in Poland has been declining from the mid-1980s and this trend has been continuing during the transition period of the 1990s. In 1997, 415,166 children were born, i.e. 25% less than in 1990, that being the lowest level in Poland since the Second World War (Table 12.9). Extramarital births are less common in Poland than in other European countries. Since the second half of the 1980s, however, the proportion of births occurring outside marriage has been rising and this trend has accelerated in the 1990s. In 1997, 11% of all live births were outside marriage. In absolute terms, it was one-third more than in 1990. At the same time, the number of children born to married women had fallen by 28% (GUS, 1986 and 1998a).

By 1990, the total fertility rate (TFR) had dropped below the replacement level. In order to reach the level required for population replacement in Polish conditions, there should be about 2.10–2.14 children per woman at the fertile age (Nowak, 1999). Since 1990, the pace of decline has accelerated. In 1997, the TFR reached a low of 1.5 children per woman (1.3 in urban and 1.8 in rural areas) and the net reproduction level was of about 0.7 (0.6 in urban and 0.9 in rural areas).

**Table 12.9: Main Indicators of Fertility, 1980–1997, selected years**

| | 1980 | 1985 | 1990 | 1995 | 1996 | 1997 |
|---|---|---|---|---|---|---|
| Total births (1,000) | 701.6 | 685.3 | 551.7 | 436.3 | 431.2 | 415.2 |
| Live births (1,000) | 695.8 | 677.6 | 547.7 | 433.1 | 428.2 | 412.6 |
| Stillbirths (1,000) | 5.8 | 3.9 | 3.9 | 3.2 | 3.0 | 2.5 |
| Crude birth rate (‰) | 19.5 | 18.2 | 14.3 | 11.2 | 11.1 | 10.7 |
| Live births outside marriage (1,000) | 33.2 | 33.8 | 34.0 | 41.0 | 43.5 | 45.3 |
| Proportion of extramarital births (%) | 4.8 | 5.0 | 6.2 | 9.5 | 10.2 | 11.0 |
| Total fertility rate | 2.28 | 2.33 | 2.04 | 1.61 | 1.58 | 1.51 |
| Net reproduction rate | 1.07 | 1.10 | 0.97 | 0.77 | 0.75 | 0.72 |
| Mean age of women at first birth | 23.0 | 23.3 | 23.0 | 22.8 | 22.9 | 23.1 |
| Mean age of women at childbearing | 26.5 | 26.4 | 26.3 | 26.9 | 26.9 | 26.9 |

Sources: GUS, 1986 and 1998a; Council of Europe, op. cit.

The decline of fertility in Poland reflected significant drop in fertility rates among all age groups of women (Table 12.10). The peak years of childbearing shifted from ages 25–29 after the Second World War to ages 20–24 in the 1960s. Recently, the rates for ages 20–24 and 25–29 have tended to be about equal. Since the pattern is still changing and the younger generation is expected to postpone marriage and childbearing, the peak may well move up again in coming years. The current transformation of the economic system may be motivating women to obtain more education and achieve a certain degree of economic stability before having a child. The shift of childbearing to a later age has raised the mean age of women at childbearing to 26.9 years in 1997, i.e. about 0.6 year more than in 1990 (Council of Europe, op. cit.)

**Table 12.10: Age-specific Fertility Rates, 1990 and 1997, per 1,000 women**

| | Age group | | | | | | |
|---|---|---|---|---|---|---|---|
| | 15–19 | 20–24 | 25–29 | 30–34 | 35–39 | 40–44 | 45–49 |
| 1990 | 31.5 | 165.2 | 121.4 | 58.6 | 24.5 | 6.2 | 0.3 |
| 1997 | 19.5 | 100.7 | 100.0 | 53.4 | 22.3 | 5.3 | 0.2 |
| Index 1997/1990 (%) | 61.9 | 61.0 | 82.4 | 91.1 | 91.0 | 85.5 | 66.7 |

Sources: GUS, 1991 and 1998a

Figure 12.5 shows differences in the age-specific fertility rate (ASFR) in urban and rural areas. The curve illustrating the fertility behaviour of the rural population is higher and more skewed to the left than that of urban population. This indicates not only higher fertility of rural women but also the fact that the peak of childbearing in rural areas is in the age group 20–24, while that in urban areas is among women aged 25–29 (GUS, 1998a).

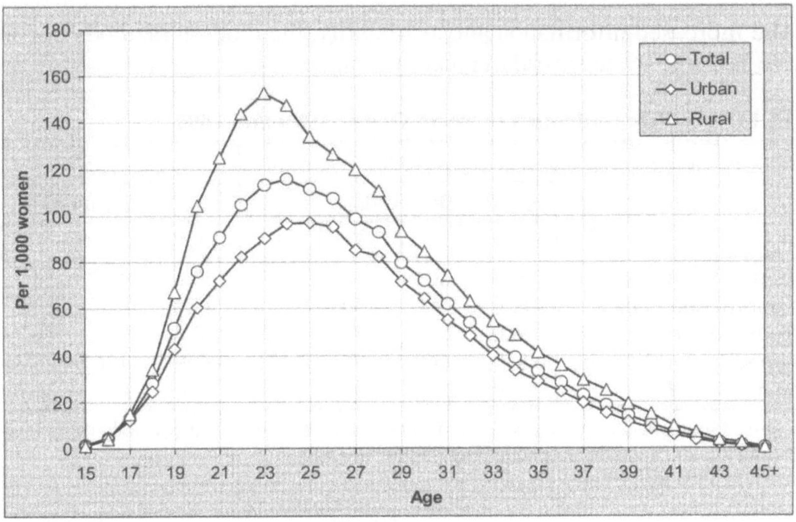


**Figure 12.5: Age-specific Fertility Rates, 1997**
Source: GUS, 1998a

The age distribution of fertility is also affected by the parity of births. Since 1990, the proportion of first births had increased from 40% to 44% in 1997, while the proportion of the second, third and fourth child had fallen. In 1997, only 63% of women were expected to have at least one child, while this proportion was as high as 85% seven years ago. Of those already having one child, 75% were expected to have the second child in 1997. Only 22% of all women were expected to have the third child and 9% were expected to have the fourth child (Table 12.11).

Until 1997, abortions were prohibited in Poland with the exception of cases when woman's health was seriously endangered, there was a strong chance of a serious defect of a child or pregnancy was the result of a rape. In January 1997, the law was liberalised. It permitted to interrupt a pregnancy for social reasons. In May 1997, the Constitutional Tribunal stated that the amendment was unconstitutional and in December 1997, the Polish Parliament accepted the statement of the Tribunal. For the understandable reasons, data on induced as well as on spontaneous abortions is not available.

As regards the methods of contraception, official data is also missing. It is worth reminding that 96% of the Polish population are Roman Catholics and the Roman Catholic Church accepts only natural methods of birth control and any other methods treats as evilly. According to the findings of the FFS, most female respondents reported that they and their partners were using traditional methods. The most common method was periodic abstinence, followed by withdrawal and then condoms. The proportions of women relying on the pill, the IUD or the diaphragm were very small. Quite a high proportion of respondents thought the question was too personal and did not give an answer (Holzer and Kowalska, op. cit.). It can be assumed that, due to the increased information and availability, the modern methods of contraception have become more spread in recent years.

**Table 12.11: Fertility Indicators by Birth Order, 1990 and 1997**

| | 1990 | | | | 1997 | | | |
|---|---|---|---|---|---|---|---|---|
| | Birth order | | | | Birth order | | | |
| | 1 | 2 | 3 | 4 | 1 | 2 | 3 | 4 |
| Total population (%) | 39.5 | 32.1 | 16.4 | 6.7 | 43.8 | 30.7 | 14.1 | 6.0 |
| Urban population (%) | 42.6 | 34.4 | 15.0 | 5.0 | 48.4 | 31.6 | 12.2 | 4.5 |
| Rural population (%) | 36.0 | 29.4 | 18.1 | 8.6 | 38.4 | 29.7 | 16.2 | 7.8 |
| Parity-specific fertility rate | 0.850 | 0.669 | 0.309 | 0.126 | 0.629 | 0.476 | 0.223 | 0.094 |
| Median age of mothers[1] | 23.0 | 26.4 | 29.5 | 31.6 | 23.1 | 26.7 | 30.0 | 32.4 |

[1]Median age of mothers is the mean age of mothers at the birth of next child; exactly the half of mothers was in this age or over and the second half was below this age
Sources: GUS, 1991 and 1998a

### 12.3.3 Mortality

In 1997, deaths numbered slightly over 380,000, i.e. about 10 thousand less than in 1990. Almost two-thirds of this fall was due to the decline in infant mortality. The number of infant deaths fell by about 60% between 1990–1997, and the crude death rate decreased from 10.2‰ in 1990 to 9.8‰ in 1997 (Table 12.12).

**Table 12.12: Mortality Indicators, 1980–1997, selected years**

| | 1980 | 1985 | 1990 | 1995 | 1996 | 1997 |
|---|---|---|---|---|---|---|
| Deaths (1,000) | 353.2 | 384.0 | 390.3 | 386.1 | 385.5 | 380.2 |
| Crude death rate (‰) | 9.9 | 10.3 | 10.2 | 10.0 | 10.0 | 9.8 |
| Infant deaths (1,000) | 17.7 | 15.1 | 10.6 | 5.9 | 5.2 | 4.2 |
| Infant mortality rate (‰) | 25.5 | 22.0 | 19.3 | 13.6 | 12.2 | 10.2 |

Sources: GUS, 1996 and 1998a

The fall in the number of deaths led to a rise in life expectancy at birth and at older ages. Until the mid-1960s, life expectancy in Poland was increasing rapidly for both males and females. During the 1970s and 1980s, male life expectancy at birth remained stable and only in the early 1990s did the situation begin to improve so that in 1997 it stood at 68.5 years. For females, the life expectancy increased only slightly during the 1970s and 1980s. The upward trend continued in the 1990s, reaching 77.0 years in 1997 (Table 12.13). The total rise in life expectancy at birth between 1990 and 1997 was 2.2 years for men and 1.8 for women. At the moment, however, the life expectancy in Poland is 4–5 years lower than that in the developed countries of Western and Northern Europe. The most often mentioned reasons for the relatively high level of mortality in Poland are the low standard of living, harmful addictions (high consumption of alcohol and smoking), unhealthy nutrition habits and deterioration of the environment (Bolesławski, 1997). An important feature of mortality in Poland is the mortality gap between the sexes: the difference in life expectancy at birth between males and females amounted to 8.5 years in 1997.

**Table 12.13: Life Expectancy by Sex and Age, 1985–1997, selected years**

| Age | 1985–1986 | | 1990 | | 1996 | | 1997 | | |
|---|---|---|---|---|---|---|---|---|---|
| | Male | Female | Male | Female | Male | Female | Male | Female | Difference |
| 0 | 66.86 | 75.33 | 66.24 | 75.24 | 68.12 | 76.57 | 68.45 | 76.99 | 8.54 |
| 15 | 53.63 | 61.83 | 53.07 | 61.84 | 54.33 | 62.66 | 54.46 | 62.94 | 8.48 |
| 30 | 39.54 | 47.16 | 39.11 | 47.16 | 40.18 | 47.95 | 40.35 | 48.23 | 7.88 |
| 45 | 26.32 | 32.94 | 26.05 | 32.97 | 26.89 | 33.66 | 27.10 | 33.91 | 6.81 |
| 60 | 15.31 | 19.90 | 15.33 | 19.96 | 15.93 | 20.52 | 16.13 | 20.80 | 4.67 |

Source: GUS, 1998a

Since the beginning of the 1990s, there has been a decrease in the level of mortality for both men and women in all age groups. Comparison of the indices of mortality by sex and age between 1990 and 1997 indicates that there was a drop of 10% to 20% for men aged 20–39 and women aged 25–44 and a lesser fall – for other age groups.

Although the level of mortality is considerably higher in Poland than in most other developed countries, the main causes of death are the same. In 1996, cardiovascular diseases were responsible for about 50% of all deaths, while about 21% of deaths were caused by malignant or other neoplasm and about 7% – by accidents, injuries or poisoning. Thus, it is realistic to assume that a reduction in the mortality from cardiovascular diseases may significantly improve the general mortality in the future. Specific mortality rates by sex, age group and cause of death are higher for males than for females: two to four times as high for circulatory diseases in the group between 15 and 69 years and twice as high for cancer between 55 and 79 years. During the 1990s, deaths from cancer were still rising, whereas there was a slight downward trend in the level of mortality due to circulatory diseases (Table 12.14).

Nevertheless, the positive changes in mortality from circulatory diseases are counterbalanced by an increase in mortality due to not specified causes. Mortality for such an extended group of causes represented 53% of total mortality for males and 65% for females in 1996 (Bolesławski, op. cit.).

The fall in the level of mortality in the 1990s – measured by the rise in life expectancy at birth – was linked with the continuing reduction in infant mortality. It experienced a decline to the level of only 10.2 infant deaths per 1,000 live births in 1997 (Figure 12.6), 7.4 of which occurred in the first 28 days of a child's life. However, the rate is still almost three times as high as that of the Scandinavian countries (GUS, 1998a).

**Table 12.14: Deaths by Sex and Cause of Death, 1980–1996, selected years, per 100,000 inhabitants**

| Year | Cancer | Circulatory diseases | Respiratory diseases | Accidents and poisonings |
|---|---|---|---|---|
| | | Male | | |
| 1980 | 271 | 725 | 103 | 129 |
| 1985 | 290 | 741 | 103 | 121 |
| 1990 | 304 | 760 | 76 | 132 |
| 1995 | 320 | 723 | 63 | 122 |
| 1996 | 322 | 714 | 66 | 116 |
| | | Female | | |
| 1980 | 200 | 751 | 58 | 45 |
| 1985 | 202 | 782 | 56 | 47 |
| 1990 | 210 | 797 | 41 | 48 |
| 1995 | 219 | 758 | 36 | 47 |
| 1996 | 221 | 756 | 41 | 45 |

Source: Bolesławski, op. cit.

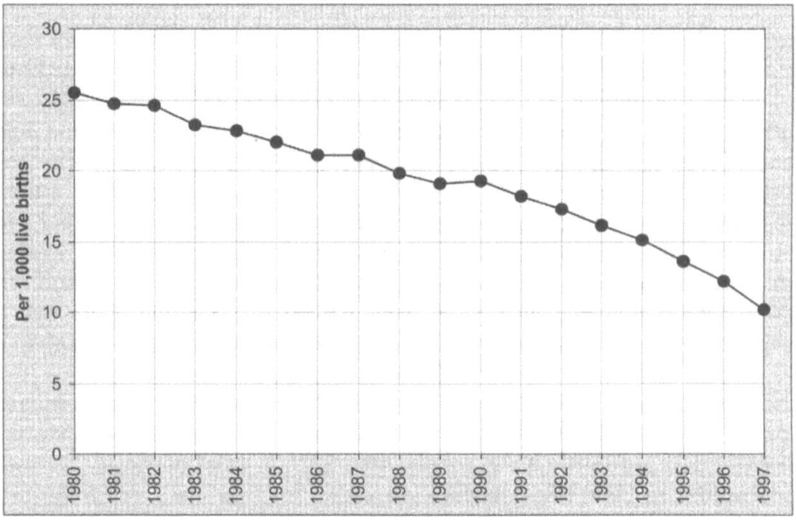


**Figure 12.6: Infant Mortality Rate, 1980–1997**

Source: GUS, 1998a

## 12.3.4 International Migration

Poland has been a country or territory of emigration since the middle of the nineteenth century and ever since 1960, emigration has greatly exceeded immigration. Official Polish statistics provide information only on permanent change of residence by Poles or foreigners. It is well known, however, that many Poles leave the country as temporary emigrants to become long-term or permanent emigrants later. Polish statistics do not have precise information on the extent of this type of emigration.

One factor traditionally contributing to emigration is the "brain drain". However, the 1990s have seen a distinct reduction of the emigration of persons with higher education. It is estimated that about 4.3 thousand of highly educated persons left Poland at that time, i.e. four times less than in the 1980s. The proportion of emigrants with higher education was 5% in the end of the 1980s but decreased to 1.5% in 1997 (Nowak, 1998). The number of emigrants with secondary school education has also decreased, although to a lesser degree. The official figures show that Poles leave the country for permanent residence mainly in Germany, United States, Canada, Austria, Sweden and France (GUS, 1998a).

In addition, an influx of people into Poland began after 1990, and in 1997 the number of immigrants reached the highest level since 1960. During 1990–1997, about 51.6 thousand persons arrived to Poland for permanent stay, which is three times more than in the whole decade of the 1980s (Table 12.15). Among immigrants, the most frequent countries of origin were Germany, United States, Canada and France ('returning migrants'), with countries that were formerly part of the Soviet Union taking on an increasing significance (Ukraine, Russian Federation, Belarus). A rise in illegal immigration has been observed in the 1990s as well. In the period 1990–1997, a negative total net migration increased to an average between 10 and 20 thousand persons a year (Nowak, 1998). Due to a small natural increase observed in the last decade, international migration has become a factor bearing a substantial impact on population development.

**Table 12.15: International Migration, 1981–1997, selected years, in thousands**

| Period/year | Immigration | Emigration | Net migration | | |
|---|---|---|---|---|---|
| | | | Total | Male | Female |
| 1981–1985 | 6.6 | 120.1 | -113.5 | -51.6 | -61.9 |
| 1986–1990 | 10.6 | 146.8 | -136.2 | -63.3 | -72.9 |
| 1991–1995 | 32.5 | 112.7 | -80.2 | -39.6 | -40.6 |
| 1995 | 8.1 | 26.3 | -18.2 | -9.0 | -9.2 |
| 1996 | 8.2 | 21.3 | -13.1 | -6.7 | -6.4 |
| 1997 | 8.4 | 20.2 | -11.8 | -5.9 | -5.9 |

Source: Nowak, 1998

## 12.4 Government Programmes and Policies

In recent years, activities of governmental institutions have focused on social fields touching upon population-related issues, in particular: social protection, social insurance, family allowance, health-care programmes, educational programmes in connection with unemployment and vocational training, targeted programmes for the disabled and so on.

The beginning of the social and economic transformation in Poland was accompanied by increasing unemployment and the rise in the proportion of population living in poverty. One of the most important tasks of the new government was, therefore, to create a more effective social protection system. The ideology behind the concept of social protection was to prevent people falling into or remaining in poverty resulting from the loss of a job, low income, shrinking of social infrastructure or occasional (unexpected) events. Within this system, series of measures have been adopted that are directed at creating decent living conditions for those individuals and families who cannot care for themselves. The Social Protection Act has been amended several times since its implementation in 1991. Among the most important amendments was the enlargement of the role of local governments (Golinowska, 1996; Rajkiewicz, 1997).

The transformation of the social insurance system in the 1990s focused mostly on the pension reform. After long debates, the new pension system was introduced at the beginning of 1999. It is a three-pillar system, starting from insurance principles. The system is self-financing and the amount of pension is related to the length of contributing period and amount of premiums. The first pillar is represented by obligatory premiums to the State Social Insurance Fund. The second pillar is an obligatory insurance in private pension funds, under surveillance of the state, based on the principle of the capitalisation of premiums. The third pillar is a voluntary insurance through private insurance companies. Importantly, there is a different social insurance system for farmers in Poland. Long-term benefits, like old-age or disability pensions, are administered by the Pension Fund, which is almost fully subsidised from the state budget (Woycicka, 1999).

The period 1990–1997 witnessed many changes in family allowance. In 1995, family allowance was excluded from the social insurance system and re-established as a grant provided by the social protection system (and, therefore, financed from the state budget). The same amendment established the family allowance as a means-tested benefit. It is paid only to families, in which the income per family member does not exceed 50% of the average working income in the national economy, beyond which the allowance is cancelled. The allowance is related to the number of children in the family, irrespective of the age of a child. In 1996, the valorisation mechanism was introduced. It enables the adjustment of the real value of the family allowance to changes in prices of consumer goods and services (Klos and Szymańczak, 1997).

The necessity of a reform in the financial system of health care in Poland became clear as early as at the beginning of the 1980s. Already then, it was obvious that the distribution of financial resources from the state budget, based on the infrastructure criterion, i.e. the number of beds and medical personnel, made any changes in the organisational system impossible. However, most of the activities aimed to reorganise the health care system began only ten years later, i.e. at the beginning of the

1990s, along with the whole societal transformation. The new system of health care based on health insurance was introduced in January 1999. Parallel changes in the financial system, the transformation of the organisational system has been under way. Up to now, most improvements have occurred in the basic health care; contracting of health services; introduction of a health service register; restructuring of hospitals; and formation of independent public health care institutions (Golinowska, op. cit.; Rajkiewicz, op. cit.).

After the political upheaval of 1989, the situation on the Polish labour market changed virtually overnight. Unemployment, previously almost non-existent, began to rise sharply. Initially, the state employment policy was rather passive, and its basic instrument was unemployment benefits. Only from 1993 onwards, different governmental measures did enable to support the formation of new job opportunities, to maximise the incentive of the unemployed to seek a job, to minimise demotivating effects of unemployment benefits, to adjust the educational system to requirements of the labour market, to solve structural unemployment by training programmes, and so on. An important element was a differentiated approach to young unemployed (up to 18 years), unemployed with dependent children and unemployed in the pre-retirement age. Special regulations were also introduced in regions strongly affected by structural unemployment (Golinowska, op. cit.).

One of the social groups strongly affected by unemployment were disabled persons. In 1995, the unemployment rate among the disabled reached 16.9%, which was more than 2 points higher than that among the whole population. The coordination of activities that could help disabled persons resulted in the establishing of the State Disabled Persons' Rehabilitation Fund at the beginning of the 1990s. Besides job opportunities for disabled, the Fund supports their therapeutic, social and cultural rehabilitation. It encourages entrepreneurs to modify working environment and conditions so that are accessible and suitable for disabled persons, subsides the production of rehabilitation aids, modernises sanatoriums, and so on (Rajkiewicz, op. cit.).

## 12.5 Population Projection up to 2020

The information presented in this section is derived from the population projection made by the Central Statistical Office in 1996, which is accepted as the official population projection for Poland until the year 2020. The projection is based on assumptions that fertility will be below the replacement level, that life expectancy at birth for both sexes will gradually increase, while net external migration will stay at the same level. Population increase will be determined by a gradual increase in the number of births, due mainly to a larger number of females in fertile age, which has been growing for the several past years. Modest intensity of increase in births teamed up with enhanced life expectancy at birth means that a rapid process of population ageing may be expected (Bolesławski and Marciniak, 1997).

With these assumptions, natural increase would be positive (slightly over 2‰ annually) in the period from 1996 to 2020 and the number of Poland's population would increase from 38.6 to 40.7 million (Table 12.16). Considerable changes will take place in the proportion of population by major age groups. The drop of births observed in the 1990s will result in a decreased number of the population aged under 18 (the pre-working age population). Its percentage share will fall from 27.6% in 1996 to 23.6% in 2020. The working-age population will be determined by an influx of numerous generations born during demographic baby boom of the early 1980s. Despite their volume, these generations will not compensate a large outflow of population to the retirement age. In the years 1996–2020, the proportion of the post-working age population (males aged 65 and over, females aged 60 and over) will grow from 14% to 19.4%. It is assumed that during this period the number of the post-working age population will rise almost by 50%. In absolute terms, this increase will be 2.6 million, i.e. from 5.4 million in 1996 to 7.9 million in 2020. The foreseen changes will have a strong impact on population ageing, which will continue to be a serious social and economic challenge to society in the beginning of the next century.

**Table 12.16: Population Projection up to 2020, selected years**

| Year | Assumptions | | | Expected numbers and structures | | | | | |
|---|---|---|---|---|---|---|---|---|---|
| | TFR | Life expectancy at birth | | Population (1,000) | | | Proportions of population at certain age (%) | | |
| | | Male | Female | Male | Female | Total | Pre-working[1] | Working[2] | Post-working[3] |
| 2000 | 1.74 | 68.0 | 76.4 | 18,878 | 19,976 | 38,854 | 24.8 | 60.8 | 14.4 |
| 2005 | 1.93 | .. | .. | 19,184 | 20,307 | 39,491 | 23.1 | 62.5 | 14.4 |
| 2010 | 1.92 | 70.0 | 77.4 | 19,538 | 20,647 | 40,185 | 23.1 | 61.7 | 15.2 |
| 2015 | 1.93 | .. | .. | 19,765 | 20,838 | 40,603 | 23.9 | 58.9 | 17.2 |
| 2020 | 1.92 | 72.0 | 78.4 | 19,828 | 20,866 | 40,694 | 23.6 | 57.0 | 19.4 |

[1]Population aged 0–17 years
[2]Include males aged 18–64 years and females aged 18–59 years
[3]Include males aged 65 years and over and females aged 60 years and over
Source: Bolesławski and Marciniak, op. cit.

## 12.6 Conclusion

At the end of 1997, the population of Poland stood at 38,660 thousand people. The ratio of population increase bottomed at about 0.5‰ (population growth by about 21 thousand) and broke long-time records as the lowest value during the whole post-war period. This has been largely determined by past and recent population trends, particularly decline in the natural increase of population reinforced by negative external net migration.

The number of births has been declining constantly since the mid-1980s and the trend toward fewer births has continued also during the period of economic transformation in the 1990s. Total fertility rate fell to only 1.51 children per woman in 1997. The decline in total fertility rate has been accompanied by an improvement in life expectancy. During 1990 and 1997, life expectancy at birth rose by 2.2 years for males and by 1.8 years for females. The continuing decline was observed also in relation to the infant mortality rate that is usually considered as a synthetic indicator of the improvement in the health situation of the population.

Undoubtedly, all the above-mentioned demographic phenomena will encourage changes in a long-term perspective. The population projection indicates that although until 2020 Poland is not threatened by depopulation, the number of population will rise only slightly. It is supposed that due to an increased number of females in reproductive age, the nearest future will bring about an increased number of births. Nevertheless, it is unlikely that Poland will achieve the level of population replacement (2.10 children per woman) until 2020. Apart from changed reproductive behaviour (less births), favourable trends in mortality and influx of numerous baby boom generations born in the early 1950s to retirement age will contribute to the ageing of Poland's population. The socio-economic pressure exerted by the elderly on the economically active population may therefore become a major demographic challenge to the Polish society in the next few decades.

## References

Bolesławski, L. (1997), *Life Tables and Mortality by Causes in 1996*, *Informacje i opracowania statystyczne*, Warszawa: Główny Urząd Statystyczny.

Bolesławski, L. and G. Marciniak (1997), *Population Projection of Poland by Voivodships 1996–2020*, *Informacje i opracowania statystyczne*, Warszawa: Główny Urząd Statystyczny.

Council of Europe (1998), *Recent Demographic Developments in Europe 1998*, Strasbourg: Council of Europe.

Duch-Krzystoszek, D. (1998), *Małżeństwo, seks, prokreacja: Analiza socjologiczna*, Warszawa: Wydawnictwo IFiS PAN.

Golinowska, S. (ed.) (1996), *Polityka społeczna w latach 1994–1996. Procesy regulacyjne i ich potencjalne skutki*, Raport IPiSS, Zeszyt nr 11, Warszawa.

GUS (Central Statistical Office) (1986), *Demographic Yearbook 1986*, Warszawa: Główny Urząd Statystyczny.

GUS (Central Statistical Office) (1991), *Demographic Yearbook 1991*, Warszawa: Główny Urząd Statystyczny.

GUS (Central Statistical Office) (1993), *Statistical Yearbook 1993*, Warszawa: Główny Urząd Statystyczny.

GUS (Central Statistical Office) (1997), *Statistical Yearbook 1997*, Warszawa: Główny Urząd Statystyczny.

GUS (Central Statistical Office) (1998a), *Demographic Yearbook 1998*, Warszawa: Główny Urząd Statystyczny.

GUS (Central Statistical Office) (1998b), *Statistical Yearbook 1998*, Warszawa: Główny Urząd Statystyczny.

Holzer, J.Z. and I. Kowalska (eds.) (1997), *Fertility and Family Surveys in Countries of the ECE Region. Standard Country Report. Poland*, New York and Geneva: United Nations.

Klos, B. and J. Szymańczak (1997), *Świadczenia na rzecz rodziny w latach 1990–1996*, Raport nr 11, Warszawa: Biuro Studiów i Ekspertyz.

Nowak, L. (ed.) (1998), *Migracje zagraniczne ludności w Polsce w latach 1988–1997, Informacje i opracowania statystyczne*, Warszawa: Główny Urząd Statystyczny.

Nowak, L. (ed.) (1999), *Basic Information on Demographic Development of Poland in 1989–1997. Demographic Changes in the Socio-Economic Transformation Period in 1989–1997*, Warszawa: Główny Urząd Statystyczny.

Rajkiewicz, A. (ed.) (1997), *Społeczeństwo polskie w latach 1989–1995/1996. Zagadnienia polityki społecznej*, Warszawa: Fundacja im. Friedricha Eberta.

Woycicka, I. (ed.) (1999), Budżet polityki społecznej. Metodologia modelu symulacyjnego, *Transformacja gospodarki*, Nr 99, Warszawa: Instytut Badań nad Gospodarką Rynkową.

# 13

# Recent Demographic Development in Romania

**Cornelia Mureşan and Traian Rotariu**

## 13.1 Introduction

Romania represents one of the middle-range European countries, both concerning its geographical surface (237.5 thousand square kilometres) and its number of inhabitants (22,581,862 people on 1 January 1997). Since 1990, similarly to the other countries of Eastern and Central Europe, Romania has been going through a transition from an authoritarian communist regime to a democratic society. It has been a period of large socio-economic changes, with definite consequences for a demographic development. The liberalisation of abortion and of the use of contraceptives, dismantling of the legal barriers for emigration and mobility within the country, the introduction of easier divorce procedures are only several of the factors with direct and immediate influence over the demographic phenomena. To all these should be added the profound changes in the way people live as a result of acquired access to Western mass culture and more and more frequent contacts with people of other countries.

At the same time, people of Romania withstand the material difficulties and the frustrations of transition. After more than 10 years since the fall of the communist rule, the country witnesses an inferior economic standard to that of 1989, while the government cannot ensure to the people the social protection offered by the previous regime, particularly a guaranteed work-place and wage as well as homes for young families. The general state of the society can be characterised, in short, as materially difficult, spiritually uncomfortable, and without a clear vision of how to solve the main problems.

This state of the society has been producing general and specific factors with an indirect or direct influence over the demographic behaviour, and has resulted in stagnation, if not deterioration, of mortality, in a severe decline in fertility and birth rate, in a rise in emigration of the population (particularly those who are qualified and of young ages), and a weakened stability of the family institution. All together, these factors have contributed to a demographic decline, that had begun in 1990, when the net migration was negative (very high for that year) and could not be compensated for by the natural increase of the population, and continued on a new level in 1992, when the natural increase was also negative (Figure 13.1).

**Figure 13.1: Population Growth (1870–1998) and Prospects (1999–2020)**
Source: based on NCS data

## 13.2 Population Structures

### 13.2.1 Sex Structure

As of 1 July 1997, the proportion of women in the population of Romania was 51%, a level that had not been recorded since right after the post-war years. Indeed, because of the war causalities, the proportion of women rose to 51.7% in 1948, then continuously decreased until the 1970s, where it remained stable for almost two decades at the level of 50.7%. Since 1992, there has been an increase of this proportion, which will probably continue due to the two factors: first, the decrease in the number of births (and, consequently, a smaller contribution to the population of the young ages, where males predominate); and second, the increase of the gap between the male and female average life expectancies in favour of the latter.

These influences are very clear with regard to the natural increase of the population. Between 1990 and 1996, the contribution of the male sex to the natural increase of the population was negative (-68,000 people), while the female influence was positive (+3,000 people). Consequently, due to different contributions during this period, the net difference between the numbers of the two sexes increased by more than 100,000 people (Gheţău, 1997). The external migration presented effects of the opposite direction, since the migratory activity of females during the same period of time was a little higher than that of males (-124,000 compared to -110,000). Therefore, the external migration was not a factor of defeminisation, but rather the contrary.

For the population of Romania, the demographic analyses of the rural and urban areas are extremely relevant, because the proportion of rural area is very high (about 45%). In contrast to common belief, the urban population is more feminised (51.5%) than the rural one (50.3%). The analysis of the sex structure by age groups reveals that the above phenomenon is mainly the result of the large differences in young adult ages (20–39), where the proportion of females in the rural area is lower, which can be explained by a more intense rural-urban migration of women.

### 13.2.2 Age Structure

The age structure represents a major component of the population also because of its social implications: it determines many features and characteristics of a society's way of life, beginning with the economic consumption and ending with cultural behaviour and mentalities. On 1 January 1997, the structure of the Romanian population by age groups was as shown in Table 13.1.

**Table 13.1: Population by Age Groups on 1 January 1997, per cent**

| | 0–14 | 15–29 | 30–44 | 45–59 | 60+ | Total |
|---|---|---|---|---|---|---|
| Percentage | 19.6 | 25.8 | 19.6 | 17.1 | 17.9 | 100.0 |

Source: based on NCS data

If we analyse the age structure over time, the increase of the proportion of the aged population and a decline of the proportion of the young population appear in a striking manner. At present, this process may be explained by the decrease of the birth rate. The comparison of the proportions of the three large age groups across the censuses (Table 13.2) gives us the dynamics of the age structure of the population from 1930 to 1992.

**Table 13.2: Age Structure According to the Census, 1930–1992, selected years, per cent**

| Age group | 1930 | 1956 | 1966 | 1977 | 1992 |
|---|---|---|---|---|---|
| 0–14 | 33.5 | 27.5 | 26.0 | 25.7 | 22.7 |
| 15–59 | 59.1 | 62.6 | 61.7 | 60.5 | 60.9 |
| 60+ | 7.4 | 9.9 | 12.3 | 13.8 | 16.4 |
| Total | 100.0 | 100.0 | 100.0 | 100.0 | 100.0 |

Source: based on NCS data

Table 13.2 shows that the proportion of the aged population (60 years and over) has grown from 7.4% in 1930, to 16.4% in 1992, and 17.9% in 1997. While in 1930 for every elderly person there were almost 8 active-age persons (the old age dependency ratio), in 1966 there were only 5, and in 1997 only 3.5, respectively. For the young population, the evolution is however reversed. The measures adopted in 1966, which are considered to be the beginning of the pronatalist policy of the Ceauşescu regime, managed until 1985 to contain the decline of the proportion of the young population. However, afterwards a decline resumed again, leading to a diminished proportion of the young population of only 19.6% in 1997 (NCS, 1996).

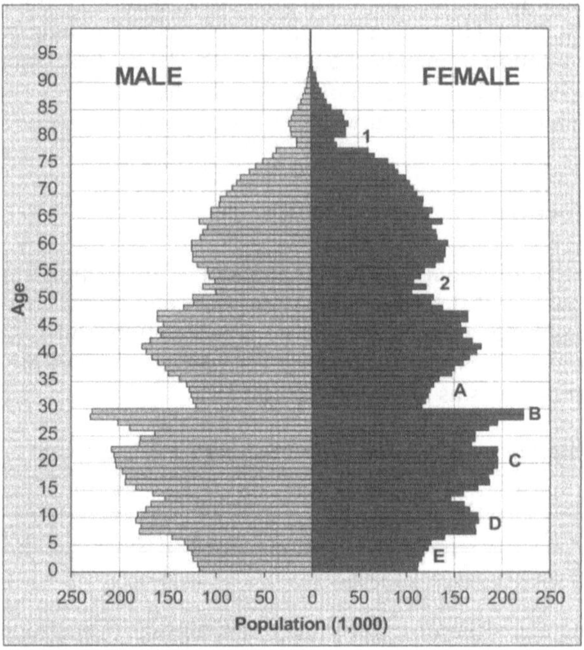


**Figure 13.2: Age Pyramid on 1 January 1997**

[1]The First World War
[2]The Second World War
[A]Liberalisation of abortion (1957)
[B]Abortion banned (1966)
[C]Measures against abortion (1974)
[D]New measures against abortion (1984)
[E]Legalisation of abortions (1989)
Source: based on NCS data

These two trends demonstrate the shift of the social burden from the young to the elderly population. The age group 15–59 for a long period of time held a constant proportion of a little over 60%. In the near future, we may witness an increase of this proportion, since the youngest sub-group aged 15–29 at present contains practically a quarter of the population of Romania. In other words, in the short run, ageing will not rise to problematic figures. Due to the relatively stable proportion of the population of working age in recent years, the age dependency ratio (the share of young and old people in per cent of the working-age population) holds constant at 59.5%.

The significant differences in the process of ageing distinguish the rural and urban areas. The common belief that the rural population is more aged than the urban is clearly confirmed by the statistics. The dynamics of the proportion of the aged population (60 years and over) across the censuses is presented in Table 13.3.

**Table 13.3: Proportion of Population Aged 60 or Over, 1930–1997, selected years, rural and urban population, per cent**

| Population | 1930 | 1956 | 1966 | 1977 | 1992 | 1997 |
|---|---|---|---|---|---|---|
| Urban | 7.2 | 9.3 | 10.9 | 11.5 | 11.6 | 13.0 |
| Rural | 7.4 | 10.2 | 13.3 | 16.7 | 22.1 | 23.8 |

Source: based on NCS data

The data shows that the divergence in the pattern of ageing between the rural and urban populations started in the 1950s, during the first stage of industrialisation. In the beginning, the differences were low, because the higher fertility of the rural population compensated for the loss in births due to migration. In the later years, the differences in the process of ageing became more pronounced, when the fertility levels of the two populations converged and the structural deficit of the rural population grew. As a result, in 1997, the proportion of aged people in rural areas was almost twice as large as the proportion of elderly in urban areas (23.8% and 13%, respectively) (NCS, 1996).

### 13.2.3 Ethnic Composition

Since the origin of the Romanian national state, the population of Romania has been composed of many ethnic groups. Along with Romanians, who were always a majority, there have lived Hungarians and Germans. Over time, the proportion of Romanians has increased. It happened not because of their higher fertility, but, first, due to the emigration of minorities, especially Germans, Jews, and most recently of Hungarians; and second, due to the process of assimilation (more exactly, through the many interethnic marriages in which children declare themselves as Romanians). According to the 1992 census, 20,408,542 persons (89.5% of the total population) identified themselves as Romanians (NCS, 1992).

Since 1930, the proportion of the German and Jewish ethnic groups has declined to their almost complete disappearance. The proportion of Hungarians has diminished too. At the same time, after experiencing a period of decline from the 1930s till the 1960s, the ethnic group of Gypsies, since the 1970s, has been growing in absolute and relative term (Table 13.4). At the last census, this minority has occupied the second place, after the Hungarians, with 401,087 persons (1.8% of the total population). Their proportion has almost doubled between the last two censuses, because their number has grown, and also because they have changed the criteria for declaring themselves as Gypsies. However, it is frequently noted that their number is underestimated. According to some experts, a more accurate number may be around one million (Mureşan, 1994; Zamfir and Zamfir, 1993).

**Table 13.4: Population by Ethnic Groups According to the Censuses Between 1930 and 1992**

| Ethnic group | 1930 | | 1956 | | 1966 | | 1977 | | 1992 | |
|---|---|---|---|---|---|---|---|---|---|---|
| | 1,000 | % | 1,000 | % | 1,000 | % | 1,000 | % | 1,000 | % |
| Romanians | 11,118 | 77.8 | 14,997 | 85.8 | 16,746 | 87.7 | 18,997 | 88.1 | 20,408 | 89.5 |
| Hungarians | 1,423 | 10.0 | 1,588 | 9.1 | 1,620 | 8.5 | 1,713 | 7.9 | 1,625 | 7.1 |
| Germans | 634 | 4.4 | 385 | 2.2 | 383 | 2.0 | 349 | 1.6 | 120 | 0.5 |
| Jewish | 452 | 3.2 | 146 | 0.8 | 43 | 0.2 | 25 | 0.1 | 9 | 0.0 |
| Gypsy | 243 | 1.7 | 104 | 0.6 | 64 | 0.3 | 227 | 1.1 | 401 | 1.8 |
| Others | 411 | 2.9 | 270 | 1.5 | 248 | 1.3 | 249 | 1.2 | 247 | 1.1 |
| Total | 14,281 | 100.0 | 17,490 | 100.0 | 19,103 | 100.0 | 21,560 | 100.0 | 22,810 | 100.0 |

Source: based on NCS data

## 13.3 Processes of Population Reproduction

### 13.3.1 Fertility

The total fertility rate shows a firm and rapid decrease in the number of children per woman. While in 1985 a woman had on average 2.26 live births, since the beginning of the 1990s, this indicator has continuously been lower than the level of generation replacement, that is 1.83 children per woman in 1990 and only 1.29 – in 1996 (NCS, 1996).

The high levels of fertility during the period 1967–1989 may be attributed to the pronatalist measures of the previous communist regime, namely strict policy of forbidding abortion and restriction of access to contraceptives (Mureşan, 1996a). After the abolishment of the restrictive legislation at the end of 1989, a decrease in the number of live births was expected. This expectation, however, should have taken into account the fact that the generations that were born immediately after the decree of 1966, which banned abortions, had entered the childbearing age on the threshold of the 1980s–1990s. The 1990s had been characterised by the changes in the timing of the births (Mureşan, 1997), and thus the completed fertility may recover in the future.

Taking into account that the mean age at childbearing in 1985 and during 1990–1996 was about 25 years, it is reasonable to analyse the fertility of the generations of women who were of that age in the periods when the changes in reproductive behaviour supposedly took place. We have therefore chosen three years as the reference points: the year 1990 as the beginning of the rapid decline in fertility, a more recent year – 1995, and 1985 as a year belonging to the "childbearing" period not very distant in time. These calendar years correspond, conforming to our criteria, to the generations of women born in 1960, 1965, and 1970, respectively.

As Figure 13.3 indicates, the generations born in 1960 and 1965 have almost the same intensity of fertility during the first years of reproductive age (around 68‰ for the age group 15–19 years and 188‰ for the age group 20–24 years), but the former one continued to give birth to relatively more children than the latter one, under the constraining effect of the pronatalist measures. The generation born in 1970 accomplishes only 70% of the fertility of the first two groups, with no sign that the postponed births will recuperate in the following years.

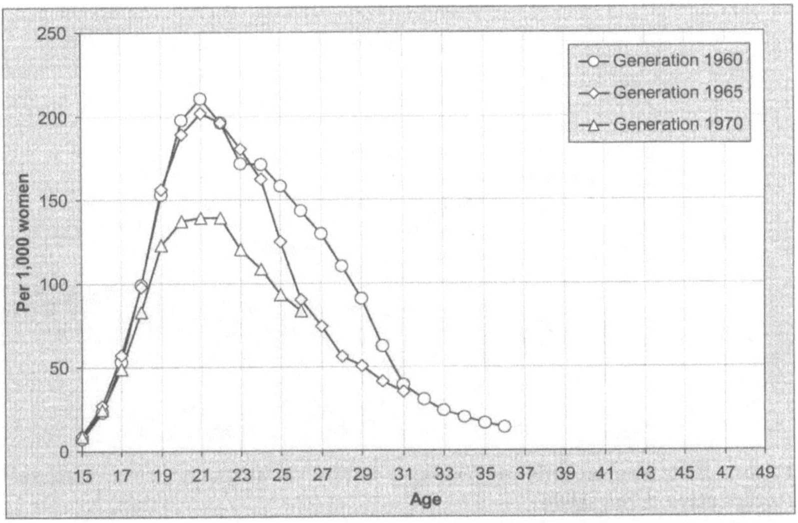


**Figure 13.3: Age-specific Fertility Rates of the Female Generations Born in 1960, 1965 and 1970**

Source: based on NCS data

### 13.3.2 Birth Order

Another indicator that cannot be ignored is the ideal model of fertility and its evolution over time. The decreasing fertility of couples, under the influence of changes in behaviour and economic factors, took also the form of an increase in the proportion of live births of the first birth order (from 38% in 1985, to 44% in 1990, and 54% in 1996). Although the proportion of children of the second birth order decreased from 32% in 1985 to 28% in 1996, it was not significant as compared to the decline in the number and proportion of the third-order births.

To identify the main factors underlying the fertility decline, we have studied the proportional distribution of mothers who have had another child (Figure 13.4).

Figure 13.4 illustrates the effect of the legislative measures on the families' reproductive behaviour throughout the 1960s–1980s. During 1974–1984, the third births were not influenced by pronatalist measures as much as the second ones. On the contrary, the periods 1967–1973 and 1984–1989 witnessed an increase in the probabilities of having a further child. After a severe decrease in the probability of having second and third child after 1990, a recovery of the *a1* curve started in 1993, followed then by a continuous decline of the *a2* curve. This proves that the preferred model of present-date families in Romania is to have one or two children.

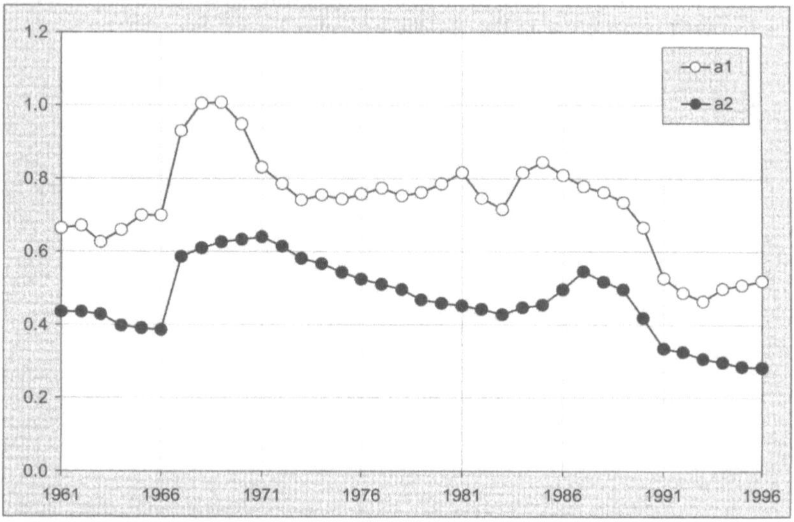


**Figure 13.4: Probabilities of Having a Further Child in a Cross-sectional Perspective, 1961–1996**

a1 shows the probability of having a second child
a2 shows the probability of having a third child
Source: based on NCS data

The longitudinal analysis based on the 1992 census data provides further evidence about the changes in the contribution of the different birth orders to the completed fertility of female generations born between 1915 and 1960. Figure 13.5 shows the contribution of the 1st, 2nd, and 3rd and higher birth orders to the formation of the completed fertility. The decline in the births of the third and higher orders and the unchanged contribution of the births of the first birth order (around 0.9 live births per 1,000 women) and of the second birth order (around 0.6 live births per 1,000 women) are quite visible for these generations.

There have been a lot of discussions concerning the significantly higher fertility of the Gypsy population in Romania. Because the census data enables to analyse the completed fertility of the generations born between 1915 and 1960 by ethnic groups, it is possible to outline the ethnic differences in fertility as well. As Figure 13.6 demonstrates, they grew up in time. The generation of Gypsy women born in 1960 has completed fertility of 2 more children than the Romanian or Hungarian women of the same generation, while the Gypsy women born in 1915 averaged only 1 child more than the Romanian women, and 1.5 children more than the Hungarian women.

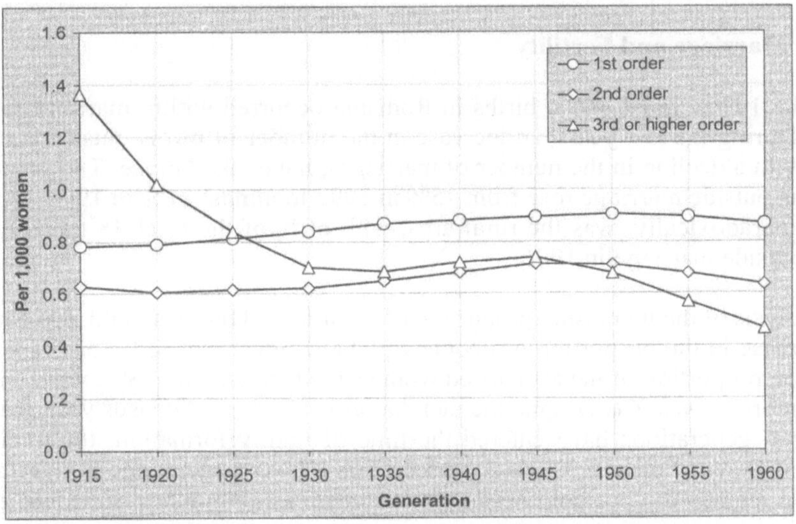


**Figure 13.5: Contribution of 1st, 2nd, 3rd and Higher Birth Orders to the Completed Fertility of Female Generations Born Between 1915 and 1960**
Source: authors' calculations based on NCS data

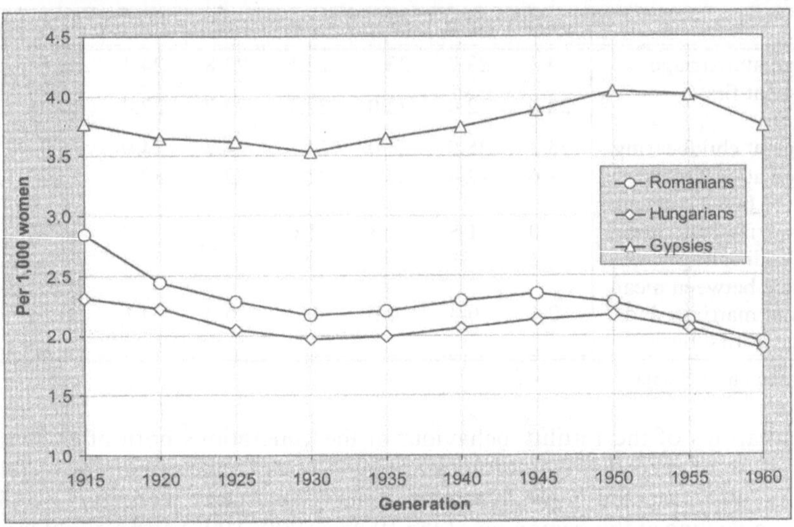


**Figure 13.6: Completed Fertility of Female Generations Born Between 1915 and 1960 by Ethnic Group**
Source: authors' calculations based in NCS data

### 13.3.2 Marriage and Fertility

Until the 1990s, most of the births in Romania occurred within marriage (around 95%). During the last years, an increase in the number of births outside marriage, along with a decline in the number of marriages, have taken place. The proportion of births outside marriage rose from 15% in 1992 to almost 21% in 1996. More affected, paradoxically, was the rural area, with 60% of the total 48 thousand live births outside marriage in 1996.

The analysis of the increasing proportion of extramarital births should also consider the increase in the proportion of people who have never married. For example, in 1977, the proportion of never-married women aged over 20 was 8%, while in 1992 this proportion was 9%. Despite the fact that in 1992, the last census year, the large post-1966 generations have entered the time of family formation, the traditional gender difference of approximately three years between mean age at marriage of men and women did not hold because of the decreasing number of people getting married.

**Table 13.5: Mean Age of Women at Marriage and at Childbearing, 1985–1996, selected years**

| | 1985 | 1990 | 1991 | 1992 | 1993 | 1994 | 1995 | 1996 |
|---|---|---|---|---|---|---|---|---|
| Mean age at marriage | 24.3 | 23.7 | 23.7 | 23.8 | 23.8 | 24.1 | 24.5 | 24.5 |
| Mean age at first marriage | 22.0 | 22.0 | 22.0 | 22.1 | 22.2 | 22.4 | 22.8 | 22.8 |
| Mean age at childbearing | 25.3 | 25.5 | 25.0 | 24.8 | 24.7 | 24.9 | 25.0 | 24.8 |
| Mean age at first birth | 22.6 | 22.4 | 22.2 | 22.3 | 22.4 | 22.5 | 22.7 | 22.9 |
| Difference between mean age at marriage and mean age at childbearing | 1.0 | 1.8 | 1.3 | 1.0 | 0.9 | 0.9 | 0.5 | 0.3 |
| Difference between mean age at first marriage and mean age at first birth | 0.6 | 0.4 | 0.2 | 0.2 | 0.2 | 0.1 | -0.1 | 0.1 |

Source: based on NCS data

The peculiarities of the fertility behaviour of the generations born after 1966 and the formation of reproductive attitudes at young ages in the condition of fertility decline are also reflected in the dynamics of the mean age of women at childbearing. After a decline at the beginning of the 1990s (1990–1993) and a slight increase after that, the value of the mean age at childbearing was about 25 years. The mean age at first birth grew slightly but constantly (Table 13.5). The difference between the mean age at marriage and the mean age at childbearing was becoming smaller and decreased from 1.8 years in 1990 to 0.3 in 1996. The difference between the mean age at first marriage and at first birth diminished from 0.4 years in 1990 to 0.1 in 1996 and thus demonstrated a shift to the demographic pattern, where the moment of conception tends to precede the moment of marriage.

## 13.4 Marriage

The state of the demographic phenomena such as the family formation and dissolution (including marriage and divorce) can be briefly characterised as generally unchanged, namely the traditional models (that value highly the family) continue to dominate the Romanian society, despite some important shifts in social and cultural norms. The family still represents the mainstay for the majority of Romanian population, bringing certain benefits (material and psychological) to those who get married, and relatively significant costs for the ones who intend to end their marriage.

The crude marriage rate (CMR) shows little changes over the last three decades. There was an obvious decrease of the CMR in the 1960s, after the marriages postponed by the Second World War recuperated. There was also a certain fluctuation in the dynamics of the CMR, mainly due to the structural changes and variations in the number of divorces. In particular, it declined from the level of over 10–11‰ in the 1950s to 7‰ in 1969, and afterwards it oscillated around 9‰. The last three years, for which data is available (1994–1996), show values under 7‰. This decline may be viewed as the beginning of a long-term downward trend, especially if we take into account the fact that numerous generations born after 1966 are just passing the ages with the highest marriage rates. Similar decline can also be observed in the total first marriage rate, since more than 85% of the marriages contracted within a given year, for both sexes, are the first marriages. Table 13.6 demonstrates that in 1996 the age-specific marriage rates for young age groups (people aged under 35), where first marriages prevailed, had lower net values as compared to 1992. Thus, it can be concluded that the marriage rates are declining mainly because of the changes in the intensity and timing of the first marriages.

**Table 13.6: Age-specific Marriage Rates, 1992 and 1996, per 1,000 inhabitants**

| Age group | Male | | Female | |
|---|---|---|---|---|
| | 1992 | 1996 | 1992 | 1996 |
| –20 | 16 | 7 | 74 | 34 |
| 20–24 | 96 | 66 | 83 | 72 |
| 25–29 | 56 | 52 | 26 | 29 |
| 30–35 | 18 | 19 | 9 | 11 |

Source: based on NCS data

## 13.5 Divorce

The crude divorce rates in Romania have never overstepped 2‰, being thus significantly lower than in Western countries. It is also noticeable, that after the government measures of 1967, which practically banned divorce (in 1967, only 48 divorces occurred in the whole country), the divorce rates increased a little, but without reaching the level seen before 1966. Even after 1989, in the conditions of general democratisation of the legislation, the number of divorces per 1,000 inhabitants as well as the total number of divorces almost did not increase, which had approximately the same absolute numbers, varying between 30,000 and 40,000 per year.

In relation to the timing of divorces, there has not been observed in recent years any significant changes too: the mean marriage duration at divorce has been fluctuating for a long period of time, however with no signs of regularity, between 10 and 10.9 years. The comparison with the period before 1966 provides a more interesting picture: while in 1963 (i.e. before the ban on abortions) more than half of the total number of divorces occurred in marriages that had lasted up to 5 years, in recent years, only one-third of marriages of such duration are dissolved by divorce (Table 13.7).

**Table 13.7: Divorces by Duration of Marriage, 1962–1996, selected years, per cent**

| Year | Duration of marriage | | | | | | Total |
|---|---|---|---|---|---|---|---|
| | 0 | 1–2 | 3–4 | 5–9 | 10–14 | 15+ | |
| 1962 | 7.4 | 26.9 | 19.0 | 25.2 | 11.3 | 10.2 | 100.0 |
| 1963 | 7.6 | 26.0 | 19.2 | 26.2 | 11.1 | 9.9 | 100.0 |
| 1995 | 2.8 | 16.1 | 16.0 | 27.6 | 14.8 | 22.7 | 100.0 |
| 1996 | 2.9 | 15.6 | 14.3 | 28.2 | 15.1 | 23.9 | 100.0 |

Source: based on NCS data

The average age difference between divorcing spouses was around 5 years during the last 15 years, with very small variations. Bearing in mind that the mean age of men at marriage is on average 3–3.5 years higher than that of women, it can be supposed that the probability of being divorced is higher when the age difference between spouses is also higher.

## 13.6 The Family and Household Structure

As demonstrated above, the first marriages predominate both for males and for females. In 1996, 85.8% of the men and 87% of the women who entered marriage were previously single; 13.8% of the men and 12.6% of the women who entered a marriage were previously divorced, and the rest were widowers. These values would have probably been relatively constant during the last 30 years, without the legislative measures of 1966, thus producing a decrease in the number of divorced, so that in the first part of the 1970s, the amount of single persons increased to 92%, then decreased back to the earlier mentioned values.

In regard to the size of the households in Romania, the data collected through the last three censuses indicates a slight reduction in the number of persons living in one household, mainly because of a more pronounced decrease of the households' size in the rural areas (Table 13.8).

**Table 13.8: Average Number of Persons per Household, 1966, 1977 and 1992**

| Year | Urban | Rural | Total |
|---|---|---|---|
| 1966 | 2.9 | 3.5 | 3.2 |
| 1977 | 2.9 | 3.3 | 3.2 |
| 1992 | 3.0 | 3.1 | 3.1 |

Source: based on NCS data

Out of the 7,288,676 households enumerated at the last census, 5,922,160 (81%) were recorded as family households, while the rest – 1,366,516 (19%) were not. Depending on the number of family cores, family households can be distributed as follows: 92.4% with one core, 7.3% with two cores and 0.3% with three or more cores. 91% of the non-family households are made up of one person and the rest – 9% (or 1.6% of the total) are made up of more than one person. The latter ones represent in many cases the households of cohabiting persons (living together without registered marriage), except for young adults who live together to share the housing costs, because due to the crisis situation in the housing sphere there is a shortage of affordable dwellings in Romania.

As official statistics do not record consensual unions, it is difficult to analyse this phenomenon. However, we can estimate that in Romania, compared with Western countries, such arrangements are not so much widespread, also because the social, economic and legislative environment that would favour the expansion of this type of living have not yet emerged.

## 13.7 Mortality: Old Trends and New Developments

The present trends in Romania, as well as in the other ex-communist countries, are different from mortality developments in Western Europe. After 1991, the factors that coincided with the transition period have directly affected the health of the population. During the six-year period between 1991 and 1996, women lost almost one month from their life expectancy at birth, and men much more: 1.26 years. In 1996, the difference between the life expectancy for men and women reached 7.8 years.

This deterioration should not be interpreted only as an effect of the changes in economic and social conditions. A deeper analysis of the changes in mortality demonstrates that the negative processes which had started as early as the mid-1970s and then developed without their effects being openly noticed are of key importance for understanding the recent decline of life expectancy at birth (Mureşan, 1996b).

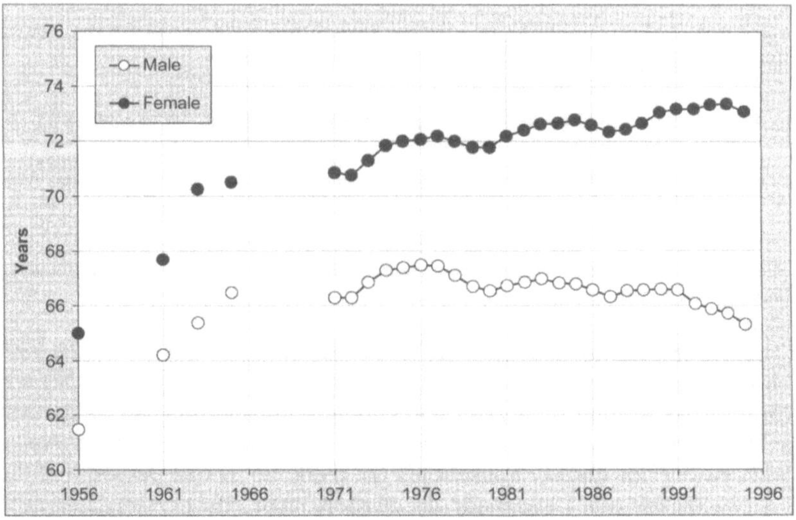


**Figure 13.7: Life Expectancy at Birth, 1956–1996, selected years**

Source: based on NCS data

For men, the probability of dying was higher in 1976 than in 1956 by 20% for the age group 35–59, and this tendency grew in intensity together with its expansion to the age group 30–70 years. Thus, for the age group 40–44, the probability of dying was almost 80% higher in 1996 than in 1956, and 35% higher than in 1991. For adult females, the increase of the probability of dying started only after 1976. It affected women between 35 and 60 years and reached a peak in 1996, though with figures better than in 1956. The amplitude of this regress does not go past 18% for any age.

Another peculiarity of the mortality development in Romania is a very high level of infant mortality, as compared to the European standards. For example, infant mortality in 1996 was 22.3‰, which is four times as high as in France in the same year. This fact, and also the fact that the life expectancy at birth is 8.5 years lower than that in France, allows us to assert that in Romania the demographic transition has not yet finished.

During 1990–1996, the decline of the infant mortality rate was due mostly to the decrease of post-neonatal mortality, from 18.1‰ to 13.5 ‰. The rate of neonatal mortality tended to increase, due to the growth of the early neonatal mortality rate, from 5.2‰ to 6.1‰ (the main causes of early neonatal mortality were births with complications resulting in deaths and congenital anomalies). The slow, but certain increase of the early neonatal mortality to the level reached before 1965 was also connected with the fact that for many Romanian women abortion was the most common (if not only) way of birth control during the period of 1957–1966. An increase of early neonatal mortality thus may be attributed to the negative consequences of abortions for women's health and for the new-born child's health.

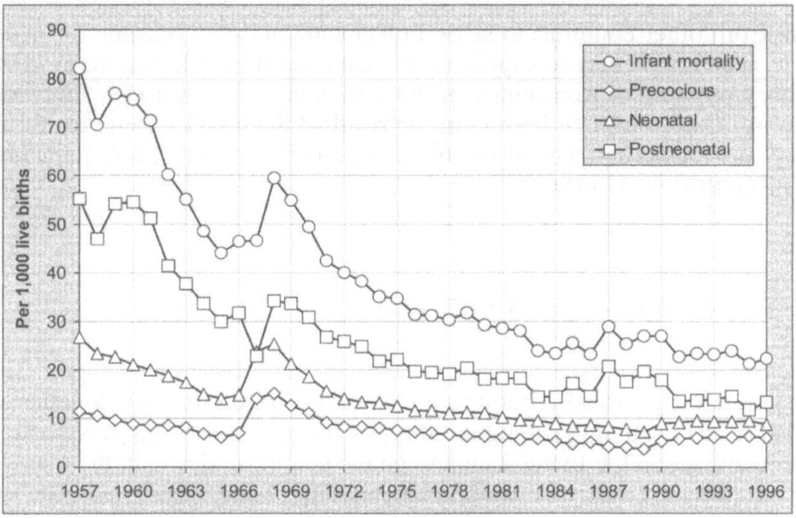


**Figure 13.8: Infant Mortality Rates, 1957–1996**
Source: based on NCS data

# 13.8 External Migration

The total number of emigrants during 1975–1995 was 595,972 people, which is an average of 28,000 per year. Over different sub-periods of time, the average values were as shown in Table 13.9

**Table 13.9: Average Number of Emigrants, 1975–1995, in thousands**

| | 1975–1979 | 1980–1989 | 1990 | 1991–1995 |
|---|---|---|---|---|
| Annual average number of emigrants | 14,942 | 28,775 | 96,929 | 27,316 |

Source: based on NCS data

The intensity of emigration doubled in the 1980s, as compared to the second half of the 1970s. In 1990, emigration witnessed a migratory wave, caused by the emigration of the German population (over 60,000 persons), and afterwards it returned to the previous level. Combining the official data and the data provided by Gheţău (1997) concerning the total migration for the period after 1990, it is possible to assess the intensity of legal immigration. During the six years (1990–1995), there were around 15,000 immigrants, with an average of 2,500 per year.

Romania was and remains a country of emigration. This situation can be explained by the fact that, despite the progress made after 1989 towards democratisation of the social and political life, the economic backwardness offers very few reasons for people from other countries to settle in Romania and few reasons for people who want to accomplish certain expectations (that cannot be fulfilled here) to stay. The migratory pressure of Romanians on Western countries is still very high, a fact that can be inferred from their hesitation to liberalise the travel regime for Romanians, as they did for the citizens of the other countries in Central Europe (Poland, the Czech Republic, or Hungary)

## 13.9 Population-related Policies

The economic and social crisis which Romania is going through, together with the fact that it has been aggravating steadily for the past few years, have had a strong negative impact on the living standard, on the health services, on the overall condition of the society, and, as a result, on the quality of life, which had been lower, by average European standards, even since the 1980s. The negative demographic "outcomes", which we described above, and especially the fall of fertility and the rise of mortality, are direct and logical consequences of the economic and social development, and are not caused by the absence of demographic policy.

### 13.9.1 Family Policy

One of the directions in which the quick changes have been made was the reconsideration of the pronatalist objectives of the former family policy, which ideology was very much rejected by the population (Zamfir and Zamfir, 1995). Logically, the law that forbade abortions was among the first laws to be abolished by the new government. Then, there were some other subtle attempts to transform the former system of child allowances from an instrument of pronatalist policy into one that would discourage families to have many children, if they cannot sufficiently support them.

This approach, however, ignored the fact that the family policy intended not only to introduce a certain demographic policy but also to help children and families, which cannot support themselves. Inflation substantially lowered the real value of child allowance and it became insufficient for families with many children, for whom it had been the major income source. The major real changes in the area of family policies were: the introduction in 1993 of child allowances for all population categories, not only for those state employed; the prolongation of maternal leave from 4 months to 1 year, and then to 2 years; and granting to fathers the right to be able to take parental leave. The value of the child allowance was readjusted from time to time, but it did not catch up with the rising inflation, and its differentiation according to birth order was cancelled.

Another reparative measure was to eliminate tax deductions (which had been substantial in the previous regime, amounting close to 20%) from the earnings of families with children. This measure had been strongly opposed by persons over 25 years who did not yet have children and, consequently, did not benefit from these tax deductions. The entire system of measures, which had been implemented before a newer system of social transfers was put in place (i.e. social allowance for families), in the context of the worsening economic situation led to a very limited growth of budgetary spending for the children and family. According to the data provided by UNICEF, in 1992, the total expenditures on funds designated for children and families (in % to the GDP) had increased since 1989 by only 39%, as compared to 110.7% for the Czech Republic, 117.5% for Hungary, and 100% for Bulgaria (UNICEF, 1993).

### 13.9.2 Pension System

The inherited pension system was considered good enough and therefore not needing any radical changes. The only problem was the ridiculously low pensions in agriculture, which were inherited from the old cooperative system. They were transferred to the jurisdiction of the Ministry of Labour and Social Security by the 80/1992 Law, and their level was reconsidered in 1994. However, the financial power of pensions has been deteriorating steadily and not catching up with inflation.

In addition, new problems appeared because the number of retired persons increased from 3.9 million in 1990 to 5.3 million in 1995 (NCS, 1996). Two factors contributed to this increase: first, the law which allowed retirement earlier than the standard age (adopted in 1991); and second, the 80/1992 Law, which became effective in 1994 and led to a rise in the number of persons who had agricultural pensions by 339 thousand, as compared to the previous year (Prisăcaru, 1996).

In sum, it can be said that currently in Romania there is no demographic policy in its pronounced way, and although its concept differs from that of the social policy, it would be problematic to raise this issue now. Some scholars argue, and it is our opinion too, that a policy with well-defined demographic objectives cannot be conceived before the economic and social crisis is solved and a secure economic growth has started, which would generate a standard of living in Romania closer to that in developed countries (see, for example, Trebici and Ghețău, 1997).

## 13.10 Perspectives of Romania's Population

To conclude, the results of the projection of the number of population and the changes in its demographic structures until the year 2020 are presented (Table 13.10). The projection is based on the assumption that the low fertility of the year 1996 will hold constant (total fertility rate is 1.29 children per woman), and that the conditions of mortality will also remain unchanged, as compared to the situation in 1996 (life expectancy at birth is 65.3 for males and 73.1 for females).

**Table 13.10: Population Projection until 2020 (constant fertility and mortality scenario), selected years**

| | 1997 | 2000 | 2005 | 2010 | 2015 | 2020 |
|---|---|---|---|---|---|---|
| Total population (1,000) | 22,582 | 22,435 | 22,130 | 21,698 | 21,112 | 20,378 |
| Index (1997 = 100) | 100.0 | 99.3 | 98.0 | 96.1 | 93.5 | 90.2 |
| Number of births in a given year (1,000) | 233.6 | 234.7 | 226.2 | 211.3 | 182.0 | 158.6 |
| Proportion of females (%) | 51.0 | 51.1 | 51.3 | 51.5 | 51.7 | 51.8 |
| Proportion of males (%) | 49.0 | 48.9 | 48.7 | 48.5 | 48.3 | 48.2 |
| Proportion of the age group 0–14 (%) | 19.6 | 18.6 | 16.0 | 15.4 | 15.0 | 14.1 |
| Proportion of the age group 15–59 (%) | 62.5 | 62.8 | 65.4 | 65.7 | 64.9 | 64.4 |
| Proportion of the age group 60+ (%) | 17.9 | 18.6 | 18.6 | 18.9 | 20.1 | 21.5 |

Source: based on authors' calculations

According to the projection, the numerical decrease of the population will continue, down to below 22 million around 2006, and below 21 million around 2016. In the year 2020, the population of Romania will represent 90.2% of the population in 1997. Based on the assumption of low and constant fertility throughout the whole projected period, there will be a systematic decline in the number of births. However, due to the influence of the age structure that is favourable for the Romanian fertility pattern (as it was observed in 1996), the number of births will slightly increase until 2000, after which there will be an obvious decrease.

The proportion of female population of Romania will continue to increase, so that the proportion of 51%, already reached in 1997, will grow to a hypothetical figure of 51.8% in 2020.

The process of demographic ageing will also continue. The main losses in this process will naturally belong to the young ages (0–14 years), whose proportion within the total population will systematically decrease. In this relation, it is interesting to analyse the beneficiary age-categories. Thus, in the year 2000, the percentage lost by the young age group is divided between the adults (+0.3%) and the aged (+0.7%). Then, until the year 2005, the Romanian population will witness exclusively an increase of the proportion of the adult population (65.4%), followed by an increase in the proportions of both beneficiary categories, the young and the aged, so that in the year 2020, the young population will represent only 14.1% of the total population, the adults – 64.5% and the aged – 21.5%.

This is how the demographic effects of the present transition will look, based on the assumption that the present fertility and mortality levels remain constant. It is almost a certainty that the respective effects will have an influence over the population of Romania, even if in a slightly different manner. And it is practically impossible to imagine a reversal of the decline of the population, especially since the current negative developments will draw long-lasting consequences.

## References

Gheţău, V. (1997), 7 ani de declin demografic, *Adevărul*, 25 March1997, Bucharest.

Mureşan, C. (1994), Changements de structures démographiques en Roumanie, *Studia Universitas Babes-Bolyai. Sociologia – politologia*, Vol. 39(1–2), pp. 44–57.

Mureşan, C. (1996a), L'évolution démographique en Roumanie: Tendances passées 1948–1994 et perspectives d'avenir 1995–2030, *Population*, No. 4–5, pp. 813–845.

Mureşan, C. (1996b), Scăderea speranţei de viaţă la naştere şi economismul reformei sanitare, *Economistul*, No. 824, pp. 813–845.

Mureşan, C. (1997), A reproduktiv magatartás változásai Romániában, *Démográfia*, Vol. 40(4), pp. 285–298.

NCS (National Commission for Statistics) (1992), *Population and Housing Census, January 7, 1992*, Vol. IV, Bucharest.

NCS (National Commission for Statistics) (1996), *Romanian Demographic Yearbook 1996*, Bucharest.

Prisăcaru, C. (1996) *Pensionarii în Perioada 1990–1995*, Bucharest: Centre for Economic Information and Documentation of Romanian Academy of Sciences.

Trebici, V. and V. Gheţău, (1997), Are nevoie România de o politica demografica?, *Populatie & Societate*, No. 3.

UNICEF (1993), *Central and Eastern Europe in Transition: Public Policy and Social Conditions. Regional monitoring Report No. 1*, Florence: UNICEF.

Zamfir, E. and C. Zamfir (1993), *Tiganii intre Ignorare si Ingrijorare*, Bucharest: Editura Alternative.

Zamfir, E. and C. Zamfir (1995), *Politici Sociale. România în Context European*, Bucharest: Editura Alternative.

# 14

# Demographic Situation and Mortality Trends in Russia

**Serguey Ivanov and Vladimir Echenique**

## 14.1 Introduction

During transition from totalitarian socialist system to democratic system with a market economy Russia has experienced dramatic transformations in its demographic development. In the period 1991–1998, the population of the country declined by more than 1.4 million people (Figure 14.1). Natural increase since 1992 has been negative and during the last few years oscillated around 705 thousand. Due to positive annual net migration, which since 1992 has been about 5 million, the total population size of Russia has been decreasing not as rapid as it could have been otherwise (Figure 14.2).

Substantial changes in social values, everyday life and in the political, social and economic conditions, inherently linked with the ongoing transition process, could not have left the demographic dimensions of society unaltered. However, in our opinion, the new type of demographic behaviour has not yet emerged. It is more likely that the demographic trends and phenomena that had formed after the Second World War have become more pronounced during the last decade. Despite some general similarities between the demographic indicators of Russia and those of the developed countries of Western Europe, significant differences in the demographic development have been present.

The similarities may be found, first of all, in the net reproduction rate, which in Russia, as in the other European countries, is less than 1.0 and therefore is not sufficient for the replacement of generations. Another similarity is the low level of fertility and of the natural population increase, which has already become negative in Russia. The latter conditions have determined dependency of the total population size on net migration. In Russia, as in Western Europe, the net migration has been positive, but nevertheless it could not compensate the losses of the population brought by the negative population increase.

The differences may be observed, first of all, in the age distribution of fertility. For example, the TFR in 1997 in Russia was 1.27, which is comparable with Germany, Spain and Italy. But, as in the Eastern European countries, the highest level of fertility in Russia is concentrated in the 20–24 years age group, whereas in Western Europe – in the 25–29 years age group (Barkalov and Kvasha, 1996). This pattern has not changed and continues to hold during the recent years (Figure 14.3).

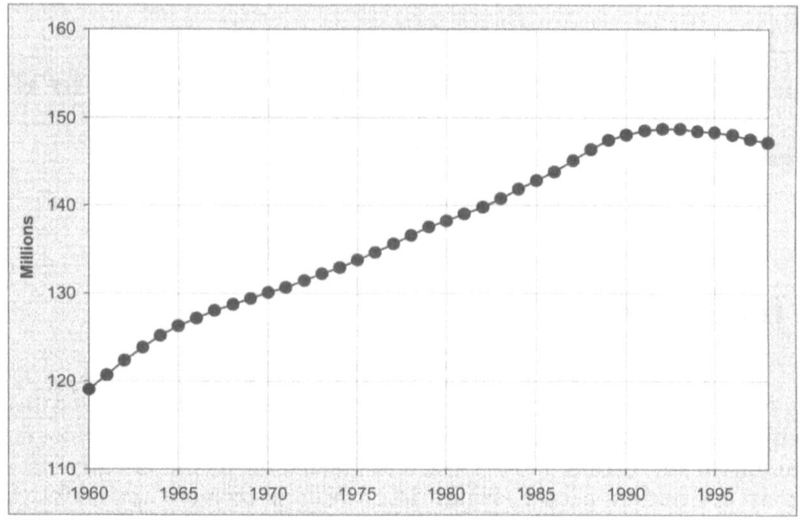


**Figure 14.1: Population Dynamics[1], 1960–1998**

[1]As of 1 January of a given year

Source: based on Goskomstat data

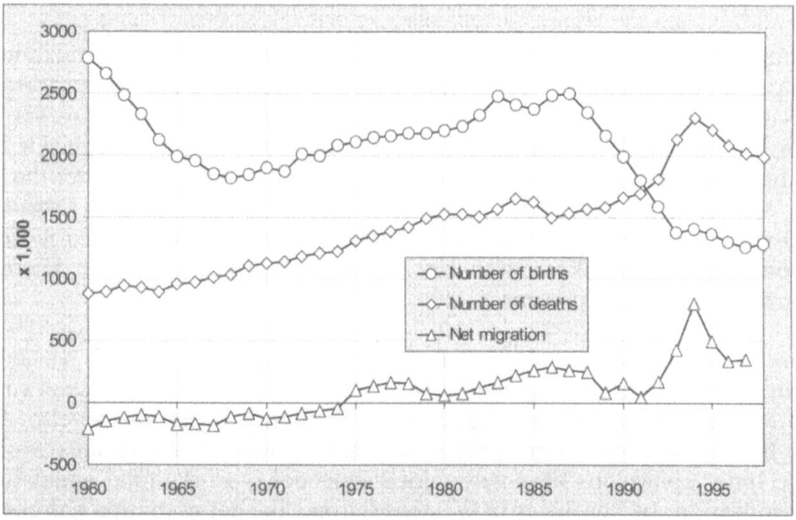


**Figure 14.2: Live Births, Deaths and Net Migration, 1960–1998**

Source: based on Goskomstat data

After a long period of relative stagnation, from the second half of the 1960s until the first half of the 1980s, when along with the significant decline of mortality in the first years of life the health condition and the mortality patterns of adult population had been deteriorating, the demographic situation in Russia has experienced a sequence of dramatic shifts (Ivanov, 1995; Vishnevsky, 1997; Zakharov, 1997b). Life expectancy at birth significantly but briefly increased during 1986–1988, then returned to the previous level during 1989–1992 and afterwards abruptly declined in 1993–1994 to the lowest level of the post-war period, and since 1995 it has been increasing rapidly (Figure 14.4). These shifts in mortality patterns have become the focus of significant research interest and public concern. Some influential political parliamentary parties even included the issue of mortality increase and fertility decline during transition period into the list of key impeachment charges posed against the President Yeltsin in 1999.

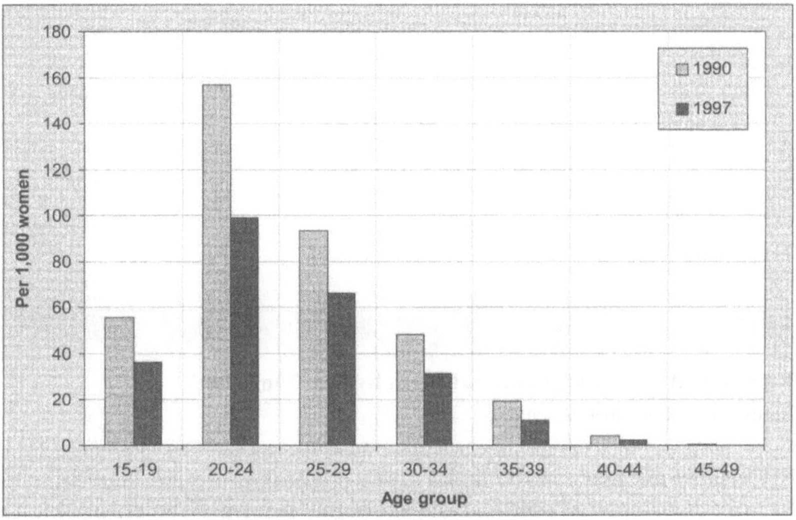


**Figure 14.3: Age-specific Fertility Rate, 1990 and 1997**

Source: based on Goskomstat data

These charges relied on the fact that the significant growth of mortality in Russia during the end of the 1980s and beginning of the 1990s has produced among the public perception that "population is dying out" and "demographic catastrophe" is immanent. This perception in turn was used by some political parties to claim that the "genocide" of the Russia's population is taking place. More neutral, but nonetheless anxious comments such as "demographic crisis", "mortality crisis", "health crisis", used extensively in academic literature (see, for example, Bobadilla, Castello and Mitchell, 1997; Shkolnikov, Meslé and Vallin, 1996), have become a cliché among journalists and part of an everyday language.

Indeed, between 1988 and 1994, life expectancy for both sexes diminished by 6 years, and by 7.2 years for men. This dramatic decline corresponds to no less dramatic increase in the absolute number of deaths. The total number of deaths during 1990–1995 period was 1.4–1.6 million higher than it would be if mortality remained at a pre-crisis level, which however by Western standards was also very high (Bennett, Bloom and Ivanov, 1998; Bloom and Malaney, 1998). The contributors to the excessive, by Western standards, number of deaths were mainly adult men: from the total 3.1 million male deaths between 1991–1995, 2.2 million deaths were of men aged between 20 and 60 years (Vishnevsky and Shkolnikov, 1997, p. 15).

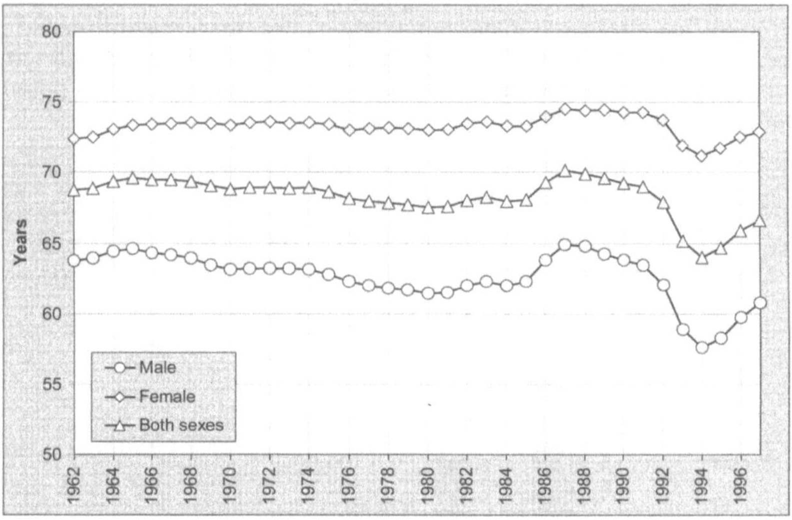


**Figure 14.4: Life Expectancy at Birth by Sex, 1962–1997**
Source: based on Goskomstat data

Mortality crisis took place in the midst of the ongoing profound, painful, contradictory and not yet completed political and economic reforms. The chronological coincidence certainly is not accidental. Causal links of mortality crisis embrace wide spectrum of particular events and processes: from frequent psychological shocks and stresses of disrupted by reforms everyday lives, to immense growth of poverty, deterioration of state health care system, and upsurge of violent crime.

A number of explanatory hypotheses of mortality crisis that have been discussed in many commentaries are often quite straightforward but limited in scope. The causes of mortality crisis in Russia could not be reduced exclusively to most often suggested, self-evident and indisputable at first glance (UNDP, 1998a, p. 46) factors such as alcoholism, smoking, malnutrition and poverty. First of all, these factors were present in society long before the onset of the crisis. Second, strong correlation between these factors and mortality tended to be short-lived, lost strength quickly and even changed the direction (Andreev, 1997; Vishnevsky, op. cit.). For instance, if the hypothesis that rapidly rising mortality during 1992–1994 was caused by the fall in the living standards of the population hold true, then the decline of mortality during 1996–1997 could not have been expected to happen. But in reality, life expectancy during these two years increased by two years. Third, mortality crisis touched not the most vulnerable and least socially protected population groups such as children, aged and handicapped people, but on the contrary – the most "strong" population segment – males of the working age (see Andreev, 1998; Ivanov, 1995; Fiedorov, 1997, 1998; Shkolnikov *et al.*, 1998; Vishnevsky and Shkolnikov, op. cit.).

The change in diet and nutrition explanatory approach is also not completely satisfactory. Undoubtedly, worsened food consumption well reflected in the government statistics (Goskomstat Rossii, 1997b) and by the Russian Longitudinal Monitoring Survey of the economic situation and population health (Zohoori *et al.*, 1998), was not accompanied by the spread of commonly understood features of severe malnutrition. Moreover, meat products traditionally have dominated Russian diet, and it appears that the lower meat consumption would have on the contrary positively influenced population health (Popkin *et al.*, 1997; Puska, 1997; Becker and Hemley, 1998).

Excessive alcohol consumption and smoking unquestionably negatively and in many ways affect health and mortality of population, of male population in particular. Still, being for a long time part of the Russian lifestyle, these factors have been experienced by few consecutive generations. Therefore, partly determining the overall high mortality of men, these factors are less likely to be responsible for its short- and medium-term fluctuations, an exception being the significant positive shift in mortality rates in the mid-1980s[1].

The attempts by some researchers to comprehend the development of the Russian mortality crisis of the last decade from a historical perspective and in the context of a complex sociological approach seem to be promising. It is suggested in some commentaries that the unusually high middle-age mortality that had been pertinent during the last four decades to the majority of the former socialist Eastern European countries and to Russia in particular had been a consequence and at the same time an indicator of the deep dysfunction of the social system, which demonstrated itself in population's apathy, stress, isolation and self-destructive behaviour (Andreev, 1998; Bobak, 1997; Becker and Bloom, 1998; UNDP, 1998a). Similar interpretation links the growth of mortality to the widespread disillusionment with the real socialism (Okolski, 1993; Andreev, 1998). Furthermore, it is not surprising that every consecutive generation which was born before the Second World War (Zakharov, 1997a) and after 1959 has been characterised by the higher mortality in the 20–60 years age group.

The radical socio-political changes of the 1990s have not yet brought any improvement in mortality patterns of this age group. Moreover, some destructive behaviours and social practices have even strengthened as a result of stressful adaptation to new, unusual economic conditions (Kennedy, Kawachi and Brainerd, 1998). The much more painful character of this adaptation in Russia may be attributed to the relatively less successful and less consistent than in the former socialist Eastern European countries market reforms and their enormous social costs, which altogether contributed to apocalyptic morale of the population, fear of galloping inflation, loss of trust in the government, and disenchantment with life.

During the last three years the level of the main mortality indicators – life expectancy and age-specific rates – have reached the values of the beginning of the 1980s and the beginning of the 1990s. However, the recovery of the population from mortality crisis has only been "a return to the previous demographic course, which was ‘normal’ only by the Soviet standards and could not stand comparison with the world standards” (Vishnevsky, op. cit.). In all former socialist Eastern European countries mortality situation during the 1960s–1980s was much worse than in the West, with Russia exhibiting the strongest deviation from mortality levels of the Western countries.

In general, low life expectancy is determined by high infant and child mortality. For example, if life expectancy is less than 50 years, more than half of all deaths occur in the under five years age group. The high infant and child mortality in turn is determined by the high incidence of infectious and parasitic diseases and their low response to treatment. During the 1940s–1960s, the Soviet health care system achieved extraordinary results in this area. The introduction of modern maternity care and medical assistance during delivery, comprehensive national system of child immunisation, the use of effective sulphanilamide drugs in treating pneumonia and intestinal infections and later introduction of antibiotics had led to the decrease of infant mortality from 200 per 1,000 live births in 1940 to 20 per 1,000 by the end of the 1960s – beginning of the 1970s.

These significant achievements of the Soviet health care system however did not go further. When life expectancy crosses the 65 years mark (which happened in Russia at the end of the 1950s), the further improvement in infant and child survival looses its predominant influence on the overall mortality level[2], while the health and mortality level of adults and ageing people acquires critical importance. During the last two decades, the countries of the West have achieved significant success in treating and prevention of cardiovascular diseases and cancer, which traditionally were the major causes of adult deaths. As a result, life expectancy in the countries of the West exceeds 75 years. In Russia, practically all gains in life expectancy throughout the 20th century were achieved due to decrease of infant and child mortality.

The Soviet health care system had been oriented mainly at the eradication of infectious diseases and diseases of the respiratory system and, while successfully dealing with them, lacked the financial resources and organisational infrastructure needed for the effective treatment of cardiovascular and other chronic illnesses. This situation along with the increasing sociopsychological stresses to a big extent affected the growth of the probability of dying in the age group 20–60 years (Andreev, 1998). From 1984 to 1994, adult mortality increased even more: for a man aged 20, the probability of not reaching age 60 jumped from 35% to 48% (Shkolnikov *et al.*, op. cit.). Furthermore, men in Russia have been dying from the cardiovascular diseases on average at the age 10–15 years younger than men in the West.

In the former USSR and Eastern Europe life expectancy had stagnated for about twenty years. At the end of the 1980s and in the beginning of the 1990s, in some of these countries life expectancy declined, while in Poland, Czechia and Slovakia it increased and even surpassed the level of the end of the 1980s. Positive correlation between life expectancy and success of the economic and social reforms is not incidental. Meanwhile, very dramatic wide-scale shifts in mortality patterns have been occurring in the European part of Russia.

The sudden leap in mortality during the first half of the 1990s and the following decline, completely reverse both in tempo and structure, happened almost in all parts of Russia. The causes of the majority of deaths fell into two groups: accidents, poisonings and trauma and cardiovascular diseases. Among both men and women, these two groups of causes were responsible for 80% of the decline in life expectancy, and if for men accidents ranked first, for women – cardiovascular diseases did (Andreev, 1997, 1998; Vishnevsky and Shkolnikov, op. cit.).

One of the key specific features of the mortality situation in Russia remains an excessive number of deaths among men. The long-term downward trend in life expectancy is mostly due to the growth in male mortality. As Figure 14.4 demonstrates, the curves of life expectancy for both sexes and for men practically follow each other, whereas the life expectancy curve for women is more stagnant.

The other important characteristic of population mortality in Russia has been very high mortality due to accidents, poisonings, trauma, homicide and suicide. In developed countries this group of causes usually ranks third, after cardiovascular diseases and neoplasms. In periods of significant increase in male mortality "unnatural" causes of death usually move to the second place, following the cardiovascular diseases. Such leap took place during 1979–1981, similar shift has been observed since 1993 up till now. In 1994, 19.2% of all male deaths were due to accidents, poisonings, trauma, homicide and suicide, while 13.4% of all male deaths were due to neoplasm. Standardised mortality rate for men in 1994 was 457.3 per 1,000, that being 4.5 times higher than similar rate for women (UNDP, 1995).

Even more unfavourable mortality situation is pertinent to men of the working age, among whom the leading cause of death are accidents, poisonings, trauma, homicide and suicide, followed by cardiovascular diseases, neoplasms and other diseases. In 1992, the proportion of male deaths due to "unnatural", external causes among all men of the working age reached 41.5%, whilst the proportion of deaths due to cardiovascular diseases was only 27.7%. From 1994 to 1997 mortality among men of working age declined by more than 27%, but still remains high and constitutes 39% of all deaths.

Persistent for quite a long time overall excessive male mortality, particularly high mortality among men of working age, and especially high proportion of male deaths due to accidents, poisonings, trauma, homicides and suicides, suggest that the peculiarities of male mortality trends in Russia may be associated to a big extent with the working conditions and employment patterns of the population.

## 14.2 Interpretation of Mortality Trends

As an explanatory framework, we suggest to consider the specific features of the population employment conditions and patterns. We argue, that the very high comparatively to the majority of the developed countries labour force participation in industry and predominantly in heavy industry along with the high labour force concentration in agriculture not only contribute to the deterioration of health and quality of life of the population because of high incidence of workplace accidents and trauma, but also indirectly affect the overall mortality situation.

The mechanisms of this indirect influence are not yet fully studied and understood, but it is reasonable to suggest that difficult and often extreme working conditions result in a continuing stressful impact on the majority of the workforce. That in turn weakens workers' immune system, resistance to external health threats and possibly leads to a higher mortality level from accidents and to premature deaths from cardiovascular diseases. In the part that follows we focus on the data that in our view confirms our hypothesis.

### 14.2.1 Structural Factors

Table 14.1 illustrates clearly that, compared to developed countries, Russia has had especially high labour force concentration in industry and agriculture and consequently very low one in service industry. In developed countries, in the beginning of the 1990s, more than two-thirds of employees worked in service sector. In Russia, at the same time, the proportion of employed in the service sector was almost twice less. Of course, the chances to get a life-threatening injury, severe trauma or work-related illness leading to premature death are much higher in heavy industry than in a service sector.

**Table 14.1: Proportion of All Workforce Employed in a Particular Sector, Russia (1990 and 1996) and selected developed countries (1990), per cent**

| Country | Agriculture | Industry | Services and other sectors |
|---|---|---|---|
| Russia, 1990 | 13 | 50 | 37 |
| Russia, 1996 | 15 | 42 | 43 |
| Japan | 7 | 34 | 59 |
| Finland | 8 | 31 | 61 |
| Sweden | 4 | 30 | 66 |
| France | 5 | 29 | 66 |
| Netherlands | 5 | 26 | 70 |
| U.S.A. | 3 | 26 | 71 |
| Canada | 3 | 25 | 71 |
| New Zealand | 10 | 25 | 65 |
| Norway | 6 | 25 | 68 |

Sources: Goskomstat Rossii, 1997a, p. 111; UNDP, 1997a

Structural peculiarities of the Russian economy, evident in comparison with the developed countries, – disproportional labour force concentration in the secondary, industrial sector – has been a legacy of the highly militarised economy of the former Soviet Union. The demilitarisation of the industry involves not only the reduction of the labour force employed in the industry, but also creation of jobs in the service sector. During the last few years the number of employed in the economy has been declining both in absolute and relative terms. The average annual number of industrial workforce has diminished by 6 million people between 1990 and 1996.

### 14.2.2 Gender Differences in Employment

The long-lasting excessive mortality of males also may be partly determined by men's employment predominantly in the heavy industry. In 1990, of all working men 60.3% were employed in industry, construction, transport and communication (secondary sector of economy), 16.3% – in agriculture and only 18.8% in service sector. For women the proportions are accordingly – 40.1%, 10.2% and 48.6% (Goskomstat Rossii, 1997a). During the last few years, an increase in employment in service sector and decline in employment in industry have been observed for both men and women, although males continue to be predominantly employed in industry (Table 14.2).

**Table 14.2: Distribution of Employed by Sector and Gender, 1990 and 1996, per cent**

| Sector | Male | | Female | |
|---|---|---|---|---|
| | 1990 | 1996 | 1990 | 1996 |
| Agriculture | 16.3 | 18.8 | 10.2 | 10.5 |
| Industry | 60.3 | 52.2 | 40.1 | 31.3 |
| Service sector | 18.8 | 24.5 | 48.6 | 57.4 |
| Other sectors | 4.6 | 4.5 | 1.1 | 0.8 |

Source: Goskomstat Rossii, 1997a, p. 112

### 14.2.3 Work-related Trauma and Accidents

Similar to the Soviet period, trauma and accident occurrence continues to remain extremely high in industry. In 1996, mortality rate due to accidents in industry was 15.5 per 100 thousand employed. Although this value is certainly significantly lower than, for example, in 1980 (18.3), since 1997 the number of deaths resulting from work-related accidents has been on the rise again.

From 1990 to 1996, the number of work-related injures leading to temporary disability (for over one day) or to death declined from 432,000 to 213,000. Although in the relative terms the situation did not demonstrate a significant improvement. If in 1990 the number of these cases was 6.6 per 1,000 of all workers, in 1996 it was 6.1 per 1,000. On the other hand, the number of those injured due to work-related illnesses or poisonings increased both in absolute and relative terms. In 1990, their absolute number was 11,525 cases (or 19.6 per 100,000), and in 1996 – 13,273 cases (or 21.5 per 100,000).

An analysis of statistical data related to work-related illnesses, poisonings and accidents should be conducted in the context of the specific features of definitions and registration of work-related injures in Russia. The Soviet judicial system that facilitated the relationships between employers and employees was based on the premise that in the majority of cases the main employer was the state, which in turn represented the interests of the society at large. Therefore, the legal practice was mainly concerned with protecting the interests of the state and not necessarily of the workers. Quite often, work-related injures were registered as not being linked to work at all and that, of course, had been altering the statistical representation of the real situation. It appears that due to inertia and lack of reform the practices of the registration of work-related injures remain unchanged.

During the Soviet period, the government policy regarding work-place safety was oriented not at the regulation and improvement of the working conditions *per se*, but mainly at establishing different systems of benefits and compensatory payments for people working in detrimental to health and dangerous working environment. All consecutive post-Soviet Russian governments have pursued the same policy.

According to 1997 data, 42.8% of all employees in industry working in unsatisfactory conditions were receiving some kind of benefits and compensations, which include additional leave, free health-maintaining prophylactic meals, free milk allowances, higher pay rates and bonuses, and right for early retirement. In 1997, of all those employed in unsatisfactory working conditions and who claimed the benefits and compensations 29.3% worked in construction industry, 38.5% – in transport industry, and 13% in communications industry (Goskomstat Rossii, 1997a, p.131).

Table 14.3 presents proportions of employees working in detrimental to health and dangerous working conditions. The data demonstrates that no significant change in this area has occurred. The proportions of people working in the conditions that do not meet safety and sanitary-hygienic standards remain at the high level of about 21% of all industry employees during the last decade. The share of people involved in heavy manual labour also remains high. The only considerable improvement took place among those working with the unsafe equipment – their share declined by more than three times between 1991 and 1997.

The working conditions in some branches of industry are particularly bad. At the beginning of the 1997, of all those employed in particular branch of industry the proportions of people working in conditions not meeting safety standards were 43.4% in coal industry, 39.1% in metallurgy, 32.5% in paper-making industry, 31.8% in energy production sector, and 30.9% in rare metals industry (Goskomstat Rossii, 1997a, p. 129).

To be employed in conditions not meeting safety standards is a male prerogative in Russia. According to authors' calculations, at the beginning of 1997, of all workers employed in conditions not meeting safety standards 71.8% in industry and 84.1% in construction were males. These statistics definitely point at possible reasons for continuing excessive mortality of men in Russia.

**Table 14.3: Proportion of Industry Employees Working in Conditions that Do Not Meet Safety Standards, 1991–1997, per cent**

| Year | Working in conditions that do not meet safety standards[1] | Involved in heavy manual labour | Working with equipment not meeting safety standards |
|---|---|---|---|
| 1991 | 17.8 | 2.7 | .. |
| 1992 | 21.4 | 2.8 | 1.8 |
| 1993 | 21.4 | 2.7 | 1.5 |
| 1994 | 21.6 | 2.9 | 1.1 |
| 1995 | 21.4 | 2.7 | 1.0 |
| 1996 | 21.2 | 2.7 | 0.7 |
| 1997 | 21.3 | 2.7 | 0.6 |

[1]Working conditions that do not meet safety standards according to Russian statistics are such work situation or place, where excessive noise levels, ultra- or infra-sounds, vibrations, dust or gases are present

Source: Goskomstat Rossii, 1997a, p. 128

As it was mentioned earlier, national statistics recently have been registering the declining number of workers employed in industry. This development, considering the working conditions predominating in industry, obviously should be regarded as a positive trend that might significantly contribute to decreasing mortality and improving health of the population. At the same time, it is possible that underestimation of the real volume of decline of workforce employed in industry is present. At many factories, plants and enterprises workers are not paid wages and salaries for few months in a row, some of them are sent into "voluntary" unpaid leaves. In these cases involvement in petty street trade, service sector or private businesses becomes the main source of the income. However, these types of employment often go unregistered by the official statistics.

That said, for Russia, the reduction of employment in industry and creation of jobs in service sector, in our view, may become the factors that could considerably contribute to the mortality decrease in a near future and in a longer term[3]. However, the shift in employment structure towards service sector, being more or less a logical outcome of market reforms, would not be enough to sustain and extend the downward trend in mortality. Given the high level of mortality among working-age men, government policies regarding work-place safety should be scrutinised and reconsidered. The emphasis of its core activities should be placed not on the further extension of benefits and compensations, but on establishing rigid work-place safety requirements and standards along with organisational mechanism to monitor compliance with them.

The need to improve safety in a work place acquires even greater meaning in the context of a weakening system of government control over the safety issues as a result of privatisation and change of ownership. In private companies, the working conditions are often less satisfactory than in state-owned enterprises. In 1997, the share of workers employed in industry in conditions not meeting the sanitary-hygienic norms was 17.2% at state-owned enterprises and 22.0% at private ones. Similar situation has formed in transport, where proportions were 8.5% and 13.5% respectively, as well as in communications (2.2% and 5.3%). The only exception has been construction industry, where the distribution is almost equal: 8.3% and 8.1%, respectively (Goskomstat Rossii, 1997a, p. 129).

Another direction for improving safety situation in industry should be achieving higher responsibility and criminal accountability of employers for breaching safety standards and employing people in dangerous working conditions.

Job environment influences directly population mortality and morbidity, which level can be estimated by data on disability, work-related deaths due to traumas and accidents and data on injures related to professional illnesses and poisoning.

The indirect impact may be however even more significant. Long-term employment in unsafe environment bears a negative impact on people's health, may lead to premature deaths due to cardiovascular diseases, neoplasm, respiratory and digestive system illnesses. Moreover, continuous work in stressful conditions weakens person's immune system resistance to external factors, impair attention and wariness, lessens demands for safety in everyday life, and all that influence the general life style of the population.

### 14.2.4 Life Safety

The level of safety and security of living environment in people's everyday lives may be estimated by the level of mortality rates due to homicide, transport accidents (auto, railway and air transport) and accidents at home or elsewhere (accidental poisonings, drowning, fire, electric shock). The share of accidents among all other "unnatural" causes is the largest – 25% (Goskomstat Rossii, 1998a). This category of causes of deaths also includes deaths due to accidents with firearms, electricity, accidental drowning or falling, and medical accidents.

The last cause represents only 0.5% of all deaths due to "external" causes. It includes the cases of deaths due to allergic reactions to medications or biological substances, injections, cuts, bleeding during therapeutic procedure or surgery as well as abnormal reaction and complications after major surgeries. To a considerable extent, accidents in a course of medical treatment may be related to the lack of professionalism of medical personnel and doctors. Though, the accountability and responsibility of medical professionals for damaging or threatening health and life of their patient remains in Russia very low. There have been very few cases when courts made decisions in favour of patients or their relatives. An absence of comprehensive legislation protecting the rights of patients and victims of medical malpractice maintains this situation and explains the lack of demand from private and public medical institutions for insurance against medical accidents or malpractice. If in developed countries almost 100% of medical practitioners and institutions are insured against cases of medical malpractice, in Russia this type of insurance is not being developed at all.

### 14.2.5 Electricity

In 1994, more than 2.5 thousand people died in Russia because of accidents related to electricity. Unfortunately deaths due to this cause are not grouped according to the place of accident at work or at home. Yet the high number of such deaths demonstrates very low requirements to safety of electric equipment and appliances at work and at home. Closely related to electric safety is fire safety. In 1994, more than 9 thousand people died in fires and fire accidents (UNDP, 1995).

Among all accidents that caused death, more than 30% (or 27 thousand deaths) were accidental drowning, strangling and accidents with firearms. Accidental drowning, which caused almost 18 thousand deaths in 1994, has a seasonal character and happens mostly in summer. Accidental falls also represent a significant share of deaths due to accidents. In 1994, there were 9.5 deaths resulting from accidental fall. More than 75% of these deaths were male deaths. Interestingly, the share of these accidents involving alcohol is extremely low – about 1% among women and 2.4% among men. Although the total proportion of men who died due to accidents, poisonings, trauma, homicide and suicide while being in a condition of alcohol intoxication in 1994 was over 16% (UNDP, 1995).

Gender distribution of deaths due to all above discussed causes demonstrates that accidental deaths in Russia mostly "choose" men. About 80% of all fatal accidents resulted in a death of man. In developed countries, distribution of deaths due to accidents by gender is more or less balanced. In France, for example, mortality due to accidental falls is almost the same among men and women (Meslé *et al.*, 1996, p. 125).

### 14.2.6 Job-related Accidents

Among above discussed causes of accidental deaths, significant proportion is directly or indirectly related to work. Low safety standards at workplace and often deliberate non-compliance with them on the part of employers and employees consequently alter system of values and attitudes towards personal and collective safety, which in turn leads to low responsibility for safety of oneself and others and eagerness to take unjustified risk.

Deaths due to accidents have a random character. Despite this, conducting some preventive measures directed at improving fire safety, reliability of electric systems and appliances, and stricter control over sale and use of firearms may significantly reduce the level of mortality due to job-related accidents. Organisation of water-safety education and rescue support network operating during summer season in major water-resort areas and beaches could help prevent many accidental drowning.

Another important factor, which could help reduce the number of accidental deaths, is further development of special professional rescue units trained to deal with natural disasters and emergencies. A small number of these units was already established during the first years of economic reforms and proved to be very effective in providing emergency medical assistance to injured people.

Among the other "unnatural" causes of accidental deaths are alcohol poisonings, homicides and suicides and transport accidents (Table 14.4).

**Table 14.4: Mortality Due to Accidents, Poisoning, Trauma, Homicide and Suicide, 1991–1997, per 1,000 deaths**

| | 1991 | 1992 | 1993 | 1994 | 1995 | 1996 | 1997 |
|---|---|---|---|---|---|---|---|
| Total number of accidental deaths, including: | 142.2 | 173.0 | 227.9 | 250.7 | 236.6 | 209.2 | 187.7 |
| Deaths due to accidental alcohol poisoning | 11.2 | 17.6 | 30.9 | 37.8 | 29.5 | 24.0 | 19.1 |
| Deaths due to all types of transport trauma | 30.7 | 30.2 | 30.8 | 28.6 | 26.2 | 22.9 | 21.5 |
| Deaths due to suicide | 26.5 | 31.0 | 38.1 | 42.1 | 41.4 | 39.4 | 37.6 |
| Deaths due to homicide | 15.2 | 22.8 | 30.6 | 32.6 | 30.7 | 26.6 | 23.9 |

Source: based on Goskomstat Rossii, 1998b

High mortality due to accidental alcohol poisonings has been a longstanding issue and serious problem in Russia. These statistics, however, should be understood not as an indicator of a poor quality of alcohol drinks and spirits, but as a reflection of the ways many people in Russia choose to deal with hardship and stress in their life. Significant number of deaths is caused not by the bad quality of drinks, but by the excessive amount of consumed alcohol. In that sense, mortality rate may serve as an indicator of country's social well being.

The growth of criminal activity during transition period has been reflected in a more than double increase in mortality due to homicide. People's reaction towards the radical changes in all spheres of life has been also manifested in an upward trend in suicide, which has been also observed in developed countries in the periods of social and economic crises.

The only mortality indicator that has not experienced any substantial change during the first half of the 1990s – is mortality due to all types of transport accidents and trauma. Interestingly, the decline of the value of this rate has been occurring in the context of steady growth of the number of cars and vehicles in the country[4]. In 1996, mortality due to transport accidents returned to the pre-reform level indicating that at least in this area people managed to adapt to new conditions.

## 14.3 Conclusion

The downward trend in mortality due to violent causes that started to shape in the mid-1990s may signify the beginning of a shift of Russian mortality towards Western mortality structure. However, it is too early to be completely sure that this positive trend will be sustainable in a longer term. On the other hand, if our hypothesis holds true, then the changes in employment structure in a direction of growing employment in service sector and declining employment in industry would contribute to the reduction in mortality of working-age men, especially due to job-related accidents.

Certainly, the poor state of Russian health care system and its slow restructuring has been detrimental to the mortality situation in Russia, but it has not been its major determinant. Moreover, as our analysis clearly demonstrated, mortality situation in Russia does not seem to be principally irreversible, nor society should complacently expect "invisible hand" of market reform to automatically eliminate all factors contributing to high level of mortality in Russia. Focused commitment of society to overcome its dire state and actively intervene in reforming of all the major spheres of its existence and reproduction (at the federal, regional and local levels, and at the level of new emerging civil institutions and organisations) is not only needed but is possible.

Given that the goal is very clear – to reduce mortality of adult population, especially of adult males, – the operationalisation of relevant policies is extremely important from both conceptual and pragmatic positions in conditions of limited resources. The principal issues here are the following. First, considerable potential for improving mortality situation lies not in the domain of health care system, but mostly in the domain of employment relations, work-place safety, social assistance, prevention of accidents and establishment of a system of societal security in a wider sense. Second, principles and goals of health care system reform should be reprioritised according to the specific mortality and morbidity situation in Russia. Desperately needed organisational and financial restructuring of health care system is not enough to address the above-mentioned complex issues. Long-term national strategy regarding protection of population health is needed (UNDP, 1998a).

In the short-term, the main priority of the health care reform should be balancing the needs of the population in medical assistance and services with the financial resources of the government. In this area the difficulties continue to arise because the process of establishing the types and levels of social guaranties is not co-ordinated enough with the planning of financial support.

## Notes

1. The government anti-alcohol campaign was started in June 1985 and lasted until the end of 1987. Its main focus was on limiting alcohol sales, increase of alcohol prices (which was done twice: in August 1985 and in August 1986), prohibition of home-based liquor production, development of medical rehabilitation centres and wide-scale mass media propaganda about harmful and destructive health effects of the high alcohol consumption. Between 1984 and 1987, the number of liquor stores declined by 80%; eight beer plants were closed and 30% of country's vineyards were destroyed. As a result, the official volume of alcohol sales shrank 2.7 times, the home-based liquor production doubled and per capita alcohol consumption declined by 25% (Shkolnikov and Nemtsov, 1997). According to expert estimates, this campaign contributed to the prevention of about 900 thousand premature deaths due to violent causes, accidents and poisonings (Ivanov, 1995).
2. From 1993, when Russia adopted the modern system of registration of live births, to 1996, the infant mortality rate decreased by 12.6% – from 19.9 per 1,000 to 17.4 per 1,000. This reduction occurred simultaneously with the decline in life expectancy (Goskomstat Rossii, 1998a).
3. It is important, that in Ukraine and Belarus, where during 1990–1995 life expectancy was declining, similar to Russia, recently the situation has changed. In Ukraine, where economic reforms have been conducted at a slower pace than in Russia, since 1996, a slight increase in life expectancy has been observed. There, as well as in Russia, the proportion of workers employed in industry significantly declined – almost by 31.9% during 1990–1996 period (UNDP, 1997c, p. 25). In Belarus, on the contrary, during the same period, there was no reduction of employment in industry and life expectancy continued to diminish (UNDP, 1998b, p. 109).
4. According to data of SAM-holding (*Kommersant-daily*), from 1993 to 1998, the number of cars in Russia increased from 11.8 million to 17.6 million.

## References

Andreev, E. (1997), The dynamics of mortality in the Russian Federation, in: United Nations and Population and Family Study Center, *Symposium on Health and Mortality*, Brussels, Belgium, 19–22 November 1997, pp. 329–367, New York: United Nations.

Andreev, E. (1998), Zdorovje i prodolzhitel'nost' zhizni, in N.B. Barkalov and S.F. Ivanov (eds.), *Osnovy izucheniya chelovecheskogo razvitiya*, pp. 51–79, Moskva: Prava cheloveka.

Barkalov, N.B. and A.Y. Kvasha, (1996), *Rozdaemost' v Rossii: obshegosudarstvennye i regional'nye tendentsii*, Preprint nauchnogo doklada, Moskva: Institut Ekonomiki Rossiiskoi Akademii Nauk.

Becker, C. and D. Bloom (1998), The demographic crisis in the former Soviet Union, *World Development*, Vol. 26(11), pp. 1913–1919.

Becker, C. and D. Hemley (1998), Demographic change in the former Soviet Union during the transition period, *World Development*, Vol. 26(11), pp. 1957–1976.

Bennett, N., D. Bloom and S. Ivanov (1998), Demographic implications of the Russian mortality crisis, *World Development*, Vol. 26(11), pp. 1921–1937.

Bloom, D. and P. Malaney (1998), Macroeconomic consequences of the Russian mortality crisis, *World Development*, Vol. 26(11), pp. 2073–2086.

Bobadilla, J.-L., C. Costello and F. Mitchell (eds.), *Premature death in the New Independent States*, Washington, D.C.: National Academy Press.

Bobak, M. (1997), Health and mortality crisis in countries with economies in transition, in United Nations and Population and Family Study Center, *Symposium on Health and mortality, Brussels, Belgium, 19–22 November 1997*, pp. 255–288, New York: United Nations.

Fiedorov, Yu.E. (ed.) (1997), *Doklad o razvitii chelovecheskogo potentsiala v Rossiiskoi Federacii. God 1997-i*, Moskva: Prava cheloveka.

Fiedorov, Yu.E. (ed.) (1998), *Doklad o razvitii chelovecheskogo potentsiala v Rossiiskoi Federacii. God 1998-i*, Moskva: Prava cheloveka.

Goskomstat Rossii (State Statistic Committee of Russia) (1997a), *Rossiiskii statisticheskii ezhegodnik. 1997*, Moskva.

Goskomstat Rossii (State Statistic Committee of Russia) (1997b), *Sotsial'noe polozhenie i uroven' zhizni naseleniya Rossii. Statisticheskii sbornik*, Moskva

Goskomstat Rossii (State Statistic Committee of Russia) (1998a), *Demograficheskii ezhegodnik. 1998*, Moskva.

Ivanov, S.F. (ed.) (1995), *Doklad o razvitii chelovecheskogo potentsiala v Rossiiskoi Federacii. God 1995-i*, Moskva: Academia.

Kennedy, B., I. Kawachi and E. Brainerd (1998), The role of social capital in the Russian mortality crisis, *World Development*, Vol. 26(11), pp. 2029–2043.

*Kommersant-daily*, No. 98, 3 June 1998.

Meslé, F. *et al.* (1996), Tendances récentes de la mortalité par cause en Russie 1965–1994, *Série Donneées Statistiques*, No. 2, Paris: INED.

Okolski, M. (1993), Health and mortality, in United Nations Economic Commission for Europe, Council of Europe and United Nations Population Fund, *European Population Conference, Geneva, Switzerland, 23–26 March 1993. Proceedings, Vol. 1*, pp. 331–334.

Popkin, B. *et al.* (1997), Nutritional risk factors in the former Soviet Union, in J.-L. Bobadilla, C. Costello and F. Mitchell (eds.), *Premature Death in the New Independent States*, pp. 314–334, Washington, D.C: National Academy Press.

Puska, P. (1997), Chronic disease prevention in the New Independent States: Finnish experiences, in J.-L. Bobadilla, C. Costello and F. Mitchell (eds.), *Premature death in the New Independent States*, pp. 335–354, Washington, DC: National Academy Press.

Shkolnikov, V. *et al.* (1998), Causes of the Russian mortality crisis: evidence and interpretations, *World Development*, Vol. 26(11), pp. 1995–2011.

Shkolnikov, V., F. Meslé and J. Vallin (1996), Health crisis in Russia, *Population: An English Selection*, No. 8, pp. 123–190.

Shkolnikov, V.M. and A.V. Nemtsov (1997), The anti-alcohol campaign and variations in Russian mortality, in J.-L. Bobadilla, C. Costello and F. Mitchell (eds.), *Premature death in the New Independent States*, pp. 238–261, Washington, DC: National Academy Press.

UNDP (United Nations Development Program) (1995), *Human Development Report 1995*, New York: Oxford University Press.

UNDP (United Nations Development Program) (1997a), *Human Development Report 1997*, New York: Oxford University Press.

UNDP (United Nations Development Program) (1997b), *Human Development Report 1997*, *Ukraine*, UNDP: Kiev.

UNDP (United Nations Development Program) (1998a), *Poverty in Transition. Economies in Transition Studies, Regional Monitoring Report*, New York: Regional Bureau for Europe and the CIS.

UNDP (1998b), *Belarus: State, Governance, People. National Human Development Report*, UNDP: Minsk.

Vishnevsky, A. (1997), Russkii krest (2), *Izvestiya*, 24 February 1997.

Vishnevsky, A. and V. Shkolnikov (1997), *Smertnost' v Rossii: glavnye grupy riska i prioritety deistviya*, Moskva: Moskovskii Tsentr Karnegi, Nauchnye doklady, vyp. 19.

Zakharov, S. (1997a), Demographicheskaya istoriya SSSR i Rossii v zerkale istorii pokolenii, *Naselenie i obshestvo*, No. 17.

Zakharov, S. (1997b), Fertility trends in Russia and the European New Independent States: crisis or turning point? *United Nations Expert Group Meeting on Below-Replacement Fertility, New York, 4–6 November 1997*, pp. 271–290, New York: UN Population Division.

Zohoori, N. *et al.* (1998), Monitoring the economic transition in the Russian Federation and its implications for the demographic crisis: the Russian longitudinal monitoring survey, *World Development*, Vol. 26(11), pp. 1977–1993.

# 15

# The Current Trends of Population Development in the Slovak Republic

**Boris Vaňo**

## 15.1 The Social and Economic Conditions of the Population Development in the Post-war Period

After the Second World War, the population development in Slovakia has witnessed two major periods, characterised by different patterns of demographic behaviour, on the one hand, and by different social, economic and cultural conditions largely shaped by the predominant political system, on the other. The first one fell on the second half of the 1960s, when the significant differences in the demographic phenomena between Western and Eastern Europe – especially between the democratic and totalitarian communist societies – became apparent. The second period has started in the early 1990s, demonstrating how fast the population development may "respond" to the radical political and economic changes in society.

In the course of the post-war development, the population dynamics in Slovakia did not differ too much from the main demographic trends that were typical for Western Europe. During the second half of the 1960s, dramatic changes in population development were occurring across most European countries: a significant decrease in nuptiality and fertility, shifts in traditional types of partnership and the rise of births outside marriage. At the same time, the mortality was declining and the life expectancy growing (see van de Kaa, 1987 and Cliquet, 1993).

However, in Slovakia – as well as in the other former communist countries – these changes had a lower intensity as compared to other European countries (EUROSTAT, 1999). In the late 1960s – early 1970s, this difference between "western" and "eastern" patterns of demographic development appeared to be more significant due to increased polarisation of social and economic environment. In that period, the dynamics of demographic processes in Slovakia seemingly stabilised: nuptiality and fertility were slightly but continuously increasing; the mortality was stagnating and showing some increase in the specific age groups, especially among males; and the orientation towards traditional forms of family and partnership was reflected, amongst others, in a low numbers of divorces and extramarital births. Thus, one may, in this respect, think that the political division of Europe manifested itself also in the two different types of demographic transition, increasingly associated with the ideological and economic polarisation.

On the other hand, even most of the former communist countries demonstrated distinct, as compared to Western Europe, dynamics of the population development, significant differences in the demographic phenomena did exist among them as well. These differences were mainly due to the peculiarities of the pre-Soviet historical, political, cultural, religious, geographic and economic development in these countries, which all together had influenced the national traditions, cultural norms and attitudes and, as a result, population reproduction patterns across the countries.

In this respect, Slovakia can be characterised as a country with strong conservative traditions reflected in prevailing orientation towards "traditional" (stable) family with many children. This general orientation was only partly modified due to pre-Soviet unification with the Czech Republic.

Although, in the context of contemporary population development, one might hear nostalgic voices praising the past, when the substantially higher fertility provided a high natural increase of population and therefore ensured the rejuvenation of the age structure, the post-war population dynamics can hardly be considered as positive. On the one hand, Slovakia belonged to the countries with the highest fertility across Europe, on the other, it was also characterised by high mortality, high numbers of induced abortions and by continuously increasing number of divorces. In addition, fertility was concentrated at the very beginning of the reproductive period, which in turn caused the low stability of the family – most people were getting married and becoming parents at a very early age.

The changes that have occurred in Slovakia since 1989 can be therefore seen as a return not only to a more human (democratic) social order but also to a more natural (unforced) type of the population development.

## 15.2 Current Population Development

In Slovakia, as in many other post-communist countries, the period of social and economic transformation of society is characterised by dramatic changes in the reproductive behaviour of population. Forty years of isolation from Western Europe had, however, led to the situation that the changes requiring under the "natural" conditions more time have been occurring with an extraordinary intensity within a very short historical period, touching upon all important components of population reproduction. Changes in nuptiality and fertility have been especially crucial as compared to other demographic processes, which exhibited more stability or have been influenced by non-demographic factors (Tirpák and Pilinska, 1999).

### 15.2.1 Age Structure of the Population

As Figure 15.1 demonstrates, today, the age structure of the Slovak population has two important features: first, it is still relatively progressive; and secondly, it is quite irregular.

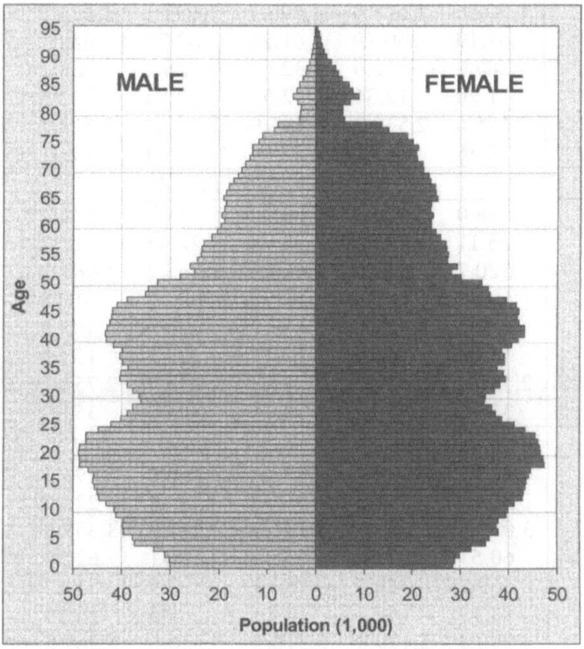


**Figure 15.1: Age Pyramid on 1 January 1998**
Source: SÚSR, 1998

The irregular age structure of population is first of all a result of the unfavourable population development in the past. Bearing in mind a relatively stable, however not very positive, dynamics of mortality, it was foremost the fluctuating fertility that had led to the mentioned irregularities in the age structure of the population. In addition, important societal changes and pronatalist policy likely have together additionally shaped the "relief" of the age pyramid resulting in the observed irregularities between the age groups of the population (KDGD, 1999).

Population ageing, representing a constant challenge for most European populations (EUROSTAT, op. cit.), is another factor, which affects the irregular age structure of the Slovak population. In Slovakia, population ageing is mainly a result of the significant decline in fertility occurring in the last decades, as the average life expectancy in the same period has not substantially increased. It means that the proportion of the elderly in all population has increased mainly due to the decrease of the proportion of children (population under 15 years).

**Table 15.1: Population by Major Age Groups, 1980–1997, selected years**

| Age group | 1980 | 1985 | 1990 | 1993 | 1995 | 1996 | 1997 |
|---|---|---|---|---|---|---|---|
| | | | | Male | | | |
| 0–14 (1,000) | 665.8 | 698.4 | 679.5 | 641.8 | 610.9 | 595.8 | 579.6 |
| 0–14 (%) | 27.11 | 27.50 | 26.18 | 24.68 | 23.37 | 22.75 | 22.11 |
| 15–59 (1,000) | 1,502.6 | 1,528.3 | 1,590.7 | 1,632.1 | 1,674.7 | 1,694.5 | 1,713.3 |
| 15–59 (%) | 61.19 | 60.19 | 61.28 | 62.77 | 64.07 | 64.72 | 65.34 |
| 60+ (1,000) | 287.2 | 312.6 | 325.7 | 326.2 | 328.2 | 328.1 | 329.2 |
| 60+ (%) | 11.70 | 12.31 | 12.55 | 12.55 | 12.56 | 12.53 | 12.56 |
| Total (1,000) | 2,455.6 | 2,539.3 | 2,595.9 | 2,600.0 | 2,613.7 | 2,618.4 | 2,622.0 |
| Mean age | 31.36 | 31.61 | 32.14 | 32.54 | 33.01 | 33.27 | 33.56 |
| | | | | Female | | | |
| 0–14 (1,000) | 638.0 | 670.0 | 651.0 | 614.2 | 584.4 | 569.1 | 554.1 |
| 0–14 (%) | 25.11 | 25.38 | 23.98 | 22.45 | 21.22 | 20.62 | 20.04 |
| 15–59 (1,000) | 1,520.7 | 1,540.8 | 1,600.3 | 1,645.2 | 1,684.1 | 1702 | 1,719.4 |
| 15–59 (%) | 59.85 | 58.37 | 58.95 | 60.12 | 61.15 | 61.66 | 62.17 |
| 60+ (1,000) | 382 | 428.8 | 463.5 | 476.9 | 485.6 | 489.5 | 492.2 |
| 60+ (%) | 15.04 | 16.24 | 17.07 | 17.43 | 17.63 | 17.73 | 17.80 |
| Total (1,000) | 2,540.7 | 2,639.7 | 2,714.8 | 2,736.4 | 2,754.1 | 2,760.5 | 2,765.6 |
| Mean age | 33.71 | 34.18 | 34.91 | 35.46 | 35.98 | 36.27 | 36.55 |
| | | | | Total | | | |
| 0–14 (1,000) | 1,303.7 | 1,368.4 | 1,330.5 | 1,256.0 | 1,195.3 | 1,164.9 | 1,133.7 |
| 0–14 (%) | 26.09 | 26.42 | 25.05 | 23.54 | 22.27 | 21.66 | 21.04 |
| 15–59 (1,000) | 3,023.4 | 3,069.1 | 3,191.0 | 3,277.3 | 3,358.8 | 3,396.5 | 3,432.6 |
| 15–59 (%) | 60.51 | 59.26 | 60.09 | 61.41 | 62.57 | 63.14 | 63.71 |
| 60+ (1,000) | 669.2 | 741.4 | 789.3 | 803.1 | 813.7 | 817.6 | 821.4 |
| 60+ (%) | 13.39 | 14.32 | 14.86 | 15.05 | 15.16 | 15.20 | 15.25 |
| Total (1,000) | 4,996.3 | 5,179.0 | 5,310.7 | 5,336.5 | 5,367.8 | 5,378.9 | 5,387.7 |
| Mean age | 32.55 | 32.92 | 33.56 | 34.04 | 34.53 | 34.81 | 35.09 |

Sources: ČSÚ, 1996; SÚSR, 1998

Both the indicator of the mean age and the index of ageing clearly illustrate the accelerating of population ageing in Slovakia. In 1997, the index of ageing was 50% higher than in 1950 (see Table 15.1 and Figure 15.2).

As a result of high fertility and high mortality in the past, the Slovak population is still characterised by a relatively large proportion of the population of young age and, consequently, a relatively low proportion of the old-age population. The ratio between these groups is however changing. It is estimated that in the near future Slovakia will witness substantial changes in the age structure of its population. After the year 2000, the bulge generations born during the post-war baby boom will enter the retirement age, heavily influencing the balance between population in the working and non-working age.

The decline in fertility that has started in the mid-1980s has also led to a relatively low number of people entering the working-age groups. As a result, the current slight increase in the population of working age, which will come to an end at the beginning of the twenty first century, would probably remain the last one, at least for a long time ahead. In the beginning of the next decade, Slovakia will not only face a loss of population in the under-working and working ages but also witness a natural decrease of the population. Furthermore, for the first time in the history of the Slovak population, the young (under-working age) population will become the smallest age group in the total population.

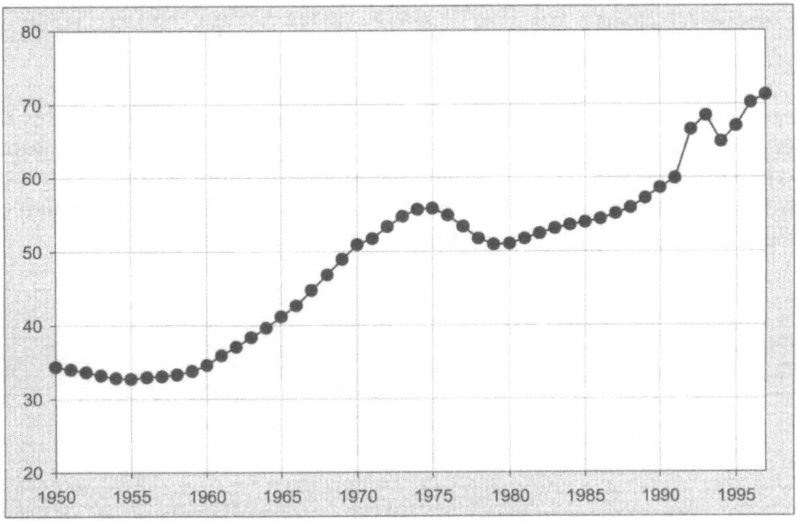


**Figure 15.2: Index of Ageing, 1950–1997**

Source: author's calculations based on ČSÚ, op. cit. and SÚSR, 1998

### 15.2.2 Nuptiality

Nuptiality appeared to be one of the most "flexible" demographic processes reflecting the transformation of society that has started at the beginning of the 1990s (KDGD, op. cit.). Forty years of progressively but slowly decreasing nuptiality have been followed by the period of dramatic change in the level and intensity of the process. After brief increase in the number of marriages in 1990, caused mostly by the announced abolishment of allowances for young families and partly by "the revolution euphoria", the number of marriages and the marriage rates started to decline substantially (Table 15.2).

Responding to the newly emerging social values and behavioural norms as well as to the aggravating social and economic problems, the apparent downward trend of the marriage rates became expressed first of all in a more frequent postponement of legal marriages and in the increasing number of consensual unions. It remains, however, a question for a time being whether young people would just delay their marriages, or they would prefer to live together without getting married.

**Table 15.2: Main Indicators of Nuptiality, 1980–1997, selected years**

| | 1980 | 1985 | 1990 | 1993 | 1995 | 1996 | 1997 |
|---|---|---|---|---|---|---|---|
| Marriages | 39,578 | 38,930 | 40,435 | 30,771 | 27,489 | 27,484 | 27,955 |
| Crude marriage rate (‰) | 7.9 | 7.5 | 7.6 | 5.8 | 5.1 | 5.1 | 5.2 |
| Mean age at marriage, male | .. | .. | 25.4 | 25.4 | 25.8 | 26.8 | 27.2 |
| Mean age at marriage, female | .. | .. | 22.7 | 22.7 | 23.1 | 23.9 | 24.2 |
| Total marriage rate, male | 0.813 | 0.836 | 0.919 | 0.708 | 0.588 | 0.564 | 0.569 |
| Total marriage rate, female | 0.871 | 0.912 | 0.942 | 0.713 | 0.590 | 0.570 | 0.581 |

Sources: ČSÚ, op. cit.; SÚSR, 1998

The development of the nuptiality in the last years (Figure 15.3) provides the evidence that, in many cases, marriages have been delayed to higher ages. Inasmuch as fertility in Slovakia is still closely related to nuptiality (approximately 60% of first-born children are born during the first year of marriage), the postponement of marriage could substantially influence the future trends of fertility.

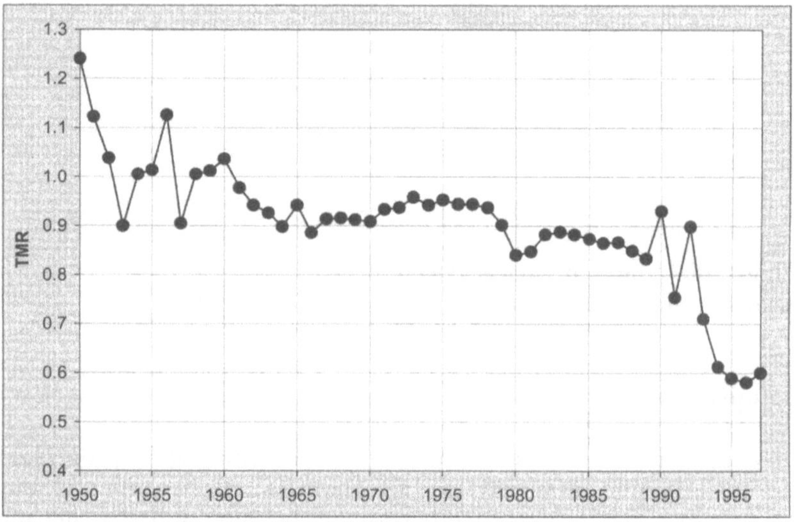


**Figure 15.3: Total Marriage Rate (TMR), 1950–1997**

Sources: ČSÚ, op. cit.; SÚSR, 1998

In the first half of the 1990s, the development of nuptiality showed some important changes in the structure of this process, especially in relation to the distribution of marriages according to the age of bridegrooms and brides. Though the marriage rates fell across all important for nuptiality age groups (younger than 35 years), the level of this decline was not similar across the specific age groups. The most affected groups for both sexes were the youngest age groups, while the decline in the age groups older than 25 years was not so significant. As a result, the mean age at first marriage has grown for both males and females (Figures 15.4 and 15.5) remaining, however, one of the lowest in Europe. Besides, the majority of marriages were the first marriages because a relatively low propensity to divorce did not create many possibilities for remarriages.

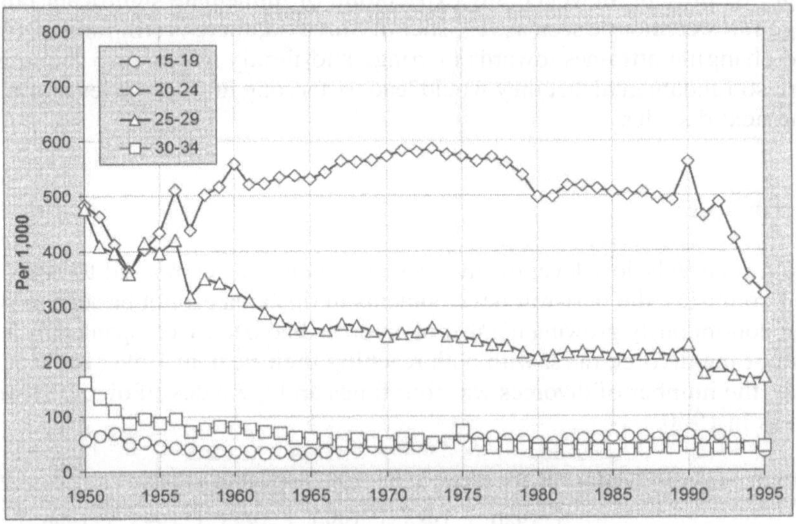


**Figure 15.4: Age-specific Marriage Rates, 1950–1995, male**
Sources: ČSÚ, op. cit.; SÚSR, 1998

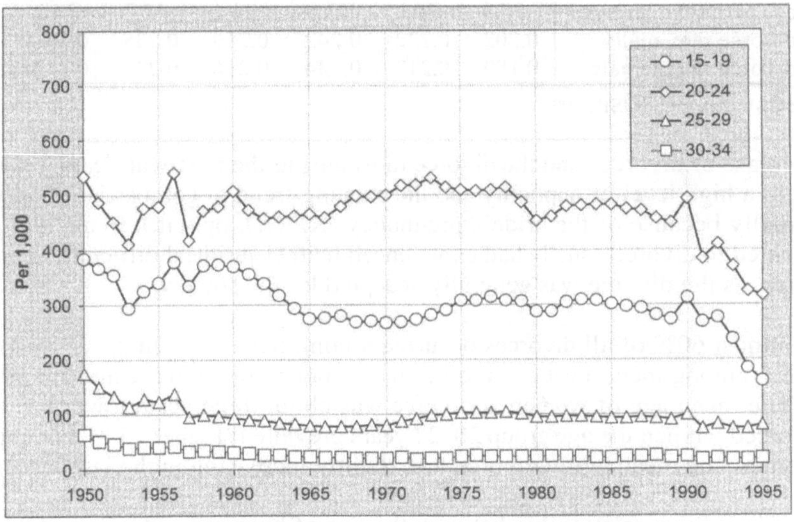


**Figure 15.5: Age-specific Marriage Rates, 1950–1995, female**
Sources: ČSÚ, op. cit.; SÚSR, 1998

The development of the nuptiality during the first half of the 1990s had led to the situation where the structure and, even more, the level of the nuptiality have approached the indicators that are typical for Western European countries. It can be suggested, therefore, that the future dynamics of nuptiality will likely take form of the continuous changes in its structure, especially in increasing mean age at first marriage. At present, however, any expectation of immediate significant fall in the marriage rates cannot be seen as realistic. In Slovakia, there is still limited evidence that the changing attitudes towards marriage and family life among young generations are so fundamental that they would lead to a strong drop in the level of nuptiality in the next decades.

### 15.2.3 Divorces

Despite a relatively low level of divorces in Slovakia as compared to other industrialised countries, the post-war developments in this area cannot be seen as stagnating. The continuously growing number of divorces had been accompanied by a steady increase of the divorce rates, with both reaching their peak in 1996 (Table 15.3). In this year, the number of divorces was four times and the index of divorce five times as high as in 1960.

**Table 15.3: Main Indicators of Divorces, 1980–1997, selected years**

| | 1980 | 1985 | 1990 | 1993 | 1995 | 1996 | 1997 |
|---|---|---|---|---|---|---|---|
| Divorces | 6,645 | 7,800 | 8,867 | 8,143 | 8,978 | 9,402 | 9,138 |
| Crude divorce rate (‰) | 1.33 | 1.50 | 1.67 | 1.53 | 1.67 | 1.75 | 1.70 |
| Divorces per 100 marriages | 16.8 | 20.0 | 21.9 | 26.5 | 32.7 | 34.2 | 32.7 |
| Total divorce rate, male | 0.202 | 0.222 | 0.242 | 0.219 | 0.238 | 0.248 | 0.244 |
| Total divorce rate, female | 0.189 | 0.212 | 0.244 | 0.216 | 0.233 | 0.242 | 0.236 |

Sources: ČSÚ, op. cit.; SÚSR, 1998

The increase of divorces and the divorce rates during the post-war years was mostly related to a high level of nuptiality and the existing trend to get married at very early age, usually because of the bride's pregnancy (KDGD, op. cit.). In addition, those who wanted to divorce usually had experienced neither juridical difficulties nor social pressures, as the divorce was generally accepted by the society.

While almost 60% of all divorces occurred among persons aged 25–39 years (Figure 15.7), among men, most of divorces were concentrated in the age group 30–34 years. The mean age of women at divorce was about three years lower, i.e. among the divorced women the age group 20–24 years prevailed (Figure 15.8). For both men and women, the mean age at divorce was slightly increasing in the last decades.

As there is a direct relationship between the age of husband and wife and the duration of their marriage, the dynamics of divorces with respect to these factors was quite similar. Most marriages were terminated within 4 or 5 years of marriage, while the mean duration of marriage at divorce was about 12 years. Among families dissolved by divorce, families with young children made up 60–75%.

**Figure 15.6: Total Divorce Rate (TDR), 1950–1997, selected years**

Sources: ČSÚ, op. cit.; SÚSR, 1998

As to the reasons for divorce, most men and women usually reported personal desperateness. It can be assumed, however, that such explanation may often serve to hide real motives such as the partner's alcoholism, infidelity, addiction problems, or the partner's indifference towards family interests.

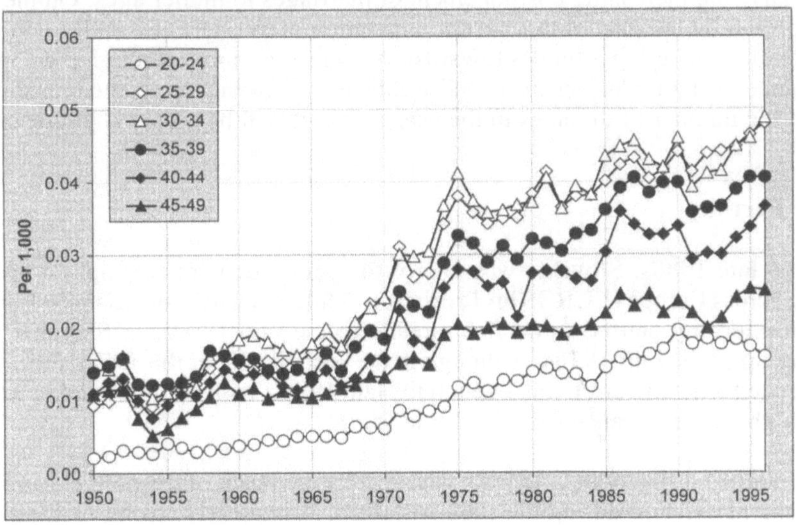


**Figure 15.7: Age-specific Divorce Rates, 1950–1997, male**

Sources: ČSÚ, op. cit.; SÚSR, 1998

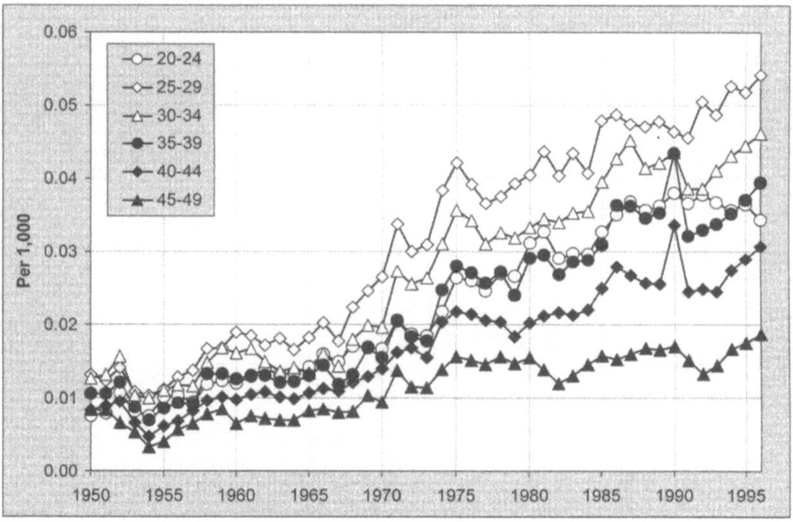


**Figure 15.8: Age-specific Divorce Rates, 1950–1997, female**
Sources: ČSÚ, op. cit.; SÚSR, 1998

In the early 1990s, there were some discussions about the likelihood of restrained growth of divorces. At present, however, it seems that any positive developments in this area can be expected only in a long-term perspective. On one hand, there have appeared already a number of factors that could contribute to the stability of marriage, particularly the increasing postponement of marriages to higher ages. On the other, the adoption by the part of the Slovak population of Western life styles and values could lead to changing attitudes towards marriage and family through placing more importance on individual interests and wellbeing. Nevertheless, if there is some decline in the number of divorces in the near future, it will be a very slight decline.

### 15.2.4 Fertility

Until the late 1980s, Slovakia was one of the countries with the highest levels of fertility across Europe (EUROSTAT, op. cit.). While in many industrialised European countries fertility started to decline already in the mid-1960s, in Slovakia it was growing up to the mid-1970s. Although in the second half of the 1970s fertility had experienced a downward trend, even in the late 1980s, its level in Slovakia was still rather high by European standards (Table 15.4).

The mentioned differences in fertility were mostly the result of the political and social environment existing during the state socialism. A relatively strong orientation towards family life among the Slovak people at that time can be explained by the fact that family not only allowed the realisation of family interests and values but also provided an important shelter from the politicised everyday reality. Moreover, pronatalist social and housing policies combined with the lack of means of family planning also strongly influenced the high level of fertility in Slovakia (Figure 15.9).

**Table 15.4: Main Indicators of Fertility, 1980–1997, selected years**

| | 1980 | 1985 | 1990 | 1993 | 1995 | 1996 | 1997 |
|---|---|---|---|---|---|---|---|
| Births (1,000) | 95.7 | 90.6 | 80.4 | 73.6 | 61.7 | 60.4 | 59.4 |
| Live births (1,000) | 95.1 | 90.2 | 80.0 | 73.3 | 61.4 | 60.1 | 59.1 |
| Crude fertility rate (‰) | 19.1 | 17.5 | 15.1 | 13.8 | 11.4 | 11.2 | 11.0 |
| Extramarital births (per 100 live births) | 5.7 | 6.6 | 7.6 | 10.6 | 12.6 | 14.0 | 15.1 |
| Mean age of women at first birth | 22.18 | 22.21 | 22.17 | 21.95 | 22.21 | 22.37 | 23.08 |
| Total fertility rate | 2.318 | 2.173 | 2.086 | 1.920 | 1.520 | 1.471 | 1.430 |
| Gross reproduction rate | 1.127 | 1.099 | 1.013 | 0.930 | 0.742 | 0.712 | 0.696 |
| Net reproduction rate | 1.098 | 1.075 | 0.993 | 0.915 | 0.730 | 0.700 | 0.685 |

Sources: ČSÚ, op. cit.; SÚSR, 1998

**Figure 15.9: Total Fertility Rate (TFR), 1950–1997**
Sources: ČSÚ, op. cit.; SÚSR, 1998

Besides the high level, another peculiarity of the fertility development in Slovakia was the timing of childbearing. The highest fertility was concentrated in the young age groups. Consequently, the proportions of births among women aged 35 and over were very low (Figure 15.10).

As in the case of nuptiality, crucial societal changes that have taken place since 1989 have had important effects on the fertility development as well. The strongest drop in fertility was observed during 1993–1995. And again, the question was whether the Slovak population would face the postponement of fertility (delaying births until higher ages) or the decline in the total fertility rate (TFR), eventually increasing planned childlessness. The most recent trends, namely the rise in nuptiality and visible stagnation of birth decline that have been recorded since 1996, support the first hypothesis – the postponement of fertility.

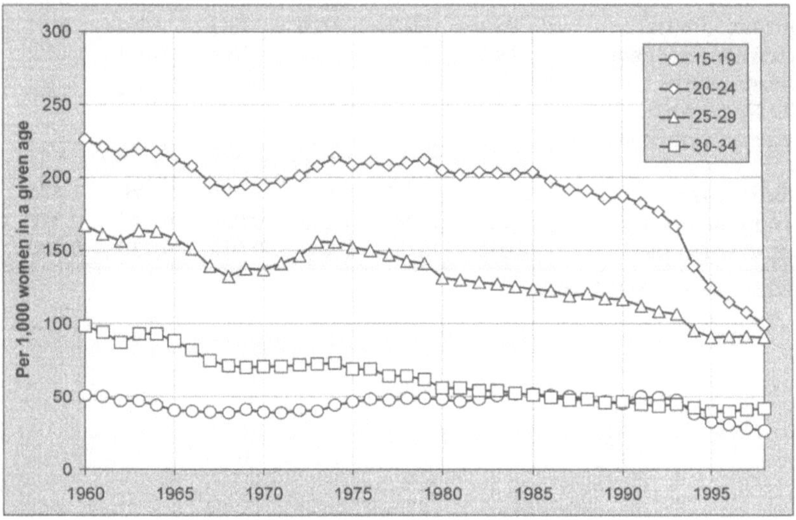


**Figure 15.10: Age-specific Fertility Rates, 1960–1998**

Sources: ČSÚ, op. cit. ; SÚSR, 1998

As far as the new family patterns have stabilised – in the course of the overall transformation of society – it can be assumed that two-children family model will be prevalent again. This in turn could be conducive to a slight increase of fertility. Although large families seemingly became the part of the past, there is still no reason to consider the planned childlessness as a factor that would strongly affect the reproductive behaviour in the future.

The impact of fertility developments in the 1990s was profound and resulted in a significant drop in the indicators of fertility in all most important (in terms of fecundity) age groups. The decline in fertility was also accompanied by a growing mean age of women at first birth, which had increased by one year during the last decade.

### 15.2.5 Abortions

Looking back on the developments in the sphere of abortions, the watershed in Slovakia would appear to be located in 1957, when the legislation allowing to make an abortion for "social" reasons was approved and the special committees aimed to manage this issue were established. One year later, the number of abortions increased by 2.5 times. This was the beginning of a forty-year period of continuously increasing number of abortions, with its peak in the late 1980s (Table 15.5). The most important factor underlying this trend was the rise of legal abortions, while the number of miscarriages was relatively stable with a slight tendency to decrease.

**Table 15.5: Main Indicators of Abortions, 1980–1997, selected years**

| | 1980 | 1985 | 1990 | 1993 | 1995 | 1996 | 1997 |
|---|---|---|---|---|---|---|---|
| Abortions (1,000) | 40.7 | 45.6 | 56.2 | 45.6 | 35.9 | 30.9 | 27.8 |
| Induced abortions per 100 births | 76.8 | 79.7 | 86.2 | 85.2 | 82.0 | 81.5 | 80.3 |
| Total abortion rate | 1.074 | 1.155 | 1.430 | 1.271 | 1.028 | 0.888 | 0.689 |
| Induced abortions per 100 registered pregnancies (%) | 29.8 | 33.5 | 41.1 | 38.2 | 36.8 | 33.8 | 31.9 |
| Index of abortion[1] | 42.5 | 50.3 | 69.9 | 61.9 | 58.2 | 51.2 | 46.8 |

[1]Abortions per 100 live births
Sources: ČSÚ, op. cit.; SÚSR, 1998

In 1958, there were 13 abortions per 100 live births, and the share of legal abortions was 11%. If we compare these numbers with the similar indicators for 1988, the dramatic increase of the number of abortions per year during thirty years would be evident. In 1988, there were 61 legal abortions per 100 live births, i.e. about 35% of all pregnancies in that year were interrupted by abortion.

Since 1989, a strong decline in the number of abortions has been observed. From 1990 to 1996, the number of legal abortions dropped almost by half; other indicators of abortion also demonstrated a significant decline. Because the intensity of the decline of the abortion rate was higher than that of the fertility rate, the number of legal abortions per 100 registered pregnancies dropped during this period by approximately 27%.

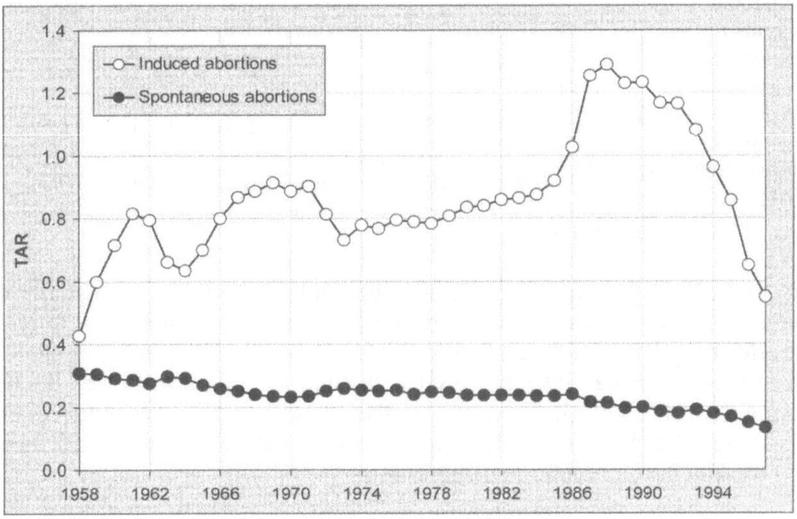


**Figure 15.11: Total Abortion Rate (TAR), 1950–1997**
Sources: ČSÚ, op. cit.; SÚSR, 1998

Slovakia still belongs to the countries with relatively high numbers of abortions. More importantly, it differs from industrialised European countries not only by the level of abortions but also by their distribution among specific age groups. Whereas in Western Europe the intensity of abortions is higher among never-married and divorced women who are 24 years old and younger and do not have children, in Slovakia, it is mostly married women aged 25–29 years with two and more children who use abortion to prevent further childbirth. Thus, the role that the abortion still plays in Slovakia – functioning as an important means of family planning – differs significantly from the role abortions play in some other European countries.

### 15.2.6 Mortality

One of the negative trends in both demographic and social development in Slovakia was and continues to be a high level of mortality. This phenomenon is well illustrated by the dynamics of almost all relevant indicators, including very slowly decreasing infant mortality rate; significant mortality rates observed among middle-aged population and the elderly (especially among men); and relatively low life expectancy at birth (Table 15.6)

**Table 15.6: Main Indicators of Mortality, 1980–1997, selected years**

| | 1980 | 1985 | 1990 | 1993 | 1995 | 1996 | 1997 |
|---|---|---|---|---|---|---|---|
| Deaths (1,000) | 50.6 | 52.5 | 54.6 | 52.7 | 52.7 | 51.2 | 52.1 |
| Crude mortality rate (‰) | 10.1 | 10.2 | 10.3 | 9.9 | 9.8 | 9.5 | 9.7 |
| Infant mortality rate (‰) | 20.9 | 16.3 | 12.0 | 10.6 | 11.0 | 10.2 | 8.7 |
| Life expectancy at birth, male (years) | 66.7 | 66.9 | 66.6 | 68.3 | 68.4 | 68.8 | 68.9 |
| Life expectancy at birth, female (years) | 74.2 | 74.7 | 75.4 | 76.7 | 76.3 | 76.6 | 76.7 |
| Life expectancy at age 60, male (years) | 15.3 | 15.2 | 15.0 | 15.9 | 15.6 | 15.7 | 15.9 |
| Life expectancy at age 60, female (years) | 19.0 | 19.2 | 19.6 | 20.5 | 20.0 | 20.2 | 20.4 |

Sources: ČSÚ, op. cit.; SÚSR, 1998

Factors that affect the unfavourable development of mortality are usually divided into three main groups such as a situation in the health care, quality of environment and the life style (KDGD, op. cit.). A long-term shortage of funds experienced by the system of health care can be considered as the major factor that caused the negative development of mortality in Slovakia. On the other hand, the basic concept underlying this system has been much debated, especially the necessity to shift focus from medical treatment to prevention of illnesses.

The practice of long-time neglect of the issues of environmental protection and emphasis exclusively on the economic rationality instead of giving priority to ecological factor has led to the significant pollution of the environment, damage to which is currently estimated in billions of the Slovak Crowns. Therefore, it is not surprising that the deteriorating quality of environment has also negatively influenced the health of population.

But probably the strongest factor contributing to the poor health situation and, consequently, to high mortality is the prevailing life style, which can hardly be seen as a healthy one. Insufficient and inadequate nutrition and, especially, high consumption of alcohol and smoking as well as increasing working stress and shortage of active leisure, are closely linked to the stability of negative mortality trends in Slovakia. As a result, the life expectancy at birth among the Slovak men is about 7 years less, compared with many other industrialised European countries; for females, this difference is approximately 5 years. The dynamics of this indicator in Slovakia is shown in Figure 15.12.

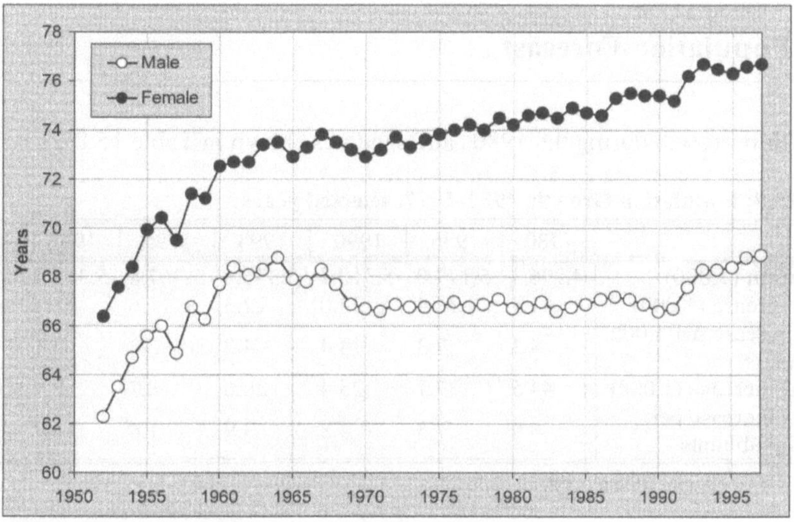


**Figure 15.12: Life Expectancy at Birth, 1952–1997**

Sources: ČSÚ, op. cit.; SÚSR, 1998

It is unlikely that the main factors contributing to the high mortality could be dealt with fast and easily. Thus, the situation in the nearest future in this respect cannot be expected to be positive. Slow and very slight increase in life expectancy at birth during the last decade of only about one year for both sexes implies that substantial long-term positive changes in mortality would require not only time but that ongoing transformation of society improves the quality of life in Slovakia.

### 15.2.7 Migration

In Slovakia, international migration does not play an important role in the demographic development. Neither in the past, when the legal emigration of Slovaks was followed by illegal emigration, nor recently, when the immigration of people from other countries has been increasing, the effect of international migration cannot be seen as significant. More important are however migration flows between Slovakia and the Czech Republic, particularly because until 1992 it was an internal migration.

After the separation, the migration between both countries significantly dropped, and, as a result, the total net migration in Slovakia is currently relatively low (Table 15.7).

**Table 15.7: Total Net Migration, 1980–1997, selected years**

| | 1980 | 1985 | 1990 | 1993 | 1995 | 1996 | 1997 |
|---|---|---|---|---|---|---|---|
| Net migration | -1,674 | -1,415 | -739 | 1,751 | 2,842 | 2,255 | 1,731 |

Sources: ČSÚ, op. cit.; SÚSR, 1998

## 15.3 Population Forecast

Population growth during the 1980s and 1990s is shown in Table 15.8.

**Table 15.8: Population Growth, 1980–1997, selected years**

| | 1980 | 1985 | 1990 | 1993 | 1995 | 1996 | 1997 |
|---|---|---|---|---|---|---|---|
| Population (1,000) | 4,996.3 | 5,179.0 | 5,310.7 | 5,336.4 | 5,367.8 | 5,378.9 | 5,387.6 |
| Total increase (1,000) | 41.4 | 34.4 | 23.0 | 22.3 | 11.6 | 11.1 | 8.7 |
| Total increase per 1,000 inhabitants | 8.3 | 7.3 | 4.4 | 4.2 | 2.2 | 2.1 | 1.6 |
| Natural increase (1,000) | 44.5 | 37.7 | 25.4 | 20.6 | 8.7 | 8.9 | 7.0 |
| Natural increase per 1,000 inhabitants | 8.9 | 7.3 | 4.8 | 3.9 | 1.6 | 1.7 | 1.3 |

Sources: ČSÚ, op. cit.; SÚSR, 1998

In Slovakia, the last official forecast of population was made in 1996 (SÚSR, 1996). It was a population projection until the year 2020 based on two variants (low and high), that identified the two possible scenarios of population development in the future. According to the low variant, until 2005 the fertility will be decreasing, whereas in the period of 2005–2020 there will be a slight increase in its dynamics. The high variant assumed that the fertility will be stabilised already in 2000 and will be increasing throughout the period 2000–2020.

In relation to mortality trends, a slight decrease was generally estimated. Both variants also suggested that the total net migration would be a low yet positive one – about 1,000–2,000 persons per year (SÚSR, 1996). Since the current demographic development has already demonstrated that the high variant cannot be seen as realistic, Table 15.9 includes results of the low variant of the projection only.

**Table 15.9: Expected Population Growth, 2000–2020[1], selected years**

| | 2000 | 2005 | 2010 | 2015 | 2020 |
|---|---|---|---|---|---|
| Population (1,000) | 5,408.7 | 5,420.2 | 5,399.0 | 5,342.9 | 5,240.2 |
| Natural increase per 1,000 inhabitants | 0.7 | -0.2 | -1.6 | -3.0 | -4.9 |
| Index of ageing (%) | 80.4 | 94.7 | 117.1 | 135.2 | 157.5 |

[1]Forecast based on the low variant
Source: SÚSR, 1996

## 15.4 Social, Family and Population Policies and Programmes

At present, the system of social security in Slovakia is undergoing principle transformation aimed at purposeful regulation of social, family and population policies to adapt them to the new social conditions and priorities. The system of social security that was operative until 1989 could hardly respond to the changing social and economic conditions, particularly to the emerging market relations. It was also insufficient with respect to the observed changes in population development. The main goal of the reform of the social security system is therefore to create conditions for a more harmonised regulation of social, family and population policies in order to effectively respond to the rights, interests and needs of specific strata and groups of the population.

Consequently, the major change in the ideology underlying the concept of social security system in Slovakia consist of shifting the focus from the state paternalism to decentralisation. This means to strengthen principles of solidarity; to support the initiative of people; and to emphasise both individual and social groups' democratic activities. With respect to the changing economic conditions, the role of social policy should be to initiate, justify and support social and economic transformation of society. Each person will be provided with a possibility to ensure his or her material and cultural needs through working incomes, whereas the state would secure wellbeing of those people and families who could not provide for themselves due to the specific circumstances.

The transformation of the existing social relationships is therefore aimed to design and implement such system that would allow the combination of personal participation and social solidarity of people with the basic social security guaranteed by the state. A main focus will however be placed on the increasing responsibility of people for their personal and family wellbeing.

A brief overview of the main spheres of social policy effective at the end of 1997 is presented below.

### 15.4.1 Social Security System

According to the existing legislation, the social security system consists of provision of pensions, health security system, social care and the state social allowances. One of the most important steps in transforming the state social security system into the public social security system was the complex tax reform undertaken in Slovakia in the recent years.

The following several types of pensions have been introduced recently. The first one is an old-age pension, which is granted to each citizen of the Slovak Republic after working for a certain number of years, or upon reaching a retirement age. Other types include a disability pension, pensions for widowers and orphans, and the so-called social pensions. The provision of social pensions relates to those cases when people are not able to support themselves during a long period of time. By the law, the minimum pension is 2,772 Slovak Crowns (US$1 was approximately 33 Slovak Crowns in 1995) for one person and 4,899 Slovak Crowns for a couple, in case it is the sole source of income. Presently, each person who would like to continue paid work after retirement (this period cannot, however, exceed one year) will get an old-age pension without any deductions (MPSVR SR, 1996).

Health security system is mainly related to short-term consequences of social events such as illness, motherhood (pregnancy and childbearing), child rearing and death in the family. In all cases, the amount of allowance is dependent on the level of earnings (or other working income). In case of illness, medical allowance cannot exceed the amount of 300 Slovak Crowns per day whereas the period of payment – one calendar year. If a person provides care for a sick child, the allowance is paid until the child reaches age 10. "Motherhood" allowance is paid during 28 weeks after delivery and its maximum amount is 90% of the salary of one of the parents (but not more than 300 Slovak Crowns per day). In addition, when the child is born, parents are given lump sum allowance of 3,000 Slovak Crowns. In case of a death in the family, the funeral allowance of 2,000 Slovak Crowns is provided (MPSVR SR, 1996).

The main purpose of the social care is to financially support those people who are not enough ensured by their earnings or allowances provided through other forms of the social security system (old-age pension, medical allowance, etc.). The system of social care is mainly focused on families with young children, handicapped people, elderly people and people with special needs.

Social provisions provided by the state mostly relate to families and aim to ensure decent living conditions for them. The child allowance generally depends on the age of the child (children) and the level of income in the family. This allowance is granted only in case when the family income does not exceed the minimal living standard by more than 2.2 times. If there is a handicapped child in the family, some additional financial aid is usually provided. Parenthood allowance is given to a mother or father who provides full-day care for the child (children) until s/he reaches age 3. According to the law, the amount of parenthood allowance is 1.68 of the sum needed to ensure basic needs of adult person (MPSVR SR, 1996).

### 15.4.2 Employment

Social measures with respect to employment and unemployment represent one of the most important and thus widely discussed spheres of population-related policies and programmes. As the recent development has demonstrated more close relationship between the labour force participation and the demographic behaviour of the population, the interest to this sphere has been clearly increasing.

Undergoing the first stage of transformation, the employment system has generally been adapted to new social and economic conditions, particularly, to the needs created by the transition to the market economy. In its further development, the main focus will be on creating a system that could provide a balanced and effective approach to labour requirements and supply, emphasising the necessity of free choice in professional career.

The state also guarantees social provisions for those who are currently unemployed. A special allowance is given to all registered unemployed for the period not longer than 12 months. The amount of allowance depends on the number of years spent in paid employment. Moreover, a monthly allowance cannot exceed the minimum monthly salary by more than 1.8 times (MPSVR SR, 1996).

### 15.4.3 Family Policy

The overall long-term goals of family policy include: to reach a relative economic independence of families; to provide conditions needed for realisation of the basic functions of the family; to support stability of marital and intergeneration relations; and to create optimal condition for population reproduction.

These goals are realised through four main spheres of family policy such as legal protection of the family and its members; social and economic security of the family; moral education of children and youth with a special focus on marital stability and parenthood; health care of family members (MPSVR SR, 1997).

## References

Cliquet, R. (1993), L'avenir de la population en Europe, *Etudes demographiques No. 26*, Strasbourg: Conseil de L'Europe.

ČSÚ (Czech Statistical Office) (1996), *Demografická příručka*, Praha: ČSÚ.

EUROSTAT (1999), *Demographic Statistics, Data 1995–1998*, Luxembourg: European Communities.

KDGD (Department of Demography and Geodemography) (1999), *Populační vývoj České republiky 1998*, Praha: KDGD, PřF, Univerzita Karlova.

MPSVR SR (Ministry of Labour, Social Affairs and Family of the Slovak Republic) (1996), *Koncepcia transformácie sociálnej sféry*, Bratislava: Ministerstvo práce, sociálnych vecí a rodiny SR.

MPSVR SR (Ministry of Labour, Social Affairs and Family of the Slovak Republic) (1997), *Koncepcia štátnej rodinnej politiky*, Bratislava: Ministerstvo práce, sociálnych vecí a rodiny SR.

SÚSR (Statistical Office of the Slovak Republic) (1996), *Projekcia vývoja obyvateľstva v SR do roku 2020*, Bratislava: Štatistický úrad SR.

SÚSR (Statistical Office of the Slovak Republic) (1998), *Vývoj obyvateľstva v SR 1998*, Bratislava: Štatistický úrad SR.

Tirpák, M. and V. Pilinska (1999), Demografický vývoj na Slovensku v roku 1998, *Slovenská štatistika a demografia*, Vol. 9(4), pp. 25–53.

van de Kaa, D.J. (1987), Europe's Second Demographic Transition, *Population Bulletin*, Vol. 42(1), pp. 1–58.

# 16

# Recent Demographic Developments in Slovenia

**Milivoja Šircelj**

## 16.1 New Country – Old Tradition

Slovenia lies on the edges of Central, Eastern and Southern Europe, where Romanic, Germanic, Slavonic and Ungaro-Finnish language groups meet. It covers 20,273 square kilometres and has nearly 2 million inhabitants.

Slovenia appeared on the European political map only in 1991, but the Slovenes settled in this part of Europe 13 centuries ago, when their first statehood was formed. The entity Karantanija, with its core in the present Austrian Carinthia, lasted for about two centuries. The territory occupied by Slovenes became soon part of the Christian Holy Roman Empire and was for more than half of the last millennium ruled by the Austrian House of Habsburg. After the First World War, the Austro-Hungarian Empire was partitioned and South Slavonic people who had lived in the Austro-Hungarian Empire joined the Kingdom of Serbia. Yugoslavia, a kingdom between the two world wars, and a Socialist Federative Republic after the Second World War, was not successful in attempts to bring people and economies of the area together. Yugoslavia disintegrated in 1991 and in June 1992 Slovenia became a member of the United Nations.

One of the consequences of such a historical background is the ethnic composition of Slovenia and the neighbouring states. In the 1990 round of censuses, there were 3,000 Italians and 8,500 Hungarians living in Slovenia (ZRSS, 1994) and about 60–180 thousand, depending on the method of estimation, Slovenes were living in Hungary, Austria and Italy (*Magyarorszag nemzetisegeinek es a szomszedos allamok magyarasaganak statisztikaja (1910–1990)*, 1994, p. 198; Zupančič, 1993). Besides autochthonous Hungarians and Italians, some other nationalities are living in Slovenia as well, mostly Serbs and Croats. According to the 1991 census, Slovenes represented 88% of the population of Slovenia. After 1991, this proportion increased as the consequence of the political changes.

In 1575, the Christian Bible was translated into the Slovenian language. Since then, the Slovenes have identified themselves with the Slovenian nationality of the modern times. Their language and culture were restrained most of the time, except in the Yugoslav period. Being the south-eastern outpost of Roman Catholicism, Slovenia has been an area of the outspoken West-European geopolitical interest for centuries. The western borders of the Islamic world were placed, for more than 400 years, close to Slovenia's borders, in Bosnia, and the Eastern-Orthodox Christianity was spread among Slavonic people of the nearby regions (Gosar, 1993). The peculiarities of this situation are reflected in religious composition of the Slovenia's population. The predominant religion in Slovenia is Roman Catholic. In the 1991 census, 71.4% of the population identified themselves as Roman Catholics, 2.2% as Orthodox, 1.5% as Muslims, and 0.9% as Protestants; 8.8% of inhabitants identified themselves as atheists or did not want to declare their religious beliefs. The religious affiliation of 15% of the population was unknown (ZRSS, op. cit.).

The economic development of Slovenia was for a long time based on the development of industry. Consequently, the proportion of persons employed in industry was increasing continually, most of all due to the decline in agriculture and immigration from southern parts of the former Yugoslavia. During 1948–1991, the proportion of population employed in agricultural sector declined from 50% to 8%. The proportion of population employed in industry reached its highest level of 50% in the 1980s, and since then it has been decreasing, while the proportion of persons employed in services has been increasing. The latter exceeded 45% in 1993 and is still increasing, especially in financial sector. In 1997, the gross domestic product per capita was US$9,163 (SURS, 1999b).

The transition from predominantly agricultural to industrial economy was accompanied by the increase of urban population (Table 16.1). Nowadays, more than half of the population live in urban settlements: 27% in the capital, 15% in cities with more than 20,000 inhabitants, while the others live in 176 small urban settlements. The second half of the population live in 5,763 non-urban settlements. Their average size is 169 inhabitants. Such dispersion of settling caused by the geographic characteristics of Slovenia, its historic development and the wilful policy of polycentric development has prevented a profuse concentration of the population and distinct polarisation into urban and rural areas.

**Table 16.1: Selected Demographic Indicators, 1931–1991, selected years, census data[1]**

| | 1931 | 1961 | 1971 | 1981 | 1991 |
|---|---|---|---|---|---|
| Total population (1,000) | 1,398 | 1,592 | 1,727 | 1,892 | 1,966 |
| Density (inhabitants per km$^2$) | 69.0 | 78.6 | 85.3 | 93.4 | 97.1 |
| Urban population (%) | .. | 33.3 | 38.7 | 48.9 | 50.5 |
| Rural population (%) | 58.8 | 31.6 | 20.4 | 9.2 | 7.6 |
| University graduates (%) | .. | 1.8 | 3.3 | 6.2 | 8.8 |
| Households (1,000) | 287.2 | 458.9 | 515.5 | 594.6 | 640.2 |
| Average size of household | 4.9 | 3.5 | 3.4 | 3.2 | 3.1 |
| Families (1,000) | .. | .. | 440.7 | 522.3 | 551.9 |
| Average size of family | .. | .. | 3.36 | 3.20 | 3.10 |

[1]Refers to the present territory of the Republic of Slovenia
Sources: ZRSS, op. cit.; SURS, 1999b

Simultaneously with economic and social development, the educational attainment of the population improved. In 1953, less then 1% of the population completed university education; by the time of the 1991 census this proportion had risen to 9%. A relatively high proportion – 17% – of the population without completed elementary education (less than 8 years of schooling) in 1991 reflected mostly the educational attainment of the older generations.

## 16.2 Stagnation and Ageing of Population

In 1857, the population within the current borders of Slovenia was 1,101,854. On 31 December 1997, Slovenia had a population of 1,984,923 residents. During this 140-year period, Slovenia's population increased by 80%, which is less than in any of the majority of European countries.

This slow increase was due to extensive emigration during the period of demographic transition, which lasted from the last decade of the 19th century until the 1970s. During this period, emigration could be observed in most European countries, but the intensity of emigration from Slovenia was among the highest. Slovenia's population began to increase faster only after the Second World War, partly due to migration as well.

The population increase was most intensive between 1971 and 1981. During this decade, the annual average growth rate was 9.1 per 1,000 inhabitants. Positive economic development and the shortage of young labour force made Slovenia attractive for emigrants from the other republics of the former Yugoslavia. In the 1980s, economic recession lowered the number of new immigrants, and the disintegration of Yugoslavia in 1991 temporarily completely stopped immigration. Net migration was negative in 1991 and 1992. Besides, in 1993, Slovenia had a negative natural increase for the first time in its recent history.

Total population of Slovenia reached almost 2 million in 1991. From then on, the total population has been steadily decreasing, while the growth rates have been mainly positive (Table 16.2). This discrepancy can be explained in the context of the political and methodological changes that occurred in the 1990s. The influence of the political changes has been twofold. Data collection was affected by changing legislative provisions on citizenship. Until 1991, the Central Population Register contained data regarding all Yugoslav citizens who had permanent residence in Slovenia, irrespective of whether they were living in the country or abroad. Since independence, the Central Population Register includes only data on Slovenian citizens. Data on foreigners have to be collected from administrative sources, which are not yet well adapted to statistical needs. In addition, in 1995 the Statistical Office of the Republic of Slovenia changed the definition of total population. The concept of *de jure* population was replaced by the definition close to international recommendations. Since then, the total population of Slovenia includes Slovene citizens, foreigners with permanent or temporary residence permits, and refugees, if they are living in Slovenia for more than three months. Those who leave Slovenia for more than three months are not counted in the total population of Slovenia.

The population of Slovenia is getting old (Figure 16.1). At the end of 1998, the mean age of men was 36.6 years and of women – 40.0 years; 17% of the population was below 15 years of age, and 14% – over 64 years of age (SURS, 1999c).

**Table 16.2: Population Growth, 1990–1999, in thousands**

| Year | Total population[1] (1,000) | Population increase (decrease) | Natural increase (decrease) | Net migration | Total increase (decrease) |
|---|---|---|---|---|---|
| 1990 | 1,996 | 3.568 | 3.813 | 2.167 | 5.980 |
| 1991 | 2,000 | -1.033 | 2.259 | -3.071 | -0.812 |
| 1992 | 1,999 | -4.828 | 0.649 | -0.387 | 0.262 |
| 1993 | 1,994 | -4.676 | -0.219 | 1.355 | 1.136 |
| 1994 | 1,989 | 0.069 | 0.104 | 0.936 | 1.040 |
| 1995 | 1,990 | 0.789 | 0.012 | 2.507 | 2.519 |
| 1996 | 1,990 | -3.277 | 0.168 | 6.510 | 6.678 |
| 1997 | 1,987 | -2.066 | -0.763 | 2.442 | 1.679 |
| 1998 | 1,985 | -6.589 | -1.183 | .. | .. |
| 1999 | 1,978 | .. | .. | .. | .. |

[1]As of 1 January of a given year
Source: SURS, 1999

The process of ageing has strongly intensified during the last 18 years. At the beginning of that period, the total fertility rate (TFR) dropped below the value of 2.1. Between 1980 and 1997, the number of births had been decreasing on average by 2.8% per year. Another important factor was the declining mortality among middle-aged and older age groups, especially women. However, the prolongation of life had almost no effect on the increase of the percentage of population aged 64 and over. Moreover, the generation effect (consequences of the First and Second World War) was so important, that the percentage of those aged 65 and over diminished in the first half of the 1980s, then stagnated and has been increasing only since 1989.

Human deficit, caused by the two world wars, was particularly pronounced in rural areas because of the significant migration flows from remote rural areas towards cities in the 1960s and 1970s. Therefore, the proportion of the elderly had been increasing constantly in rural areas, while in urban areas it had been decreasing between the 1981 and 1991 censuses. In 1991, the share of population aged 65 and over was 9.8% in urban and 12.1% in rural areas. From then on, the proportion of elderly has been increasing in both areas and the difference between urban and rural settlements is getting smaller. In the future, this difference will probably continue to diminish, because rural-urban migration flows are complemented by migration flows of opposite direction. Besides, external immigration, very important in the second half of the 1960s and in the 1970s and oriented towards urban areas, is not so significant any more.

The influence of migration on the age structure fluctuated according to the prevailing immigration or emigration. A relatively short period of positive net migration, from 1957 to 1990, temporarily slowed the process of ageing. The reduction of the volume of net migration after 1990, older age structure of immigrants, hardly positive or even negative natural population growth – these are the elements that will accelerate the ageing of the Slovenia's population in the near future.

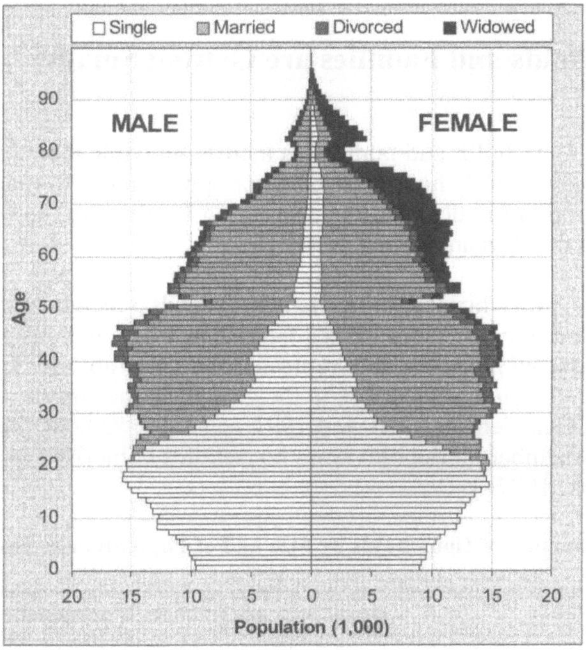


**Figure 16.1: Slovenia's Citizens by Age, Sex and Marital Status**[1]

[1]As of 1 January 1997
Source: based on data from Central Population Register

The expected consequences of such developments are higher expenses for old-age insurance and the increasing costs of health and social services. Therefore, some principle changes in the pension and disability insurance system have been made after 1991. The retirement age was extended by three years, and it became possible to join the pension and disability insurance on a voluntary basis or under certain conditions (if individual is taking care of a child of up to 7 years of age or an elderly person). However, these measures are not sufficient to cope with financial problems arising from the population ageing. A complex reform of the pension and disability insurance system is needed. The Government of Slovenia has already prepared two new proposals for parliamentary approval (MLFSA, 1998), but none was yet accepted as trade unions are against them.

The growing number of elderly, one-fourth of whom are living alone, forced the Government to accept the programme which anticipates the expansion of the institutional care network so that institutions could take care of 4.5% of elderly, the creation of day-care centres and centres for help at home. Special apartments and apartment homes for elderly will be offered as well.

## 16.3 Households and Families are Getting Smaller

The number of households and families is increasing while their size is decreasing. Preferences for one-family households, higher opportunities to realise these preferences (housing opportunities) and the decreasing fertility are the main reasons that households and families are getting smaller.

At present, the average household size hardly exceeds 3 members. Households with two, three and four members represented three-quarters of all households in Slovenia in 1991, and those with one member represented 18% (Table 16.3). The proportion of the latter is increasing, mainly due to the growth in the number of households of elderly people. Between the 1981 and 1991 censuses, 73% of the increase of the number of one-member households were households comprised of persons aged 65 and over (Šircelj, 1997b).

**Table 16.3: Proportion of Households by Size and of Population by Household Size, 1991, per cent**

| | Household size (number of members) | | | | | | | |
|---|---|---|---|---|---|---|---|---|
| | 1 | 2 | 3 | 4 | 5 | 6 | 7+ | Total |
| Households | 18.0 | 21.0 | 21.4 | 25.0 | 8.6 | 3.8 | 2.2 | 100.0 |
| Population | 5.9 | 13.6 | 20.9 | 32.7 | 14.3 | 7.4 | 5.2 | 100.0 |

Sources: SURS, 1998; author's calculations

According to the 1991 census, 74% of households consisted of one single family, 6% – of two or more families and the rest were households without family nucleus. The average number of family members was 3.1. Nearly 80% of families had children; 37.2% of families with children had only one child, 32.2% had two children and only 7.6% had three or more[1]. There is no data available for the recent years (the next census will be carried out in 2001), but given the progressively decreasing fertility, the share of families with two or more children is certainly diminishing.

In the past 20 years, Slovenia's families experienced important changes. Married couples with children accounted for 60% of all families in 1991, which is less than in 1981, while the share of one-parent families and unmarried couples with children increased in the same period. The number and the share of unmarried couples with children more than doubled. Almost all children in these families were younger than 26 (Table 16.4). These changes continued after 1991 but can be illustrated only by the changes in marital status of total population and the proportion of children born outside marriage. The proportions of single and divorced persons as well as of the children born outside marriage are increasing. The decreasing proportions can be observed only for married persons, men and women.

**Table 16.4: Family Structure, 1981 and 1991, per cent**

| Family type | Proportion of families by family type | | Proportion of children under 26 living at parental home by family type |
|---|---|---|---|
| | 1981 | 1991 | 1991 |
| All families | 100.0 | 100.0 | 100.0 |
| Married couples without children | 20.4 | 19.9 | .. |
| Married couples with children | 63.3 | 59.0 | 81.3 |
| Unmarried couples without children | 0.9 | 0.9 | .. |
| Unmarried couples with children | 1.1 | 2.2 | 2.9 |
| Mothers with children | 12.5 | 15.4 | 13.5 |
| Fathers with children | 1.8 | 2.6 | 2.3 |

Sources: ZRSS, op. cit.; author's calculations

## 16.4 Postponement of Events Related to Family Formation

The process of family formation experienced important changes in the last 20 years (Table 16.5). First of all, the proportion of those who have never married decreased to less than 8% in generations born during the Second World War. It seems that this percentage will remain the lowest for a longer time, because the number of marriages as well as the total marriage rates, which were relatively stable from the end of the Second World War to the mid-1970s, began to decrease continually. In 1991, the total first marriage rate for women under 50 was for the first time equal to 0.50. In 1991 and 1992, a slight increase was observed. It is not clear if this increase could be attributed to minor methodological changes in data collection or to the postponed marriages preceded by cohabitation. Since 1994, the decrease has been continuing.

Cohabitation is particularly widespread among young people. Unfortunately, statistical data on cohabitation is very poor, although consensual unions were legally equalised with marriages already twenty years ago. It is estimated that in 1991 about 5% of women aged 20–34 years lived in consensual unions (Table 16.6).

The drop in the number of marriages and the total marriage rates began at the same time as the growth of the number and proportion of extramarital births. Until the 1970s, only about 10% of children were born outside marriage. Since then, their number had increased, and proportion reached 30% of all births and 43% of births of the first order in 1995. The majority of births outside marriage occur to women aged below 20 and above 35. The proportion of extramarital births registered by both parents is increasing: from 55% in 1970 to over 90% from 1993 on. This suggests that a large proportion of extramarital births occurs within a stable partnership.

**Table 16.5: Main Indicators of Nuptiality, 1980–1998, selected years**

| | 1980 | 1985 | 1990 | 1995 | 1998 |
|---|---|---|---|---|---|
| Marriages per 1,000 inhabitants | 6.5 | 4.5 | 4.3 | 4.2 | 3.8 |
| Divorces per 1,000 inhabitants | 1.2 | 1.3 | 0.9 | 0.8 | 1.0 |
| Total first marriage rate | 0.71 | 0.58 | 0.49 | 0.51 | 0.45 |
| Total divorce rate | 0.16 | 0.19 | 0.14 | 0.13 | 0.19 |
| Total fertility rate | 2.11 | 1.68 | 1.46 | 1.29 | 1.23 |
| Extramarital births per 1,000 live births | 13.1 | 19.1 | 24.5 | 29.8 | 33.6 |
| Mean age of women at childbearing | 25.3 | 25.5 | 26.0 | 27.2 | 27.8 |
| Mean age of women at first birth | 22.9 | 23.2 | 23.9 | 25.0 | 25.8 |
| Mean age at first marriage | 22.4 | 22.8 | 23.8 | 25.2 | 25.8 |

Source: SURS, 1999a

Slovenian brides and grooms are young. Since 1960, the mean age at marriage was decreasing continuously, reaching the lowest values in the first half of the 1980s. At that time, the mean age of women at first marriage was between 21.0 and 21.5 years, the same as in many Eastern European countries. In the last ten years, however, the mean age of women and men at first marriage increased by more than 3 years. During the same period, the mean age at first birth increased by only 1.5 year, reaching 25 years of age, which is more than in the compensation period after the Second World War. Since 1994, the mean age of women at first birth has been already lower than the mean age of women at first marriage (Šircelj, 1997a).

**Table 16.6: Cohabited Women by Age, 1991**

| Age group | Cohabited women | | |
|---|---|---|---|
| | Total | Per 100 women | Proportion of those having children (%) |
| -20 | 513 | 0.72 | 54.4 |
| 20–24 | 3,360 | 4.68 | 72.3 |
| 25–29 | 4,210 | 5.48 | 81.0 |
| 30–34 | 3,038 | 3.95 | 84.1 |
| 35–39 | 2,123 | 2.59 | 82.5 |
| 40–44 | 1,297 | 1.84 | 75.4 |
| 45–49 | 775 | 1.38 | 59.1 |
| 50+ | 2,058 | 0.65 | 26.6 |

Sources: SURS, 1999a; author's calculations

Besides the increasing mean age at marriage and at childbearing, very young generations also postpone leaving parental home to a later age. According to results of the *Family and Fertility Survey* (FFS) conducted in 1994–1995[2], the median age at leaving home was 21.6 years for cohorts born before 1970 and 24.5 for those born in 1970–1974 (Kožuh-Novak *et al.*, 1998). Shortage of housing in terms of costs and space is usually considered to be the main reason for late departure from the parental home. In addition, relatively high unemployment among young generations in recent years may also contribute to a later formation of one's own household.

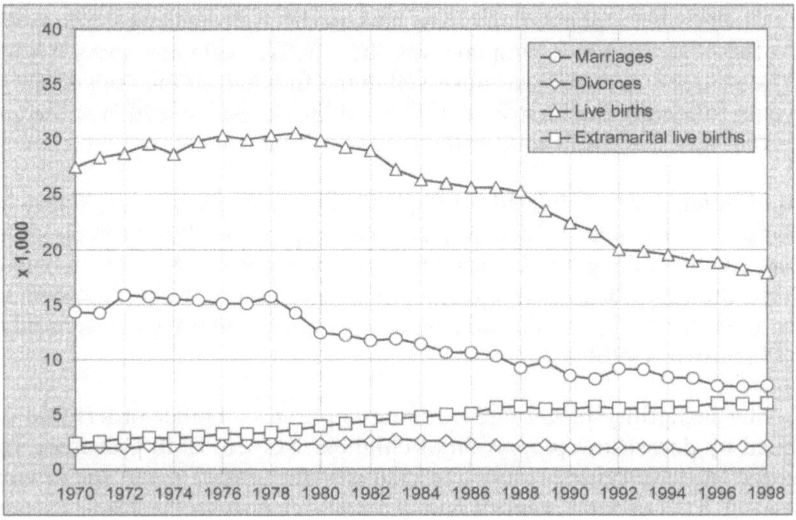


**Figure 16.2: Marriages, Divorces, Total and Extramarital Live Births, 1970–1998**

Source: SURS, 1999a

The sequence of events related to marriage and procreation has changed considerably in young generations. It seems that two types of family formation are prevailing: "traditional" and "modern". In the first one, the eventual cohabitation and the marriage precede the birth of the first child. Couples preferring "traditional" arrangements are, however, more and more postponing the arrival of the first child. In 1989, 68% of first legitimate children were born in the first year of marriage, while in 1997 the proportion hardly reached 55%. The second type of family formation starts with cohabitation, birth of child (children) and then eventually marriage. This behaviour, which was in the past known and accepted by population only in certain parts of Slovenia, gradually spread among the wider population, probably partly under the influence of developments in other European countries. But this influence, if any, refers mostly to family formation and not to family dissolution.

In spite of quite liberal legislation concerning divorce, marriages are relatively stable. Total divorce rate is among the lowest in Europe and quite stable. The changes occur in the timing of divorce; the proportion of divorces after 15 years of marriage is increasing. This fact and decreasing fertility are probably the reason for the decreasing proportion of divorces among families with dependant children. According to the unpublished data of the Ministry of Justice, about 70% of requests for divorce are submitted by women.

## 16.5 Almost Half of Live Births are Births of the First Order

Fertility of Slovenia's population is low and has been decreasing continually since 1880. At that time, the crude birth rate was about 35‰, while nowadays it is less than 10‰. The sharpest decrease was observed in the first half of the 20th century. Only in the years following the First World War and the Second World War the compensation effect was so significant that the crude birth rates increased for a few years.

Expressed in terms of completed fertility, this decrease gives us the following picture: women born around 1875 delivered an average of 4.7 live-born children, their daughters 3.0, granddaughters 2.1 and great-granddaughters 1.8. Women born around 1930 were the first not to have enough children to assure the replacement of generations. Cohort fertility for female generation born in 1964 will be certainly lower than 1.77 (Šircelj, 1998).

The decline in fertility began with limiting children of higher orders and was accompanied by decreasing proportion of childless women. Both processes, together with rejuvenation of brides, resulted in gradually decreasing mean age of women at childbearing. This process stopped with generations born in the 1960s. Women began to postpone childbearing to a more advanced age. These changes in the schedule of births in relation to women's age have resulted in an underestimation of period fertility rates in Slovenia for the last eighteen years.

Total fertility exceeded 2.1 live births per woman until 1980, when it started to decline steeply (Figure 16.3). After the decline of 22% in only 6 years (1980–1986), the stagnation was observed for three years, then a new decrease has begun. In very recent years, the decrease slowed down. Total fertility for 1998 was 1.23. Total fertility has been decreasing for all birth orders: the most – for births of fourth and higher orders and the less – for births of third order. As the proportion of first and second births among all births is very high (85–87% after 1990), total fertility has been decreasing at the same rate as births of first and second order (Table 16.7).

As already mentioned, the main reason for the rapid decrease of the period fertility is the postponement of childbearing to mother's older age. In the post-war period, the mean age of women at childbearing reached the lowest values at the second half of the 1970s and at the beginning of the 1980s, then it began to increase. The mean age at childbearing increased from 25.3 in 1980 to 27.8 in 1998 and the mean age at first birth – from 22.9 to 25.8 years. This trend has accelerated after 1990 and is also reflected in the dynamics of the age-specific fertility rates. From 1980 to 1991, fertility rates were decreasing in all ages, but mostly for teenagers. Since 1992, fertility rates at ages 15–24 are still decreasing, while fertility rates for women in their 30s have increased, however not enough to counteract the declines in younger ages (Figure 16.4).

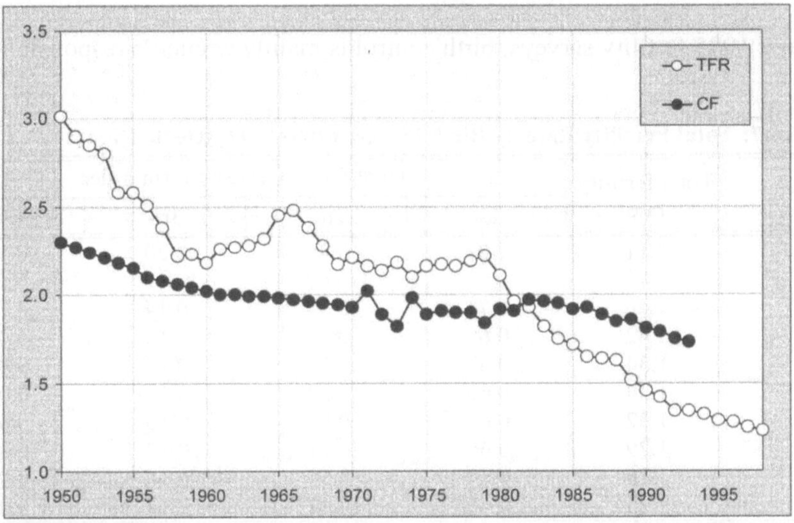


**Figure 16.3: Total Fertility Rate (TFR) and Completed Fertility (CF), 1950–1998**

Sources: SURS, 1999a; author's calculations

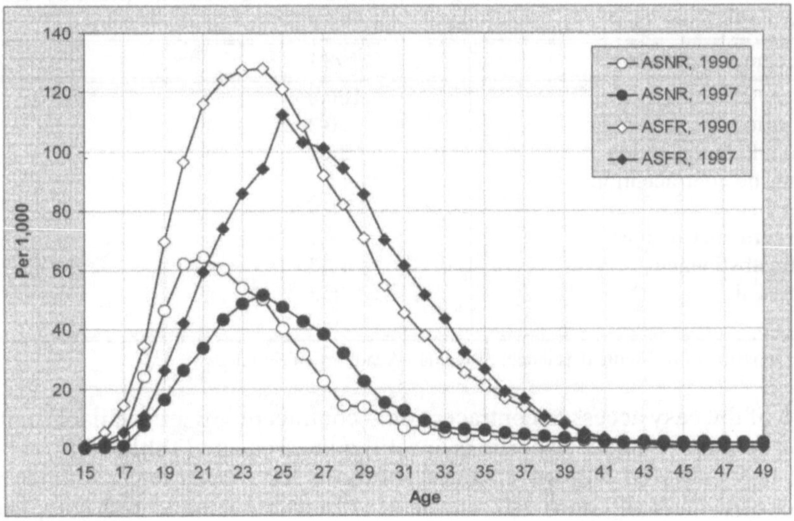


**Figure 16.4: Age-specific Nuptiality (ASNR) and Fertility (ASFR) Rates, 1990 and 1997**

Sources: SURS data; author's calculations

In Slovenia, the deliberate and planned birth control began towards the end of the 19th century, first among the higher social classes and among educated and employed women. It spread to other social classes and groups progressively. In 1955, the first family planning clinic was established. But reliable data on contraceptive methods used by the population is not available for such a long period of time. According to

1989 and 1995 fertility surveys, birth control is mainly women's responsibility and concern.

**Table 16.7: Total Fertility Rate by Birth Order, 1980–1997, selected years**

| Year | Total fertility rate | Total fertility rate by birth order | | | |
|---|---|---|---|---|---|
| | | 1st | 2nd | 3rd | 4th+ |
| 1980[1] | 2.11 | 1.02 | 0.81 | 0.20 | 0.08 |
| 1985 | 1.77 | 0.87 | 0.67 | 0.17 | 0.06 |
| 1990 | 1.46 | 0.71 | 0.57 | 0.14 | 0.04 |
| 1991 | 1.42 | 0.69 | 0.55 | 0.14 | 0.04 |
| 1992 | 1.34 | 0.67 | 0.50 | 0.13 | 0.04 |
| 1993 | 1.34 | 0.65 | 0.52 | 0.13 | 0.04 |
| 1994 | 1.32 | 0.63 | 0.52 | 0.13 | 0.04 |
| 1995 | 1.29 | 0.60 | 0.51 | 0.14 | 0.04 |
| 1996 | 1.28 | 0.60 | 0.50 | 0.14 | 0.04 |
| 1997 | 1.25 | 0.60 | 0.47 | 0.14 | 0.04 |

[1]According to the 1981census, the values are as follows: 2.01, 0.97, 0.77, 0.19, 0.12
Sources: SURS, 1996, 1997, 1998, 1999a-c; SURS, unpublished data; author's calculations

**Table 16.8: Distribution of Women Aged 15–45 and Using Contraception by Method, 1989 and 1995, per cent**

| Contraceptive method | 1989 | 1995 |
|---|---|---|
| Total | 100.0 | 100.0 |
| Sterilisation | 0.3 | 1.1 |
| Hormonal contraception | 25.8 | 32.4 |
| Intrauterine contraception | 11.3 | 14.3 |
| Condom | 6.7 | 13.5 |
| Diaphragm/spermicide | 4.1 | 4.6 |
| Periodic abstinence | 11.5 | 10.4 |
| Withdrawal | 36.3 | 15.7 |
| None | 6.0 | 8.0 |

Source: Department of Medical Science, Slovenian Academy of Sciences

Despite of the easy access to contraception – contraceptives are available and mostly free of charge – induced abortions are still quite frequent (Table 16.8), especially among less educated women. Induced abortions have been legal without restrictions, except medical, since 1977. Data is therefore available and complete. The number and the rate (legal abortions per 1,000 women aged 15–49) of induced abortions was increasing until 1982, mainly due to the increase of the immigrant population, whose reproductive behaviour is very different from the native population. From then on, the age-specific induced abortion rates have been decreasing in all age groups, including teenagers. In 1997, the induced abortion rate for Slovenia was 18.7 per 1,000; i.e. 0.54 abortions per one live birth. More than 95% of induced abortions are done in the first ten weeks of pregnancy (IVZRS, 1997, 1998).

## 16.6 Stagnation of Life Expectancies is Coming to an End

In 1930, life expectancy at birth was 50 years for men and 54 for women, while in the middle of the 1990s it was 71 and 78, respectively. These latter values place Slovenia somewhere in the middle of the European scale: about 6 years of life separate it from the countries with the lowest mortality and 6–7 years from those with the highest mortality.

Since 1930, mortality has been declining steadily, whereas the decline in the male mortality has been interrupted from time to time, especially in the 1960s. In the first half of the 1990s, stagnation in life expectancies was observed again, this time for both sexes. It is generally attributed to the social changes of the transitional period.

The values of life expectancies at birth are influenced by mortality experience at all ages. Therefore, the increase or decrease in the value of life expectancy at birth does not mean that mortality increased or decreased in all ages: in the period from 1990–1991 to 1993–1994, the values of life expectancy at birth stagnated due to the increase of probabilities of dying in almost all ages, but not for children up to 15 years of age. Mortality continued to decrease only for children, above all for infants. In 1997, infant mortality was 5.2 ‰ (Table 16.9).

**Table 16.9: Live Births and Infant Mortality Rates, 1980–1997, selected years**

| Year | Live births | Infant mortality rate | Early neonatal mortality rate | Late neonatal mortality rate | Post-neonatal mortality rate |
|---|---|---|---|---|---|
| | | Per 1,000 live births | | | |
| 1980 | 29,902 | 15.3 | 8.7 | 2.0 | 4.5 |
| 1985 | 25,933 | 13.0 | 7.0 | 1.6 | 4.4 |
| 1990 | 22,368 | 8.4 | 4.1 | 1.0 | 3.3 |
| 1991 | 21,583 | 8.2 | 4.6 | 1.1 | 2.5 |
| 1992 | 19,982 | 8.9 | 4.7 | 1.2 | 3.0 |
| 1993 | 19,793 | 6.8 | 3.4 | 1.2 | 2.2 |
| 1994 | 19,463 | 6.5 | 2.8 | 1.2 | 2.5 |
| 1995 | 18,980 | 5.5 | 2.6 | 0.4 | 2.5 |
| 1996 | 18,788 | 4.8 | 2.5 | 0.7 | 1.6 |
| 1997 | 18,165 | 5.2 | 2.9 | 0.9 | 1.4 |

Sources: SURS, unpublished data; author's calculations

In 1994–1995, life expectancy at birth increased again because of improved survival rates in almost all age groups and for both sexes. In spite of that, the survival rates for men aged 15–34 and for women aged 15–49 were still lower than in the years 1990–1991. Life expectancy at birth was prolonged due to decreasing mortality rates of children and old persons (dependent population) and not because of the decreasing mortality rates of economically active population. Only in 1996–1997, survival rates finally exceeded those for 1989–1990 in almost all age groups for men and women (Figure 16.5).

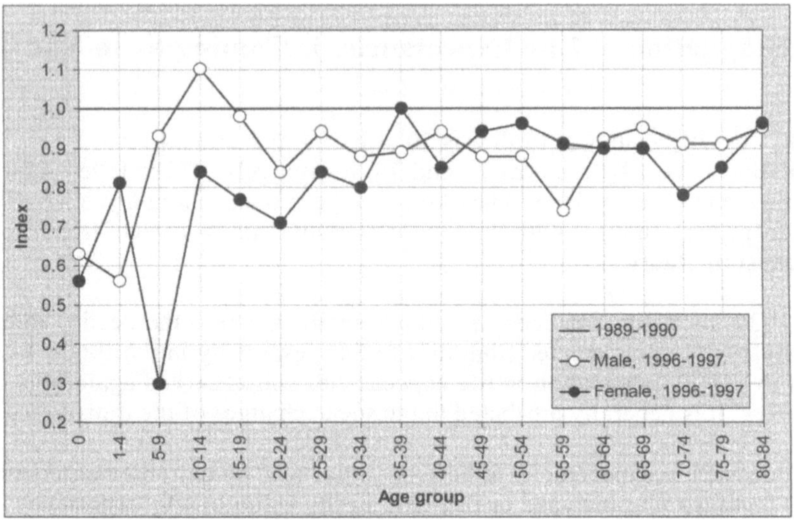


**Figure 16.5: Changes in Probability of Dying by Age and Sex Between 1989–1990 and 1996–1997[1]**

[1] 1989–1990 as 100

Sources: SURS, 1999a; author's calculations

The difference between male and female life expectancy at birth due to premature deaths of adult men was increasing until 1990–1991, when the difference was 7.84 years. In recent years, the gap has been getting smaller, but is still exceeding 7.4 years (Table 16.10). The improving of survival rates has been slightly quicker for men than for women.

**Table 16.10: Life Expectancy at Certain Ages by Sex, 1988–1997, in years**

| Period | Male at age | | | | | Female at age | | | | |
|---|---|---|---|---|---|---|---|---|---|---|
| | 0 | 1 | 45 | 60 | 65 | 0 | 1 | 45 | 60 | 65 |
| 1988–1989 | 68.86 | 68.54 | 27.35 | 16.11 | 13.03 | 76.72 | 76.36 | 33.73 | 20.58 | 16.55 |
| 1989–1990 | 69.38 | 69.02 | 27.68 | 16.36 | 13.24 | 77.19 | 76.75 | 34.03 | 20.78 | 16.70 |
| 1990–1991 | 69.54 | 69.26 | 27.86 | 16.38 | 13.22 | 77.38 | 76.87 | 34.01 | 20.76 | 16.68 |
| 1991–1992 | 69.45 | 69.15 | 27.91 | 16.29 | 13.22 | 77.25 | 76.80 | 33.99 | 20.80 | 16.76 |
| 1992–1993 | 69.40 | 69.02 | 27.83 | 16.23 | 13.17 | 77.29 | 76.81 | 34.06 | 20.82 | 16.18 |
| 1993–1994 | 69.58 | 69.08 | 27.29 | 16.37 | 13.26 | 77.38 | 76.85 | 34.13 | 20.85 | 16.82 |
| 1994–1995 | 70.27 | 69.70 | 28.36 | 16.64 | 13.49 | 77.76 | 77.22 | 34.45 | 21.15 | 17.06 |
| 1995–1996 | 70.79 | 70.22 | 28.66 | 16.81 | 13.59 | 78.25 | 77.58 | 34.71 | 21.45 | 17.34 |
| 1996–1997 | 71.01 | 70.43 | 28.89 | 17.01 | 13.80 | 78.62 | 77.94 | 35.00 | 21.68 | 17.55 |

Sources: Šircelj, 1997c; SURS, 1997, 1998

The vast majority of deaths (80%) occur due to circulatory diseases, neoplasms and deaths caused by accidents, poisonings and violence. Their frequency varies according to the age. In young ages, road accidents are the leading cause of deaths, especially among men. Persons aged 15 to 49 most frequently die from injuries; men five times more often than women do. Neoplasms and circulatory diseases take at this age only the second and the third position. In the age group 50–64 years, neoplasms become the most frequent cause of death, followed by circulatory diseases, injuries and diseases of the digestive system. Compared with women in the same age group, the risk of dying from those diseases is 1.5 (neoplasms) to 3.4 (injuries) times higher for men in recent years. According to analyses of differential mortality, it is the less educated segment of the population who is markedly exposed to premature mortality from circulatory and digestive diseases and from accidents (MLFSA, 1998).

One of the specific characteristics of mortality in Slovenia is the high frequency of suicide. As it is the most common among the aged, the number of suicides has been increasing slowly and constantly, but no change occurred in the transition period. For men, the proportion of suicide among other causes of deaths ranges between 4 and 5%. Men prevail among traffic casualties as well. The mortality due to road accidents was the highest at the end of the 1970s, then it has been decreasing, but is still high, about 20 per 1,000 deaths in recent years. The intention of the new law on road transport safety – brought into force in 1998 – is to reduce the number of road accidents considerably.

The excess mortality of men is an acute health problem and a social problem as well. Namely, the frequency of dying is the highest at the ages of family formation. The disintegration of families is, especially for children, a bitter experience, which – more frequently than we usually imagine – is brought about by the death of one of the parents. It is estimated that in 1994 the death of one of parents, mostly father, affected about 500 children aged under 19 (SC UNICEF, 1995).

After 1990, many countries undergoing transition have experienced a sharp decline in life expectancies, while the mortality in other parts of Europe continued to decline. In these developments, Slovenia has an intermediate position. Despite that, experts are concerned about the potential impact of high unemployment, caused by transition to free market economy, on the mental health of middle-aged people, whom the political and other changes of the early 1990s have driven into social insecurity, which they had never experienced before.

## 16.7 Old Migration Pattern Recovered

Slovenia has for a long period been a region of emigration. Emigration was the most significant between 1880 and the First World War, when annual net migration amounted to one-half of the natural increase. After 1930, this trend subsided, but emigration was still greater than immigration until some years after the Second World War. According to official statistics, net migration became positive at the end of the 1950s. However, if persons who have temporarily, but for more than one year, lived and worked abroad (in accordance with the UN recommendations on international migration) are included among emigrants, Slovenia would become a country of immigration only towards the end of the 1970s.

Slovenia received the greatest immigration flow between 1971 and 1981, when net migration represented 41% of population growth. The immigration flow originated from the parts of the former Yugoslavia, especially from Croatia and Bosnia and Herzegovina, and was in fact considered as internal migration, while the emigration flow was directed towards western and northern Europe, mainly towards Germany, Austria, Switzerland and Sweden (Šircelj *et al.*, 1992).

Emigration touched mainly the less developed regions of Slovenia, while the immigration flow was directed mainly to the cities and industrial centres, which resulted in the ageing of the population of the first and the rejuvenation of the latter. This process was accelerated by internal migrations, also oriented towards urban areas. Regional distribution of the population was changing quickly.

Immigration was slowly changing the ethnic composition of Slovenia's population, especially in urban areas. The former Italian and German minorities, progressively diminishing after the First and the Second World War, were replaced by ethnic groups of a similar size, mostly of Slavonic origin (Croats, Serbs, Muslims). The problems of attitudinal, cultural, social and linguistic nature have emerged (Gosar, 1993). With regard to demographic phenomena among immigrants, the most evident different patterns compared to native population occurred among women of reproductive age. Lower mean age at childbearing and higher prevalence of induced abortions as the method of birth control were characteristic for immigrant women.

Since 1991, the immigration and emigration flows diminished considerably (Table 16.11). Simultaneously, their nature changed as well. Migration flows caused by different levels of economic development were for a few years replaced by migration flows with political and ethnic background. From strictly demographic point of view, this modification was expressed in very quick increase of the mean age of migrants. The data for recent years, however, indicates that the former migration pattern is being restored. In 1996, net migration already exceeded that of 1990 and the mean age of migrants began to decrease. Although the borders of East European countries opened after 1989, the main direction of migrant streams remains the same: from Southeast (successor states of the former Yugoslavia) to Northwest (West and Central European countries) and back. Besides this main stream, the most important is the one coming from the successor states of the Soviet Union. The immigrants from these states are mainly women.

In 1992 and 1993, Slovenia received more than 30 thousand refugees (persons under temporary protection) from Croatia and Bosnia and Herzegovina. At the beginning of 1999, there were still about 3.3 thousand of them living in Slovenia with a status of refugee (SURS, 1999c), while others had returned to their home countries or immigrated to other European countries or have acquired a temporary residence in Slovenia. Since 1995, the refugees who have got a temporary residence in Slovenia are included in the total population of Slovenia. In 1999, according to the data of

Administrative Internal Affairs Directorate of the Ministry of Interior, 2,600 refugees from Kosovo got a temporary protection in Slovenia.

**Table 16.11: External Migration, 1990, 1991 and 1996**

| Country | Immigrants | | | Emigrants | | |
|---|---|---|---|---|---|---|
| | 1990 | 1991 | 1996 | 1990 | 1991 | 1996 |
| Total | 7,075 | 5,989 | 1,500 | 4,908 | 9,060 | 803 |
| Austria | 21 | 25 | 72 | 48 | 70 | 111 |
| Bosnia and Herzegovina | 3,232 | 1,884 | 301 | 1,601 | 3,507 | 47 |
| France | 11 | 13 | 16 | 5 | 8 | 12 |
| Croatia | 2,094 | 2,860 | 562 | 1,704 | 1,852 | 177 |
| Italy | 17 | 16 | 40 | 30 | 23 | 33 |
| Yugoslavia | 1,214 | 861 | 206 | 1,266 | 3,225 | 87 |
| Macedonia | 302 | 164 | 27 | 149 | 276 | 11 |
| Germany | 84 | 96 | 136 | 59 | 52 | 174 |
| Sweden | 10 | 7 | 9 | 3 | 1 | 4 |
| Switzerland | 8 | 5 | 18 | 9 | 9 | 52 |
| Canada | 12 | 11 | 19 | 11 | 8 | 17 |
| United States | 13 | 4 | 27 | 6 | 3 | 29 |
| Other countries | 57 | 43 | 67 | 17 | 26 | 49 |

Source: SURS, 1998

With the establishment of an independent state and the changing political situation in Europe, Slovenia has been facing new types of international movements and various problems have been arising in this relation. In particular, the increasing number of people try to use Slovenia – situated at the border of EU – as a transitional post on their way to the West. As the issue of refugees, asylum seekers and illegal migrants became more acute, Slovenia started implementation of a specific immigration policy. In 1997, the Law on Temporary Refuge and in 1999 the Law on Asylum were adopted. In 1998, the Government of Slovenia adopted the Resolution on Immigration Policy.

In sum, the Government adopted an immigration policy that respects international agreements while encourages economic and social development of Slovenia. According to the 1998 Resolution, the immigration policy aims to preserve balance between the immigration and labour force demand; enable family reunion; and encourage immigration of Slovenia's citizens. Social and economic integration of immigrants is considered to be a common responsibility of Slovenian society and the immigrants themselves. In accordance with the 1999 Law on Foreigners, the Parliament is obliged to adopt the Resolution on Migration Policy every second year. In the future, quotas for stay permits of foreigners will be provided on the basis of this resolution.

## 16.8 Population Policy

In Slovenia, a comprehensive and integrated population policy has not been yet introduced. There were some attempts to establish such a policy in the 1980s and in 1993, but without success. In 1993, the Government of Slovenia set up the National Committee for Population Policy. It has prepared the Slovenian National Report for Cairo conference in 1994 (MLFSA, 1998) and started the elaboration of the report on demographic situation in Slovenia, including suggestions for appropriate population policy. Though the work of the Committee has been stagnating for almost two years, many elements of social policy can be considered as elements of population policy as well. Furthermore, changes introduced after 1991 are generally in line with the population-related policy measures being put forward already in the pre-transition period.

Awareness of the consequences of the declining fertility was solely a matter of experts until the spectacular drop of the TFR after 1980. Population policy measures have been requested although Slovenia has been gradually introducing numerous measures of social policy. Maternity leave had been extended two times in the last 20 years: in 1975 from 3 to 8 months and in 1986 to 12 months. From 1975 on, it is divided into maternal leave (105 days) and parental leave (260 days). Fathers are entitled to parental leave if they agree upon with child's mother, but only a negligible number of fathers have taken this opportunity. Financial supplement for maternity and parental leave amounts to 100% of the average wage or salary received by the person during the 12 months before the beginning of maternity or parental leave. This supplement is the right derived from employment. Mothers who are not in the paid employment (15% in 1997) are entitled to parental supplement, which is about 19% of the average net monthly earnings.

Parent(s) get layette or financial assistance for every new-born child from 1980 onwards. They also receive child allowances. The amount of these allowances has always been related to the family income, but the threshold has been changing. In the 1980s, the proportion of children receiving child allowances was very low, while at present it is about 80% due to changes in legislation in 1993.

In addition to direct benefits, the state provides families with indirect benefits such as subsidies for transport of school students, school meals, scholarships, textbooks, kindergartens and tax relief. Progressive tax relief for families with children was introduced in 1991. It depends on the level of family income and the child order. The amount of all (direct and indirect) state benefits provided to families represents about 5% of the GDP. This proportion will be increased if the Parliament approves the government proposal (1998) to gradually extend the parental leave up to 305 days; to introduce paternity leave (45 days); to make fiscal changes in favour of low-income social strata; and to establish more flexible working arrangements for parents of pre-school and school children.

The aim of the government proposal is: to reduce income inequalities among families which have been increasing during the transition period and are expected to enlarge with the introduction of the new tax system (VAT); to make parenthood more equally shared by mothers and fathers; and to enable better combination of professional and family activities. The first step towards the achievement of these goals was made in May 1999. Child allowances have been raised and, as a result, the total sum of state benefits paid in the form of child allowances has increased by 30 % (based on MLFSA data). In addition, their amount is now related to the birth order of the child as well.

While some political parties are in favour of longer parental leave and more support to large families, as proposed by the Government, many experts, especially women, do not agree with the prolonging parental leave because this could reduce employment opportunities for women. Indeed, female labour force participation is traditionally very high. According to the 1991 census, 46.9% of the total female population was economically active, while among women aged 25–44 this indicator was 90%[3]. As the part-time employment is still rare among working women, the proportion of children enrolled in pre-school child-care institutions is also high and was 58% in 1996–1997. Day-care facilities gradually developed in the socialist period have not significantly changed during the transition period. Private day-care institutions, which have been developing since1993, accept only small proportion of pre-school children.

The adoption of the new Constitution in 1991 – according to which, the free choice of childbearing is the basic human freedom and no more the basic human right as it was before – did not affect the legal regulations adopted in 1977 in regard to family planning. According to the Constitution, "Persons shall be free to decide on the births of their children. The State shall ensure that persons have every opportunity to exercise this freedom and shall create such conditions as enable parents to freely choose on the births of their children".

## 16.9 Conclusion

Together with independence won in 1991, Slovenia got a new political and economic system. These novelties involved, among other, temporary change in the migration pattern, temporary stagnation of life expectancy and rapid increase of unemployment.

Changes in size, direction, sex and age composition of migration flows were caused by Slovenia's independence, by conflicts emerged from disintegration of the former Yugoslavia as well as political changes in Eastern Europe. On the other hand, it seems that the previous pattern of migration flows is going to be restored, although this time on the level of international migration. Kin relationships originating from the former Yugoslavia, related languages and higher standard of living are most likely to attract immigrants from the other successor states of the former Yugoslavia to Slovenia.

The period of stagnating life expectancies was relatively short and no changes were observed in cause-specific mortality rates. The detailed study conducted by the National Institute of Public Health, which investigated the influence of transition period on mortality risks, did not find any relevant influence. But the proportion of household expenditures on health services and voluntary health insurance has been increasing considerably since 1992. As Slovenia's GDP is the highest among the countries undergoing transition, it may explain why the transition process, which involves such changes in health care system as a shift in the responsibility for health care costs from institutions to the individual, did not affect mortality risks in Slovenia as much as in other transitional countries.

The decline of fertility has been continuing during the transition period, but at present it is less pronounced than it was in the 1980s. According to population projections elaborated in 1993 by the Statistical Office, a slight increase of the TFR was expected after 1995 as a consequence of changes in timing of births, however, this assumption has not been proved right (Šircelj *et al.*, 1995). It seems that the negative influence of social and economic changes, especially in terms of increasing unemployment rates after 1990, has affected the fertility level. Although in 1995 the financial supplement for maternity and parental leave was extended to mothers (fathers) whose paid employment is terminated without their violation or fault during pregnancy of the mother, the fear of unemployment and unemployment itself seem to play an important role in decision-making about childbearing.

All the above mentioned changes can be considered as short-term, related to transition process, while first signs of long-term changes, i.e. changes in the demographic behaviour, could be observed already in the second half of the 1970s. The most important ones refer to family formation and dissolution: increasing cohabitation and proportion of children born outside marriage; increasing mean age at marriage and childbearing; decreasing frequency of marriages and very recently – increasing frequency of divorces. When the first demographic transition hardly came to an end, the first signs of the second one have already emerged.

## Notes

1. According to Slovenia's statistics, a family consists of parents (both or one) and their unmarried children whatever their age living in the same household, or of husband and wife (or man and woman living in consensual union) without children.
2. *Fertility and Family Survey* (FFS) was conducted in Slovenia in 1994–1995 by the Institute of Public Health in cooperation with the Statistical Office of the Re-

public of Slovenia and University Clinical Centre – Clinic for Gynaecology and Obstetrics.

3. Economically active population was defined as persons who worked and who were paid in-kind or money at the time of the census. Economically active were also all those who were looking for their first or new employment at the time of the census and those who temporarily ceased to be employed due to serving in the army or serving a prison sentence. In Slovenia, part-time jobs are possible only for medical reasons.

## References


Gosar, A. (1993), Nationalities of Slovenia – Changing ethnic structures in Central Europe, *Geo Journal*, July.

Kožuh-Novak, M. *et al.* (1998) *Rodnostno vedenje Slovencev*, Ljubljana: Znanstveno-raziskovalni center SAZU-Založba ZRC.

IVZRS (Institute of Public Health) (1997), *Zdravstveni statističeni letopis Slovenije 1997*, Vol. 37(1), Ljubljana: Institut za varovanje zdravja Republike Slovenije.

IVZRS (Institute of Public Health) (1998), *Zdravstveno varstvo 1998*, Ljubljana: Institut za varovanje zdravja Republike Slovenije.

(1994), *Magyarorszag nemzetisegeinek es a szomszedos allamok magyarasaganak statisztikaja (1910–1990)*, Budapest.

MLFSA (Ministry of Labour, Family and Social Affairs) (1994), *Slovenian National Report*, Presented at the International Conference on Population and Development, Cairo, 1994, Ljubliana: MLFSA.

MLFSA (Ministry of Labour, Family and Social Affairs) (1998), *Slovenia – National Report*, Presented at Regional Population Meeting, Budapest, December 1998, Lubljana: MLFSA.

SC UNICEF (Slovenian Committee for UNICEF) (1995), *Situation Analysis of the Position of Children and Families in Slovenia*. Ljubljana: SC UNICEF.

SURS (Statistical Office of the Republic of Slovenia) (1996), *Rezultati raziskovanj št. 664*, Ljubljana: Statistični urad Republike Slovenije.

SURS (Statistical Office of the Republic of Slovenia) (1997), *Rezultati raziskovanj št. 685*, Ljubljana: Statistični urad Republike Slovenije.

SURS (Statistical Office of the Republic of Slovenia) (1998), *Rezultati raziskovanj št. 703*, Ljubljana: Statistični urad Republike Slovenije.

SURS (Statistical Office of the Republic of Slovenia) (1999a), *Rezultati raziskovanj št. 730*, Ljubljana: Statistični urad Republike Slovenije.

SURS (Statistical Office of the Republic of Slovenia) (1999b), *Statistične informacije št. 93*, Ljubljana: Statistični urad Republike Slovenije.

SURS (Statistical Office of the Republic of Slovenia) (1999c), *Statistične informacije št. 112*, Ljubljana: Statistični urad Republike Slovenije.

Šircelj, M. (1997a), *Demographic Situation in Slovenia*, Strasbourg: Council of Europe.

Šircelj, M. (1997b), Living arrangements and demographic characteristics of elderly population in Slovenia, In: *Social and Economic Aspects of the Ageing Societies. Proceedings of 5th biannual European IUCISD Conference*, Ljubljana.

Šircelj, M. (1997c), *Tablice umrljivosti prebivalstva Slovenije, 1980–1982 – 1994–1995*, Ljubljana: Statistični urad Republike Slovenije.

Šircelj, M. (1998), Demografski razvoj Slovenije, *IB revija*, Vol. 32, pp. 1–3, Ljubljana: Urad Republike Slovenije za makroekonomske analize in razvoj.

Šircelj, M. *et al.* (1992), *Vrednotenje dosedanjega razvoja ter na inov in metod spremljanja selitev v Slovenijo*, Ljubljana: Zavod Republike Slovenije za makroekonomske analize in razvoj.

Šircelj, M. *et al.* (1995), *Projekcije prebivalstva Republike Slovenije 1995–2020*, Ljubljana: Statistični urad Republike Slovenije.

Zupančič, J. (1993), Socialgeographic Transformation and National Identity – the Case of the Slovene Minority in Carinthia (Austria). In: *Geo Journal.* July.

ZRSS (Statistical Office of the Republic of Slovenia 1994) (1994), *Statistični letopis 1995 Statistical Yearbook*, Ljubljana: Zavod Republike Slovenije za statistiko.

# 17

# Demographic Situation in Ukraine in the Transition Period

Valentyna Steshenko

## 17.1 Introduction

Ukraine belongs to the group of the largest countries of Europe in terms of land area (603.7 thousand kilometres) and size of population (50.1 million); 67.9% of the Ukrainian population lives in urban settlements. At the beginning of 1998, 2,346.5 thousand people lived in the territories polluted by radiation as a result of the Chernobyl disaster. Ukraine is a multinational country. According to the last population census (1989), Ukrainians make up 72.7%, Russians – 22.1%, Jews – 0.9%, Belarus – 0.9%, and other nationalities – 3.4% (SSCU, 1999a).

Ukraine became independent in August 1991 and is currently developing towards a market economy and democracy. But its economic situation is in deep crisis resulting from the transition to a model different in principle from the previous state of the economy, and the dismantling of the former Soviet economic system.

## 17.2 Dynamics, Sex and Age Composition of the Population

The size of the population of Ukraine systematically increased after the Second World War (Figure 17.1). Recently this tendency has changed. For the first time, the population of Ukraine began to decline during peacetime.

This is mostly conditioned by the socio-economic crisis engulfing Ukraine. Ukraine's economic experience has been characterised by a significant decline of production and a decrease of labour productivity. Prices have been rising but real wages were falling. All these factors are leading to a fall in the living standards of the vast majority of population and to the spread of poverty. Low pensions of the elderly also exacerbate the poverty. Rising unemployment further contributes to lower living standards. Poverty is the main complicating factor in the formation of both the quantitative and qualitative parameters of population reproduction (UNDP, 1997).

The main negative socio-demographic consequence of this economic crisis is depopulation. While initial population decrease due to death rates rising above birth rates was compensated by immigration, after 1993 such compensation ceased and the absolute number of people in Ukraine began to decline. At the beginning of 1993, the actual population was about 52.2 million; at the beginning of 1999 it was 50.1 million (SSCU, 1999a, 1999b), that is a population decrease of 2.1 million, including 83.6% due to natural decrease and 16.4% due to net migration.

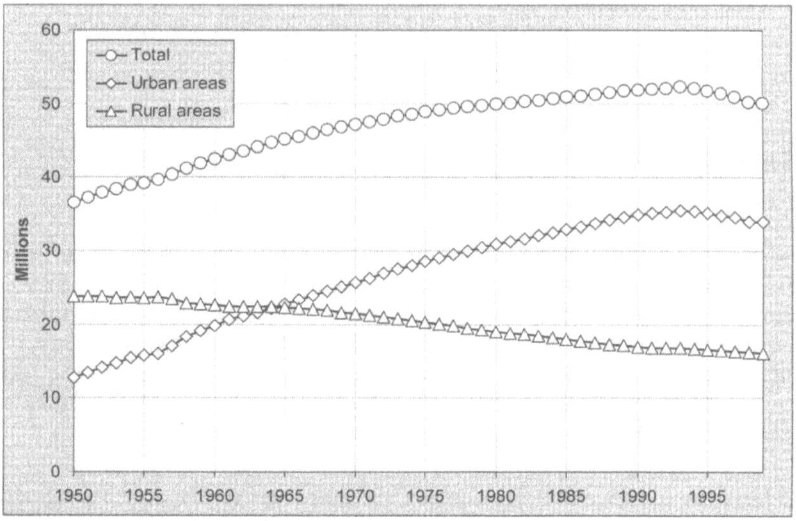


**Figure 17.1: Population, 1950–1999**

Source: based on SSCU data

The proportion of males in Ukraine was 46.5% (46.7% in urban areas and 46.1% in rural areas) at the beginning of 1999. The sex composition that was strongly influenced by the Second World War has improved gradually. The sex ratio (number of men per 1,000 women) in 1999 was 868 (1,046 for ages 0–14; 944 for ages 15–59; and 556 for ages 60 and older). The men's numerical superiority is observed up to age 31 (28 in urban areas and 43 in rural areas) (SSCU, 1999b).

Age composition of the population is the result of the main demographic processes and is a major precondition for their further development. The essential feature of lasting changes in the age composition of the population in Ukraine is ageing. The main cause of population ageing is low fertility. A high level of ageing is characteristic for the Ukrainian population (Table 17.1). According to data on the age composition of the population by three large groups (children, population aged 15–59, and people aged 60 years and older), the proportion of the population under 15 decreased by 14.4% during 1989–1999, while the proportion of those aged 60 years and older increased by 11.7%. The most significant decrease among children was seen in urban areas (18.3%). The share of children is declining both in males and females, especially in cities, as a result of the fertility drop. The proportion of the population aged 15–59 is relatively stable, but it should be noted that large differences between percentages of men and women aged 15–59 exist in rural and urban areas. It is much lower in rural areas. The proportion of women aged 60 and older is 56.5% higher than that of men in all types of areas. That is caused, most of all, by a higher life expectancy of women. The proportion of rural women aged 60 and older is very high – 31.4%.

**Table 17.1: Population by Age Groups, 1989 and 1999[1], per cent**

| Age group | Total | | Urban | | Rural | |
|---|---|---|---|---|---|---|
| | 1989 | 1999 | 1989 | 1999 | 1989 | 1999 |
| | | | Total | | | |
| 0–14 | 21.6 | 18.5 | 21.9 | 17.9 | 20.9 | 19.7 |
| 15–59 | 60.4 | 61.4 | 63.2 | 64.7 | 54.9 | 54.6 |
| 60+ | 18.0 | 20.1 | 14.9 | 17.4 | 24.2 | 25.7 |
| | | | Male | | | |
| 0–14 | 23.8 | 20.4 | 24.0 | 19.7 | 23.4 | 21.9 |
| 15–59 | 63.4 | 64.2 | 65.1 | 66.6 | 60.0 | 59.1 |
| 60+ | 12.8 | 15.4 | 10.9 | 13.7 | 16.6 | 19.0 |
| | | | Female | | | |
| 0–14 | 19.7 | 16.9 | 20.1 | 16.4 | 18.8 | 17.9 |
| 15–59 | 57.9 | 59.0 | 61.6 | 63.0 | 50.7 | 50.7 |
| 60+ | 22.4 | 24.1 | 18.3 | 20.6 | 30.5 | 31.4 |

[1]As of 1 January of a given year
Source: SSCU data

According to a scale created by French scholar J. Garnet, and then developed by Polish demographer E. Rosset (1968), the level of population ageing in Ukraine is high in urban areas, and very high in rural areas, which, by far, are at the highest stage of demographic ageing. The mean age of the rural population was 39.8 years, while of the urban population – 37.2 years in the beginning of 1999. The level of ageing of both urban and rural women can be characterised as very high and urban men are presumed to be at the entry level of demographic ageing. Rural men can be characterised as a population with a very high level of ageing and rural women – as being at an extremely high level of the demographic ageing. This is confirmed not only by the high proportion of the population aged 60 and older, but also by such measure of ageing as the ratio of the population aged 60 and older to the population aged 80 and older. For urban men that index at the beginning of 1999 was 6.7, for rural men – 8.0, for women – 11.9 and 15.2, respectively. The situation of demographic ageing looks much more unfavourable, if the distribution of the population by age groups, which make up the work force, is considered (retirement age in Ukraine is 60 years for men and 55 years for women). The population of working age made up 59.9% of urban population in Ukraine and only 49.5% of rural population in 1999, while the population of retirement age was 20.5% and 29.9%, accordingly. Therefore, it may be concluded that Ukraine is becoming one of the most aged populations in the world.

A much higher proportion of elderly population – and a somewhat higher proportion of children – in rural areas than in urban, leads to much higher dependency ratio of the rural population (Table 17.2). In 1999, there were 669 persons of non-working age in urban areas per every 1,000 persons of working age in 1999, while in rural areas there were 1,019. So, the dependency ratio was 1.5 times higher in rural areas as compared to urban. This is an important demographic factor determining the living standards in urban and rural areas.

**Table 17.2: Dependency Ratios[1], 1989 and 1999[2]**

| | Total | | Urban | | Rural | |
|---|---|---|---|---|---|---|
| | 1989 | 1999 | 1989 | 1999 | 1989 | 1999 |
| Non-working population | 791 | 768 | 696 | 669 | 1,017 | 1,019 |
| Of which: | | | | | | |
| Young-age population | 412 | 356 | 397 | 327 | 447 | 430 |
| Population of retirement age and older | 379 | 412 | 299 | 342 | 570 | 589 |

[1]Per 1,000 working-age population
[2]As of 1 January of a given year
Source: SSCU data

Considerable differences between urban and rural areas are also observed in the structure of the dependency ratio. In urban areas, in 1999 it consisted of 327 children and 342 persons of retirement age and older, while in rural areas it was 430 children and 589 persons of retirement age and older. In other words, in the structure of the dependency ratio in rural areas, the number of children was 1.3 times higher than in urban areas, and of elderly population – 1.7 times. This situation creates not only different demographic prerequisites for living standards formation in urban and rural areas, but also a different level of home workload for women, because upbringing of children and care of elderly family members is considered to be a primarily woman's responsibility.

The age pyramid (Figure 17.2) shows particularities of the sex and age composition of the Ukrainian population. It also provides an overview of the impact of the decline in birth rates in recent years on the sex and age composition of population. A shrinkage of the base of the pyramid means a reduction in favourable demographic and, consequently, social and economic prospects for Ukraine.

Ageing of the population results in a number of demographic and socio-economic problems in Ukraine. First, it diminishes "the demo-reproductive potential", which resides in the age structure of a population, as well as the labour potential of the population (Steshenko and Piskunov, 1996a). The reduction of the demo-reproductive potential will create problems in overcoming depopulation. Second, the deepening of the population ageing is an extremely important phenomenon not only from a demographic but also from an economic point of view, as it results in a decline of the percentage of the young working age group of the population as well as in the other changes in its composition, which do not promote social and economic development.

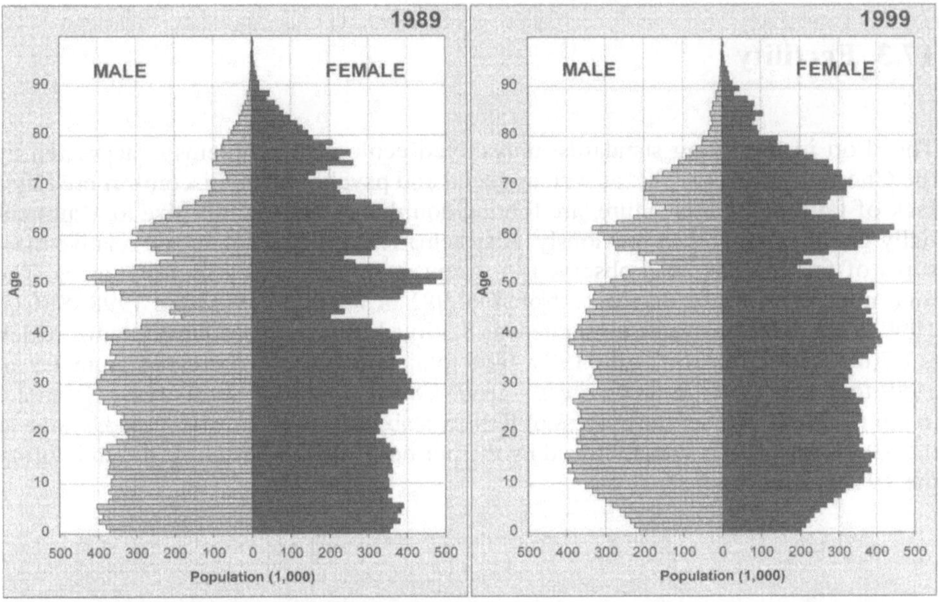


**Figure 17.2: Age Pyramid, 1989 and 1999[1]**

[1]As of 1 January of a given year

Source: author's calculations based on SSCU data

Though there is no concrete evidence about the correlation between age and labour productivity, it is customary to consider that young population is the producer of innovation, who quickly perceive novelties in the production, have higher dynamism, i.e. have those qualities, which are necessary for scientific and technical progress. At the same time, the preconditions for the more effective participation of seniors in the process of production and public life are not found yet. So, now societal labour productivity, to a great extent, depends on the age composition of the economically active population.

Moreover, the ageing of the population requires a constant increase in pension funds. However, to do so under the conditions of an overall drop in economic productivity reduces the opportunities for reconstruction and modernisation of the economic base. The living standards of the elderly in Ukraine are below the basic survival level (World Bank, 1996). The current situation is the result of the fact that the overwhelming part of state "pension capital" and all pensioners' personal savings "disappeared" during the unsuccessful attempt to reform the economy during the transition period. Thus, in the case of Ukraine, the population ageing is a factor, which hinders overcoming both the depopulation and socio-economic crisis.

## 17.3 Fertility

The drop in the living standards, unresolved ecological problems exacerbated by the Chernobyl catastrophe, as well as social and psychological discomfort bred by a lack of faith in a better future, are forcing couples to limit family size to a substantially greater degree than previously. A systematic drop of absolute and relative measures of fertility has been observed in recent years, especially in urban areas. The total number of births decreased from 690,981 in 1989 to 419,238 in 1998 (SSCU, 1999a). In 1998, the crude birth rate was 8.3 live births per 1,000 inhabitants, which is 37.6% less compared with 1989. The total fertility rate decreased from 1.9 in 1989 to 1.2 in 1998, in urban areas – from 1.8 to 1.0, and in rural areas – from 2.4 to 1.6 (Table 17.3). So, the process of fertility stabilisation at a low level in Ukraine in the 1970s and 1980s was followed by the period of further downward trend during the 1990s (Figure 17.3).

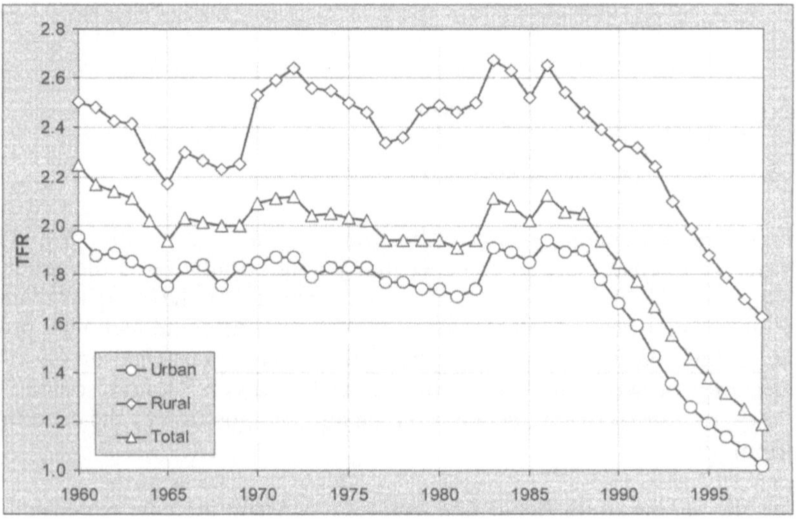


**Figure 17.3: Total Fertility Rate (TFR), 1960–1998**

Source: author's calculations based on SSC USSR and SSCU data

The continuing decline of fertility means the loss of favourable demographic prospects for Ukraine. Even in the rural areas, where fertility was traditionally higher than in urban areas, since 1993 it has fallen below the level necessary for population replacement. The difference between this indicator in urban and rural areas during the years of economic and social crisis has increased, as fertility was declining in urban areas faster than in rural areas. The lowest fertility is observed in industrially developed regions and in the Autonomous Republic of Crimea. At the same time, in the regions where fertility is at a very low level, abortions are most spread, and losses from these are extremely large, compared to other countries. On average, annually in Ukraine 119 abortions take place per every 100 live births (SSCU, 1998).

**Table 17.3: Main Indicators of Fertility, 1989–1998**

| Year | Crude birth rate[1] | | | General birth rate[2] | | | Total fertility rate | | |
|---|---|---|---|---|---|---|---|---|---|
| | Total | Urban | Rural | Total | Urban | Rural | Total | Urban | Rural |
| 1989 | 13.3 | 13.6 | 12.9 | 55.8 | 52.1 | 66.0 | 1.935 | 1.781 | 2.390 |
| 1990 | 12.7 | 12.7 | 12.7 | 53.3 | 49.0 | 65.1 | 1.848 | 1.682 | 2.328 |
| 1991 | 12.1 | 11.9 | 12.6 | 51.3 | 46.2 | 64.8 | 1.771 | 1.590 | 2.317 |
| 1992 | 11.4 | 11.0 | 12.5 | 43.8 | 42.6 | 64.1 | 1.667 | 1.465 | 2.242 |
| 1993 | 10.7 | 10.1 | 12.0 | 44.4 | 38.6 | 60.8 | 1.551 | 1.353 | 2.096 |
| 1994 | 10.0 | 9.3 | 11.6 | 41.2 | 35.3 | 57.9 | 1.453 | 1.259 | 1.984 |
| 1995 | 9.6 | 8.8 | 11.1 | 38.7 | 33.0 | 54.7 | 1.379 | 1.192 | 1.879 |
| 1996 | 9.1 | 8.4 | 10.7 | 36.6 | 31.1 | 51.7 | 1.315 | 1.135 | 1.787 |
| 1997 | 8.7 | 8.0 | 10.3 | 34.6 | 29.4 | 48.8 | 1.250 | 1.079 | 1.699 |
| 1998 | 8.3 | 7.6 | 9.9 | 32.8 | 27.8 | 46.2 | 1.188 | 1.019 | 1.626 |
| Index[3] | 62.4 | 55.9 | 76.7 | 58.8 | 53.4 | 70.0 | 61.4 | 57.2 | 68.0 |

[1]Total number of births per 1,000 inhabitants
[2]Total number of births per 1,000 women 15–49 years
[3]1998 (1989 = 100)
Source: SSCU data

The percentage of children born out of wedlock is growing due to a decreasing number of marriages and increasing divorce rates: in 1989 that percentage was 10.8%, in 1998 – 16.2%. If in 1989–1992 the percentage of children born out of wedlock was higher in rural areas than in urban, since 1993, it has become higher in urban areas (Table 17.4).

**Table 17.4: Extramarital Births, 1989–1998, per cent**

| Population | 1989 | 1990 | 1991 | 1992 | 1993 | 1994 | 1995 | 1996 | 1997 | 1998 |
|---|---|---|---|---|---|---|---|---|---|---|
| Total | 10.8 | 11.2 | 11.9 | 12.1 | 13.0 | 12.8 | 13.2 | 13.6 | 15.2 | 16.2 |
| Urban | 10.1 | 10.5 | 11.6 | 12.0 | 13.1 | 13.0 | 13.4 | 13.8 | 15.4 | 16.5 |
| Rural | 12.4 | 12.6 | 12.5 | 12.4 | 12.8 | 12.6 | 12.8 | 13.3 | 14.8 | 15.5 |

Source: SSCU data

The overwhelming majority of children (84.1% in 1998) are being born by women aged under 30. In urban areas, this share amounts to 83.3%, in rural – to 85.4%. In 1989, these percentages were accordingly 81.1%, 80.4%, and 82.6%. Compared to the pre-crisis period, fertility decreased in all age groups, both in urban and rural areas. An increase of fertility among the youngest women, which was observed for a long time, stopped in the crisis years. Fertility dropped to the greatest extent among women aged 30–44, and the least significant decrease was among the youngest women (Figure 17.4). That is, we can conclude that the trend of declining age-specific fertility rates, which is considered to be a common feature of historical changes in fertility patterns, persists in the crisis conditions as well: the older the women, the more significant decrease in fertility they have.

Data on changes in the distribution of births by order is of great interest but, unfortunately, data for such analysis is not available in state statistics of Ukraine since

1995. The Ministry of Justice of Ukraine revised and shortened the programme of vital events registration, which is the primary source of demographic statistics. The last year for which the data on the distribution of births by order can be obtained is 1994. In 1994, as compared to 1989, the share of first children increased, while of the second and third – decreased. The proportion of first children was 56.9% in 1994 (in urban areas – 62.7% and in rural areas – 47%) (SSCU, 1995). Families with more than the average number of children were more common among rural population, however, the age and sex composition of rural population, unbalanced by migration processes, conditioned the situation, when under higher intensity of fertility in rural areas, crude fertility rates there were lower than in urban areas. Since 1991, that correlation has reversed due to a more rapid drop in the age-specific fertility rates in urban areas under crisis conditions.

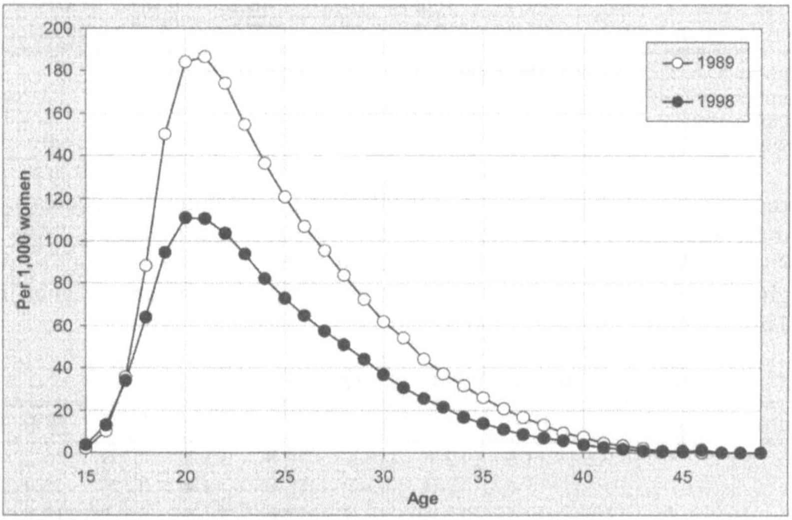


**Figure 17.4: Age-specific Fertility Rates, 1989 and 1998**

Source: SSCU data

The declining birth rates are reflected in changing family structures. Even in 1989, among 56% of families with children under 18 years, the majority, 52%, were one-child families. In urban areas, this proportion was 55% and in rural areas – 44.0%; 39.5% of the families with children under 18 years had two children and only 8.4% had three or more children. As early as in 1990–1994, first and second children comprised 87.4% of all newborn children (SSCU, 1995). The proportion of single-parent families and families without children is growing. According to survey data, about 20% of all women of childbearing age do not have children (UNDP, 1997, pp. 110–111).

Another specific pattern of demographic behaviour has been forming during the transition period. The average childbearing age decreased from 24.9 years in 1989 to 24.1 years in 1994. The corresponding values for the first child were 22.1 and 21.7

years, for the second child – 29.3 and 29.2 years (SSCU, 1995). The fall in fertility was thus accompanied by a rejuvenation of childbearing. In 1994, compared to 1989, the total fertility rate (TFR) decreased by 24.9%. The TFR calculated for the first child declined by 15.3%, for the second child – by 36.2%, and for the third child – by 34.6%. Indeed, it is reaffirmed one more time that unfavourable conditions have a greater influence on births of the second and following order, than on the births of the first children. Contribution of the first births to the TFR increased from 51.2% in 1989 to 57.8% in 1994. The contribution of the second births declined from 36.2% to 30.7%, and of the third births – from 8.2% to 7.2%.

It is argued, that one of the causes of a drop of fertility to a level insufficient for population replacement under current conditions may be the fact that for many people realisation of their desire of parenthood and of having children is limited by and competes with a string of other needs, i.e. maintaining existing living standard. In our view, this hypothesis may apply to the pre-crisis period as well as to the current crisis situation. In pre-crisis conditions wages and salaries, being the fundamental source of supporting and bringing up children, never met the needs of population reproduction, as they could not cover adequately all the necessary expenditures for having and rearing of second or third child in a family.

In the transition period, the conditions for bringing up children are evidently getting worse. For the majority of population, the level of salaries (as a principle source of income) is insufficient to cover maintenance and upbringing of the desired number of children. The most important consequence of the socio-economic crisis is, however, the deterioration of the economic wellbeing of existing and potential parents themselves: the realisation of desire to be a parent and to have children in a current crisis situation competes with the need for bare survival. Population reproduction on the level desirable for family and society is therefore not economically ensured. As a result, most families opt for one child or often remain childless.

Poverty in Ukraine has a "women's profile": average women's salaries and wages are lower than those of men, although women's educational level is not less than men's. In 1997, an average monthly salary and wage was 156 Hryvna for both sexes, 182 Hryvna for men and 132 Hryvna for women (UNDP, 1998, p. 37). Sociological survey data indicates that the average number of children that married women wish to have is two, but current difficulties are making realisation of this wish almost impossible. The conditions, which might enable women to have the number of children they wish, are difficult to achieve, given the current economic situation has already pushed the majority of the population to the poverty line. According to a survey conducted by the Kiev International Institute of Sociology in 1996, 43% of women indicated inadequate income level as the main reason why they do not have as many children as they would want (UNDP, 1997, p. 116).

Unemployment also has a great influence on fertility. According to the State Statistical Committee's survey on the economic activity of the population (based on ILO methodology) carried out in October 1997, only 64.5% of the population aged 15–70 is currently employed (68.4% of men and 61.2% of women), far less than in pre-crisis times (SSCU, 1998). According to the data of the surveys of 1995–1998, the unemployment rate in 1995 was 5.6%, in 1996 – 7.6%, in 1997 – 8.9%, and in 1998 – 11.3% (SSCU, 1995–1999a). So, the *de facto* unemployment rate is increasing. The basic component of unemployment in Ukraine is hidden unemployment in the form of compulsory unpaid leave and a shortened work time. The level of hidden unemployment is evaluated now to be around 30%. Such a situation creates social tension and a feeling of helplessness. Women make up the majority both among those who received the status of unemployed and those who work under conditions of forced part-time employment (SSCU, 1998).

The additional factors of declining fertility are the crisis of the pre-school education system and poor housing conditions. Moreover, pensions for elderly, which are being paid at a level far below the poverty line, also have become a factor that depresses the already low birth rate: the middle-aged generation has to support not only their children, but also parents and/or other elder relatives.

## 17.4 Marriages and Divorces

Fertility decline during crisis years is connected also to some extent with the drop in the number of marriages and the increase of divorces. The marriage rate has decreased from 9.5‰ in 1989 to 6.2‰ in 1998. The divorce rate was especially high in 1992–1993: 4.0–4.3‰, while in 1989 – 3.8‰, and in 1998 – 3.6‰. (SSCU, 1994–1999a). If in 1989 the difference between the crude marriage and divorce rates was 5.7‰, in 1998 it was only 2.6‰.

## 17.5 Mortality and Life Expectancy

The 1990s – the years of societal transformation accompanied by socio-economic crisis – are characterised by a growing deterioration of population health, caused by a drop in living standards, a decay of the public health care system, and economic preconditions for its development. Today, there is practically no preventive medicine, and curative medicine is degrading. The quality of the medical services is declining. Weakened by the crisis, the health care system, existing in extraordinarily difficult conditions, cannot neutralise the negative influence of the numerous socio-economic factors on public health and that has raised the risks of illness and death. Private and fee-for-service medicine does not compensate for the decline of state health care establishments because these services are too expensive to be used by a large share of the population. The decline in public health is reflected in increasing morbidity and mortality.

Mortality has grown significantly. The total number of deaths increased from 600,590 in 1989 to 719,954 in 1998. While in 1989, the number of deaths per 1,000 population was 9.8 in urban areas and 15.2 in rural areas, in 1998 these numbers were 10.2 and 18.4, accordingly (SSCU, 1999a). The sharp increase in the crude death rate in recent years is related not only to the growth of the proportion of the elderly but also to the rise in premature deaths. Especially a great increase was observed in urban areas (Table 17.5), although the mortality rate in Ukraine is traditionally higher in rural areas. Women have somewhat lower crude mortality rate than men, although their ageing level is higher. That is accounted for by lower age-specific mortality of women compared to men. It should be noted that rural men and women have higher crude mortality rates, than their urban counterparts. That is determined, first of all, by a higher ageing level of rural population.

**Table 17.5: Crude and Infant Mortality Rates, 1989–1998**

| Year | Crude mortality rate[1] | | | Infant mortality rate[2] | | |
|---|---|---|---|---|---|---|
| | Total | Urban | Rural | Total | Urban | Rural |
| 1989 | 11.6 | 9.8 | 15.2 | 12.9 | 12.9 | 12.9 |
| 1990 | 12.1 | 10.2 | 16.1 | 12.8 | 12.5 | 13.5 |
| 1991 | 12.9 | 10.8 | 17.2 | 13.9 | 13.5 | 14.7 |
| 1992 | 13.4 | 11.4 | 17.6 | 14.0 | 13.8 | 14.4 |
| 1993 | 14.2 | 12.2 | 18.5 | 14.9 | 14.7 | 15.4 |
| 1994 | 14.7 | 12.8 | 18.8 | 14.5 | 14.1 | 15.2 |
| 1995 | 15.4 | 13.6 | 19.1 | 14.7 | 14.3 | 15.3 |
| 1996 | 15.2 | 13.3 | 19.2 | 14.3 | 14.4 | 14.3 |
| 1997 | 14.9 | 12.9 | 19.0 | 14.0 | 14.2 | 13.8 |
| 1998 | 14.3 | 10.2 | 18.4 | 12.8 | 12.9 | 12.7 |
| Index[3] | 123.3 | 127.6 | 119.7 | 99.2 | 100.0 | 98.4 |

[1]Number of deaths per 1,000 inhabitants
[2]Number of deaths among children during their first year of age per 1,000 live births
[3]1998 (1989 = 100)
Source: SSCU data

In the early 1990s, infant mortality in Ukraine was lower than in the other CIS states, and even those of Central and Eastern Europe, but was double that of the European Union (EU). While infant mortality has been decreasing in the EU, it is not decreasing in Ukraine (Table 17.5). Currently, the infant mortality rate in Ukraine is considerably higher than in developed countries (12.8‰). The most common causes of death in the first year of life are congenital anomalies, situations arising in the perinatal period, and respiratory diseases.

There are some striking gender differences in infant and child mortality. The death rate among infant boys in their first year of life exceeded that of girls by 30%, among 1–3 year olds – by 20%, among 4–7 year olds – by 44%, and among 8–14 year olds – by 77%. Moreover, mortality among rural boys of this age is 1.2 times higher than that of their urban counterparts. There is a tendency for mortality among boys to be higher than among girls. While the death rate of boys is usually higher than that of girls, this difference does not generally increase with age. Factors contributing to this discrepancy in Ukraine may include the difficulties of upbringing children and the increasing number of the orphaned and homeless children. The maternity death rate is also high in Ukraine – 29.5 per 100,000 live births in 1998 (SSCU, 1999a).

An increase in the total annual number of deaths is accompanied by a rise of mortality in all age groups (excluding 1–14 age group) and an increase of premature deaths, especially among men. The rise of age-specific death rates in the crisis period was particularly considerable in the population of working age (Figures 17.5, 17.6 and 17.7). In all age groups between 15–70, death rates for men are 2–3 and more times higher than that of women. The biggest differences between mortality of men and women are observed in the working ages (Figure 17.8), especially in the group of 30–39 years, which is possibly more exposed to adverse influences of industrial factors and working conditions. In that group, the mortality of men is 3.6–3.8 times higher than that of women.

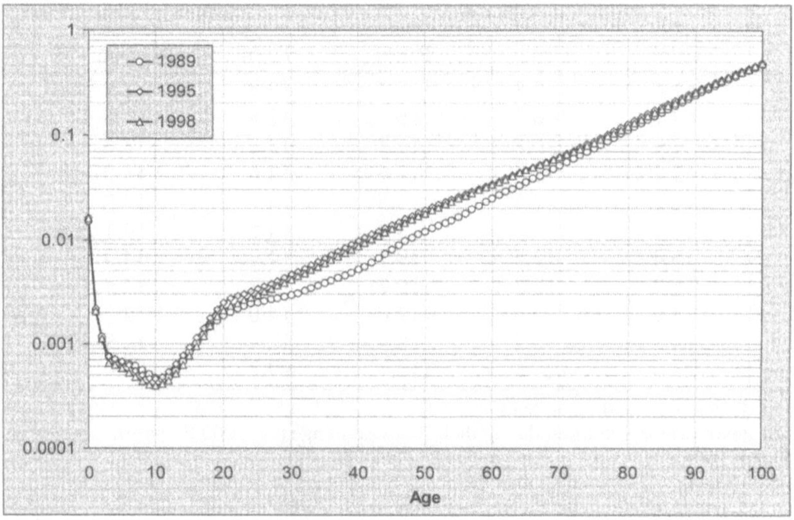


**Figure 17.5: Probability of Dying by Age, 1989, 1995 and 1998, male**

Source: author's calculations based on SSCU data

As a result, the life expectancy for men decreased from 66.2 years in 1989 to 61.3 years in 1995. Females faired somewhat better, their life expectancy declined from 75.2 years in 1989 to 72.6 years in 1995 (Table 17.6). Life expectancy for men decreased particularly in urban areas, although regional variations are also evident. During 1989–1995, the life expectancy decreased by 4.9 years for men and 2.6 years for women. A principal part of that decrease was conditioned by an increase of mortality from circulatory system diseases. While in 1989 the life expectancy for women was 9 years higher than that for men, in 1995 it was 11.3 years higher. This difference show that women, suffering more than men from a crisis state of society, seem to be more viable in adverse conditions compared to men. Such unhealthy phenomena as hard drinking and drug use, which have gained an unseen scale, are much less spread among women.

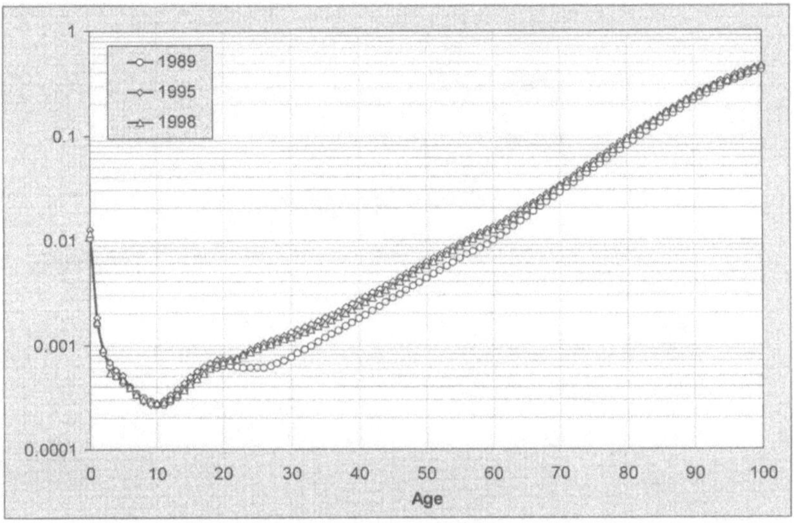


**Figure 17.6: Probability of Dying by Age, 1989, 1995 and 1998, female**

Source: author's calculations based on SSCU data

**Table 17.6. Life Expectancy at Birth, 1989–1998, in years**

| Year | Total | | Urban | | Rural | |
|---|---|---|---|---|---|---|
| | Male | Female | Male | Female | Male | Female |
| 1989 | 66.2 | 75.2 | 66.8 | 75.2 | 64.8 | 75.0 |
| 1990 | 65.4 | 74.9 | 66.3 | 74.9 | 64.2 | 74.6 |
| 1991 | 64.7 | 74.3 | 65.5 | 74.4 | 63.0 | 73.9 |
| 1992 | 63.9 | 74.1 | 64.5 | 74.1 | 62.5 | 73.7 |
| 1993 | 63.3 | 73.4 | 63.7 | 73.4 | 62.1 | 73.1 |
| 1994 | 62.5 | 73.0 | 62.9 | 72.9 | 61.6 | 72.8 |
| 1995 | 61.3 | 72.6 | 61.5 | 72.4 | 61.0 | 72.6 |
| 1996 | 61.6 | 72.8 | 61.9 | 72.8 | 61.0 | 72.7 |
| 1997 | 62.3 | 73.2 | 62.8 | 73.2 | 61.3 | 72.9 |
| 1998 | 63.2 | 73.8 | 63.7 | 73.8 | 62.2 | 73.6 |
| | Difference | | | | | |
| 1995–1989 | -4.9 | -2.6 | -5.3 | -2.8 | -3.8 | -2.4 |
| 1998–1989 | -3.0 | -1.4 | -3.1 | -1.4 | -2.6 | -1.4 |

Source: author's calculations based on SSCU data

There was some increase of life expectancy in 1996–1998 compared to 1995 (1.9 years for men and 1.2 years for women). However, now we have reason to conclude that this increase was not influenced by a decrease in mortality caused by shifts in life standards. It was connected with the fact that in hard conditions, people with the weakest health are dying more intensively. That fact caused specific selection, after which mortality was lower for some period than in previous years. Evidence of such situation in Ukraine is an increase in mortality in 1999.

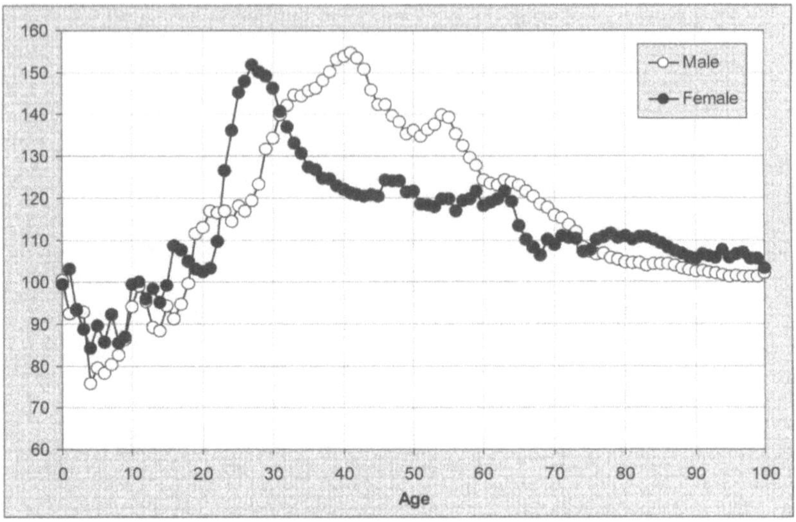


**Figure 17.7: Change in Age-specific Probability of Dying Between 1989 and 1998 by Sex, index (1989 = 100)**

Source: author's calculations based on SSCU data

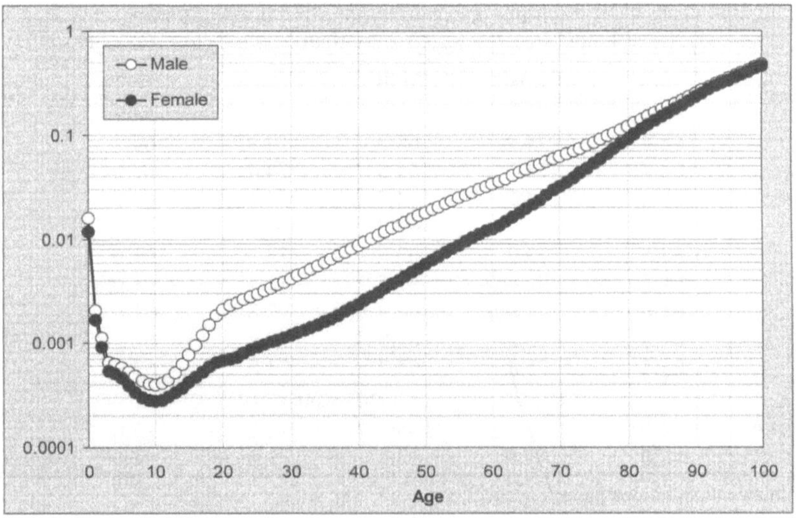


**Figure 17.8: Probability of Dying by Sex and Age, 1998**

Source: author's calculations based on SSCU data

In 1998, male life expectancy at birth was 4.5% lower than in 1989, and female life expectancy was lower by 1.9%. A loss of life expectancy rises considerably with age. Corresponding percentages for age 65 are 7.1 and 4.4. Life expectancy at retirement age has substantially declined (Table 17.7).

**Table 17.7: Life Expectancy at Certain Ages by Sex, 1989 and 1998, in years**

| Age | Male | | | Female | | |
|---|---|---|---|---|---|---|
| | 1989 | 1998 | Difference | 1989 | 1998 | Difference |
| 0 | 66.2 | 63.2 | -3.0 | 75.2 | 73.8 | -1.4 |
| 1 | 66.2 | 63.1 | -3.1 | 75.0 | 73.6 | -1.4 |
| 15 | 52.8 | 49.7 | -3.1 | 61.5 | 60.1 | -1.4 |
| 30 | 39.2 | 36.1 | -3.1 | 47.0 | 45.6 | -1.4 |
| 45 | 26.3 | 24.1 | -2.2 | 32.8 | 31.7 | -1.1 |
| 60 | 15.7 | 14.4 | -1.3 | 19.9 | 19.0 | -0.9 |
| 65 | 12.7 | 11.8 | -0.9 | 16.0 | 15.3 | -0.7 |

Source: author's calculations based on SSCU data

Cardiovascular disease is the leading cause of death in Ukraine, neoplasm is the second, and the third most common cause of death includes accidents, homicides, suicides and other external causes. Women have a considerably higher mortality from circulatory system diseases, but much lower from neoplasms than men. Deaths from external causes have the largest contribution to the increase of death rates. Male mortality from unnatural causes such as accidents, poisonings, and trauma also increased greatly. They have reached the second place in male mortality (after circulatory system diseases), and the third among women. The incidence of alcohol poisonings is increasing, as well as of suicides and homicides. Psychological stress connected with unsuccessful social and economic reform may well have contributed to the increase in the latter causes of death. Male mortality from all causes became considerably "younger".

The structure of mortality among the population of Ukraine indicates its poor state of health relative to that of the EU. Compared with other countries, Ukraine has a relatively high number of people classified as invalids. In addition, outbreaks of infectious diseases such as cholera and diphtheria have been observed at rates unprecedented in peacetime. There has also been a gradual increase of tuberculosis. An increase in mortality due to infectious and parasitic diseases is likely to be associated with the whole complex of deteriorating living conditions, exacerbated hygienic and epidemiological situation. Alcoholism, drugs, and substance abuse are spreading. Prospects of life expectancy are therefore difficult to predict not only because of the yet unknown possible consequences of Chernobyl catastrophe, but also because of HIV/AIDS epidemic losses. There has been a rapid rise in the number of HIV/AIDS cases since 1995 (Barnet *et al.*, 1997).

## 17.6 Natural Increase (Decrease)

Ukraine had the highest fertility in Europe and a longer life expectancy compared with European Russia at the end of the 19th century. The total fertility rate in Ukraine was 7.5 children per woman, and the net-reproduction rate was 1.95 in 1896–1997 (Kuchynsky, 1931). Now Ukraine belongs to the group of the most "unfortunate" countries of the world in the demographic respect.

The crude rate of natural increase became negative in Ukraine as a whole since 1991 (Table 17.8). Depopulation mostly influences male population in urban areas and females in rural areas. The most significant depopulation is now characteristic for rural women and to some lesser extent – for rural men. Also we should note that the depopulation, which began in rural areas in 1979, for a long time was conditioned by depopulation among women, while among men it has begun only in 1989. Therefore, the deterioration of the demographic situation among women began 10 years earlier than among men. In urban areas, depopulation began simultaneously for both sexes – in 1992. Demographic losses due to depopulation in urban areas are mostly conditioned by a decreased number of births, and in rural areas – by an increased number of deaths, compared to trends which were prevalent prior to the social and economic crisis.

**Table 17.8: Crude Rate of Natural Increase, Vital Index, and Net Reproduction Rate, 1989–1998**

| Year | Natural increase (decrease) per 1000 inhabitants | | | Vital index[1] | | | Net reproduction rate | | |
|---|---|---|---|---|---|---|---|---|---|
| | Total | Urban | Rural | Total | Urban | Rural | Total | Urban | Rural |
| 1989 | 1.7 | 3.8 | -2.3 | 1.151 | 0.846 | 1.382 | 0.914 | 0.845 | 1.105 |
| 1990 | 0.6 | 2.5 | -3.4 | 1.044 | 0.786 | 1.240 | 0.873 | 0.800 | 1.079 |
| 1991 | -0.8 | 1.1 | -4.6 | 0.941 | 0.732 | 1.100 | 0.839 | 0.758 | 1.063 |
| 1992 | -2.0 | -0.4 | -5.1 | 0.856 | 0.708 | 0.965 | 0.791 | 0.699 | 1.042 |
| 1993 | -3.5 | -2.1 | -6.5 | 0.752 | 0.649 | 0.825 | 0.735 | 0.642 | 0.986 |
| 1994 | -4.7 | -3.5 | -7.2 | 0.682 | 0.615 | 0.729 | 0.687 | 0.595 | 0.933 |
| 1995 | -5.8 | -4.8 | -8.0 | 0.622 | 0.583 | 0.647 | 0.651 | 0.564 | 0.883 |
| 1996 | -6.1 | -4.9 | -8.5 | 0.602 | 0.557 | 0.632 | 0.619 | 0.536 | 0.832 |
| 1997 | -6.2 | -4.9 | -8.7 | 0.587 | 0.541 | 0.619 | 0.591 | 0.511 | 0.795 |
| 1998 | -6.0 | -4.9 | -8.3 | 0.582 | 0.545 | 0.608 | 0.563 | 0.485 | 0.759 |
| Index[2] | x | x | x | 50.6 | 64.4 | 44.0 | 61.6 | 57.4 | 68.7 |

[1]Ratio of births to the number of deaths of the same year
[2]1998 (1989 = 100)
Source: author's calculations based on SSCU data

The decrease of fertility and the deteriorating health status of the population, which led to increasing mortality, caused a decline of the net reproduction rate (which shows to what extent a generation of parents is replaced by a generation of children) during 1989–1998 by 38.4% (by 42.6% in urban areas and by 31.3% in rural). Both in urban and rural areas, it became lower than 1.0 (0.485 and 0.759, accordingly), which is much below replacement level (Table 17.8).

The decrease of the vital index was even higher than of the net reproduction rate. From 1989 to 1998, the ratio of births to deaths in Ukraine, as a whole, decreased by 49.4%, in urban areas – by 35.6%, and in rural areas – by 56%. In 1998, births compensated the number of deaths in total population – by 58.2%, in urban areas – by 54.5%, and in rural areas – by 60.8%. The contemporary population age composition in rural areas negatively influences the levels of vital indices, so that they are much lower than the net reproduction rates

Depopulation in Ukraine as a whole began in 1991 (Figure 17.9). The total number of deaths in 1991 exceeded the total number of births by 39.2 thousand. In the following years, this trend grew rapidly (300.7 thousand in 1998). During 8 years, because of natural decline, the population of Ukraine decreased by 1,788.3 thousand.

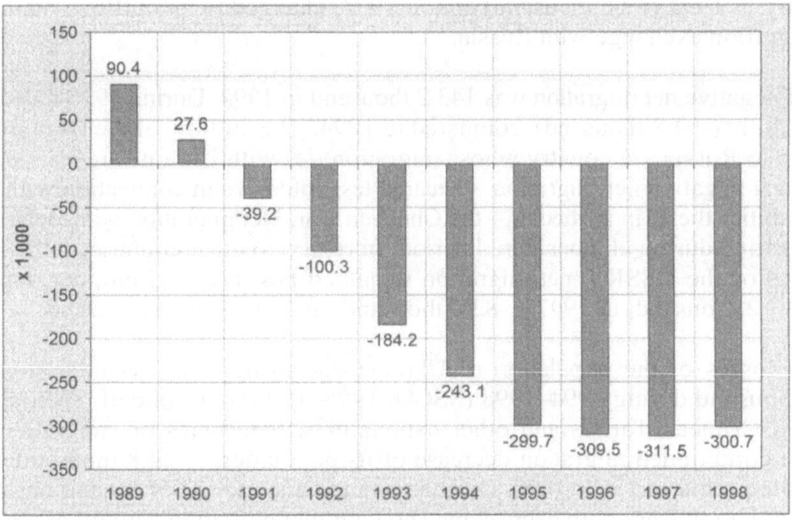


**Figure 17.9: Natural Increase (Decrease), 1989–1998**

Source: SSCU data

For the first time in Ukraine's history, depopulation began to develop and accelerate in peacetime. Previously, such demographic phenomena took place only during relatively short periods of world or civil wars. Depopulation gained spontaneous character and no indication of its end is in sight. An important feature of depopulation in Ukraine resides in the fact that it is accompanied by deterioration in qualitative characteristics of the population and especially of its health.

## 17.7 Migration

During many decades of the post-war period, Ukraine was characterised by positive external net migration, which increased considerably after Ukraine gained independence. A mass return migration of ethnic Ukrainians and migration from Ukraine of other nationalities was observed. Ethnic Ukrainians were the most numerous group among the people arriving to Ukraine. According to the data of state statistics on registered migration, positive net migration during 1989–1990 was 118.2 thousand and 436.5 thousand during 1991–1992.

However, an aggravation of the economic situation conditioned a decreasing number of those who want to return to Ukraine and caused more active emigration to Russia, where living standards were higher at that time. Following the fall in living standards in Ukraine, migration from the former Soviet republics, which slowed significantly in 1993 (49.6 thousand) and in 1994, changed to an outflow, mainly due to a migration exchange with Russia.

Overall negative net migration was 143.2 thousand in 1994. During 1995 it decreased significantly (-94.8 thousand), compared to 1994. The outflow of the Ukrainian population to Russia – a country whose migration ties with Ukraine are characterised by highest negative net migration – became less intensive in connection with political instability there, in particular – the Chechen war. Net migration with Belarus was also negative during all considered period. In regard to other countries – the former republics of the USSR – net migration remained positive. In 1996, net migration was -117.2 thousand, in 1997 – -82.1 thousand, in 1998 – -93.6 thousand.

Overall losses of the population of Ukraine due to negative net migration were 530.9 thousand during 1994–1998 (SSCU, 1995–1999a). In spite of repatriation of deported Crimean Tartars and other nationalities, tendencies of emigration from Ukraine conditioned migration decrease of its population – -44.8 thousand during the whole period of 1991–1998. During recent years, indices of in- and out-migration from Ukraine are both decreasing, showing that migration activity of a population in unfavourable economic conditions is declining (Figure 17.10).

Among persons arriving to Ukraine from Central Asia, Trans-Caucasian and the Baltic States, the numerous are ethnic Ukrainians. Among those who leave Ukraine, the most numerous group is Russians. That is connected, first, with the fact that Russians, like other nationalities, after disintegration of the USSR were captivated by an aspiration to return to their ethnic motherland, and, second, with a change for the worse of economic situation in Ukraine against background of more favourable situation in Russia. Emigration of Russians from the other former Soviet republics continues. Positive net migration was observed for ethnic groups of Georgians, Armenians, Azeris, and Tajiks, that is, people whose homelands had complicated political, social, and economic conditions. Migrants representing these nations are mainly forced migrants.

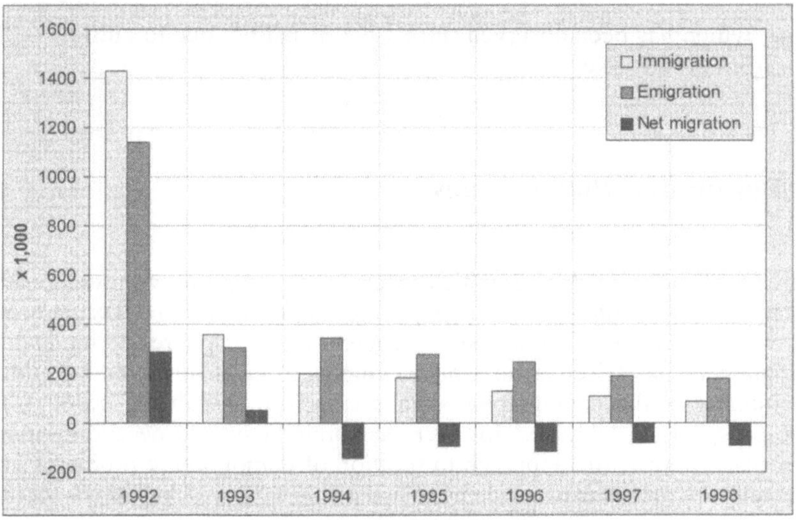


**Figure 17.10: Registered External Migration, 1992–1998**
Source: SSCU data

It should be mentioned that migration to countries other than former Soviet republics has the character of irrevocable emigration. Its volume was the highest in 1990, when it reached 95 thousand (Malinovska, 1997). After Ukraine has declared its independence, the level of emigration to these countries began to decline. The main country of destination is Israel (about 40% of emigrants). Almost a half of the emigrants to countries other than former republics of the USSR go to USA and Germany, and migration to these places is growing. The majority of emigrants going in that direction are Jews, but their share is decreasing. The share of Ukrainians is growing even among emigrants to Israel. The share of emigrants to Israel is declining but the share of emigrants to developed countries of the West is increasing. It is an indicative illustration of growing economic migration compared to ethnic migration.

The main reason of migration is family circumstances both among emigrants and immigrants. This cause was indicated by about half of migrants (Malinovska, op. cit.). Changes of the working place ranks second (approximately 20% of migrations). People of working age are most common among migrants. The share of the economically active persons among emigrants to former Soviet republics is considerably higher than among emigrants to other countries. The educational level of migrants is higher than the average educational level of the total population of Ukraine. This supports the suggestion that there exist a "brain drain" from Ukraine.

The character of internal migration has also changed. Traditionally, there had always been positive net migration in urban areas and a negative one in rural areas. In 1992–1996, net migration was negative in urban areas and positive in rural areas. This demonstrates that the urban population, which had not lost its connections with the countryside, sought to save themselves from poverty not only by external migration but also by returning to work on the land. Thus, negative external net migration in

Ukraine, which has been observed since 1994, is mainly due to outflow of the population from urban areas.

## 17.8 Population Policy Issues

Negative tendencies in demographic processes are laying down prerequisites for a protracted unfavourable situation in population reproduction in Ukraine, which will have a wide spectrum of undesired consequences in all spheres of societal life. An immediate need has arisen to carry out a complex of measures, which could prevent the worsening of the demographic situation, as well as halt the ruining of demographic prospects of Ukraine. However, economic crisis and decentralisation of resources make a systemic approach to solution of demographic problems unaffordable, as relevant mechanisms or agencies being able to provide resources for measures regarding the improvement of a demographic situation are absent.

The crisis situation in the economy thus calls for concentration of limited resources to solve the most pressing problems. The most urgent and major task in Ukraine is prevention of the deterioration of the population's health. Therefore, the basic aim of population policy in conditions of resource deficiency during the transition to a market economy should be the maintenance and improvement of health as one of the nation's most important priorities. The state of the population's health is an integral indicator of demographic and overall societal welfare. The strategy of socio-economic reform should envision orienting all spheres of society to healthy living conditions, especially work conditions, everyday life, and childbearing activity. *De facto*, this should be the strategy embodied in many countries under the name "Health for All" (WHO, 1991).

Incorporating into public policy the "Health for All" concept is not only humane but also may be economically worthwhile because it does not necessarily require additional expenditures and could significantly reduce costs to society, as a result of lowering morbidity and number of disabilities. The main task is to improve health care policy. Among priorities, it is necessary to develop measures aimed towards better conditions for the upbringing of children in families and in educational institutions, especially in pre-school institutions, to reform the health care system, devoting special attention to lowering mortality and morbidity among mothers and children and among men of working age. Demographic expertise of major economic projects, laws and programmes should also be introduced to avoid harm to population reproduction and, first of all, to its health.

Extraordinary steps are needed to improve child-rearing conditions. Significant deterioration of the living conditions of the overwhelming majority of the population had an immediate effect on fertility level. The main means of social support of families having children in Ukraine are family allowances. But their size is inadequate.

For example, mothers on maternity leave receive 16.6 Hryvna per month (US$4.2 in June 1999) to care for child under 3 years. In fact, population-related policy is reduced to social policy with measures on extremely low level. It is therefore necessary to reinforce social protection for mothers and children, by carrying out relevant measures on a level not below the poverty line. It is very important that, in the reform of wages in state-owned enterprises, the adequate cover of the expenses of supporting and raising the number of children, needed by family and society, is established as a principle of remuneration. It is equally important to improve living standards of retired people.

Family policy stipulated that working women, and particularly those with young children, were given privileges by enterprises. These privileges no longer correspond with market economic conditions, resulting in exclusion of women from enterprises. Women comprise the majority of those working in forced part-time employment. Their low wages in general, coupled with high levels of underemployment or unemployment are encouraging women to stay on maternity leave as long as possible. The poor quality of pre-school education further encourages this choice, so that about 10% of working-age women are on maternity leave at any given time, substantially more than in other countries, although the birth rate in Ukraine is too low.

While the increase in mortality of both men and women was caused mainly by aggravation of living standards, the principal factor for the unprecedented decrease of fertility is, in our view, a change of women's status in society and worsening of the conditions for children upbringing. This is connected not only with circumstances, which have emerged due to crisis (unemployment, drop in salaries etc.), but also with the fact that in present conditions even those women's achievements that were gained prior to the crisis, are disappearing. For instance, an important role, which was earlier played by the system of pre-school child care institutions is declining, thus one of the important prerequisites of combining women's professional activities with bringing up children is being lost.

From 1990 through 1998, the number of such institutions fell from 24.5 thousand to 17.6 thousand and the number of children in them – from 2,428.3 thousand to 1,102.6 thousand. The quality of services in the majority of pre-school institutions has also dropped substantially, but their costs have increased. Now pre-school institutions are too expensive for a significant segment of the population and unattractive to another segment. In connection with this, it is necessary to take measures to end the decline of the pre-school child-care system, since it is an important condition for women to be able to combine their professional work with motherhood.

## 17.9 Conclusion

In general, a reversal of the unfavourable dynamics of demographic processes could be expected, first of all, with overcoming of the socio-economic crisis. But even today, measures should be taken to carry out the basic idea of "demographisation" of all branches of social and economic policy. Measures for improving the demographic situation have an interdisciplinary character. Inasmuch as any part of social policy directly or indirectly influences how the population reproduces itself, demographic problems in general should be dealt with by strengthening the demographic emphasis and increasing the demographic effectiveness of social and economic measures in all spheres of social life, most of all in the labour sphere (Steshenko and Piskunov, 1996b). Reinforcement of "demographisation" of all directions of social and economic policy, primarily wages and salaries, privatisation, social security, housing, and tax policy may all be especially effective in the context of population policy. It is necessary to strengthen the "demographisation" of the programme for overcoming the crisis, that is, to attach more closely the solving of the urgent problems of demographic development to solution of the problems of creating a socially oriented market economy.

## References

Barnet, T. *et al.* (1997), *The Social and Economic Impact of HIV/AIDS in Ukraine*, Kyiv: UNAIDS/British Council.

Kuchynski, R.R. (1931), *The Balance of Births and Deaths. Volume 2. Eastern and Southern Europe*, Washington, D.C.: The Brookings Institution.

Malinovska, O. (1997), Migraciya movoyu statystyky, *Problemy migraciyi (Ukrayinskiy informaciynyi analitychnyi zhurnal)*, Vol. 1, pp. 8–13.

Rosset, E. (1968), *Process starenia naselenia*, Moskva: Statistika.

SSCU (State Statistics Committee of Ukraine) (1993), *Naselennya Ukrayiny 1992. Demografichnyi zhorichnyk*, Kyiv.

SSCU (State Statistics Committee of Ukraine) (1994), *Naselennya Ukrayiny 1993. Demografichnyi zhorichnyk*, Kyiv.

SSCU (State Statistics Committee of Ukraine) (1995), *Naselennya Ukrayiny 1994. Demografichnyi zhorichnyk*, Kyiv.

SSCU (State Statistics Committee of Ukraine) (1996), *Naselennya Ukrayiny 1995. Demografichnyi zhorichnyk*, Kyiv.

SSCU (State Statistics Committee of Ukraine) (1997a), *Naselennya Ukrayiny 1996. Demografichnyi zhorichnyk*, Kyiv.

SSCU (State Statistics Committee of Ukraine) (1997b), *Ekonomichna aktyvnist naselennya Ukrayiny v 1996 roci. Statistichnyi zbirnyk*, Kyiv.

SSCU (State Statistics Committee of Ukraine) (1998), *Ekonomichna aktivnist naselennya Ukrayiny v 1997 roci. Statistichnyi zbirnyk*, Kyiv.

SSCU (State Statistics Committee of Ukraine) (1999a), *Naselennya Ukrayiny 1998. Demografichnyi zhorichnyk*, Kyiv.

SSCU (State Statistics Committee of Ukraine) (1999b), *Department of Population Statistics Database* (data on magnetic media), Kyiv.

SSC USSR (State Statistics Committee of the USSR) (1988), *Naseleniye SSSR 1987. Statisticheskiy sbornik*, Moskva.

Steshenko V. and V. Piskunov (1996a), Demografichna cina suchasnoyi socialno-economichnoyi crysy v Ukrayini, *Viche*, Vol. 8, pp. 86–96.

Steshenko V. and V. Piskunov (1996b), Pro koncepciyu nacionalnoyi demografichnoyi polityky v Ukrayini, *Demografichni doslidzhennya*, Vol. 18, pp. 3–42.

UNDP/UNICEF/WHO/World Bank (1997), *The Health of Women and Children in Ukraine*, Kyiv: UNDP Office in Ukraine.

UNDP (United Nations Development Programme) (1998), *Ukrayina. Prava lyudyny ta lyudskyi rozvytok*, Kyiv: UNDP Office in Ukraine.

WHO (World Health Organization) (1991), *Zadachi po dostizheniyu zdorovja dlya vsekh*, Copenhagen.

World Bank (1996), *Bidnist' v Ukrayini*, Kyiv.

# 18

# Changes in Fertility and Mortality in the Czech Republic: An Attempt of Regional Demographic Analysis[1]

**Boris Burcin and Tomáš Kučera[2]**

## 18.1 Introduction

During the current decade the debate concerning commonalties and variations in population development has been thrust into the national and international arenas. Of those interested in diversity among the populations, most have concentrated on cross-national comparisons, but only little attention has been given to sub-national characteristics of population, i.e. those observed at the level of a country's regions and districts. This can be attributed to, first of all, the seemingly insignificant (or hidden) differentiation of demographic patterns observed across the country, as compared to more obvious general population trends and dynamics. Second, it can be at least in part explained by the shortage of comprehensive cross-regional data, especially in the countries where the population registers have not been introduced.

The third consideration is pertinent to the methodological apparatus. A review of literature reveals that there are also inadequacies in theory and research: insufficient exploration of the relationships among the concept, the indicators, and the analysis employed leaves open the question as to whether the research findings reflect the phenomenon under study or are merely artefacts of a mismatch between concept, indicators and method. Specifically, when regional differentiation is seen as an outgrowth of some intrinsic, "natural" (e.g. geographical) characteristics *per se* and universal processes working consistently across all or most regions, the existing analytical tools would be sufficient, yet the complexity of the phenomenon ("regionalisation") would be probably lost. However, when it is examined as a phenomenon that emerges from spatial, social, economic, cultural, ecological, administrative etc. organisation of the entire society also through region-specific processes of differentiation and evolution, then new models may need to be developed that adequately consider the effect of "regionalisation" in structuring both the options and choices of people (individuals or families) with respect to their demographic behaviour.

In the absence of such a model – elaboration of which is indeed needed, but is beyond the scope of this paper – we will address recent trends in fertility and mortality, focusing on their cross-regional variation and, partially, on the mechanisms involved. Although our emphasis in this discussion will be primarily on quantitative data, we would argue that qualitative research might provide greater depth in addressing the complexity of the described issues – what we suggest could help systematise this complexity. We begin by briefly reviewing some of the regional characteristics of the social and economic development in the Czech Republic in order to explain why we accept certain characteristics (factors) to be more important in some contexts and how certain characteristics are related to recent changes in demographic patterns cross-regionally.

## 18.2 An Overview of Recent Regional Development in the Czech Republic

After 1989, the issues of regional development have been gaining political importance and media attention. On the other hand, scholars as well as practitioners are still pondering over how to define regional diversity, how to measure it, or how to manage it (cf. Hampl, 1998, 1999; Murphy, 1991; Nir, 1990; Paddison, 1997). Measuring regional differences has come to mean more than identifying, describing, and counting specific regional characteristics, especially when they depend on both relatively static (territory, population, ecosystem, etc.) and dynamic (economic, social and public structures) elements. In addition, these elements are not independent constructs, but may be interrelated with each other.

Moreover, in the Czech Republic, the regional economic and social differentiation has a deep historical background regardless the fact that for more than forty years the regional development has been strongly influenced by specific political and socio-economic conditions. This differentiation is linked to the history of industrial revolution in the Czech lands, particularly to extensive development of the industry and other progressive economic activities, as well as to the geopolitical changes that resulted in a more favourable positionality of some Czech regions towards major economic areas or large centres. Although there have been quite extensive efforts to eliminate the differences between rural and urban areas (between the core and peripheries) made by the previous regime, "the territorially homogenous society" has not appeared. On the contrary, significant diversity of social, economic and population development became apparent by the end of the forty-year communist era.

The reforms that have taken place since 1989, particularly re-establishment of free market relations, had led to the weakening of the previously used redistributive principles and, consequently, to the reinforcement of differences between separate regions, districts and other territorial units within the country. Regional studies undertaken in the 1990s have shown, amongst others, a pronounced trend towards both the restoration of some historically originated differences and emergence of the new ones, that is generally in line with the concept of societal transition (Hampl, 1999). With respect to population development, the most important outcome of these trends was an increasing variation in life conditions across the regions (districts).

There are obviously a large number of factors that may influence the population development at the regional level. And, as above mentioned, it is quite difficult to identify which factors and during which period of time have had most or limited influence on regionally based changes (and variation) in demographic behaviour. "Regionalisation" of population has many dimensions – it is not only a territorial, rural/urban, or socio-economic arrangement; it also goes far beyond pure historical developments. In this respect, the question of what are the main "push factors" of regional differences in demographic indicators is a vital issue. In this paper, we discuss some of these factors based on Mellens's (1999) classification of variables that determine the differentiation of population patterns across the countries, yet applying it at the regional level (such assumption seems to be appropriate bearing in mind the general character of Mellens's model).

In his study of determinants of demographic behaviour, Mellens distinguishes between the *socio-economic dimension* and the *cultural dimension*. The first dimension is linked to the socio-economic variables including both *fixed* – for example, geographical or climatic characteristics – and *dynamic* ones (economic, education, health, technology etc.). The cultural dimension refers to the values, norms and customs that lead to common attitudes and patterns of behavior. Mellens also argues, that "the actions of policy-makers form a separate third dimension" (Mellens, op. cit., p. 5). In view of the relatively small influence of this dimension in the Czech context (there still has not been any pronounced population-related policies or programmes implemented at the regional level in the Czech Republic) we will not consider it as a variable underlying differentiation of demographic patterns (We may however assume that this issue will undoubtedly gain more importance in the future). On the other hand, the increasing differentiation in lifestyles, particularly between the central and peripheral parts of the country, may be seen as factors that may be attributed to recent changes in demographic behaviour.

Since cross-regional analysis particularly relies on the availability of information, another critical issue is the quality of data. Though there have been efforts to identify and measure socio-economic and, to a lesser extent, socio-cultural variables underlying the regional differentiation, the knowledge in this area is still scarce. In a regional perspective, economic development alongside with changes in life conditions have been well studied with respect to the dynamics of educational attainment, labour opportunities, income and earnings (wages and salaries), unemployment, labour productivity, or the overall economic growth. On the other hand, these were mostly quantitative aspects that have been monitored: the qualitative aspects of these variables have usually received far less attention. For example, the differences in the quality of the education across the regions, which may further cause variations in economic growth, are still a "blank space".

Likewise, the role of technology, especially the access to information, which seems to have a great impact on the lifestyles of people, has on the whole remained peripheral to both professional and public debate. The underestimation of the qualitative aspects has in turn caused the situation where foremost direct effects have been analysed. But many of the socio-economic and cultural determinants demonstrate also indirect effects on population development by putting different pressures on people's values, attitudes and life strategies. In particular, economic and cultural barriers for migration to urban areas may be smaller, as compared to migration to the rural areas.

Given the purpose of this article and for practical reasons (the availability of data), we nevertheless have to limit our discussion to a small number of factors (determinants) that, in our view, could have the relatively strong impact on the recently emerged regional differences in population patterns. We argue that the variation in demographic indicators across the regions or districts reflects not only the existence (absence) or direct (indirect) influence of such factors, but increasing regional differentiation (irregularity) as well. In fact, the co-existence of these two possible effects on the variation of demographic behaviour across the regions has become even more obvious in the recent years.

More specifically, we examine the changes in such characteristics as: territorial organisation of population and its educational and socio-economic structures; economic structure and labour market; income distribution and poverty; public expenditures and public services (social welfare); and the overall level of prosperity (potential for transformation). The shift to the economic characteristics is not only due to the difficulties related to measuring of qualitative, cultural characteristics; it is also based on findings of a number of regional studies and reports which documented that the most pronounced effect on recent changes in demographic behaviour was brought by material conditions of life, especially by the worsening of some social-economic indicators already evident under previous regime and emerging, new welfare problems (UNDP, 1997; UNICEF, 1995).

In our analysis, we refer to the existing administrative division of the Czech Republic (see Appendix) and consider region (district) as a socio-territorial subsystem of the country characterised by specific composition, surroundings and structure (Murphy, 1991).

### 18.2.1 Territorial Organisation of Population

Being strongly related to the level of urbanisation and, consequently, more advanced economic structures and social welfare, population density can be seen as not only a quantitative but also qualitative indicator of territorial organisation of population. More specifically, people living in less inhabited areas more often encounter difficulties (limitations) with respect to both availability and quality of education, employment and social infrastructure, as compared to those living in a more inhabited areas, especially large cities and urban agglomerations. The lesser density of population may also put obstacles to information exchange and, consequently, limited access to technological changes and innovations. All these have resulted in a relatively high variation in the quality of life across the more and less inhabited regions on the whole, and population development in particular.

Generally, it seems that in the Czech Republic, especially over the last decade, disadvantages caused by "isolation" have prevailed over possible benefits, such as a relatively better quality of physical environment, lower stress, more healthy lifestyle, etc. The privatisation has led to disintegration processes in rural regions (under the previous regime, rural areas were integrated by collective farms), thus new sectors connected with technological innovations and progressive infrastructures have to be located in more advanced urban agglomerations (Enyedi, 1996, p. 132). In addition, after 1989, the state discontinued the previous policy of "spatial justice" (Blažek and Kára, 1992, p. 80) aimed at the unification of life conditions across the country. Consequently, the growing differences in quality of life among rural and urban regions, reinforced by irregularities in territorial distribution of population (Figures 18.1 and 18.2), have become even more apparent in the recent years (Swain, 1996).

Having said that, we nevertheless recognise that the increasing cross-regional differentiation may be only a short-term trend and will not necessarily persist, at least to the same extent, in the future. Moreover, a territory-based differentiation may also be modified ("compensated") by geographical factors, particularly region's positionality in relation to major urban centres, industrial zones and other axes of economic development (Hampl, 1996), as well as towards the Austrian and Bavarian borders. The "near-border location" may bring less urbanised areas new education and work opportunities, additional investments, benefits related to tourism and so on.

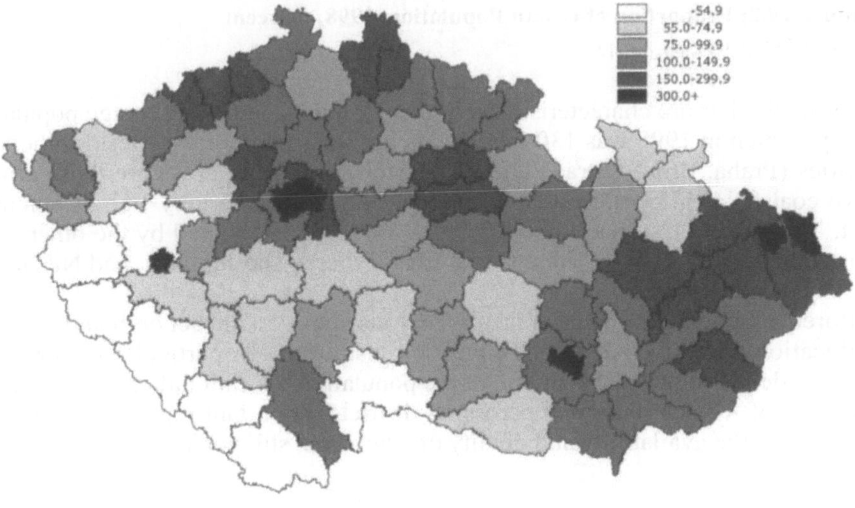


**Figure 18.1: Population Density, 1998, inhabitants per km²**
Source: ČSÚ, 1999, pp. 12–13

By the end of 1998, almost 7.3 million out of 10.3 million, or about 70%, of the Czech population lived in urban areas. The highest concentration of population was registered in traditional administrative and industrial centres and their agglomerations such as: Central region, particularly Praha and its environs (Praha-východ, Praha-západ, Kladno and Mělník); Northern Moravia (Ostrava-město, Karviná and

Frýdek-Místek); Southern Moravia (Brno-venkov); Plzeň-město, the center of Western Bohemia; coal-mining communities in Northwest Bohemia (Chomutov, Most, Teplice, Ústí nad Labem and Děčín); Northern Bohemia (Liberec and Jablonec nad Nisou); and in Mid-East Bohemia (Hradec Králové and Pardubice).

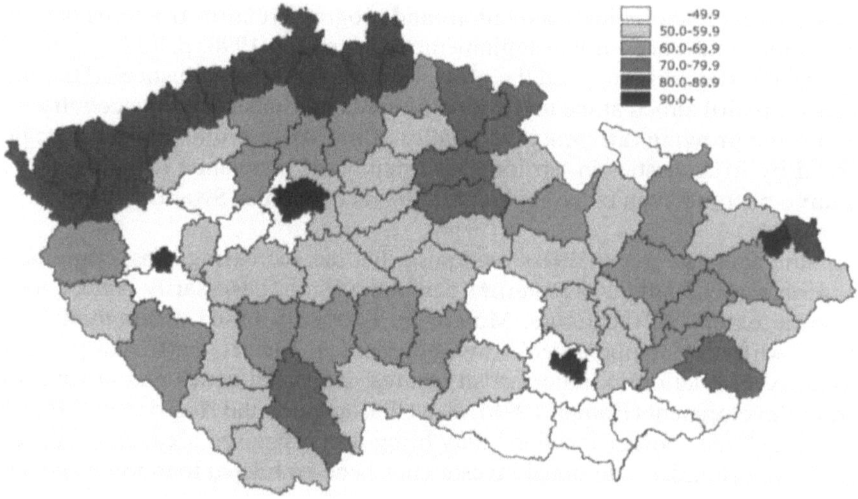


**Figure 18.2: Proportion of Urban Population, 1998, per cent**
Source: ČSÚ, 1999, pp. 12–13

All these districts are characterised by higher than the country's average population density, which in 1998 was 130 inhabitants per square kilometre. Besides the largest cities (Praha, Brno, Ostrava and Plzeň), most inhabited areas are those around brown coal-fields in Northwest Bohemia (Cheb, Sokolov, Karlovy Vary, Chomutov, Most, Teplice and Ústí nad Labem), which are further followed by the other "old" industrial districts such as Děčín, Česká Lípa, Liberec and Jablonec nad Nisou.

As aforementioned, geographical factors may also have an impact on both the access to education and effectiveness of education institutions in particular regions. The recent evidence suggests that although the population educational attainment, especially that of women, has risen across all districts, important regional differences, especially in the availability and quality of education, still persist.

### 18.2.2 Educational and Socio-cultural Structures of Population

According to the last (1991) census, the level of educational attainment of the population was strongly related not only to the location of industries more prone to technological innovations (including military industry) or presence of the government/public administration bodies, but also to the fact whether there were universities or other equivalent degree granting institutions, or not. The latter relationship seems to be even stronger. Another factor that has affected the regional variation in educational level was the policy mainly implemented in the 1970s and aimed to decentralise the academic institutions (research institutes of the former Czechoslovak Academy of Sciences). As a result, the significantly higher educational attainment of population was registered in Praha and in the other administrative centres, i.e. the main cities of the former administrative regions (*kraj*) and their districts and environs. Amongst them, the vanguard positions were occupied by such districts as Brno-město, Olomouc, Ostrava-město, Plzeň-město, Hradec Králové, Pardubice, České Budějovice, Ústí nad Labem and Liberec (Figure 18.3).

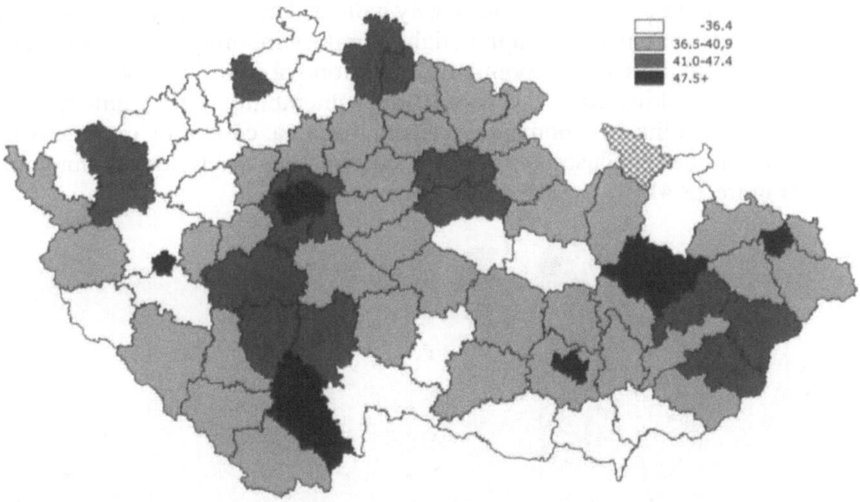


**Figure 18.3: Population by Attained Education, 1991, index of educational level[1]**

[1]Index is defined as proportion of population with completed secondary education + twice proportion of population with a university degree among the population aged 25 and over
Source: Hampl, 1999, p. 49

The differences in the attained level of education have in turn caused the socio-economic differentiation of the population: people with higher education tend to have occupied more qualified jobs and to earn higher wages. The education also enables people a better access to information, which implies that they are more prone to further professional advancement and, as surveys indicated, to more responsible life strategies and healthier lifestyles as well (Mellens, op. cit., pp. 12–13). In view of demographic outcomes, education is becoming a crucial factor affecting people's values and behaviour.

Regional differentiation of socio-cultural structures of the Czech population is still to a great extent affected by the post-war (1945–1947) forced migration (repatriation) of ethnic Germans, who before the Second World War represented the absolute majority of the population living in a relatively large area, bordering with today's Germany and with Austria and Poland – the so-called *Sudetenland*. In the following years, the less attractive parts of the former Sudety have been settled mainly by people belonging to the lower social strata of the post-war Czechoslovak society, by members of the ethnic minorities and by repatriates, the Czechs and Slovaks coming from the former Soviet Union and some other countries of Eastern and Southeast Europe. For example, only from the former Liberec region (today's districts of Liberec, Děčín, Česká Lípa, Jablonec nad Nisou and Semily) almost 455,000 Germans had been transferred and replaced by 205,000 inhabitants from the other parts of the country (Kopačka, 1994, p. 48).

The first wave of immigrants to this area consisted of people who were, on average, less educated, had low occupational status, and who seemingly did not have any special concern about the land they had easily gained. The poor assimilation capacities of newcomers were manifested in a high migratory mobility and, consequently, an extensive fluctuation of the population (Bartoňová and Čermák, 1999). The negative effects resulting from the population vulnerability were reinforced by a long-term neglect of the environmental crisis in this area, caused by extremely high concentration of heavy industries and some other nature-deleterious technological activities (Figure 18.4).

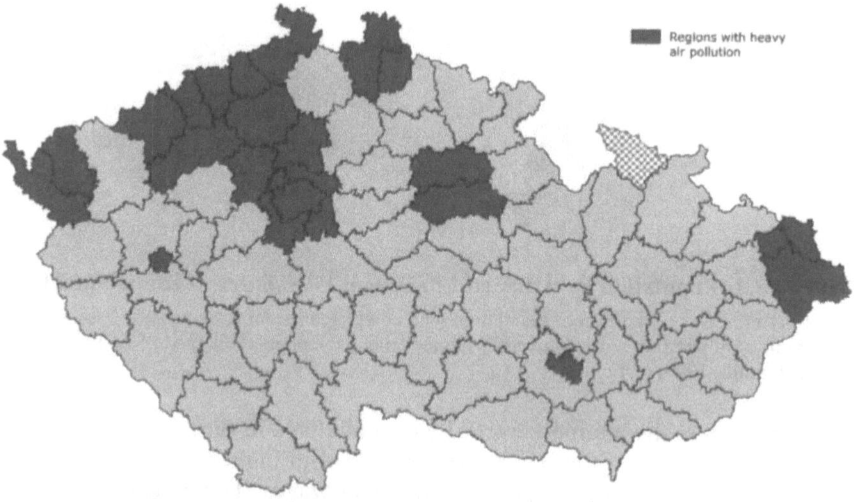


**Figure 18.4: Regions with Heavy Air Pollution, 1992**

Source: Blažek and Kára, op. cit., p. 89

As a result, a very high, compared to the country's average level, mortality was registered in this region as well. In fact, the post-war developments in the former *Sudetenland* might be seen as a good illustration of well-known hypothesis about a positive relationship between personal health and socio-economic status – the lower the social-economic status or educational attainment, the higher the risk of contracting various diseases (Garssen *et al.*, 1999). Parallel high mortality, also the higher prevalence of socio-pathological phenomena was also registered here (Bartoňová, 1996). Thus, the population in this area has never been restored, both from a quantitative (in 1950, the population of the former Liberec region reached only 68% of that living in 1930) and qualitative point of view.

Though one may speak about a nation's culture (see Mellens, op. cit., p. 17), diversity in cultural values, attitudes and behaviours existing across the country (and nation) cannot be avoided, when the regional demographic patterns are examined. In the Czech context, it appears first of all to be the proportion of Gipsy (Roma) population in the regional populations that underlies the cultural (ethnic) dimension of cross-regional variation in demographic patterns. Moreover, the real effect of "Gypsy component" is likely to be even stronger than the simply linear progression, since the Gipsy population traditionally has higher, as compared to the rest of population, intensity of both fertility and mortality.

According to the 1971 and 1980 censuses and local data base, the Gypsy population made up between 1% and 2% of the total population. Based on the estimations provided by Kalibová (1996), in the period 1971–1989, life expectancy of the Gipsy males was about 55.3 years, while the corresponding indicator for the whole Czechoslovak population reached in 1980 66.8 years; for females it was 59.5 and 74.0 years, accordingly. The difference in fertility levels may be illustrated by the numbers of ever-born children: in 1991, by age 49 the Gipsy married females had 5.03 children per woman, as compared to the country's average number of 2.17 children (Kalibová, 1996).

The highest proportion of Gypsies has continuously been registered in Northern and Northwest Bohemia, in a belt-type region consisting of 12 districts (between Cheb in the West and Jablonec nad Nisou in the North). Other regional "centres" of the higher concentration of the Gypsies, were, according to the 1991 census: Kladno (Central Bohemia); Rakovník and Plzeň-město (Western Bohemia); Český Krumlov (Southern Bohemia); and Bruntál, Přerov, Ostrava-město and Karviná (Northern Moravia) (Figure 18.5).

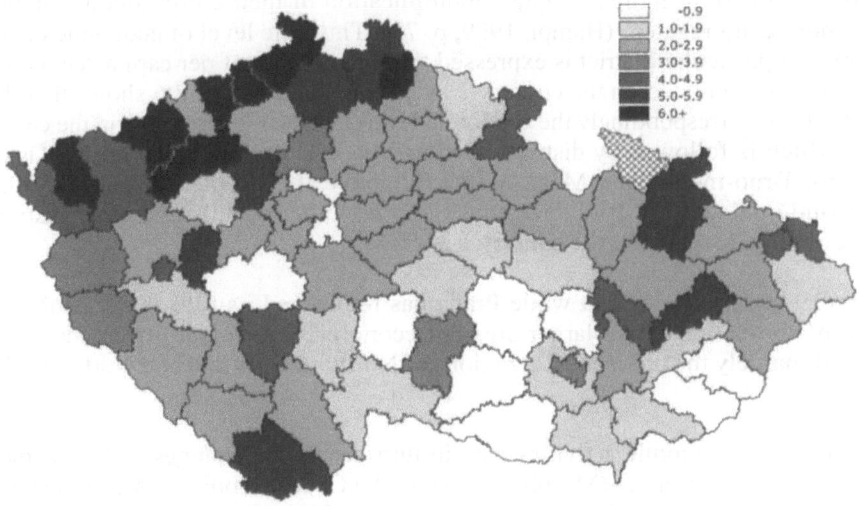


**Figure 18.5: Proportion of the Gypsy Population, 1991, per mille**

Source: Kalibová, 1996, p. 76

The lower proportion of the Gypsy population in Most (Northern Bohemia) in Figure 18.5 is the result of incomplete registration. The 1980 census, when the census data collectors ticked off the forms filled by people "looking (or living) as Gypsies" (Kalibová, 1999), indicated higher (more than 3%) proportion of this ethnic group in the total population, especially in districts such as Most, Sokolov and Teplice (Kučera M., 1996, p. 340). In Most, the Gypsies were, for example, concentrated in the micro-district called Chánov, where data collectors had almost no access.

### 18.2.3 Economic Structures and Labour Market

The socio-economic environment in the 1990s not only crucially differed from that in the 1980s, but also witnessed a more pronounced differentiation in its regional levels: whereas some of districts have enjoyed a relatively high economic growth, the others have faced an economic retraction resulted in the general worsening of social conditions for its populations. It appears that the main factors underlying the regional distinctions in economic development are a pronounced decline in the industrial sector (including the light industries such as textile, clothing, or glass production) and the increasing spatial disparity with respect to newly formed industries and services. Also, changes in trade patterns, particularly, markedly weakening trade ties with the former USSR and, on the other hand, a strong intensification of cross-border trade activities with Germany and Austria, have caused further shifts in regional economic structures.

Because the Czech official statistical data still does not enable direct comparison of the economic development across the districts, we use for this purpose the indirect estimations based on the values of the GDP in relation to wages and employment, considering them, or more accurate – multiplication of their corresponding values, as "economic aggregates" (Hampl, 1999, p. 73). Thus, the level of economic development of a particular district is expressed through a value of per capita "economic aggregate" recalculated on the country's average level. Figure 18.6 shows that this indicator (and correspondingly the economic level) has the highest value in the capital Praha, which is followed by districts such as Mladá Boleslav, Plzeň-město, Ostrava-město, Brno-město, and Most. Markedly above the average level are further České Budějovice, Zlín, Pardubice, and Ústí nad Labem, whilst the other districts have economic level under the country's average.

Vozáb (1998) also notes that while Praha has reinforced its role as the economic engine of the country, two larger areas of economic and social differences have appeared, namely the old industrial regions of Northern Bohemia and Northern Moravia.

Fluctuations in economic activities may in turn accelerate changes in labour markets and working practices (Murphy, 1994). In the Czech Republic, one of the basic features of the economic restructuring during the 1990s was a decrease of industrial output in the heavy sectors and textiles. The Czech military industry, previously being a major employer in many districts, has also witnessed a drastic decline over the recent decade. On one hand, all these can be seen as positive developments restoring the balance between heavy industry and the market-oriented sectors. On the other, employment reduction in the declining industrial branches has not been compensated by a job growth in the remaining and/or emerging industries and tertiary sector. For example, though the financial service sector has been rapidly expanding during the same period, it has mainly been concentrated in large cities with already existing "institutional framework" (Sharp and Barz, 1996, p. 205).

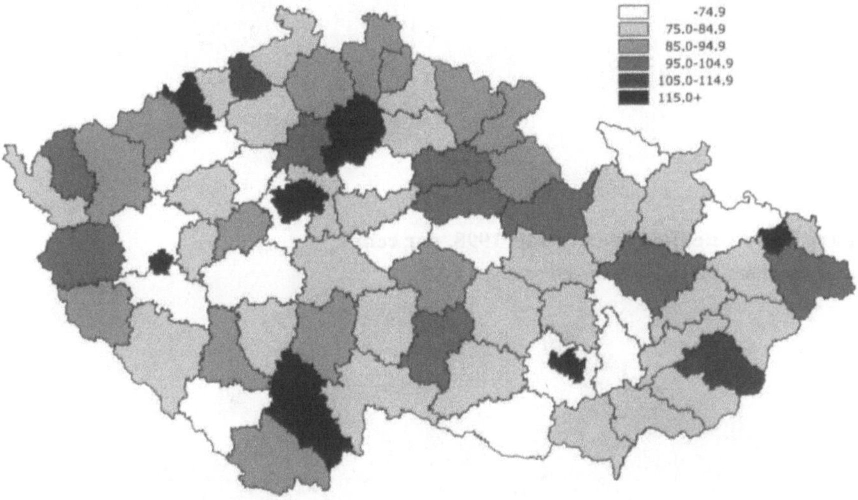


**Figure 18.6: Economic Level[1], 1998, index (Czech Republic = 100)**

[1]Economic level is evaluated on the basis of economic aggregate, i.e. the average of wages and salaries multiplied by the number of employees, related to the total population (per capita)
Source: Authors' calculations based on ČSÚ, 1999

As a result, paradoxically, unemployment has been particularly concentrated in such districts as Most, Ostrava-město, Karviná and some others, despite the fact that several of them enjoyed a relatively high level of economic development (Figures 18.7 and 18.8). By the end of 1998, the highest (between 16% and 18%) unemployment rates were registered in the coal-mining districts, namely Chomutov, Most and Teplice, and in the neighbouring district Louny as well as in most Moravian districts, except Brno (city and countryside) in Southern Moravia and Uherské Hradiště and Zlín.

On the whole, the transition well demonstrates that the newer industries and services would be created first of all in the areas with an easier access to markets, banks, specialist suppliers, i.e. large cities or urban agglomerations, yet not necessarily in the areas which are losing jobs (Figure 18.9). This observation supports other international studies which have also identified a close link between the amount of new jobs and the level of infrastructure available (see, for example, Gorzelak, 1996; Kortus, 1996).

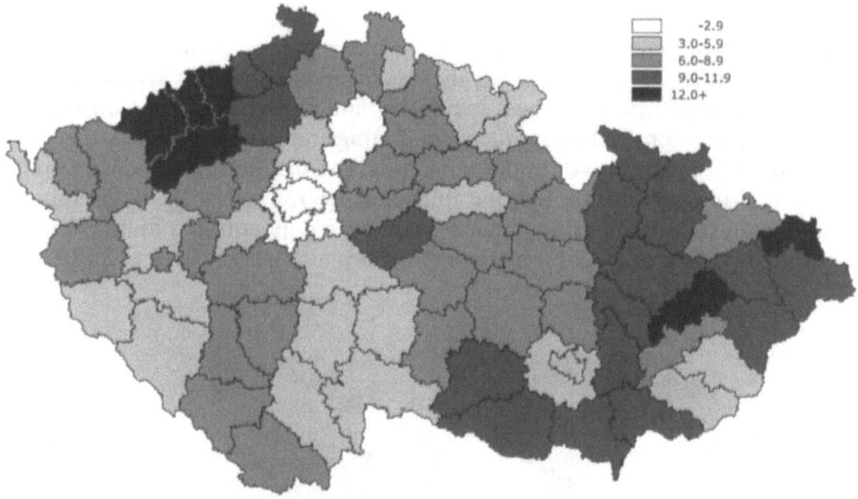


**Figure 18.7: Unemployment Rate, 1998, per cent**

Source: Authors' calculations based on ČSÚ, 1999

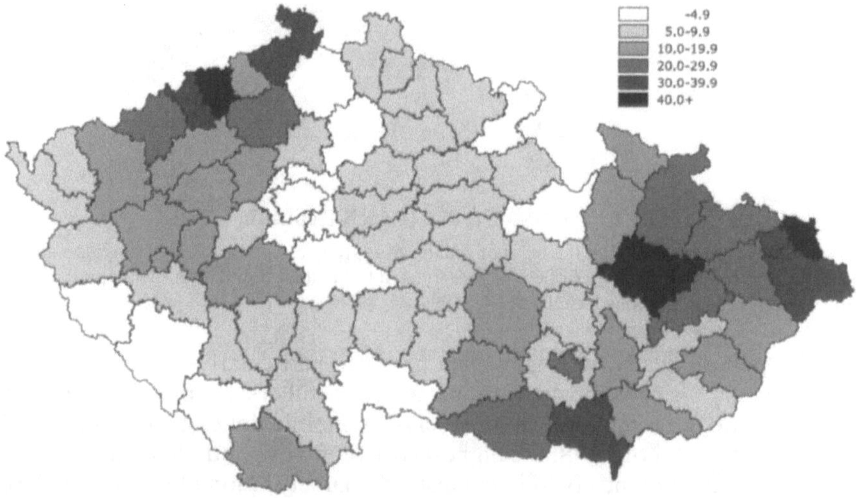


**Figure 18.8: Job Seekers per Vacancy, 1998**

Source: Authors' calculations based on ČSÚ, 1999

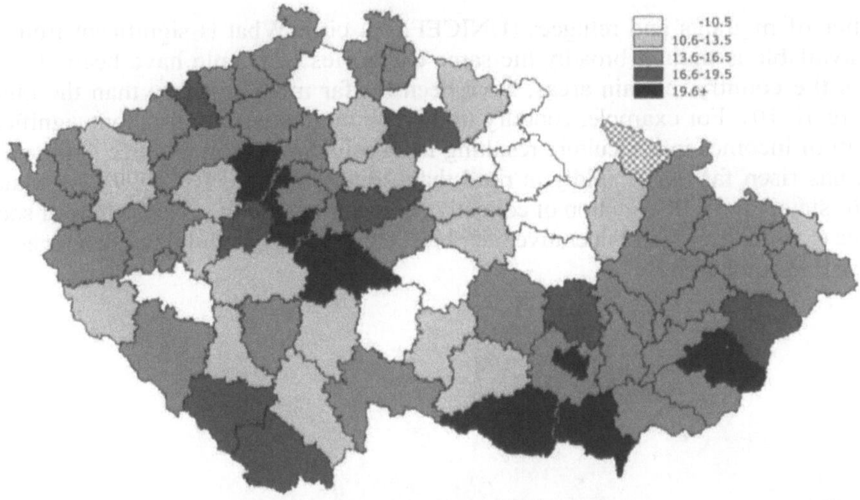


**Figure 18.9: Absolute Increase in Percentage of Jobs in Services Between 1989 and 1996**

Source: Hampl, 1999, p. 88

### 18.2.4 Income Distribution and Social Welfare

Though many demographic studies focus on the relationship between average income and demographic developments, there has still been no definitive answer to this question (see, for example, Lesthaeghe and Surkyn, 1988; Mellens, op. cit.). In advanced industrial societies, characterised by transition from material to post-material values (Inglehart, 1990), one may assume both positive and negative relationship, depending on specific circumstances as well as individuals' (families') motives and values. In the so-called transition societies where the economic security and material aspects of life, on the whole, seem still to be most important with respect to demographic outputs, decline in incomes may lead to the decreasing fertility and deteriorating of the population health. This is, of course, not to say that post-material values have no effect on people's behaviour in the Czech society at all. We would however emphasise that the overall population trends observed in the last decade have obviously been in line with the level of economic and social welfare. It is perhaps also worth noting that the similar trend has been documented in most post-communist countries (Council of Europe, 1999).

As regards income distribution, there is an increasing evidence that the economic difficulties caused by the transition to a free market have most affected such population groups as large and single-parent families; the elderly living on minimum pensions; people with severe disabilities and some minority (marginalised) people. These groups were often near the poverty line already during the socialist regime. Also, some new "risk groups" have recently appeared including young people in search of first employment, the unemployed, low-skilled workers, and a growing number of migrants and refugees (UNICEF, op. cit.). What is significant from the data available is though broadly the same categories of people have been affected across the country, certain areas, have been hit far more severely than the others (Figure 18.10). For example, contrary to the common expectations about significant growth of incomes in agriculture resulting from privatisation, in practice impoverishment has risen far more rapidly in rural than urban areas (AERI, 1999). As Maurel (1996) stated, the redistribution of collective ownership among several kinds of social groups (former owners, cooperative members, etc.) brought about new social inequalities within rural areas.

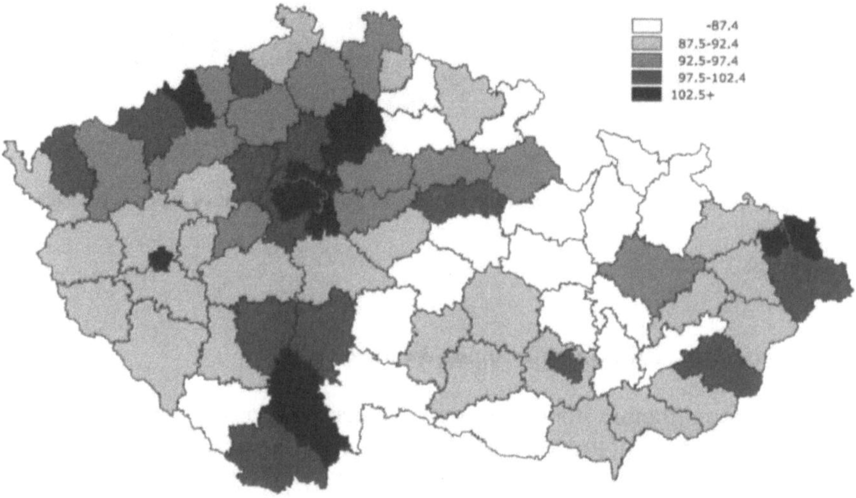


**Figure 18.10: Average Wages and Salaries of Employees, 1996, index (Czech Republic = 100)**

Source: Hampl, 1999, p. 70

It is important to note that, on the whole, privatisation introduced a new basic distinction between people, dividing them into owners and non-owners. And if the macro consequences of this phenomenon are well known, micro-level adjustments at the individual and local level seem to have been still underestimated (Maurel, op. cit.). It could be however assumed that districts with the higher privatisation rates may witness more significant and rapid social stratification of its populations and, consequently, higher levels of social tension and disorder.

Under the previous system, all redistribution took place mainly along the sectoral perspectives and "within the overall interconnected budgetary system" (Blažek and Kára, op. cit., p. 84), thus not primarily taking into account regional issues. In the first years of transition, the so-called "problem regions" – i.e. regions that experienced economic difficulties, environmental problems, or infrastructure shortage – have received some priority in the distribution system of grants for local governments (Figure 18.11). However, as some research indicate, general grants have not always had the levelling-off effects (Blažek, 1994, p. 87).

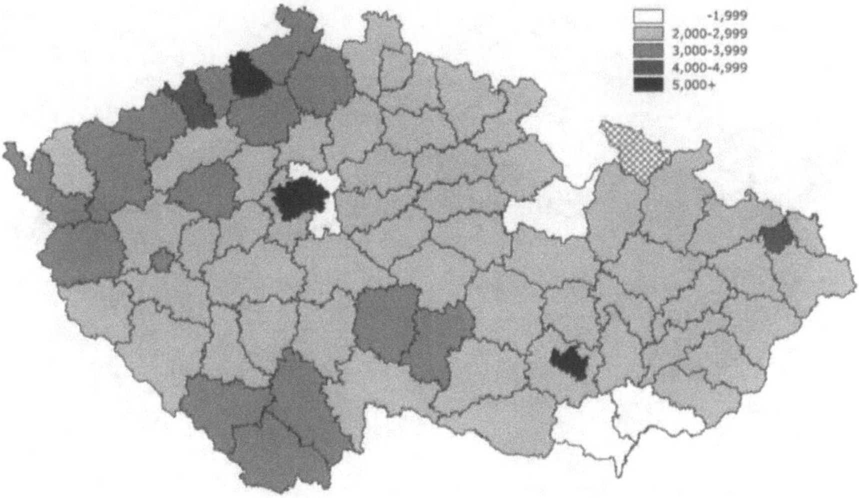


**Figure 18.11: General Grants per Capita, 1991, in the Czechoslovak Crowns**
Source: Blažek, op. cit., p. 87

But even if a general similarity among regions in total spending would exist, variation may persist in how resources are used and distributed in practice. In particular, regions may differ in the priority given to cash transfers (i.e. through various social payments and allowances) relative to services, and among services – in the priority given to community services relative to institutional care. On the whole, it can be suggested that community services would have lower priority in regions with less mature level of socio-economic development, and high priority in regions enjoying a relatively high economic growth (Figure 18.9). In addition, the variation in level of community services may also illustrate how local welfare policies are formed by individual choices (e.g. political orientations, religious believes etc.) than by the needs and resources.

Regardless the variation across the regions, the demands for services are, however, now growing and will be accelerating in the coming years because of socio-demographic changes in all regions. For instance, the prolongation of life and the ageing of population have produced more old people in need of care, while social changes have reduced the family capacity for caring. Moreover, women's increasing educational attainment and occupational careers are producing further needs for institutional supportive arrangements. The availability and standards of services may thus become the critical issue with respect to current and future population development. Regions or districts that have established services to meet these new challenges and/or reformed the already established social support systems would be more to withstand the negative effects of recent demographic development, as compared to those having less developed services (Figure 18.12).

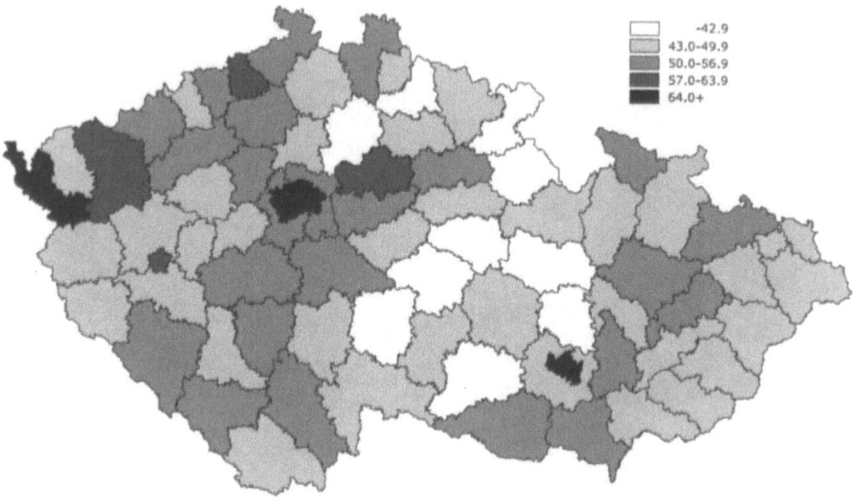


**Figure 18.12: Share of Services in the Total Number of Jobs, 1996, per cent**
Source: Hampl, 1999, p. 89

### 18.2.6 The Potential of Economic Growth (Transformation)

Progress in economic and social development, linked with the privatisation process and economic restructuring, also has its regional dimension and implications. The economic transformation reduces the role of traditional industrial agglomerations (e.g. coal-minning districts in Northern Bohemia), prioritising new modern industry, trade activities and tertiary facilities. As aforementioned, the latter ones are usually located in the areas with higher transformation possibilities (potential), i.e. in the areas with higher privatisation rates, larger concentration of foreign capital and with higher level of human capital (Figure 18.13). Moreover, foreign investments often mean putting further considerable resources in training local staff, both white and blue collar.

To sum up, it would seem at present that ongoing spatio-economic transformation will have led to increasing differentiation among the districts, also with respect to their potential of future growth. This disparity is also evident through the cross-regional differences in concentration of financial sector registered over the last decade (Table 18.1).

Several studies further indicate that the differences between districts with strong, on one hand, and weak, on the other, potential of economic growth (or transformation potential) tend to rise, particularly with respect to unemployment rates and income distribution (see, for example, Bičík and Kupková, 2000). Obviously, new work opportunities could hardly appear in the "problem areas", usually based on industrial "mono-culture" or on a one large plant. Figure 18.14 shows the variation between districts in distribution of jobs, which generally confirms the disparity between the wealthier Western and Southwest districts and the border regions and less affluent Eastern and Northeast districts.

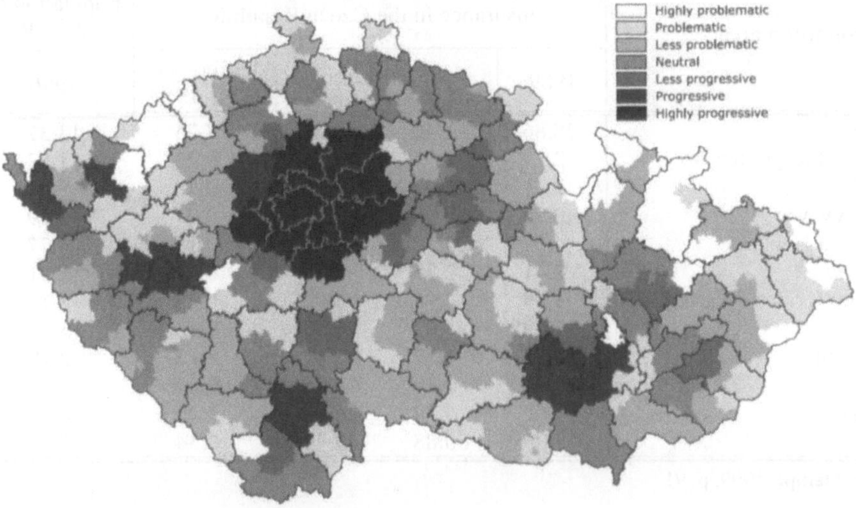


**Figure 18.13: Economic Potential**

Source: based on internal materials of M. Hampl (unpublished)

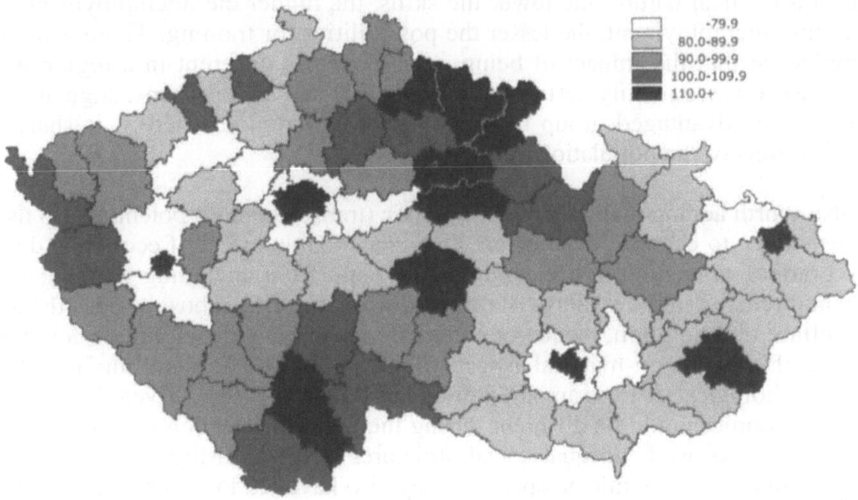


**Figure 18.14: Intensity of Working Opportunities[1], 1998, index (Czech Republic = 100)**

[1]Intensity of working opportunities is defined as a share of the number of working opportunities to the total population

Source: Hampl, 1999, p. 64

**Table 18.1: Concentration of Financial Sector, 1989–1996, selected years, per cent**

| Metropolitan area | Share of the number of jobs in finance and insurance in the Czech Republic | | | | Share of population of the CR |
|---|---|---|---|---|---|
| | 1989 | 1992 | 1996 | Difference 1996–1989 | 1996 |
| Praha | 28.86 | 31.40 | 36.61 | 7.75 | 13.32 |
| České Budějovice | 2.11 | 1.95 | 2.31 | 0.20 | 1.72 |
| Plzeň | 3.31 | 2.96 | 4.29 | 0.98 | 3.01 |
| Karlovy Vary | 0.96 | 0.99 | 0.95 | -0.01 | 1.19 |
| Ústí nad Labem | 4.02 | 3.80 | 3.83 | -0.19 | 4.77 |
| Liberec | 2.41 | 2.38 | 2.30 | -0.11 | 2.41 |
| Hradec Králové-Pardubice | 3.59 | 3.93 | 4.02 | 0.43 | 3.15 |
| Brno | 5.49 | 5.02 | 5.62 | 0.13 | 5.28 |
| Olomouc | 1.55 | 1.72 | 1.67 | 0.12 | 2.19 |
| Zlín | 1.14 | 1.39 | 1.78 | 0.64 | 1.91 |
| Ostrava | 5.62 | 5.34 | 6.02 | 0.40 | 8.13 |
| Total | 59.06 | 60.88 | 69.40 | 10.34 | 47.08 |

Source: Hampl, 1999, p. 91

As far as new investments usually not only create new jobs, but also significantly improve the quality of human capital in the area, the above relationship would seem to be of a cyclical nature: the lower the skills, the higher the unemployment – the higher the unemployment, the lesser the possibilities for training. There is no need to emphasise that the impact of being unemployed is different in a region where such an experience mainly pertains to a rather selected and, perhaps, stigmatised or otherwise disadvantaged group in society than in a region where it is shared by large fractions of the population.

It is also worth adding that the lower economic (transformation) potential also means less resistance to economic recession. One unavoidable effect of economic decline is the gradual worsening of life conditions of population, including growing uncertainty and tension in the society (Blažek and Kára, op. cit.). Thus, besides the absolute welfare deterioration, the lower potential of economic development could have negative effects on non-material aspects of the quality of life, resulting in high levels of psychological distress among individuals (Glasová, 1999). Even the impact of earnings/incomes could be different during the period of economic growth than in harder times. As well, unequal social structures – e.g. housing, which is usually strongly linked to economic prosperity – may also have led to different demographic outcomes with respect to family formation and childbearing (a close relationship between life strategies and housing opportunities and constrains was discussed, for example, by Mulder, 1993).

In order to illustrate our hypothesis about the increasing cross-regional variability of population patterns as a result of both universal and specific trends in socio-economic development occurred at the level of regions (districts), we next discuss regional differences in fertility and mortality.

## 18.3 Regional Differences in Fertility Development

In the 1980s, the total fertility rate (TFR) – as well as the other indicators of fertility – has steadily slowed down. The crucial changes in the political system together with new social and economic climate that emerged in the early 1990s have influenced demographic behaviour of the population, albeit with a time-lag. For instance, the most significant drop in the TFR after 1989 occurred for the first time in 1992. This year became the beginning of the new important period in the post-war population development in the Czech Republic characterised by unexpectedly strong and sharp fall in the level of fertility. The intensity of fertility drop was culminated already in 1994, when the value of the TFR fell by 0.23 live-born children per woman as compared to 1993. From 1987 to 1998, the TFR has fallen from 1.91 to 1.16, i.e. by 40%.

Similar and even more dramatic changes have been occurring at the regional level of population development. During the period of 1987–1998, among 76 districts including the capital Praha (since 1996 – among 77 regions including the newly established Jeseník district), the maximum value of the TFR had fluctuated between 2.12 and 1.32, while its minimum value – between 1.72 and 1.02 (Table 18.2). Until 1992, the most significant drop in the level of fertility was observed among districts where the values of the TFR were the lowest, yet their proportion was relatively small at that time. The acceleration of fertility decline could therefore be connected with the growing number of districts experiencing the decreasing fertility.

**Table 18.2: Cross-district Variation in the Total Fertility Rate, 1987–1998, selected years**

| | 1987 | 1990 | 1993 | 1994 | 1995 | 1996 | 1997 | 1998 |
|---|---|---|---|---|---|---|---|---|
| Minimal value | 1.72 | 1.71 | 1.44 | 1.26 | 1.13 | 1.05 | 1.05 | 1.02 |
| Maximal value | 2.12 | 2.13 | 1.91 | 1.64 | 1.47 | 1.38 | 1.37 | 1.32 |
| Range | 0.40 | 0.42 | 0.47 | 0.38 | 0.34 | 0.33 | 0.32 | 0.30 |
| Standard deviation | 0.086 | 0.094 | 0.090 | 0.075 | 0.067 | 0.062 | 0.066 | 0.058 |
| Coefficient of variation | 4.4 | 4.9 | 5.3 | 5.1 | 5.2 | 5.2 | 5.6 | 4.9 |

Source: Authors' calculations

In the beginning of the 1990s, as a result of the above-mentioned asymmetry in the fertility development, there had been a pronounced regional differentiation in the TFR values; it has however started disappearing, and since 1992 the fertility decline is becoming continuous and rapid in most districts. The changes recorded in the evolution of fertility in the first half of the 1990s allow us to identify some general principles (features) of the transformation of demographic behaviour patterns, particularly a short-term heterogeneity as regards the level and intensity of the fertility development, which likely to appear in course of the transition to a new, qualitatively different fertility model.

Yet some direct and quite profound relationships between the differentiation in fertility level and the whole economic and social status of a region could be found, one has to recognise that the previous heterogeneity reflected rather the unity of economic and social conditions of the regional development than its differentiation. This can be supported by the data presented in Table 18.2, which demonstrates that the opposite trend – the weakening of regional differences – has recently become more obvious. On the other hand, the issue of expected regional differentiation cannot be seen as absolutely ill posed. It seems that general assumptions about accelerating differences among districts in the population development have underestimated the effect that the crucial societal changes may have on the evolution of demographic phenomena, especially in the initial stage of the transformation. Moreover, it is reasonable to suppose that such differences could appear and, moreover, increase in the future. A final point is that though under current conditions no significant relation has been observed between the level of fertility, on one hand, and social and economic indicators of a region, on the other, the possibility of stronger link in the coming years should not be disregarded.

The latter hypothesis concerning the time frame of achieving regional homogeneity with respect to the fertility levels is also supported by the results obtained on the basis of a more in-depth analysis. In particular, the fact that the currently observed "period of convergence" could be only the beginning of a more fundamental and long-term change in the regional demographic development, which may result in renewed diversity, is well illustrated by the changes in the distribution of the districts on both sides of the array (Table 18.3).

Parallel to general statistical regularities in the distribution of the TFR values, one may observe substantial and sustained cross-district variations based on the more specific structural conditions. For example, the higher (as compared with the average for the Czech Republic) fertility levels can be observed extensively among some Moravian districts (Žd'ár nad Sázavou, Třebíč, Svitavy). In Bohemia, districts with more-than-average values of fertility registered in the long run are traditionally concentrated in the East, mostly in the rural areas (Ústí nad Orlicí, Chrudim), and in some districts near the Western border (Prachatice, Sokolov, Chomutov and Děčín). Similarly, among the districts with the lowest levels of fertility, Praha and surrounding areas as well as the districts of Brno-město and Plzeň-město have historically prevailed. Recently, five other units such as Strakonice, Klatovy, Domažlice, Vyškov and Přerov have joined these "traditional" districts with a low fertility. Tables 18.4 and 18.5 demonstrate the changes in the levels of TFR (both minimal and maximum values) that occured during the three most important in terms of fertility development years – 1987, 1993 and 1998.

**Table 18.3: Distribution of Districts by the Total Fertility Rate, 1987–1998, selected years**

| TFR | Number of districts in a given interval | | | | | | | |
|---|---|---|---|---|---|---|---|---|
| | 1987 | 1990 | 1993 | 1994 | 1995 | 1996 | 1997 | 1998 |
| 1.01–1.08 | - | - | - | - | - | 1 | 5 | 6 |
| 1.09–1.16 | - | - | - | - | 2 | 16 | 17 | 31 |
| 1.17–1.24 | - | - | - | - | 9 | 40 | 39 | 44 |
| 1.25–1.32 | - | - | - | 3 | 39 | 18 | 13 | 6 |
| 1.33–1.40 | - | - | - | 11 | 20 | 2 | 3 | - |
| 1.41–1.48 | - | - | 1 | 34 | 6 | - | - | - |
| 1.49–1.56 | - | - | 3 | 19 | - | - | - | - |
| 1.57–1.64 | - | - | 15 | 9 | - | - | - | - |
| 1.65–1.72 | 1 | 1 | 30 | - | - | - | - | - |
| 1.73–1.80 | 2 | 9 | 21 | - | - | - | - | - |
| 1.81–1.88 | 19 | 19 | 3 | - | - | - | - | - |
| 1.89–1.96 | 32 | 27 | 3 | - | - | - | - | - |
| 1.97–2.04 | 12 | 14 | - | - | - | - | - | - |
| 2.05–2.12 | 10 | 3 | - | - | - | - | - | - |
| 2.13–2.20 | - | 3 | - | - | - | - | - | - |

Source: Authors' calculations

As already mentioned, from 1987 through 1998, a general downward trend was accompanied by significant regional differences in the tempo and intensity of fertility decline. Most significantly, it has been manifested in Strakonice, where the TFR during this period fell by 51%, and also in the districts, where the fertility level was previously over the average, such as Tachov, Česká Lípa and Semily. The smallest decline was observed in the districts Svitavy and Prachatice, where the TFR decreased by about one-third. The comparison of cross-year indexes provides, in addition, evidence that the strongest drop in the level of fertility was in 1994 (on the average, by 14%), with the maximum value of decline (21%) registered in Svitavy and Vyškov.

**Table 18.4: Districts with the Lowest Total Fertility Rate, 1987, 1993, 1998**

| 1987 | | 1993 | | 1998 | |
|---|---|---|---|---|---|
| Plzeň-město | 1.70 | Praha | 1.44 | Strakonice | 1.02 |
| Brno-město | 1.74 | Plzeň-město | 1.48 | Praha | 1.05 |
| Praha | 1.76 | Cheb | 1.50 | Kolín | 1.07 |
| Cheb | 1.80 | Brno-město | 1.56 | Domažlice | 1.07 |
| Ostrava-město | 1.81 | Jablonec nad Nisou | 1.56 | Brno-město | 1.08 |
| Praha-západ | 1.81 | Ostrava-město | 1.58 | Plzeň-město | 1.08 |
| Kladno | 1.82 | Nymburk | 1.58 | Klatovy | 1.08 |
| Pardubice | 1.82 | Beroun | 1.58 | Zlín | 1.10 |
| Pelhřimov | 1.84 | Rakovník | 1.59 | Přerov | 1.11 |
| Mladá Boleslav | 1.84 | Pardubice | 1.60 | Vyškov | 1.11 |

Source: Authors' calculations

**Table 18.5: Districts with the Highest Total Fertility Rate, 1987, 1993, 1998**

| 1987 | | 1993 | | 1998 | |
|---|---|---|---|---|---|
| Česká Lípa | 2.12 | Svitavy | 1.91 | Ústí nad Orlicí | 1.32 |
| Chomutov | 2.10 | Třebíč | 1.90 | Prachatice | 1.29 |
| Semily | 2.09 | Jindřichův Hradec | 1.88 | Děčín | 1.29 |
| Tachov | 2.08 | Žďár nad Sázavou | 1.87 | Sokolov | 1.26 |
| Český Krumlov | 2.07 | Vyškov | 1.83 | Pelhřimov | 1.26 |
| Ústí nad Orlicí | 2.07 | Blansko | 1.82 | Svitavy | 1.25 |
| Strakonice | 2.06 | Znojmo | 1.80 | Žďár nad Sázavou | 1.24 |
| Svitavy | 2.05 | Semily | 1.78 | Chomutov | 1.24 |
| Louny | 2.04 | Český Krumlov | 1.78 | Třebíč | 1.24 |
| Znojmo | 2.04 | Bruntál | 1.78 | Louny | 1.23 |

Source: Authors' calculations

Both the prolonging diversity in fertility trends and the resulting regional differentiation of the relative values of TFR (to the average TFR numbers) are shown in Figure 18.15. Besides differentiation in fertility development observed from 1987 through 1998, it demonstrates the basic characteristics of fertility transition relevant to regional populations.

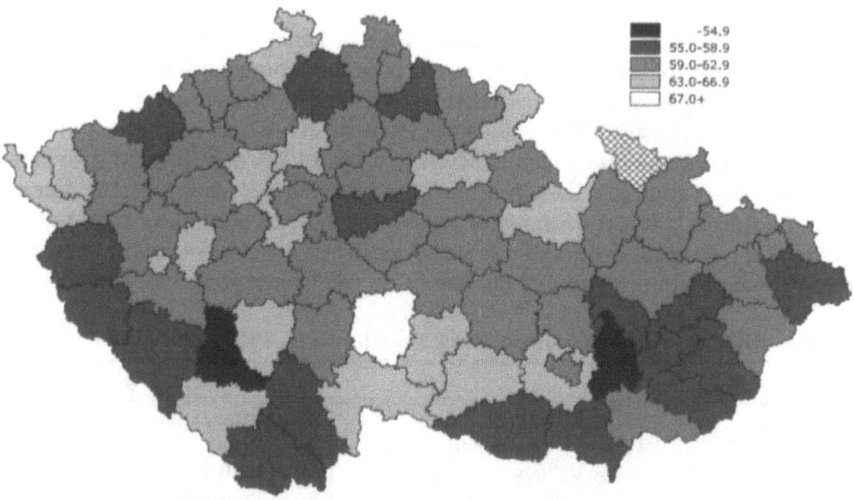


**Figure 18.15: The Change of the Total Fertility Rate Between 1987 and 1998, index (1987 = 100)**

Source: Authors' calculations

In the 1990s, not only the level of fertility has reached its historically low values. Important changes have also taken place with respect to the fertility distribution among age groups of the population. In the recent years, the model of fertility has been crucially transformed: the postponement of marriage and, consequently, the motherhood became more and more widespread among young women, and that has significantly influenced the "traditional" distribution of fertility by age. The mean age of women at childbearing has increased by two years; the number of childless women has also grown. In addition, the transformation of age-specific distribution of fertility was accompanied by some irregularities with respect to different age groups of women: while in the age groups 15–19, 20–24 and 25–29 the fertility rates in the period 1987–1998 dropped not only in relative but also in absolute terms, among women aged 30 or over, it experienced stagnation or even slight increase during the same period of time.

The most pronounced fall in the relative values was registered among women aged 15–19. In 1998, their fertility amounted to only as much as 37% of the value registered in 1987. This decrease was not however so important in view of the overall fertility because the contribution of this age group has never been significant, representing about 7% of the total value. The rapidly decreasing level of fertility has mostly been the result of the fertility decline among women aged 20–24. From 1987 through 1998, the fertility rate for this group fell by more than 55%, whereas the TFR – by 40%. In the course of the above-mentioned fertility development, the 20–24 age group has therefore lost its decisive role in forming the total fertility both on the national level and in most regions – in 1998, the contribution of this age group to the TFR was 34%, compared to 47% in 1987 (Figures 18.16–18.18).

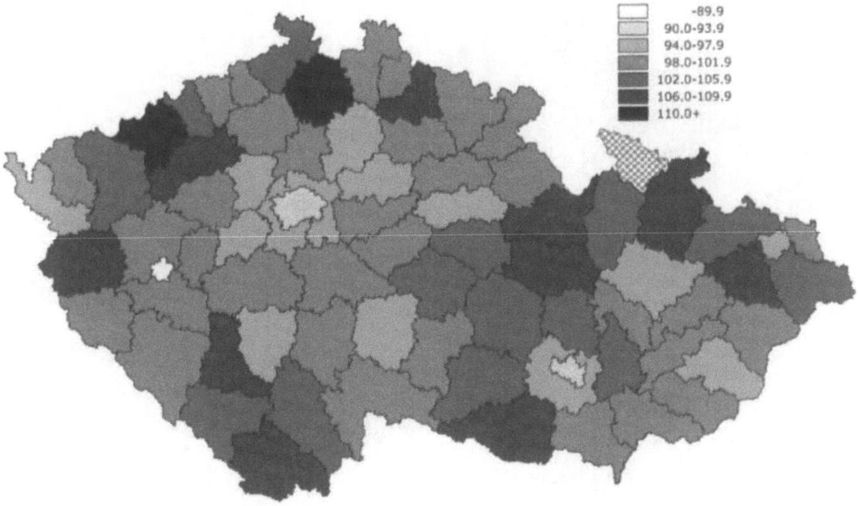


**Figure 18.16: Regional Differentiation of the Total Fertility Rate, 1987, index (Czech Republic = 100)**

Source: Authors' calculations

It should be taken into account that measuring the regional variation in the age-specific indicators of fertility may complicate the interpretation of the TFR as the average number of children per woman. For example, since 1995 the indicators showing the variation across the values of age-specific fertility rate for women aged 20–24 (Table 18.6) have been reaching the levels, which are almost twice as much as those of the TFR.

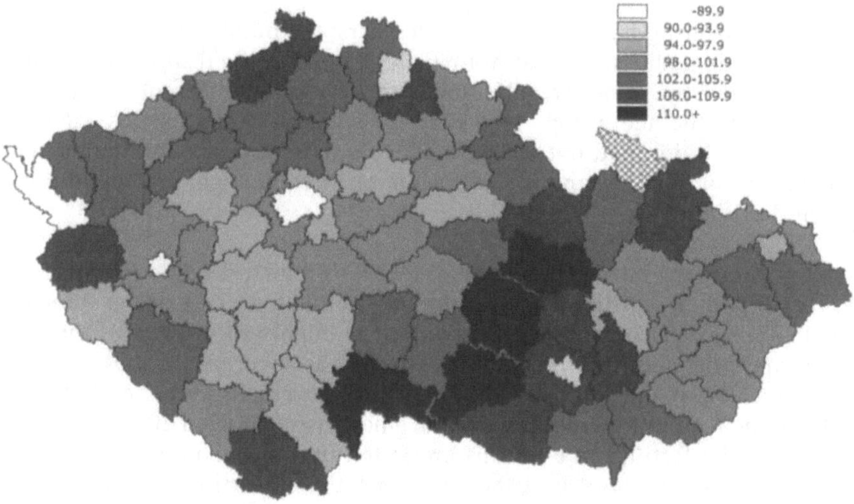


**Figure 18.17: Regional Differentiation of the Total Fertility Rate, 1993, index (Czech Republic = 100)**

Source: Authors' calculations

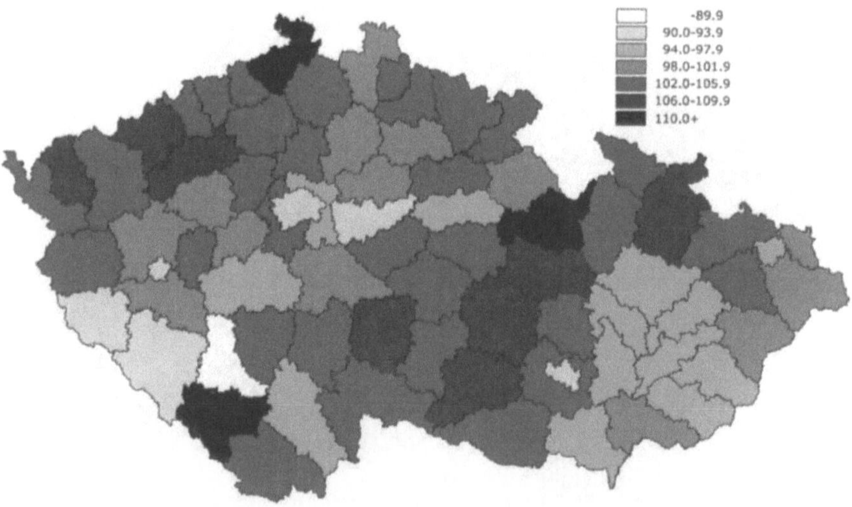


**Figure 18.18: Regional Differentiation of the Total Fertility Rate, 1998, index (Czech Republic = 100)**

Source: Authors' calculations

**Table 18.6: Cross-district Variation of the Age-specific Fertility Rate for the Age Group 20–24, 1987–1998, selected years**

| | 1987 | 1990 | 1993 | 1994 | 1995 | 1996 | 1997 | 1998 |
|---|---|---|---|---|---|---|---|---|
| Minimal value | 140 | 133 | 99 | 84 | 68 | 59 | 53 | 49 |
| Maximal value | 205 | 212 | 182 | 147 | 129 | 114 | 117 | 103 |
| Range | 65 | 79 | 83 | 63 | 61 | 55 | 64 | 54 |
| Standard deviation | 13.2 | 14.5 | 13.8 | 11.4 | 11.2 | 10.2 | 9.6 | 9.0 |
| Coefficient of variation | 7.2 | 8.0 | 9.1 | 9.0 | 10.3 | 10.6 | 10.6 | 10.6 |

Source: Authors' calculations

In the first stage of the fertility transition that had started in 1990, the differences in the fertility of the age group 20–24 have been gradually increasing across the regions. The growth of the variability alongside with the widening of the range suggested that in various districts the transformation of the fertility model – reflected foremost in the changes of the level and structure of fertility – was undergoing different stages. On the contrary, the narrowing of the range and the stagnation of values of the coefficient of variation over the last three years (1996–1998) can be seen as a sign of the formation of a "new" regional structure according to the age-specific fertility level. However, in view of the continuous decrease of extreme values, these developments could also have led to the decline (supposedly, a slight and short-term) of the fertility among women aged 20–24 and thus a certain modification of the present regional fertility structure (Figures 18.19–18.21).

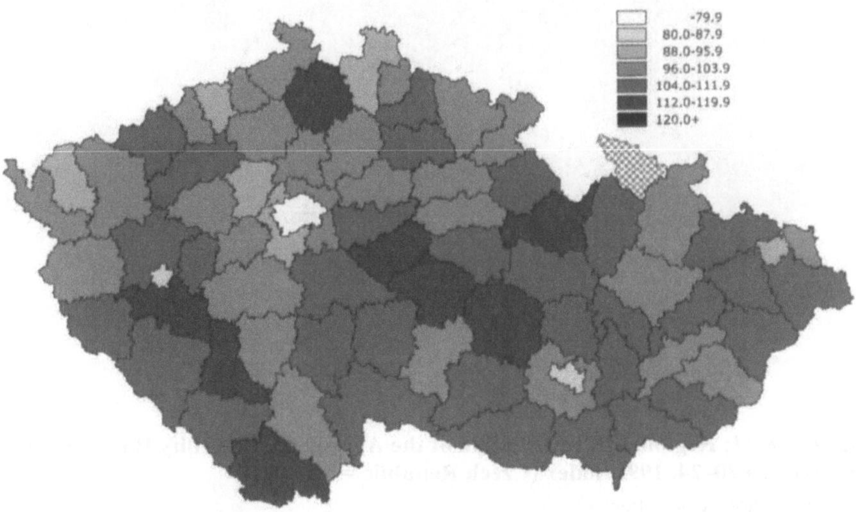


**Figure 18.19: Regional Differentiation of the Age-specific Fertility Rate for the Age Group 20–24, 1987, index (Czech Republic = 100)**

Source: Authors' calculations

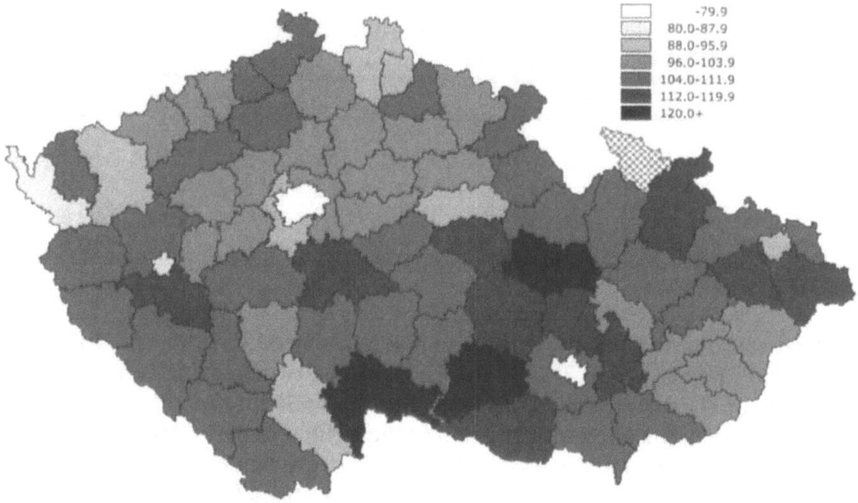


**Figure 18.20: Regional Differentiation of the Age-specific Fertility Rate for the Age Group 20–24, 1993, index (Czech Republic = 100)**

Source: Authors' calculations

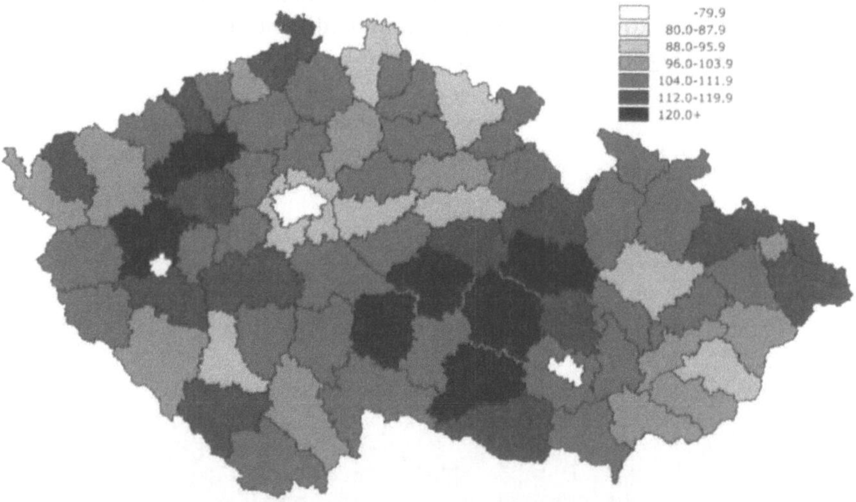


**Figure 18.21: Regional Differentiation of the Age-specific Fertility Rate for the Age Group 20–24, 1998, index (Czech Republic = 100)**

Source: Authors' calculations

The decline of fertility in the age group 20–24 has been observed in all districts, with a relative value of decline varying between 42% (Sokolov) and 64% (Strakonice and Praha). The sequences of regional structures with respect to selected time-periods reflect, besides the above-mentioned increasing regional differentiation, the regional structure based on the comparison of the districts' levels of fertility and the average country's level. With respect to the latter structure (resulting indeed from the first one), the most striking evidence is a special status of the three "city-districts" – the capital Praha, Brno-město and Plzeň-město. The drastic fall of fertility among young women observed here suggests that the further decline of fertility across the other districts is still possible.

After 1989, the fertility in the age group 25–29 has also experienced important changes. First, the contribution to the total fertility of this group has increased, gaining the first position and replacing the age group 20–24. In 1998, the contribution of women aged 20–25 to the age-specific fertility was 36%, i.e. by one-tenth larger than in 1987, though the level of fertility in this age group had fallen by 17% during the same period of time. Yet the decline in the two other age groups (under 20 and 20–24 years) was even higher, resulting thus in the increasing contribution of the 25–29 age group.

In the period 1987–1998, the variation of fertility among women aged 25–29 was (as in the case of the age group 20–24) larger than the variation of the TFR (Table 18.7). It may be argued that the growth of the range between 1996 and 1998 represents a first sign of the expected fertility compensation that is the realisation of the postponed childbearing by women aged 25–29 years.

**Table 18.7: Cross-district Variation of the Age-specific Fertility Rate for the Age Group 25–29, 1987–1998, selected years**

| | 1987 | 1990 | 1993 | 1994 | 1995 | 1996 | 1997 | 1998 |
|---|---|---|---|---|---|---|---|---|
| Minimal value | 88 | 85 | 78 | 65 | 68 | 64 | 68 | 73 |
| Maximal value | 117 | 116 | 113 | 103 | 93 | 94 | 96 | 97 |
| Range | 29 | 31 | 35 | 38 | 25 | 30 | 28 | 24 |
| Standard deviation | 6.5 | 7.9 | 7.6 | 6.3 | 5.1 | 6.0 | 5.9 | 5.6 |
| Coefficient of variation | 6.5 | 7.8 | 8.1 | 7.4 | 6.3 | 7.6 | 7.2 | 6.6 |

Source: Authors' calculations

In terms of regional differentiation, the fertility rate in the age group 25–29 has experienced the largest decline in districts such as Semily and Karlovy Vary (over 30%); on the contrary, the smallest decline of the fertility rate was registered in districts of Kutná Hora, Pelhřimov and Havlíčkův Brod. Based on the recent evidence, i.e. that over the last years there has been observed the realisation of the postponed motherhood in the age group 25–29, we can also assume that it will be women aged 25–29 who will mostly compensate the decreasing fertility in the younger age groups. Data shows that while in almost all regions the lowest fertility rates for women aged 25–29 were registered in 1996, in the following years the minimal values have been growing faster than the maximal ones. And though none of the districts had reached the pre-1987 level of fertility, in 1998 some of them demonstrated values which were close to it. As far as this trend to be continued, it can be expected that the fertility rate in this age group will reach the level of 1987 and even exceed it. As a result, the contribution of the age group 25–29 to the TFR will also have grown. Figures 18.22–18.24 show the development of fertility in this age group in relation to the country's average level.

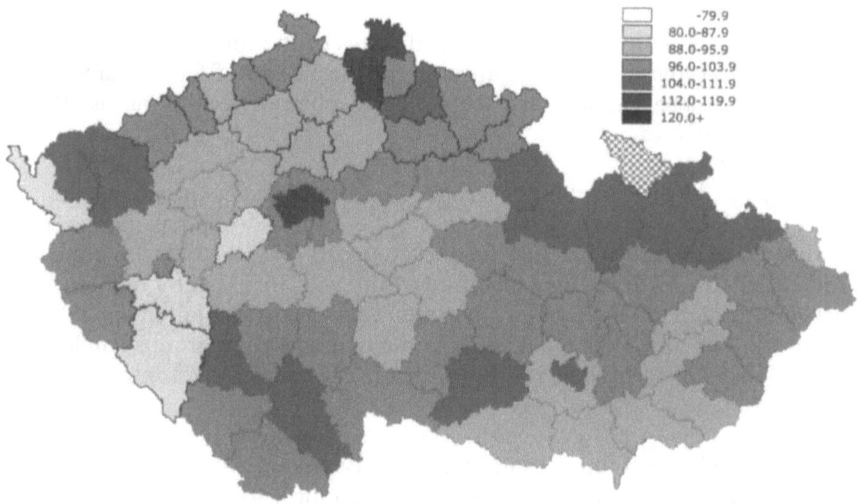


**Figure 18.22: Regional Differentiation of the Age-specific Fertility Rate for the Age Group 25–29, 1987, index (Czech Republic = 100)**

Source: Authors' calculations

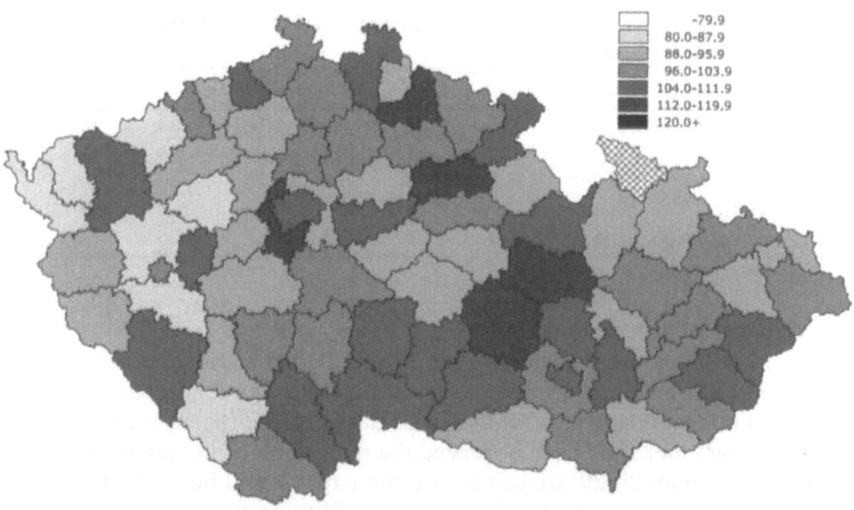


**Figure 18.23: Regional Differentiation of the Age-specific Fertility Rate for the Age Group 25–29, 1993, index (Czech Republic = 100)**

Source: Authors' calculations

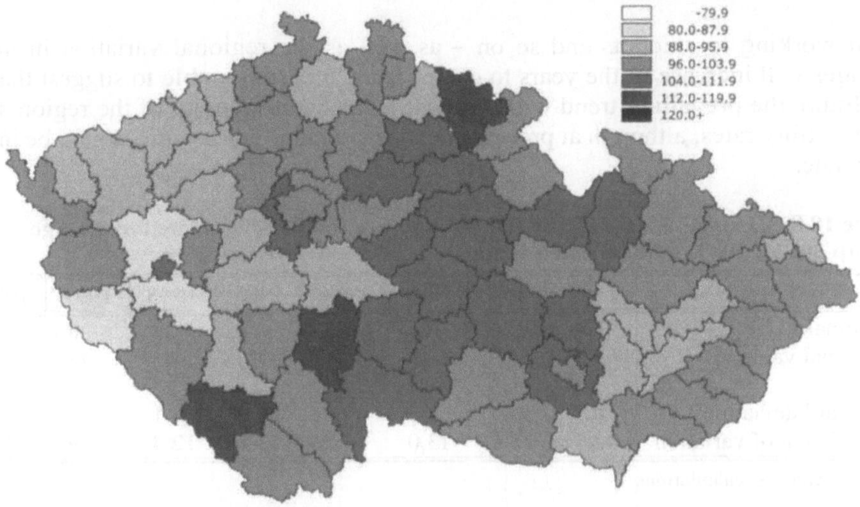


**Figure 18.24: Regional Differentiation of the Age-specific Fertility Rate for the Age Group 25–29, 1998, index (Czech Republic = 100)**

Source: Authors' calculations

During 1987–1998, the contribution of previously less "important" age group 30–34 to the total fertility had grown by two-thirds (16% in 1998), whereas the variation across districts – by one-third, being accompanied by slightly increasing age-specific fertility rates (Table 18.8). With respect to this age group, the variation in rate values is striking – both minimal and maximum positions are occupied by the districts that have the lowest levels of the TFR. On one hand, maximum values have been registered in the districts where the process of age-specific fertility transition has entered the major stage, characterised by the very low values of the TFR as well as by higher mean age of women at childbearing (Praha, Brno-město, Liberec, Semily and some others). On the other, minimal levels of fertility in this age group were registered among the districts where the transformation of fertility pattern has had a shape of a more or less unified (for all age groups) decline of fertility without any significant rise in the mean age of women at childbearing (Strakonice, Rakovník, Kolín, Domažlice).

To conclude, though over the 1990s there has been an impact on fertility from some general change in the social climate for childbearing in the country (that affects practically all districts and all groups of women simultaneously), this does not imply that there has been no effect of economic, social, cultural and other variables on fertility trends existing in particular regions. The almost universal drop in the TFR can be interpreted in a way that more fundamental changes in the reproductive behaviour have temporarily blocked or limited the influence of the region-specific conditions, particularly the cross-regional changes in population educational, occupational or income structures. It may be argued, however, that the effect on childbearing of such compositional changes – e.g. the shift of large segments of individuals (families) from high- to low-income groups, from employed to unemployed, from working to students and so on – as well as the regional variation in these changes will increase in the years to come. Thus, it is reasonable to suggest that in the future the prevailing trend will be towards the heterogeneity of the region-specific fertility rates, although at present one may consider this assumption to be inappropriate.

**Table 18.8: Cross-district Variation of the Age-specific Fertility Rate for the Age Group 30–34, 1987–1998, selected years**

| | 1987 | 1990 | 1993 | 1994 | 1995 | 1996 | 1997 | 1998 |
|---|---|---|---|---|---|---|---|---|
| Minimal value | 24 | 26 | 25 | 24 | 23 | 22 | 26 | 27 |
| Maximal value | 47 | 49 | 49 | 49 | 46 | 45 | 48 | 50 |
| Range | 23 | 23 | 24 | 25 | 23 | 23 | 22 | 23 |
| Standard deviation | 4.2 | 4.4 | 4.5 | 4.5 | 4.0 | 4.1 | 4.5 | 4.9 |
| Coefficient of variation | 12.1 | 12.0 | 13.0 | 13.2 | 12.1 | 12.4 | 12.9 | 13.4 |

Source: Authors' calculations

## 18.4 Regional Differences in the Development of Mortality

As in the case of fertility, the late 1980 – early 1990s also became the beginning of a new stage in the development of mortality. After long-term stagnation, distinguished first of all by mortality level lagging behind the values characteristic to Western industrialised countries, from the mid-1980s mortality has started improving. In 1987, life expectancy at birth achieved about 68 years for men and 75 years for women. Since then on, these have been gradually increasing, reaching in 1998 values of 71 and 78 years, respectively (i.e. have increased by 3 years). The similar trend has been evident in most regions. While at the beginning of the considered period (1987–1989) the male life expectancy at birth varied across districts between 65 and 70 years, by the end of the period (1996–1998) it oscillated between 68 and 73 years; for women, life expectancy at birth increased from 73–77 years to 75–79 years, depending on the district. Figures 18.25 and 18.26 show differentiation of regions according to life expectancy at birth based on the average levels for three-year intervals, both for males and females (the interval indicators are used to avoid possible drawbacks of using small samples of died, especially in case of small territorial units).

At first sight, the differentiation of values of life expectancy at birth considered on the sub-national level could be seen as insignificant, mainly due to relatively low values of some coefficients of variation. However, any consideration of the regional differences in mortality should be based on the previous analysis of the commonalities as well as causality of this process. Being quite a stable demographic phenomenon, mortality is inasmuch less influenced by "external" conditions (and their variability), as compared to the other demographic processes. Thus, it may be hypothesised that low values of both standard deviation and coefficient of variation have made the real differences in the life expectancy across the districts hidden from view. The evidence that may further support this is the observed higher values of the range (Table 18.9).

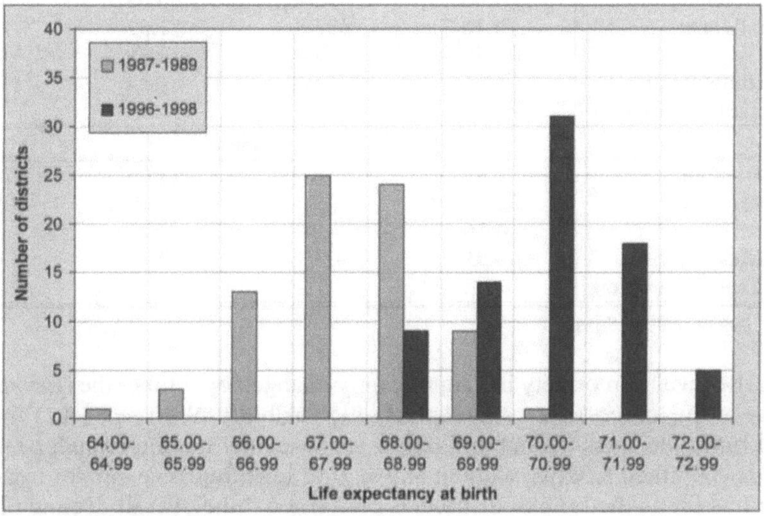


**Figure 18.25: Distribution of Districts by Life Expectancy at Birth, 1987–1989 and 1996–1998, male**

Source: Authors' calculations

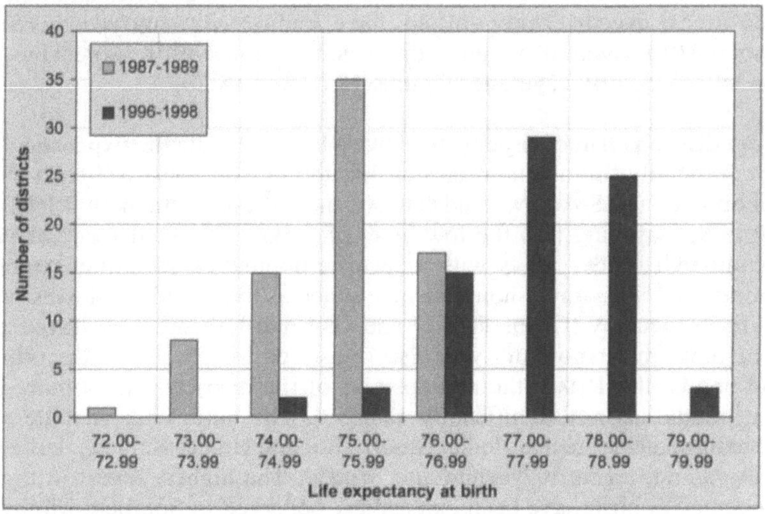


**Figure 18.26: Distribution of Districts by Life Expectancy at Birth, 1987–1989 and 1996–1998, female**

Source: Authors' calculations

**Table 18.9: Cross-district Variation in Life Expectancy at Birth by Sex, 1987–1998**

| | 1987–1989 | 1990–1992 | 1993–1995 | 1996–1998 |
|---|---|---|---|---|
| | Male | | | |
| Minimal value | 64.86 | 65.34 | 66.68 | 68.18 |
| Maximal value | 70.26 | 69.98 | 71.57 | 72.57 |
| Range | 5.40 | 4.64 | 4.89 | 4.39 |
| Standard deviation | 1.05 | 1.04 | 1.04 | 1.05 |
| Coefficient of variation | 1.6 | 1.5 | 1.5 | 1.5 |
| | Female | | | |
| Minimal value | 72.83 | 73.16 | 73.66 | 74.70 |
| Maximal value | 76.99 | 77.34 | 78.09 | 79.31 |
| Range | 4.16 | 4.18 | 4.43 | 4.61 |
| Standard deviation | 0.91 | 0.93 | 0.93 | 0.96 |
| Coefficient of variation | 1.2 | 1.2 | 1.2 | 1.2 |

Source: Authors' calculations

Though the level of mortality has significantly changed over time, the regional differentiation of this process shows a relatively high stability. With respect to life expectancy at birth, the cross-district differences are evidently not increasing; on the other hand, they continue to exist, without any sign of levelling. The similar trend can be observed as far as the rank of districts is concerned – the overall decline of mortality has not changed the cross-district differentiation in the level of this process. While Northwest and Western regions of Bohemia and Northern Moravia have had extensively less favourable dynamics of mortality, the districts situated in the Czech Moravian Highlands, Northeast Bohemia as well as the large cities and other highly urbanised areas, except Ostrava-město, have traditionally enjoyed more positive development in this area. In the other districts, the values of life expectancy at birth are close to the country's average (Figures 18.27 and 18.28).

Among ten districts characterised by the lowest levels of male life expectancy at birth, one can continually find the four districts located in Northwest Bohemia – Teplice, Most, Chomutov and Sokolov – and Ostrava-město (except the period 1993–1995). The first ones, enjoying also the low level of female life expectancy at birth, are typical industrial border zones with a specific population structure. Among their neighbouring districts, three should be mentioned as those with the lowest values of female life expectancy (Cheb, Tachov and Ústí nad Labem). Less favourable dynamics of the female mortality was also registered in Děčín. On the other hand, since the end of the 1980s, the composition of the districts with a more positive mortality trends has not significantly changed. The latter ones include not only highly urbanised areas such as Praha, Brno-město and Hradec Králové, but also Žďár nad Sázavou and, recently, Náchod and Semily. The highest levels of the female life expectancy at birth have been extensively observed in Southern Moravian districts such as Žďár nad Sázavou, Třebíč, Brno-venkov and Vyškov, and also in Hradec Králové (Tables 18.10 and 18.11).

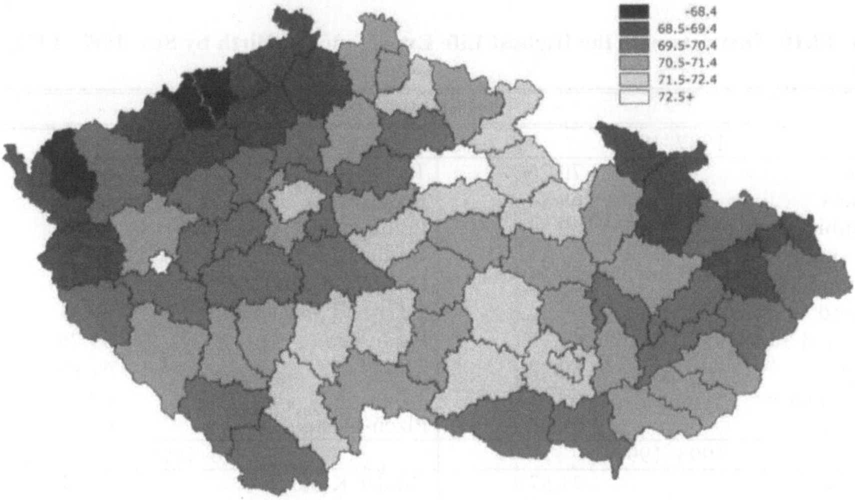


**Figure 18.27: Regional Differentiation of Life Expectancy at Birth, 1996–1998, male**

Source: Authors' calculations

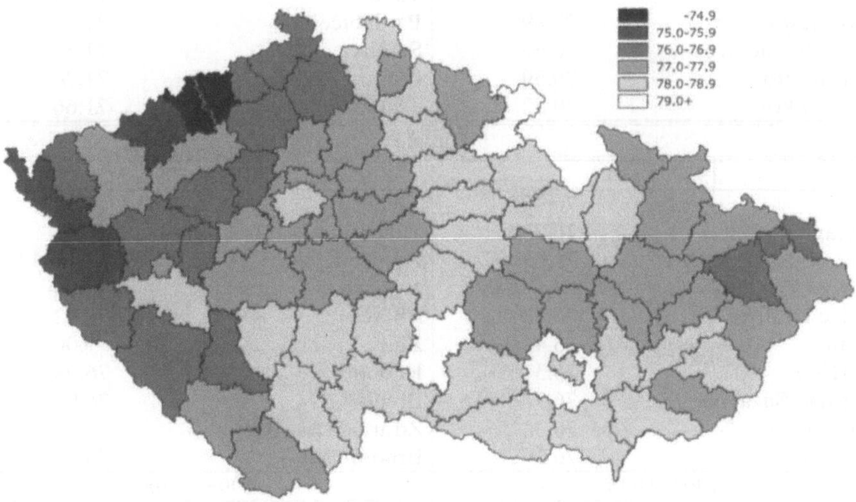


**Figure 18.28: Regional Differentiation of Life Expectancy at Birth, 1996–1998, female**

Source: Authors' calculations

**Table 18.10: Districts with the Highest Life Expectancy at Birth by Sex, 1987–1998, in years**

| Male | | | |
|---|---|---|---|
| 1987–1989 | | 1990–1992 | |
| Třebíč | 70.26 | Třebíč | 69.98 |
| Vyškov | 69.74 | Brno-město | 69.69 |
| Pardubice | 69.59 | Praha | 69.68 |
| Brno-město | 69.51 | Hradec Králové | 69.58 |
| Hradec Králové | 69.42 | Havlíčkův Brod | 69.52 |
| Náchod | 69.34 | Žďár nad Sázavou | 69.33 |
| Žďár nad Sázavou | 69.33 | Pardubice | 69.25 |
| Praha | 69.32 | Zlín | 69.16 |
| Brno-venkov | 69.31 | Tábor | 69.15 |
| Blansko | 69.23 | Plzeň-město | 69.13 |
| 1993–1995 | | 1996–1998 | |
| Náchod | 71.57 | Hradec Králové | 72.57 |
| Hradec Králové | 71.43 | Plzeň-město | 72.57 |
| Žďár nad Sázavou | 71.00 | Praha | 72.28 |
| Praha | 70.95 | Náchod | 72.27 |
| Semily | 70.86 | Brno-město | 72.15 |
| Jičín | 70.72 | Tábor | 71.94 |
| Brno-město | 70.69 | Pardubice | 71.88 |
| České Budějovice | 70.63 | Semily | 71.84 |
| Plzeň-město | 70.59 | Ústí nad Orlicí | 71.76 |
| Brno-venkov | 70.52 | Třebíč | 71.66 |
| **Female** | | | |
| 1987–1989 | | 1990–1992 | |
| Třebíč | 76.99 | Třebíč | 77.34 |
| Břeclav | 76.73 | Tábor | 77.32 |
| Zlín | 76.67 | Hradec Králové | 77.11 |
| Vyškov | 76.57 | Vyškov | 77.04 |
| Hradec Králové | 76.52 | Jihlava | 77.02 |
| Vsetín | 76.44 | Zlín | 77.00 |
| Prostějov | 76.37 | Hodonín | 76.98 |
| Žďár nad Sázavou | 76.32 | Břeclav | 76.98 |
| Brno-město | 76.32 | Žďár nad Sázavou | 76.90 |
| Hodonín | 76.29 | Brno-město | 76.72 |
| 1993–1995 | | 1996–1998 | |
| Hradec Králové | 78.09 | Náchod | 79.31 |
| Zlín | 78.00 | Jihlava | 79.17 |
| Žďár nad Sázavou | 77.98 | Brno-venkov | 79.03 |
| Třebíč | 77.83 | Pardubice | 78.92 |
| Vyškov | 77.73 | Vyškov | 78.88 |
| Blansko | 77.70 | Hradec Králové | 78.86 |
| Brno-venkov | 77.69 | Šumperk | 78.79 |
| Pelhřimov | 77.62 | Jičín | 78.74 |
| Jičín | 77.53 | Semily | 78.56 |
| Tábor | 77.50 | Chrudim | 78.51 |

Source: Authors' calculations

**Table 18.11: Districts with the Lowest Life Expectancy at Birth by Sex, 1987–1998, in years**

| | | | |
|---|---|---|---|
| **Male** | | | |
| 1987–1989 | | 1990–1992 | |
| Teplice | 64.86 | Chomutov | 65.34 |
| Most | 65.56 | Teplice | 65.42 |
| Cheb | 65.68 | Most | 66.08 |
| Chomutov | 65.94 | Děčín | 66.17 |
| Louny | 66.15 | Sokolov | 66.24 |
| Litoměřice | 66.32 | Louny | 66.27 |
| Český Krumlov | 66.50 | Ostrava-město | 66.39 |
| Ostrava-město | 66.54 | Karviná | 66.45 |
| Sokolov | 66.62 | Rakovník | 66.49 |
| Česká Lípa | 66.63 | Tachov | 66.56 |
| 1993–1995 | | 1996–1998 | |
| Teplice | 66.68 | Teplice | 68.18 |
| Most | 67.12 | Most | 68.19 |
| Chomutov | 67.38 | Sokolov | 68.38 |
| Karviná | 67.56 | Jeseník | 68.61 |
| Sokolov | 67.62 | Karviná | 68.76 |
| Děčín | 67.68 | Chomutov | 68.77 |
| Tachov | 67.77 | Tachov | 68.82 |
| Ústí nad Labem | 67.80 | Děčín | 68.87 |
| Litoměřice | 67.84 | Česká Lípa | 68.96 |
| Louny | 67.89 | Ostrava-město | 69.06 |
| **Female** | | | |
| 1987–1989 | | 1990–1992 | |
| Teplice | 72.83 | Teplice | 73.13 |
| Sokolov | 73.12 | Sokolov | 73.26 |
| Most | 73.39 | Most | 73.61 |
| Česká Lípa | 73.62 | Děčín | 74.08 |
| Cheb | 73.68 | Cheb | 74.24 |
| Tachov | 73.93 | Tachov | 74.25 |
| Chomutov | 74.00 | Karlovy Vary | 74.27 |
| Český Krumlov | 74.00 | Rakovník | 74.40 |
| Karviná | 74.00 | Ústí nad Labem | 74.53 |
| Litoměřice | 74.05 | Chomutov | 74.55 |
| 1993–1995 | | 1996–1998 | |
| Teplice | 73.66 | Teplice | 74.70 |
| Most | 74.26 | Most | 74.83 |
| Chomutov | 74.77 | Chomutov | 75.78 |
| Děčín | 74.77 | Cheb | 75.79 |
| Sokolov | 74.87 | Tachov | 75.86 |
| Cheb | 74.89 | Děčín | 76.27 |
| Benešov | 74.91 | Ústí nad Labem | 76.29 |
| Ústí nad Labem | 75.29 | Sokolov | 76.31 |
| Karlovy Vary | 75.45 | Česká Lípa | 76.37 |
| Tachov | 75.47 | Rakovník | 76.34 |

Source: Authors' calculations

From 1987 through 1998, parallel to the regional differentiation, the dynamics of mortality trends has also varied with respect to sex and age. First, the male mortality has improved most. During 1996–1998, the country's average for male life expectancy at birth increased by 2.7 years, compared to the period 1987–1989; while across districts, the corresponding values varied from 1.4 up to 4.2 years. The most rapid increase (about 4 years) of male life expectancy at birth was documented in Plzeň-město, Strakonice, Jablonec nad Nisou, Kolín and Kutná Hora. On the contrary, districts such as Třebíč, Praha-východ, Vyškov, Prostějov and Děčín showed the lowest increase, reaching about 1.5 years. During the same period, female life expectancy at birth has been raising slower than that of males. On the average, it has increased by 2.3 years, with a cross-district variation 0.9–3.7. Jihlava, Kutná Hora, Náchod and Plzeň-město have had the most significant increase (approximately 3.5 years), whereas Rakovník, Klatovy, Rokycany and Prostějov – the smallest (less than one year). Both for males and females, the dynamics of mortality improvement has been only insignificantly influenced by the initial values of mortality indicators; this can be illustrated through the changes in the regional mortality differentiation as well as the observed developments in the districts demonstrating both minimal and maximum values of life expectancy at birth (Figures 18.29 and 18.30).

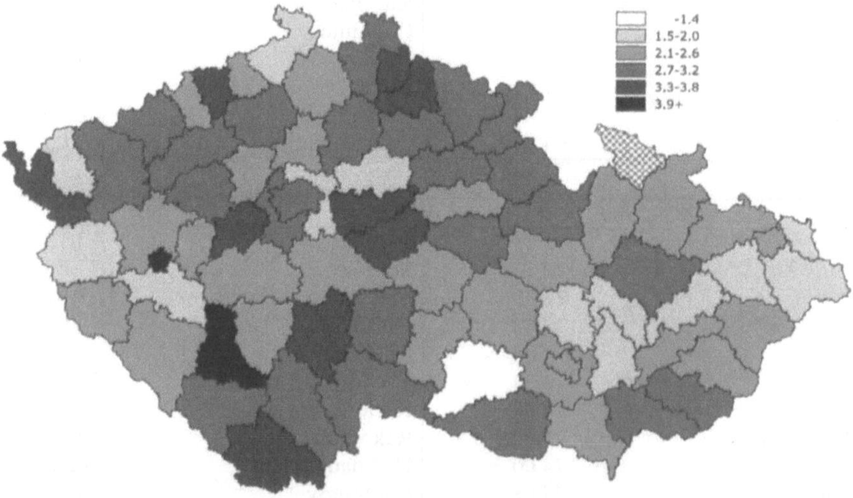


**Figure 18.29: Change in the Life Expectancy at Birth Between 1987–1989 and 1996–1998, male, in years**

Source: Authors' calculations

As far as mortality rates for males and females have been dropping to a different extent, in some districts the convergence in the life expectancy by sex has been observed. In 1996–1998, the sex difference in life expectancy at birth fluctuated between 5.2 and 8.4 years, while in half of the districts it was more than 7 years. A relatively small difference (about 6 years) was traditionally observed in Praha and Plzeň-město, where also the most favourable indicators of male mortality were registered. During the same period, the difference less than 6 years was observed in

Plzeň-sever and Strakonice, yet it was mainly a result of the lower life expectancy among women than the higher life expectancy of men. Most significant differences (8 years and over) were identified in six districts, among which four (Jičín, Znojmo, Břeclav, Plzeň-jih) were characterised by the above-average life expectancy for women and two (Jeseník and Karviná) – by the lower than average mortality of men (Figure 18.31).

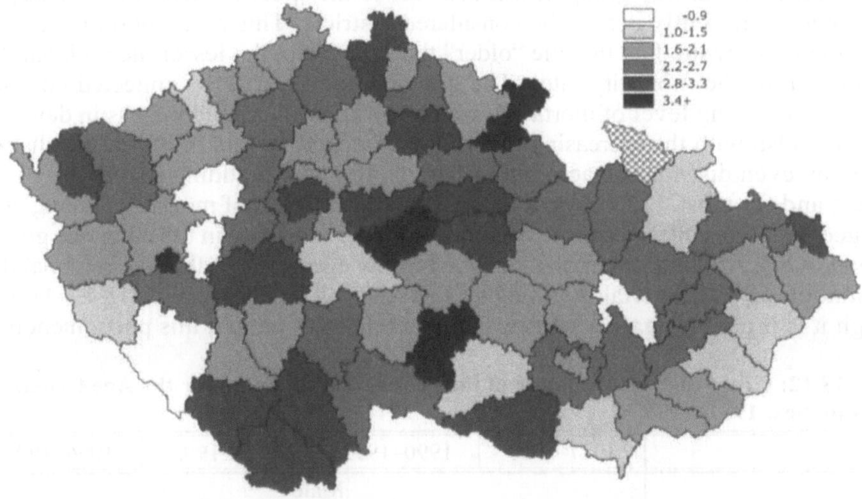


**Figure 18.30: Change in the Life Expectancy at Birth Between 1987–1989 and 1996–1998, female, in years**

Source: Authors' calculations

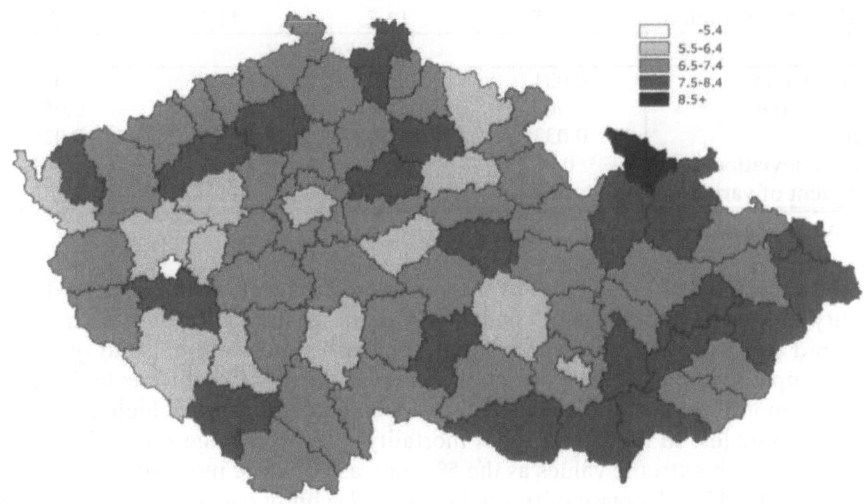


**Figure 18.31: Difference Between Female and Male Life Expectancy at Birth in 1996–1998, in years**

Source: Authors' calculations

Similar to fertility, behind the overall positive development of mortality lies the fact that there have been diverse trends in its age-specific structure. In some age groups, regional variability of the age-specific mortality rates was considerably larger than that for the life expectancy at birth. In particular, the most pronounced differentiation was observed within the age group 40–54. It may be assumed that though such a high variation was partly a statistical artefact resulted from a relatively small number of deaths in this age group, it was also due to the specific factors which may be functioning differently across the considered districts. This assumption is in addition supported by the fact that the "older" the age group, the lesser the regional differentiation of the mortality rates. The growing age is closely connected not only with the increasing level of mortality, which works against randomness in development, but also with the increasing role of the universal factors of mortality, characterised by even distribution across the districts. It is worth adding that in the Czech context and for most regional populations, the higher level of mortality among people aged 40–54 usually means the consequent higher mortality in the older age groups (55 and over). Another common evidence for this age group is that the regional differentiation of male mortality is smaller than that of female (Tables 18.12–18.14), though it is probably again a statistical artefact that lies behind this phenomenon.

**Table 18.12: Cross-district Variation of the Probability of Dying for the Age Group 40–54 by Sex, 1987–1998**

| | 1987–1989 | 1990–1992 | 1993–1995 | 1996–1998 |
|---|---|---|---|---|
| | Male | | | |
| Minimal value | 0.084 | 0.086 | 0.070 | 0.066 |
| Maximal value | 0.145 | 0.147 | 0.131 | 0.126 |
| Range | 0.061 | 0.062 | 0.061 | 0.060 |
| Standard deviation | 0.01 | 0.01 | 0.01 | 0.01 |
| Coefficient of variation | 11.5 | 12.7 | 12.7 | 13.2 |
| | Female | | | |
| Minimal value | 0.031 | 0.033 | 0.028 | 0.025 |
| Maximal value | 0.063 | 0.063 | 0.056 | 0.053 |
| Range | 0.033 | 0.030 | 0.028 | 0.028 |
| Standard deviation | 0.01 | 0.01 | 0.01 | 0.01 |
| Coefficient of variation | 16.2 | 14.9 | 15.4 | 17.0 |

Source: Authors' calculations

During the period 1987–1998, all of the considered districts witnessed the drop of mortality in the age groups 55–69 and 70–84 years. In the majority of districts, the most rapid decrease was observed among the people who were close to retirement age, as compared to the elderly population. As far as the regional differentiation of the changes in mortality rates is concerned, females again demonstrated higher values, as compared to males. In the evolution of mortality rates in the age group 40–54, one may observe such extreme values as the 5% increase of male mortality registered in Benešov, or the 45% decrease of this indicator in Rychnov nad Kněžnou. As already mentioned, for women of the same age, the cross-district fluctuation in mortality rate was even higher – from the 27% increase in Strakonice to the 54% decrease marked in Prachatice. For the age group 55–69, the ratio of mortality decline was, for example, varied for males – between 4% (Praha-východ) and 28% (Plzeň-město) and for females – between 2% (Klatovy) and 35% (Semily). The similar developments – universality of the overall trends of mortality, but higher variability observed across female mortality rates – were also evident in the oldest considered age group 70–84. For instance, between the periods 1987–1989 and 1996–1998, the decline of the probability of dying has been fluctuating between 3% (Plzeň-jih) and 15% (Brno-město) for males, and between 2% (Klatovy) and 18% (Kutná Hora) for females. The regional differentiation of these changes is shown in Figures 18.32–18.37.

**Table 18.13: Cross-district Variation of the Probability of Dying for the Age Group 55–69 by Sex, 1987–1998**

| | 1987–1989 | 1990–1992 | 1993–1995 | 1996–1998 |
|---|---|---|---|---|
| | Male | | | |
| Minimal value | 0.319 | 0.332 | 0.291 | 0.256 |
| Maximal value | 0.468 | 0.452 | 0.417 | 0.391 |
| Range | 0.149 | 0.120 | 0.126 | 0.135 |
| Standard deviation | 0.03 | 0.03 | 0.03 | 0.03 |
| Coefficient of variation | 7.6 | 7.9 | 7.7 | 9.2 |
| | Female | | | |
| Minimal value | 0.158 | 0.151 | 0.131 | 0.127 |
| Maximal value | 0.260 | 0.248 | 0.231 | 0.216 |
| Range | 0.102 | 0.097 | 0.100 | 0.089 |
| Standard deviation | 0.02 | 0.02 | 0.02 | 0.02 |
| Coefficient of variation | 10.2 | 10.9 | 12.4 | 11.8 |

Source: Authors' calculations

**Table 18.14: Cross-district Variation of the Probability of Dying for the Age Group 70–84 by Sex, 1987–1998**

| | 1987–1989 | 1990–1992 | 1993–1995 | 1996–1998 |
|---|---|---|---|---|
| | Male | | | |
| Minimal value | 0.778 | 0.771 | 0.738 | 0.701 |
| Maximal value | 0.883 | 0.871 | 0.855 | 0.836 |
| Range | 0.106 | 0.101 | 0.117 | 0.135 |
| Standard deviation | 0.02 | 0.03 | 0.03 | 0.03 |
| Coefficient of variation | 2.8 | 3.2 | 3.3 | 3.7 |
| | Female | | | |
| Minimal value | 0.621 | 0.611 | 0.593 | 0.552 |
| Maximal value | 0.770 | 0.731 | 0.715 | 0.699 |
| Range | 0.149 | 0.120 | 0.122 | 0.147 |
| Standard deviation | 0.03 | 0.03 | 0.03 | 0.03 |
| Coefficient of variation | 4.4 | 4.3 | 4.7 | 5.1 |

Source: Authors' calculations

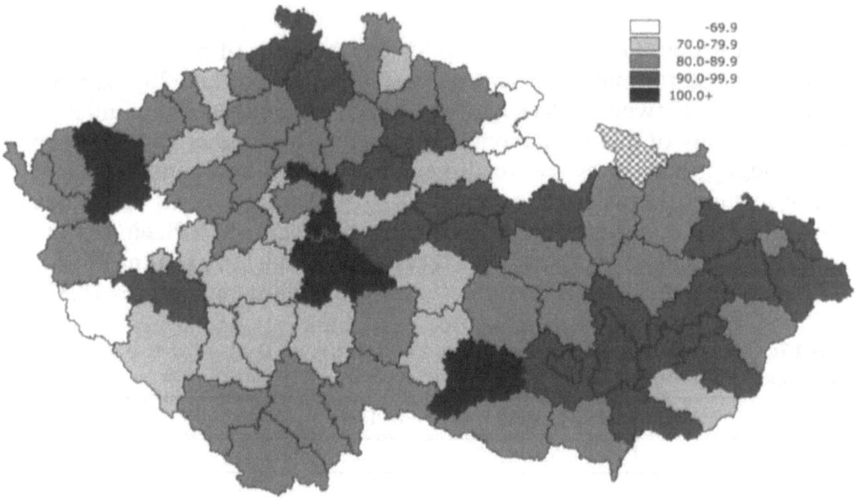


**Figure 18.32: Changes in Probability of Dying for the Age Group 40–54 Between 1987–1989 and 1996–1998, male, index (1987–1989 = 100)**

Source: Authors' calculations

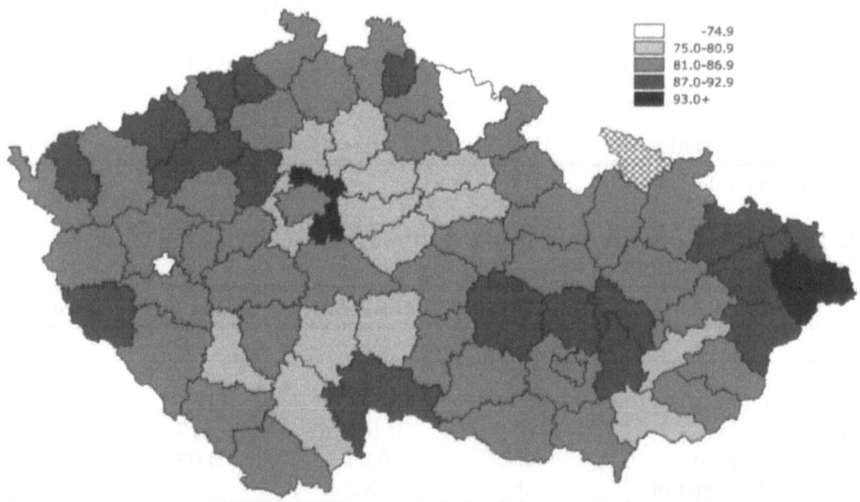


**Figure 18.33: Changes in Probability of Dying for the Age Group 55–69 Between 1987–1989 and 1996–1998, male, index (1987–1989 = 100)**

Source: Authors' calculations

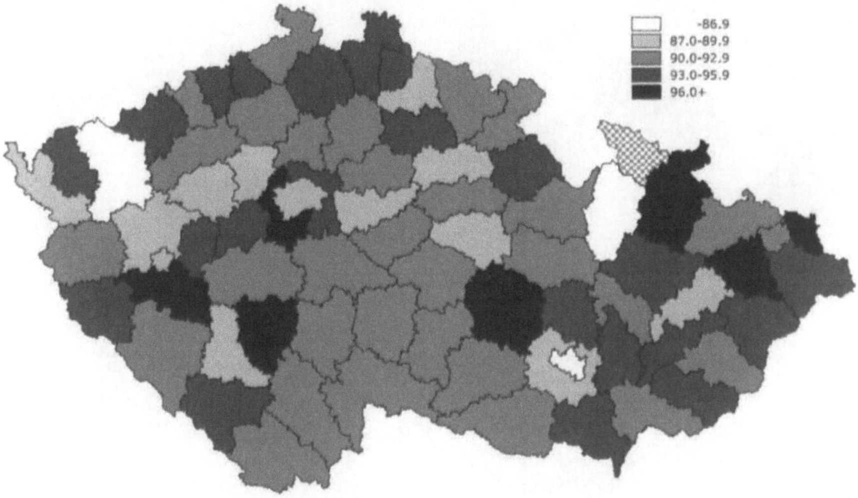


**Figure 18.34: Changes in Probability of Dying for the Age Group 70–84 Between 1987–1989 and 1996–1998, male, index (1987–1989 = 100)**

Source: Authors' calculations

The regional analysis of mortality by sex demonstrates that since the end of the 1980s life expectancy at birth has grown in all districts, while its improvement was most pronounced among the male population. In the majority of districts, the increase of male life expectancy was mostly due to the declining mortality among men aged 55 and over. However, with respect to the regional differences in male mortality there have not been any significant shifts in the considered period; in other words, previously existing regional differentiation of the male mortality has remained almost unchanged. Insomuch as female mortality enjoyed the same dynamics (overall decline), its regional differentiation has not changed very much too.

In sum, although some of the observed regional variations in mortality trends can be attributed to differences already existing before 1989 (Dzúrová, 1996), the other ones have appeared recently. According to some medical surveys, districts with a higher rate of the economic growth can also be characterised by a more pronounced transition to healthier life style (i.e. lower consumption of saturated fat, tobacco and alcohol, more fitness activities etc.). On the other side, there has been evidence that regions with higher than average unemployment rate have also a lower life expectancy.

It is easy to think of at least a few other regionally differentiated factors that could be important in explaining the increasing variation in the mortality trends in the 1990s. Among macro factors, the quality of environment, especially air pollution, seems to be one of most important. Finally, the changes in social and educational structures of the population at the regional level could increase further the variation in mortality indicators, beyond that currently is observed.

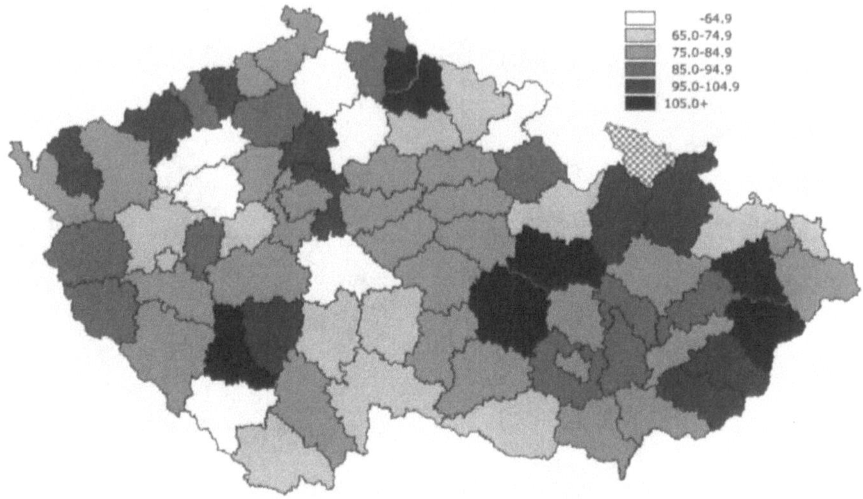


**Figure 18.35: Changes in Probability of Dying for the Age Group 40–54 Between 1987–1989 and 1996–1998, female, index (1987–1989 = 100)**

Source: Authors' calculations

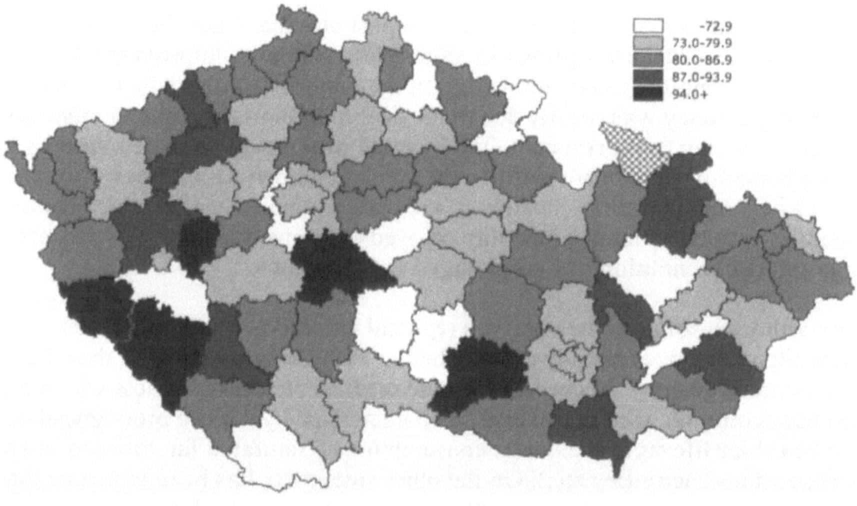


**Figure 18.36: Changes in Probability of Dying for the Age Group 55–69 Between 1987–1989 and 1996–1998, female, index (1987–1989 = 100)**

Source: Authors' calculations

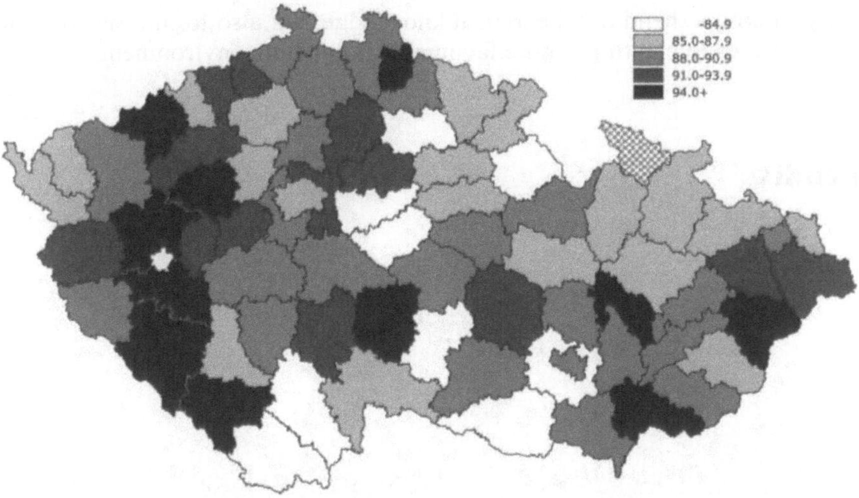


**Figure 18.37: Changes in Probability of Dying for the Age Group 70–84 Between 1987–1989 and 1996–1998, female, index (1987–1989 = 100)**

Source: Authors' calculations

## 18.5 Conclusion

Our preceding discussion of cross-regional changes in fertility and mortality was provided to illustrate that though general dynamics and basic features of these demographic phenomena seem to be unified across the country, diverse variations may exist in social and economic conditions as well as specific socio-cultural environments underlying the seemingly common trends. We further assume that the influence of these specific factors may have increased in the nearest years, particularly as the Czech society moves through the transition process.

This is not to abandon the importance of cross-country or cross-national research but reexamine the limits of standard nation-based indicators that have become almost instutionalised as proxies for analysing population development in a country. We would emphasise that the demographic expertise should be sensitive also to cross-regional differences in population patterns and try to go beyond what standard indicators say about them, looking to sub-national sources for indicators, especially for indicators that can sensitise us to the socio-cultural and economic contexts from which we draw our indicators.

Finally, it is already evident that in further analysis of regional population development various factors that might work on sub-national level in a way that easily could produce different patterns of demographic behaviour has to be studied in a view of not only to comprehend our theoretical knowledge, but also to increase the role of local authorities in creating a more favourable population environment.

## Appendix

**Figure 18.A1: Districts of the Czech Republic (since 1 January 1996)**

## Notes

1. The research reported in this article was supported by a National Grant Agency (Grant number: 205/97/0229) and a research grant from the Ministry of Education, Youth and Sport of the Czech Republic (Grant number: MSM 11310007). Authors acknowledge the Institute of Health Information and Statistics for providing unpublished data on vital statistics.
2. We would like to thank Dr. Olga Kučerová for helpful comments and suggestions.

## References


AERI (Agricultural Economy Research Institute) (1999), *The Social and Economic Position of Rural Women, Particularly Those in Agriculture. Report on a project of the Czech Grant Agency*, Brno and Praha: AERI.

Bartoňová, D. (1996), Regionální diference sociálně-demografických znaků obyvatelstva, in M. Hampl *et al.*, *Geografická organizace společnosti a transformační procesy v České republice*, Praha: PřF UK.

Bartoňová, D. and Z. Čermák (1999), Územní rozdíly sociálně-demografických znaků obyvatelstva Česka, *Geografické rozhledy*, Vol. 9(2), pp. 52–53.

Bičík, I. and L. Kupková (2000), Sektorová struktura a vybrané charakteristiky okresů Česka, *Geografické rozhledy*, Vol. 9(3), pp. 82–83.

Blažek, J. (1994), Local financing and settlement structure, in M. Barlow, P. Dostál and M. Hampl (eds.), *Territory, Society and Administration. The Czech Republic and the Industrial Region of Liberec*, Amsterdam: Instituut voor Sociale Geografie.

Blažek, J. and J. Kára (1992), Regional policy in the Czech Republic in the period of transition, in G. Gorzelak and A. Kukliński (eds.), *Dilemmas of Regional Policies in Eastern and Central Europe*, Warszawa: Europejski Instytut Rozwoju Regionalnego i Lokalnego.

Burcin, B. and T. Kučera (1996), Perspektivy reprodukce demografických struktur v nových podmínkách, in M. Hampl *et al.*, *Geografická organizace společnosti a transformační procesy v České republice*, Praha: PřF UK.

Council of Europe (1999), *Recent Demographic Developments in Europe 1999*, Strasbourg: Council of Europe.

ČSÚ (Czech Statistical Office) (1999), *Okresy České republiky v roce 1998*, Praha: ČSÚ.

Dzúrová, D. (1996), Zdravotní stav obyvatel: regionální rozdíly, in M. Hampl *et al.*, *Geografická organizace společnosti a transformační procesy v České republice*, Praha: PřF UK.

Enyedi, G. (1996), New Regional Processes in Post-Socialist Central Europe, in F.W. Carter, P. Jordan and V. Rey (eds.), *Central Europe after the Fall of the Iron Curtain: Geopolitical Perspectives, Spatial Patterns and Trends*, Frankfurt am Main: Peter Lang GmbH.

Garssen, J. *et al.* (1999), *Vital events: Past, present and future of the Dutch population*, Voorburg: Statistics Netherlands.

Glasová, A. (1999), Porovnání života před a po listopadu 1989, in M. Tuček *et al.*, *Odraz společenských změn ve veřejném mínění 1990–1998 (analýza dat IVVM)*, Praha: Sociologický ústav AV ČR.

Gorzelak, G. (1996), *The Regional Dimension of Transformation in Central Europe, Regional Policy and Development Series No. 10*, London: Regional Studies Association and Jessika Kingsley Publishers.

Hampl, M. (1996), Transformační procesy a předpoklady dalšího vývoje systému osídlení, in M. Hampl *et al.*, *Geografická organizace společnosti a transformační procesy v České republice*, Praha: PřF UK.

Hampl, M. (1998), *Realita, společnost a geografická organizace: hledání integrálního řádu*, Praha: PřF UK.

Hampl, M. (1999), The development of regional system and societal transformation in the Czech Republic, in M. Hampl *et al.*, *Geography of Societal Transformation in the Czech Republic*, Prague: Faculty of Science, Charles University of Prague

Inglehart, R. (1990), *Culture Shift in Advanced Industrial Societies*, Oxford: Princeton University Press.

Kalibová, K. (1996), Demografické a geodemografické charakteristiky romské populace v České republice, in *Populační vývoj České republiky 1995*, Praha: KDGD, PřF UK.

Kalibová, K. (1999), Romové z pohledu statistiky a demografie, in H. Balabánová *et al.*, *Romové v České republice*, Praha: Socioklub.

Kopačka, L. (1994), Industrialization and regional industrial structures, in M. Barlow, P. Dostál and M. Hampl (eds.), *Territory, Society and Administration: The Czech Republic and the Industrial Region of Liberec*, Amsterdam: Instituut voor Sociale Geografie.

Kortus, B. (1996), Spatial-Economic Transformations in Poland, in F.W. Carter, P. Jordan and V. Rey (eds.), *Central Europe after the Fall of the Iron Curtain: Geopolitical Perspectives, Spatial Patterns and Trends*, Frankfurt am Main: Peter Lang GmbH.

Kučera, M. (1996), Obyvatelstvo Českých zemí ve 20 století, in L. Fialová *et al.*, *Dějiny obyvatelstva Českých zemí*, Praha: Mladá fronta.

Lesthaeghe, R. and J. Surkyn (1988), Cultural dynamics and economic theories of fertility change, *Population and Development Review*, Vol. 14(1), pp. 1–45.

Maurel, M.-C. (1996), Post-Collectivist Local Societies in Central Europe, in F.W. Carter, P. Jordan and V. Rey (eds.), *Central Europe after the Fall of the Iron Curtain: Geopolitical Perspectives, Spatial Patterns and Trends*, Frankfurt am Main: Peter Lang GmbH.

Mellens, M. (1999), Determinants of Demographic Behaviour, in J. de Beer and L. van Wissen (eds.), *Europe: One Continent, Different Worlds. Population Scenarios for the 21st Century*, Dordrecht: Kluwer Academic Publishers.

Mulder, C.H. (1993), *Migration Dynamics: A Life Course Approach*, Amsterdam: Thesis Publishers.

Murphy, A.B. (1991), Regions as social constructs: the gap between theory and practice, *Progress in Human Geography*, Vol. 115(1), pp. 22–35.

Murphy, R. (1994), Regional restructuring, local government and small firms sector in England, in M. Barlow, P. Dostál and M. Hampl (eds.), *Territory, Society and Administration: the Czech Republic and Industrial Region of Liberec*, Amsterdam: Instituut voor Sociale Geografie.

Nir, D. (1990), *Region as a socio-environmental system*. Dordrecht: Kluwer Academic Publishers.

Paddison, R. (1997), Political Geography at the Subnational Scale: Spatial Implications of Local and Regional Government, in R.D. Dikshit (ed.), *Developments in Political Geography: A Century of Progress*, London: Sage Publications Ltd.

Sharp, M. and M. Barz (1996), Multinational Companies and the Development and Diffusion of New Technologies in Eastern and Central Europe and the Former Soviet Union, in A. Kukliński (ed.), *Production of Knowledge and the Dignity of Society*, Warsaw: European Institute for Regional and Local Development, University of Warsaw.

Swain, N. (1996), *Rural Transformation in Central Europe*, Budapest: CEU Press.

UNDP (United Nations Development Programme) (1997), *Human Development Report. Czech Republic 1997*, Praha: Institute of Sociology, Academy of Sciences of the Czech Republic.

UNICEF (1995), *Poverty, Children and Policy: Responses for A Brighter Future*, Florence: UNICEF.

Vozáb, J. (1998), Regional Development Agencies in the Czech Republic, in H. Halier, M. Danson and C. Damborg (eds.), *Regional Development Agencies in Europe, Regional Policy and Development Series, No. 21*, London: Regional Studies Association and Jessika Kingsley Publishers.

# List of Authors

| | |
|---|---|
| **Atis Berzins** | Centre of Demography, Faculty of Economics and Management, University of Latvia, Riga, Latvia |
| **Isabella Buber** | Institute for Demography, Austrian Academy of Sciences, Vienna, Austria |
| **Maria Bulgaru** | Department of Sociology and Social Work, State University of Moldova, Chişinău, Moldova |
| **Oleg Bulgaru** | Department of International Relations, State University of Moldova, Chişinău, Moldova |
| **Boris Burcin** | Department of Demography and Geodemography, Faculty of Science, Charles University in Prague, Czech Republic |
| **Vladimir Echenique** | Faculty of Economics, Moscow State University, Russia |
| **Jochen Fleischhacker** | Max Planck Institute for Demographic Research, Rostock, Germany |
| **László Hablicsek** | Demographic Research Institute, Central Statistical Office, Budapest, Hungary |
| **Hans Oluf Hansen** | Institute of Economics, University of Copenhagen, Denmark |
| **Serguey Ivanov** | Population Division, Department of Economic and Social Affairs, United Nations, New York |
| **Kalev Katus** | Estonian Interuniversity Population Research Centre, Tallinn, Estonia |
| **Tomáš Kučera** | Department of Demography and Geodemography, Faculty of Science, Charles University in Prague, Czech Republic |
| **Olga Kučerová** | Department of Demography and Geodemography, Faculty of Science, Charles University in Prague, Czech Republic |
| **Miroslava Mašková** | Prague, Czech Republic |
| **Cornelia Mureşan** | Department of Social Work, Faculty of History and Philosophy, Babeş-Bolyai University, Cluj-Napoca, Romania |

| | |
|---|---|
| **Oksana Opara** | Women's Studies Programme, The University of Auckland, New Zealand |
| **Dimiter Philipov** | Max Planck Institute for Demographic Research, Rostock, Germany |
| **Asta Põldma** | Estonian Interuniversity Population Research Centre, Tallinn, Estonia |
| **Alexia Prskawetz** | Max Planck Institute for Demographic Research, Rostock, Germany |
| **Allan Puur** | Estonian Interuniversity Population Research Centre, Tallinn, Estonia |
| **Traian Rotariu** | Department of Social Work, Faculty of History and Philosophy, Babeş-Bolyai University, Cluj-Napoca, Romania |
| **Luule Sakkeus** | Estonian Interuniversity Population Research Centre, Tallinn, Estonia |
| **Eberhard Schaich** | Lehrstuhl für Statistik, Ökonometrie und Unternehmensforschung, Wirtschaftswissenschaftliche Fakultät, Eberhard-Karls Universität in Tübingen, Germany |
| **Liudmila P. Shakhotska** | Department of Demography, Research Institute of Statistics, Minsk, Belarus |
| **Milivoja Šircelj** | Statistical Office of the Republic of Slovenia, Ljubljana, Slovenia |
| **Tomáš Sobotka** | Department of Demography and Geodemography, Faculty of Science, Charles University in Prague, Czech Republic |
| **Vlada Stankuniene** | Demographic Research Centre, Lithuanian Institute of Philosophy and Sociology, Vilnius, Lithuania |
| **Leona Stašová** | University of Pedagogics, Hradec Králové, Czech Republic |
| **Valentyna Steshenko** | Department of Demography, Institute of Economics, National Academy of Sciences, Kiev, Ukraine |
| **Boris Vaňo** | Infostat, Bratislava, Slovakia |
| **Petra Vojtěchovská** | Warsaw, Poland |
| **Kryštof Zeman** | Department of Demography and Geodemography, Faculty of Science, Charles University in Prague, Czech Republic |
| **Peteris Zvidrins** | Centre of Demography, Faculty of Economics and Management, University of Latvia, Riga, Latvia |

MIX
Papier aus verantwortungsvollen Quellen
Paper from responsible sources
FSC® C105338

If you have any concerns about our products,
you can contact us on
**ProductSafety@springernature.com**

In case Publisher is established outside the EU,
the EU authorized representative is:
**Springer Nature Customer Service Center GmbH**
**Europaplatz 3, 69115 Heidelberg, Germany**

Printed by Libri Plureos GmbH
in Hamburg, Germany